Satan
Christianity's Other God

Satan
Christianity's Other God

Legend, Myth, Lore, or Lie

Historical and Biblical proof of how man created Satan and made Satan to be a god.

VOLUME I

By James R. Brayshaw

www.scog.ca

www.scog.ca

ISBN: 978-0-595-48640-3 (pbk)
ISBN: 978-0-595-60735-8 (ebk)

Printed and bound in Canada

ArtBookbindery.com
Empowering Writers to Self-Publish™

Table of Contents

PREFACE

For many of us, the teachings of man that we have received have become so much a part of our lives that we believe our beliefs are truth, at the very depth of our being.
At any point in our lives any one of us could be deceived, however, a person who is deceived does not know they are deceived, otherwise they would not be deceived.
If we think that our own heart cannot deceive us then God would not have had His prophet Jeremiah say;

"The heart *is* deceitful above all *things*, and desperately wicked: who can know it?"
Jeremiah 17:9 KJV[1]

When I was a child and was taught about Satan, I always wondered, as many of us have, how an all-powerful God can allow such an evil being as Satan to exist. If God is sovereign, why doesn't He just wipe Satan out? How can this loving God allow an afflicter to continue to exert his cosmic powers upon the faithful and the innocent to bring destruction, chaos, and harm? Today I would like to share some answers to those questions and others about the existence of Satan. The answers shared in the following pages are able to free people from fear, confusion, and misunderstanding about Satan and evil. The following is a work intended to prove that Satan does not exist as a cosmic

---

1 Throughout this work the letters KJV after a Scripture verse identify that verse as taken from the King James Version Bible. Where required to indicate which Strong's Dictionary number has been assigned to a specific word the Strong's numbers will be incorporated into the verse after each word. This is known as "inline Strong's". Here is an example of that practice; *In the beginning[7225] God[430] created[1254 (853)] the heaven[8064] and the earth.[776] Genesis 1:1 KJV+*

supernatural being, who is intent on destroying humanity and thwarting the plans of the Most High God.

In arriving at a clear understanding of the non-existence of a Satan, I have learned from many teachers on the subject. The problem with the existence of a Satan is that the sovereignty of the Creator is in question. The question has long been asked; If God is sovereign then why does Satan have so much power to harm humans? I agree that is a question needing to be answered and in short, it can be answered by saying there is no Satan and that man is the primary purveyor of evil in this world. The subject becomes even more serious when one considers that ascribing supernatural power to anything elevates that thing to the status of a God.

Yahweh is God and He claims that there is no other supernatural force in the universe, saying there is none like Him. Thus, we are left with the problem of trying to remove the other God, Satan, from the throne that he has been given by the heart and mind of humanity. If Satan truly does not exist, then those who believe he does have a conflict of interest with the concept of believing in One God. So consider the following very carefully.

INTRODUCTION

Whether "Satan" exists or not is an issue that has huge implications for humanity and religion today. If "Satan" does not exist, then you and I have been taught a very ancient and complicated lie, at the hands of the religious institutions of this world. From the time the Israelites left Persia until today, those who are the leaders and teachers of these religious institutions have almost unanimously heralded the message that there exists a cosmic being that is like God but is not the One God who is sovereign over the entire Universe.

Probably the most serious repercussion of a culture coming to terms with the non-existence of a cosmic Satan is the impact this information will have on the individual when they fully realize what it is they are responsible for. By there being no "Satan", you and I are then left as the party who must take the full responsibility for sin. We can then dismiss the idea that an evil influencing force has secretly introduced sin to us and we are not hapless participants in behavior that is not approved by the Almighty.

The fault for evil then is not to be laid on a supernatural, mind controlling, satanic spirit; the fault lies with the individual who submits to the original propensity to choose sin, which is a potential that is inherent in the human psyche. Sin changes the human mind and there are many theories and hypotheses as to how the actual neurological wiring is altered when a person continually chooses to sin. The change in our brain physiology becomes the primary factor why sin gets easier and easier. The liar finds it easier to lie, the rager finds it easier to rage and the porn addict finds it easier to choose to look at porn. Eventually the brain and emotions control the person because of the cellular changes to the areas in the brain, which have been continually stimulated by whatever sin has persistently occurred.

Admittedly, we all sin regularly but many who are in a cycle of habitual sin may be there because of the first time they justified their actions. Now that person no longer has to work to justify their action because that "principality," is the driving force of their choice to sin. A principality here is the primary drive or original impetus to choose to disobey, it has taken over, and the person has effectively "lost" control in areas of their life where sin becomes an almost automatic behavior. I will not use such a broad brush as to paint every person, without exception, as being able to have lost control to his or her propensity to sin. It is true that some of us have a propensity to commit one sin or another because of things that may have happened in our childhood. Trauma changes us and is particularly efficacious on the brain of a child, as are various forms of negative programming that might be foisted on a child in one way or another. For excellent teaching and understandable scientific explanations in this area, you may want to look at the work of Dr. Paul Hegstrom.[2] He is a premier researcher and teacher in the way our brains have been changed by situations and stimulus from our early years as well as how neurological changes occur from repeated sin choices.

Admitting that there is no cosmic "satan" is only one step in the journey of faith which leads us to a true monotheism that fears God only. Imagine how safe we will feel instead of feeling fear when we are able to dismiss the concept of being inhabited by a demon as is portrayed in certain movies. Or when we concretely embrace the fact that a midnight walk on a pagan high holy day will not place us at risk of being attacked by a demonic spirit who wants to drag a soul to hell. Let me testify to the freedom that comes from knowing there is only One God and no evil, cosmic force that has any power to affect your life in any way. There is amazing freedom that comes with learning that all ideas of demonic, transient spirit beings are the fabrications of men's minds, which find their origins in ancient mythology. For others, you can expect peace to be found in the area of fear that may come in the night, thinking a horned beast with fangs and breath of sulfur is going to appear when you awake from a bad dream.

When we learn there is no Satan we can begin to help our children more when they awake from a nightmare or we find them emotionally trapped in an irrational fear of being separated from Mom and Dad at a sleep over with friends. When parents are able to see these fears as not coming from a demonic source, they will be liberated to begin meeting the real emotional needs of the child by a proper logical and intuitive assessment, leading to true emotional support for that child. The benefits of recognizing that there is no Satan are multiple. Western nations would no longer have to think

2 Dr. Hegstrom's work can be accessed through his organization called Life Skills International. www.lifeskillsintl.org

of Mid East terrorist groups as working for Satan and the terrorists could be free to no longer believe that the West is being driven by Satan. All who are parties in a situation where one country is against another, would then be able to recognize the source of evil is the wicked hearts of man in the conflict and perhaps come to the realization that their own heart is equally as wicked. A conflict that brings pain and death is driven by human desires and although many blame "satanic" influence for these conflicts, great benefit will be realized by seeing man is the source of the evil perpetrated against another people group. The list of freedoms we get from changing our belief in a cosmic Satan can go on and on, but the bottom line in all this is that he does not exist, so we humans are going to have to take responsibility for all the evil in the world.

Some state that if you say there is no Satan then you are in danger of hell yourself, I say; "If you say *there is a Satan*, then you are in danger of having two Gods." The greatest danger one faces by saying there is no Satan is the danger that comes with taking full responsibility for their sin and evil. To embrace a "One God" mindset frees the mind from the subtle trap which always wants to find someone or something to blame for the evil in the world. One only stands to benefit, by once and for all taking full responsibility for the sin in their life which so easily deceives the mind.

In the following pages, we will find many thoughts and concepts that would have been difficult to arrive at had we used the Scriptures alone. I have tried to be thorough in the explication of this idea and yet the entire study of this concept is far from being exhausted. We will look at mountains of Scripture, assess the words of the Apostles and the Messiah as recorded in the "New Testament", and we will receive testimony and instruction from many sources to add to our historical and cultural understanding. Ahead I will claim some really difficult ideas to be true and will deny and dismantle some of the most commonly accepted beliefs in the Christian religion, citing evidence, logic and the fact that our perspective is not even close to the Hebraic thinking of those who were the first and earliest hearers of the words in the Bible. Concepts that are considered include; if there is a Hell, and what is Heaven for. Another concept that is addressed is the question of where the dead go.

The concepts shared in this work are flexible and a life-long learning process will continue for me long after I have signed off on this book. That stated, It is entirely possible that an understanding which I have provided, for a particular verse or passage may not be the only and complete understanding. I thoroughly enjoy hearing other interpretations of the material I have covered in this work. You will see however, it would be unlikely an interpretation that includes a Cosmic Satan would be accepted as correct, based on the information shared in the arguments of the two volumes of *Satan, Christianity's Other God.* I will present a plethora of arguments however, I do understand that more could be added in some instances to the thoughts and information I have shared. Even when faced with one interpretation of a passage there undoubtedly are other ways the passage could be explained to illuminate the truth of a non-existent Satan.

Men such as Origen, Plato, Philo, and Augustine have come to accept that sin is from an internal drive in man and is driven by the pleasure of the senses. These men are just a few of the historical figures who make allusions to the "serpent in the Garden" as being an allegory for man's potential to choose sin, called by some the *yetzer ha ra,* or the evil inclination. In Augustine's work titled, *Confessions,* we are given this comment regarding how we are able to fall into sin;

> For first comes a suggestion, whether through thought, or through the bodily senses, by sight, or touch, or hearing, or taste, or smell. When the suggestion is made, if our cupidity does not move us to sin, then the cunning of the serpent will be excluded. If this movement happens, however, then we will be persuaded, just as the woman was.

Augustine recognized sin was from the internal drive of man but he could not find a way around the Greek mythology of his day to disclude Satan from his theology. Many men have identified the inborn ability to choose sin as an internal influence that comes because of the "pleasures of the senses". Some have tried to place a cosmic Satan in the picture while others have tried to minimize Satan and show that underneath the surface is rebellion bent humanity itself.

In chapter 12 and 13, we will discuss the thought that the "serpent" in the garden is not Satan nor is it a real serpent that was inhabited by Satan. What we have found is that the writer of the garden story was capable of using current mythological images, in a type of mytho-poetic language, to instruct the hearers as to what man's fall from perfect obedience looked like. It is possible that the events said to have transpired in Eden are somewhat of an allegory, intended to teach the Israelites how wonderful life could have been without sin. I would be fooling myself if I was to claim that all the images and stories in the Scriptures are either literal or all allegorical. They cannot all be either or. If the Scriptures are true and we serve a God who transcends the natural, then some of what appears to be symbolical imagery may in fact end up being real and true in a physical sense. It is likely that many of the elements of numerous stories are allegorical but other elements will actually prove to be literal. Logic and diligent study can assist in forming a conclusion on at least some of these components of the Scriptures.

We will see some history related to the development of the common idea of a cosmic Satan. It is realized that this idea truly flourished in the 6th century BC exile of the Hebrew people under Persia and Babylon. The concept grew in the minds of the generations in exile and was then added to the belief system of certain "religious sects" that came out of exile in about 539 BCE. It was there, as we will discuss, that the dual-God philosophy of the Zoroastrian cult was embedded in what was to be the exclusively monotheistic faith of the Israelites. The thought of there being a good god and an evil god took root at that time and was filtered through the Parsi, who were Persian Magi, down through the Pharisees who developed Rabbinic Judaism. The two-God thinking traveled on into the first century, past the advent and ascension of Christ and into the cult of Christianity. This concept has had almost 3000 years of development and is so deeply embedded that we now see millions of dollars spent on information and amulets which are designed to keep "demons" from getting close enough to humans so that they can affect their lives. The multi-billion dollar media industry now drives this false idea deeper into the mental, emotional and spiritual fibers of all who drink in the high action high graphic demonstration of the powers of Satan. These intense, mind numbing portrayals are displayed in literally thousands of movies, TV shows and video games. All the while the innocent user of said media is left to believe that forces such as they are seeing on screen, actually exist and do the things that "Hollywood" has them doing.

In these pages we will note how there is only One God and if you or I profess there is another supernatural being performing humanly impossible tasks, then we are ascribing to a dualistic, two-God philosophy. This is a philosophy that is against the God of the Scriptures and Universe, because He claims to be the only God. In the Torah this God teaches that all the other Gods, yes this would include "Satan," are nothing and do not even exist but are fabrications from the minds of men. As a way of emphasizing their non-existence, the Revelation of John says "they neither see nor hear nor walk."

We will discuss how the writer also called the angel who prevented Balaam from proceeding to curse the Israelites "Satan". Also in the Torah, (1 Kings 22) we will see how Yahweh sent a "satan" to Ahab to be a "lying spirit" so that Ahab would decide to go to war and suffer destruction. In the vision had by Jehoshaphat, a satan was clearly recorded but does this vision of a "spirit" have to be taken literally or is it symbolic of human messengers that came to Ahab? Both of these examples show us that "the Satan" is simply an adversary that has been sent by Yahweh and the "lying spirit" was dispatched by Yahweh as well. This type of adversary can be either human or some manifestation of a divine presence from the Creator. We see clearly in the Torah that the "adversary" is not an archenemy of Yahweh but in these instances it is a tool of Yahweh's.

Another privilege we have by studying the words of the Torah is to see that it is man's heart which is continually inclined to choose evil. There is no recognition of a fallen spirit being who has caused man to choose evil in the Scriptures. Man makes choices out of the wickedness that is in his heart and if man chooses righteousness, he will overcome that inclination to do evil. Along with that instruction from the Torah, we find in the Books of Leviticus and Deuteronomy that devils and demons are simply man-made, hairy goat-idols. Again if one looks carefully at the context, the history, and the language, it is clear the false gods made by men's hands, were believed to be supernatural forces that were being worshipped by the Israelites. The syncretizing(combining faith practices from varied religions) of Israelite worship took place because of the seductiveness of the varied gods of the pagan nations around them. The nation of Israel often took on these false gods as "lesser gods." Yahweh accused them of idolatry because they acknowledged these gods and He said they are impotent and amount to absolutely nothing. The only power they had is what is believed to exist as power in the minds of those who engaged in false worship and acknowledgment of these worthless idols.

Together we will look at the supposed appearance of "satan" in the book of Job. You will be shown that the term "before the LORD" is a term describing an Earthly Temple environment and the word "Satan" seen in Job, is speaking of a human adversary. Job's troubles were brought on by a few jealous men who found ways to influence the human forces around them so that Job was the recipient of great suffering. True Yahweh allowed this to happen, but it happened by the hands of humans, not by supernatural agents who can beg Yahweh to let them harm a human and Yahweh allows the attacks to happen. Job himself attributes all the evil that befell him, to Yahweh.

The problem with most commentators accepting the "Satan" in Job as a literal being; is that they reduce the writing to a mere historical account when it has been written as a separate genre of writings called "wisdom literature." Wisdom literature is designed to express deep concepts using metaphor and allegory, while still employing the elements of humanity which would be familiar to the hearer. Job had recognized that the men, who brought evil upon him and the natural events which rendered Job a victim of circumstance, all occurred at the permission of Yahweh. Of course Yahweh could have supernaturally subverted the evil will of Job's "adversaries" but we serve a God who operates at times by allowing one man's evil choices to affect another man who may be righteous.

After looking at the concepts of the "adversary" as found early on in Scripture, light will be shed on the identity of "Lucifer" in Isaiah 14. It will be shown that "Lucifer" was not the name of Satan prior to his fall, as scholars have claimed for years. The term "son of the dawn" also said to be equivalent to "the bright and morning star" was what was originally meant by the Hebrew term "*helel.*" The phrase was a well know appellation for the Kings of Pagan nations. This speech against the king of Babylon by Isaiah is set in a series of words against pagan nations, know to be; *The Oracles Against the Nations.* The fact that the context of this passage clearly identifies this "Lucifer" as a man and that the term itself had no fallen angel meaning until after it arrived in Jerome's Latin translation of 346 CE, indicates strongly that Isaiah 14:12 is about a man who thought himself to be God, was given power and authority from the Creator, but abused it in thinking he answered only to himself. The subsequent "fall from heaven" is a reference to this pagan king's fall from power. The idea of this person being the actual "satan" of common religious thought, never entered the realm of theological scholarship until sometime after Jerome translated the Hebrew word for "morning star," in the fourth century, with the Latin word *Lucifer,* a word that means light bringer.

The Book of Isaiah also revealed that Yahweh is the one who creates evil and calamity. Isaiah had been given the charge by God to speak to the people coming out from exile. He was to inform them that Yahweh is the one responsible for the evil which has befallen them. The exiled Israelites were incorporating ideas they had adopted from Persian theology into their faith system. The idea which came from Persian, Zoroastrian religion claimed that good came from one God and the evil came from another God who was constantly at odds with the supreme God. George Knight, a past professor of Old Testament in McCormack Theological Seminary speaks about this two-God religion in his work on *The Prophets of Israel;*

> Zoroastrianism at that time was a fine new religion spreading out of Persia over all the East. Faced with the complexity and mystery of human life, it sought to present man with a clear and

> logical explanation of the problem of evil and of pain. There are two powers, two Gods, this faith proclaimed, a God who is good, and a God who is evil. In the end however, after the long struggle between the two is over, Light will win over Darkness, so that man can look forward to a glorious future.[3]

This two-God system is probably the most subtle form of dualism that is present in Christianity and other religions today. It forces the believer to attribute things that only Yahweh can do, to another source, even though the other source does not really exist and was made up in a "vision" by an ancient Persian man. Perhaps God sees the belief in that source as idolatry and for this reason, He stated over and over again that He is God and there is none else.

A great deal of mythological lore has been used by writers of the Scriptures and subsequently misunderstood by interpreters of those same Scriptures. As we look at the prophetic books, we will begin to see signs of mythology sewn into the fabric of numerous stories. Many of the characters from myths are seen in visions had by the prophets. A major mythological connection will be found in the Serpent in the Garden story however, we will become familiar with the use of mythical imagery by the prophets before we embark on our study of the Genesis 3 serpent. Our study of the Ezekiel 28 passage, which is about the human King of Tyre and not a cosmic being, will reaffirm to us the importance of being careful to not interpret the visions of all prophets, as literal. True some visions have literal application for parts or individual components of the vision. But out of what almost seems to be instinct, we interpret most of the content of most visions literally. This practice has hamstrung the typical student of the bible by, inhibiting them from receiving the message the prophet intended to send through articulating his vision. The International Standard Bible Encyclopedia relates how visions in the Scripture should be recognized as containing elements that are familiar in daily life;

> The objects of vision, diverse and in some instances strange as they are, have usually their points of contact with experiences of the daily life. Thus Isaiah's vision of the seraphim (Isa_6:2) was doubtless suggested by familiar figures used in the decoration of the temple at Jerusalem; Paul's "man of Macedonia" (Act_16:9) had its origin in some poor helot whom Paul had seen on the streets of Troas and who embodied for him the pitiful misery of the regions across the sea; and "Jacob's ladder" (Gen_28:12) was but a fanciful development of the terraced land which he saw sun-glorified before him as he went to sleep. Among the recurring

3 Bible Guides, Prophets of Israel (1) Isaiah, page 75

> objects of vision are natural objects - rivers, mountains, trees, animals - with which man has daily and hourly association. [4]

Much will be gleaned from exploring the reasons that 2 Samuel 24 tells us Yahweh caused David to number the tribes of Israel, while the same account of the story in 1 Chronicles 21 reveals "Satan" as being the inciter of David. This apparent contradiction can be seen by some as a reason to discount the writings of Scripture. However, a closer examination reveals that the writer of Chronicles was writing the story about 300 years after the return of the Israelites from the Persian exile. The perspective that the writer spoke from was one of understanding that Yahweh was acting as an adversary; therefore, the writer used the Hebrew word for adversary, *sawtawn*. This term was subsequently translated into English as "Satan" and given a capital letter at the start to seemingly identify it as a proper noun as the name of the mythical, cosmic evil one. The occurrence of terminology that would have been understood by the ancient hearers but misunderstood by hearers today is a common situation and one that has led to many misunderstandings of the meaning of Scripture.

As we look on in the Scriptures, we will be presented with a more plausible understanding of Zechariah's vision of Joshua the High Priest being accused by the "satan." This situation seems to smack of a real life Satan, but turns out to be, first of all, a vision. A vision which when viewed along with the remainder of the Book of Zechariah is not to be taken literally as not one of the visions he had was to be taken literally. Zechariah's visions are as much metaphorical as any of the visions in the Scripture. It will be shown that once again the Hebrew word used for "Satan" means adversary. The use of this term for an adversary, or one who opposes the will of Yahweh, helped to express the fact of Zechariah not seeing a cosmic satanic being, but was receiving a vision of adversarial men trying to keep Joshua from acting as the High Priest.

Our overview of the inter-testamental period will shed light on the development of the supernatural Satan concept. This period is understood to have been the three or four hundred years before Christ came on the scene. Many religious and apocalyptic documents were penned during this period and the Hellenized thinking of the writers was widely sown into religious thought. From a couple of hundred years after the release of the Persian exiles, the formation of a "living spirit entity concept," as the counter-Yahweh force in the cosmos, became popular. This ideology influenced Judaism in numerous

4 From the article, Visions, in the International Standard Bible Encyclopedia

ways and became part of first century religious life. Some believed that if you spoke of a demon you were talking about one of the evil minions of a very real, evil cosmic leader; while others were able to maintain the understanding that to speak of a person having a demon, meant they were sick, insane or entertaining false beliefs. In its simplest form, the theory of a supernatural being at odds with Yahweh became a concrete belief, causing passages like Isaiah 14:12, about a human man, to be infused with mystical interpretations. None of the commonly identified passages about Satan was interpreted as such until the Hebrews left Persia and apocalyptic literature flourished in the inter-testamental period. The inter-testamental period played a huge role in the history of developing theology. It was a period that was largely influenced by Greek thinking and had been given a huge launching pad by expanding on the borrowed concepts of Persia. Many of the dualistic concepts that are deeply woven in the fabric of religion today were still strongly embedded in the spiritual psyche of the people who came out of the Persian Empire.

Another deeply embedded belief in the spiritual hard drive of today's culture that was not present until well into the fourth century CE, is the belief that says the New Testament is Scripture. Our forthcoming discussion will bring to light many reasons why the "New Testament" is not Scripture and is not to be given the same authority as the Old Testament. One of the most convincing arguments for that theory is the absolute lack of internal evidence for that body of Apostolic literature. The New Testament never calls itself Scripture and only refers to the Hebrew Scriptures as Scripture. Being considered Scripture has brought men to raise the "New Testament" to a status that parallels the Hebrew Scriptures. Because this has been done by religious leaders for thousands of years does not make it right. The passage of time does not turn an error into a truth, so we have the privilege of considering how the writings of the Apostles were used in the first centuries of the Common Era. Yeshua and Paul never used the "New Testament" as Scripture and they only ever affirmed the authority of the ancient Hebrew canon as Scripture. Though the Apostolic Testimony is not Scripture used for designing doctrine, it is a body of literature that helps clarify numerous difficult issues and concerns within the early assemblies of believers. We have in the New Testament a valid witness to the happenings of the first century apostles and certain believing communities. Honestly assessing the value of this personal mail for what it is quickly diminishes it as words that have authority to develop new doctrine, particularly on such as a doctrine of a cosmic "satan." These documents were at best, written by various men who would be mortified to hear their letters that were intended for assemblies and friends, are raised to equality with Torah and being used for defining and designing doctrines. The evidence against some of these letters being written by the alleged authors whose names appear as the title of the "book," is manifold and should be considered when we stake our faith on these letters as words which are said to show how to live a life of faith in the God of the Universe and His Messiah. One major issue with the writings of the New Testament is how to reconcile the apparent contradictions it has with the writings of the Old Testament. When the writings are studied through the lens of their correct historical, cultural, and linguistic context, any apparent contradiction that surfaces can soon be explained so that the writings are not held in contrast to each other any longer.

I will say however, we are fortunate to have the Apostolic writings as a witness to major happenings in the development of the Faith of Israel during and after the Messiah's appearing. Using these documents as a means to comprehend some of what happened in the first century as it pertains to the Messiah and His followers has been of great value to the believing community, the Israel of God. The difficulty with using these documents is that unless one sees them through the eyes of a first century Hebrew believer in Messiah, they practically have their hands tied to correctly understand and apply the precepts and instruction contained in this body of literature. Many will claim that you are throwing out the Messiah if you refuse to believe the "New Testament" is Scripture. The fact is, Messiah is not going to be using this body of literature as His textbook in the millennial age; is He therefore guilty of the same charge? I am reminded that the present format and order of the New Testament that we have today was only put into one compendium in the year 367 by the Bishop Athanasius, who was a right hand man of the pagan Christian Emperor Constantine.

The handlers of these early Apostolic documents had long been divorced from a Hebraic heritage. Had these Greco-Roman philosopher-theologians been properly trained to rightly divide the word of Yahweh, they would have interpreted and used these documents in a proper context. They then would have had much success at making use of these documents which were intended to be aids to assemblies of those with faith in Yeshua. Quite the contrary though, they set off a stream of erroneous teaching based on their incorrect understanding of much of this literature. Their teaching brought millions into the false religion of Christianity, and the Gnostic flavor of their system of religion was sent throughout the world. In Volume Two of *Satan, Christianity's Other God,* the issue of the New Testament not being Scripture is dealt with thoroughly.

Our journey then will take a different turn, as we carefully look at all the passages in the Apostolic Testimony, which pertain to sin, evil and "satan." If there is no "satan," as I posit, there then has to be a comprehensive explanation for all the verses where it appears Satan is being spoken of. The personification of sin, evil, sickness, and insanity was related to the hearer using the words, demon, devil, Satan, and unclean spirit. Interpreting and understanding the Apostolic Testimony through the eyes of the Hebrew Scriptures is essential to perceiving these terms correctly. Each New Testament use or instance of "Satan" must draw on the "Old Testament" precedents for this so called Satan. The Old Testament Satan was almost always an adversarial force sent by Yahweh. At times, this force might have been inspired of itself to go but it was typically a human force with the infrequent exception of the force appearing as some manifestation of the celestial workings of the Creator Himself. The frequency with which commentators and scholars have not correctly understood a passage in the Apostolic Testimony has grown to epidemic proportions due to almost a complete lack in seeing the verses in the Apostolic testimony through "Old Testament" glasses.

Many of the potential understandings of most passages that will be shared with you are just that, "potential". I will not claim to be the final authority on these words because we are all still learning and the distance in time that we find ourselves from the workings of that culture is vast, thus making it difficult to state a hypothesis as final authority. I will say though, the correct path is one similar to the one I have taken you on and not a path that points the modern reader to the existence of a cosmic Satan. The path presented in Volume II of *Satan, Christianity's Other God,* where the New Testament is surveyed and expounded on as it pertains to Satan, is a path that indicates that Scripture must define Scripture. All Apostolic Testimony must completely support the words of Scripture or else it is the words of false prophets. I encourage you to continue exploring the meaning of the difficult words of the Apostolic Testimony beyond that which is presented in this book. You will find the pieces of the puzzle falling into place the more you commit to ask yourself, "*I wonder what the original hearer understood these words to mean.*"

Even with correct hermeneutics and a mind that thinks more in the manner of an ancient Eastern person rather than a present-day, Greco-Roman thinker, we still arrive at a slight problem. What are we to do with all the experiences? Experiences of credible people who claim to have made "contact" with the evil spirit realm. Many will say that they have seen demons and watched people fly across the room during an "exorcism." Some will tell of experiences they have had with ghosts and others will swear they have encountered "satan" himself. All these are difficult to explain, but if we start with the foundational concept that is taught in the Holy Scriptures which can be called the Torah, that there are no other living Gods except Yahweh, we will then be prepared to not force the Bible, which is the teaching and instruction of God, to fit into one's experiences. That is to say, if I have an experience of seeing a seven-headed dragon, I don't force that vision to define what the Scriptures could possibly mean. I try with my entire mind, to understand that experience through the eyes of Torah. The Torah is specifically the first five books of the common Old Testament and according to some, can loosely refer to the entire Christian Old Testament. Letting our experiences be the thing that defines Torah and truth is a backwards manner of living one's faith. If the Torah says there is no supernatural evil being in existence and I see a supernatural evil being, I must try to comprehend how that can be understood without building a dualistic theology.

If I accept the truth of Torah and I have an experience that seems to oppose a truth of the Torah, then I might have developed that experience out of my own mental and emotional resources. Many people follow their experiences thinking that because they have had a certain experience; they then are in the truth. The possibility of being deceived is a very real possibility for all of us as we wander through life trying to make sense of what is truth and what is lie. Often experiences that seem very real are only tangential images and when taken too literally, they will lead one into deception. The challenging thing though is that the deceived do not know they are deceived unless they realize that it is possible their beliefs are inconsistent and possibly wrong. We only need one wrong belief to enable a whole bunch of opportunity for future deception in our lives. That is why Paul the Apostle suggests we prove all things and hold fast those which are good. Dr Margaret Singer has made many aware, that because we think our minds are invulnerable to wrong thought, does not make it so.

> **"Just as most soldiers believe bullets will hit only others, not themselves, most citizens like to think that their own minds and thought processes are invulnerable. "Other people can be manipulated, but not me,' they declare." -- Margaret Singer, Ph.D.**

We are all "other people," to someone and we all have the potential to be deceived. To see someone who is manifesting signs which suggest "demon possession," is usually thought to be a sure representation that there exists a cosmic "satan" who is able to inhabit a person's psyche in a similar fashion to one being inspired by the Holy Spirit. What appears to be spiritual possession by a netherworld resident, is only an activity which is brought about by certain mental conditions, postures and positions one places themselves in via some form of self induced hypnosis or hysteria. In his book, *Occult and Supernatural Phenomenon,* D. H. Rawcliffe tells of the ancients experiencing what is probably one of the earliest forms of ecstasy, which brings on a state likened to the common pattern thought to be "demonic possession."

> There is little doubt that the Dionysiac frenzy and similar forms of "ecstasy" were hysterio-epileptoid in character. Such ecstatic states manifest themselves in rigidity of the body, contortions, tremors, frothing at the mouth are often accompanied by visual and auditory hallucinations and extreme euphoria. The hallucinations and euphoria provide the component of visions and exaltation, which in Thrace, used to take the form of mystical union with the god and which in later times, was followed by wild sexual orgies. The soul of the ecstatic was supposed to leave the worshipper's body and hold communion with distant gods and daemons.[5]

We can come to terms with the fact that ecstatic behavior, such as is mentioned of the Dionysiacs, is a state of instability that is self-induced as a response to a hysterical environment. The person today who enters such a state, perhaps not even quite as pronounced as what is told of the Dionysiacs, is no less guilty of self-induction of the desired state which they themselves developed and then believe is a sign they are connecting with God's Spirit. There is much to be said of those who today might manifest the signs of being out of control and therefore controlled by another entity. This is commonly thought to be a demonic possession but is more likely a form of dissociation, hysteria or self-hypnosis.

As a former Pentecostal "prayer warrior", I have been involved in a number of situations where a person is said to be under the influence of a satanic spirit, defined as "a spirit of anger" or "a spirit of jealousy." In these situations, I had been part of the "deliverance" team and we began the prayers and anointing with oil, to cast out this "demon". The engagement was placid, not eliciting the manifestation that would have affirmed "possession" and thus would have indicated we were making a serious dent in the hold this "demon" had on an individual. With success not yet in our grasp, our intensity and fervor would increase. These manic deliverance sessions would often bring us to the point of being fully embroiled in a frenzied situation that was fueled by our beliefs that there existed a real "demon" and this person would eventually be liberated from the clutches of it because of our spiritual authority. None could

---

5 *Occult and Supernatural Phenomenon,* D H Rawcliffe, pg274

deny that we truly thought that what we were experiencing was real. So we pressed on until the subject, or perhaps I should say victim, was lying on the floor grimacing as if he or she were trying to pass a gall stone and then finally would become calm once again. In our minds and the mind of the innocent victim, there was a "demonic spirit" which had now been removed. We had accomplished what we had set out to accomplish and our belief system was affirmed and made still stronger by the experience. I now understand this and other situations like it, to be cases of hysteria where the participants caused some type of physical manifestation to occur. Both the deliverer and the deliveree were giving themselves over to the experience and had such a deep belief as to how things should go, that they unwittingly cooperated with each other to produce a faux deliverance on a person who came to believe that he had a "demon" and subsequently brought on all the manifestation that he truly accepted to be part and parcel with being "demon possessed."

These types of experiences are not uncommon. Our culture is prone to the power of suggestion and to becoming a slave to our beliefs. So much so that some actually "experience" such impossibilities, as seeing a "demon" or "spirit." Perhaps the experience a person has is that they sense a presence or feel a touch of the "spirit," somewhere on their body. In Volume One, we will mention the work of the great illusionist Harry Houdini. I am not referring to his masterful illusions and feats of escape but to his work that found him investigating the spirit realm. Houdini discloses that people are extremely prone to the power of suggestion and the paranormal becomes the normal which is magnified and pronounced in their mind. Houdini had the privilege of exposing numerous famous and internationally renowned paranormal charlatans. Many of these deceivers of men exposed themselves by their own admission at the end of a long career. Houdini could find absolutely no evidence of actual paranormal activity during the entire 30 years he investigated this art. It is a fact though, that the power of suggestion, such as has been utilized in indoctrinating various religious groups for thousands of years, has amazing power to become reality in the minds of the initiate. What the subconscious accepts, it will act on and forms a belief which becomes a reality in the mind of many. It may be that a person truly believes they see a certain demonic representation or perceives a convincing spiritual presence, and I believe they are sincere in what they have seen. This sight or sense is real to them and they may actually visualize it in the minds eye. It is no more real though than if I say to someone, "Look, a fire truck just went by!" You see a fire truck, your mind processes the words I have spoken and you, on some level, picture a big red, shiny Fire Apparatus but in fact one had not just driven by. The mere suggestion of something will generate an image in the mind of most people. This is the case for someone who doesn't even have an intense desire to witness the said fire truck. Imagine how strong this process would be for the person who is told there are ghosts in their house or that a certain part of their town is under control of demonic forces. Most hyper-spiritual people will actually see that which is suggested and when shared by another person of the same persuasion, they often have corroborating stories as they fuel each other's tales by emphasizing the vague similarities to what each person has seen in the mind's eye. By conforming the elements of their story to correspond to the other person's story, as a way of confirming that what they saw is real, they then are able to feel affirmed as truly "spiritual" persons; both "seeing" the same apparition. This type of phenomenon of the mind is plentiful in our over stimulated culture where images of ghosts, demons, gargoyles and witches unceasingly bombard us via the medium of motion pictures. This same mental phenomenon occurs for untold thousands who seek the skills of a "medium" to contact a dead relative or friend. Rawcliffe tells of the amazing deception performed by mediums who are commissioned by sincere seekers of contact with the dead. The tricks are very difficult to detect by the uninformed and the medium provides no assistance for one to uncover his or her charade. Rawcliffe says;

> Men as well as women have been known to recognize a dead father, mother, sister or cousin in the figure of a thinly disguised medium....
>
> Many descriptions have come from observers who have looked on aghast at the success of the most flagrant deceptions: before their eyes stands the most patently disguised figure of the medium, and with each insignificant change of apparel a bereaved mother or daughter or wife cries out a heart-rending greeting to one long since dead and buried. The illusion brought about by frustrated longing and the overwhelming will to believe, is complete. One is inevitably reminded of the collective hallucinations that have occasionally occurred at moments of religious fervor.[6]

Rawcliffe's words ring true for the belief of Satan and demons as well. If we would completely accept the teaching of Scripture that declares convincingly, "there is only one God and none else," we could more properly address the tricks of the mind that are able to fool even the intellect into believing something exists when it actually doesn't. If we could dampen down our overwhelming "will to believe" in Satan and demons, which we too often couple with "religious fervor," I am certain that we would come to the correct conclusion that we humans with an unchecked potential to choose evil, are

6 *Occult and Supernatural Phenomenon,* D H Rawcliffe, pg 312

the only force of evil in this world. We would then understand that as long as man rebels against good, that evil men will wax worse and worse.

The Apostolic Testimony, known as the New Testament, ultimately identifies the "Satan" with three main bodies of apostates who are adverse to the truth. They are; the leaders of the Jews who oppose Yeshua, the false brethren who oppose Yeshua's true followers and the false religious systems and institutions who oppose Yeshua's system of faith. Many principles can be gleaned from the Apostolic Testimony as to what the metaphorical terms, "devil and satan" are intended to mean. These can be stated as declarations which are found in various letters of the Apostles and Prophets. They are;

1. THE SOLE SOURCE OF TEMPTATION IS THE LUSTS OF MAN - James 1:12-17

2. ALL LUSTS ARE ORIGINATED BY THE WORLD - 1 John 2:15-17

3. THE SOLE SOURCE OF SIN IS THE PASSIONS OF MAN'S FLESH - Romans 7:5-25

4. THE THINKING OF MAN'S FLESH IS THE ENEMY OF GOD - Romans 8:7

5. THE HEART OF MAN IS THE SOURCE OF ALL WICKEDNESS - Mark 7:18-23

6. MAN'S HEART IS THE MOST DECEITFUL OF ALL THINGS – Jeremiah 17:5-11

7. THE DRIVE TO CHOOSE SIN HAS BEEN CANCELLED OUT THROUGH YESHUA'S DEATH - Hebrews 2:14

For all the time spent fighting Satan and all the prayers spoken against the "work of satan" it is amazing that the supposed "satan" still has any power at all to affect humanity. I heard one man when told that the concept of "satan" not existing was thousands of years old said; "Well what is going to happen to my prayer life if there is no Satan?" The reason that Satan has not gone away in response to the millions of prayers against him, is because it is the satan inside us that we must battle against, not a cosmic external force that was dreamed up in the mind of some mystic.

It doesn't have to be difficult to simply eliminate Satan from your life. Just remove him by thinking of him now as an old dog that passed away. Like the memories of the dog you've lost, you may have lots of memories about Satan being a part of your past life, but when held up to the light of Scripture and History, "Satan" holds no power anymore to be a part of your life, from this moment on. In many ways Satan is like an imaginary friend from childhood that never existed anyway.

As you read this book I hope that you will be able to truly believe in One God and become the responsible citizen of His kingdom that you were created to be. Ultimately, we will be able to lift our head high, look in a mirror and see ourselves as people who are sometimes satan, like the Apostle Peter was when he opposed the plan of God and was rebuked by the Messiah. It is my hope that every individual who cares to believe in the One Creator, can boldly claim that there is One God and no Satan.

CHAPTER 1

Considering Why We Have a Doctrine of Satan

Presently there are many who claim the days are approaching of swift judgment; beyond that a time of redemption and renewal. This thought has been articulated for thousands of years. Many throughout the world view the time of the Messiah's return as very near. Many who believe the return of the Messiah is imminent, also see a different power approaching, and not only approaching but currently, actively involved in opposing the work of the Creator. Much of Catholic Christianity, Protestant Christianity, and Judaism believe this power is working to prevent the rescue of the inhabitants of the earth by the Messiah. The Catechism of one of the great faiths of the world has this to say;

> *In this petition, evil is not an abstraction, but refers to a person, Satan, the Evil One, the angel who opposes God. the devil (diabolos) is the one who "throws himself across" God's plan and his work of salvation accomplished in Christ.*[7]

Many who call this evil power Satan say that "Satan" [8] is working secretly to thwart the purposes of God (called Yahweh in the Hebrew Scriptures).

---

7 #2851 Catechism of The Catholic Faith; VII. OUR FATHER PRAYER - "BUT DELIVER US FROM EVIL

8 Satan will be written with a small letter "s" in many places in this document from here on. To begin to come to correct understanding and use of the term it is helpful for the learner to begin to see this name for a cosmic being, spelled without a capital to indicate that it is not a name. The name Satan has been wrongly applied as a proper noun when it was originally and throughout the history of the Hebrew Scriptures, used as a simple noun or a label to describe an adversarial force which comes from Yahweh or from another human. The Hebrew word itself is a verb and the International Standard Bible Encyclopedia makes this observation***; We are thus enabled to note in the term "Satan"***

Terms such as "demonic activity," "satanic activity," "the work of satan", are very often used by believers in the God of the Scriptures, to refer to the evil that is ongoing in the world. Martin Luther said much on the subject, he too thought that the "Devil" was able to afflict humanity with his spells.

> *"Our bodies are always exposed to Satan. The maladies I suffer are not natural, but Devil's spells." (Martin Luther)*

Luther had an odd relationship with the Satan in his mind. Satan was said to have slept with Luther more than Luther slept with his wife Katie.[9]

Although evil occurs at the hands of men, there is a prevailing view in many religions that evil is propagated by unseen spirit beings that must be stopped using spiritual ammunition such as the sign of the cross, or holy oil or water. The graphic 1974 thriller "The Exorcist", showed the spiritual battle against a demonically inhabited girl with the Priest chanting, "The power of Christ compels you" repeatedly at the foot of the bed of the apparently demonized girl. Demonic spiritual activity against a person is often attributed for the hardships of individuals and of nations. It is often seen as the cause for problems here and abroad. By some, the alleged power of Satan is claimed to be the active force that makes life difficult or the force that prevents us from performing the will of God. World-renowned spiritual leader Billy Graham has this question and answer posted on his organization's web site to explain their concept of "satan" to an inquirer;

> *Q: I know Satan is real, but does he have supernatural beings under his control the same way God does, with His angels? I've always been curious how Satan gets his work done, because he sure seems active. — D.P.*
>
> *A: **Dear D.P.,** Yes, Satan certainly is active today—and he always has been active, because his goal has always been to block God's work. Whenever God is at work, you can be sure Satan also will be at work, counterattacking and trying to stop whatever God is doing.*
>
> *The Bible doesn't go into great detail about Satan and how he works; after all, our focus should be on God, not Satan. (If we concentrate mainly on Satan we'll become either overly-fearful or*

(and Devil) the growth of a word from a general term to an appellation and later to a proper name.

9 Page 172, The Prince of Darkness, Jeffrey Burton Russell 1988 Cornell University Press.

> *overly-fascinated—and both are wrong.) But the Bible does tell us that the devil has a multitude of demons under his authority, just as God has the angelic hosts under His control to do His will*[10]

The Bible teaches no such thing as a Satan that has a multitude of demons under his authority. Satan is often seen as a force diametrically opposed to Yahweh[11] and as fighting feverishly to claim as many souls for the kingdom of darkness as possible. Feverishly working to claim a victory before the end of the age when Messiah returns to rescue His faithful remnant and destroy the "devil and his demons" forever in a cataclysmic, apocalyptic battle. A battle that is said to take place between two great cosmic forces. This can be seen in the Book of Revelations where the writer tells of his vision of a great dragon hurled into the lake of fire. Both of the symbols for this apocalyptic battle are full of meaning and metaphor. It is virtually impossible to enumerate all the conditions, situations, issues, and incidents that are attributed to the alleged creature Satan. However, one thing we know for certain is that the character of Satan possesses a personality and supposed physicality that is so shrewd and deceptive, yet so sinister and horrifying that at the mention of the supposed orchestrater of evil mental images of the "evil one" often come to mind. The thought of this torturous creature of hate makes the proverbial hair on the back of the neck stand up. Is this the character that is said to be found in the Scriptures or is legend and myth largely responsible for designing the form, features, and attributes of the "Prince of Darkness"?

There are truly many, many diversified concepts of "Satan" and just who he is, what he does, what he looks like and what kind of authority he has. These are questions that I believe can be answered. For some the answers have been found through contemporary media, colorful graphic images, or

10 Billy Graham Evangelical Association website; http://www.billygraham.org/MyAnswer_Article.asp?ArticleID=1698

11 YAHWEH is known to be one possible pronunciation of the Hebrew spelling of the name of the Creator. This option for pronouncing the name is contested by numerous scholars and linguists who advocate a number of different forms for the appellation of the Most High. One of the closest pronunciations in my opinion is Ye-hovah, pronounced as Jehovah but replacing the J with the letter Y sound. There was no letter J in the English language until the 16th century and the 1611 King James Version of the Bible testifies to that through its use of the letter I sound and character where one would commonly see the letter J in English today. Webster's 1828 Dictionary states; **J**. This letter has been added to the English Alphabet in modern days; the letter I being written formerly in words where J is now used. It seems to have had the sound of y, in many words, as it still has in the German. The English sound of this letter may be expressed by dzh, or edzh, a compound sound coinciding exactly with that of g, in genius; the French j, with the articulation d preceding it. It is the tenth letter of the English Alphabet.

lively literature. For still others the answers have been found through tales from parents and grandparents, regaling by friends or siblings at a young age or even through subjecting oneself to a medium or spiritist, seemingly who possessed powers to contact the spirit world. For most though, whatever concept of Satan they currently hold to, is a concept that has in many ways, been imposed upon them rather than one they have concluded by engaging in diligent questioning. It seems that a belief in Satan is somewhat of a second-hand belief that has not been discovered by each individual but has been passed on by those who have gone before us. Perhaps, when their concept of Satan is scrutinized under the light of Scripture and the microscope of historical understanding and consideration of the formation of thought, some will see the holes in a belief system that includes a Satan. Recognizing that indeed, they have in fact received their particular understanding of Satan through ideas that have not been true to Scripture, instead of adopting the ancient understanding of satan such as would have been common to Christ, known as Yeshua[12], and those grounded in the available Scriptures of the first century.

For those of you who have been looking for the answers to your questions regarding the character of Satan through any of the aforementioned sources such as metaphysical practitioners or traditional church teachings, I laud you for desiring to find answers and for being an active seeker. However, the answers to the difficult question of whom or what Satan is will be found in much more stable sources. Numerous scholars have written major works on the topic of Satan and evil. Scholars such as Paul Carus and Neil Forsythe have brought major insight to the origins of Satan. I am also grateful to the prolific author, Professor Elaine Pagels who has added yet another layer to the dynamic topic of Satan in her book *The Origin of Satan.* Pagels makes us aware of the Gnostic Writings that contain such assertions that claim the serpent may have had sex with Eve. In her work, she also brings to light the fact that Satan as we know of him today, was created by Christianity. Pagels testifies that the ancient Hebrews knew nothing of the cosmic being that is now seen by many to be the epitome of evil. She relates the social implications of a figure Satan and how he is invoked to express human conflict and characterize human enemies, as she puts it in her introduction.

In *The Old Enemy; Satan and the Combat Myth,* by Neil Forsythe, we are privileged to read of the ancient belief in a cosmic evil force. Forsythe intricately elaborates on the development of varied Combat Myths from ancient history. These myths in his opinion have been rolled into the concept of Satan as we typically hear it today. Forsythe too recognizes the deeply poetic, metaphoric,

12 The name Yeshua is the Hebrew name for Jesus.

and symbolic writing of the Biblical authors when relating his understanding of Satan as myth that became reality in the minds of the faithful.

It is worth mentioning the monumental work of Paul Carus in 1900, *The History Of The Devil And the Idea of Evil From the Earliest Times to The Present Day.* Carus' work shows the path of the concept of evil from ancient Egypt up until the period of the Reformation. Carus' clarity on the influence of Persian dualism on the Christian concept of Satan is illuminating. In his chapter titled *The Dawning of a New Era,* he writes;

> *Since the lower classes began to make their influence felt, it is natural that in the Apocryphal Books of the Old Testament the conception of Satan grew more mythological and at the same time more dualistic. He developed into an independent demon of evil, and now, perhaps under the influence of Persian views, the adversary of man became the adversary of God himself.*

Prior to this statement by Carus in his work, we are given a sizeable treatise on the Persian religion of Zoroaster. We are shown how this ancient religion was a primary catalyst for religion to move towards a two-God philosophy. Zoroastrianism remains known as the most consistent form of dualism. This Persian dualism, we are taught, is intricately connected to major religions today by the nature of a philosophy of an evil, supernatural being, and a good supernatural being. These beings are known as Ahura Mazda and Ahriman respectively. Much of common religion has conformed to the Persian philosophy with the most notable of the conformists being found in Christianity. A religion that has turned the Persian good God and evil God into the entities that are called God and Satan. Carus writes;

> *THE TRANSITION from Devil-worship to God-worship marks the origin of civilisation; and among the nations of antiquity the Persians seem to have been the first who took this step with conscious deliberation, for they most earnestly insisted upon the contrast that obtains between good and evil, so much so that their religion is even to-day regarded as the most consistent form of dualism.*[13]

If one is willing to take the time, I assure you the answers can be found through the Scriptures, through history and with the help of scholars such as those mentioned above. Resources such as these will prove to be the most likely candidates for our task of showing that Satan is not real. Yes that is the plight and as I set forth to prove to you that Satan does not exist I will

13 Pg 50, History of the Devil, in the chapter titled Persian Dualism. By Paul Carus 1900

cover as much ground as possible related to the topic, yet piecing together a corrected understanding of long held erroneous beliefs and concepts. Beliefs and concepts such as, where the dead are, and the idea of a literal hell that is set apart for the eternal torture of the unfaithful. Although topics such as these will creep into our study out of necessity to establish that there is no Satan, they are not the primary objective and will only be treated cursorily.

So to be clear, this book is intended to show how Christianity has adopted an ancient pagan myth in the concept of Satan and further to that, how this evil being is mistakenly believed to literally exist by untold millions in many diverse religious sects. That is the truth that will be shared here with all who choose to explore further. With that, I must give two caveats. Regarding the use of source materials, the caveats are as follows;

1) **In utilizing the Scriptures one must take extra caution to ensure that the Scriptures they are studying from are studied from a properly placed cultural, historical, linguistic, social, and religious perspective, based on the period of the writing.**

The Scripture, in fact any ancient writing must be assessed through the eyes and ears of a hearer from the period in which it was written. This is proper historical and cultural context. Too many have assigned grievously improper interpretation to many Biblical writings because they failed to place the writings in the proper period to gain an understanding of the context they were written in. For instance, many of you reading this will have at one time or another (probably in High School) been forced to study Shakespeare.

If you are at all like I was, when my High School English teacher, Mr. Sigstad had the class read Shakespeare orally it was so very interesting but frustratingly difficult to comprehend. Once we were given some knowledge as to the cultural context of the writings in their proper historic period our ability to engage in constructive thought about the writings started to blossom. When we were assisted in understanding the language of the period and many of the meanings, which were complicated to our ears because of the distance from the period of their writing, we began understanding Shakespeare afresh.

Therefore, I submit, that some knowledge of the language, the culture, the history and the religion of the period wherein the writings originated, will be the only way to arrive at a correct understanding of any ancient text. Consideration of the respective Hebrew and Greek languages and trying to perceive the prevailing thoughts of the people from the periods those texts were written in is vital to understanding the message of the text.

The second caveat in regard to utilizing sources such as Scripture, history and the work of other scholars to answer our question about Satan is this;

> **2) We must not reject any source in our search that will aid in "Proving all things". If you or I believe a source is rife with heresy and anti-messiah sentiment, yet it provides a nugget of truth to assist in achieving the goal, then we ought to take that nugget and blow away the rest as chaff.**

We as a culture continue, and I am generalizing here, to be profoundly lacking in our ability to adopt a theological concept that is not generally accepted and approved by the laity. This being the case, I would like to make a suggestion. I suggest that for the reader to begin to ingest the information I will provide in the following pages, he or she must at least agree that because a concept or opinion is obscure does not mean it is wrong or heresy. If all obscure concepts, unapproved by the masses of faithful followers of a religious philosophy are rejected on some level, then we must reassess the value and significance for today of the ninety-five theses of Martin Luther.

If you are unfamiliar with the situation, I will encapsulate it for you by saying this; Martin Luther was a German Monk in the fifteen hundreds who came to realize many of the doctrines and practices of the Catholic Church were not in agreement with Scripture. He believed that Scripture had the final word on matters of faith and religion and composed ninety-five arguments that systematically refuted many Catholic doctrines. Take for instance thesis number thirty-two. Luther writes;

> *Those who believe that they can be certain of their salvation because they have indulgence letters will be eternally damned, together with their teachers.*

The general Catholic populous throughout the world were taught that they might purchase eternal salvation with the payment of monetary amounts to the Catholic Church, called indulgences. This belief was common and the leaders of Catholicism saw Luther's refutation of it as obscure and very unwelcome. Luther posted a multitude of theses, decrying the efficacy and integrity of the act of advocating indulgences and collecting them to build the Pope's empire. Today we see the sense in Luther's position but looking back we might ask; "Were some of Martin Luther's concepts obscure"? Yes they were. Were they incorrect because of this obscurity? No!

If a concept disagrees with Scripture, no matter how many church councils have met and upheld it, it is wrong. Conversely, if a concept is in agreement with Scripture, no matter how obscure it is in relation to the practice and understanding of the time, it is still a correct concept. One might conclude that it is difficult to assign a concept from Scripture as either correct or incorrect, based on the contradictory statements made in the Bible. However, I assert that the appearance of contradictions in the Bible is not a problem with the Bible, but it is a problem with the understanding of the reader. All apparent contradictions can be brought into a state of reconciliation if the reader makes the effort to adequately understand the passages in the fullness of their original intent and context. We must accept the obligation to carefully accept truth from any source if that truth adds to our much needed paradigm shift about the person of "satan".

Many concepts of Satan and his demons abound in common thought and literature. The most common thought seems to be the one that proceeds from organized religion, which claims to follow the Bible's teachings. Oddly, the majority who believe Satan is somewhat of a symbolic entity and a metaphor are quick to believe that demonic possession is common. The Barna research group supplies us with some of its poll statistics.

> Six out of ten Americans (59%) reject the existence of Satan, indicating that the devil, or Satan, is merely a symbol of evil. Catholics are much more likely than Protestants to hold this view - 75% compared to 55% - although a majority of both groups concur that Satan is symbolic.
>
> The rejection of Satan's existence seems to conflict with the fact that a slight majority (54%) also contends that, "a human being can be under the control or the influence of spiritual forces such as demons." People 57 or older were the group most likely to doubt Satan's existence (64%) and also emerged as those least likely to accept the notion of demonic influence (39%, compared to 55% among Baby Busters and 62% of Baby Boomers).[14]

There are many arguments on whom or what Satan is. Through this book, I hope to assist the reader in coming to an understanding of various points in regard to satan. As we walk through this concept, we will be discussing satan as seen in the Tanak, known by many as the Old Testament and by a growing segment of the faithful as the Hebrew Scriptures. These Scriptures, by the way, are the Scriptures used by Yeshua the Messiah in the first century C.E., as well as by all of the apostles and first century believers.

We will be discussing Satan in history. We will be discussing the history of who it is Satan answers to. What does pagan mythology have to do with

14 http://www.barna.org/FlexPage.aspx?Page=BarnaUpdate&BarnaUpdateID=122

Satan? What does the New Testament seem to say about Satan? Is there a difference in the treatment of Satan from the Tanak to the New Testament? Why do the Greek writings known as the New Testament appear to show a doctrine of a personal and physical Satan yet they are so different from the doctrine of Satan seen in the Tanak, the Bible Yeshua taught from?

Other thoughts and questions that will be considered are;

Where is Satan? What or who are Satan's demons? Is the first century Hebrew concept of Satan the same as the first century Greek concept of Satan? The concept of Satan today is not the same as the concept of Satan in the first century. One could look at the many perspectives of the late first century and the 2nd to 4th century "Church Fathers" on Satan such as Clement, Irenaeus, Origen, Tertullian and Augustine, however, that exercise will not serve the purpose of determining what the pre-Christian understanding of Satan was. The post first century view of Satan became entwined with Greek and Roman thought, which still is a prevalent perspective in society today.

Jeffery Burton Russell expands on this thought in his book *Satan; An Early Christian Tradition.* Russell speaks of the inconsistent modalities of thought by some of the most notable Apostolic Fathers. We are told "Irenaeus was less concerned with the mythology of demons than with the alienation of humanity from God, a concern that led him to tie the sin of the devil closely to the sin of Adam and Eve"[15]

It is however important that we explore what Yeshua understands about satan based on a first century perspective? If the ancient and present cultural concepts differ, where and when did the divergence occur? How much power does Satan have? Is the word "satan" a noun or perhaps is the name/word "satan" supposed to be an adjective?

There is a distinct need to focus on the belief in Satan if one is going to find the answer as to whether he exists or not. Many pious writers, speakers, and teachers have often said, "Don't focus on Satan; focus on Jesus". So if you feel that through attempting to understand who, what, where and why Satan is, is too much of a focus on "Satan" then it is your prerogative to choose not to explore this topic. However, allow me to inform you that the Greek word *satanas,* the word that is translated as satan, occurs 37 times in the Greek New Testament and plays a significant role in the revelation of Yeshua the Messiah as relayed to us in the Greek, by John the Revelator. The word devil occurs 61 times in the New Testament. By the sheer number of

15 Satan: The Early Christian Tradition, By Jeffrey Burton Russell pg 82

times the words Satan and devil are used in the New Testament (from here on I will also refer to the New Testament as "the Second Testament" or the "Apostolic Testimony") it is clear that if there is a Satan, someone wanted us to know and understand the matter. Further to that, if you are interested in acquiring more truth on this issue or you are a follower of the Messiah, I suggest you take the time to consider the matter on a level you may have not considered before. Unless the God of the Universe specifically instructs you from His word by His Spirit to not investigate this topic, there is no chance that you will be overcome by the wicked deeds of darkness by simply engaging in a search for the truth. In other words, by engaging in a study on "Satan" you are not at risk of becoming "filled" with demons as some have suggested. Although an odd thought to many intellectuals, the thought that a person might fear studying a topic out of a chance of becoming possessed by a demonic entity, is a real concern. We find this belief prevalent and testified to in an exhortation from C.S. Lewis. Lewis warned the faithful to be wary of becoming too interested in "demons". Perhaps this philosophy suggests the idea that becoming influenced by demonic powers is a real concern for some. C.S. Lewis wrote in "*The Screwtape Letters*";

> ***'There are two equal and opposite errors into which our race can fall about the devils. One is to disbelieve in their existence. The other is to believe, and to feel an excessive and unhealthy interest in them. They themselves are equally pleased by both errors. "***

So as one seeker of the truth to another, don't believe anything I say, unless the Scriptures prove to you that what I am saying is true. Ultimately, you are left to find your own conclusions and not adopt another man's ideas unless you are confident that you can prove them yourself. It is from the standpoint of Scripture being accurate, in its original manuscript form, that I meet the teaching and doctrine of a literal Satan head on. If you want proof of the validity and accuracy of Scripture then you need to take time to study Scripture. The Scriptures can be shown to be historically accurate as archeology continues to reveal large quantities of proof, as the years pass by. If you are interested in what it is the Scriptures and the Apostolic testimony truly speak and mean on this topic, then we need not argue as to the authority of Scripture. I am not able to show you that Scripture is 100% accurate although that is my belief when understood in its original form and intent. I am willing to show where man has adopted an inaccurate understanding of many parts of Scripture and the "New Testament" as it regards Satan. This pursuit will naturally lead to various other topics that will be presented in the following pages.

I simply ask of you that you come with me on a journey for the truth, a journey that for the time being sets our current understanding, as given us by other men, on the shelf. I ask that you would resist the urge to pull one or two verses out of the Greek, New Testament writings to use them as proof that your present understanding of a topic is rock solid. I respectfully ask that you will allow me the liberty to elaborate at length on associated topics that I feel might be necessary to establish a point, a point that will affect our thinking on the non-existence of Satan. I ask that your mind on the matter would not be made up before truly proving to yourself the matter from an ancient Hebraic perspective, the perspective of the Messiah who in fact is Yahweh and does not change, as is indicated by John and Malachi respectively.

> *In the beginning was the Word, and the Word was with God, and the Word was God.... And the Word was made flesh, and dwelt among us....John1:1 and 13*
>
> *For I am the LORD, I change not...Malchi3:6*

I ask that you take the full counsel of God on the matter, which is the entire Scripture and the inspired writing contained in the Second Testament, as understood in their proper context of their first century setting. I ask that you would be patient, that if there seems to be an apparent contradiction, that is to say where one verse appears to oppose another verse in different places in the Scripture and Apostolic writing, that you will see through and attempt to reconcile all the verses so that they agree with each other. This practice to move toward understanding Scripture is not often taught. Christianity as we know it appears to have decided to stop searching for answers in many theological areas. Beliefs such as; 'the dead go to heaven', or 'that Jesus died on a Friday and was resurrected on a Sunday, a period consisting of 3 days and only 2 nights', have become common and unquestioned by the masses. Three days and two nights is not possible according to the words of Messiah that tell us He will be in the heart of the earth three days and three nights in Matthew 12:40.

It seems many in Christianity, in its typical form, have settled on a reasonable answer for many inconsistencies and questions about its beliefs. Perhaps this is done to simply placate the masses. Christianity has in effect, settled for some dead-man's theology, which we will come to see is often opposed to the theology of Yeshua the Messiah. Men such as Augustine, Dante, and John Milton have been among those who have been dead for centuries yet are found to have been pivotal in the development of satanology. In many ways man's theology and doctrine has broken the true theology of the Scriptures. Yeshua tells us that Scripture cannot be broken, as is testified in John 10:35 and the implication is that anything taught in the "Old Testament" must be held to be true in the period of the "New Testament" and beyond.

Included in this axiom is the teaching in the Hebrew Scriptures that clearly eliminates the potential for a cosmic satanic entity existing apart from the Creator and existing to thwart the Creator and mankind. So please read on and understand that to find the underlying cause of understanding Satan there will be the need to utilize many tools. I will employ some theology, some philosophy, some history, some chronology some linguistics and some logic. This will involve a rudimentary assessment of particular Greek and Hebrew wording at times, as well as considering the fallibility of many of the English translations of the Greek and Hebrew writings. To purport to be a theologian, philosopher, historian, chronologist, linguist or logician would be foolish, therefore, I simply purport to be a lover of the truth and a follower of the Messiah who died and was resurrected. I also claim to believe Yeshua when He said He would ensure that we would be guided into truth after He left to resume His office in the Heavens. This is how he put it in John 16:13;

> *Howbeit when he, the Spirit of truth, is come, he will guide you into all truth: for he shall not speak of himself; but whatsoever he shall hear, that shall he speak: and he will show you things to come. KJV*

So, as we continue our search I would like you to be aware that this is neither just a scholarly work, nor an opinion put to ink, but it is a little of both.

Are we open to new ideas?

Almost everyone on the planet knows that we are in an age where so much knowledge is available that we often presume we have all things figured out. In 1899, the Commissioner of the U.S. patent office suggested the government close down that office because there was nothing left to invent. Charles H. Duell reportedly announced, "*everything that can be invented has been invented.*"

Today inventors and inventions continue to prosper and we are no closer to knowing everything there is to know in the field of inventions than we are in knowing all there is to know about Scripture and history. We still have a lot to learn and develop in our societies around the world. It is ever more important today that we do not claim the ideas we have received to be accurate and correct for the past hundreds of years are the conclusion of the matter. Rather we ought to be willing to look at many things once thought to be "gospel," from a different perspective.

It may seem implausible that our understanding of Satan as handed down from the Greek thinking Church fathers of the first centuries of this Common Era might need some adjusting. It may be difficult to believe that the common Satan doctrine that is maintained by North American Christianity is in fact not exactly as it seems. Is it possible that we, who believe we have been taught correct Biblical perspective of Satan, are the victims, in a sense, of an erroneous concept and understanding of Satan that has evolved since the pre-exilic period of the Israelites? Do we have the ability to look at a concept or doctrine that has been established for millennia and rethink it from a more advanced perspective? Our understanding of Satan is not the same as the understanding the Messiah had in the first century when He walked the earth in human form.

In his book tilted *The Art of Making Sense,* Lionel Ruby puts forth a truly profound statement. Ruby says;

> *It is difficult to think well in a field which involves our emotions and self-interest. We often simply forget that we ought to exercisc our critical powers. We become dogmatic and make positive and arrogant assertions without proof. We may become blind fanatics and stop thinking all together. We become followers of authorities without ever inquiring as to whether their pronouncements can be justified by the evidence*

The claim of the existence of a literal Satan cannot be justified by evidence. It is very likely we can benefit spiritually from perhaps a more Biblically correct understanding of an issue that is incorrectly understood by the masses. Are we at risk of accepting the present understanding of "Satan" and being content with our belief because it keeps us at a comfortable level of understanding with little challenge to our established belief system? All we need ask ourselves is, "Is it possible?..... Is it possible we are wrong on who or what satan is?"

The truth is hidden in mountains of time and buried under piles of Greek and Greco-Roman philosophy handed down and continually spun through the ages. It is possible that once the "Early Church Fathers" became disconnected from a Hebraic pattern of worship and understanding of Old Testament theology that they endorsed and expounded a concept of "Satan" which was never found in the Faith of Yeshua. The Church Fathers worked hard to explain what the demons of other religions were and they decided at one point, that the demons were fallen angels and to be placed in the same category as "Satan". Clement of Alexander (circa 150-213 CE) was the first major Christian writer to claim that the gods of other religions were demons: "*The verdict of the prophets is that the gods of all the nations are images of demons.*"[16]

Is it possible that the Creator of the Universe has remained the same on the concept of Satan, and we the creation, have changed the concept and in so doing we ourselves have changed? Within this change, we may have in some form minimized the fact that there is one God and none else[17] by intimating Satan has the power to thwart, change, or alter the will of the King of the Universe. This attitude towards Satan, when honestly weighed, indicates that Satan has the power to create, making Him a "Creator". Not to mention the inherent idea in the Satan theology that Satan's demons have the power to procreate as is incorrectly understood of the "sons of God coming in unto the daughters of men," in Genesis Chapter Six[18] by many in Christianity and

---

16 Saint Clement, "*Exorcism to the Greeks*," quoted in G. Messandé,"*The History of the Devil*", p. 262

17 Isaiah 45:5 KJVR
I *am* the LORD, and *there is* none else, *there is* no God beside me: I girded thee, though thou hast not known me:
Isaiah 45:6 KJVR
That they may know from the rising of the sun, and from the west, that *there is* none beside me. I *am* the LORD, and *there is* none else.
Isaiah 45:21 KJVR
Tell ye, and bring *them* near; yea, let them take counsel together: who hath declared this from ancient time? *who* hath told it from that time? *have* not I the LORD? and *there is* no God else beside me; a just God and a Savior; *there is* none beside me.

18 **Genesis 6:4** There were giants in the earth in those days; and also after that, when the sons of God came in unto the daughters of men, and they bare *children* to them, the same *became* mighty men which *were* of old, men of renown.
The concept of the "sons of God" referring to the fallen angels who then spawned demons with the women of the earth is a concept that, if true, indicates Satan's demons have the power to procreate and have organs for sexual function. These notions will not stand up to the light of Scripture and the following excerpt from a popular bible commentary sheds some light on the matter. Please peruse the topic on your own if you need more answers to this issue.
Gen 6:4 - There were giants in the earth in those days,.... That is, in the days before the sons of God took the daughters of men for wives, in such a general manner as before declared, or before the declension and apostasy became so universal; even in the times of Jared, as the Arabic writers (n) understand it, who say that these giants were begotten on the daughters of Cain by the children of Seth, who went down from the mountain to them in the days of Jared, see Gen 5:20 the word "Nephilim" comes from a word which signifies to fall; and these might be so called, either because they made their fear to fall upon men, or men, through fear, to fall before them, because of their height and strength;

Judaism. In an article on the textual controversy surrounding this issue we are given a brief explanation of this theory and its relevance to early Rabbinic and Christian thinkers.

> The strange events recorded in Genesis 6 were understood by the ancient rabbinical sources, as well as the Septuagint translators, as referring to *fallen angels* procreating weird hybrid offspring with human women-known as the "*Nephilim.*" So it was also understood by the early church fathers. These bizarre events are also echoed in the legends and myths of *every* ancient culture upon the earth: the ancient Greeks, the Egyptians, the Hindus, the South Sea Islanders, the American Indians, and virtually all the others.[19]

Ancient mythology has long put forth the belief that the gods impregnated human women to bring forth their progeny. The Scriptures are clear that there is only one God; therefore, there is only one power with the attribute and ability to create. This would very likely render the probability of a" fallen angel" procreating as a far stretch from the purpose in Yahweh's created angelic order. The desire to imbue an ancient Biblical narrative with mystical meaning has led scholars far off the mark on Genesis 6. Many of those men and women have deceived themselves by the desires in their own heart.

Is it not accurate that the heart is deceitfully wicked above all else, just as Jeremiah tells us?

> *The heart is deceitful above all things, and desperately wicked: who can know it? Jeremiah 17:9*

Perhaps we cannot trust even our own hearts to give us clear guidance on concluding what the truth is about Satan but what we can trust is the word of Yahweh that stands forever.

Revealing the truth about the non-existence of satan has its advantages. There are a number of folks that I have had the privilege of dialoguing with about the issue of Satan. As they have come to an understanding that there is likely no horned, spike tailed, celestial nemesis to attack and oppress us as

---

or rather because they fell and rushed on men with great violence, and oppressed them in a cruel and tyrannical manner; or, as some think, because they fell off and were apostates from the true religion, which is much better than to understand them of apostate angels, whom the Targum of Jonathan mentions by name, and calls them Schanchazai and Uziel, who fell from heaven, and were in the earth in those days:

19 Mischievous Angels or Sethites? *From John Gills Entire Exposition of the Bible by Chuck Missler http://www.khouse.org/articles/1997/110/*

believers of Yahweh in Messiah, they enjoyed a renewed liberty in their walk of faith and no longer presume that all the negative "karma" is from Satan. They soon found that they no longer feared him and his works. Fear has been a result of a belief in Satan for far too long.

The little child that is told that Satan will be watching for him or her to slip up and sin so he can find a way into the crack in the door to their heart is not an uncommon way to invoke fear of a supernatural demon in a small child. Images from the renaissance period that depict the dogs of hell devouring innocents bring people to their knees with rosary beads and prescribed prayers intended to be used to chase away the attacking satan. The fear of encountering a demon or a devil in the night has kept young women from enjoying a midnight walk with a friend or husband. Even the most faithful in the Christian faith have been given near panic attacks, supposing that they haven't been righteous enough to warrant protection from God against the horned beast of malevolence.

Undoubtedly, fear has its purpose in any person's life and properly placed fear serves a person well if they manage it well and allow fear to be a factor in keeping them safe from harm. Are we supposed to fear a Satan creature? Who and what are we told to fear in the Scripture? One certain thing is, if there is a Satan we are nowhere told in the Bible to fear him. As you may know, we are told to fear the God of the universe only. The following verses are a sampling of passages that indicate who it is we are to fear. The fear spoken of here is not a paralyzing spine tingling fear of evil one might experience when manifesting a fear of Satan. It is a fear of awe that is worthy of a Creator who spoke and the earth was created and who brought plagues on Egypt to mock its false gods. Let's hear these statements encouraging us to fear God.

> *Ecclesiastes 12:13*
> *Let us hear the conclusion of the whole matter: Fear God, and keep his commandments: for this is the whole duty of man.*

> *1Samuel 12:24*
> *Only fear the LORD, and serve him in truth with all your heart: for consider how great things he hath done for you.*

> *1Peter 2:17*
> *Honour all men. Love the brotherhood. Fear God. Honour the king.*

> *Revelations 19:5*
> *And a voice came out of the throne, saying, Praise our God, all ye his servants, and ye that fear him, both small and great.*

The difficulty that many have with leaving behind an incorrect understanding of satan is that evil has to be attributed to a source. With Satan out of the picture, as the man hating bad guy, we are left with only two sources to blame for evil.

Dare I be so bold as to say a primary source of evil is the Creator of the universe, Yahweh, God Almighty? I ask that you trust what the Scriptures say on this and not the words of my pen. We stand to gain immensely by understanding that there are no other Gods and any who believe in a cosmic Satan are at risk of being guilty of idolatry, for their beliefs testify that there is more than the One God of the Universe. Isaiah speaks expressly of there existing only one supernatural force in the entire universe and both Isaiah and Amos repeat the claim that evil comes from that One God. This is stated in the following passages from these prophets.

> *That they may know from the rising of the sun, and from the west, that there is none beside me. I am the LORD, and there is none else.*
> *I form the light, and create darkness: I make peace, and create evil: I the LORD do all these things. Isaiah 45:6-7*

> *Shall a trumpet be blown in the city, and the people not be afraid? shall there be evil in a city, and the LORD hath not done it? Amos 3:6*

In the above passages the Hebrew word for "evil" is the word *rawah* and is translated elsewhere as *adversity, affliction, badness, calamity, distress, displeasure, misery, naught.* The concept of a satanic being[20]exerting some measure of control over the world is so interwoven in our culture that the concept becomes elusive in trying to pin it down to a point in history where it started. Ancient Egypt, Accadia, and Persia all had a philosophy of an evil force that must be appeased or it would turn on humanity, however the Persians were the truly dualistic culture that moved the idea of a good god and bad god forward. This was noted in the previous pages as Paul Carus was quoted. Here is his statement again for reflection:

---

20 "satanic being"- This term will throughout this paper refer to the contemporary understanding of Satan. This means that it refers to an alleged angel created by Yahweh before the earth was created and this angel rebelled against Yahweh because of his pride, was cast down to earth, and now is the ruler of hell committed to destroying mankind and drawing mankind away from a relationship with the Creator through tempting mankind to sin and in essence to rebel against the Creator as well

> *Since the lower classes began to make their influence felt, it is natural that in the Apocryphal Books of the Old Testament the conception of Satan grew more mythological and at the same time more dualistic. He developed into an independent demon of evil, and now, perhaps under the influence of Persian views, the adversary of man became the adversary of God himself.*[21]

The vagueness about the whole idea will prove to be an adequate adversary itself in preventing the unearthing of a simple answer or solution to the question and problem. Meaning, if the clues were clearly recognizable and easily found, we would not be faced with the daunting task of re-assessing the entire Scripture to see how it lines up the fact that Satan does not exist as a literal entity. Although thousands in the past and millions in the present have propounded this concept, it is seen as impossibility and is readily rejected as a ridiculous theory by most in religions like Christianity today. It is an intriguing exercise to consider what Christianity, and Judaism, or Islam for that matter, would be like if there proves to be no Satan. One suggestion would be that a lot of people would be teetering on questionable faith to find out that all the evil done against them was done by men with wicked hearts. Even more striking is the thought that God has done the evil to them just as those hearing Isaiah were shocked to know that God creates evil.(See Isaiah 45:6-7)

I encourage you though not to be too hasty to dismiss what seems to be a "new idea" when in fact it is a very old idea revisited. We must remember that the world was flat according to some in the ruling empire at one point in time and evidence suggested for a few hundred years that this was a verifiable fact. Although the Greeks and others had understood that the Earth was round centuries before the flat Earth proponents began their work, the thinking that the Earth was flat, seemed to be based on all the mainstream science and literature at that time. Therefore, seeing that something once known to be true can be lost and then reclaimed, I contend that it is possible to reclaim a truth and eliminate an error that has been embedded in our minds and culture through pervasive and persuasive ideas, thoughts and concepts which were brought into mainstream thought from ancient mythology and paganism. That truth is of Satan not existing as a cosmic force but that "satan" is an adversarial force from Yahweh or an adversarial force from man.

As we embark on this journey of learning what "satan" really is, I will provide a couple of house keeping points, so to speak, to aid in the process. Firstly, where Scripture is quoted at length, it will be done so in line with the

21 Paul Carus. *The History Of The Devil And the Idea of Evil From the Earliest Times to The Present Day, from chapter, The Dawning of a New Era*

body of the text at times and at other times, it will be placed in the footnotes. Secondly, because of the obscure and difficult nature of the topic, I will state my conclusion in a very general sense in this first chapter and then articulate the position and its intricacies throughout the pages of this discussion. So in order to diligently pursue the truth, let's be faithful and do as Paul told the Thessalonians in his letter to them when he told them to test, examine, prove, scrutinize to see whether a thing is accurate or not;

> Prove[22] all things; hold fast that which is good. 1Thessalonians 5:21

It is prudent to make an effort to prove those beliefs that are held as sacred cows so to speak. That means every person interested in truth must test the things believed to be true, which have not been thoroughly investigated with each of us taking the time to prove to ourselves that they are true.

Most North Americans and many from other continents have been subject to a default education about Satan but have not chosen to pursue it further. It is by default that so many of us have even learned a concept or understanding about Satan. I say this concept is by default because there was little to no choice for the learner as to whether or not they would receive an education on the topic, but rather, they were simply subjected to the predominant point of view of the social group they are most exposed to. Once taught incorrectly, time caused the roots of that incorrect teaching to go very deep.

The point is, that what we are taught about someone or something from the beginning is often the only reality that we know. All our decisions and conclusions about a person are solely based on the information we believe about them. More likely than not, the first thing we are presented with about a person or concept is received as the truth. It is not until the scales of proof are loaded with enough evidence that they are tipped in the opposite direction and a new truth begins to replace a previously believed concept. So many neglect the duty to examine all of their beliefs in a critical manner that therefore a paradigm shift for them is next to impossible.

Bob McCue, the ex Mormon, current exposer of Mormonism, writes in numerous articles about the extreme difficulty humans have in changing a belief that has been part of their life for an extended period. He writes; "Once we have a particular belief and have built a life around it, we are highly resistant to any information that suggest our belief is incorrect."

---

22 According to Thayer's Definition, prove means;:
1) to test, examine, prove, scrutinize (to see whether a thing is genuine or not), as metals

McCue goes on to explain that evidence must be piled up high on the side of our scale that is opposite to the dogmatic belief we once held. I agree with McCue that the tipping point often takes mountains of information, thought, and time. Often the result in a dramatic paradigm shift is a wonderful experience of celebrating the insight one has received. Often with this fundamental change in a belief come many emotions that cause the newly "enlightened" one to question their decision. The principle is the same for most people who adhere to a long held belief on practically any subject.

For instance, when my son Olli was about 4 or 5 years old he had seen me playing chess with his big brother Cass. It was easier for me to teach Oliver how to play checkers than it was to play chess, so we started using the chess set to play checkers. Soon he was jumping my men diagonally across the board to victory. A little over a year later after numerous games of checkers had been played with the chess pieces; we acquired a new chess set. Oliver was now ready to learn how to play chess. So we sat down on the floor and I showed Olli how to set up the pieces. At first, Oliver endeavored to correct me but after a lengthy explanation, I convinced him that this was a different game. Oliver continued to move his pieces diagonally, just as I had taught him in the games of checkers we had played previously using these same pieces. I quickly saw that Oliver had been taught a specific way to use the pieces and for him to change made for a challenging time of convincing him otherwise. This is little different with the religious concepts many of us have been taught early on in our religious walk. People taught a specific practice or concept generally believe that first concept to be true and correct. Many of us have been taught certain aspects of our faith and belief system, and because they were the first concepts we were fed, we now believe and accept those concepts as true and find it unnecessary to question them.

The resistance to changing core beliefs is not only common in today's society, it has been a formidable barrier to overcome for most, if not all, of known history. There was a time when the Roman Catholic institution was battling over the issue of whether the Sun or the Earth was the center of our solar system. Until that point, it was common knowledge that everything revolved around the Earth. The story of Copernicus shows the difficulties he went through to present the truth to some very entrenched people with a much-solidified belief that claimed the Earth was the center of the universe. Copernicus brought his research that testified to a heliocentric universe but the religious leaders who played a major role in politics, demanded Copernicus was wrong and that he had better "lose" his information because the Earth, they said, is the center of the universe. Copernicus was silenced, and the Ptolemaic view of the Earth being a fixed immovable object continued to be taught by the leaders who rejected

Copernicus and placed a moratorium on his scholarly predecessor Galileo.[23] Often, people have been led to believe incorrect information about a person or idea, only to be introduced to more correct information later on. At that point, they are faced with the challenge of having or rejecting a paradigm shift.

In countless cases, we have been given information about "Satan" that has led us to conclude that Satan is a fallen angel. Because of his pride and rebellion, he is trying to defeat Yahweh and rule the world through destruction of all that is good and those people that are good. The most prolific of religious institutions in the world is arguably the Catholic Church. We find in the widely published *Catechism of the Catholic Faith,* a statement of the fallen "satan" which is mirrored and mimicked in most of protestant Christianity, and seen in Islam and Judaism. In the section titled *The Fall of The Angels*, the message is as follows;

> **391** Behind the disobedient choice of our first parents lurks a seductive voice, opposed to God, which makes them fall into death out of envy.[266] Scripture and the Church's Tradition see in this being a fallen angel, called "Satan" or the "devil".[267] The Church teaches that Satan was at first a good angel, made by God: "The devil and the other demons were indeed created naturally good by God, but they became evil by their own doing."[268]

---

23 In 1530, Copernicus completed and gave to the world his great work *De Revolutionibus*, which asserted that the earth rotated on its axis once daily and traveled around the sun once yearly: a fantastic concept for the times. Up to the time of Copernicus the thinkers of the western world believed in the Ptolemiac theory that the universe was a closed space bounded by a spherical envelope beyond which there was nothing

Copernicus died in 1543 and was never to know what a stir his work had caused. It went against the philosophical and religious beliefs that had been held during the medieval times.

Two other Italian scientists of the time, Galileo and Bruno, embraced the Copernican theory unreservedly and as a result suffered much personal injury at the hands of the powerful church inquisitors. Giordano Bruno had the audacity to even go beyond Copernicus, and, dared to suggest, that space was boundless and that the sun was and its planets were but one of any number of similar systems: Why! -- there even might be other inhabited worlds with rational beings equal or possibly superior to ourselves. For such blasphemy, Bruno was tried before the Inquisition, condemned and burned at the stake in 1600. Galileo was brought forward in 1633, and, there, in front of his "betters," he was, under the threat of torture and death, forced to his knees to renounce all belief in Copernican theories, and was thereafter sentenced to imprisonment for the remainder of his days.

http://www.blupete.com/Literature/Biographies/Science/Copernicus.htm

> **392** Scripture speaks of a sin of these angels.[269] This "fall" consists in the free choice of these created spirits, who radically and irrevocably *rejected* God and his reign.[24]

As we continue through this book, the concepts I express will be elaborated on thoroughly. Some who have difficulty accepting the view presented here may ask if it is sensible to try to prove that the devil does not exist. I am not certain how Poet Charles-Pierre Baudelaire came to his conclusion, but somehow in his works he decided that the "Devils deepest wile was to persuade us that he does not exist."

I cannot say that I agree with Baudelaire as it seems that his premise is to assume that there is a "Satan" and if this mythological evil being can trick us into thinking that he doesn't exist, then we will find ourselves wandering aimlessly into sin because we will think that there is no sin. Although Baudelaire was not a theologian but a masterful poet, he clearly expressed many theological views in his poetry as all great poets are inclined to do. It seems in his statement telling of the devil's deepest wile, that he believed what he wrote. It seems Baudelaire also believed the reason the devil existed was to fool humankind into sin.

I think one might want to consider the very opposite of his words and realize that to believe Satan doesn't exist is one of the most liberating of conclusions and not a "wile" at all. The person is then able to truly live a monotheistic faith and accept the complete sovereignty of the Creator. This result is so because, as we will discuss often in this work, the belief in another supernatural power whether or not it is assigned a lesser role than the Supreme Being, is a form of dualism and testifies that there are at least two Gods. That person will experience the solemn realization that there is nothing in the cosmos that causes them to sin but that they themselves are responsible for all the sin that they have chosen to do, and that there does not exist a Satanic influencing force, which has the power to move man to choose evil. Admittedly, there are proponents of a cosmic Satan who do not claim Satan made them do it. However, they are in effect only slightly closer to a true monotheism than are those who attribute sin and evil acts to the supposed "Satan".

---

24 **Catechism of the Catholic Church PART ONE THE PROFESSION OF FAITH** ; **SECTION TWO**
THE PROFESSION OF THE CHRISTIAN FAITH; CHAPTER ONE; I BELIEVE IN GOD THE FATHER; **ARTICLE I**
"I BELIEVE IN GOD THE FATHER ALMIGHTY, CREATOR OF HEAVEN AND EARTH" Paragraph 7. The Fall

CHAPTER 2

Satan, Evil Force at Creation or Man Created with a Potential for Evil?

Is It Even Logical To Have A Satan In God's World?

In proving there is no Satan, I am left with no other choice but to assess the logic of the mythical concept of a Satan and to consider some of the inconsistencies in the general North American belief about "satan". In the "New Testament", we are told that Christ came to destroy the works of the devil. If *the Son of God was manifested, that he might destroy the works of the devil,* should we not attempt to correctly understand just what that work of the Messiah is supposed to have accomplished and what or who the devil is? First take a look at the whole verse, which tells of the reason, or at least one of the reasons, Christ, came.

> *He that committeth sin is of the devil; for the devil sinneth from the beginning. For this purpose the Son of God was manifested, that he might destroy the works of the devil. 1John 3:8*

The entire concept of a devil and the existence of "Satan" is inextricably wrapped up in theology and the Bible. Therefore, I am presenting an argument against the existence of "satan" and the "devil", which are seen as one and the same. This can only be done using the theological work that is most commonly employed in developing a doctrine of the person of "satan. The use of the Bible in this work will be extensive and at times overwhelming to some who have not built a familiarity with the Bible to any degree. If you must, feel free to excuse yourself from sections of this study that become clunky due to the need to process Biblical information. Although most authors want the reader to ingest every word they have penned, it is completely understandable for certain readers to have less need or desire to consume entirely every word placed before them in this book.

What then are the works of the devil that Christ came to destroy in the above verse? In short, the "*works of the devil*" are the sin and rebellion that is inherent in humanity. The *devil, satan, the serpent, the dragon, the evil one, the enemy of our souls* are in fact references to various things that all relate to the wickedness in man. Satan as a noun is shown in the Scriptures to be an agent of the Almighty. The word in the Hebrew is *ha sawtawn* [25]or *the satan,* and is properly translated as opposer or adversary. The Holy Scriptures, the Hebrew Scriptures, are the only documents that are said by apostles like Paul to be good for making doctrine. According to that fact, any doctrine on Satan must be derived from a thorough and correct understanding of the doctrine found in the Hebrew Scriptures. In his letter to the young protégé, Paul tells Timothy that the Hebrew Bible is the choice of writings to find and understand doctrine. Here Paul teaches that doctrine is to be found in the Hebrew Scripture. Paul means to remind Timothy that any doctrine that is used in the faith community must be found in the Old Testament. I have added emphasis to the key statement below;

> *And that from a child thou hast known the holy scriptures, which are able to make thee wise unto salvation through faith which is in Christ Jesus.*
> ***All scripture is given by inspiration of God, and is profitable for doctrine,*** *for reproof, for correction, for instruction in righteousness: That the man of God may be perfect, throughly furnished unto all good works. 2Timothy 3:15-17*

In the Holy Scriptures, "Satan" or the adversarial force called at times an evil spirit or a lying spirit, is always dispatched by Yahweh, and must submit to His will. This force is seen specifically in Numbers 22 as a "*sawtawn*" but is not called Satan in the English. Rather it is called *adversary* and is sent from Yahweh to be an adversary to Balaam as he goes out to curse the children of Israel for money. In addition, in Judges 9:23 while not specifically called *sawtawn,* there is an evil spirit sent from God between Abimelech and the

---

25 **H7854**שׂ טן
śạtan *saw-tawn'*
From H7853; **an *opponent*;** especially (with the article prefixed) *Satan*, the archenemy of good: - adversary, Satan, withstand.

men of Shechem. Also recognized as an evil spirit from Yahweh, we see in first Samuel 16 that when the Spirit of the Lord is taken from Saul an evil spirit from the Lord is given to the rebellious king.

Satan, or the Hebrew term *sawtawn,* is a title for a particular office or ministry and can be the title of any manifestation that is used by the Father to place obstacles and choices in the path of His people, to cause His will to be played out and cause the human to make a choice. Just as the title Adonai or LORD in English, has been taken to be the name of the creator, so too has the term "satan" been taken to be the name for the supposed archenemy of God and man. The Hebrew word *sawtawn,* has mistakenly been used as a name for what is often thought of as the opposite power to the Creator. Here is the definition as the International Standard Bible Encyclopedia gives; it is given for the Hebrew and then the Greek;

> **Satan**
>
> **sā´tan (שׂ טן, *sāṭān*)**, "adversary," from the verb שׂ טן, *sāṭan*, "to lie in wait" (as adversary);
>
> **Σατᾶν, *Satán*, Σατανᾶς, *Satanás***, "adversary,"
>
> διάβολος, *diábolos*, "Devil," "adversary" or "accuser," κατήγωρ, *katḗgōr*

The word "Satan" as a verb is referring to that power or characteristic that is active in every human being who opposes the will of the Almighty Creator. Satan as a verb is referring to the human will that chooses to disobey the will of the Father. The word satan is intended to indicate behavior that is born out of rebellion, as well as behavior or attitudes that oppose the plan of Yahweh and His Messiah. Anyone can be Satan, particularly if one is acting against the will of Yahweh.

When the God of the Universe calls you "Satan", are you Satan?

Consider the logic in Yeshua calling Peter, Satan, and saying that the Pharisees were devils. I would like to explore the importance of the words that proceeded from the mouth of Yeshua. First, we must make note of the thinking that Yeshua is God in the flesh. Consider for a moment that you are the God of the Universe. If you were the God of the Universe and had come down to walk with your creation in the flesh, would you not hope that the words that came from your mouth would be taken seriously? Would it be fair to assume your words would be seen as "gospel", to use a common phrase? If you were the Messiah of Israel or claimed to be, and you knew that there is a prophecy about you in Deuteronomy 18, that said Israel was supposed to listen to you, would you not expect that those who hearkened to the prophecy and then to your words would likely take very seriously any words that passed from your lips? Deuteronomy 18 tells us that God will raise up a prophet from among the children of Israel and that they are to listen to Him;

> *God will raise up unto thee a Prophet from the midst of thee, of thy brethren, like unto me; unto him ye shall hearken;*[26]

We are also told in Deuteronomy that this prophet, who I am suggesting is Yeshua, *will speak all that Yahweh commands Him to speak*[27]. Therefore, the children of Israel would always be waiting for the one who makes claim, by word or by deed, to be that prophet... Enter Yeshua...

In the Book of John, Yeshua makes it very clear in his clever rabbinic style of revealing who He is, that he is that prophet. Yeshua says; "*For I have not spoken of myself; but the Father which sent me, he gave me a commandment.*"[28] Moreover, He reiterates the point by saying; "*whatsoever I speak therefore, even as the Father said unto me, so I speak.*[29]"

Yeshua, in making these statements, has just dropped an irrefutable clue that He is the one who was said to come. He is the one to be heard and therefore the words that He spoke held far greater authority than if He were just another man claiming to have wisdom. Notice the prophecy says *He will speak that which the Father commands him* and then in the gospel of John the Messiah says, "*He gave me commandment*"; and he also said, "*even as the Father said unto me so I speak.*" Those looking for the Messiah, the one they knew to be God incarnate, would not miss the connection. The Messiah often performed acts and made statements that pointed to words about Him in the Holy Scriptures so those in His presence could find out who He was. The

---

26 Deu 18:15 YAHWEH thy God will raise up unto thee a Prophet from the midst of thee, of thy brethren, like unto me; unto him ye shall hearken;

27 Deu 18:18 I will raise them up a Prophet from among their brethren, like unto thee, and will put my words in his mouth; and he shall speak unto them all that I shall command him.

28 John 12:49 For I have not spoken of myself; but the Father which sent me, he gave me a commandment, what I should say, and what I should speak

29 John 12:50 And I know that his commandment is life everlasting: whatsoever I speak therefore, even as the Father said unto me, so I speak.

point is arguable according to some, but there is no doubt that the Apostles and followers of Messiah came to believe that He is the incarnate God of the Universe and therefore, He was worthy to be heard and His words were like gold. Holding this divine office as the Messiah of Israel and being aware that those you were speaking to knew of the prophecies from the Torah about you, you would be extremely intentional with the words you used and the names and descriptors you called people. You are the God of the Universe. Your words matter and not one of them is an idle word. Therefore if you were to call a group of people a brood of vipers either that group of people would actually be a literal brood of vipers, which are snakes or serpents, or you would be using a current metaphor to describe a type of behavioral pattern for the said group of people. The logic of the issue is that Yeshua was a master of metaphor and many of His words were not to be taken literally. He used metaphor in a way that illuminated a deeper truth for those who were perceptive. Calling someone a viper was not to say they are a viper but was speaking about their behavior. If one decides to assign a literal meaning to most uses of the words *satan* and *devil* in the Apostolic Testimony, then one should be consistent and do the same in the instances we are presently discussing. However, logic does not always dictate how one interprets the New Testament writings that seem to speak of a "Satan". What one has been taught previously becomes the filter through which most people interpret these passages. If one is going to be logical and consistent in his interpretation of these passages then when Yeshua said He saw "Satan" fall from heaven like lightning, and elsewhere He calls Peter "Satan", then a consistent assessment of these sayings would conclude that Peter was Satan that fell from Heaven.

Consider this thought further. If you, the Sovereign over all, were to call a friend and companion Satan, with a capital "S" according to the manner seen in the New Testament, and because you are God in the flesh, should one not expect that Peter your companion and disciple is then Satan? After all, the convenient choice to accept other references to Satan as literal should apply in this instance as well; that is if interpretation of passages is consistent and logical. Let's look at the verse where Peter is called Satan.

> *But he turned, and said unto Peter, Get thee behind me, Satan: thou art an offence unto me: for thou savourest not the things that be of God, but those that be of men. Matthew 16:23*

As you see, the Messiah just called Peter "Satan." Could it be possible that Peter is Satan, the fallen angel that works feverishly to thwart the plan of God? Or is it more likely that Yeshua understood the concept of satan as a term to describe a person's anti-god behavior and was in fact using the word properly as a term referring to Peter's desires and not to declare an appellation? Yeshua was using the term "satan" with the frame of reference that anyone who opposes the will of the Father is an adversary or opposer, hence can be, and in fact is then considered Satan or a satan.

Yeshua was not confused about what satan was when he called Peter "Satan". Yeshua understood, as He knew Peter would, that calling Peter satan was simply in this instance a scolding to a student. Peter was a follower of Yeshua, therefore the rabbi Yeshua intended to admonish the student in a way that would cause the student to realize that he is opposing the plan of Yahweh when Peter made the statement *"...this shall not be unto thee,"*[30] in reference to the upcoming execution of Yeshua. If logic is to prevail in this discussion we must consider how one of us might feel if we were in Peter's position. Say we believed Satan was the archenemy of Yahweh and our master then called us Satan, would we feel uplifted and encouraged by such a comment? No, being called Satan would be crushing. The power of suggestion alone from a man who taught with so much authority would cause deep feelings of insignificance. Can you picture the face of a 5 year old that makes a statement to his daddy saying; "Daddy, you're like Superman!" Then the daddy turns around and says, "Don't be stupid, I'm nothing like Superman!"

The child's face and heart would sink just like Peter's heart must have sank if he was a believer in a cosmic Satan and was just then told that he was Satan by the greatest Rabbi he ever had the privilege of sitting under. I feel weakened just thinking about it. If it were I in Peter's shoes, I can only imagine how crushed I would be. Thankfully the Greek term Yeshua used, was not understood by Peter as the name of a cosmic super-being, fallen angel. What a discouraging picture for Peter. Peter had just shared some intensely deep and meaningful moments with his Rabbi Yeshua, who has just asked who the disciples thought he is. There were plenty of indicators who He was; He had been performing some potent miracles. If you or I were Peter, we knew Yahweh could perform miracles through anyone. We've read the scrolls and heard the teaching in the synagogues. As Jewish Disciples of Christ, we knew that Yahweh controls everything and has done countless miracles since the day of creation. If I were Peter, I would have been in the situation where I had been walking with this amazing Rabbi who has performed miracles for a few years now. This Rabbi was not like other rabbis, he was the Messiah, God in the flesh. I could see no reason why he might want to spend time with me, a fisherman with a kind of unpredictable edge. And if I'm being honest, I'm not even really that smart. The Rabbi I love asks me and the guys, "*Who*

30 Mat 16:22 Then Peter took him, and began to rebuke him, saying, Be it far from thee, Lord: this shall not be unto thee.

do men say that I am?" Some did think He was John the Baptist or Elijah or Jeremiah or one of the prophets but I knew better.[31] Deep down inside I knew that this Rabbi was more than that and I knew there was no other like him. Then, He asked us, *"But who do you say that I am?"*

In a moment, less than a second, my answer came. It was as if my answer was deep, deep down inside me, just waiting for a chance to come out. Something this monumental often is not fully realized until it is spoken. Often an incredibly, profound piece of information or nugget of truth doesn't really sink in until it comes off our lips. Yeshua asked the question and out popped the answer, *"Thou art the Christ, the son of the Living God."* I didn't understand everything but I did know for 100% certain that I was walking with the Messiah. God in the flesh and I guess we both knew that I wasn't all that brilliant and that's why He said; "*Blessed art thou Simon Bar Jonah, for flesh and blood has not revealed it unto thee, but my father which is in heaven.*" The Messiah just said I'm blessed and that Yahweh has revealed the fact of who He is to me. I don't think I have ever felt so...so warm and so filled with gratitude, yet feeling so special. My Messiah just blessed me and what next? He actually tells me he is giving me the keys of the kingdom of heaven. This means he trusts me and wants me to carry on and spread His message, the message of who he is and the gospel of the kingdom [32]. Then soon after my Messiah tried to tell us of his soon coming death at the hands of the leaders, I told him that it can't be so and He rebuked me and called me Satan. This is almost too much for me to take. I thought I had been given the keys to the kingdom of heaven and now I'm told I'm Satan, how could this be? Blessed

31 Mat 16:13 When Jesus came into the coasts of Caesarea Philippi, he asked his disciples, saying, Whom do men say that I the Son of man am?
Mat 16:14 And they said, Some *say that thou art* John the Baptist: some, Elias; and others, Jeremias, or one of the prophets.
Mat 16:15 He saith unto them, But whom say ye that I am?
Mat 16:16 And Simon Peter answered and said, Thou art the Christ, the Son of the living God.
Mat 16:17 And Jesus answered and said unto him, Blessed art thou, Simon Barjona: for flesh and blood hath not revealed *it* unto thee, but my Father which is in heaven.
Mat 16:18 And I say also unto thee, That thou art Peter, and upon this rock I will build my church; and the gates of hell shall not prevail against it.
Mat 16:19 And I will give unto thee the keys of the kingdom of heaven: and whatsoever thou shalt bind on earth shall be bound in heaven: and whatsoever thou shalt loose on earth shall be loosed in heaven.
Mat 16:20 Then charged he his disciples that they should tell no man that he was Jesus the Christ.

32 Mat 4:17 From that time Jesus began to preach, and to say, Repent: for the kingdom of heaven is at hand.

by the Messiah in one breath and called Satan in another. That would be awfully difficult to take, especially if I believe in a cosmic Satan and neglect to perceive the real meaning of the term "Satan".

We must consider the magnitude of such an event in light of the absence of a literal being called "satan". It is utter lunacy to think that the God of the Universe is calling His number one boy "Satan", particularly if the concept of Satan as a literal being fighting against God and His people is factual. Obviously, the Messiah knew what it meant to call someone Satan. It meant that someone is not presently performing the will of the Father and for the moment at least, is an adversary. That is exactly how He defines the term "satan" in the very sentence that he called Peter Satan; the definition is as follows;

> *for thou savourest not the things that be of God, but those that be of men.*

Yeshua knew a "satan" was anyone or anything that opposes the will of God. Peter too knew Yeshua didn't believe him to be the archenemy of Yahweh, but I am certain Peter knew that he needed to alter his thinking and get in line with the plan of the Father for under his current mode of thought Peter was being an adversary to the perfect plan of the creator and therefore was being a 'satan". A satan can be one who does not savor the things of God perhaps for the moment or perhaps for a lifetime.

I am afraid we have been taught wrongly who or what Satan is instead of being taught that Satan is a God-appointed and dispatched minister. A minister that acts as an adversary to force one's hand, so to speak, to make a choice to come in line with the will of God. or satan is that behavior of rebellion that is deep within the heart of mankind and desires that we as human beings with the power to choose, are continually bent on doing evil and in essence our own will. Therefore, Satan is not a being but is a feature or aspect of human behavior.

The illogical and inconsistent interpretation of the uses of the word "satan" has brought many to wrongly conclude that a reference to a literal created being is made when mention of the word "satan" occurs. From here, we will take a look at how the concept of Satan is developed in the Scriptures from the beginning and what better place to start than the beginning.

Does the Scripture Show that Satan Fell at Creation?

Satan was supposedly an angel who predated the creation of man and is said by some to have been in heaven at the beginning of creation. The concept of an angel that was exalted above all other angels has been taught for centuries and if this is the case then we should be able to see some mention of this pre-existent creation in the Genesis account. Clues of this belief are only found in the eisegesis of certain biblical texts. Eisegesis is reading into a text and developing a theological understanding of it based on information that is not mentioned in the text. Many have searched and searched the Genesis account of creation but have not been able to come up with a comprehensive indication of a special angel in the heavenlies that had abilities and powers that caused him to think he could rival God. What does come through though in the Genesis account is that Yahweh created man with an ability to choose good or evil. We also see that Yahweh placed the choice for evil before man and a little beyond the Garden of Eden story we see that God identifies man's heart as the seat of evil as it is said to be inclined towards evil continually in Genesis chapter 6;

> *And GOD saw that the wickedness of man was great in the earth, and that every imagination of the thoughts of his heart was only evil continually. Genesis 6:5*

Assessing the creation account to see where the root of evil is will help us formulate an informed conclusion on the non-existence of satan. There are definite indicators that inform us of evil being a product of humanity and therefore not being attributed to Satan. Notice in the opening verses of the book of Genesis that there was only darkness before God decided to create light. Could this darkness be the Satan that religions like Christianity so feverishly search for in the Scriptures? Let's explore.

> *In the beginning God created the heaven and the earth. And the earth was without form, and void; and darkness was upon the face of the deep. And the Spirit of God moved upon the face of the waters. And God said, Let there be light: and there was light. And God saw the light, that it was good: and God divided the light from the darkness. And God called the light Day, and the darkness he called Night. And the evening and the morning were the first day. Genesis 1:1-5*

This then, is the very start of the entire plan of God the creator of all things and the one who brings order from chaos. God is the one who works a purpose that is not always understandable to our frail and limited human minds. The creation and the Garden of Eden story could very well be the story of time as we know it. It always has been and always will be argued by scholars when and how it happened, and how long this "day" was.

I will not enter into the debate at this time but I will simply state that I believe it is a literal 24 hour day. Aside from espousing numerous arguments in support of my belief, I will simply ask you to take note of the part where we are told, "t*he evening and the morning were the first day.*" As simplistic as this one argument is, even at the time of creation before the sun and the moon were created, Yahweh gave us a huge clue that this was a literal day. Through the hand of the writer of these words, God just may have inferred that creation took place in six literal, 24 hour days. Affixing a contrived, mystical and allegorical meaning to the term "*evening and the morning*", may produce a convincing argument against the literal day idea. However, for the Creator of the universe to use the phrase,, "the *evening and the morning*", one may find means the same thing as that which clearly happens during every 24 hour day since recorded time; there is an evening and a morning in the daily 24 hour period.

As was stated above, the debate of the literal day versus another theory for what a creation day was, is not mine to engage in and the reader will have to pursue that issue on his or her own to gain a proficient understanding. There are multitudes of teachings on the days of creation; one teaching in particular that I have heard in the past is thus:

On the first day of creation when Yahweh separated light from darkness, Satan was expelled from heaven. This teaching suggests that Satan was the "darkness" that was separated from the "light". It is a concept that comes out of rabbinic, Kabalistic thought and is riddled with numerous inconsistencies and difficulties. Inconsistencies such as the problem that arises when the timing of the fall from Heaven is called into question. Gnostic lore posits that Satan fell from his position in Heaven, after man was created, which is days after the separation of light from darkness. The biblical creation order was like this; God created the heavens and the earth, He created light and then separated the light from the darkness on the first day. The second day had God separating the waters above from the waters below and He pooled the waters together that day. Vegetation was created on the third day and then the lights in the sky were brought into existence the next day, day four. On day five, He added fish and marine life to the waters and fowl and flying things to the sky. On the sixth day, the beasts and creeping things of the Earth were made and man was created by the end of the sixth day. The order that is given in Genesis shows darkness separated from light right at the beginning of creation. A biblical view of this is often such that God performed the acts of creation in six literal days and rested on the Sabbath.

Specific to how long a creation day was we hear of another concept that is put forward called the *Gap Theory*. A theory that claims there was a huge amount of time that intervened between the first verse of the book of Genesis and the second verse. The Gap theory asserts that Satan knew about the upcoming creation of man and became jealous and prideful only to be cast out of heaven with all the rebellious angels. There is no reference to either of these thoughts in Genesis and revisionist interpreters imposed the idea backwards on the creation story. The idea of Satan being cast out when light was created suggests that evil and rebellion had now entered the world and did so because Yahweh kicked the evil one out of His presence, the darkness that was separated from the light was representative of "Satan", and the light was representative of God. This is an exceptionally brief encapsulation of this teaching. A teaching which has gained speed out of a misunderstanding of Ezekiel 28 where the King of Tyre is referred to as being in a paradisiacal environment. The topic in Ezekiel is the King of Tyre, a human man, and not a celestial being that rebelled and was ejected from the throne room of the Creator. I quote here excerpts from the text of Ezekiel. (This concept will be addressed in Chapter 9)

> *Son of man, take up a lamentation upon the king of Tyrus, and say unto him, Thus saith the Lord GOD; Thou sealest up the sum, full of wisdom, and perfect in beauty...*
>
> *Thou wast perfect in thy ways from the day that thou wast created, till iniquity was found in thee. Ezekiel 28: 12 and15*

This teaching on an alleged celestial entity being ejected from heaven is also buoyed up by Yeshua's statement in Luke 10 verse 18 where He says, "I saw Satan fall like lighting". These misunderstood passages are viewed through the eyes of one who believes in a cosmic "Satan" and they are tragically infused with a meaning that was not intended by the writer. We will discuss them fully in chapters 8 and 9 and I will also address a loosely associated passage in Isaiah chapter 14, which is said to be speaking of Satan but is talking about the King of Babylon.

Suffice it to say that the theory of Satan being cast out of heaven at the point where Yahweh separated light from darkness does not hold up to a critical examination of the Scriptures. Satan was not the darkness that was separated from light at the beginning of creation. The fact that Yahweh saw and called the light good would indicate that He had just made something new and not something that was pre-existent. God was pre-existent therefore light must not be a reference to His goodness anymore than darkness is a reference to an evil presence. The more plausible understanding would be that there was only darkness and now upon the creation of light Yahweh saw it was a good thing and that the darkness that was there already was simply the absence of light in the universe. In this theory, evil pre-existed everything. Darkness then must not be a representation of Satan because Yahweh certainly did not exist in a universe that contained only evil. The mistaken understanding of the so-called fall from heaven of an angelic being is based on metaphor, that being darkness means evil and Satan, while light means good and God. Surely if both were pre-existent and light being God while darkness was Satan, then Yahweh would not have had to state His approval of the light as if it was appearing for the first time.

The theory that Satan was ejected from Heaven when Yahweh separated light from the darkness is simply another revisionist interpretation that adopts a mystic, Gnostic idea for an ancient Hebraic account of creation.

We will not go through the entire creation account but I will bring you to the next indicator that evil does not emanate from a so-called satanic being. Let's look at the next verse in Genesis, which I ask that you simply keep in mind when we discuss the "Serpent" and for the moment recognize that man's dominion over everything is stated quite explicitly.;

> *And God said, Let us make man in our image, after our likeness: and let them have dominion over the fish of the sea, and over the fowl of the air, and over the cattle, and over all the earth, and over every creeping thing that creepeth upon the earth. Genesis 1:26*

If there were an animal that came up to Adam and Eve in the garden and attempted to get Adam and Eve to do its will then was God mistaken to have said *man will have dominion over all the animals*? To have dominion over the animals means that the animals will be subjugated and ruled over by man. For one of the animals to exhibit behavior that expresses other than the creator's will for man to have dominion, would not be the case. If we are dealing with a real serpent in the Garden of Eden then that animal was not under man's dominion as was supposed to be the case. Therefore, the serpent must be something other than the English word depicts. A thorough study of the serpent in the garden reveals that particular symbol of evil, to be just that, a symbolical representation of the evil inclination that is created in man from the start. In chapters 12 and 13, on the Serpent in the Garden in Genesis, I will unfold the entire concept for you so you will be able to see how Adam and Eve were not confronted by a literal serpent or by a cosmic Satan.

For now, we will continue to discuss how man was created with an inherent potential to choose evil and that this potential to choose evil did not come as a result of an outside, influencing force. In Genesis 1:31, we will see that the Creator has finished His work of creation and proclaims that everything He has created is good.

> *And God saw every thing that he had made, and, behold, it was very good. And the evening and the morning were the sixth day. Genesis 1:31*

This now, is the end of the first account of the days of creation. We see a second account in Genesis chapter 2. Like many dual accounts of activities in the Scripture and the Gospels, we receive slightly different and supplemental information in comparison to the first account. Like any good detective, counselor, or principal that interviews more than one child after an incident or altercation, they combine all the pieces to understand the puzzle as best as can be understood. So too we must take the sum of all the parts. When given additional information in more than one account of a story we should use both stories to build the best possible compilation that is not given too many textual contradictions from pitting the information in one account against the information in the other.

If there is an evil inclination in man, what is it and what is its purpose? In answer to that, I will provide a few quotes from the rabbinic writings of the sages. The first quote below that is found in the Talmud is one of the more controversial statements about the evil inclination because it asserts that the evil inclination is "Satan". In saying this, the message identifies satan not as a cosmic entity but as an attribute or behavior of man;

> R. Simeon ben Lakish said: Satan, impulse to evil, and angel of death: all three are the same thing.[33]

This next quote is part of an article on the Birth of the Good Inclination and speaks of the need for the evil inclination to cause man to make choices that move humankind forward in areas of necessity. In this thought lies the philosophy that the evil inclination is a good thing and Yahweh created man with it so that man would be able to have a free will and find his own path to loyalty and obedience to the God of the Universe.

> The rabbinic duality of *yetzer hara*, the so-called "evil inclination," and *yetzer hatov*, the "good inclination," is more subtle than the

33 Babylonian Talmud, BabaBatra16a:, Reish Lakish

> names connote. Yetzer hara is not a demonic force that pushes a person to do evil, but rather a drive toward pleasure or property or security, which if left unlimited, can lead to evil (cf. Genesis Rabbah 9:7). When properly controlled by the yetzer hatov, the yetzer hara leads to many socially desirable results, including marriage, business, and community.[34]

Many years of Biblical studies have taken place in the Hebrew Union College, the oldest Jewish seminary in the Americas. Rabbi Geoffrey Dennis, ordained at that institution, is of the mind that the evil inclination is for the ultimate good of man. He teaches that were it not for the evil inclination, nothing would get accomplished in this world. Geoffrey says;

> Another such harsh but necessary force in God's creation is the *Yetzer ha-Ra*, which is variously translated as the "Evil Impulse," the "Evil Desire," the "Selfish Desire" or just "Desire." It is that aspect of nature, but especially human nature, which drives us to compete, to fight, to possess, but most of all to desire sexual gratification.

Geoffrey goes on to explain that this necessary force of God's creation would be missed if it were completely overcome so as to have no effect on humanity.

> Without the *Yetzer ha-Ra*, the world as we know would cease – people [and animals] would no longer be driven to build, to create, to have children. In short, life as we know, including not only evil aspects but all that is beautiful also, would cease. Without Desire, Life itself would slowly wither away, and that would be a sad thing. So the goal of the spiritual person is not to destroy the selfish-sexual-evil impulse, but rather to sublimate it to God's purpose.[35]

---

34 The Birth of the Good Inclination By Jeffrey A. Spitzer; http://www.myjewishlearning.com/lifecycle/Bar_Bat_Mitzvah/AboutBarBatMitzvah/HowOld/barmitzvahpsychology.htm

35 Saturday, December 30, 2006; A Necessary Evil: The Yetzer ha-Ra ; Jewish Myth, Magic, and Mysticism; http://ejmmm2007.blogspot.com/2006_12_01_archive.html

Is Satan a Creator?

Therefore, with the answer to what the evil inclination is and what is its purpose is simple. It is the aspect of human nature that prompts us to make a choice by pricking the desire for pleasure. Another question about Satan is, if there is an alter-God in the form of a Satan, does he have the power to create or to add in any way to the creation of God? It is agreed upon almost universally that this Satan can only pervert that which God has created. This belief has been prolific in religious circles for hundreds of years. In a book titled *Rules of Engagement* by Charles Kraft and David M. Debord, we are told of the belief that "Satan" is able to pervert what God does. An interesting affirmation of common religious, Christian thinking is revealed in this book, as these men outline numerous principles of their faith and in doing so they admit to believe that there are two Gods by claiming there are two dispensers of superhuman spiritual power. Here is the full principle as stated in their work.

> ***Principle One**: There are Two Dispensers of Superhuman Spiritual Power - God and Satan*
>
> In observation 1.1 and 1.2 of this book, we are told the following;
>
> Just as God's desire is for the allegiance of the hearts of humankind, so Satan desires that same goal. Just as God requires obedience from those who would have a relationship with Him and be recipients of His authority and protection, so Satan demands obedience from those who are under him and who receive his power and protection. Just as God empowers words for good through blessings, so Satan empowered words for evil through curses.
>
> Satan can only copy, counterfeit or pervert what God has created for His purposes.[36]

If it is true that Satan can only pervert what God has done, then the answer to my second question asking whether or not Satan can create, would be 'No', Satan does not have the power to create. If you find you cannot agree that Satan does not have the power to create, then you will find yourself in the camp that has more than one God. Even the writer of the above book,

---

36 "The Rules of Engagement", published by Wagner Publications (2000) Charles Kraft and David M. Debord

in their admission that they believe Satan has superhuman powers like God; agree that their "Satan" cannot create?

> Even though Satan is a created being, he is sterile and, unlike God, cannot create something from nothing.[37]

A sound conclusion based on most common demonology would agree that "Satan" cannot create. Even if he exists as many posit, he is not a Creator.

If Yahweh placed a choice in the garden for the first man and women would it make sense that He created them with the power, attribute, or ability to choose? Exploring the question of "Free Will" is a much larger subject than I am willing or prepared to tackle at this time, however, why would a Creator place an opportunity for choice in the midst of a perfect environment if He had not imbued His creation, which is man, with the power to make a choice. In fact, we are told that Adam named all the creatures. This would have involved many, many choices so Yahweh would have placed what I'll call a "choosing gene" in humans. The inherent ability to choose evil was built into man from the moment that Yahweh formed man from the dust of the ground and breathed life into him. Now we see that through the days of creation Yahweh saw what He created and called it good. At the end of the sixth day after man was created, Yahweh sees His creation and says it is "very good". So here, we have the Creator of Heaven and Earth, peering down upon His creation, a creation that includes humanity and because Adam was created as a mature adult and complete, he would have both the desire to choose good and the desire to choose evil, pre-programmed within him. Yahweh knew man was created with the genetic potential for "choosing good or evil" and then Yahweh proceeds to call man "very good". In no way does the Creator indicate He is displeased with any single, miniscule part of His creation. Therefore, in essence the ability to choose evil that was placed in man at creation is referred to as "very good", along with the rest of creation. There is no force that possesses creative abilities outside that which emanates from Yahweh. I am not saying that Yahweh is calling evil "very good", but I am saying that He is calling the characteristic in man that allows him to choose evil "very good". This potential to choose evil has been in man since the moment Yahweh created man and I remind you that if we believe this potential to choose evil entered the human spectrum of attributes, as a result of Satanic influence on humanity, then we are saying "Satan" has the power to create. It seems by suggesting that Satan imparted the potential to choose sin into humans, that he then possesses similar creative power as Yahweh. If we

37 ibid

believe and are saying Satan has the power to create, then we have just placed ourselves in a position that opines that there are two Gods. True monotheism becomes impossibility in a faith that believes a Satan can impart anything to a human, a creation of Yahweh. Isaiah dealt with this concept when Israel was in exile and adopting a Babylonish philosophy about dual cosmic forces that supposedly were in opposition to each other. We are shown in the book of Isaiah that the Israelites who were in exile began to attribute their situation to other "Gods" and Isaiah was commissioned by Yahweh to set them straight. Isaiah proclaims that the evil that came upon them is from Yahweh and there is nothing or no one else who can bring evil upon humanity.

George Knight has learned from a serious study of the writings of Isaiah as well as from historical records pertaining to the religious movements of the period Isaiah is said to be writing in about the efficacious philosophy of Persian dualism. Knight identifies Persian dualism as one of the most accelerating religions of the period. It was a religion that took the concept of there being One God who is responsible for all the good and another evil God who is responsible for evil to a new level. Knight responds to this conjecture by saying:

> But such a faith flatly contradicts the faith of the prophets of Israel. If Cyrus believed such nonsense, thought our particular prophet in 540 B.C., then Cyrus must be told the truth. "I am Lord and there is no other," declares Israel's God in 45:6, "I am not just one half of the Reality, the other half being Evil. I form Light and create Darkness: I make weal (or 'peace' i.e. all that is positively and constructively good), and create woe (all that is the opposite of what is good): I am the Lord who do all these things." That then is the essence of Israel's faith, the faith with which she is to confront Zoroastrianism and later on all the religions of Greece and Rome. Her God is none other than the LORD, and as such is responsible for creating a world where men are free, free to rend and tear and rape and murder, and bring all manner of evil upon themselves.[38]

Knight understood that Isaiah was intent on declaring the message that one should not claim anything, good or bad is the product of any God but Yahweh.

The extent to which the Persian influence on Israel and the idea of a "Satan" is so significant, that we will see it treated fully in chapter 7, The *Post-Exilic, Persian Influence On The Idea of Satan.* We will see in that chapter how Zoroastrian Dualism was pervasive throughout the exile period of the

---

38 Bible Guides: Prophets of Israel (1) Isaiah by George Knight pg 75

Hebrews, but for now I will quote two verses that tell us where evil comes from. The prophet Isaiah is telling the hearer at this moment that Yahweh brings both the good and the evil to pass.

> *That they may know from the rising of the sun, and from the west, that there is none beside me. I am the LORD, and there is none else.*
> *I form the light, and create darkness: I make peace, and create evil: I the LORD do all these things. Isaiah 45:6-7*

This is a well-known passage and most scholars treat it delicately so as not to imply Yahweh is the creator of moral evil. The reason for the delicacy is that their explanations are most commonly made through the predetermined grid that there is God (Yahweh) and there is Satan. One does good and the other does evil. This is such a prevalent concept that few even bring into question the history of Satan and how the Scriptures portray this supposed Dark Angel in the pre-Babylonian exile period. However, if we believe that there is one God and none else, as the Scriptures claim[39], a belief which includes understanding that there is no Satan that is given the status of a God by the activities it is claimed he can perform, such as giving diseases and controlling peoples minds as well as other behaviors of creating, then we can come to a correct understanding of the above verses in Isaiah 45. Then we can accept that yes, even evil comes from Yahweh. Evil that so often is said to be from "Satan". The very fact that Isaiah has been charged with the duty of announcing that there is "One God and none else" informs the reader that the people of the period were entertaining the notion that there is another power which influences and affects humanity, and is therefore seen as a God. To be told there is "One God and none else" is clearly a statement that shows Yahweh thought that any other obeisance paid to any other force was to have another God.

Albert Barnes is one of the many scholars who recognize what Yahweh is trying to get across in His message through Isaiah but he has failed to conclude that the "Satan" featured in contemporary Christianity, is a product

---

39 *(Isaiah 45:21) Tell ye, and bring them near; yea, let them take counsel together: who hath declared this from ancient time? who hath told it from that time? have not I the LORD? and there is no God else beside me; a just God and a Saviour; there is none beside me.*
This is only one example in scripture of the Creator emphasizing that there is no God beside Him. He had just 14 verses previous told us he creates darkness and evil. In verse 21 among others Yahweh wants to clearly state that the only cosmic ,supernatural force in existence is Himself.

of Israel's association and acceptance of Persian philosophy. Barnes stresses in his commentary on this passage in Isaiah that moral evil, meaning man's choice to sin, does not come from Yahweh.

> The parallelism here shows that this is not to be understood in the sense of all evil, but of that which is the opposite of peace and prosperity. That is, God directs judgments, disappointments, trials, and calamities; he has power to suffer the mad passions of people to rage, and to afflict nations with war; he presides over adverse as well as prosperous events. The passage does not prove that God is the author of moral evil, or sin, and such a sentiment is abhorrent to the general strain of the Bible, and to all just views of the character of a holy God.

Is Evil Placed Before Man By God?

We are moving along nicely in coming to an understanding that man was created with an evil inclination and that evil, which falls upon humanity, often comes at the hand of God, I move now to the issue of how an opportunity to choose evil comes before a man.

Many, who assert the reality of a cosmic Devil, think that the devil places opportunity before man to sin. It is this idea that underlies the statement, "The Devil made me do it". Genesis chapter 2 however, reveals that this is not the case and one can witness the fact that Yahweh, the Creator, places the choice for either good or evil before humanity and the choice is left up to us.

> *And out of the ground made the LORD God to grow every tree that is pleasant to the sight, and good for food; the tree of life also in the midst of the garden, and the tree of knowledge of good and evil. Genesis 2:9*

Note the names given the two trees in the midst of the garden that God caused to grow. The first is the tree of life and the second is the tree of the knowledge of good and evil. We see that the trees in the midst of the garden were special. They were set apart in a sense from all the other trees in the garden. What is the tree of life? According to the International Standard Bible Encyclopedia, the answer to that is clear.

Tree of Life

> The expression "tree of life" occurs in four groups or connections: (1) in the story of the Garden of Eden, (2) in the Proverbs of the Wise Men, (3) in the apocryphal writings, and (4) in the Apocalypse of John...
>
> The meaning seems to be that the gratification of good and lawful desires produces those pleasures and activities which make up life and its blessings.[40]

It appears that this phrase, "The Tree of Life" is a metaphor; it is a special tree that represents eternal life. Through the account of its existence we come to realize that were Adam and Eve to have embraced the privilege of partaking of this unique tree they would become immortal. Our story reveals this information to us because the first man and woman disobeyed Yahweh and ate of the other tree in the garden that was forbidden to them, the tree of the knowledge of good and evil. Genesis clearly displays the consequences and the result of eating from the forbidden tree. We will see that the choice for evil was not instilled after Adam and Eve ate the fruit but that deciding to eat the fruit was the choice for evil in and of itself. Whether one views the Genesis story as myth, history, science or theology matters little to finding clarity as to the meaning of the story and to where the choice for evil comes from. The story tells who it was that placed the trees in front of man. Who was it that caused the knowledge of good and evil to be a part of the equation in the garden? Look at Genesis 2:9 again to see the answer, this time I have bolded the words that reveal the answer to the question of who caused the trees to grow.

> *And out of the ground made the* ***LORD God to grow*** *every tree that is pleasant to the sight, and good for food; the tree of life also in the midst of the garden, and the tree of knowledge of good and evil. Genesis 2:9*

Therefore, we see in the above verse, that it was "***the LORD God"*** who caused the tree of knowledge of good and evil to exist as a possible choice for man. God specifically placed that opportunity in front of Adam and Eve and they then had the privilege of choosing whether or not they would justify eating of it and contravene the Creator's command to not eat from it.

40 International Standard Bible Encyclopedia.

Adam and Eve were commanded not to eat something, and when they gave in to their own desires and disobeyed, the results had a huge impact that have rippled throughout all of history and have an effect on humankind to this day. Genesis 3 tells of the ejection of man from the garden. These words might be seen as Satan falling like lighting in that man fell from his position of perfection once he sinned and acted as an adversary to Yahweh. It is possible that Yeshua had this situation in mind when he spoke of something falling like lightening in Luke.

> *And the LORD God said, Behold, the man is become as one of us, to know good and evil: and now, lest he put forth his hand, and take also of the tree of life, and eat, and live for ever: Therefore the LORD God sent him forth from the garden of Eden, to till the ground from whence he was taken. Genesis 3:22, 23*

Adam and Eve became as Yahweh, knowing good and evil. Yahweh wants his children to choose the good and reject the evil as is found to be written about the Messiah in the book of Isaiah.

> *Therefore the Lord himself shall give you a sign; Behold, a virgin shall conceive, and bear a son, and shall call his name Immanuel.*
> *Butter and honey shall he eat, that he may know to refuse the evil, and choose the good. Isaiah 7:14 -15*

Evil proliferates not because of a sinister satanic being, weaving a devious plan throughout the world, but because of humanity not keeping God's commands, a practice that is known as iniquity in the Scriptures and Apostolic letters. Paul has written to Timothy of the degradation of humanity as time progresses but he exhorts Timothy, as seen below, that Timothy ought to keep practicing what he learned as a child in the Torah, the Psalms and the Prophets, the "Holy Scriptures".

> *But evil men and seducers shall wax worse and worse, deceiving, and being deceived.*
>
> *But continue thou in the things which thou hast learned and hast been assured of, knowing of whom thou hast learned them; And that from a child thou hast known the holy scriptures, which are able to make thee wise unto salvation through faith which is in Christ 2 Timothy 3:13 -15*

In the Old Testament who is considered an evil man? In Job 1, Proverbs 14, Isaiah 56 and Jeremiah 26 you will find that it is the one who disobeys God's commands, decrees, statutes, ordinances, and judgments that is shown to be the evil one by the context of those writings. The book of Proverbs teaches us that this is a rebellious man. This man rebels against that which is asked of him by Yahweh. As we see in the Proverbs what an evil man is, we note the word "messenger" in the following verse. It is the word "*mawlawk*" in Hebrew, often translated as "angel". We see from this verse that the person who is rebellious against the word of God has a cruel angel sent against him.

> *An evil man seeketh only rebellion: therefore a cruel messenger (angel) shall be sent against him. Proverbs 17:11*

According to those words, Yahweh sends a cruel angel to the rebellious person who rejects obedience to God and sees that one as evil. We just read in Genesis 3 that God expelled the disobedient from paradise, the Garden of Eden, because they had become like Him. Man now knew good and evil, just like the Creator knows good and evil. It is almost impossible to perceive of Yahweh as having an intimate, experiential knowledge of evil; however, the text of Genesis tells us He knows good **and evil.** Therefore, on some level evil and good are both facets of the only Holy One. For God to expel man from paradise because of the altered condition of man's knowledge seems to show us that now that man had chosen evil, man would struggle with making wrong, sinful choices throughout his existence. Moreover, now tainted by only one sin, man was not an eligible candidate for immortality. Therefore, Yahweh would continue with His plan of the ages. The term "tree of life" is found throughout Scripture and again in the Apostolic writing called Revelations, which is the Revelation of Yeshua the Messiah that God gave to John.

What is the Tree of Life?

The term, "tree of life," is often known to refer to the Torah and by extension refers to humanity keeping the commands of God. Speaking of wisdom, which is found in the Torah, the writer of Proverbs says: *She is a tree of life to them that lay hold upon her: and happy is every one that retaineth her.* (Pro 3:18). In the synagogue liturgies of the Jews, for hundreds of years, we are able to hear a recitation of the proclamation that accompanies the replacement of the Torah scroll to its proper cabinet called the ark, after the public reading. The liturgy is as follows;

"Return O LORD, to the myriads of Israel's families. Arise The LORD to Your resting place, You and Your mighty ark. Clothe Your priests with righteousness. May those who have experienced Your faithful love shout for joy. For the sake of Your servant David, don't delay the return of Your Messiah."

"I give you good instruction; do not forsake My Torah. A tree of life it is for those who take hold of it, and blessed are the ones who support it. Its ways are ways of pleasantness, and all its paths are peace. Long life is in its right hand, in its left are riches and honor. The Lord was pleased for the sake of His righteousness, to render the Torah great and glorious."

In the book of Revelations, we read of the access to the "tree of life" being the privilege of those who keep the commands of God;

Blessed are they that do his commandments, that they may have right to the tree of life, and may enter in through the gates into the city. Revelation 22:14

Adam and Eve forfeited the right to eat of the tree of life on the day they chose to disobey God and become sinners.

What we are being shown in the Revelation is that we come to the end of the plan of redemption of Yahweh and are sent back to the beginning in the true circular fashion of the Creator God. Having this made apparent is to see that Yahweh still wants us to return to Him. It is understood that one must overcome the evil inclination to gain access to the tree of life, just as Adam and Eve were given the opportunity to eat from the "tree of life" had they not succumbed to their evil inclination. What we are being told is only those who diligently, out of love for the Messiah, keep the commandments of Yahweh will be able to live forever with the King of the universe in paradise, which is simply the restored Earth according to Revelation 21 where God comes down and makes His dwelling among men. Many believe that paradise is a place of perfection up in heaven where a soul goes after the physical body dies and that the righteous will eventually go there to live for eternity, in a city of gold with beautiful mansions that are unimaginably exquisite. The Hebrew and Greek understanding of the term "Paradise" however, both acknowledge that the term is referring not to a place up above the clouds but a place that was once perfect and where Yahweh walked. Easton's Bible Dictionary indicates that this word speaks of the Garden of Eden originally but came to be known as something else.

Paradise

A Persian word (pardes), properly meaning a "pleasure-ground" or "park" or "king's garden." (See EDEN.) It came in course of time to be used as a name for the world, happiness, and rest hereafter.[41]

Paradise is in fact the Garden of Eden. Adam and Eve disobeyed God and lost the opportunity to eat of the tree of life and live forever. We must learn from that lesson and strive to enter in at the narrow gate by not disobeying the unchanging Creator.Through submitting to the inherent desire to rebel, man has been forbidden to eat of the "tree of life". Man has become culpable for his choice that proceeded from his own desire and there was no external cosmic, anti-God Satan coercing man. We must come to grips with the fact that moral evil proceeds from the human heart and opportunity for evil choice, is placed before man by the Creator. All nations who have kept the commandments of God and have accepted the Messiah, will be given access to this "tree of life".

In the midst of the street of it, and on either side of the river, was there ***the tree of life****, which bare twelve manner of fruits, and yielded her fruit every month: and the leaves of the tree were for the healing of the nations. Revelations 22:2*

In this verse, we are told of the great benefit of obeying the commands of the Father. Any who partake of the tree of life will receive that healing. Any who choose to know evil and not do good will find themselves in a constant struggle against the sin that is personified as a crouching beast in Genesis and again as a roaring lion in the Epistles.

Sin is Always Ready to Pounce!

The roaring lion is not to be seen as "Satan" but is to be seen as the sin that subtly overcomes us when we begin to practice sin in our lives. You will see below in Genesis that the writer expressly identifies "sin" as that which is waiting to take over the one who does not "do well". A comparison of the statement in Peter about "the devil being a roaring lion" (shown below) can be made and when it is made one can conclude that Peter was drawing attention to the statement found in Genesis that indicates the intensity of

41 These Dictionary topics are from M.G. Easton M.A., D.D., Illustrated Bible Dictionary, 1897.

sin. Peter does so using common metaphorical terms in calling the "devil" a lion. The "devil" is simply "sin". The English term "*couching*" is the Hebrew word *rawbawts* and means to *crouch* on all four legs folded, like a recumbent animal, according to James Strong. The nuance of this word is that of a lion waiting to pounce and Peter's use of the lion imagery for sin as seen below reflects the Hebraic understanding of the sin that was ready to pounce on Cain if he did not "rule over it". Looking here at both verses will show that the writer of each was trying to impress upon the hearer that sin will take over if we do not do something about in our lives.

> *If thou doest well, shall it not be lifted up? and if thou doest not well, sin coucheth at the door; and unto thee is its desire, but thou mayest rule over it.' Genesis 4:7 (Jewish Publication Society Version)*

> *Be sober, be vigilant; because your adversary the devil, as a roaring lion, walketh about, seeking whom he may devour: 2 Peter 5:8 KJV*

Therefore, in Genesis, we are given a personification of sin and disobedience as a predatory beast, waiting to "devour" and like any predatory beast it is personified as preying on us at the moment we are weak, that moment is once we have sinned.

An axiom many know of or have heard is, "Like begets Like". This means that dogs beget dogs, fish beget fish, humans beget humans. The same is true of sin. When the Scriptures tell us "*if thou doest not well, sin coucheth at the door; and unto thee is its desire*", we can conclude that sin begets sin. This is clearly displayed when Yahweh tells Cain that if Cain is to do well the propensity to sin will be lessened. However if Cain "does not do well", which means he is disobeying the commands of God, sin will inevitably overtake Cain and as Peter puts it, devour him.

Consider what we are shown of sin even in the Genesis account when sin was in its infancy in the existence of humanity. We are shown that sin is a product of man's wickedness and not a product of a powerful, god-like "Satan". It is vital to see that the Hebrew Scriptures are absolutely replete with symbols, metaphor, allegory, and personifications, often by using animals and animal characteristics as comparisons. If there is any doubt as to the profound and prolific use of symbols we only need read the blessing of Jacob over his sons Manasseh and Ephraim to see how much symbolism and metaphorical reference to animals Jacob makes in the tribal blessings. Here we also see the use of the term "couching". In Genesis 49 verse 9 Judah is a "*lion's whelp*" and is referred to as couching; Issachar is seen as a "*strong ass*" in verse 14, again being said to be couching. In verse 21 Naphtali is a "*hind*", which is a doe. In Verse 22 Joseph is a "*fruitful bough*". In Chapter 49 verse 17 Dan is "*a serpent*". Here we are not told "as a serpent" but just straight up, a serpent. To many the serpent is a bad thing but I guess Yahweh has a different concept of the serpent than you and I have been handed down by religious thought that seems to connect a serpent with the "satan" that is believed to exist by many. In many ancient and present cultures, the serpent is connected to wisdom and knowledge, which would connect the use of the serpent in Genesis to the "knowledge" that Adam and Eve gained by eating from the forbidden tree.

If we continue to apply a misunderstanding of the personification and metaphor found in Scripture, we will be in trouble. When we see a tangible entity, such as a human man, described using a metaphor or if we see a behavior of a human or group of humans personified as a living being or entity, and we take the words of the description literally, then we are in danger of false doctrine. In danger because we then will interpret the message of a passage through our misunderstanding of the metaphorical meaning intended by the author. This has been done by applying a literal interpretation to the "roaring lion who seeks to devour us". When misapplying metaphors occurs in Biblical interpretation we will be driven towards believing there is some force other than our own human, rebellious, selfish, disobedient will and nature that is opposing the creator. This belief is anti-scripture and when taught it is heresy. The fact that if we sin, more sin will come, is why this world is so messed up today. Not because there is a satanic plan to have the hordes of hell and all the demonic minions feverishly toil to thwart the plan of the Sovereign. Through choosing sin, evil men wax worse and worse. Second Timothy 3 teaches us that it is men that are the deceivers, not "satan"; *But evil men and seducers shall wax worse and worse, deceiving, and being deceived.* Those men that sin will wax worse and will be sent a strong delusion because by their sin they have proven to not be lovers of the truth according to 2nd Thessalonians 2 which says; *because they received not the love of the truth, that they might be saved. And for this cause God shall send them strong delusion, that they should believe a lie:*

This delusion is not from a mythical satanic being but it comes straight from God just as many adversarial (satanic) outworkings came from Yahweh in the Old Testament scriptures. Old Testament principles state that man's heart is inclined towards evil from His youth (Genesis 8) and that man seems to be continually given to choosing evil.

> *I also will choose their delusions, and will bring their fears upon them; because when I called, none did answer; when I spake, they did not hear: but they did evil before mine eyes, and chose that in which I delighted not. Isaiah 66:4 KJV*

Common perspective on the issue of where delusion comes from is that delusion, which can be said to be deception, comes from "Satan" but the letter from Paul to the Thessalonians states that God sends the strong delusion. It is very clear that the delusion is from Yahweh. Those that refused to embrace the truth, that is receive the love of the truth, were sent a strong delusion. This delusion comes from no one else but the Creator Himself. In understanding this concept, it seems sensible to show a love for the truth and in particular, a love for the truth of there being only One God and not a series of lesser "god-like" entities, such as Satan. These are nothing more than imagined, supernatural creatures that are credited for things that they are unable to accomplish because they simply don't exist.

Delusion Sent From God

I would be remiss to not mention a classic account in the Scriptures displaying the principle of a delusion being sent from Yahweh. If we look back on the story of the Exodus, we see a clear account of a belligerent, obstinate, selfish, and prideful Pharaoh. The Pharaoh was given multiple opportunities to humble himself and let the people of God go out of Egypt, into the wilderness to worship Yahweh. If you follow the tale carefully, you will note that Pharaoh in five of the plagues hardened his own heart. After the repeated occurrences of self- hardening, God then hardened Pharaohs heart. Moses and Aaron went to Pharaoh and confronted him on his stubborn pride. The account in Exodus makes clear the fact of Yahweh sending the delusion to Pharaoh, which is to say, "God hardened his heart";

> *And I will harden Pharaoh's heart, that he shall follow after them; and I will be honoured upon Pharaoh, and upon all his host; that the Egyptians may know that I am the LORD. And they did so. Exodus 14:4*

Pharaoh did not receive a love for the truth and in essence Pharaoh received a strong delusion. Yahweh was now the active ingredient in hardening Pharaoh's heart. If having your heart hardened by God is not being sent a strong delusion then I don't know what is. The connection can be made to man having a potential to choose evil. If he does not choose well then sin becomes what he is controlled by in many ways and in so choosing this man proves not to be a lover of the truth which then subjects him to a great delusion from the Creator. No satan, no devil no demons, just man rejecting a path of obedience to Yahweh because of the hardness of his heart and then man is "devoured" by his own sin which is uncontrollable to the man who has chosen this path. In the story of Pharaoh, we are given a picture of a powerful leader who chooses his plan and path for a situation rather than receiving a love for the truth and choosing Yahweh's path for the situation.

It is a common Messianic and Christian ideology to believe that a delusion comes from Satan and to attribute evil choices one makes to the influence of the same Satan. This belief is rife with theological and historical problems that point to a contrived doctrine or philosophy that has proven to spawn confusion, fear, and control of millions of so-called believers. Yeshua reminded His hearers of where all the wicked thoughts and their following actions came from. The Messiah was quite succinct in telling us it all comes from our hearts. This is how He described it in Matthew and again in Mark;

> *But those things which proceed out of the mouth come forth from the heart; and they defile the man. For out of the heart proceed evil thoughts, murders, adulteries, fornications, thefts, false witness, blasphemies: Matthew 15:18-19*

> *And he said, That which cometh out of the man, that defileth the man. For from within, out of the heart of men, proceed evil thoughts, adulteries, fornications, murders, Thefts, covetousness, wickedness, deceit, lasciviousness, an evil eye, blasphemy, pride, foolishness: All these evil things come from within, and defile the man. Mark 7:20-23*

These two accounts of the Messiah's response to being confronted by the Pharisees about the accusation that the disciples were defiled because of eating with unwashed hands end with very clear statements as to from where it is that evil proceeds. Yeshua's statements are made in a response to yet another of the rigid commands that were added to Scripture by the Pharisees. Perhaps one of the real "Satans" in religion is those men and women who add to or take away from the eternal Word of Yahweh; some fabricating commandments that are simply the doctrine of men. The addition and deletion of commands by Christianity and Judaism has been infecting the true faith of Israel for many centuries.

If we are willing to add commands as the Pharisees and many rabbis do, or take away commands, as the Christians and Catholics do, then we have chosen to obey man rather than Yahweh the Creator of the universe. We have broken the first commandment by putting other Gods before him and have chosen not to fear Him in adding to or taking away from His words. How can man be so arrogant? Just think of the implications of adding to the words of the Sovereign Creator of the universe. Yet additions have occurred with regularity by Judaism and Catholicism, making their respective ecclesiastical authorities out to be equal with God by believing they have the authority to write commandments as Yahweh has done. Even in today's context, it is quite unacceptable to take the words of a great author and add to or take away from them. Plagiarism itself is a taboo act and one implicates himself to be a liar if one goes further still and adds to the words he has plagiarized.

Just pause and think for a moment of the great and absolute idiocy one must be floundering in if he were to remove or add to the text of a particular Bill from Senate or legislation from the government. Can you think of the response you would receive had you added to or taken away from the words of G W Bush's edict against terrorism or edict on economic sanctions with China? How much worse should it bode for us to add to or diminish the words of the Most High? Have we minimized Him so much in this age that we no longer fear Him? Scripture is clear we are to fear Him and the primary manner in which we display that proper fear is through keeping His commandments. The message of fearing God, connected to obeying Him is continually presented in the Scriptures and the Apostolic testimony as is shown by the following examples;

> *Therefore thou shalt keep the commandments of the LORD thy God, to walk in his ways, and to fear him. Deuteronomy 8:6*

> *Ye shall walk after the LORD your God, and fear him, and keep his commandments, and obey his voice, and ye shall serve him, and cleave unto him. Deuteronomy 13:4*

> *The secret of the LORD is with them that fear him; and he will shew them his covenant. Psalms 25:14*

> *Behold, the eye of the LORD is upon them that fear him, upon them that hope in his mercy; Psalms 33:18*

> *And fear not them which kill the body, but are not able to kill the soul: but rather fear him which is able to destroy both soul and body in hell. Matthew 10:28*

One who fears God as told to does not add to or take away from his words but they keep all His commandments because they love Him, as is made clearing Exodus and John.

> *And shewing mercy unto thousands of them that love me, and keep my commandments. Exodus 20:6*
>
> *If ye love me, keep my commandments. John 14:15*

If there is no Satan and only one God as I am claiming, you might ask; how does Jesus fit into the picture. Isn't He one like God? That is an excellent question and the answer is found in both the Old Testament Scriptures and the Apostolic writings. There you will find it taught that Yeshua is not simply "one like God" but that He is God. Yeshua is God manifest in human form. Yeshua the Messiah is God in the flesh as John 1 tells us, and that is why the statement "*love me and keep my commandments*" proceeds from both the mouth of God the Creator and of Yeshua the incarnate God at different times in history. Yeshua did not change the commandments, He is renewing the covenant that is made with the house of Israel and the house of Judah as described in Jeremiah 31:31-33 and in Hebrews chapter 8 and came to do so as God in the form of a human. One who changes the word of God by adding to it or taking away from it, is seen as being a "satan". This is so because they have chosen to be adversarial to Yahweh and have given in to their evil inclination, which places their person and the desires of their heart before the desires of the heart of the Creator of the Universe.

The Sin Comes From Within

So far, we have seen that man was given a choice to obey and choose life, or disobey and choose death. Man was created with the ability to choose and this ability was the potential that is within each human being from the beginning of creation. In theory, man could live forever immortally if he would not have disobeyed and eaten of the tree that he was not supposed to eat of. However, the opportunity to receive something he didn't have was too great and man fell. It is quite the attribute of man, to want what he does not already possess. Man already possessed the presence of Yahweh, man possessed a perfect trouble-free life of peace, and beautiful surroundings while in the garden. Now that desire that was within man saw something that he did not yet possess and he wanted it. Man's fall involved the desire to have something he did not presently posses. If you think about all the things you want; SUV, bigger house, more money, more hair, more sex, more chocolate, more time, a Swiffer™, new dishes, a PSP™(Play Station Portable), a plate of cookies, new job, recognition from others, love from your spouse; you will see that these are things that you do not have. So, it soon becomes apparent that we want the things we do not have. I am not sure how small this trait was in Adam and Eve, yet it was apparently present or man would not have desired the only tree in the garden that man was not allowed to eat. One thing I would like us to understand completely though, is where this impetus to desire that which we do not have comes from. Let me give you some of the thoughts of James the brother of Yeshua the Messiah, who affirms that these desires are our own lusts that reside within each of us and not a desire that is given us by Satan.

> *But every man is tempted, when he is drawn away of his own lust, and enticed. Then when lust hath conceived, it bringeth forth sin: and sin, when it is finished, bringeth forth death. Do not err, my beloved brethren. James 1:14-16*

Yet to be covered are many of the other verses in the Scriptures that show us the propensity we have as humans, to follow what is in our own hearts. In *Satan, Christianity's Other God-Volume 2,* the companion volume to this work, you will find a catalogue of the "New Testament" passages related to this topic with explanations of how these difficult passages are to be understood when considering the underlying Hebraic context of the words. For now let's discuss the above verses in light of my position on the non-existence of a fallen angel and leader of the demons named "Satan", coupled with the position that sin originates in the heart of man because of a desire to have that which we do not presently posses and the lust that flows from that.

James is telling us not that a satanic being tempts us, but that we are tempted by our own lust, which is the lust of the flesh, lust of the eyes and the pride of life. So once I have lusted for something, such as that Mississippi Mud Pie dessert that was sitting on the counter, if I dwell on it long enough then the lust will seize me, or clasp hold of me, which is what James means by using the Greek word in his letter translated as conceived.

> *Then when lust hath conceived(clasped or taken hold of), it bringeth forth sin James 1:15*

Therefore, when I get to the point in my battle against lust of the flesh that I am no longer mastering sin but sin has become my master, I have essentially succumbed to this lust or desire. Now that I have committed myself to this sin and once I have performed this sin in heart and deed, it will bring death and I am now a slave to sin. Paul tells of the hazard with yielding ourselves to sin, he says we then are the servant of sin in the following quote;

Know ye not, that to whom ye yield yourselves servants to obey, his servants ye are to whom ye obey; whether of sin unto death, or of obedience unto righteousness? Romans 6:16

Paul wisely instructs us that if we obey sin then we are led to death. Of course most sins we submit to do not bring instant heart stopping death, but any sin we sin by choice or by ignorance separates us from God, who is life. To be separated from life means we are in death. Death is a result of a chronic problem when it comes to unrepentant sin. So to put it plainly, the problem starts in our heart when we lust for something that Yahweh has not set apart for us to have. That lust takes hold of us, in a sense it is roaming about, seeking to devour. After the lust takes hold on us, we then commit the sin. Of course we know that the wages of sin is death. First John 3:4 tells us *sin is the transgression of the Torah*; Paul tells us in Romans 7:7 that *without the Torah we cannot know what sin is*[42]. Again, 1 John 3:9[43] tells us if we are born of Him, we stop sinning. Many of God's children think they can redeem themselves through perfect adherence to all His commands, thus effectively not sinning, but that is not possible unless you are the Creator and this becomes even more vivid and realizable to the children if they see the Creator come down and the fullness of the Godhead appear bodily[44] who was the sinless, sacrifice Yeshua, the salvation of God. In Deuteronomy 30 verse 15, we are told God set life and good before us, as well as death and evil, we read in the King James Version that this "life and blessing" was realized when the Children of God kept His commandments faithfully.

See, I have set before thee this day life and good, and death and evil; In that I command thee this day to love the LORD thy God, to walk in his ways, and to keep his commandments and his statutes and his judgments, that thou mayest live and multiply: and the LORD thy God shall bless thee in the land whither thou goest to possess it. Deuteronomy 30:15-16

---

42 (Rom 7:7) What shall we say then? *Is* the law sin? God forbid. Nay, I had not known sin, but by the law: for I had not known lust, except the law had said, Thou shalt not covet.

43 (1Jo 3:9) Whosoever is born of God doth not commit sin; for his seed remaineth in him: and he cannot sin, because he is born of God.

44 (Col 2:9) For in him dwelleth all the fullness of the Godhead bodily.

Of course, the God of the Universe doesn't want us to choose evil. He simply placed both before us at Sinai as He did in the Garden of Eden with the "tree of the knowledge of good and evil", providing us with the free will to choose to do the good; exhibiting that we choose life. He wants us to make the best choice and when we do, we fulfill His desire to have a willing and loyal servant rather than a servant forced into a choice or given no choice at all. To be given no choice at all proves nothing in the way of loyalty and love, nor does it allow the servant to see inside him or her self that I, the servant, chose Yahweh because He first chose me. Yahweh is a God that wants us to make the choice to serve and obey Him and to see that we made the choice not by force but by our will to choose. Still today, just as in the garden of Eden, God would not place a choice in front of us and tell us what not to choose, unless we had the potential to disobey. Had man not had an evil inclination the day he was created there would have been no need to give an instruction to not eat from the tree of the knowledge of good and evil. You don't tell the family dog not to speed when he drives the car because it is not possible for him to commit this infraction. You do however tell him "No!" when he is eyeing up the burgers that have just come off the barbeque and are sitting on a plate right beside the grill. The fact of giving a command is that the potential to break that command must really exist.

Desires are Lusted After Before They Become Sin

As we near the close of this chapter, we will take some time to look closely at the theme of James' verses about lust when conceived becoming sin and then bringing death. We are going to assess these statements through the eyes of a Hebraic studier, one who would have received James' correspondence and then heard it read to the assembly. As we do I would like you to understand a few points about James; these points are as follows;

1- James was a first century Hebrew believer.

2- James was a pillar of the First Century assembly according to Paul.

3- James was a Hebrew scholar and a great teacher of Torah.

4- James knew what sin was, according to the Tanak, breaking the commands of Yahweh.

5- James did not teach from nor use the Apostolic Testimony/ New Testament as it was not even close to being penned at the time. James had none of Paul's letters and only taught from the "Old Testament" and the "Old Testament" perspective on sin, which he knew to be breaking the commands of Yahweh.

Let's look now at James' statement in chapter 1.

> *My brethren, count it all joy when ye fall into divers temptations; James 1:2*

First off, in verse 2 of chapter one James tells us to count it a joy when we fall into divers temptations. Unless James is saying, be happy when you sin, then falling into temptations is not sin. James knew sin means the breaking or disobeying of the Torah commands. Falling into divers temptations means coming upon the many testings that Yahweh puts upon us to "prove" us. The diverse testings are designed not to cause us to sin but to cause us to choose life, to choose to obey God and to choose that which is good. The prophecy of the Messiah in Isaiah that informs us there is a process of learning to choose the good and reject the evil also shows that our potential for good is balanced by our potential for evil, we must know to do good, which indicates an active and intentional process to reject the evil.

> *Butter and honey shall he eat, that he may know to refuse the evil, and choose the good. Isaiah 7:15*

Refusing to sin is refusing the evil. The Messiah taught us that in Him we have the power to refuse to sin. Also, we through Him, have the power to choose good. What then is "good"? Paul tells us in Romans 7:12 that the *Torah and the commandment is holy and good.* [45]That is why the book of Revelation tells us that the unswerving character of the saints is that they keep the commands of God and have the testimony of Yeshua. In making that statement, John is saying that to make it into and be a part of the eternal Kingdom of God, one must choose the good by doing commands of the unchanging God and believe that Yeshua is the Messiah in whom and through whom we have been redeemed to God. James knew to refuse evil, Paul knew to refuse evil, and we too must choose to refuse evil. Evil in the Torah and the Prophets and the Psalms is clearly taught to be disobeying the commands of

---

45 (Rom 7:12) Wherefore[5620] the[3588] law[3551] *is* holy,[40] and[2532] the[3588] commandment[1785] holy,[40] and[2532] just,[1342] and[2532] good.[18]

Yahweh. So what then are the diverse temptations James talks about? They are those temptations and testings to prove us and strengthen us to know to refuse evil and to choose good.

> *My brethren, count it all joy when ye fall into divers temptations; Knowing this, that the trying of your faith worketh patience. But let patience have her perfect work, that ye may be perfect and entire, wanting nothing. James 1:2-4*

The above verses explain "diverse temptations" as testing or trying of your faith for the purpose of bringing us to maturity and to become whole or complete; termed as "*be perfect and entire*" in the English translation of James. This maturity brings us to a point of "wanting nothing". Many commentators are clear on the point of wanting nothing. This statement refers to the future when we are reigning with Messiah for in this present state we are wanting things. "Things" may be seen as wanting love, fellowship, and closeness with the Father. So for the statement to mean we can achieve a type of Nirvana[46] in this age cannot be so. The statement, "wanting nothing" means being tested and proved, to direct us to maturity in the faith. This maturity means we are in a process of accepting Messiah as our salvation and choosing to refuse evil or in other words choosing not to break Torah. This process will bear the fruit of us reigning with Messiah where we will be fellowshipping in love and truth and therefore "wanting nothing." It simply is a nutshell teaching from James that when we come to faith in Yeshua we will be tested in order to help us mature and ultimately come to the end goal, which will be realized when we are dwelling in His kingdom in peace and safety. James gives us a depiction of an orderly progression of our faith to our reward. Ultimately if we do not succumb to our lusts and choose not to sin, we exercise our authority in Messiah to choose life and not death. Let's read that section of verses again that teach us how sin begins;

> *Let no man say when he is tempted, I am tempted of God: for God cannot be tempted with evil, neither tempteth he any man: But every man is tempted, when he is drawn away of his own lust, and enticed.*
> *Then when lust hath conceived, it bringeth forth sin: and sin, when it is finished, bringeth forth death. James 1:13-18*

46 **Nirvana:** Complete peace, a mind state of complete awareness or enlightenment. Reached or understood after one frees oneself of all desires and worldly things. (http://www.whitneystewart.com/HHDL/Glossary.htm)

As for verse 13, James is simply helping us to come to terms with the fact that Yahweh does not tempt us in order that we will choose evil and fall. The point of the matter James addresses is that Yahweh is testing us so we would learn to refuse the evil and choose the good, thereby building within ourselves a faith that is strong and moving toward maturity that we might at some point receive a crown of life as shown in James 12;

> *Blessed is the man that endureth temptation: for when he is tried, he shall receive the crown of life, which the Lord hath promised to them that love him. James 1:12*

We find then that evil is a product of the inclination of man and that the core issue for humanity is to recognize opportunities to choose evil as testing from the Creator. It is the Creator who places opportunities to make a choice in front of man. We are to embrace the opportunity to express our free will and make the choice to do good so that it will go well with us. We also can conclude by assessing the Scriptures that resisting the opportunity to choose good will result in sin metaphorically working in your life to eventually "devour" you.

Finding the source of our evil choices to be the lust that is already in us, allows us the opportunity to become free of any two-God thinking and reject the concept of a satanic influence, an evil force that has a celestial origin and is working to try to get man to commit sin. Paul teaches that it is the human mind bent on things of the flesh that is opposed to God and therefore we find that one can no longer attribute opposition to God as coming from Satan. Paul states it this way asserting that each person has a mind that finds ways to justify sin and disobey God;

> *Because the carnal mind is enmity against God: for it is not subject to the law of God, neither indeed can be. Romans 8:7*

The entire Bible confirms that man was not only created with the potential to make choices and the ability to choose to sin but that man will struggle with this potential for his entire existence. The concept of free-will comes to mind when we think on the reality of man being given a choice from the beginning. If Yahweh had not made an opportunity for man to choose, then He is no God at all but a ruthless dictator who prefers programmed responses to a response by man to His unfathomable love. This response is one that leads man to choose, as best as man can, to serve and obey the only God in the universe.

CHAPTER 3

God, Creator of All Things Good and Evil.

We pick up our story in the Garden of Eden where God has discovered Adam and Eve in their disobedience, which we know to be sin. Taking a closer look at this recounting of the fall of man, which is thought to be written by Moses sometime just before the children of Israel entered the Promised Land, we see a theme developing. We will discuss the serpent in chapters 12 and 13; *The Serpent In the Garden: Understanding the Foundations of Why We Believe a Myth;* and, *Answering The Serpent In The Garden Questions*

In those chapters, a thorough explanation will be put forth as to what the "serpent" possibly could have been, what the curse upon the serpent means and how it could be that the Israelites never considered the serpent in the garden to be the Satan of common lore.

We are somewhat restrained by present thinking on the Serpent in the Garden, due to the force of a 2000 year old concept that is embedded in North American religion. The concept of Satan being the cosmic being that is represented in a number of Old Testament stories was projected backwards on the story of the serpent, after the Babylonian exile period of the 6th century BC.

Once "theologians" took to interpreting the wisdom writings and other Biblical texts through the framework that had them believing in Satan, the system of demonology that we are familiar with today, forcefully migrated into Judaism. Due to strongly mythological thinking and a desire to make sense of Scripture from a Greek perspective, Zoroastrian cosmic-dualism nestled itself in the cradle of the religious world where Christianity is said to have sprung from.

The Hellenistic, mythical demonology that was developed by Plato, who lived from 427 BC to 347 BC, was then strengthened by the Greek philosopher Xenocrates, a student of Plato, as well as others.

Plato maintained that "*There must always remain something that is antagonistic to good*" and his successors adopted Plato's concept, agreeing that this thing in opposition to good is the evil cosmic entity known as Satan. The transfer of an originally Persian philosophy of good and evil into a Greek philosophy was seamless. In the minds of many Jews who were assimilated by these cultures, this myth had taken on a force of its own and had become to them, a reality. Many Jews of the first century and scores of Gnostics, who fed the Christian theme a steady diet of errors, provided the fodder for what would eventually become the world's most populous religion.

There is hope however. When we refuse to accept the practice of projecting backward the belief in a Greek myth such as Satan, onto ancient Hebrew writings, we are more likely to find the meaning and intent of the writers of Scripture. We see that the writers used a language and style that was understandable to the culture they were writing to. Therefore, we must continue to look at Scripture from the fresh perspective that says, "What is understood today from a Greek-thinking mindset, may not equate to what was understood way back then in a world much different from the Greco-Roman world that most of us are familiar with. Perhaps our interpretations would be more accurate if we strove to understand the ancient words of an ancient Eastern-Hebraic writer, through the eyes and mind of an ancient Eastern-Hebraic mindset. As we look on in the Scriptures to learn where evil comes from we will find clues that identify the source of the "evil". At this time we will look at another passage in Genesis. The following passage helps us to learn that there is a God and it is He that foists such things as evil curses upon humanity. There is nowhere and at no time that we find a curse on a human, coming from a cosmic evil entity. As we look at the first curses delivered in history, we are able to conclude that they were given by the Creator. This is a Creator who said of Himself that He knows good and evil.

One cannot even begin to perceive of an all-good God being responsible for evil unless one chooses to see that this God uses the evil He administers to bring about His ultimate plan for good. We must consider this very serious proposal by looking to the curses that were meted out at the Hand of God as a result of the disobedience of the first man and woman. Two humans that were given a choice by God to choose life or to choose death. Here from Genesis is the account of the curse from Yahweh on the serpent, the woman, and the man.

And I will put enmity between thee and the woman, and between thy seed and her seed; it shall bruise thy head, and thou shalt bruise his heel.

Unto the woman he said, I will greatly multiply thy sorrow and thy conception; in sorrow thou shalt bring forth children; and thy desire shall be to thy husband, and he shall rule over thee.

And unto Adam he said, Because thou hast hearkened unto the voice of thy wife, and hast eaten of the tree, of which I commanded thee, saying, Thou shalt not eat of it: cursed is the ground for thy sake; in sorrow shalt thou eat of it all the days of thy life;

Thorns also and thistles shall it bring forth to thee; and thou shalt eat the herb of the field; In the sweat of thy face shalt thou eat bread, till thou return unto the ground; for out of it wast thou taken: for dust thou art, and unto dust shalt thou return. (Genesis 3:15-19)

We see in Genesis 3:15 that the serpent is something worthy of Yahweh pronouncing enmity between the woman and her seed. Does this mean that women will have an unusual fear of snakes or does it mean something else? It is interesting to note that right after the curses from Yahweh were laid upon Adam and Eve. Adam named his wife and called her *Chavah* in the Hebrew language, or as we have it in English, "Eve". The curse is shown in the verse below;

And I will put enmity between thee and the woman, and between thy seed and her seed; it shall bruise thy head, and thou shalt bruise his heel. Genesis 3:15

The fact that the name Eve/Chavah means the mother of all living and that this verse is juxtaposed promptly after the curses are pronounced seems to reveal to us that the enmity was with the human seed and every human life that would come after Eve. Some may say that the "seed" referred to is Yeshua, however, there is much ambiguity in the term and it may be interpreted as "descendants" or "offspring". That lends itself to understanding the curse of "the enmity" being passed on to not only the Christ but also to the descendants of the first woman, throughout time. One should note that we finished the last chapter with Paul telling us that the carnal mind is at enmity with God and now we see reference to something else that is at enmity with the seed of the woman. Where Paul calls the carnal mind as that which is at "enmity", the writer of Genesis claims that the serpent is that which is at "enmity". This is our first clue that the "serpent" of Genesis and the carnal mind that Paul talks about are the same thing. This curse applies to the Messiah as well because He is "seed of the woman" and the carnal mind is at enmity with Him because He was fully man and fully God, the express image of the Godhead in bodily form.[47] As a human He would have struggled to some degree with that which is common to man. The Apostle affirms this understanding for us in the letter to the Hebrews;

> *For we have not an high priest which cannot be touched with the feeling of our infirmities; but was in all points tempted like as we are, yet without sin. Hebrews 4:15 KJV*

I think we need to keep the fact of where the cursing comes from in our minds or we may slip into the habit of blaming "satan" for curses as well. The curse on the woman comes from the Creator not from the nefarious "Satan" of mythology. Sorrows multiplied, pain in childbirth and a woman "desiring" her husband are easily seen as evil things. Which of us experiencing these things in our life would not be ready to identify them as evil? The evil things placed upon the woman sometime after creation are placed there by the Father. This is part of the Father's promise to us. If we disobey, we get death and cursing. The curse of Eve desiring her husband and the curse of the husband ruling over her was not the ideal for the relationship between a husband and wife. The intent was that they become one, as the Father and Son are one, without any separation or division. So many today see this curse as the "reason" that a man should dominate his wife, yet part of the curse, is that the husband shall rule over her. A husband "ruling" over the wife is not a positive thing because it is brought to pass by way of a curse from Yahweh. This was the beginning of power struggles in a marriage. Anyone who has been married for any length of time knows that power struggles are imminent. We all know that sometimes he wants things his way and she wants things her way. In a marriage, unconditional love often comes with lots of conditions. This is why we are instructed to love our wives as Messiah loved the body of believers "the church", for that is the only way that we can give ourselves up for her, that we would have her best interests in mind.

---

47 Who being the brightness of *his* glory, and the express image of his person, and upholding all things by the word of his power, when he had by himself purged our sins, sat down on the right hand of the Majesty on high;
Hebrews 1:3

How much more clearly can it be said? The cursing that brought strife into the perfect Edenic relationship was not placed on man by a cosmic Satan but was placed there by God because man chose to disobey and fowl the covenant that the Creator had made with the man. Marital strife happens not because of satanic attack on marriages to try to destroy what God has joined together, but because of the wicked heart of man that deep down wants to serve itself and has trouble getting to the place of sacrificial love. A love that always has the spouse's best interests in mind.

After the woman is cursed, we are given a look at the curse that was placed on man. Man's curse covers the way he relates to the creation. We see again that this supposed evil thing that is instituted for man is not done by a cosmic "Satan" but by the God of the universe. Man is sentenced, so to speak, to a difficult time sowing, harvesting, and earning a living as is stated in verses 17 to 20 below;

> *And unto Adam he said, Because thou hast hearkened unto the voice of thy wife, and hast eaten of the tree, of which I commanded thee, saying, Thou shalt not eat of it: cursed is the ground for thy sake; in sorrow shalt thou eat of it all the days of thy life; Thorns also and thistles shall it bring forth to thee; and thou shalt eat the herb of the field; In the sweat of thy face shalt thou eat bread, till thou return unto the ground; for out of it wast thou taken: for dust thou art, and unto dust shalt thou return. And Adam called his wife's name Eve; because she was the mother of all living. Genesis 3:17-20*

The cursing ends with the most tragic of statements. Recall with me what God said in the first commandment to Adam, "In the day you eat of it you will die". Well, that was stated because if man chose to refuse the evil and embrace the good we would be able to eat of the tree of life and live forever. However, as you know, that was not the case. Therefore, we are told that we will die, for returning to dust is precisely that; we die, decompose, and then become dust, the very material we were created from. Death is the consequence, instead of living forever in the Edenic relationship with our Creator and with our spouse. Death did not come into the world by "Satan" as many believe but it came into this world by the sins of one man as Paul teaches in the following verse;

> *Wherefore, as by one man sin entered into the world, and death by sin; and so death passed upon all men, for that all have sinned: Romans 5:12*

Who does Paul state as the responsible party for "death" entering God's creation? We are told it is man and we are not given any indication of a cosmic being called "Satan" bringing death into the world.

Had there been a serpent or even a Satan that was truly present in the garden and responsible for the sin that took place there; then Paul would not have stated that sin and death came into the world by a man. Had there been a serpent Adam and Eve would have been able to take some solace in the fact that they were duped by a creature that was more intelligent than they were and would have possibly not had felt the need to hide from God. It is likely that Adam and Eve had only themselves to blame and therefore, out of the guilt they had for submitting to their evil inclination, referred to as the serpent, they hid. Man's propensity to hide when he is responsible for an act that he is feeling guilty about is a common trait of humanity. Adam and Eve hid because they knew they had no one to blame but themselves for their disobedience.

Adam and Eve's hiding was an indictment of their actions so after Yahweh had pronounced the curses on the first man and woman, Because the sin that was committed was enough to bring death to the man and woman, God spoke of the issue of immortality and took action to remove the gift of immortality. In Genesis 3:22 God declares this strong edict;

> *And the LORD God said, Behold, the man is become as one of us, to know good and evil: and now, lest he put forth his hand, and take also of the tree of life, and eat, and live for ever: Therefore the LORD God sent him forth from the garden of Eden, to till the ground from whence he was taken. Genesis 3:22-23*

Yahweh did not remove the "tree of life" from man; He removed man from accessing it to eat of it. One simple rule was broken but Yahweh "knows evil" and He knows that this sin will permanently affect man's heart. In the following verse, we see the Creator take note of the tragic choice of man but as you read this verse, I would like to point out another significant thing. What is so significant in this verse is that knowing good and evil is seen as an attribute of the Almighty Creator.

> *And the LORD God said, Behold, the man is become as one of us, to know good and evil: and now, lest he put forth his hand, and take also of the tree of life, and eat, and live for ever: Genesis 3:22*

Both good and evil are part of Yahweh's portfolio as a sovereign God. "Satan" has been given the credit for being pure evil for thousands of years but evil is an attribute of Yahweh and we are told that there is none like God. This sovereign Creator is being proactive in punishing man to keep him from now eating of the tree of life. After man ate of the tree of the knowledge of good and evil and came to know evil, God did not want immortality to be granted to the unredeemed man. And this all because man had a choice to make and made the one that served himself instead of the one that served his Creator.

If we believe Yahweh is the one and only Creator and if we believe there is no other entity in existence that has the power to create, we then must conclude, evil came to be by the work of Yahweh. After the creation of man, Yahweh placed an opportunity for choice before man. We must understand man then had been given the ability to choose by his Creator. I hope that we are able to see that the greatest gift we have been given by Yahweh is the power to choose. He never leaves us guessing what is good and evil, He has told us all through the Torah and Psalms and the Prophets what is good and what is evil. God sets both of them before us and wants us to choose good so that ultimately we may receive life.

Once again, we see the profound placement of choice between life and death given the Children of Elohim when they receive instruction from Moses on how to live their lives in the time period just before their entry into the Promised Land. The book of Deuteronomy gives us this instruction.

> *I call heaven and earth to record this day against you, that I have set before you life and death, blessing and cursing: therefore choose life, that both thou and thy seed may live: Deuteronomy 30:19*

Some would opine that death is set before humanity by one they think to be the "angel of death" but death as a choice is clearly set before the Children of Israel by God. It is the Creator that put death before them and it is the Creator that gave them the opportunity to make a choice. This gift of choice is once again magnified in the spiritual and physical journey of Yahweh's people. The children of Israel knew that obedience to the commands of Yahweh would lead to life. The death that comes from disobedience to God was clearly portrayed in the object lesson of the two mountains stood upon by the tribes of Israel when the curses and blessings, the life and death, were pronounced over all Israel. These mountains were Mount Gerazim and Mount Ebal the excerpt of the verse as seen below identifies both mountains;

These shall stand upon mount Gerizim to bless the people, ... And these shall stand upon mount Ebal to curse;... Deuteronomy 27:12-13

Yahweh was using a huge object lesson to teach us how desolate and barren and lifeless we as individuals and as a people are if we do not follow all the commands of the Torah relayed to us by Moses. Mount Gerazim was a green mountain with a vital, healthy appearance. Vegetation was covering this mountain up to the top and was a visual representation of blessing and in appearance was a huge contrast to Mount Ebal. Mount Ebal was a desolate and barren piece of rock. Ebal had no "life" on it above the lower regions of the Mount and visually represented death. All Israel easily made this connection and knew which choice was the right choice. Through placing a choice before His people, Yahweh is imparting the responsibility for one's spiritual life to the individual and none on the mountains that day would have been thinking that they knew they had a chance for either blessing or cursing but sure hoped "Satan" didn't mess things up for them. A choice is essential to spiritual growth. If we do not have a choice of how to behave, we don't have the opportunity to overcome sin and volitionally yield to righteousness, thus proving our desire is to serve Yahweh. Of course when one compares the choice between life and blessing with death and cursing, it seems that one would be compelled to choose the former. When a child is taken to a toy store and begins looking for a special toy, it may not be decided for the child what to choose but there is value in directing the child to a wise and meaningful choice. After looking at dozens of toy options, a child may have the choice narrowed down to two attractive but different toys. As the child weighs his or her desire for each toy with the other advantages of having a certain toy, he or she will eventually come to a decision. Once the decision has been made and the toy is paid for and taken home, we can see the pride of ownership and the responsibility the child takes for that choice by guarding and playing with the new toy. Because care was taken in making the choice, the toy is often assigned a special place in the child's room for a time and the diligence the child displays in knowing where the toy is at all times and carefully playing with it is all part of the outworking of the child making the choice himself. The choice was compelled in a sense by many factors and hopefully the factors considered were not based merely on pleasure but on the benefits of one choice versus another. A child being wisely compelled to make the best choice for a new toy is much like our choice of "life and blessing" versus "death and cursing". The choice for the former is so compelling when set in the context of the lush Mount Gerazim versus the desolate Mount Ebal, that when we make the right choice it is clear we have chosen wisely. We have chosen life. The serious consequence of choosing sin, which is disobedience, was very apparent to all of Israel when they saw the difference between a mountain with the appearance of life where blessings were pronounced and a mountain with the appearance of death, where curses were pronounced.

Here is an excerpt from the International Standard Bible Encyclopedia that speaks of Mount Ebal where the curses were spoken to Israel by the Levites;

> The lower slopes of Ebal as one ascends from Nablus are covered with gardens and orchards, the copious streams from the fountains under Gerizim washing its foot, and spreading fertility and beauty. The vine, the fig and the olive grow luxuriantly. Higher up we scramble over rough rocky terraces, where grow only the ubiquitous thistles and prickly shrubs.

As Israel was given a choice for life or death, so too had Adam and Eve been given a choice. Adam and Eve, through the act of sinning, initiated the human creature into the deception of sin.

The letter to the Corinthians in chapter 15 verse 26 tells us that *the last enemy to be destroyed is death.* Watch carefully to see how the following fits together:

If death came into the world by a man, and death is the result of sin, and sin is disobeying God's commands and man made the choice to disobey, then the final enemy to be destroyed is that desire for man to disobey by choosing to sin, which brings death. Yeshua came so that man's propensity to sin will be destroyed. There is no destruction of a mythological being called Satan who is said to be responsible for all the sin and evil in the world. As Genesis 6 tells us, it is every inclination of man's heart that was continually evil; once death, meaning man's desire to choose to sin is destroyed, our heart's desire will be to continually choose life.

Sin initially invokes shame on the sincere and sensitive heart of the less corrupted individual. The person who experiences little to no corruption or corrupt behavior in their lives is less able to tolerate sin and corruption. This evolving tolerance to sin is quite apparent in the evolution of today's entertainment industry. Ten years ago, many of us who endeavored to live a righteous and moral life did not tolerate profanity and sexual images and content. Many today still adamantly reject this type of imagery and behavior in the entertainment industry and they are to be lauded. However, many who have come from a moral lifestyle in the past, whether they are religious or secular people, have become tolerant of these images and behaviors. Tolerance has grown not because we have become more intelligent, but in large part due to the fact that we have agreed with the purveyor of these concepts by not resisting the devil, which I posit in the context of James' writings, is the opportunities and choices for sin that are ever present in our world and environment. Were we to habitually resist the "devil" and submit to God, which is submitting to the Torah (not sinning), as James tells us in his epistle, sin, "the devil" would seemingly flee from us. In the quote below we see James writes his thought concisely using "the devil" as a metaphor for sin which must be actively resisted by humanity;

> *Submit yourselves therefore to God. Resist the devil, and he will flee from you. James 4:7*

We have seen Yahweh caused evil to exist or at least placed evil as an option before mankind, in growing the tree of the knowledge of good and evil. We have seen that the knowledge of evil acquired by man did not please Yahweh. God was not pleased that man became like Him in the area of good and evil. Perhaps the Creator was not pleased that man now knew good and evil because God knew man did not have the same capacity as Him to resist the draw to do evil.

Let's look at other references to the resident evil and sin in man. Since sin is so often connected to Satan, it is prudent for us to see more information that reveals where sin and evil actually do come from. In Genesis 6, we are given more than a clue that should lead us away from thinking that a "Satan" creature has anything to do with sin or evil.

> *And GOD saw that the wickedness of man was great in the earth, and that every imagination of the thoughts of his heart was only evil continually. And it repented the LORD that he had made man on the earth, and it grieved him at his heart. And the LORD said, I will destroy man whom I have created from the face of the earth; both man, and beast, and the creeping thing, and the fowls of the air; for it repenteth me that I have made them. Genesis 6:5-7*

In taking an honest look at these verses, we are able to see man is destroyed because every inclination of his heart is evil continually. Yahweh had been patient since the garden disappointment. Now He was ready to destroy mankind. Wouldn't it make sense however, to destroy the evil "Satan" if there was so much evil on the earth? After all, wasn't Satan the cause of all the evil? The answer is no! The evil was the result of man's choices. Man's heart is where the evil comes from. The words of Jeremiah 17:9 say the heart is deceitfully wicked above all else. Who can know it? Moreover, in the words of Yeshua in Mark 7 and Matthew 15… the Messiah says, *"out of the heart proceeds evil"*.

Yeshua knew exactly where evil came from. It came from man's heart, just as was known when the Earth was destroyed with a flood. In no way do these verses attribute evil to any entity other than man and his choices. Man's sins affected the whole creation. This is proven through seeing that it was Yahweh who brought the destruction of everything on the face of the earth because of man's sin. Here God decides to destroy the man and not "Satan". He is a just God and if "Satan" existed as the cause of sin and evil, then why wasn't "Satan" destroyed?

> *And GOD saw that the wickedness of man was great in the earth, and that every imagination of the thoughts of his heart was only evil continually. And it repented the LORD that he had made man on the earth, and it grieved him at his heart. And the LORD said, I will destroy man whom I have created from the face of the earth; both man, and beast, and the creeping thing, and the fowls of the air; for it repenteth me that I have made them. Genesis 6:5-7*

According to the statement in Genesis 6:5, it is man's heart that is bringing forth, producing and choosing evil, not some alleged satanic being.

Evil, or at least the opportunity for man to choose evil, appears to emanate from Yahweh. Moving to the end of the Book of Genesis, one would think that if there is a "Satan" he should have been clearly revealed in those writings. However, that is not the case. It is so much so not the case, that we learn from reading Genesis chapter 50 that God was the force who orchestrated Joseph's sale into slavery so the family of Jacob would go down to Egypt and ultimately end up in slavery so He could redeem them for a people to be a light to all nations. In verse 20 of that chapter, we see the patriarch Joseph gives credit where credit is due for all the evil that happened to him;

> *But as for you, ye thought evil against me; but God meant it unto good, to bring to pass, as it is this day, to save much people alive. Genesis 50:20*

In all the Torah, the mention of "Satan" is conspicuously absent and even in the above verse; Joseph recognizes **his brothers** had intended evil, not some cosmic Satan. Joseph was a profound dreamer and interpreter of dreams through Yahweh. He, being one who understood Egyptian mythology, symbology, and symbolism did not even hint at a satanic being as the one who caused his troubles. Joseph knew categorically that Yahweh is the one who causes all things to happen. Yahweh used Joseph's brothers and their evil hearts to get Joseph to Egypt. The concept of evil becomes almost surreal when one thinks that God allows the evil hearts of man, not Satan, to work within the framework of His plan of redemption for the ages.

CHAPTER 4

The First Use of the Word "Satan" in the English version of the Hebrew Scriptures

Paging through Genesis in the Torah we come to the first use of the word "satan". It is well known that the story of the serpent in the garden did not use the word "satan" in describing the deception of Adam and Eve. The use of the word "serpent" or as the Hebrew has it *nachash* is not comparable to the term "satan" in the Torah. Below is the list of verses where the Hebrew word "satan" appears in the Old Testament. Throughout this book, I will endeavor to concisely state how each one is used. I will address the term *sawtawn* as found in the book of Job at length separately, in Chapter 10; *The Satan In Job is Just a Human Adversary.* At this time, information on the rest of the uses in the Tanak[48] will be shared. I would like to start by listing all the Scripture verse that contain the Hebrew word for adversary.

Scripture Verses that use two of the Hebrew words for "satan" given the number 7854 and 7853 as reported in James Strong's Hebrew and Greek Dictionary.

The Total number of occurrences of 7854, pronounced saw-tawn, in the KJV is 27.

The word is translated as Satan 19 times and is seen in the following verses; 1Chronicles 21:1, Job 1:6-9 (5), Job 1:12 (2), Job 2:1-4 (5), Job 2:6-7 (2), Psalms 109:6, Zechariah 3:1-2 (3)

48 Tanak is a Hebrew acrostic of three letters with two vowels added in to aid in pronunciation. The word is made up of TNK as taken from the words *Torah* which is the instruction of God , the *Nevi'im*, which is the Prophets and the *Kethuvim*, which is the Psalms

The word is translated as adversary 6 times and is seen the following verses; Numbers 22:22, 1Kings 5:4 (2), 1Kings 11:14, 1Kings11:23, 1Kings 11:25

The word is translated as adversaries 1 time in the following verse; 2Samuel 19:22

The word is translated as withstand 1 time in the following verse; Numbers 22:32

The total number of occurrences of Strong's 7853, pronounced '*saw-tan*', is 6.

The word is translated as adversaries 5 times in the following verses; Psalms 38:20, Psalms 71:13, Psalms 109:4, Psalms 109:20, Psalms 109:29

The word is translated as resist 1 time in the following verse; Zechariah 3:1

Looking at the list of occurrences of the word "satan", we are able to note the various ways the word is translated. We first see the use of the word in the book of Numbers. The word occurs in chapter 22, two times; verses 22 and 32. The emphasis I have added shows where these words occur in the quote below. I have left the inline Strong's numbers in place to help you in identifying the focus words.

Numbers 22:22 And God's[430] anger[639] was kindled[2734] because[3588] he[1931] went:[1980] and the angel[4397] of the LORD[3068] stood[3320] in the way[1870] for an ***adversary[sawtawn]***[7854] *against him. Now he[1931] was riding[7392] upon[5921] his ass,[860] and his two[8147] servants[5288] were with[5973] him.*

Numbers 22:32 And the angel[4397] of the LORD[3068] said[559] unto[413] him, Wherefore[5921, 4100] hast thou smitten[5221] (853) thine ass[860] these[2088] three[7969] times?[7272] behold,[2009] I[595] went out[3318] to ***withstand[sawtawn]***[7854] *thee, because[3588] thy way[1870] is perverse[3399] before[5048] me:*

In the above passages, the English word "adversary" is the word "*sawtawn*" in the Hebrew text. As you are able to see, the Strong's number assigned to this word is 7854.

Strong's 7853, which carries the same meaning but is predominantly used when referring to a plural entity in opposition to God, is mostly used in the Psalms with one reference in the book of Zechariah.

For the benefit of the reader, I will place the text as given in the story in the book of Numbers below, and then continue my thoughts on the use of "satan" in this text.

> *Numbers 22:20-33 And God came unto Balaam at night, and said unto him, If the men come to call thee, rise up, and go with them; but yet the word which I shall say unto thee, that shalt thou do. 21 And Balaam rose up in the morning, and saddled his ass, and went with the princes of Moab. 22 And God's anger was kindled because he went: and the angel of the LORD stood in the way for an adversary* [7854] *against him. Now he was riding upon his ass, and his two servants were with him. 23 And the ass saw the angel of the LORD standing in the way, and his sword drawn in his hand: and the ass turned aside out of the way, and went into the field: and Balaam smote the ass, to turn her into the way. 24 But the angel of the LORD stood in a path of the vineyards, a wall being on this side, and a wall on that side. 25 And when the ass saw the angel of the LORD, she thrust herself unto the wall, and crushed Balaam's foot against the wall: and he smote her again. 26 And the angel of the LORD went further, and stood in a narrow place, where was no way to turn either to the right hand or to the left. 27 And when the ass saw the angel of the LORD, she fell down under Balaam: and Balaam's anger was kindled, and he smote the ass with a staff. 28 And the LORD opened the mouth of the ass, and she said unto Balaam, What have I done unto thee, that thou hast smitten me these three times? 29 And Balaam said unto the ass, Because thou hast mocked me: I would there were a sword in mine hand, for now would I kill thee. 30 And the ass said unto Balaam, Am not I thine ass, upon which thou hast ridden ever since I was thine unto this day? was I ever wont to do so unto thee? And he said, Nay. 31 Then the LORD opened the eyes of Balaam, and he saw the angel of the LORD standing in the way, and his sword drawn in his hand: and he bowed down his head, and fell flat on his face. 32 And the angel of the LORD said unto him, Wherefore hast thou smitten thine ass these three times? behold, I went out to withstand* [7854] *thee, because thy way is perverse before me: 33 And the ass saw me, and turned from me these three times: unless she had turned from me, surely now also I had slain thee, and saved her alive.*

So, the story goes that Balaam was asked to go and curse the Israelites, Yahweh's chosen people. First, if there is to be any cursing on the Israelites, history up until that point and beyond had shown that Yahweh will be the smiter with a curse. Secondly, Yahweh explicitly told Balaam to go with the men that would come in the morning but to speak only the word that He would give him. Yahweh's anger was kindled towards Balaam and He sent the angel of Yahweh to be a **satan against** Balaam because of this. Who or what is the "angel of Yahweh" that is being a "satan" to Balaam? This adversarial force has been written as being the "angel of the Lord" in our English bibles. However, Scriptural evidence is plentiful to reveal to us that the "angel of the Lord" may in fact be Yahweh Himself. Following are some occurrences of this term and you may notice this "being" appears to be one and the same as Yahweh. The reader will have to search this topic out as they see fit, as there are 66 verses in the Old and New testaments where this phrase appears.[49] By way of an example we will look at the account of Hagar, the excommunicated concubine of Abram, being spoken to by a fountain of water in the wilderness, when she had fled from her mistress Sarai;

> *And the angel of the LORD[50] found her by a fountain of water in the wilderness, by the fountain in the way to Shur. (8) And he said, Hagar, Sarai's maid, whence camest thou? and whither wilt thou go? And she said, I flee from the face of my mistress Sarai. (9) And the angel of the LORD said unto her, Return to thy*

---

49 Below I provide you with a list of all occurrences of the phrase "Angel of the Lord" and the reader may come to a conclusion through his or her own study of the topic._ Gen_16:7; Gen_16:9; Gen_16:10; Gen_16:11; Gen_22:11; Gen_22:15; Exo_3:2; Num_22:22; Num_22:23; Num_22:24; Num_22:25; Num_22:26; Num_22:27; Num_22:31; Num_22:32; Num_22:34; Num_22:35; Jdg_2:1; Jdg_2:4; Jdg_5:23; Jdg_6:11; Jdg_6:12; Jdg_6:21; Jdg_6:22; Jdg_13:3; Jdg_13:13; Jdg_13:15; Jdg_13:16; Jdg_13:17; Jdg_13:18; Jdg_13:20; Jdg_13:21; 2Sa_24:16; 1Ki_19:7; 2Ki_1:3; 2Ki_1:15; 2Ki_19:35; 1Ch_21:12; 1Ch_21:15; 1Ch_21:16; 1Ch_21:18; 1Ch_21:30; Psa_34:7; Psa_35:5; Psa_35:6; Isaiah_37:36; Dan_3:23; Dan_12:13; Zec_1:11; Zec_1:12; Zec_3:1; Zec_3:5; Zec_3:6; Zec_12:8; Mat_1:20; Mat_1:24; Mat_2:13; Mat_2:19; Mat_28:2; Luk_1:11; Luk_2:9; Act_5:19; Act_7:30; Act_8:26; Act_12:7; Act_12:23;

50 You will notice at times throughout this work I have chosen to leave the word LORD in scripture references as opposed to replacing it to the name of God, Yahweh. In the Hebrew text the letters that appear at places where LORD is found are the letters that compose the name of the Creator, **יהוה**. These letters are said to be Yod, Hay, Vav, Hay , commonly pronounced Yahweh or Yehovah. The purpose in the choice to not replace LORD with the proper Hebrew letters for God's name or name of God, is that I feel there is a greater likelihood my point is clearly communicated to the reader. Language and word choices for deity are very personal and if one's mind begins to disconnect due to the use of the Hebrew and therefore Biblical name of God, a point may be missed. I will use a word, which although is not the name of the Father, has come to represent Him in the minds of so many.

> *mistress, and submit thyself under her hands. (10) And the angel of the LORD said unto her, I will multiply thy seed exceedingly, that it shall not be numbered for multitude. (11) And the angel of the LORD said unto her, Behold, thou art with child, and shalt bear a son, and shalt call his name Ishmael; because the LORD hath heard thy affliction. Genesis 16:7-11*

In that account, we see numerous references to the "angel of the Lord" however, that same angel is the one who is promising to multiply Hagar's seed. In verse 10, we see that the "angel of the LORD" has to be Yahweh because it is He who is the one who can promise to multiply seed and then fulfill that promise.

The Book of Acts makes a similar claim about God when the story of Moses speaking to Yahweh on the Holy Mountain is recounted by Stephen. Stephen says;

> *This is he, that was in the church in the wilderness with the angel which spake to him in the mount Sina, and with our fathers: who received the lively oracles to give unto us: Acts 7:38 KJV*

Please consider exploring the possibility of an omnipresent Creator representing Himself or a facet of Himself as an "angel of the LORD" in a personal study that I am not intending to engage in, in this book.

Aside from the angel of the LORD being Yahweh in some manifestation, it is clear in verse 22 of chapter 22 in the book of Numbers, the *sawtawn* which means "adversary", is a direct dispatch from God. There is no "satan" who opposes God at work here. At the very least we see a *sawtawn* who is nothing more than an adversary to Balaam under the employ of God and even a diligent servant, quick to do the will of the Father and act with His authority when the anger of Yahweh has been kindled as is stated in verse 22. Many will ignore the clear evidence that the adversary, which is a satan, is sent from Yahweh once and continue to define "Satan" by their own belief system as a real being that Yahweh allowed to go and oppose Balaam. The text is clear, the messenger sent from Yahweh to Balaam was a "satan", and thus one should think of amending their current belief about Satan to one that agrees with the teaching in the Torah that teaches "the adversary" comes from God. Adhering to another philosophy of a fallen satanic angel as the one who brought the evil upon Balaam, forces one into a position where Isaiah 45:7 becomes difficult at best, to explain. Agreeing with the message of Yahweh as spoken by Isaiah maintains that there is nothing else in existence that can do evil to man except Yahweh. In this instance where the adversary is sent to Balaam as well as in many others, it is done when His anger is kindled. The following verse identifies Yahweh as the one doing evil when evil is enacted upon man.

> *That they may know from the rising of the sun, and from the west, that there is none beside me. I am the LORD, and there is none else. (7) I form the light, and create darkness: I make peace, and create evil: I the LORD do all these things. Isaiah 45:6-7*

Another fact in the story of Balaam is that the angel who was a "satan" came to oppose Balaam for opposing Yahweh's will. If "satan" takes the lead part in any way in stopping people from opposing the will of the Father then he, "satan", no longer is the archenemy of Yahweh. Satan then becomes a loyal servant of God. If Satan is stopping a man from breaking the will of the Father then we have just seen Satan divided against Satan. Therefore, this adversarial force from Yahweh could not have been a literal "Satan" who was simply allowed to go and get in the way of Balaam; otherwise, we have an evil entity stopping an evil activity. This behavior would effectively divide a "satanic" kingdom and bring it to desolation. The Master's words on what happens to a kingdom that divides against itself were cleverly stated to expose the illogic of the Pharisees to an onlooking crowd.

> *But when the Pharisees heard it, they said, This fellow doth not cast out devils, but by Beelzebub the prince of the devils. And Jesus knew their thoughts, and said unto them, Every kingdom divided against itself is brought to desolation; and every city or house divided against itself shall not stand: And if Satan cast out Satan, he is divided against himself; how shall then his kingdom stand? (Mat 12:24-26)*

Based on Yeshua's words above and the fact that the adversary in Numbers 22:22 is "the satan", we could see this incident with Balaam as an account of "Satan" casting out "Satan". This is seen in the way Balaam, who was opposing the will of Yahweh, was prevented from opposing Yahweh's will. It is "the satan" that goes to stand in the way of Balaam so Balaam could not be operating under the influence of "Satan".

Looking at verse 22 and 32 of the Numbers 22 passage, it is true we see the word "sawtawn", but should we stop at a literal definition of the word as we have come to know the word Satan today? Doing so in an effort to understand the passage places a limit on the writer's ability to relate a story using common colloquialisms. We will glean mountains more truth from Scripture if we allow ourselves to interpret the words the way the writer meant them to be heard. Making the decisions of rigid interpretation of Hebrew words alone may cause one to decide "*sawtawn*" means other than an agent of Yahweh. Only reading the words is not adequate to seeing what is spoken here. The word "withstand", you may have noted, is Strong's number 7854, *sawtawn*. This angel of Yahweh clearly says three times of himself, "He" went out to be a satan. The reason being was that Balaam's way is perverse. A perverse way is a way that is contrary to Yahweh. The kindling of Yahweh's anger is a result of the perverseness of Balaam's way. Would the unchanging God of the universe still have His anger kindled if our ways are perverse, that is if our ways our in opposition to His way? I would highly expect His anger to be kindled and in His time to dispatch a "satan", an adversary to oppose us in some way. Repeatedly when an adversary or evil spirit is sent upon a person or people group it is because the anger of Yahweh has been kindled and He then responds accordingly.

Without a doubt, the satan in the story of Balaam is not some cosmic, archenemy of the Creator but it is something or someone that is a direct employee or ministering angel from Yahweh. If *sawtawn* in the Torah is not speaking of a literal Satan, then is it possible that the appearance of the words "*devil" and "demons*" refer to a cosmic satan? Appearances initially seem that that is the case however, there is much more to the words than meets the eye.

"Devils" in the Torah and Why They Are Not What You Have Been Told

Through diligent, critical study, we find that there is no representation of Satan in the Torah, yet the Torah has not been silent on identifying that an adversarial force can come from Yahweh. The Scriptures typically use the words *sawtawn* or *sawtan* to describe this force. If the Torah does not teach a concept of a cosmic "Satan" then does the Torah provide us with any information about devils that may be an indication that Satan does exist as many believe him to exist today? We will look at some clues to finding answers to that question by looking at the use of another word found in the Torah. The English word "devils" is used four times in the King James Version, translated from two Hebrew words with slightly different meanings. The Strong's words are 8163- "*sá'iyr*", and 7700- "*shade*". Although these words are translated only four times as "devils", the appearance of the Hebrew originals occurs frequently in other passages that will help to clarify the meaning. The words are both referring to a shaggy goat that was worshipped in the desert. Albert Barnes elaborates on the use of this word in Leviticus 17 by saying;

> **Devils -** The word in the original is the "shaggy goat" of Lev_4:23. But it is sometimes employed, as here, to denote an object of pagan worship or a demon dwelling in the deserts 2Ch_11:15; Isa_13:21; Isa_34:14. The worship of the goat, accompanied by the foulest rites, prevailed in Lower Egypt; and the Israelites may have been led into this snare while they dwelt in Egypt.[51]

The total number of occurrences found in the Hebrew Scriptures of the word *saiyr* (8163) is 59 and translated variously. The number of times it is translated for each English word is as follows;

> It is translated as **kid 26** times in the following verses; Genesis 37:31, Leviticus 4:23, Leviticus 9:3, Leviticus 23:19, Numbers 7:16, Numbers 7:22, Numbers 7:28, Numbers 7:34, Numbers 7:40, Numbers 7:46, Numbers 7:52, Numbers 7:58, Numbers 7:64, Numbers 7:70, Numbers 7:76, Numbers 7:82, Numbers 15:24, Numbers 28:15, Numbers 28:30, Numbers 29:5, Numbers 29:11, Numbers 29:16, Numbers 29:19, Numbers 29:25, Ezekiel 45:22-23 (2)
>
> It is translated as **goat 21** times in the following verses; Leviticus 4:23-24 (2), Leviticus 10:15-16 (2), Leviticus 16:9-10 (2), Leviticus 16:15, Leviticus 16:18, Leviticus 16:20-22 (5), Leviticus 16:26-27 (2), Number 29:22 (2), Numbers 29:28, Numbers 29:31, Numbers 29:34, Numbers 29:38, Ezekiel 43:25
>
> It is translated as **goats 3** times in the following verses; Leviticus 16:7-8 (2), 2Chronicles 29:23
>
> It is translated as **devils 2** times in the following verses; Leviticus 17:7, 2Chronicles 11:15
>
> It is translated as **hairy 2** times in the following verses; Genesis 27:11, Genesis 27:23
>
> It is translated as **kids 2** times in the following verses; Leviticus 16:5, Numbers 7:87
>
> It is translated as **rough 1** time in the following verse; Daniel 8:21

51 Albert Barnes' Notes on the Bible, Albert Barnes (1798-1870)

It is translated as **satyr 1** time in the following verse; Isaiah 34:14

It is translated as **satyrs 1** time in the following verse; Isaiah 13:21

The "shaggy goat" was known as a satyr to some of the prophets of Israel such as is seen of Isaiah. Below are the two occurrences of the word "devils" and then the Isaiah 13:21 occurrence of the same Hebrew word being translated as satyr. The Strong's dictionary reference numbers are left in place to help in identifying where the word "*saiyr*" is found.

And they shall no[3808] more[5750] offer[2076 (853)] their sacrifices[2077] unto ***devils,[8163]*** *after[310] whom[834] they[1992] have gone a whoring.[2181] This[2063] shall be[1961] a statute[2708] forever[5769] unto them throughout their generations.[1755] Leviticus 17:7*

And he ordained[5975] him priests[3548] for the high places,[1116] and for the ***devils,[8163]*** *and for the calves[5695] which[834] he had made.[6213] 2Chronicles 11:15*

But wild beasts of the desert[6728] shall lie[7257] there;[8033] and their houses[1004] shall be full[4390] of doleful creatures;[255] and owls[1323, 3284] shall dwell[7931] there,[8033] and ***satyrs[8163]*** *shall dance[7540] there.[8033] Isaiah 13:21*

Above we see "devils" were sacrificed to in the Israelites' history. This was spoken against by God and even the stranger who was sojourning with the Israelites was clearly taught to no longer sacrifice in the fields as they had been doing but to bring the sacrifice to the tabernacle where the priests would perform their religious duty with it. We see the word *saiyr* is most frequently given the meaning of "kid" and "goat." Although the concept may not be familiar to our 21st Century Western Christian mindset, there was plenty of worship of goat-like, man-made, and man-imagined creatures in the wilderness period. Our culture today is so far removed from the eastern culture of the wandering Israelite in the wilderness periods, that we have difficulty understanding the varied entities worshipped and the frequency with which Israel adopted the worship practices and icons of the nations they became exposed to. Jamieson, Fausset, and Brown in their commentary say this about the satyr;

> Satyrs
>
> *seirim*. Lev_17:7, "they shall no more offer ... sacrifices unto devils" (*seirim*) i.e. to the evil spirits of the desert, literally, "shaggy goats," hence applied to an object of pagan worship or a demon dwelling in the desert (2Ch_11:15; Isaiah_13:21; Isaiah_34:14). At Mendes in Lower Egypt the goat was worshipped with foul rites. Israel possibly once shared in them. Compare Jos_24:14-15; Eze_23:8-9; Eze_23:21.[52]

We find more information in the International Standard Bible Encyclopedia that explains the Hebrew word for *satyr* is translated as the Greek word *daimonia* in the Septuagint. Daimonia became "demon" in the English language.

> The question is whether *sa'ir* and *s^e'irim* in these passages stand for real or for fabulous animals. In Lev_17:7 and 2Ch_11:15, it is clear that they are objects of worship, but that still leaves open the question of their nature, though it may to many minds make "devils" or "demons" or "satyrs" seem preferable to "he-goats." In Isaiah_13:20 we read, "neither shall the Arabian pitch tent there; neither shall shepherds make their flocks to lie down there." This may very likely have influenced the American Committee of Revisers to use "wild goat" in Isaiah_13:21 and Isaiah_34:14 instead of the "he-goat" of the other passages. In the American Standard Revised Version, no fabulous creatures (except perhaps "night-monster") are mentioned here, but the Septuagint employs *daimonia*, "demons" in Isaiah_13:21[53]

Therefore, the Septuagint employed the word demons when faced with the choice to use he-goat or another related word. I contend, this choice was critical in the formulation of the demonology concept of the present day and the past. The concept has been imposed on us through the use of a word that is full of meaning in many ages, but the present meaning is not the intended meaning in the age of its original use. Today when we read certain passages in the English Bible, we are presented the concept that a cosmic entity is employed by certain worshipers because the word "demon" is in the text. Very few readers will actually recognize that the "demon" which is being spoken of in those instances is nothing more than a shaggy goat that was given the

52 Robert Jamieson, A. R. Fausset and David Brown Commentary Critical and Explanatory on the Whole Bible

53 International Standard Bible Encyclopedia, under heading;"Satyr"

elevated status of being worshipped by a culture that had lost its way in many respects.

One need not be confused as to the meaning of the word *saiyr* in the Scriptures. The occurrence of the word "devils" in 2 Chronicle 11:15, aids in clearing up much confusion. We are given a list of what was implemented for false worship by Jeroboam when the house of Israel was separated from the house of Judah. Jeroboam was a son of King Solomon who had been exiled to Egypt and upon his return was raised to be the king of the Northern Tribes of Israel as seen in 1Kings 12:1-20.

Jeroboam was a master at manufacturing false worship and even at one point declared a different festival for the House of Israel to celebrate in Jeroboam's kingdom in an effort to keep them from returning to Jerusalem for worship. The list given in 2 Chronicles 11:15, tells us Jeroboam made his own priests. Priests that were not the God appointed Levites of the Holy Temple. We are also told that he made devils. These devils would have been goat-like idols to worship. As well as making devils to worship, Jeroboam also made calves. This action is reminiscent of the golden calf Aaron constructed for the Israelites as they waited for Moses to descend the Mountain with the commandments. The text that makes the point distinctly says; "*which he had made*," referring to Jeroboam as the originator of the worship item called "devils."

> *And he ordained him priests for the high places, and for the devils, and for the calves* ***which he had made****. 2Chronicles 11:15 KJV*

Jeroboam built these devils and in this case, the "devils" were not cosmic supernatural beings actively pursuing the worship and allegiance of Israelites. This is yet another instance where a man chooses to abuse power because of the corruption of his heart. The heart is always the point from were evil behaviors proceed. Remember Yeshua's words about where defilement comes from.

> *But those things which proceed out of the mouth come forth from the heart; and they defile the man. For out of the heart proceed evil thoughts, murders, adulteries, fornications, thefts, false witness, blasphemies: Matthew 15:18-19*

It becomes clear that what was made by Jeroboam for worship was simply a goat-like idol and was considered a blasphemy. John Gill's Exposition of the Entire Bible provides us with this comment regarding the use of the word "devils" in 2 Chronicles 11:15;

> *...and for the devils; demons in the shape of goats, as this word signifies, in which form many of the Heathen deities were worshipped; idols of whatsoever kind are so called; for whosoever worships them worships not God, but devils, 1Co_10:21 the images which Jeroboam set up may be meant, and the next clause may be rendered as explanative of them:*

Adam Clark in his Commentary on the Bible says the following:

> 2Ch 11:15 -
>
> *And he ordained him priests - for the devils -* שעירים seirim, the hairy ones; probably goats: for as the golden calves, or oxen, were in imitation of the Egyptian ox-god, Apis; so they no doubt paid Divine honors to the goat, which we know was an object of religious veneration in Egypt.

It seems clear from the word *saiyr,* used in the text of Lev 17:7 and 2 Chronicles 11:15, which is translated in the KJV bible as devils, is not meaning anything more than a fabricated, goat-like, man made article of veneration. Jeroboam did nothing different from the surrounding cultures and nations, by designing a system of worship to entice the Israelites in his kingdom into staying with him and therefore not returning to the "Holy Land" where they could participate in true biblical worship according to the manner and design that Yahweh had prescribed for His covenant peoples. Jeroboam believed that to mimic the pagan nations' worship style, practices, and false deities, was an effective mode of maintaining the subjects of his kingdom and preventing an exodus from his geographic area.

I think it is now safe to conclude the "devils" of the Leviticus 17:7 and 2 Chronicles 11:15 passages are not referring to anything supernatural at all but are referring to a totally powerless inanimate object, designed and built by man. Once again we are able to set aside an understanding of a word in Scripture that has been thought by many to refer to Satan by peering into the culture surrounding the incident in the text and looking at the meaning of the words as they would have been understood by a listener in the time they were written.

The other two occurrences of the word devils in the English do not have the same definition of goat as the occurrences in Leviticus 17:7 and 2 Chronicles 11:15 but they do refer to the goats that were sacrificed to by the Israelites and the pagans. The two verses which contain the Strong's Hebrew word #7700 *"shade"*, but are translated as the word "devils" are given here;

Deuteronomy 32:17
*They sacrificed[2076] unto **devils,**[7700] not[3808] to God;[433] to gods[430] whom they knew[3045] not,[3808] to new[2319] gods that came[935] newly up,[4480, 7138] whom your fathers[1] feared[8175] not.[3808]*

Psalms 106:37
*Yea, they sacrificed[2076] (853) their sons[1121] and their daughters[1323] unto **devils,**[7700]*

Briggs, Driver, Brown Hebrew Lexicon and James Strong both assign the definition of "demon" to this word but the context of the word used, reveals that a *shade*(pronounced shed), is a pagan-hairy-goat-idol and was not a supernatural entity at all. The literary context reveals that this *shade* was nothing but a mythological character that was imbued with power by the actions of man through man designing the goat-idol to fit the imagined characteristics and physical attributes of their highly superstitious thinking. Man had a belief and man fabricated an icon to fit that mythological belief.

Although scholars such a Briggs, Driver, Brown define the word #7700 as "demon", we must be careful to not stop at that and neglect to explore the ancient meaning underlying the word. As simple as it is, the definition should lead us to determine what exactly the demon that is spoken of here is. Just as the Hebrew word for "tree", *etes,* when used by the writer, can be further explored to determine what kind of tree was being spoken of. Such as in Ezekiel when Yahweh is telling of the fall of a mighty political ruler and there speaks of him as a tree, so too can the definition of the word *shade* as demon, be investigated further to determine what the demon was. Words do not always mean what they literally can be defined as in the Scriptures

And all the trees of the field shall know that I the LORD have brought down the high tree, have exalted the low tree, have dried up the green tree, and have made the dry tree to flourish: I the LORD have spoken and have done it. Ezekiel 17:24 KJV

Understanding the words of Scripture is not always the simple matter of being told what a word means to us today in the English language, rather one must consider what the words in the original Hebrew would have meant thousands of years ago. Following that path leads us to find the "demon" is the *saiyr*, a shaggy kid.

Reading the definition of the word alone, one might be inclined to say, "There, the definition of this word is demon!" So there is the concept of demons given in the Old Testament".

In thinking this, one might take that simple definition as the proof that demons do exist and are part of the theology of the Israel of God. I can see where one could take these verses and devise doctrine from them; however, I posit that these two verses are simply employing a different word for the same concept. The concept is explained in verse 17 of Deuteronomy 32 by informing us that the "devils" came up new. This indicates that these "devils" were not the so-called fallen angels who allegedly were cast down from heaven with Satan.

Rashi, the 11th Century Bible commentator gives fairly lucid insight on the issue.

Here is the translation from a 1992 Israel Research Society English translation of the Bible. Rashi's comments follow where I have placed an emphasis on his point that makes a connection to the word *shade* in Isaiah 13.

> *They provoked him to jealousy with strange gods, with abominations provoked they him to anger:*
>
> *They sacrificed to powerless spirits, not to God; to gods whom they knew not; to new gods that came newly up, whom your fathers feared not: Deuteronomy 32:16-17*
>
> **RASHI'S COMMENTS**:
>
> (Verse 17) **LO ELOHA.**
>
> understand this as the Targum does - they sacrifice unto devils in which is no utility, for if there were at least any utility in them to the world (as e g, the sun, moon and stars) the provocation to anger would not be so intense (lit, double) as it actually is now (Siphre):
>
> **THEY SACRIFICED— TO GODS THAT CAME UP REGENTLY.**
>
> i e with which even the heathen nations were not familiar; Indeed, if a heathen saw them he would say, "This is a Jewish idol" (Siphre):
>
> **WHOM YOUR FATHERS REVERENCED NOT.**
>
> this means, which your fathers feared not; more literally it means - their hair did not stand up on end because of them - for it is the

> nature of a person's hair to stand up out of fear; Thus is it (the word "Se'arum") explained in Siphre; **But it is also possible to explain it as being connected with the noun in (Is:13:21)** "And Se'irim shall dance there"; "Se'irim" are demons (satyrs), and the meaning of our verse would then be - your fathers never made these satyrs:

Rashi notes the devils that were sacrificed to, were satyrs and had no past existence, such as would be of any real demonic angels called devils. Even the heathen nations saw these "devils" as specifically Jewish idols, says Rashi. Please look at the Young's Literal translation of this verse below, which helps us by supporting Rashi's understanding of this passage.

> *They sacrifice to demons--no god! Gods they have not known--New ones--from the vicinity they came; Not feared them have your fathers! Deuteronomy 32:17 YLT*

The Jewish Publication Society Translation states the concept in a very similar manner;

> *They sacrificed unto demons, no-gods, gods that they knew not, new gods that came up of late, which your fathers dreaded not. Deuteronomy 32:17 JPS*

So we see from these two versions of this Scripture that the devils or the demons that were sacrificed to are not gods at all. Rashi commented on the originality of these demons being specifically associated with the Israelites and I believe the reason why we are told our fathers, the Patriarchs of Israel, did not dread these demons is because they, the demons, did not exist and there was therefore nothing to dread. The picture we are seeing expressed here in the Torah is a picture of the Israelites, perhaps in their ignorance but more likely in their rebellion, fashioning idols, called here demons, with their own hands. This is what made them new. They were not called new because they were recently created by the Father, nor because they were recently fallen from heaven and now are part of a satanic minion. We are able to see this concept reiterated in the book of Isaiah where he states that these things were created recently by the hands of men.

> *I have even from the beginning declared it to thee; before it came to pass I shewed it thee: lest thou shouldest say, Mine idol hath done them, and my graven image, and my molten image, hath commanded them. 6 Thou hast heard, see all this; and will not ye declare it? I have shewed thee new things from this time, even*

> *hidden things, and thou didst not know them. 7 They are created now, and not from the beginning; even before the day when thou heardest them not; lest thou shouldest say, Behold, I knew them. Isaiah 48:5-7*

Isaiah tells us, any idols that are given credit for the things that Yahweh says and does, were not present from the beginning, and were not present a long time ago. Israel is told that they should not say they are ancient and they knew them long before this present time, mistakenly attributing a supernatural characteristic to these empty and powerless idols.

In looking at this passage in Isaiah 48, you may see Yahweh is chastising Israel once again, for living hypocritically. The people profess their holiness and speciallness because they are inhabitants of the Holy City and are called by the name of the Holy One of Israel. For this, God rebukes the Israelites. He tells them that it was He who declared things to happen in the future but had declared them to happen a long time ago, from the beginning.

What Yahweh declared did indeed happen and now the Idols that were created newly by the hands of the Israelites are given the credit. What an abomination to Yahweh. In fact, for three chapters Isaiah is rebuking and exhorting the Israelites because of their propensity to attribute acts of Yahweh to another power. Isaiah is very clear to inform them as Yahweh imparts to him, that there is no other power. Israel has been in exile and spent time in Babylon and Persia. Simply by their intermingling with the culture many of the pagan spiritual concepts have been adopted and put into practice by the Israelites.

Israel the people had found themselves so integrated with the pagan culture of their captor; they adopted much of the philosophy of that region. I believe this point in Israel's history is a fulcrum in our quest to understand how "Satan" became another god in the minds and practice of the faithful. It is here we see the ancient understanding of "the satan", which is the adversarial force from God or man, evolve into a cosmic dualistic philosophy.

Cyrus is a Messiah who Led Israel Towards a Two God System

History is quite clear on when the Israelites were taken captive and when they were sent back to Jerusalem to rebuild the temple. It was under King Cyrus in the 6th Century BCE. Cyrus is the one who sent Israel to their homeland to rebuild. Cyrus is even called Yahweh's anointed in the prophecy foretelling of his purpose in the 45th chapter of Isaiah, verse one.

Thus saith the LORD to his anointed, to Cyrus, whose right hand I have holden, to subdue nations before him; Isaiah 45:1

Cyrus is a pagan king who is set apart for the purpose of defeating the Babylonians and releasing the captive Jews. It is poignant that the Creator of all things calls Cyrus His Mashiach. The Septuagint translates this term for Cyrus as Christos or Christ. What an incredible concept! Cyrus, a pagan king of Persia, is called Yahweh's Christ. Albert Barnes in his Notes on the Bible commentary says this about Cyrus as the anointed;

Isaiah 45:1 -

Thus saith the Lord to his anointed - This is a direct apostrophe to Cyrus, though it was uttered not less than one hundred and fifty years before Babylon was taken by him. The word 'anointed' is that which is usually rendered "Messiah" (מש יח mashiyach), and here is rendered by the Septuagint, Τω χριστω μου Κύρω To christo mou Kuro - 'To Cyrus, my Christ,' i. e, my anointed. It properly means "the anointed," and was a title which was commonly given to the kings of Israel, because they were set apart to their office by the ceremony of anointing, who hence were called οι χρυστοὶ Κυρίου hoi christoi Kuriou - 'The anointed of the Lord' 1Sa_2:10, 1Sa_2:35; 1Sa_12:3, 1Sa_12:5; 1Sa_16:6; 1Sa_24:7, 1Sa_24:11; 1Sa_26:9, 1Sa_26:11, 1Sa_26:23; 2Sa_1:14, 2Sa_1:16; 2Sa_19:22-23. There is no evidence that the Persian kings were inaugurated or consecrated by oil, but this is an appellation which was common among the Jews, and is applied to Cyrus in accordance with their usual mode of designating kings. It means here that God had solemnly set apart Cyrus to perform an important public service in his cause. It does not mean that Cyrus was a man of piety, or a worshipper of the true God, of which there is no certain evidence, but that his appointment as king was owing to the arrangement of God's providence, and that he was to be employed in accomplishing his purposes. The title does not designate holiness of character, but appointment to an office.[54]

The above quote identifies clearly the role of Cyrus, the great King of Persia. As the Messiah he was of course, not the Savior as is spoken of elsewhere in the prophets but nonetheless he was indeed anointed by God to perform certain actions as a ruler that would bring about the plan of God to return the exiles to Israel.

---

54 From Albert Barnes Notes on the Bible

As I stated previously it is at this point in Israel's history that Isaiah is telling the Israelites about the nature of Yahweh and is often addressing the concept that all things, good and evil, come from the only Power, the Creator; God. Isaiah spoke of a time in the future where Israel eventually had bought in to the Zoroastrian cosmic dualism philosophy of the Persians. Zoroaster was a Persian theologian from about the 6th Century BCE. King Cyrus was a Zoroastrian and ascribed to his philosophies. Cyrus also is noted in history for his many conquests and the success of the growth of his kingdom through the adoption of many philosophies of those lands he conquered. The philosophy which was foundational to Cyrus and his Persian Kingdom, believed that there was a good god called Ahura Mazda and a bad god Ahriman. Ahriman was intent on thwarting the plans of Ahura Mazda and was given the dubious distinction of being the cause of all the evil and bad in the world of the ancient Persians. Isaiah was responding to God by issuing statements of truth to the Israelites, who would inevitably accept the Zoroastrian philosophy that claims there exists two supernatural beings; one of them was in control of the good while the other was responsible for the evil. Although this prophecy of Isaiah is spoken about one hundred and fifty years before the time of Cyrus, Israel's path was clear to Yahweh and He warned them of a time when they would adopt a philosophy that attributed the things God does to an imagined cosmic entity.

A special notice here of Isaiah 45:7, seen below, intimates that Yahweh wanted Israel to know that it was He who was responsible for the evil in their world. Other prophets have taken on the charge to speak a similar message as is seen from Amos in chapter 3 of his Book, where he also shares the concept of evil coming from God through his rhetorical question.

> *Shall a trumpet be blown in the city, and the people not be afraid? shall there be evil in a city, and the LORD hath not done it? Amos 3:6*

There is much that will be said on the topic of Zoroastrian influence on religions, in chapter 7, for now here is a short list of the occurrences in Isaiah 44 to 48 which demonstrate Isaiah's effort in teaching the Israelites that there is no power but one, and it is Yahweh.

Isaiah 44:6	*Thus saith the LORD the King of Israel, and his redeemer the LORD of hosts; I am the first, and I am the last; and beside me there is no God.*

Isaiah 44:8	*Fear ye not, neither be afraid: have not I told thee from that time, and have declared it? ye are even my witnesses. Is there a God beside me? yea, there is no God; I know not any*
Isaiah 44:10	*Who hath formed a god, or molten a graven image that is profitable for nothing?*
Isaiah 45:5	*I am the LORD, and there is none else, there is no God beside me: I girded thee, though thou hast not known me:*
Isaiah 45:6	*That they may know from the rising of the sun, and from the west, that there is none beside me. I am the LORD, and there is none else.*
Isaiah 45:7	*I form the light, and create darkness: I make peace, and create evil: I the LORD do all these things.*
Isaiah 45:14	*Thus saith the LORD, The labour of Egypt, and merchandise of Ethiopia and of the Sabeans, men of stature, shall come over unto thee, and they shall be thine: they shall come after thee; in chains they shall come over, and they shall fall down unto thee, they shall make supplication unto thee, saying, Surely God is in thee; and there is none else, there is no God.*
Isaiah 45:18	*For thus saith the LORD that created the heavens; God himself that formed the earth and made it; he hath established it, he created it not in vain, he formed it to be inhabited: I am the LORD; and there is none else.*
Isaiah 45:21	Tell ye, and bring them near; yea, let them take counsel together: who hath declared this from ancient time? who hath told it from that time? have not I the LORD? and there is no God else beside me; a just God and a Saviour; there is none beside me.
Isaiah 45:22	*Look unto me, and be ye saved, all the ends of the earth: for I am God, and there is none else.*
Isaiah 46:9	*Remember the former things of old: for I am God, and there is none else; I am God, and there is none like me,'*

In this chapter, we have looked at verses in the Hebrew Scriptures that contain the word "devils." We talked about how Rashi, the 11th Century commentator on the Torah, understood them to be satyrs and the heathen nations around the Jews recognized the "devils" to be specifically Jewish idols. This then gives strong evidence that these particular "devils" were not familiar to other cultures and therefore not existing prior to the fabrication of them by the Jewish/Hebrew/Israelite people. Even though these concepts seem quite self-explanatory, I would still like to consider the possibility of these "devils" being newly brought into existence or were angels that recently rebelled for any number of reasons. Is it even a logical possibility to suppose devils are new in the sense that they are just recently created? Is Yahweh or Satan developing more angels or demons? If that scenario is possible then any of a number of dynamic activities which must be questioned are going on; these are posed below;

1) either God is creating new angels that rebel, or

2) He is creating new demons to tempt and attack man or

3) "Satan" is creating more devils; or

4) "Satan" is drawing more angels away from the service of the Sovereign Creator.

There may be more possibilities to consider but we will deal with the ones I state here. It is clear after considering each of them that not one of them is a plausible possibility. None of them fit the concept of one Creator who finished His work of creation on the 6th day of the creation account. Let's look at the possibilities one by one.

1) Yahweh is creating new angels that rebel;

Is it possible that Yahweh is still creating? If we are to believe God is still performing a creation act, then we loosen, that is to weaken, the biblical fact that Yahweh finished His work of creation on the sixth day. He rested on the Sabbath, the seventh day because His work of creation was completed. I am not saying that a fruit tree does not rise up from a seed or an infant is not developed from a fertilized egg in the womb of a fertile mother. What I am saying here is all things that come into existence after the sixth day of creation come about through the reaction of already existing matter. The fruit tree must have a seed to be developed from, and the infant must come from an egg, which needs to be fertilized. Even the conception of the Messiah came to be through the use by God, of existing matter. The unfertilized ovum in the womb of Mary the Mother of Yeshua was a material that was already in existence. Yahweh chose to act upon this existing tangible material to manifest Himself in the flesh. Was this necessary or could not the God of the Universe have simply materialized as a full-grown man? In fact, if we assess many of the appearances of Yahweh, we see a pattern of the Creator using the created to express himself. This is evident in the continued manifestation of Yahweh through things like fire and wind, two elements that exist because of the act of creation and need not be created especially for a demonstration of the power and presence of Yahweh. No, Yahweh is not still performing creative acts that might involve the creation of "demons".

2) He (Yahweh) is creating new demons to tempt and attack man

We have discussed the plausibility of creation being an ongoing act of Yahweh. I claim it is not a plausible dynamic. To carry the thought further; is it then plausible Yahweh, a God who desires that none should perish but all would come to the knowledge of the Messiah and receive eternal life, would continue to create an opponent who has proven to be successful at killing and destroying the work and people of Yahweh? What kind of a loving Father would we be beholden to and called to honor, if He continues to create more creatures that will undoubtedly be the harbingers of death and destruction causing people world wide to be deceived resulting in eternal damnation? It is by far a more consistent belief to believe there are no demons being created by Yahweh.

As I stated, He finished His work of creation on the sixth day and due to the fact that the Messiah overcame the works of the devil, why would He then create more devils or demons? It is totally illogical to believe He would, therefore, I emphatically believe and declare He would not. New demons are not being created and there is a lack of proof to say that there ever will be.

3) Satan is creating more devils;

This one is an easy one. We see movies and read stories of the forces of darkness spawning demons and spirits with fairly regular frequency. This situation lends us the theory that "Satan" has the power to create. Is there any force in the universe besides Yahweh with the power to create? If there is another force in the universe with the power to create, then there are more gods than one and now we have a viable option to choose a god other than Yahweh with real creative power. We then can choose a God with the ability to answer us and respond to us in the way he or she chooses. This is in total opposition to the Scriptures which clearly state there is no god but one. We may be inclined to think that Yahweh "allows" this "Satan" the power to create demons. If one is inclined to believe this then one doesn't believe creation is complete. Why would Yahweh prove He is God and perform the act of creation, which He chose to cease on the sixth day, and then give another supernatural being the ability to be like God? I believe He wouldn't and He helps us with that concept by telling us in Isaiah that there is none like Him. I have added emphasis in the quote below.

> *Remember the former things of old:* ***for I am God, and there is none else; I am God, and there is none like me,*** *Isaiah 46:9*

It is highly unlikely that there is another supernatural entity that has the ability to create more demons as he finds need for reinforcements in his sworn battle against all that is good.

The final possibility we put forth for discussion is that;

4)"Satan" is drawing more angels away from the service of the Sovereign Creator.

If we believe the "new" gods are angels recently drawn away by "Satan" then we encounter a completely new set of problems. These problems would involve the angels in heaven never having a true sovereignly ordained position of worship and ministry to the Father. In fact if we really begin to understand the glory and majesty of the throne room of Heaven and get a picture of the Creator's brilliance, which is too amazing for us to behold, we see His radiance is so awe inspiring that no man can see Yahweh and live. The writer of Exodus states his point as seen below and we see in the following passage Paul the apostle is providing us with similar information as he tells Timothy that the Creator is unapproachable in the true physical sense of someone approaching Him;

> *And he said, Thou canst not see my face: for there shall no man see me, and live. Exodus 33:20*

Who only hath immortality, dwelling in the light which no man can approach unto; whom no man hath seen, nor can see: to whom be honour and power everlasting. Amen. 1 Timothy 6:16

In seeing how inexplicable the true presence of Yahweh is, we may begin to understand how improbable it is that an angel, which is created as a minister [55]of Yahweh, would have its own will and choose to leave the presence and duty that it was created to do. Of course, to have a Satan philosophy that expresses itself as is currently typical in North American Christianity and folklore, as well as many other continents in the world, we are forced to believe that angels do in fact have a free will to choose to maintain their position or to choose to leave it and rebel against the Father.

This book is not a treatise on angels and their roles according to their created purpose. However, I posit that if there are angels which are ministering spirits for Yahweh, created to do His will as it pertains to Him and His relationship with mankind, that there is no indication in Scripture that they posses a free will as was given to man. Man was created with a free will to choose to fear and worship Yahweh only as was demonstrated in the Garden of Eden when Adam and Eve chose to place their own desires ahead of Yahweh's will for them. If in fact angels exist in the manner of common belief, they are created beings given the charge of praising Yahweh and would not have the impetus derived from an evil inclination, to do otherwise. The Psalms identify the role of angels as being one of praise as seen below; a praise that is decreed to last forever and is even assigned to the dragon which would show a connection to any being that is thought to be evil;

Praise ye him, all his angels: praise ye him, all his hosts. Psalms 148:2

---

55 For a study on the purpose of angels you may be inclined to start with a search of the word in a concordance and follow the verses listed. For a little extra help here are some verse references on the topic. Although I do not endorse all the content on the page quoted from or the website as mentioned below, I provide the list of references and the web site address for the reader. If the link is not available at the time of your search please feel free to email me and I will forward the copy saved in my databank on the subject.
The Ministry of Angels:
Nehemiah 9:6
Psalms 148:2
Isaiah 6:2-4
Matthew 18:10
Luke 2:13
Hebrews 1:6
Revelation 5:11, 12; 7:11
Taken from ; http://dianedew.com/angels.htm

> *Let them praise the name of the LORD: for he commanded, and they were created*
> *He hath also stablished them for ever and ever: he hath made a decree which shall not pass.*
> *Praise the LORD from the earth, ye dragons, and all deeps: Psalms 148:5-7KJV*

It is a theological and philosophical stretch to claim angels ever were able to or are presently able to rebel out of a choice or act of their will, and choose to remove themselves from the role they are created for and from the presence of Yahweh. It is not logical thinking nor is it Biblical thinking to say angels would choose to give up their designated position of servitude to the Creator, in a deluded attempt to overthrow Him. This alleged overthrow is attempted through oppressing and attacking humans whom God loves and wants to be with Him for eternity. Can we see the stretching required to believe that an angel has even been given the capacity to choose to exit heaven? An angel can no more make that choice than can a human who becomes a citizen of the Millennial Kingdom[56] when wickedness is done away with and beyond, when God makes His dwelling place with men on the new earth[57]. We at that point will no more be able to choose to leave His magnificent presence than can the angels choose now or ever were able to choose to emancipate themselves from an eternal position in the presence of the Glorious One.

Simply put, any creature who is allowed to have access to the physical presence of Yahweh and His throne room would by no means choose to remove him or her self from that environment. For one to believe that a cognitive being could purposely choose to exit the presence of the Creator, is to fall tragically short in their understanding of just how majestic, magnificent and

56 The Millennial Kingdom is referenced in the book of Revelations Chapter 20 verses 5 and 7. There, we are told of those who cross over from this age to the Millennial age and how they will not be subject to the second death, which is the death of the wicked resurrected, who enter into judgment upon their resurrection. We who are alive at the appearance of Messiah Yeshua and those who are the resurrected righteous will spend 1000 years with Mashiach before the wicked are resurrected, judged and will be rewarded with eternal death, which is a destruction from the presence of Yahweh according to 1 Thessalonians 1:9

57 Rev 21:1-3 And I saw a new heaven and a new earth: for the first heaven and the first earth were passed away; and there was no more sea. 2) And I John saw the holy city, new Jerusalem, coming down from God out of heaven, prepared as a bride adorned for her husband. 3) And I heard a great voice out of heaven saying, Behold, **the tabernacle of God *is* with men, and he will dwell with them**, and they shall be his people, and God himself shall be with them, *and be* their God.

Holy that experience is. Once a created being is in the presence of Yahweh, that being will remain in the status that allowed him or her to enter that environment and would not choose to leave.

As for the "devils" and "demons" in the Torah, we can see that they are just satyrs in the form of goats that are dreamed up by man and imbued with power by the human mind. The ancient god "Pan" comes to mind when one hears of a goat idol, as Pan was an Eastern God that possessed the characteristics of a goat such as hooves and horns. A devil or demon is nothing and there is only one God. Paul tried to teach the polytheistic Corinthians this truth in 1 Corinthians chapter 7. A version of the Bible called *The Message* provides a clear translation indicating how certain Paul is that there is no other Gods but One.

> *Some people say, quite rightly, that idols have no actual existence, that there's nothing to them, that there is no God other than our one God, that no matter how many of these so-called gods are named and worshiped they still don't add up to aything but a tall story. 1 Corinthians 8:4-5 MSG*

CHAPTER 5

If Satan Exists He is a God according to Yahweh

There is only One God as you have seen testified to throughout this book several times already. However, you might ask, "how can you state that if there is a Satan, then there is another God?" Some will opine that because they believe there is a "Satan" does not mean that they have a two-god belief system. The facts though are contrary to their thinking and simply put, if one ascribes any supernatural power to anything, be it an imagined character or a wood carving on a mantle, they are proclaiming that there is at least one other god. To address this question we must explore the Scriptures to see if Yahweh calls lesser gods "Gods" and if Yahweh charges that those who claim their power is real are guilty of idolatry. These typically become the demons of religions such as Christianity. This "transfer of false gods of nations to demons of satan" thinking is a very dangerous ideology and one which has been evolving into multiple streams of mystical interpretation. The perception of many over the history of Christianity has been one that sees the belief in a devil by the faithful, as an abandoning of monotheism. In *The Origin of Satan,* Pagels reports the thought of Celsus, a second century doctor, historian and philosopher, with these words;

> What makes the Christians' message dangerous, Celsus writes, is not that they believe in one God, but that they deviate from monotheism by their "*blasphemous*" belief in the devil. For all the "*impious errors*" the Christians commit, Celsus says, they show their greatest ignorance in "*making up a being opposed to God, and calling him 'devil.' or in the Hebrew language, 'Satan.*" All such ideas, Celsus declares, are nothing but human inventions, sacreligious even to repeat: *"It is blasphemy…to say that the greatest God…has an adversary who constrains his capacity to do good."* Celsus is outraged that the Christians, who claim to

worship one God, "*impiously divide the kingdom of God, creating a rebellion in it, as if there were opposing factions within the divine, including one that is hostile to God.*"[58]

Do we stand then on the words of Celsus and look no further for the understanding that claims adding a "satan" to one's faith is equal to adding another God? Although insightful, the words of a first century rhetorician who was not know to be a follower of Messiah are not to be the foundation for our understanding, a good foundation for this topic is to consider the words of the Creator spoken to Moses as given in the Torah. These words were given upon the occasion of God explaining to Moses the purpose in bringing plagues on the Egyptians and mocking all their gods in order to bring the Israelites out of their bondage in Egypt. In Deuteronomy 4:35 and 39 below, while on the brink of stepping into the Promised Land after 40 years of wandering in the wilderness, Yahweh says;

Unto thee it was shewed, that thou mightest know that Yahweh he is God; there is none else beside him. Deuteronomy 4:35

Know therefore this day, and consider it in thine heart, that the LORD he is God in heaven above, and upon the earth beneath: there is none else. Deuteronomy 4:39

There is none else besides Him! What an absolutely powerful and clarion statement. Some could see this statement as an arrogant taunt aimed at diminishing the plethora of gods that are utilized by many polytheistic, spiritual types. How can anyone say there is only One God? That statement could also be seen to mean, that Yahweh is saying there are no other Gods, that is to say, deity type personalities who work in the lives of the people and work through the creation to affect the universe and enact the divine plan. One less often considered possibility in this statement is that it may be possible Yahweh is attempting to teach His followers that there is no other supernatural force but Him.

At the time of this statement, the Israelites who were privy to His deliverance, protection and Torah, had just spent a couple of hundred years in bondage in Egypt and they had not known the name of God as it was first revealed to Moses on the Holy Mountain from the burning bush. We are told of this in Exodus 6 when Yahweh dramatically introduces Himself to Moses;

---

58 Quoted from page 143, *The Origin of Satan,* by Elaine Pagels, the Celsus quotes are referenced to *Origen, Contra Celsum 6.42*

> *And I appeared unto Abraham, unto Isaiah, and unto Jacob, by the name of God Almighty, but by my name Yehovah was I not known to them. Exodus 6:3 KJV*

It is here Yahweh is affirming to the Israelites that He is the only existing force in the entire creation. He is omnipotent, all-powerful and will not allow His children to believe there is any other force that directs their lives but Him. The children of Israel had spent hundreds of years in Egypt with a large portion of that time under cruel bondage as slaves of Egypt. During this time, what type of input from Egyptian culture might they have experienced? Would their experience with the Egyptian cultural gods, who are believed by the Egyptians to produce both good and evil, affect their perceptions of the God of Abraham, Isaac, and Jacob? Apparently, the God who brought them out of Egypt with an outstretched arm and a mighty hand, and had recently been fully revealed to them, believed that they would be affected by this association.

The revelation included such things as the Torah given at Mount Sinai where all the Israelites heard the voice and were afraid. The revelation of the only God included a parting of a sea resulting in their safe passage to dry land and the decimation of all of Pharaoh's horses and chariots. The start of this revelation included ten intense and unforgettable plagues that ended up bringing mighty Egypt to its knees. These plagues culminated in the angel of death passing through all of Egypt and taking the life of every first born in the country who was not under a roof that bore the mark of the Passover blood over the doorpost and lintel. Illuminated to the power and judgment of the only and true God, the Israelites had a real God to compare with all their concepts of Egyptian Gods. It is not extraordinary to perceive that after so many years of harsh bondage and forced submission amid the numerous gods of the Egyptians that the Israelites are in need of a revelation. What better way to provide them with a revelation and to eliminate false concepts that cause one to entertain the notion that there may be other supernatural powers at work, than to see the true God mock numerous Egyptian Gods through plagues related to each of those Gods.

Although the Gods of Egypt are not supernatural entities, they were believed to be Gods by the Egyptians, just as other nations believed their national deities to be Gods in the most literal sense of the word. Both the Egyptians and the Israelites could benefit from having the revelation that the Egyptian Gods not only amounted to nothing, but also by their complete silence during the plagues, were proven to not even exist. In Deuteronomy, Yahweh makes it clear that the conceptual entities that are worshipped by the heathen are "gods". The Hebrew language uses the term Elohim in the following verse;

> *And the LORD shall scatter you among the nations, and ye shall be left few in number among the heathen, whither the LORD shall lead you. And there ye shall serve gods, the work of men's hands, wood and stone, which neither see, nor hear, nor eat, nor smell. Deuteronomy 4:27-28*

The fact remains though, that the Gods of opposing religions, which would be called "demons" by many, meet the criteria required to be given the status of a God. Any who agree that one religion's Gods are to be considered as their religion's demons, are precariously positioning themselves to be seen as one who does not believe what Yahweh says of Himself. Frequently the Creator God told us in Scripture that He is the Only God. Justin Martyr is quoted in *The Origin of Satan* by Elaine Pagels, saying that the Gods of his past are now allies of Satan;[59]

> For Justin, conversion changed all this. Every god and spirit he had ever known, including Apollo, Aphrodite and Zeus, whom he had worshipped since childhood, he now perceived as allies of Satan.-....
>
> Justin saw the universe of spiritual energies, which pious pagan philosophers called *daimons*, as, in his words, "*foul daimons.*"[60]So Justin says,
>
> *We, who out of every race of people, once worshipped Dionysius the son of Semele, and Apollo the sons of Leto, who in their passion for human beings did things which it is shameful even to mention, who worshipped Persephone and Aphrodite... or some other of those who are called gods, now through Jesus Christ, despise them, even at the cost of death.... We pity those who believe such things, for which we know that the daimons are responsible.* [61]

We see then that Justin testifies to the concept of the gods of other nations being viewed as demons by the Christian nations. One is able to see the unchallenged power of the only God, Yahweh, when He brought plague judgments on the Egyptians who had multiple gods, one of which was the

---

59 From *The Origin of Satan* pg 120, by Elaine Pagels

60 Justin Martyr, First Apology 5, passim.

61 Justin Martyr, First Apology 5, passim.

god *Set-an,* who is understood to have been a forerunner of the current *Satan.* In an internet article by David Padfield, we are told of the numerous gods of Egypt and told of Yahweh proving them to be no gods at all in His acts of the plagues. The use of the gods was complicated for the Egyptian. Egyptian polytheism was so prolific and weighty, that an Egyptian would have trouble figuring out which god to pacify in the event that it was believed that a god was angry. The confused Egyptian would work diligently to ensure he or she was not doing anything to anger the "gods" if at all possible, however, due to the huge number of gods utilized by the Egyptians, the chance of angering one god by performing an action to please another god was often a concern. Yahweh wanted to make Himself clearly known as the only God, the God that controls all things and even has the power over life and death as was seen through the unfortunate but necessary plague of death where the angel of death was the angel of the LORD.

Here are some excerpts from Padfield's excellent article, take note as you read how many Gods and how specific the portfolio of each of the false gods was as we see the directness of Yahweh in also being very specific to confront each god individually;

Against All The Gods Of Egypt (#1)
by David Padfield[62]

In all likelihood, the first nine plagues were similar to plagues that have stricken the land of Egypt from the dawn of time. It appears as though God Divinely intensified these plagues and brought them to pass at the time of His choosing.

These plagues were not just against Pharaoh and his people, but also "against all the gods of Egypt" (Exo. 12:12). Every one of the plagues was a direct insult to the gods of Egypt. It has been my observation that many people study the plagues and focus only on the plague itself, and totally ignore that fact that these plagues were directed "against all the gods of Egypt" (Exo. 12:12).

First Plague: Water Changed To Blood (Exo. 7:14-25)

The Nile was the heartbeat of Egypt -- all trade, commerce, and crops depended upon the Nile. In the first plague the water of the Nile was changed to "blood." It is not clear from the original text

62 Copyright ,David Padfield, 2002; http://www.padfield.com/2002/egypt_1.html(used by permission)
http://www.padfield.com/2002/egypt_2.html

whether the water was changed to literal blood or just changed to a "blood red" color -- in either case, the fish in the Nile would have died. Not only was the Nile "red," but other waters as well, even the water that was drawn for use in houses and stored in stone or wooden jars.

This plague was an affront to many of the greatest gods of Egypt.

"It was appropriate that the first of the plagues should be directed against the Nile River itself, the very lifeline of Egypt and the center of many of its religious ideas. The Egyptians considered the Nile sacred. Many of their gods were associated either directly or indirectly with this river and its productivity. For example, the great Khnum was considered the guardian of the Nile sources. Hapi was believed to be the 'spirit of the Nile' and its 'dynamic essence.' One of the greatest gods revered in Egypt was the god Osiris who was the god of the underworld. The Egyptians believed that the river Nile was his bloodstream. In the light of this latter expression, it is appropriate indeed that the Lord should turn the Nile to blood! It is not only said that the fish in the river died but that the 'river stank,' and the Egyptians were not able to use the water of that river -- imagine the horror and frustration of the people of Egypt as they looked upon that which was formerly beautiful only to find dead fish lining the shores and an ugly red characterizing what had before provided life and attraction. Crocodiles were forced to leave the Nile. One wonders what worshipers would have thought of Hapi the god of the Nile who was sometimes manifest in the crocodile." (John Davis, *Moses and the Gods of Egypt*p. Pg 102).

Second Plague: Frogs (Exo. 8:1-15)

Frogs were so sacred in Egypt that even the involuntary slaughter of one was often punished with death. Imagine the people of the land as they went out to gather the decaying bodies of the frogs, and put them into heaps. The fact the Pharaoh entreated Moses to intercede with Jehovah to take away the frogs was a sign that he recognized the God of Israel as being the author of the plague -- Pharaoh realized this was not a natural occurrence.

Third Plague: Lice (Exo. 8:16-19)

The word "lice" is rendered as "sand flies" or "fleas" in some translations. The Hebrew word kinnim comes from a root word meaning “to dig”; it is probable that the insect in question would dig under the skin.

This plague would have been an embarrassment to Geb, the great god of the earth. Egyptians gave offerings to Geb for the bounty of the soil -- yet it was from “the dust of the soil” that this plague originated.

Fourth Plague: Swarms (Exo. 8:20-32)

In the fourth plague, Pharaoh was warned that God would “send swarms of flies on you and your servants, on your people and into your houses. The houses of the Egyptians shall be full of swarms of flies, and also the ground on which they stand” (Exo. 8:21).

It is important to note that Moses did not use the phrase “of flies” in this passage -- he simply used the word “swarms” -- the phrase “of flies” was added by the translators, and it is very possible the translators did not help with our understanding of this passage.

It is very likely that the “swarms” in this passage were swarms of the scarab beetle. The scarab was actually a dung beetle -- an insect that feeds on the dung in the fields. The plague of swarms of scarabs, with mandibles that could saw through wood, was destructive and worse than termites!

Deification of the scarab beetle is still seen in Egypt today. Amon-Ra, the creator and king of the gods, had the head of a beetle. “Ra, the Sole Creator was visible to the people of Egypt as the disc of the sun, but they knew him in many other forms. He could appear as a crowned man, a falcon or a man with a falcon’s head and, as the scarab beetle pushes a round ball of dung in front of it, the Egyptians pictured Ra as a scarab pushing the sun across the sky.” (Geraldine Harris, *Gods & Pharaohs from Egyptian Mythology,* p. 24).

Fifth Plague: Livestock Diseased (Exo. 9:1-7)

The fifth plague was directed against the domestic animals in the land of Egypt. Horses and cattle were not only highly valued in the land of Egypt, but they were also sacred. “All Egyptians use bulls and bull-calves for sacrifice, if they have passed the test for ‘cleanness’; but they are forbidden to sacrifice heifers, on the ground that they are sacred to Isis.” (Herodotus, *The Histories,* p. 101).

Sixth Plague: Boils (Exo. 9:8-12)

This medical malady was also an affront to Imhotep, the god of medicine -- this alone must have led to great despair in the land. "The first real person in known history is not a conqueror or a king but an artist and a scientist -- Imhotep, physician, architect and chief adviser of King Zoser (ca. 3150 B.C.). He did so much for Egyptian medicine that later generations worshiped him as a god of knowledge, author of their sciences and their arts; and at the same time he appears to have founded the school of architecture which provided the next dynasty with the first great builders in history." (Will Durant, *The Story of Civilization,* Volume One, p. 147). It is very likely that Imhotep was the architect who planned Egypt's first large-scale stone monument: the Step Pyramid at Saqqara.

This plague would have also been an affront to Serapis, the deity in charge of healing, and to Thoth, the ibis-headed god of intelligence and medical learning.

Seventh Plague: Hail (Exo. 9:13-35)

The seventh plague was directed at the "very heart" of Egypt so the Egyptians would "know that there is none like Me in all the earth" (Exo. 9:14). Jehovah was going to cause "very heavy hail to rain down, such as has not been in Egypt since its founding until now" (Exo. 9:16). This would have been a very unusual occurrence, for the region around Cairo normally receives only two inches of rain per year.

Since this plague originated from the sky, it would have been an insult to Nut, the sky goddess. "Her most general appearance, however, is that of a woman resting on hands and feet, her body forming an arch, thus representing the sky. Her limbs typified the four pillars on which the sky was supposed to rest. She was supposed originally to be reclining on Geb, the earth, when Shu raised her from this position." (Lewis Spence, *Ancient Egyptian Myths and Legends,* p. 173).

Eighth Plague: Locusts (Exo. 10:1-20)[63]

Again, as with the preceding plagues, the gods of Egypt were silent. You have to wonder what their worshippers thought as they

63 Copyright, David Padfield 2002; http://www.padfield.com/2002/egypt_3.html

saw the devastation. Where was Nepri, the god of grain? Where was Ermutet, the goddess of childbirth and crops? Isis is silent once again. Thermuthis, the goddess of fertility and the harvest was speechless. Seth, another god of crops, was also mute.

Ninth Plague: Darkness (Exo. 10:21-29)

The ninth plague consisted of a "thick darkness in all the land of Egypt" for three days. The darkness was so severe that "they did not see one another; nor did anyone rise from his place for three days. But all the children of Israel had light in their dwellings" (Exo. 10:23).

"The moon was a god, perhaps the oldest of all that were worshiped in Egypt; but in the official theology the greatest of the gods was the sun. Sometimes it was worshiped as the supreme deity Ra or Re, the bright father who fertilized Mother Earth with rays of penetrating heat and light; sometimes it was a divine calf, born anew at every dawn, sailing the sky slowly in a celestial boat, and descending into the west, at evening, like an old man tottering to his grave. Or the sun was the god Horus, taking the graceful form of a falcon, flying majestically across the heavens day after day as if in supervision of his realm, and becoming one of the recurrent symbols of Egyptian religion and royalty. Always Ra, or the sun, was the Creator: at his first rising, seeing the earth desert and bare, he had flooded it with his energizing rays, and all living things -- vegetable, animal and human -- had sprung pell-mell from his eyes, and been scattered over the world." (Will Durant, *History of Civilization, Vol. 1: Our Oriental Heritage*, p. 198).

Once again, the gods of Egypt were silent. Where was Ptah, the chief god of Memphis, and the one who created the moon, the sun and the earth? Where are Atum, the sun god and creator who was worshiped at Heliopolis, the major center of sun worship? Where was Tem, the god of the sunset? Where was Shu, the god of sunlight and air?

Tenth Plague: Death Of The Firstborn (Exo. 11:1-12:30)

> This plague was directed against "all of the gods of Egypt" (Exo. 12:12) and would show the total inability of the gods of Egypt to protect their subjects. In the face of unparalleled tragedy, "all of the gods of Egypt" were silent. Where was Meskhenet, the goddess who presided at the birth of children? Where was Hathor, one of the seven deities who attended the birth of children? Where was Min, the god of procreation? Where was Isis, the goddess of fertility? Where was Selket, the guardian of life? Where was Renenutet, the cobra-goddess and guardian of Pharaoh?

The Egyptian people and subsequently many of the Hebrew people came to believe that there were in existence multiple supernatural entities possessing power. A belief in anything that is claimed to have supernatural God-like abilities is a belief in multiple Gods. The work of understanding the process and function of each of the plagues is quite remarkable in the way the Creator, the only God, showed the Egyptians, the Israelites, and now the world through the recounting of the events; that there is no other power in the entire universe that in any way compares to Yahweh. This in short, would have been understood by those willing to believe, during the period of plagues, and those willing to believe in the present period looking back, that there is in fact no other supernatural power that affects the earth. Yahweh causes all things to happen, good and bad, prosperity and adversity as we are told in Ecclesiastes.

> *In the day of prosperity be joyful, and in the day of adversity consider; God hath made even the one as well as the other, to the end that man should find nothing after him. Ecclesiastes 7:14 Jewish Publication Society*

There either is a tendency to believe Yahweh does not bring evil on anyone but that He is only allowing it or the alleged "fallen angel" is orchestrating it. It is so difficult to accept that the loving God, who is revealed in the incarnate Yeshua, could inflict evil on a people. Aside from Isaiah 45:7 where Yahweh tells us He creates evil, the scriptures are replete with accounts of the "evil", being directly inflicted on the recipients from Yahweh. Below are merely a couple of examples that clearly portray the concept of Yahweh as the source of evil as well as the source of good. In the following two references, we see the first, "evil" is being put on those who hate His people and nation and the second the evil is being inflicted upon His people for transgressing the covenant. I have added the emphasis that identifies clearly that the evil was placed upon the recipients by Yahweh

*And Yahweh will take away from thee all sickness, and will put none of the **evil diseases** of Egypt, which thou knowest, upon thee; but **will lay them upon all them that hate thee.** Deuteronomy 7:15*

*Therefore it shall come to pass, that as all good things are come upon you, which Yahweh your God promised you; **so shall Yahweh bring upon you all evil things**, until he have destroyed you from off this good land which the LORD your God hath given you.*

When ye have transgressed the covenant of Yahweh your God, which he commanded you, and have gone and served other gods, and bowed yourselves to them; then shall the anger of Yahweh be kindled against you, and ye shall perish quickly from off the good land which he hath given unto you.

Joshua 23:15-16

The reference in Deuteronomy points us again to a common stream in Yahweh's judgment and use of the *satan,* meaning the adversarial action that comes from Him. In the above Joshua reference, we are given another clear statement that the false god that the heathen attributed good and evil to as an entity with supernatural powers, is called a god. In the above verse, we can also detect that the "satan" is a response from Yahweh when "*the anger of Yahweh be kindled against you*". In the Hebrew Scriptures, the pattern is evident that when Yahweh gets angry *ha satan* or "evil" upon someone is often the result. We previously discussed this and saw the connection to "*the adversary*" being commissioned, upon the occasion of a people repeatedly angering Yahweh. It is evident that Yahweh's anger brings such a result in Joshua and it was evident that the result of Yahweh's anger towards David occurred in 2 Samuel 24:1 and in Numbers 22:22 as a result of Balaam cursing Israel. It is time to give credit where credit is due and when calamity or evil falls upon a nation or people, or even an individual, we ought to be certain it is from God instead of being so quick to credit the devil for it. After all, should there be evil in a city and Yahweh has not done it as Amos poses to the rebellious Israelites?

Shall a trumpet be blown in the city, and the people not be afraid? shall there be evil in a city, and Yahweh hath not done it? Amos 3:6

There is a comparative unbiblical viewpoint from the second century that we can look at in considering the danger of a two-god view where one of the Gods is responsible for the evil. To hold to the view that only good can come from God is likened to the 2nd century heretic Marcion.

History testifies that Marcion was a Greek theologian who lived in the latter half of the second century C.E. (A.D). Marcion decided to separate the Hebrew Scriptures from the "Greek Scriptures." Marcion was intent on the philosophy that the Old Testament God was for the Jews and was a bad god who could enact judgments and inflict pain and evils upon people, while the "New Testament" God was the God of the Christians and would prove to be the merciful, kind and gentle deity, who treated "Christians" only with kindness. Marcion was labeled a heretic at his death. Regardless of the heretic label Marcion received, the keepers of true monotheism gradually had their Scripturally based philosophy polluted with the mythologically based ideology of Marcion and other Greek thinkers.

It is surprising to see that so many today believe a similar philosophy to Marcion's in thinking that Yahweh does not do evil acts. The Scriptures testify otherwise and along with Isaiah 45:7 and Amos 3:6, there are many, many instances where Yahweh either promised to inflict evil on people or in fact does inflict evil upon people. After all, is not the "Angel of Death" a manifestation of God performing evil or at the very least the implement of evil in the hands of a just God? One does not have to dig very deep to come to terms with the fact that without a doubt, there were some first borns in Egypt who were innocent in their knowledge of the true God, and that they died the night of the first Passover does not portray the picture of kindness upon the recipient. Tradition amplifies this evil act by testifying that there were numerous Hebrew first borns that died that night because of the failure of certain families to apply the lamb's blood to their homes in the prescribed manner. These acts of callous killing would be difficult to see as acts of kindness. Evil was "created" by God and a cosmic "satan" had nothing to do with it. The biblical account does not lie when the text attributes the *angel of death* to Yahweh and not "Satan".

Let's explore the Angel of Death concept for a few moments. The phrase "Angel of Death" may not be an exact biblical term, but it has come to be seen as a term for the death angel that went through Egypt on the first Passover and slew all the firstborn males of Egypt, both humans and animals. The ***Jewish Heritage Online Magazine*** has a few interesting things to say about the angel of death. The JHOM even translates a passage in Isaiah 37, which refers to Yahweh killing thousands of Assyrians with the "Angel of Death". The verse from Isaiah is quoted below and comments from the JHOM article follow;

And the Angel of Death went out and attacked the Assyrian camp;
One hundred eighty-five thousand.
And when they arose in the morning, they were all dead bodies. (Isaiah 37:36)

While Jewish monotheism rejected the polytheistic concept of a specific deity responsible for death on earth (as was popular, for example, among the Canaanites), remnants of the polytheistic influence is evident in biblical descriptions of God's host of angel servants in general, and of the angel of death in particular. The "Angel of the Lord" who smites human beings is called the destroyer and is described as standing between earth and heaven, with a drawn sword in his hand. This angel, however, is a temporary messenger, and even the verses where death is personified do not point to a permanent angel responsible for terminating life on earth.

In post-biblical times the concept of an Angel of Death as an independent being emerged. The Angel of Death came to be associated with not only those episodes of death, cruelty, and wretchedness described in the Bible — such as the plagues in Egypt — but also with the dreadful ogres and demons which make their way into the oral tradition (as it does into the ancient Near Eastern and medieval European traditions). This Angel of Death is an active supernatural being who acts independently of God's will; he fights, harms and destroys man at his own initiative. [64] *(emphasis added)*

Just to reiterate the sentence I have in bold type above, it was in post biblical times that the "Angel of Death" emerged as an independent being and was not independent at all in the prior periods of history. The belief that Satan can literally kill, has led millions to believe that he is an angel of Death yet the Scriptures show it is Yahweh who is or sends the "Angel of Death". The Creator Himself has told us in Deuteronomy that He is the one who kills.

See ye, now, that I--I am He, And there is no god with Me: I put to death, and I keep alive; I have smitten, and I heal; And there is not from My hand a deliverer, Deuteronomy 32:39

64 Excerpt taken from document titled "Angel of Death", which can be found at; http://www.jhom.com/topics/angels/death.htm

When Yahweh's angel went through the land of Egypt, it certainly was not an angel of life. Could it have been an angel of bad news or an angel of discipline for a disobedient Pharaoh? Of course, it is quite clear in the biblical account that this was God's angel and it did indeed bring death. There is no mistaking, that all those who chose not to display their faith in the God of Abraham through their act of smearing blood on the doorposts and lintels of their homes, would die by the hand of God. This selective culling was meted out by the death angel that was sent through the land and Yahweh was completely and utterly at the helm of this activity. Yahweh desired that only He would get the glory or credit for such an act of judgment and calamity. After all, Yahweh is the creator of evil and there is none like him in all the earth. If Isaiah 45:7 and Exodus 9:14 are true, then evil can come from no other supernatural source and Yahweh is responsible for every evil act aside from the evil that proceeds from the rebellious heart of man.

If There Is None Like Him—Then Why is Satan Like Him in so Many Ways?

To apply the logic behind the thought of there being none like Him, it is fair to conclude that if He makes peace and creates evil (Isaiah 45:7); and if He is the one who causes calamity in a city (Amos 3:6); and if He is the one who makes the day of adversity, according to King Solomon (in Ecclesiastes 7:14); then for there to be another one like Him who causes evil, brings evil or creates evil, there would have to exist another God. Believing this "other one" exists is to believe in a second God. To restate that point; it is not possible for Yahweh to be telling the truth when He says in Exodus 9:14 that there is *"none like Him in all the earth,"* if there is another entity in the earth who has the ability to be one who orchestrates evil. If there is a "Satan" who kills, and propagates and brings evil to pass, then Yahweh is not the only God. Here again is how it is stated in Exodus;

> *For I will at this time send all my plagues upon thine heart, and upon thy servants, and upon thy people; that thou mayest know that there is none like me in all the earth. Exodus 9:14 KJV*

From very ancient times, it was understood that the "gods" would and could bring good and would and could bring evil on their servants if the god saw it as needed. The ancient Hebrew writing of Job expresses Job's knowledge that the evil that had befallen him, had come from Yahweh. Early in the story we are told of "satan", an adversary, afflicting Job, however the end of the tale concludes that it was Yahweh who had brought Job to within striking distance from total destruction. We are not told that Job was wrong in telling his wife that it is acceptable to receive evil at the hand of Yahweh as well as good, but he makes his factual statement to correct his wife for asking Job not to be so accepting of his tribulations. Notice where blame/credit is laid for Job's woes in the verse below.

> *But he said unto her, Thou speakest as one of the foolish women speaketh. What? shall we receive good at the hand of God, and shall we not receive evil? In all this did not Job sin with his lips. Job 2:10*

Then again, in chapter 42, the narrator of Job's story explains that the evil that had befallen Job had come from Yahweh.

> *Then came there unto him all his brethren, and all his sisters, and all they that had been of his acquaintance before, and did eat bread with him in his house: and they bemoaned him, and comforted him over all the evil that the LORD had brought upon him: every man also gave him a piece of money, and every one an earring of gold. Job 42:11 KJV*

This is such a telling picture of where evil comes from. I for one believe all the Scripture in its original language, context, and authorial intent can be correctly understood and shown to be true. That said, one must conclude that if there is a God then He must be culpable for the evil and the good.

The dilemma we will work to understand is the puzzling question of who the "adversary" in Job is. A thorough explanation to this question is shared in an upcoming chapter (Chapter 10) which is fully devoted to this question. The adversary is learned to be two fold; it was man as an adversary and it was God as an adversary. Therefore, man and God are the "Satan" of Job. We learn through the Scriptures that "satan" the adversary, is either another human being who takes up a position against us or it is a manifestation of Yahweh Himself or His angel, dispatched for the purposes of enacting judgment or testing us. Yahweh often tests His people to determine their loyalty and love towards Him, as is seen in Deuteronomy 13.

> 1 *If there arise among you a prophet, or a dreamer of dreams, and giveth thee a sign or a wonder,*
> 2 *And the sign or the wonder come to pass, whereof he spake unto thee, saying, Let us go after other gods, which thou hast not known, and let us serve them;*

3 *Thou shalt not hearken unto the words of that prophet, or that dreamer of dreams: for the LORD your God* ***testeth*** *you, to know whether ye love the LORD your God with all your heart and with all your soul.*
4 *Ye shall walk after the LORD your God, and fear him, and keep his commandments, and obey his voice, and ye shall serve him, and cleave unto him.*
5 *And that prophet, or that dreamer of dreams, shall be put to death; because he hath spoken to turn you away from the LORD your God, which brought you out of the land of Egypt, and redeemed you out of the house of bondage, to thrust thee out of the way which the LORD thy God commanded thee to walk in. So shalt thou put the evil away from the midst of thee. Deuteronomy 13:1-5*

In the above passage, there was no mention of evil coming from a cosmic Satan. Very significant points are seen in Deuteronomy that support the case of "evil" coming from Yahweh or evil being an act of the will of a human. Firstly, we see that this passage is about the false prophet, a man. One who speaks to encourage us to go after other Gods. This is the equivalent to discouraging someone from following the dictates, which includes the commands, ordinances, and statutes, of the One God. In that passage the prophet/dreamer, gives a sign or wonder that comes to pass. They are not directing us toward Yahweh, the only God by the sign or wonder they enact but are directing us to go after other gods. We are told not to listen to that prophet/dreamer because Yahweh is testing us by the false prophet's words. God wants to see if we love Him with all our being and will not go after some false prophets' Gods who did not bring us out of the bondage of Egypt.

In verse five, we see that the false prophet/dreamer has spoken to turn us away from Yahweh. Now here it is very clear that it is referring to a man who is intending to turn me away from God, there is nothing in this statement to have me believe there is a supernatural, cosmic "Satan" trying to turn me away from God. The deceiver is a man and it is God who uses the deceptive person to test those who claim they are wanting to be loyal to Yahweh. It is solely the actions of a human false prophet, being used by Yahweh to test us, which is the active force in trying to turn us from Yahweh. Our part in this three-act play is to not hearken to that false prophet/dreamer but to seek after and follow God only. The entire structure of this passage only addresses three entities. They are Yahweh, the human false prophet and the human conscience, responsible for choosing whether or not one will go after other gods or go after Yahweh. This mode of operations is characteristic of Yahweh right from the beginning of time. In the beginning, Yahweh caused the tree of the knowledge of good and evil to be placed before the first man and woman and their obedience and loyalty was tested. In telling about the false prophet, we are to understand that Yahweh is placing a test before His people through the false prophet with signs and wonders

Testing comes by way of choices. Choices come by Yahweh providing them. When a person is challenged to choose between good or evil or between the false prophet's words and the truth, that is a test. Often an evil consequence is the result of choosing the evil that is placed before us. This evil consequence can be called a curse. It is very clear who sets the curses before Israel. The curses are equivalent to evil coming from Yahweh and here, once again He places the evil before the children of Israel. Death and evil, testing and opportunity, to choose sin come from God.

> *I call heaven and earth to record this day against you, that **I have set before you life and death, blessing and cursing**: therefore choose life, that both thou and thy seed may live: Deuteronomy 30:19 KJV*

There is no indication that the curses will come from some type of a cosmic Satan, but the curses are clearly from the Father and they come upon us as a result of our own choice for evil and death. Every choice we make in our faith walk and in life has a result or a consequence. Yahweh wants to teach us that we must grow to the place where it is a choice to serve Him. It is not good for us to flippantly expect we are in good standing with the Creator if we don't consciously "choose" the blessing. If we are not choosing life and blessing, then death and cursing will be the default choice. Once again, Yahweh is placing the equivalent of the tree of Knowledge of Good and Evil before His children and saying in a sense, "I love you, and I want you to choose to love me back. I have given you the formula to show that you love me and want to serve me now it is up to you to choose" If we choose death and cursing we will obviously be the recipients of what many would call "evil." In Exodus 20, [65]we are told there is a blessing to a thousand generations for those who love God and keep His commandments.

Scripture does not indicate in any way that there is a "Satan" who is causing us to go after other Gods. The one attempting to get us to go after other gods is a man according to Deuteronomy 13. And if we do go after another god, then we are choosing death; and evil in the form of cursing from Yahweh, will be what comes upon us.

---

65 Exo 20:6 KJV
And shewing mercy unto thousands of them that love me, and keep my commandments.

Thou shalt not hearken unto the words of that prophet, or that dreamer of dreams: for the LORD your God proveth you, to know whether ye love the LORD your God with all your heart and with all your soul. Deuteronomy 13:3 KJV

The patterns that reveal themselves in the Torah and the rest of the Hebrew Scriptures show that evil is brought on man as an act of the Creator and is brought as a response to man for His choices that are contrary to the choice to serve Yahweh and to love Him with all his heart soul and strength. King Saul was the recipient of an evil spirit, which did not originate from a cosmic "Satan," but the Scripture is very clear the evil spirit came from God. (See 1st Samuel 16 or the next chapter) We see this stated of the evil Spirit sent between Abimelech and the men of Shechem in Judges 9:23 and then six times the evil spirit that is foisted upon Saul is said to be from God. It is very clear that the evil entity is from Yahweh and there is no indication, inference, nor reference to a "Satanic" entity who is able to, nor does in any way, foist the evil upon Saul. It was because of Saul's anti-God behavior that the evil spirit was sent from Yahweh to Saul.[66]

Choosing to believe that evil comes from an entity other than Yahweh is a failure to believe that there is only one God. The monotheistic faith of the Messiah and in the Messiah who was God in the flesh chooses to dismiss all notions of otherworld cosmic deities, whether derived from ancient mythology or some form of Neo-paganism. These imaginations of men's minds are seen as nothing and as not existing at all. This must be so if the words of Yahweh in His Torah are true when He says, "*I am God there is none else, there is none like me.*"

In the next chapter, we will take a close look at the evil spirits that Yahweh has sent upon individuals at different points in the biblical narrative. In doing so, one will be able to cement even more securely the concept that evil spirit "inhabitation" occurs from God and not in the sense of demonic possession as an act of "Satan's" will as many have believed throughout history.

66 The evil spirit as told to come from Yahweh is not only found in 1 Samuel 16 and 18. We also see an occurrence of the evil spirit coming from Yahweh in *Jdg 9:23 KJV Then God sent an evil spirit between Abimelech and the men of Shechem; and the men of Shechem dealt treacherously with Abimelech:*
I am only mentioning it here as an added reference to the concept for the reader.

CHAPTER 6

Evil and Lying Spirits, How God is the Origin

The Evil Spirit

For many centuries, many individuals have been labeled as having a demonic spirit of one sort or another inhabiting them. This charge has been magnified through the teaching of many religious leaders who assert themselves by speaking against, teaching against and praying against the various sprits they believe are affecting a person or situation. The Scriptures claim to be the text of Holy writ from where all doctrine is supposed to be taken. These Scriptures reveal a somewhat different teaching on the issue of spirits such as the evil spirit or a lying spirit.

In the pages of the Scriptures, we see that Yahweh is the one who sends the evil and lying spirit upon an individual and we are hard pressed to see any indication that a cosmic "satan" is involved. If we are able to come to the understanding that the evil and lying spirit in the Scriptures is a product of God's direct actions then we move one-step closer to comprehending the non-existence of Satan. This is so in the way that we can see what the Hebrew Scriptures teach on the issue and then move to apply that thinking to what is generally believed about evil spirits in the "New Testament".

We are prepared now to look at the evil spirit that came from Yahweh and was imparted to King Saul. As mentioned in the previous chapter, there are mentioned six times the evil spirit that is foisted upon Saul is said to be from Yahweh. Below are all those occurrences as seen in the book of First Samuel.

1 Samuel 16:14 KJV
But the Spirit of the LORD departed from Saul, and an evil spirit from the LORD troubled him.

1 Samuel 16:15 KJV
And Saul's servants said unto him, Behold now, an evil spirit from God troubleth thee.

1 Samuel 16:16 KJV
Let our lord now command thy servants, which are before thee, to seek out a man, who is a cunning player on an harp: and it shall come to pass, when the evil spirit from God is upon thee, that he shall play with his hand, and thou shalt be well.

1 Samuel 16:23 KJV
And it came to pass, when the evil spirit from God was upon Saul, that David took an harp, and played with his hand: so Saul was refreshed, and was well, and the evil spirit departed from him.

1 Samuel 18:10 KJV
And it came to pass on the morrow, that the evil spirit from God came upon Saul, and he prophesied in the midst of the house: and David played with his hand, as at other times: and there was a javelin in Saul's hand.

1Samuel 19:9 KJV
And the evil spirit from the LORD was upon Saul, as he sat in his house with his javelin in his hand: and David played with his hand.

What we see in the six occurrences of the evil spirit coming from Yahweh in the book of 1st Samuel is that the writer, who was inspired by Yahweh, understood where the evil spirit came from and was not reticent to indicate that it was from God. Some interesting things to note about this concept as seen in the book of 1st Samuel are;

- Chapter 16 verse 15 Saul's servants knew the evil spirit was from Elohim.

- Verse 16 reveals this evil spirit was affecting Saul's mind and that the anointed music from the cunning harp player was seen by the servants as a way to treat this mental malady, which is called an "evil spirit".

- Verse 23 shows Saul becoming well and the "evil spirit" departing are synonymous.

- Chapter 18 verse 10 informs us that the evil spirit was re-occurring on Saul. It had departed but due to the fact there were multiple times that David had played to "exorcise" the evil spirit, we can conclude this evil spirit must be closely related to Saul's mental condition. Verse 18 also informs us that Saul prophesied while afflicted with the evil spirit,

- Chapter 19 verse 9 shows us the evil spirit would return after it had "left" Saul. We had previously seen in Chapter 16 the evil spirit had left Saul then three chapters later the evil spirit is once again "upon Saul."

It becomes almost irrefutable when taking the information given us in the book of 1st Samuel, that evil, in the form of an "evil spirit" comes from Yahweh. When looking at the story of Saul, the anointed King of Israel, it is sad to see how Saul's disobedience caused him to lose the anointing as king and to spiral into a downward slide which exhibits itself as a form of mental and emotional madness.

The sad story goes that Saul was commanded to destroy the Amalekites completely. That is a command to destroy everything. Saul decides to spare King Agag and the choicest animals for sacrifice. This disobedience is confronted by the prophet Samuel and Saul says "sorry", to some degree. Saul's apologetic response, although repentant, is too little too late and Yahweh has Samuel go find David and anoint him as the next king. I find it an amazing coincidence in the text, that as soon as David is anointed by Samuel the prophet; Saul receives the evil spirit from Yahweh as 1st Samuel 16 shows;

> *Then Samuel took the horn of oil, and anointed him in the midst of his brethren: and the Spirit of the LORD came upon David from that day forward. So Samuel rose up, and went to Ramah.*
> *But the Spirit of the LORD departed from Saul, and an evil spirit from the LORD troubled him. 1Samuel 16:13-14 KJV*

The correlation between these two events is unmistakable. God removed His spirit from the King of Israel, and at the same time, He imparted His Spirit to the upcoming king of Israel. This is the moment Saul is afflicted with the evil spirit and how ironic (as if there is any irony in Yahweh's script) that it is David the newly anointed one who is brought in to soothe the king with his fantastic harp playing. Let me share a bit of the background to Saul's story that brought him to the place where he received an evil spirit.

The account tells us that the armies of Saul are going to war with the Philistines who are flaunting their notorious bad boy, the uncircumcised Philistine, Goliath. David goes out to take provisions to his brothers and David, certainly under twenty years of age, which is the age of military service in Israel, hears this Goliath bad mouthing the God of Israel, so he tells Saul that he will take Goliath out, believing that he can slay this insulter of the Children of Israel. Well as the story goes, David sinks one stone from his sling into the giant's forehead and then cuts off his head with Goliath's own sword while Goliath is laid out on the ground before both armies.

This heroic feat catapults David socially, and he is now brought to the king's house and dwells there where he becomes extremely tight friends with the Kings son Jonathon. All this is good but the exploits of David and the accolades of the people are enough to stir up major jealousy in King Saul. Saul wants to kill David and at one point Jonathon dissuades his father King Saul and Saul relents. This reprieve for David only lasts a short time. Jonathon soon ends up warning David of his Fathers renewed plan to have David killed. Meanwhile David has paid the requested dowry of 100 Philistine foreskins for Michal, Saul's daughter. David then becomes the son in law of the King and it is not easy for him to find the approval usually sought from a father in law. David is loved by all of Judah and Israel, as well as by the King's son Jonathon and the King's Daughter Michal. At this, Saul is apparently quite jealous.

I have seen this numerous times in the lives of people. One who had been walking in an anointing and authority from God is slowly replaced, in a sense, by a younger representative of Yahweh's plan and purpose. The jealousy that is latent in the older servant of Yahweh often causes much grief to both parties.

In this story, a message can be seen quite clearly. David walks in humility, not even thinking himself worthy to be the son-in-law of the King, while Saul walks in pride, thinking himself to be the one worthy of honor. Samuel the prophet of God, at one point earlier in this drama, rebuked Saul for his arrogant attitude, reminding Saul of his past and how he became the mighty king because of Yahweh not because of Saul. Saul needed to hear that all his kingliness came from Yahweh, not from his own abilities. This is seen in chapter 15 of 1 Samuel

> *And Samuel said, When thou wast little in thine own sight, wast thou not made the head of the tribes of Israel, and the LORD anointed thee king over Israel? 1Samuel15:17 KJV*

Saul lost the favor of Yahweh because he did not heed the word of Yahweh. After seeing David walking in the favor of Yahweh, we are told Saul continues to grow in fear of David because the spirit of Yahweh is with David but has left Saul.

> *And Saul was afraid of David, because the LORD was with him, and was departed from Saul. 1Samuel 18:12 KJV*

> *And Saul saw and knew that the LORD was with David, and that Michal Saul's daughter loved him. And Saul was yet the more afraid of David; and Saul became David's enemy continually. 1Samuel 18:28-29 KJV*

In the end of this tale, we are left with many lessons of how God sets up and brings down kings. We are left with lessons that teach us of the fallout from walking pridefully as well as lessons that teach about loyalty and humility as it pertains to Jonathon and David. However, the important point for our present discussion and the pertinence of this story in relation to evil is that we see where the "evil spirit" comes from. It is abundantly clear that the evil, in the form of an evil spirit, came from Yahweh. But does that mean Yahweh sent a ghost-like, intangible entity into the heart of Saul or does that mean Yahweh's Spirit, which brought authority and favor to Saul, was lifted from Saul because of the sin and disobedience of one who was called to be an obedient servant of the Creator?

The impartation of an "evil spirit" is probably not as mystical as we have been led to believe. I am inclined to question the likelihood of God actually imparting a supernatural spirit being into a human heart/soul. Would it be likely that Yahweh now placed an evil entity in the space where He once occupied? Is it perhaps more likely that the metaphor of the "evil spirit" represents the result of Saul's disobedience, pride and sin? Or, does God just plop His spirit in and out of a human being every time He pleases based on His level of displeasure with His servant?

The "evil spirit" is seen to come and go from Saul in this story. What kind of a God throws a human in and out of evil spirit possession or inhabitation whenever He sees fit? It is difficult to not see the evil spirit from God as a metaphor for the mental, physical, and emotional consequences of sin choices in Saul's life. After all, doesn't God promise to give us a peaceful existence if we keep His commands and love Him with all our heart, soul, mind, and strength? This Saul, who had an evil spirit from God, did not remain in that state. We are told after Saul sent his servants three times to take David, the Spirit of Yahweh was upon them, and then when Saul actually went himself to get David the Spirit of Yahweh was upon Saul. This indicates that the "Spirit of Yahweh" was returned to Saul yet again. It returned so much so that Saul then prophesied and lay around in his underwear for a whole day.

This is a great testament to an "evil spirit" being from God, coming upon Saul when we see in the text that now the Spirit of Yahweh was upon Saul. Both were not given to Saul at the same time and it is not realistic to think that Saul was under the power and influence of Satan for a time, then under the power and influence of Yahweh, indicating that Saul was subjected to being flip flopped between forces that he was consigned to submit to. The following verse tells of Saul's "naked" prophesying after the spirit of God returned to him.

> *And he went thither to Naioth in Ramah: and the Spirit of God was upon him also, and he went on, and prophesied, until he came to Naioth in Ramah.*
>
> *And he stripped off his clothes also, and prophesied before Samuel in like manner, and lay down naked all that day and all that night. Wherefore they say, Is Saul also among the prophets? 1Samuel 19:23-24 KJV*

These verses lend strength to the argument that the supposedly tangible spirit of evil from Yahweh could be a metaphor for the results of sin choices in Saul's life. However, Yahweh in His sovereignty is still able to impart His spirit, which here is His inspiring breath to prophecy, into any of His sinful people.

There is little I can add to the fact that whatever the evil spirit is, it did not come from some "satan" who is the cosmic archenemy of Yahweh and all the children of Yahweh. The evil spirit was known biblically to come from Yahweh.

The Lying Spirit

Concluding that the "evil spirit" on Saul was not a product of "satanic" work or influence is helpful in seeing that it is okay to accept the concept that evil comes from God. We are however confronted in life with lies that occur and with lies that we ourselves may sometimes propagate. I have sat under many religious teachers who have adamantly pounded the pulpit with their fist and proclaimed "satan is a liar". True, the "New Testament" does inform us that Satan is a liar and the father of lies but that statement is not to be taken to mean that there exists a cosmic "satan" as much as it is intended to mean that the evil inclination which is adversarial to God and his truth is the place where lies begin. This passage about Satan being the father of lies is addressed in volume Two of *Satan, Christianity's Other God*, where each New Testament passage is given full treatment. Part of the puzzle can be put together on this issue of where lies come from by looking at the Lying Spirit found in the book of 1 Kings. As with the "evil spirit" that came from Yahweh, we will see in the following verse that the Lying Spirit also comes from Yahweh. Our exploration of this concept will lead to the conclusion that man chooses to lie and to use lies at times but that also God chooses to have a person who is stubbornly bent on doing things according to their own plan instead of His, led down a destructive path. The stubborn person is told the very thing that will lead the rebellious individual into the path that is designed to afflict that individual with a judgment either to destroy him or to have him turn to the Father and the Father's ways. 1st Kings and 2nd Chronicles both relate the story of the "Lying Spirit" from God.

> *And the LORD said unto him, Wherewith? And he said, I will go forth, and I will be a lying spirit in the mouth of all his prophets. And he said, Thou shalt persuade him, and prevail also: go forth, and do so.*
> *Now therefore, behold, the LORD hath put a lying spirit in the mouth of all these thy prophets, and the LORD hath spoken evil concerning thee. 1Kings 22:22-**23***

> *And he said, I will go out, and be a lying spirit in the mouth of all his prophets. And the LORD said, Thou shalt entice him, and thou shalt also prevail: go out, and do even so.*
> *Now therefore, behold, the LORD hath put a lying spirit in the mouth of these thy prophets, and the LORD hath spoken evil against thee. 2Chronicles 18:21-22*

The original story initially told in 1st Kings is repeated in the post-exilic book of 2nd Chronicles, which is a mirror of the story first told. I am not planning to answer the question of why the story is told twice. I will say that much of the repeated material in the books of the Chronicles is very helpful in establishing chronology and is also very useful for establishing different names and ruling periods of Kings of Israel and Judah. The fact that Yeshua used the entire Hebrew bible in the first century and therefore condoned it as the Word of Yahweh, allows us the freedom to accept the dual accounts of certain stories as necessary and beneficial for our understanding of Yahweh and His word.

What I will address here is quite simple. The "lying spirit" is used to deceive King Ahab of Israel into engaging in a losing battle against the Syrians. This King of Israel was intent on going to war against Syria. He gathered some 400 prophets of Israel to himself and asked of them if it was sensible to engage in the campaign against the Syrians. The entire body of prophets certainly affirmed the King's desire by stating that he would decisively win the battle against the enemy.

> *Then the king of Israel gathered the prophets together, about four hundred men, and said unto them, Shall I go against Ramothgilead to battle, or shall I forbear? And they said, Go up; for the Lord shall deliver it into the hand of the king. 1Kings 22:6*

Therefore, Ahab heard from the lying prophets that he would win the battle against the Syrians. At the testimony of four hundred prophets, it seemed like a no-brainer that it was prudent to go forth to war. This would likely be the conclusion of most leaders in the world. If they had called 400 advisors to consult with about a specific campaign, most leaders would invariably act in agreement with the counsel of the advisors that had been called together. However, for Ahab the King of Israel, this was not so. Ahab and Jehoshaphat, the king of Judea, were now in league together. Jehoshaphat had agreed to come along side Ahab and the Israelite army. This, on first sight, seems like a winning combination, Judah and Israel together, in the battle against Syria. Is that not the way God would want things? His 12 tribes had not been united since the days of King Solomon, now they had a common enemy and were hooked up to take the enemy out.

Although the concept looks like it will reap great rewards in the way of victory and prosperity, we come into a little snag in the plan when Jehoshaphat, the King of Judah, makes the next statement. Both Ahab and Jehoshaphat had set up their thrones in the "void place." This is a place where multitudes can gather to hear edicts and statements and in this instance, prophecies by the prophets about the current issue. It is kind of like a big town square where a group of activists might congregate to generate interest in their cause and hear from representatives of their group. Promptly after the prophets of Israel said; *"Go up; for the Lord shall deliver it into the hand of the king"*.... Jehoshaphat said to Ahab;

> *And Jehoshaphat said, Is there not here a prophet of the LORD besides, that we might enquire of him? 1Kings 22:7*

Jehoshaphat wanted to hear from someone else besides the prophets who already affirmed the next military move of Ahab. Perhaps Jehoshaphat did not see these prophets as true prophets of Yahweh so he asked Ahab if there was another prophet of Yahweh around. In the Jamieson, Fausset and Brown Commentary we are told the following regarding this situation:

> Previous to declaring hostilities, it was customary to consult the prophets (see on 1Sa_28:8); and Jehoshaphat having expressed a strong desire to know the Lord's will concerning this war, Ahab assembled four hundred of his prophets. These could not be either the prophets of Baal or of Ashteroth (1Ki_18:19), but seem (1Ki_22:12) to have been false prophets, who conformed to the symbolic calf-worship of Jehovah. Being the creatures of Ahab, they unanimously predicted a prosperous issue to the war. But dissatisfied with them, Jehoshaphat inquired if there was any true prophet of the Lord. Ahab agreed, with great reluctance, to allow Micaiah to be summoned. He was the only true prophet then to be found residing in Samaria, and he had to be brought out of prison (1Ki_22:26), into which, according to JOSEPHUS, he had been cast on account of his rebuke to Ahab for sparing the king of Syria.

One probability could be that Jehoshaphat had a strong inkling these men were not totally in line with the philosophy that Yahweh is the only God. These prophets were under the rule of Ahab and He may have perceived them not to be the true prophets who would be worth heeding. Ahab reluctantly sends for the prophet Micaiah. While Micaiah is being summoned, it seems there ensues quite a show in front of the allied kings by the false prophets of the hour.

> *And all the prophets prophesied so, saying, Go up to Ramothgilead, and prosper: for the LORD shall deliver it into the king's hand. 1Kings 22:12*

One of the prophets, Zedekiah, even used an object lesson style of prophesying to add force to his words through visual effect. This "prophet" made horns of iron and said; "it is by these that the Syrians will be pushed until Ahab and Jehoshaphat have consumed them." While the prophets of Ahab are going on, Micaiah is summoned and told to say what the King wants to hear. Now Micaiah being a true prophet of God, of course says he will only speak what Yahweh tells him to speak. Upon arriving at the place where the Kings are sitting, Micaiah is asked by Ahab if he should go up against Ramoth-Gilead. If you read the entire story it is clear Micaiah's answer affirming the 400 prophets' approval of the war quest, is somewhat tongue in cheek. Ahab scolds Micaiah for not speaking only the truth from Yahweh on this issue. Micaiah then goes on to tell Ahab just what the word of God is at this time for Ahab and his campaign. Listen to what the text says in the King James Version of 1st Kings Chapter 22;

1Kings 22:16-28
16 And the king said unto him, How many times shall I adjure thee that thou tell me nothing but that which is true in the name of the LORD?
17 And he said, I saw all Israel scattered upon the hills, as sheep that have not a shepherd: and the LORD said, These have no master: let them return every man to his house in peace.
18 And the king of Israel said unto Jehoshaphat, Did I not tell thee that he would prophesy no good concerning me, but evil?
19 And he said, Hear thou therefore the word of the LORD: I saw the LORD sitting on his throne, and all the host of heaven standing by him on his right hand and on his left.
20 And the LORD said, Who shall persuade Ahab, that he may go up and fall at Ramothgilead? And one said on this manner, and another said on that manner.
21 And there came forth a spirit, and stood before the LORD, and said, I will persuade him.
22 And the LORD said unto him, Wherewith? And he said, I will go forth, and I will be a lying spirit in the mouth of all his prophets. And he said, Thou shalt persuade him, and prevail also: go forth, and do so.
23 Now therefore, behold, the LORD hath put a lying spirit in the mouth of all these thy prophets, and the LORD hath spoken evil concerning thee.
24 But Zedekiah the son of Chenaanah went near, and smote Micaiah on the cheek, and said, Which way went the Spirit of the LORD from me to speak unto thee?
25 And Micaiah said, Behold, thou shalt see in that day, when thou shalt go into an inner chamber to hide thyself.
26 And the king of Israel said, Take Micaiah, and carry him back unto Amon the governor of the city, and to Joash the king's son;
27 And say, Thus saith the king, Put this fellow in the prison, and feed him with bread of affliction and with water of affliction, until I come in peace.
28 And Micaiah said, If thou return at all in peace, the LORD hath not spoken by me. And he said, Hearken, O people, every one of you.

Micaiah, when demanded to tell Ahab what Yahweh speaks on the issue of the pending battle, speaks of the vision he has had from Yahweh. In the text above, we first hear Micaiah prophesy the same success in war with the Syrians, as did all of the previous 400 prophets. Micaiah was seemingly being noticeably sarcastic so to speak, in stating the prophecy that said victory will be yours.

When Ahab challenges Micaiah, Micaiah then proceeds to tell the king and all who are able to hear just what Yahweh says on this matter. Micaiah's job is not to dissuade the King from going to war as that is how Yahweh will have Ahab killed, but his job is more to let Ahab know that the word from his prophets predicting victory was an untrue prophecy. Micaiah first tells Ahab that he saw Israel scattered as sheep with no master therefore they should return to their homes. This statement undoubtedly means many things, but the one thing for certain King Ahab would have seen it to mean would be that he should not go to war and the Israelites , who are to be sent to their homes should not go to battle for him either. This concept does not sit well with the stubborn and arrogant king Ahab who had just received many encouraging prophesies from his prophets and now Micaiah is saying do not go to war. Ahab speaks to Jehoshaphat and tells him, "I told you so. This prophet always says bad things and that's why I don't like hearing from him." Now Micaiah is free to give Ahab the rest of the prophecy. This part is to let Ahab know that his prophets had told a lie to him and to let Ahab know why His prophets spoke a lie about the pending war.

In Micaiah's vision from God, Yahweh has the host of heaven standing beside him while He is on His throne. While on His throne Yahweh asks the host who will go and persuade Ahab to go up to war at Ramoth-Gilead and subsequently fall, which means be killed in battle. Micaiah relays the vision in such a manner that Ahab would see a bit of the picture that there is numerous ways suggested to have him go and be persuaded to go to battle where he would die. This may suggest that Ahab had various issues along with his pagan worship and pride filled heart that could be played against him to go fall in battle. However, in the vision one spirit comes forth and says to Yahweh. "Hey, I will go and persuade Ahab." Yahweh asks, "How?" The spirit, who is a servant of Yahweh, says, "I will go and be a lying spirit in the mouths of all of Ahab's prophets."

We notice a few things in respect to this "spirit's" statement. One; is that the false prophets are Ahab's and are not called Yahweh's prophets. Two; is the fact that the "spirit" understands that Ahab will listen to the counsel of his false prophets. And three: Micaiah is revealing that the plan to get Ahab killed in battle was decided on by Yahweh before Ahab even decided to go to battle. The influence for this decision making process is the lying spirit which came from Yahweh. It seems odd, when attributing lies to the one and only "Satan" that such a lying spirit is actually sent from Yahweh. Not only does Micaiah stick his neck out on this one in a very literal sense with Ahab. But here he is in front of some 400 prophets of Ahab saying," Oh yeah, these were prophets who all spoke with one voice, well, you should know that they all lied because Yahweh put a lying spirit in their mouths." This must have been an inflammatory statement to make to hundreds of men, who have the backing of their community, the power of their numbers, and the approval of the King. Micaiah states it in no uncertain terms that the prophets of Ahab prophesied to go to war because a lying spirit from Yahweh was telling them to say so. Micaiah's job is to tell Ahab that his prophets were given a lying spirit from Yahweh to entice him to war. Part of this prophecy is spoken of in a slightly veiled manner. Micaiah tells Ahab that Yahweh agreed to send the lying spirit and that indeed the lying spirit would prevail, which means the lying spirit would convince Ahab, through the false prophets to go to war where he would be killed. In verse 28 Micaiah says, if Ahab comes back from war alive, then Micaiah's words are not from Yahweh. Before that point in the text Micaiah had provided a picture of what Yahweh has orchestrated to deal with Ahab, and clearly depicts the *lying spirit* was given from Yahweh with no mention of a cosmic "Satan".

These false prophets had chosen evil in their form and practice of worship. They were serving the syncretistic King of Israel, Ahab and were now able to be candidates for the strong delusion. They were used by Yahweh to carry out his plan that Ahab would be killed. The choice for sin by the prophets of Ahab, gave Yahweh the right to speak through them by putting a lying spirit in their mouths. Perhaps this was a real manifestation of God's power imposed upon the lives of men, or perhaps we are seeing a written depiction of the heart of man estranged from the Creator, showing the resulting choice to lie. By their actions they had already chosen to surrender to the latent evil potential within themselves, therefore they were now vessels to be used for ignoble purposes and fulfill Yahweh's will so that Ahab would die as prophesied by the prophet earlier in the story of Ahab. Where we are told, "His blood will be licked up by dogs".

> *And thou shalt speak unto him, saying: Thus saith the LORD: Hast thou killed, and also taken possessions? and thou shalt speak unto him, saying: Thus saith the LORD: In the place where dogs licked the blood of Naboth shall dogs lick thy blood, even thine.' 1Kings 21:19*

To be sure, there are multiple issues we might be inclined to discuss from this story, however, I will only go on for a short bit to talk of Yahweh's use of the false prophets to bring about evil in the life of Ahab. These men were supposedly men who spoke truth and heard from God. According to the Scriptures, they were servants of Ahab and thus they would have worshipped in the way of the Amorites, as Ahab was accused of. It is often the manner of God to adversely affect the lives of those who have made a choice to not humble themselves in service to Him. These prophets of Ahab were simply not serving Yahweh only. Much like the Pharaoh of Egypt during the exodus, these prophets were not humble before God.

If you recall there are a number of times in the Exodus story that we are told God hardened Pharaoh's heart. We are often quick to say, well that doesn't seem fair, and Pharaoh didn't have a hope if his heart had been hardened by God. This would be true if Yahweh had not repeatedly given the opportunity for submission to Pharaoh before He hardened Pharaoh's heart. In fact, if you follow the story of the 10 plagues from the beginning you will see that Pharaoh hardened his own heart a number of times before Yahweh hardened it too. This represents God, after seeing the choice of His servant for evil, actively getting involved in hardening Pharaohs heart. Why does Yahweh do this in Pharaoh and likewise use the false prophets of Ahab to have His will performed? I suggest the reason Yahweh acts in this manner is because all things are created by Him, through Him, and for Him and He will orchestrate all activities in the universe so ultimately He will get the glory and all will know that He is God. This is seen in Exodus 7.

> *And I will harden Pharaoh's heart, and multiply My signs and My wonders in the land of Egypt.*
> *But Pharaoh will not hearken unto you, and I will lay My hand upon Egypt, and bring forth My hosts, My people the children of Israel, out of the land of Egypt, by great judgments.*
> *And the Egyptians shall know that I am the LORD, when I stretch forth My hand upon Egypt, and bring out the children of Israel from among them.' Exodus 7:3-5*

Therefore, God's use of the prophets of Ahab is not an arbitrary choice to impart a lying spirit to a group of otherwise innocent men. It would be more in line with Yahweh's character that due to the choices in the false prophets' lives to not serve God only; they were then used, to put into motion a judgment upon a wicked king. Yahweh has used evil men to bring about evil on other evil men all through the scriptures. In this case the lying spirit was explicitly sent from God and affected the prophecies of a group of evil men.

In other cases, the evil that comes from man stems from his own heart, as is seen in the verses below.

> *Jeremiah 17:9 The heart is deceitful above all things, and desperately wicked: who can know it?*

> *Matthew 15:19 For out of the heart proceed evil thoughts, murders, adulteries, fornications, thefts, false witness, blasphemies:*

> *Mark 7:21-23 For from within, out of the heart of men, proceed evil thoughts, adulteries, fornications, murders, 22 Thefts, covetousness, wickedness, deceit, lasciviousness, an evil eye, blasphemy, pride, foolishness: 23 All these evil things come from within, and defile the man.*

> *James 1:14-15 But every man is tempted, when he is drawn away of his own lust, and enticed. 15 Then when lust hath conceived, it bringeth forth sin: and sin, when it is finished, bringeth forth death.*

Suffice to say that at this point in the history of the people of God, neither the prophets nor the Kings recognized evil and a lying spirit as coming from "Satan." The fact is that even as Ahab was branching out in pagan worship, as his fathers did, he still did not attribute evil to someone other than Yahweh. The lying spirit is not spawned of Satan but is a term that represents the influence of the Creator over a situation that involved evil men counseling the wicked King of Israel to go to war so that God could enact a judgment upon him.

Abimelech's evil Spirit

There is a story in the book of judges where yet another evil spirit is sent from Yahweh. This is the story of Abimelech. The story is quite interesting from a literary standpoint. It is also interesting to note that the entire story can be seen in one chapter of the Scriptures. The key verse that identifies the evil spirit as coming from Yahweh is in Judges Chapter 9;

> *Then* ***God sent an evil spirit*** *between Abimelech and the men of Shechem; and the men of Shechem dealt treacherously with Abimelech: Judges 9:23*

Abimelech was one of the seventy sons of Jerubbaal according to the Scriptures. Jerubbaal is know to be Gideon (Judges 6:32 and Judges 7:1) who destroyed the altar of Baal earlier in the book of Judges and was given the name Jerubbaal, which means, "let Baal plead" or "contender with Baal." After the death of his father Gideon, Abimelech wants to become king. He ends up murdering his 70 brothers, the sons of Gideon and is elected king by a group of people from Shechem.

Now as the uncontested , man-appointed King of Israel, Abimelech enjoys a three year reign until he is killed after responding to an insurrection against the Shechemites, the very people who elected him king in the first place. It is interesting to note that the King of Israel is to be appointed by Yahweh and not to be chosen and installed by the people. However, this Abimelech was not one to follow the rules of God, he wanted to be king, and had it done his way. Ultimately, there is a coup, or uprising against Abimelech and when his army chases down the insurrectionist Shechemites, he has the pagan temple hold of the false god Berith burned down and kills all the rebelling Shechemites and their women as well.

> *And all the people likewise cut down every man his bough, and followed Abimelech, and put them to the hold, and set the hold on fire upon them; so that all the men of the tower of Shechem died also, about a thousand men and women. Judges 9:49*

Abimelech then sets off on a campaign against Thebez. The people of the region made their way up into a strong tower for protection from Abimelech and his army. While Abimelech was standing near the entrance, a woman hurled a piece of the upper millstone off the tower and struck Abimelech in the head. Knowing this was a fatal wound Abimelech told his armourbearer to run him through with his sword so that it is would not be said that a woman killed Abimelech. The armourbearer did as requested by Abimelech and Abimelech died. The last two verses of Judges 9 are an excellent summary of the evil King Abimelech and the wicked men of Shechem who aided in the murder of 70 of Abimelech's brothers.

> *Thus God rendered the wickedness of Abimelech, which he did unto his father, in slaying his seventy brethren: 57 And all the evil of the men of Shechem did God render upon their heads: and upon them came the curse of Jotham the son of Jerubbaal Judges 9:56-57*

We are told in the story, that the bad Shechem murderers received the curse of Jotham. Jotham was the only surviving son of Gideon after Abimelech's culling. Jotham had prophesied the Shechemite murderers would receive the fire from Abimelech. It happened exactly according to the curse of Jotham, the Shechemites died by a fire that was set by Abimelech and his soldiers outside the hold of the house of Berith. And as mentioned, Abimelech also died. His death came about as a consequence for the murder of the sons of Gideon and as prophesied by Jotham, his brother, the fire from Shechem and Millo did devour Abimelech. This was not a literal fire as was the fire from Abimelech that burned the Shechemites to death. This fire was the symbolic representation of the strife and contention, the rebellion and seething bitterness that was caused to grow from the Shechemites towards Abimelech, their once happily elected king.

Therefore, all in all, Jotham's prophecy in Judges 9 about both Abimelech and those who consorted with him came true.

What I would like to bring to your attention for our discussion on the non-existence of "Satan" as an independent, cosmic, archenemy of Yahweh, is what happened to Abimelech and the Shechemites following Jotham's prophecy. It appears Abimelech had been reigning for three years and then after three years, things between Abimelech and the Shechemites who placed him in power went sour. However, who was the orchestrater of the souring of that relationship? Once again, if we believe the words of the Scriptures it was Yahweh who orchestrated the bad feelings between ruler and people. Moreover, Yahweh did so by use of an evil spirit. Here is what he Scriptures say;

> *When Abimelech had reigned three years over Israel, 23 Then God sent an evil spirit between Abimelech and the men of Shechem; and the men of Shechem dealt treacherously with Abimelech: 24 That the cruelty done to the threescore and ten sons of Jerubbaal might come, and their blood be laid upon Abimelech their brother, which slew them; and upon the men of Shechem, which aided him in the killing of his brethren. Judges 9:22-24*

If we believe what we are reading, then it was Yahweh who sent an evil spirit in this instance. He did so because He wanted to enact a judgment upon Abimelech and the men of Shechem for the heinous, murderous acts they committed together in the killing of the 70 brothers of Abimelech. Through sending an evil spirit to stir up the relationship between the two guilty parties, God would see a plan to judge the parties fulfilled. I am not sure if Yahweh does this manner of evil spirit sending by infusing a human spirit with the exact program and behaviors He wants and gets them to act exactly in the manner that will best suit His purpose of marching them to their death. OR, Does God take part in orchestrating situations and issues which will systematically deteriorate the good relations that had been enjoyed by both parties previous to sending the evil spirit? I would suggest it is through the latter of the two methods Yahweh operates.

It seems possible in understanding that part of the Creator's intent in creating humanity was to get us to be humans and to act accordingly. That then speaks to the fact that we will respond to situations and people and their issues toward us in ways that often aid in deteriorating relationship. I believe God will make use of the evil inclination of man to assist His plan to bring another man or group of humans along the path to receive the judgment He is prepared to mete out to them. All through Israel's history in the Scriptures Yahweh utilizes a foreign nation or pagan people to exact His punishment on the Israelites through war. Yet again, the Holy Scriptures that were used by Yeshua and the early believers, speak of the evil spirit as a force that comes from Yahweh. There are many, many mysteries that the Creator has yet to reveal to His creation, and although I would dearly love to have the answer to all God's mysteries, it is clear to me presently that no one is ready to posses all that Yahweh has to impart to His creation. The impartation of His truth and mysteries happens at the time He sees fit and to the ones He desires to reveal it to. For now though, I do see clearly the force of evil in the story of Abimelech and the Shechemites is not being sent from Satan. In this story, there is no cosmic Satan who has a desire to thwart Yahweh's plans that possesses supernatural powers to affect humanity and to destroy all humans. The evil force in the story of Abimelech and Shechem came from God.

> *Then **God sent an evil spirit** between Abimelech and the men of Shechem; and the men of Shechem dealt treacherously with Abimelech: Judges 9:23*

Yahweh is credited for the evil, not an Egyptian god

If then, an "evil spirit" comes from God and a "lying spirit" is also sent from God, are we able to find convincing testimony in the Torah that there is only the Creator who is responsible for the evil? Do we see any examples of any other, such as a patriarch crediting Yahweh for the evil that happened to him? Or is there an inclination to blame another god such as "Satan" for evil that is experienced by a patriarch? We find in the book of Genesis the story of Joseph with all the dramatic raising to and removal from power that goes with the beloved son of Jacob, the father of the twelve tribes of Israel. In the story of Joseph, we are shown the many evils that this great leader suffered on his rise to the second from the top in all of Egypt, yet the tale of tragedy and betrayal does not end with an evil cosmic force being blamed for any of the unpleasantness and evil that befalls Joseph.

Would Joseph have been wrong to lay blame on another force for the affliction he endured throughout the years? Had he suggested that the Egyptian God "Set-an" was responsible for the evil in his life, would Joseph have been guilty of blaspheming the Holy Spirit by attributing the unfortunate incidents of his journey to another source, when it was Yahweh who orchestrated each situation? Some in the realm of religion today are quick to tag people as blasphemers of the Holy Spirit for various reasons. A common derivation of this charge is said to be that if someone attributes to Satan what God has done or to God what Satan has done, they are blaspheming the Holy Spirit and are now guilty of the unpardonable sin.

This judgment is levied, based on a poor understanding of the verse in Mark that says*; But he that shall blaspheme against the Holy Ghost hath never forgiveness, but is in danger of eternal damnation:* Mark 3:29

What if there is no Satan to mistakenly attribute God's works to? That changes the weak interpretation of this verse and it therefore must mean something else? If there is no Satan as the Scriptures disclose, then the above verse from Mark cannot mean that there is a real Satan who can perform acts of evil and result in some suggesting that God has done the act. John Gill understands this charge directed at the Pharisees as a charge to not attribute the good that comes from the Creator, to a diabolical power. That power does not have to have a real existence but one must not believe that there is a power that can enact good works except for God. Gill says it like this; "*Against his person, and the works performed by him, by ascribing them to diabolical power and influence, as the Scribes did,*"

As we search for the truth in our lives, there are times when a confrontation may occur as different opinions are expressed. Perhaps Joseph was familiar with confrontation from the views he apparently had of there being only one God, perhaps too, those who heard him credit God for all the evil that he had suffered might have said that he was blaspheming the Holy Spirit out of a heartfelt belief that God did not cause evil but some other cosmic force did. One must always consider what they say, but when one gains the understanding that "Satan" does not exist, to blaspheme the Holy Spirit becomes a charge that means a great deal more than attributing to "Satan" what God has done.

Can Satan Be Credited for What God Does If Satan Doesn't Exist?

Over the course of the years, as I have journeyed out from Christianity I have come to accept there are many things to agree with in most religions. That is to say, every religion has some truth in their belief system and I am always willing to agree with the truth. However, of all the religions in the world that claim to follow the Bible, which one is "the truth"? It is likely that most of us can agree on lots of things but is it not odd that so many of us disagree on enough things to have such a large number of different "Christian" sects in the world? According to a recent study on religions and Christianity, there are almost 34000 different flavors of Christianity since 30 CE. According to the *World Christian Database, Center for the Study of Global Christianity*[67] , presently there are over 9000 brands of Christian religious denominations in the world. Recent research on world religions and history has tagged the number of Christian flavored religions that have existed at over a whopping 33,800. Which one is right? David Barret writes of these monstrous proportions in his work; *"A Comparative Survey of Churches and Religions,"*

> There are 19 major world religions which are subdivided into a total of 270 large religious groups, and many smaller ones. 34,000 separate Christian groups have been identified in the world. "*Over half of them are independent churches that are not interested in linking with the big denominations.*"[68]

Thirty four thousand differing views on what the truth is, is a huge number of different "religious sects". A religious sect becomes a religious sect because those who make it so believe that they have more truth than others of a similar religious mindset do. Even of the 9000 that are said to presently exist in the world, which one has the truth?

Some could look at the preposterous numbers of Christian groups and say one might as well scrap the faith idea all together; I mean "why bother to try to decide which one is right, with so many to choose from they must be screwed up", some might say. I agree in very large part with that line of reasoning and would support the concept that they must be skewed, at least in some areas of doctrine and practice. As for scrapping the pursuit of faith and therefore of truth altogether, well I heartily disagree with taking that

67 http://www.worldchristiandatabase.org/wcd/about/denominationlist.asp

68 According to David Barrett et al, editors of the "*World Christian Encyclopedia*:

position. It is a simple fact that every religion has some truth; it is also a simple fact that Yahweh is the author or source of all truth.

It may be a little less of a simple fact but I believe a fact nonetheless, that all the faiths which claim to follow the Messiah and the "Holy Bible" sprung from first century belief in Yeshua as Messiah. This premise therefore should lead us to understand that all we have to do to have truth and not be a doctrinally diverse and fractured variety of religion, is to find out how the Messiah taught His apostles to live their faith and subsequently how the first century believing community and individual followers of "The Way" lived their faith. Once we figure out the manner and practice of the first century believers who we read of in the Apostolic Testimony (the New Testament), then we have the opportunity to live and walk out faith in the same manner and practices. Living a faith life, in such a manner, usually finds those doing so enjoying agreement with the Scriptures rather than compromising in order to agree with a man or a denomination just to keep the peace and remain in step with others who have found the same need to agree. It is with this in mind that I relate the situation I found myself in at a showing of *The Rape of Europe*. A situation where I was in agreement with a deeply disturbing religious sect called the Nazis on an issue that the Scriptures agreed with.

An example of a skewed belief that has migrated deep into the Christian fiber of certain sects is seen in what is taught about the "gift of tongues". A couple of years ago I was facilitating a meeting with a group of believers where we had watched a film called *The Rape of Europe*. This film is a production by David Hathaway, a Christian minister who did an excellent job in the film of informing the viewers how Europe and the European Union more specifically, appear to be the seat of the Anti-messiah spirit which wants to dominate the world and impose its ungodly agenda on the world. The film was excellent for revealing some of the concepts of end times, which elucidate who are the world's major players and nations to be watched and to be weary of as we await the return of Messiah.

A Christian ministry produces this film as I have said and although I found many things to agree with in the film I do not claim to be a Christian and there were some things I did not agree with, things that are presumed as true by much of Christianity.

When the film ended, I began the discussion with a statement that indicated I agreed with the Nazis about the Pentecostal movement. The Pentecostal movement was a move into hyper-spiritualism and not a move of holiness led by the spirit of Yahweh. Its followers breaking out in ecstatic, unintelligible-babble, known as "tongues", mark this early 1900's movement. The reason I can state this, is that the Spirit of God would not have people speaking in unintelligible tongues and claiming it was like the Day of Pentecost spoken of in Acts because that incidence of tongues was very different from the tongues found in Christian sects such as Pentecostalism. In chapter 2 where "tongues" are reported as happening during a biblical festival, all the languages spoken were intelligible and understood as the native tongues of the hearers. Without embarking on a complete argument as to why I agreed with the Germans on that one issue, I will submit, that the Acts 2 account of "tongues" was an account where the apostles spoke perfectly understandable language, and the general "tongue talking" in the Pentecostal movement is not. "Tongues" as we know it today in Charismatic religion, is not a biblical practice at all. Because the Pentecostal movement is marked by unintelligible babble, it begins to be a suspect movement and I believe it was not a "Move of God". Upon stating my opinion of "tongues" during discussion that day, there were a couple of individuals who disagreed with my perspective and made it known to the entire group. In short, I was told that in saying the Pentecostal move with "tongues" was not a move of God; I had committed the unforgivable sin and could be seen as blaspheming the Holy Spirit. The explanation that followed was that if one attributed to Satan what God had done and to God what Satan had done, then they were blaspheming the Holy Spirit. This accusation was made on a misunderstood basis of Matthew 12:32.

I did not get the opportunity to elaborate at that time nor share with the group that the unintelligible tongues movement of the Pentecostals is a man-produced and generated phenomenon that can be compared to early Gnostic worship festivals that involved the same behaviors as those of the Pentecostals. I was in no way attributing the move to a Satan but was not allowed the privilege of clarifying my position at that time and was then accused of "the unpardonable sin" of blaspheming the Holy Spirit.

After a few weeks, I had the opportunity to sit down with one of the young men who had stated his concern regarding my statements. At that meeting, He came to somewhat of an understanding that the unpardonable sin did not mean what many have believed it to mean. That is, it did not mean specifically, the behavior that attributes certain activities to the wrong God.

A more comprehensive explanation of blaspheming the "Holy Spirit", would be the persistent and rebellious denial that Yeshua is Messiah and refusal to accept that He is to be recognized as such and worshipped and believed as such. We agreed that if the unforgivable sin was simply the concept that he and many considered it to be, then most of us have committed it. For who of has not blamed some evil force such as Satan for a natural disaster or the choice of a lecherous man to commit adultery and leave his wife and children husbandless and fatherless? Some may have blamed the unfair death of an infant or child on Satan. Who has not blamed the loss of an income or the infirmity and illness of another or ourselves on Satan at some point in life, when God may well have given it? If we are all subject to the standard that I was held to at that meeting, where I was said to be "blaspheming the Holy Spirit", then most of us are beyond pardoning. What then is the sense in even attempting to show the Master we love Him by our obedience if we are unpardonable anyway?

The truth is, if one of your loved ones today was betrayed by his family members and sold into slavery where you had no idea of what end may come of him, many of us would be inclined to blame some "satanic force" for his misfortune? If there exists a Satan who is the purveyor of evil, then one could expect if evil has fallen on a man of God in the Scriptures, that the purveyor of evil should be blamed. However we see in more than one instance that there is no blaming of Satan when evil is issued to a man of God. Had the man of God understood there to be a Satan that caused evil, then they would be guilty of blaspheming the Holy Spirit in attributing the evil that happened to them, as coming from God.

A scenario of betrayal, and slavery did happen to Joseph in the Torah (Genesis 37) but at the end of the tale credit is given to God for the evil. Besides the story of Joseph, there are numerous accounts and situations where Yahweh sends evil. He sends evil in some cases on the Israelites and in other cases, He sends evil on those who are opposed to the Israelites and the God of the Israelites. In addition, it was Yahweh who sent evil on Joseph. We will see that Joseph knew nothing of another cosmic force and unless one existed that was responsible for evil, Joseph was right to blame God for the evil that he walked through.

Joseph was apparently the favored son of Jacob the patriarch. After telling his seemingly self-vaunting dreams to his brothers and then to his father, Joseph was pretty much despised by his brothers. At one point in Joseph's teenage life, he is given a special coat from his Father. This is the coat that is known by contemporaries to be the coat of many colors. It may have been a colorful coat but many scholars suggest that although it was special, it was not the multi colored coat one would see in the Broadway production of *Joseph and the Amazing Technicolor Dreamcoat*. Regardless of the number of colors on this special coat, the point is that it was a special gift from Jacob to Joseph and the brothers all recognized this and were then even more jealous of their young brother. As time progressed Joseph, who at one point had snitched on his brothers for the poor care they were providing for Jacobs flocks, was sent out to check on them. As the brothers saw Joseph coming in the distance, they conspired to harm him and did so with the result of Joseph being thrown into a pit coatless to die. Rueben the eldest son was not present at the pit confinement of Joseph and upon his return to the group, he tore his clothes and was quite distressed at the thought of his father's son dying in the pit that the brothers had sentenced Joseph to. Reuben, not wanting his little brother to be left to die, convinced the brothers to sell Joseph to a band of Ishmaelite merchants from Midian who were traveling through the area. So far, the maliciousness Joseph was exposed to was certainly perceived as evil.

Joseph was then taken to Egypt were he became the slave of Pharaoh's captain of the guards. We all know the rest of the story, which can be seen in Genesis 39. Joseph rises to power in Egypt through hard work, wise counsel, and ultimately interpreting the Pharaoh's dreams after a lengthy stay in prison. He may have been imprisoned for as many as 12 years before he was released to interpret Pharaoh's dream of the upcoming famine and then he was raised to second in command, answering only to Pharaoh in the land of Egypt. Many of us, if we had been there, would likely have believed that some evil force such as Satan was causing all of Jacob's trouble, at least up until Joseph's miraculous catapult to power. While Jacob was going through years of spirit-breaking imprisonment, he did not know the end of the story. For us to candidly say after the fact, "Oh it was God's will for Joseph to go up to Egypt," is meaningless. It is meaningless due to the fact that we know the entire story and how it ended by God bringing the tribes of Israel to Egypt so that they would not starve during the widespread famine and ultimately go into slavery for years only to be delivered by Yahweh through Moses and given the eternal Torah at Mount Sinai. Easy for us to see it as Yahweh's will now, but it would be real hard for the one going through it to think Yahweh was doing it…or would it? Still no mention in the story of any Satanesque being as the perpetrator of the evils that came upon Joseph. If, and that's a huge IF, if Joseph knew there was only the God of His fathers and hadn't been taught to believe there were some other evil force trying to bring harm and thwart the plan of the God of the universe, would he have thought what was happening to him was of "the Devil"? On the other hand; without consideration, would he have believed the bad string of events that led to the ultimate good for him and his family was all courtesy of God?

Conspicuously absent from the entire Torah including the story of Joseph, is the idea of blaming anyone other than Yahweh for the bad situations and calamities that Yahweh's people go through. When unexplainable, bad things happened to the Hebrew people, they understood Yahweh to be the one who had done it. When the Israelite people are attacked and defeated by other nations, it is always clear that it happened because Yahweh caused it to be so. Absent from the story of Joseph is any mention of "Satan" as the one causing his troubles. It is hard to find any suggestion that Joseph thinks his situation, which appeared evil and treacherous for the most part, is the result of the actions of some evil entity opposed to Yahweh. If Joseph believed there to be a "Satan" figure, then all the evil that happened to him, would undoubtedly be blamed on him. Much to the contrary though, when Joseph finally reveals himself to his brothers who had made multiple trips to Egypt for provisions, he tells them something very poignant. Joseph says in Genesis 45:5;

> *"Now therefore be not grieved, nor angry with yourselves, that ye sold me hither: for God did send me before you to preserve life."*

Joseph does not tell his brothers it was "Satan" who sent him to Egypt as if he was one who believed in a Satan as the cause of evil. Joseph tells his brothers that they should not be angry **with themselves** because "God" was the one who sent him to Egypt. If the children of Israel/Jacob, believed in some Yahweh-opposing force, other than the evil inclination within themselves, then they might be able to blame that force and not be angry with themselves only. However Joseph exhorted them not to be angry with "themselves" which indicates that neither Joseph, nor his brother were even considering there was a supernatural force other than the God of their fathers who was orchestrating every aspect of their existence. Only one of two forces was to be blamed for the evil Joseph had experienced, either humans or Yahweh. Joseph of course understood that the human will could be a force to bring about actions that are opposed to the will of God. This would be the understanding that moral evil comes from the heart of man as there is no moral evil in Yahweh, while tangible, physical evil that comes as an act of Yahweh often utilizes the moral evil in mans' heart as a tool to bring about His plan. Either Joseph lied to his brothers about who brought him to Egypt or Joseph knew that Yahweh was in control of and orchestrating everything. Surprisingly enough, after all the years Joseph spent in Egypt, he still was not attributing any of the circumstances or situations in his life to any force other than the Creator of the Universe.

Why Didn't Joseph Adopt a Cosmic Evil Enemy Philosophy?

As my wife put it recently when we were discussing this topic, Joseph's clear stand on the non-existence of an evil cosmic being after being so enmeshed with the pagan culture of Egypt for so long, is likely because of proper Torah training for him in his youth. Training that results in a firm stand in the truth when faced with challenging situations. Even when the young man is placed in the midst of the fiery trials of pagan life with all its seductive ways and feeling and sensory-based activities, the young man who has been grounded in and taught the truth will very likely choose the good and refuse the evil.

What a model of uncompromising resolve we see in Joseph. Aside from the fact that he never used his positions of favor for self-gain but remained a man of integrity all along his Egyptian sojourn, Joseph even rejected the draw to blame an unknown, false Egyptian god for his trials and times of less-than abundant life. If we had the privilege of having had solid training in areas of truth such as that a "Satan" does not exist, the same philosophy would hold true for us as we move through life. We would be far better equipped to also reject the ancient and distorted notion that there is any force other than Yahweh acting upon this universe. Today we are surrounded by the essence of Egypt. With all the influences from media and culture which endeavor to prick our heart's deepest desires to follow and participate in worship of concepts and things that are contrary to the worship of the only Creator. We are constantly bombarded with ungodly philosophies, however here in North America we are privileged to be able to take refuge in the freedom of religion. A freedom that provides us with some manner of support system to strengthen our walk, as we are able to meet with like-minded believers.

I think many of us may have a hard time imagining the total lack of support system Joseph had in Egypt. Granted the Egyptian culture had such a diverse multitude of false gods that for Joseph to be worshipping or allied to yet another intangible god would not have been cause for persecution. Still though, the intensity of the acts of worship that were going on around him in honor of the false gods of Egypt were often very convincing arguments for true power being available through these gods. Joseph obviously maintained a very real relationship with Yahweh who was known as the God of his fathers at that point in history. How many of us today could marry the daughter of the pagan priest of Egypt as Joseph had done and not then gravitate toward worshipping the pagan gods alongside the God of our Fathers? One of the biggest risks to the person who is assimilated with pagan culture is to adopt a polytheistic view, which adds lesser gods to the faith in the One God. I can almost say for certain I would see myself drifting away from the truth of monotheism from time to time with a risk of a having a dangerous slide down the slippery slope of compromise. No wonder Joseph is such a clear anti-type of the Messiah. Joseph was truly a deliverer and walked in purity as much as is possible for a man to walk in. In fact, there is even no mention of more than one wife for Joseph, which is a testimony to monogamy. When confronted with the chance to fulfill the desires of the flesh through sexual sin with Potiphar's wife, Joseph chose the good once again. Oh to be like Joseph in displaying integrity and as strong in Godly choices.

One thing is for certain, Joseph had a very dramatic journey as he went from the favored son of Jacob to the despised brother of Jacobs's sons. Being stripped and thrown into a pit, then sold into slavery could easily be seen by some as Joseph being the recipient of evil. Again, Joseph was favored, this time by the chief of guard of Potiphar. Favored enough so as to be regarded as worthy enough to run his household, then to be cast into prison for a crime he didn't commit could also be construed as and believed to be evil from the hand of the minions of a cosmic Satan. When left for two more years after the release of the baker and butler, surely one could construe the apparent neglect of a release as the actions of some kind of cosmic Satan blocking the work of Yahweh. However, Joseph, because he understood there is no other God but one, unabashedly proclaimed to his brothers in Genesis 50 verse 20 that Elohim was the one responsible for sending him before them to be able to preserve life in the future. In that statement, Joseph is admitting that all that happened to Him was by the hand of God. Neither he nor his brothers, the patriarchs of the 12 tribes of Egypt, were inclined to attribute the events that resulted in Joseph ending up in Egypt to a supposed evil entity.

After the death of his father when the brothers come before him, afraid Joseph will harm them now that Jacob is dead; Joseph tells them that it was God who put the pieces of his story together.

> *But as for you, ye thought evil against me; but God meant it unto good, to bring to pass, as it is this day, to save much people alive. Genesis 50:20*

A cosmic "Satan" plays no part in the "evil" which came upon Joseph at the hand of his brothers and slave masters. All the "evil" done to Joseph came from Yahweh. Because Joseph knew that evil was not the product of a secondary god he gave credit where credit was due in naming "God" as the axis of evil in his story.

Moral evil is not from Yahweh

The evidence that suggests Yahweh "creates" evil could not be more clear throughout the Scriptures. Looking at only one or two instances of evil coming from God gives somewhat of a picture of where evil proceeds from. But as we piece together the concepts found in the Hebrew Scriptures that pertain to evil and "satan", it begins to be irrefutable, that evil is brought on God's creation, by none other than the Creator Himself. Being reminded of the verse in Isaiah 45, in which God says, "*I make piece and create evil.*" or the statement in Amos chapter 3 verse 6 where Yahweh asks the rhetorical question through the prophet, *that if there is evil in a city has God not done it*; helps us to come to an understanding of other statements made in the Scriptures about this topic. Are there different types of evil in the Scriptures?

Understanding that though, is it then sensible to suggest that the Creator of the Universe is capable of evil such as the genre of evil that comes from the thoughts and heart of man?

Addressing the place of "moral evil" in humanity, we need to consider if this is the "evil" that proceeds from Yahweh. Would the God of Creation be indictable for an evil that can be defined as coveting or murdering or any sin resulting from a moral choice? Yahweh is clearly not guilty of sin, so to suggest He makes moral, or immoral choices which are classified as evil and subsequently "sin" is to say He is less than a perfect and Holy Creator. Nor does He place choice in front of man to give man an excuse to choose evil only then to justify the evil choice by saying that God made him do it. This is the discussion James engages in, in the book of James.

> *Let no man say when he is tempted, I am tempted of God: for God cannot be tempted with evil, neither tempteth he any man: But every man is tempted, when he is drawn away of his own lust, and enticed. Then when lust hath conceived, it bringeth forth sin: and sin, when it is finished, bringeth forth death. James 1:13-15 KJV*

One could make contentions on how perfect the Creator is if He is perfect at all and one might contend that any effort to perceive the Creator's morality is flawed due to the fallibility of the Scriptures that have been passed down to us by fallible humans. These contentions will not disappear as a result of this book but I am only able to conciliate the contentious reader with a statement of my belief in the infallibility of the words in Scripture. The infallibility only exists for Scripture when the Scriptures are understood according to their original tongue and the original intent of the author. Standing on this premise when exploring the morality of Yahweh, one can come closer to a true and accurate understanding of Gods perfection in all He does. If you are inclined to believe the Scriptures are invalid due to the seeming flaws in transmission of the truth found in them, then please take the time to explore both sides of the debate on the Scriptures' validity. Try to be fair enough to honestly investigate the most read book in the world to determine not only where it might be seen as wrong but to also determine where the Scriptures might be right and therefore then, accurate. Take into account that the Messiah, who is allegedly God in the flesh, approved the Holy Scriptures by using a compilation of books that are almost identical to the Old Testament used today.

For instance, based on the belief that the message in the Garden of Eden story and "fall of man" is an accurately written account of the beginnings of man, certain conclusions can be drawn. And based on the belief that it was written using spiritually-rich metaphor aimed at teaching the concept of man's ability to choose to sin or choose not to sin as an ability that was placed in man from the beginning of man's existence; it seems logical to conclude that man has the latent potential to choose to do evil. How this relates to the moral evil, which affects humanity becomes a factor of man's ability to choose evil not being the same as Yahweh's ability to bring evil on man. There is a difference in the type of "evil" Yahweh is responsible for and the type of evil that comes from the heart of man. Jeremiah 17:9 told us that *The heart is deceitful above all things, and desperately wicked* and Yeshua told us that *out of the heart proceed evil thoughts, murders, adulteries, fornications, thefts, false witness, blasphemies.*

Yeshua knew that every inclination of man's heart was continually evil before the flood. That is why Yahweh destroyed the earth with a flood, as Genesis teaches;

> *And GOD saw that the wickedness of man was great in the earth, and that every imagination of the thoughts of his heart was only evil continually. Genesis 6:5*

Looking at these references we start with the one made by Jeremiah who confirms that the heart of man is still the most wicked thing in creation and Yeshua is affirming once again that evil proceeds from man's heart. The verse in Genesis has proclaimed it is man's heart that is inclined to do evil continually. The wisest man to walk the face of the earth, King Solomon, recognizes that due to the fact evil work is not always judged speedily, men's hearts are fully set on doing evil.

> *Because sentence against an evil work is not executed speedily, therefore the heart of the sons of men is fully set in them to do evil. Ecclesiastes 8:11*

The concept of the wickedness of man's heart is a very large reason why God wants to give us a new heart, a heart of flesh. This is a circumcised heart that obeys His commands out of love for Him and appreciation for the great sacrifice of the only begotten son, Yeshua. So clearly according to Yeshua, Jeremiah, and Genesis, the evil that comes from a man is the inclination that is right there in the heart of man. It is an inclination to do wickedness and this wickedness is not an attribute of Yahweh. Yahweh does not do wickedly nor does He battle with making moral choices as does man, but Yahweh, as we have seen, does enact evil in some instances. Therefore, my position is this;

Man has an evil and wicked heart that has the potential to make wicked choices, this results in a moral type of evil.

Yahweh has a pure heart and does not make wicked choices but He creates evil, which can be seen as a type of evil likened to calamity. It is calamities such as defeat at the hands of enemies, or pestilences or diseases that represents the evil that comes from the Creator. Perhaps the evil Yahweh brings upon man is a natural disaster. For instance, in Joshua there is a warning of the consequence of transgressing His ways. The consequence is that He will lay evil upon those who "transgress";

> *Therefore it shall come to pass, that as all good things are come upon you, which the LORD your God promised you; so shall the* ***LORD bring upon you all evil things****, until he have destroyed you from off this good land which the LORD your God hath given you. 16 When ye have transgressed the covenant of the LORD your God, which he commanded you, and have gone and served other gods, and bowed yourselves to them; then shall the anger of the LORD be kindled against you, and ye shall perish quickly from off the good land which he hath given unto you. Joshua 23:15-16*

In Nehemiah, God is credited with bringing evil on the city due to the profaning of the Sabbath.

> *Did not your fathers thus, and* ***did not our God bring all this evil upon us****, and upon this city? yet ye bring more wrath upon Israel by profaning the sabbath. Nehemiah 13:18*

It can't be emphasized enough, that God brings evil on His people when they are persistent in their disobedience and He also brings evil on those who are opposed to His people. By not being a respecter of persons and delivering His evil upon any one He decides deserves to be punished, there is no confusion that He is a God who wants to be seen as the only one who creates evil. It is due to a somewhat myopic view of God as the Creator of absolutely everything; orchestrating every situation in the entire earth so that ultimately He gets the glory, that we confuse bad happenings as happenings which came from "satan." The following list of verses clearly states He is sending/bringing evil. They all provide the same statement of Yahweh enacting evil; perhaps you need only read a few of the verses I provide here to see the clear statement of "evil" being rendered by God.

> **Joshua 23:15 Therefore it shall come to pass, *that* as all good things are come upon you, which the LORD your God**

promised you; so shall the LORD bring upon you all evil things, until he have destroyed you from off this good land which the LORD your God hath given you.

2Samuel 17:14 And Absalom and all the men of Israel said, The counsel of Hushai the Archite *is* better than the counsel of Ahithophel. For the LORD had appointed to defeat the good counsel of Ahithophel, to the intent that the LORD might bring evil upon Absalom.

1Kings 14:10 Therefore, behold, I will bring evil upon the house of Jeroboam, and will cut off from Jeroboam him that pisseth against the wall, *and* him that is shut up and left in Israel, and will take away the remnant of the house of Jeroboam, as a man taketh away dung, till it be all gone.

1Kings 21:21 Behold, I will bring evil upon thee, and will take away thy posterity, and will cut off from Ahab him that pisseth against the wall, and him that is shut up and left in Israel,

1Kings 21:29 Seest thou how Ahab humbleth himself before me? because he humbleth himself before me, I will not bring the evil in his days: *but* in his son's days will I bring the evil upon his house.

2Kings 22:16 Thus saith the LORD, Behold, I will bring evil upon this place, and upon the inhabitants thereof, *even* all the words of the book which the king of Judah hath read:

2Kings 22:20 Behold therefore, I will gather thee unto thy fathers, and thou shalt be gathered into thy grave in peace; and thine eyes shall not see all the evil which I will bring upon this place. And they brought the king word again.

2Chronicles 34:24 Thus saith the LORD, Behold, I will bring evil upon this place, and upon the inhabitants thereof, *even* all the curses that are written in the book which they have read before the king of Judah:

2Chronicles 34:28 Behold, I will gather thee to thy fathers, and thou shalt be gathered to thy grave in peace, neither shall thine eyes see all the evil that I will bring upon this place, and upon the inhabitants of the same. So they brought the king word again.

Nehemiah 13:18 Did not your fathers thus, and did not our God bring all this evil upon us, and upon this city? yet ye bring more wrath upon Israel by profaning the sabbath.

Isaiah 31:2 Yet he also *is* wise, and will bring evil, and will not call back his words: but will arise against the house of the evildoers, and against the help of them that work iniquity.

Jeremiah 4:6 Set up the standard toward Zion: retire, stay not: for I will bring evil from the north, and a great destruction.

Jeremiah 6:19 Hear, O earth: behold, I will bring evil upon this people, *even* the fruit of their thoughts, because they have not hearkened unto my words, nor to my law, but rejected it.

Jeremiah 11:8 Yet they obeyed not, nor inclined their ear, but walked every one in the imagination of their evil heart: therefore I will bring upon them all the words of this covenant, which I commanded *them* to do; but they did *them* not.

Jeremiah 11:11 Therefore thus saith the LORD, Behold, I will bring evil upon them, which they shall not be able to escape; and though they shall cry unto me, I will not hearken unto them.

Jeremiah 11:23 And there shall be no remnant of them: for I will bring evil upon the men of Anathoth, *even* the year of their visitation.

Jeremiah 17:18 Let them be confounded that persecute me, but let not me be confounded: let them be dismayed, but let not me be dismayed: bring upon them the day of evil, and destroy them with double destruction.

Jeremiah 19:3 And say, Hear ye the word of the LORD, O kings of Judah, and inhabitants of Jerusalem; Thus saith the LORD of hosts, the God of Israel; Behold, I will bring evil upon this place, the which whosoever heareth, his ears shall tingle.

Jeremiah 19:15 Thus saith the LORD of hosts, the God of Israel; Behold, I will bring upon this city and upon all her towns all the evil that I have pronounced against it, because they have hardened their necks, that they might not hear my words.

Jeremiah 23:12 Wherefore their way shall be unto them as slippery *ways* in the darkness: they shall be driven on, and fall therein: for I will bring evil upon them, *even* the year of their visitation, saith the LORD.

Jeremiah 25:29 For, lo, I begin to bring evil on the city which is called by my name, and should ye be utterly unpunished? Ye shall not be unpunished: for I will call for a sword upon all the inhabitants of the earth, saith the LORD of hosts.

Jeremiah 32:42 For thus saith the LORD; Like as I have brought all this great evil upon this people, so will I bring upon them all the good that I have promised them.

Jeremiah 35:17 Therefore thus saith the LORD God of hosts, the God of Israel; Behold, I will bring upon Judah and upon all the inhabitants of Jerusalem all the evil that I have pronounced against them: because I have spoken unto them, but they have not heard; and I have called unto them, but they have not answered.

Jeremiah 36:31 And I will punish him and his seed and his servants for their iniquity; and I will bring upon them, and upon the inhabitants of Jerusalem, and upon the men of Judah, all the evil that I have pronounced against them; but they hearkened not.

Jeremiah 39:16 Go and speak to Ebedmelech the Ethiopian, saying, Thus saith the LORD of hosts, the God of Israel; Behold, I will bring my words upon this city for evil, and not for good; and they shall be *accomplished* in that day before thee.

Jeremiah 42:17 So shall it be with all the men that set their faces to go into Egypt to sojourn there; they shall die by the sword, by the famine, and by the pestilence: and none of them shall remain or escape from the evil that I will bring upon them.

Jeremiah 45:5 And seekest thou great things for thyself? seek *them* not: for, behold, I will bring evil upon all flesh, saith the LORD: but thy life will I give unto thee for a prey in all places whither thou goest.

Jeremiah 49:37 For I will cause Elam to be dismayed before their enemies, and before them that seek their life: and I will

> **bring evil upon them, *even* my fierce anger, saith the LORD; and I will send the sword after them, till I have consumed them:**

> **Ezekiel 5:17 So will I send upon you famine and evil beasts, and they shall bereave thee; and pestilence and blood shall pass through thee; and I will bring the sword upon thee. I the LORD have spoken *it*.**

Reading the above verses shows that certainly there is a type of evil that comes from Yahweh and it seems to be meted out to "evildoers", as Isaiah 31:2 above states. In so many cases where there has been sin and disobedience or simply plain old rebellion out of a stubborn heart, Yahweh responded by sending evil. So many people have believed that no evil could come from God, however, if God creates evil, and if God created man with the potential to choose evil; then God must have a purpose for the evil that He uses. The depth one could go, in pondering the purpose of a righteous God creating and using evil for His righteous purposes is profound. Again though, I am not intending to plum that depth of the diverse expressions of evil that come from Yahweh at this time but I will say it is possible Yahweh created and uses evil in His plan so that His plan, which ultimately glorifies Him and draws us to Him, will be worked out. Is it possible that the type of evil Yahweh imposes upon humanity is actually intended to bring about results that complement His desires and will? It is without a doubt that Yahweh is sovereign and His use of evil is absolutely designed to bring about His plan. His plan often includes judgment and the destruction of those who will stubbornly refuse to turn from following the "evil inclination", as well as turning those to repentance who are willing to humble their hearts and receive His forgiveness while they endeavor to overcome the evil inclination that internally draws us away from making the good choice.

> **The evil, which comes from Yahweh, is not a choice for evil in the sense of personal morality; it is a response by Yahweh to a choice for evil by humans. That choice for evil when acted upon by man is known to be referred to as wickedness. Then, when God sees that pattern of choice as the predominant choice by man, He eventually takes action by administering evil in some form that causes man to rethink his choices.**

If the first type of evil we have discussed in this chapter is seen to be the process of God using His powers to orchestrate situations which cause distress for man, such as sending a young man as Joseph into the land of Egypt as a slave or wreaking havoc upon a disobedient nation; the second type of evil is the moral evil that comes from man choosing to do wickedness. To be clear, this type comes from man and is not the actions of Yahweh on sinful man.

What is Moral?

Morality is sometimes difficult to define and is often alluded to in culture, with a reference to what is acceptable behavior in a given society for that social period. Webster's 1828 Dictionary states the following in its definition of morality;

> Morality
>
> MORAL'ITY, n. The doctrine or system of moral duties, or the duties of men in their social character; ethics.
>
> The system of morality to be gathered from the writings of ancient sages, falls very short of that delivered in the gospel.
>
> 1. The practice of the moral duties; virtue. We often admire the politeness of men whose morality we question.
>
> 2. The quality of an action which renders it good; the conformity of an act to the divine law, or to the principles of rectitude. This conformity implies that the act must be performed by a free agent, and from a motive of obedience to the divine will. This is the strict theological and scriptural sense of morality. But we often apply the word to actions which accord with justice and human laws, without reference to the motives from which they proceed.

In Webster's point number 2 in the above definition, it is good to see included, some reference to the motivation surrounding a moral action. According to the Scriptures, morality or the choice to do what is considered "good" must be based out of the correct motivation, if it is to be credited to the performer of the particular action as a righteous act that is pleasing to the Creator. Secondly, morality in the above definition at point 2 by Webster recognizes the connection of morality to the divine law and therefore one would be performing acts in accordance with the divine law. The divine law complements and can be complemented by societal rules and laws. For instance, the divine law does not state that you are not allowed to walk around naked in public whenever you desire. Therefore based on the verse in 1 John 3:4 which tells us that sin is the transgression of the divine Torah law, one would not be guilty of sinning if he or she chose to walk around naked in public based on simply a strictly semantical reading of the rules and words. However, there are other issues that would present themselves if you, I, or many of us were to wander through the streets of our town or mow our lawn in the nude. Simply because Adam and Eve were created and existed naked in the Garden of Eden, does not give us an inalienable right to subject those around us to the discomfort of witnessing us naked. It may be traumatic in some instances. Or perhaps impure thoughts by a witness of the nakedness may be a result of seeing a naked person performing their daily activities in full view of the entire world. Therefore, in this instance societal law coupled with biblical law can be seen as morality. This is just a brief point on the matter and there are many biblical reasons why public nudity should not be practiced.

Now as I stated earlier, Yahweh is not a candidate for participating in or producing moral evil. This type of evil is strictly the domain of the creatures Yahweh created with the power to choose good or evil. He gave us the choice in the Garden of Eden and told us we would die if we ate of the Tree of The Knowledge of Good and Evil. This was reiterated in the second reading of the law near the end of the Book of Deuteronomy. Yahweh placed an option before us that could bring us death if we decide to choose accordingly.

> *I call heaven and earth to record this day against you, that I have set before you life and death, blessing and cursing: therefore choose life, that both thou and thy seed may live:*
> *That thou mayest love the LORD thy God, and that thou mayest obey his voice, and that thou mayest cleave unto him: for he is thy life, and the length of thy days: that thou mayest dwell in the land which the LORD sware unto thy fathers, to Abraham, to Isaac, and to Jacob, to give them. Deuteronomy 30:19-20*

So the choice is always before us and if we choose other than life, other than the good choice for morally acceptable decisions, we then are choosing evil and are participants in wickedness by our own decision. By choosing wickedness, we have consciously chosen evil and therefore we are open to the evil from Yahweh as a judgment, punishment or act which is designed to bring us to repentance. Sin does not open a person to the attack of the Devil as is often taught, sin wakens part of our humanness to become more apt to choose sin in the future and opens us to retribution and corrective judgments from the Creator who asks that we obey Him. As for repentance, it is not to be over explained, because it is simply an action described from the Hebrew word *teshuva,* which means to turn or change directions, and it carries the contextual meaning in the Scriptures of one turning from wicked ways and returns to Yahweh and following His ways. The evil that is from man's heart is never credited to a cosmic Satan. This type of evil is simply man deciding to disobey God and not keep His commands. This is wickedness and if we turn from this wickedness, we can return to God and He will return to us. The context of the following verses reveals wicked ways are in fact disobedience to Yahweh's commands as laid out in the Hebrew Scriptures.

> *If my people, which are called by my name, shall humble themselves, and pray, and seek my face, and* ***turn from their wicked ways****; then will I hear from heaven, and will forgive their sin, and will heal their land… 14*
> *And as for thee, if thou wilt walk before me, as David thy father walked, and do according to all that I have commanded thee, and shalt observe my statutes and my judgments; …17*
> *And it shall be answered, Because they forsook the LORD God of their fathers, which brought them forth out of the land of Egypt, and laid hold on other gods, and worshipped them, and served them: therefore hath he brought all this evil upon them. 22*
> *2 Chronicles 7:14, 17, and 22 KJV*

> *Say unto them, As I live, saith the Lord GOD, I have no pleasure in the death of the wicked; but that* ***the wicked turn from his way and live****: turn ye, turn ye from your evil ways; for why will ye die, O house of Israel?*
> *Ezekiel 33:11*

To wrap up a few thoughts on the types of evil and from where they proceed, let me just say Yahweh sends evil in the form of an "evil spirit" or a "lying spirit" sometimes. Other expressions of evil occur through pestilences, wars, calamities, famines, judgments, disease and other things we typically want to avoid in our lives. Wickedness is the evil that proceeds from the rebellious heart of man who chooses to do evil by sinning. These acts of evil can be temporary and isolated or they can be perpetual and habitual.

In our journey to find what pleases the God of the Universe we can boil it down to the simple process of learning to refuse the evil and choose the good. Evil is a choice that stems from the heart of man. That is why Yahweh continually puts evil before us. He wants us to choose. This opportunity for choice is stated in the Scriptures and seen variously including the placing of the tree of the knowledge of evil and good before Adam and Eve. We have looked at it before and I think another look is an excellent reminder that it is God who not only causes evil in many ways but also places evil before us that we would make the decision to choose life.

See, I have set before thee this day life and good, and death and evil; 16 In that I command thee this day to love the LORD thy God, to walk in his ways, and to keep his commandments and his statutes and his judgments, that thou mayest live and multiply: and the LORD thy God shall bless thee in the land whither thou goest to possess it. Deuteronomy 30:15-16

CHAPTER 7

The Post-Exilic, Persian Influence On the Idea of Satan

So far, in our discussion, we have seen there is little if not any true reference to a Satanic being in the Torah or the judges or the history of the kings of Israel. We have seen the Hebrew Scriptures clearly reveal that a lying spirit comes from Yahweh and that an evil spirit comes from Yahweh. It is necessary that we discuss for a while, how the changes in the understanding or philosophy of a being called Satan came to be.

For this task, I would like to ask you to view the Hebrew Scriptures, the Old Testament not as an anthology that was constructed in one distinct period; rather I ask that you see the Scriptures in sections. The sections I am asking you to recognize will be seen as two individual periods of history and are understood to have a very distinct chronological position in the development of the Hebrew Scriptures and the mindset of the Hebrew people as it pertains to "Satan" and to evil. In the simplest form of the sectioning, we can separate the Hebrew Scriptures as the pre-exilic and the post-exilic books. Some writings were complete before the Hebrew people went into the Persian exile while others were not written until the time of the Persian exile and beyond. The Israelites had a very profound and intense history. A history of kings who would lead them in the ways of the most High and of kings who, as the scriptures put it, "did evil in the sight" of God and caused the children of Israel to break God's commands and engage in sin thereby walking after the ways of their wicked Fathers. Here is one example of this concept from the Hebrew Scriptures where we are told that King Zechariah was considered a King who did evil.

> *And he did that which was evil in the sight of the LORD, as his fathers had done: he departed not from the sins of Jeroboam the son of Nebat, who made Israel to sin. 2Kings 15:9*

A quick search of the phrase, "*did evil in the sight*" on the e-sword[69] bible software program resulted in 37 verses that contain almost the exact phrase. So the Israelite history was a very up and down history and journey in respect to walking in a manner that was pleasing to God by keeping the Torah of Yahweh and refusing the evil. A major portion of this journey for the Israelites was written about in the Scriptures and compiled in the books of Genesis through Kings. These books were written prior to the 6th Century BC when Israel went into exile as a result of the sin they had walked in for so long.

During the period of exile, the children of Israel learned many things from their Babylonian and Persian hosts. Many beliefs and practices were taken from their captors and subtly applied to the Israelite religious culture. We will talk more of what was learned to their detriment shortly. For the present, it is helpful for you to note that portions of the major and minor prophetic books were written after the exile to Babylon. Those writings that were penned during this period then, is the second section of the Hebrew Scriptures I would like to consider within the context of the development of a Satan doctrine.

Essentially, we have the pre-exilic writings and the postexilic writings. Often times the reader of the Bible will confuse the time that the books were written with being the same time as what was written in the books. This error would be tantamount to a present day historian writing about the First World War and a reader thinking that he was recounting the events from a first person perspective. For instance, the Book of Isaiah was written to cover a period of history that is quite large and the writers often write of things that happened far in the past in relation to the day they wrote the information on the page.

In the Book of Isaiah, we are given prophesies in the days of Uzziah, Jotham, Ahaz, and Hezekiah; all kings of Judah. The period of these Kings covered around 120 years.[70] If Isaiah were a history book I could see the intent in covering such a large chunk of time but it is not identified as a history book although it contains much history amid the prophesies, warnings, exhortations

69 E-Sword can be downloaded for free on the internet at the following web address; http://www.e-sword.net/index.html

70 Below is a chart indicating the approximate years of the reigns of each of the 4 kings of Judah mentioned in Isaiah. It is to be noted these dates are approximate and could conceivably be open to correction based on various chronology and archeological data. However the dates indicated, show the reader there was a significant time period covered by the writings which are labeled as the Book of Isaiah.

Uzziah	786-758
Jotham	758-742
Ahaz	742-726
Hezekiah	726-697

and encouragements. Some sections speak in the present while others speak of the future. So to be clear, the occurrences written about in the particular texts of the individual biblical books often are written down at one point in history but are referring to a time before that in which they were written. It is also quite regular to have a statement made as a prophecy, which will occur hundreds of years in the future. Nonetheless, one must attempt to place the statements found in Scripture, into their historical context by determining at what point of Israel's history the statement was made. In *Prophets of Israel,* George Knight says;

> *"Thus for example we owe an unqualified debt of gratitude to those scholars who were able to show that the book of Isaiah covers a period of some 250 years of Hebrew thought. It is only as a result of their labors that we are able to place the great majority of passages in their historical setting. Till we were in the position to do so, much of "Isaiah" was virtually meaningless.*[71]

It is quite important that the notable prophecy in Isaiah 45 given to King Cyrus, is placed in its proper historical setting if we are to attempt to understand it correctly. In this prophecy, we are told Cyrus is Yahweh's Messiah. I am using the English understanding of the Hebrew term Mashiach; this is a term which is affixed to Yeshua the Messiah/Mashiach and is a title and descriptor of the role of the individual honored with it. In Scofield's Reference Notes to the Bible, he has this to say of Cyrus as a Messiah;

> The only instance where the word is applied to a Gentile. Nebuchadnezzar is called the "servant" of Jehovah (Jer_25:9); (Jer_27:6); (Jer_43:10) This, with the designation "My shepherd" (Isaiah_44:28) also a Messianic title, marks Cyrus as that startling exception, a Gentile type of Christ. The points are:
>
> (1) both are irresistible conquerors of Israel's enemies. (Isaiah_45:1); (Rev_19:19-21).
>
> (2) both are restorers of the holy city (Isaiah_44:28); (Zec_14:1-11).
>
> (3) through both is the name of the one true God glorified (Isaiah_45:6); (1Co_15:28).

71 Bible Guides, Prophets of Israel (1) Isaiah, page 25. By George Knight

The study of a Gentile King being called Yahweh's Messiah, is full of interesting implications. Yahweh chooses to use any creature in His creation to accomplish His will. The fact a pagan King can be called His Messiah lends well to the argument that it would also be probable that evil could be stated to be coming from Yahweh. Both of these concepts can be equally inane if considered through the ideas that Yahweh does only the good, whilst the evil is under the control of "Satan." However, as has been shown through the Scriptures, evil in a type that is different from the wickedness in man's heart, can and does proceed forth from Yahweh.

To move on from the discussion of Cyrus as Messiah I would like to have you consider further the different sections of the bible and their periods of coming into existence as mentioned above. Specifically for our discussion, we will look at the Books of 1st and 2nd Samuel and 1st and 2nd Chronicles. These books repeat vast amounts of information and are used to cross-reference each other when one studying is looking into the issue of a King or perhaps a King's reignal period. There is so much repetition of information between these two books that one might ask the question of why they are both in the Scriptures? I might suggest they are both extremely valuable as a tool to establish chronologies which when compared to secular history and ancient Kings' chronologies, aids in proving the accuracy and historicity of the Scriptures.

If you are to read from a copy of the Hebrew Bible today, you will find that the Chronicles are intentionally placed at the back for certain reasons as opposed to closer to the front as in English Bibles. There are multiple other reasons why they are both contained within the Hebrew Scriptures and true there is also large quantities of unrepeated information between the two accounts, however, for our purposes I believe there is at least one glaring difference between these two amazingly similar books that can be used to help us understand the transition period. This transition period is the period when the well-understood concept of the adversary coming from God evolves with a serious twist. It is in this pivotal period of biblical history that the adversary starts to become a character called "Satan", a character who many believe is an actual distinct personality.

The Adversary is God According to One Writer and is Called The Sawtawn By Another

The books of 1st and 2nd Samuel cover much of the same information as the Books of 1st and 2nd Chronicles, however they were written in very different periods. The Samuel duo was written prior to the exile of the Israelites to Babylon and the Chronicles duo was written sometime after the exile to Babylon. Both were written to aid in giving a historical account of the timeline of the Kings of Judah and Israel. Now both sets of books may have been written with a very similar purpose, however the mindset of the writers may have been dissimilar in some areas.

When the book of Samuel was penned, it was clearly understood by the Israelites that both good and evil came from Yahweh. In the pre-exilic version of our target verses, Yahweh moves David to number Israel; quite opposite to that is the blaming of "Satan" as the one provoking David to number Israel in the book of Chronicles. The clear language used in the Hebrew is calling the inciter an adversary. However, although I believe the Chronicler simply used a different word to describe the action of God inciting David, the question could be raised asking if the Chronicler was in fact equating Yahweh with the adversary or if he thought that the adversary was a different force than the God spoken of in the Samuel account. Giving the benefit of the doubt to the writer of Chronicles I suspect he was simply using a different term for what God was doing when He incited David to number the tribes of Israel. Samuel says "*God*" and the Chronicler says "*sawtawn*"- meaning adversary. Putting these two passages in the same Bible must not be seen as a contradiction rather it is to be seen that the God of 2nd Samuel 24 is the adversary of 1st Chronicles 21

This theosophical shift reveals itself in the account of David numbering the tribes of Israel as inspired to do so by Yahweh so that a judgment on the Israelites may be brought about. Numbering Israel in the manner of Kings is against the Torah. The Torah prescribes numbering through the collection of the half-shekel temple tax each year. Every male over the age of 20 was to bring their half-shekel to the temple. By Yahweh moving David to number the Israelites in a manner that is against the prescribed manner, the judgment of Yahweh is brought upon the sheep, those who are servants of the King. The appearances in the Scriptures of two different sources of the inspiration to number Israel are given in the verses quoted below. The subject has been highlighted.

> *2Samuel 24:1-2 And again the anger of **the LORD** was kindled against Israel, **and he moved David** against them to say, Go, number Israel and Judah. 2 For the king said to Joab the captain of the host, which was with him, Go now through all the tribes of Israel, from Dan even to Beersheba, and number ye the people, that I may know the number of the people.*

> *1Chronicles 21:1-2 **And Satan stood up against Israel, and provoked David** to number Israel. 2 And David said to Joab and to the rulers of the people, Go, number Israel from Beersheba*

even to Dan; and bring the number of them to me, that I may know it.

Notice the apparent huge theological discrepancy in the above two passages. Both of these passages are contained in every bible whether it is a Christian Bible or the Hebrew Tanak. One passage clearly indicates God moved David and the other clearly states it was Satan. How could the Bible confuse such a clear concept? Was Yahweh or was Satan responsible for moving David to count the people? How are we to reconcile these two conflicting statements? Is it possible the many commentaries which state God let "Satan" have his way, by removing His hand from the situation, have failed to asses the cultural understanding and historical context at the time of the writing of the two passages? If we are planning to believe the words of the Hebrew Scriptures then we are left with little option but to see that according to the words in the two accounts in question, either Satan is God or God is Satan in some manner and sense. We can easily reconcile the words by understanding that Yahweh has always been and is in these accounts, the only force in the universe; therefore, He is the inciter on both accounts. The Satan in the Chronicles account is simply the Hebrew words *ha sawtawn* and should be translated into English as "the adversary". This concept of the adversary might be the same adversary that proceeded from Yahweh in the story of Balaam when Balak attempts to have Balaam curse Israel (see Numbers 23). In fact, in 1st Samuel 26 more understanding of evil being either from man or from God is given us, when David asks Saul to consider whom the one is that is stirring up against him. The two options for who the antagonist is are presented as either God or men.

Now therefore, I pray thee, let my lord the king hear the words of his servant. If the LORD have stirred thee up against me, let him accept an offering: but if they be the children of men, cursed be they before the LORD; for they have driven me out this day from abiding in the inheritance of the LORD, saying, Go, serve other gods. 1Samuel 26:19

This verse is an extraordinary statement about the origin of evil by David the soon to be king of Israel. If we are willing to recognize David's ancient understanding of there being no supernatural force but Yahweh, then you might see why David does not attribute Saul's pursuit of him to a cosmic Satan. In the above verse, David is calling out to Saul and Saul's camp after creeping into the camp of Saul with his companion warrior, Abishai. David calls out to Saul and puts forth the statement that Saul is pursuing David for one of two reasons. David states that either Yahweh has stirred Saul against

David or it is humans who have stirred Saul against David to hunt David like an animal.

David, knowing the persecution he was enduring came from either Yahweh prompting Saul or from men, who were prompting Saul, gives no indication he is considering his persecution as an action from a character such as Satan. David even goes so far as to say that he will make a sin offering to Yahweh in an attempt at expiation which will bring Yahweh to turn from His act of using Saul to persecute David. If however it is men responsible for the persecution coming through Saul, David rightly speaks a curse on them, as they will be responsible for David being driven from the holy land wanting David to engage in false worship in a nation where Yahweh is not the only honored deity. David is the recipient of Saul's persecution through the relentless pursuit Saul engages in. David's life is made to be miserable and he is continually running for his life. He has had more than one chance to kill King Saul but as a man of integrity, he will not touch Yahweh's anointed. I might add here a note about the common cliché thrown out to people who speak a negative word against certain, supposedly anointed Christian pastors and leaders. The "Lord's anointed" is nothing more than a reference to the man who is anointed by Yahweh to be King. David and in fact the people of God (Elohim), had a correct view of Yahweh and did not possess a belief in a supernatural, created being, who is in obstinate, wicked rebellion against the Creator.

When we look at the discrepancy between the 2nd Samuel use of "God" as the inciter and the 1st Chronicles use of "Satan" as the inciter of David, we are able to understand the shift in the thinking of who is responsible for evil. Addressing the question of timing and when, in Israel's history, the book of Samuel and the book of Chronicles were authored, will help us understand the reason for the different terminology. The book of Samuel is accepted to have been authored and edited to its completion by the early 7th century Before Christ. The book of Chronicles is understood to have been authored and edited by the early 4th century BC. Even a ballpark dating of these two books will still reveal the "Samuel" compilation was penned before the exile of the Israelites into Babylon and the book of Chronicles was penned after the return from exile in Babylon.

Allow me to share a bit of information on how the book of Chronicles was compiled. This should provide us with the clear understanding that the book of Samuel long preceded the book of Chronicles. And help us to conclude that the wording used by the Chronicler in this verse about Satan inciting David, is only descriptive terminology aimed at explaining what the actions of God were as outlined hundreds of years earlier in 2nd Samuel. We find this testimony about the book of Chronicles in the Nelson's Study Bible under the heading ***Author and Date.***

> Originally First and Second Chronicles were one book. The overall consistency of style in the book indicates that although several contributors might have worked on it at various stages, one editor shaped the final product.
>
> Jewish tradition identifies the editor as Ezra. However, some have argued that the genealogies in 3:17-24 may include as many as eleven generations past Zerubabbel. To include such information, the book would have to have been written as late as the middle of the third century B.C.
>
> On the other hand it is possible that 3:17-24 may embrace only three generations. If so a date of approximately 425 B.C for the completion of Chronicles is quite reasonable. Ezra was active between 460 and 430 B.C.and thus could have incorporated this particular genealogy into the book.
>
> **Under the heading *Sources and Historicity* in the Nelson Study Bible;**
>
> It is evident the Chronicles is the result of a compilation process. The chronicler made use of the books of Samuel and Kings for about half the narrative.
>
> ......
>
> Writing about the same event, the compiler of First Chronicle simply emphasized a different perspective on them than did the authors of Samuel and Kings.
>
> ......
>
> **Under the heading Purpose in the Nelson Study Bible;**
>
> Writing approximately when the Israelites returned from captivity...[72]

The view of the editors of the Nelson Study Bible is not contested in biblical scholarship. We find supporting testimony in the much-used text

72 Pg 659 In the introduction to the book of First Chronicles, Nelson's Study Bible, Nelson's Complete Study System; NKJV version

titled, *Surpassing Wonder The Invention of the Bible and Talmuds; By Donald Harman Akenson.* This textbook is intense in its information about the history of the world's holiest book and profound rabbinic writings. It clarifies many extremely important points regarding the evolution of the Scriptures and it also confuses and perhaps distorts many points regarding the divine authorship of the Scriptures. However, one cannot argue with most of the historical perspective on the writing of the Bible. The author lucidly demonstrates that the known books that returned from exile included Genesis to Kings as a major portion of their kitbag.[73] This testified to the fact that 2 Samuel was written prior to the exile in Babylon. The book *Surpassing Wonder* states numerous interesting suggestions about the book of Chronicles. Among those is found the following;

> ***Pg 72****...Both the Book of Ezra-Nehemiah and of Chronicles rewrite the estimate of the editor-writer of Genesis-Kings...*
>
> **Pg 73***...On the surface it is the least necessary book in the Bible. For the most part, it is merely a précis of the Genesis-Kings unity, a fact that it's author tangentially acknowledges (II Chron.24:27). Fully 95 percent of the text is an abstract of material found in Joshua-Judges-Samuel-Kings and therefore, Chronicles appears to be intended to supplant these volumes.*[74]

Akenson's statement about the Chronicler of the Book of Chronicles intending to supplant Joshua to Kings can be argued against. However, I can see clearly from what was stated in the Nelson's Study Bible, "*Writing about the same event, the compiler of First Chronicle simply emphasized a different perspective on them than did the authors of Samuel and Kings...*"[75] that the book of Chronicles was not a pre-exilic book and it was authored through the use of the book of Samuel, among others. The books of 1st and 2nd Samuel are pre-exilic books. Understanding that Chronicles was penned centuries after Samuel leads the reader to decide if the writer was infusing a Persian dualistic philosophy on the story of God causing David to number the tribes of Israel in 2nd Samuel 24 and attempting to introduce a cosmic Satan into the biblical record. If the writer was not introducing a cosmic Satan then one must decide that the writer simply used his literary license to describe Yahweh as a type

73 page 65, *Surpassing Wonder The Invention of the Bible and Talmuds; By Donald Harman Akenson. Published by McGill Queens.*

74 Surpassing Wonder The Invention of the Bible and Talmuds; By Donald Harman Akenson. Published by McGill Queens. From Chapter 3 Returning with Yahweh to Jerusalem Pages72 and 73

75 ibid

of adversarial force that influenced David to take action in order for God to test David and subsequently administer justice. Agreeing that the writer of Chronicles likely was not referring to a cosmic Satan by using the word for adversary, allows us to now move on to the question of What happened in Babylon?.....that is, as it pertains to the concept of Satan.

What Was Different About the Babylonian and Persian Philosophy of Good and Evil?

The situation in Babylon was typical of any exiled person's situation and involved social, cultural, and theological assimilation to a large degree. The period of exile in Babylon was a period of longing for the restoration of the temple and the return to the land, by the Hebrew people. Israel had been told they would be punished for the wickedness and the way they had neglected to obey Yahweh in accordance with the way He was asking to be obeyed. Because of disobedience to the Creator, the Israelites were exiled. Once they were in exile, it did not become any easier for the Israelites to be obedient but through the change of circumstances, the Israelites realized what they had lost in being ejected by Yahweh from the Holy Land. They now missed it and wanted it back. Incidentally, there is never a Hebrew prophet who equated Israel being sent into exile, an apparently evil situation, and circumstance, with the actions and desires of a satanic entity. The prophets completely understood that Yahweh was responsible for all the bad that had come upon Israel. Now, while they were in their exile they began to fulfill a prophecy about themselves that was given in the Torah. In Deuteronomy 4, the prophecy speaks of the eventual scattering of the Children of Israel as a result of their sins. In the places they are scattered they will serve the false gods of the heathen whom they are scattered amidst. God calls the false gods of the nations "gods" and a supernatural embodiment of evil such as Satan, would fit into the same category as these other false gods. Just as Molech was seen to be another God of those who served it so too would Satan be another God by those who serve him through crediting him with the evil that God causes. The following passage from the Torah explicitly explains that Yahweh will scatter the disobedient among heathen nations where they will serve those nations' gods.

> *And the LORD shall scatter you among the nations, and ye shall be left few in number among the heathen, whither the LORD shall lead you. And there ye shall serve gods, the work of men's hands, wood and stone, which neither see, nor hear, nor eat, nor smell. Deuteronomy 4:27-28*

So according to the eternal words of the Torah, the people of God did just as was told of them. They corrupted themselves, were removed out of the land of their inheritance, they were scattered among the heathen and served other gods. Just a reminder that these gods are not some supernatural demons, spirits or devils; these gods are the work of men's hands, if we believe verse 28 above. The fact that the exile to Babylon resulted in worship of false gods and false worship practices to false gods is no surprise. It in fact was "destined" to happen. Destined to happen not because of the powerful "satanic" influence of the heathen; but it was destined to happen because Yahweh knew the hearts of the people. God knew that they would eventually drift away from Yahweh and His ways, which left them, open to worship after the imaginations of their hearts.

Israel has been exiled, are worshipping other gods and end up adopting Babylonian worship practices as well as adopting the Babylonian/Persian philosophy that there is a good God and then there is the antagonist bad God. These were likely introduced to the Israelites in the form of the gods of Zoroastrianism. Ahura Mazda was the all-powerful good god and Ahriman was the antagonistic and evil producing god, according to Zoroastrianism. Let's explore this Zoroastrian philosophy a little more…no… a lot more

First, let's get a few simple definitions from Webster's World Encyclopedia 2004, of some of the key characters in Zoroastrianism.

Zoroaster

Sex: Male

History; Greek form of Zarathustra

Life: 6th –c B.C.

Iranian prophet and founder of the ancient Parsee religion which bears his name. He had visions of Ahura Mazda, which led him to preach against polytheism. He appears as a historical person only in the earliest portion of the Avesta. As the centre of a group of chieftains, he carried on a struggle for the establishment of a holy agricultural state against Turainian and Vedic aggressors.

Ahura Mazda

History (Persian "Wise Lord")

The name for God used by Zoroaster and his followers. The world is the arena for the battle between Ahura Mazda and Ahriman, the spirit of evil- a battle in which Ahura Mazda will finally prevail and become omnipotent.

Ahriman

The supreme evil spirit, Angra Mainyu, the lord of darkness and death in Zoroastrianism. Ahriman is engaged in a continuing struggle with Ahura Mazda, Zoroaster's name for God

Avesta

The scriptures of Zoroastrianism, written in Avestan, a language of the E-branch of the Indo-European family. Traditionally believed to have been revealed to Zoroaster, only the Gathas, a set of 17 hymns, may be attributed to him. Few portions of the original survive

The Zoroastrian concept of more than one Supreme Being was foreign to the Israelites. The faith of Israel as handed down by Moses was to be an explicitly monotheistic faith. As Israel became more and more engrossed and engulfed by the culture they were exiled to and flourishing in many ways, they naturally became more syncretistic. Syncretism is the process of adopting, accepting, and merging pagan practices that are not original to the faith of the God of the Scriptures, with the faith of the God of the Scriptures. I say Israel "naturally" became more syncretistic, due to the fact that Yahweh told us we were to remain isolated from the cultural melting pot of heathen nations because if we didn't we would inevitably be drawn to adopt their gods and practices. While the nation of Israel was engaged with other pagan nations on a fairly intimate level, they "naturally" became more syncretistic. If Yahweh knew we were inclined to move in this harmful direction then I think it is fair to say it happened naturally. "Naturally", simply means this was the expected outcome of having a close association with nations who were not worshipping Yahweh.

Assimilation Brings Compromise and New Beliefs

In the exceptional book *Peoples of the Old Testament World,* [76] a book given a Publication award in 1995 by the Biblical Archeology Society, we are provided some excellent information on the religion of the Persian King, Darius, who followed Cyrus in continuing the return of the Jewish exiles to the Holy Land.

76 Peoples of the Old Testament World; Edited by; Alfred J. Hoerth, Gerald L. Mattingly and Edwin Yamauchi. Published By Baker Books. Pages 122-123

This great Persian world leader was a devout Zoroastrian according to the testimony of the above-mentioned book. The order of ruler-ship during the years of Israel's exile were Cyrus II for approximately 29 years, Cambyses II for only about 7 years and Darius I for a period of about 36 years. The Persian religion of these time-periods has been well documented to be the religion of Zoroastrianism. The Israelites had not been known to have a doctrine similar to the good entity verses an evil entity doctrine that was taught to them in their exile. We find through the study of the religion of Darius the Zoroastrian, that he was a ruler with amazing morals and ethic. This great leader was eager to allow the exiled Israelites, the Judahites who were now a group of people beginning to be labeled as Jews, to return to their homeland and rebuild the Temple that was destroyed in their captivity. On the surface, it seems this act by the Persian ruler was a noble act in heartfelt service to Yahweh. Would that not be an astounding move for a leader to make as an act of service to the one Creator? I agree it would, however this particular ruler, as a worshipper of Ahura Mazda the Zoroastrian god, was simply doing what good Zoroastrian rulers did. He was being tolerant and supportive of other religions. A real ecumenical flare was common to the religion of Darius. It was a common practice to allow the worshippers of other gods to build their temples and practice their worship.

This was such a wise political move. For a people who are under a particular ruler to be given freedom of worship by that ruler, it follows that the people will remain content with their ruler and it can be expected in many cases that this people will show support to the ruler who provides them with religious freedom. The tragedy in the religious freedom concept lies in the fact that when a group is privileged with being part of a religious, cultural mosaic, they are then exposed to all the other religions that are practiced in their culture. Now exposure in and of itself may not be bad; however the exposure coupled with a slow slide into compromise over a long period will always improve the odds that a group who are purely intending to worship Yahweh in the manner He prescribes , will take on some of the practices of the culture they are in. In a sense, tolerance breeds syncretism. Take for example the use of a Christmas tree by Bible believing Christians in North America.

Now history proves that Christmas and the Christmas tree are both a holiday and a decoration borrowed from ancient pagan religion. In fact Christmas was never celebrated by the early 1st Century believers and in particular the festivities which occurred at the winter solstice were categorically pagan and neither the Messiah nor any of the apostles who walked with Him ever condoned or celebrated this festival. The trappings that are associated with this festival are not practices prescribed by Yahweh as ways to worship Him, nor are they original to any early Bible believing, Messiah following group. This was understood by differing religious groups at different points in history and some as recently as the Mennonites in the early to mid 20th Century.

In my family, I have an aunt and uncle who are arguably from a Mennonite background. I mention them not because of a prejudice against Mennonites but because of the traditional view many in the Mennonite culture have had regarding pagan festival practices.

This particular aunt and uncle were instrumental about 38 years ago, in directing and encouraging my parents to pursue the God of the Bible. My Aunt and Uncle had been very strong in their stand to not erect a Christmas tree at Christmas, because they knew it was a custom drawn from a pagan worship practice and it in no way was associated with the celebration of the Messiah's Birth.

Incidentally, the Messiah Yeshua whom is called Jesus by many, was not born on December 25 or anytime near that date. The December 25th date of the celebration of His birth is not connected to the historical Yeshua or to His followers for hundreds of years after His death and resurrection. It has been proven that Yeshua was born in the fall of the year 3 BC. Recognizing the origins of the Christmas tree as being non-biblical, my Aunt and Uncle would teach against the use of the "pagan" Christmas tree, until slowly, after years of exposure to it and years of seeing that the use of it brought no harm on the users, they began to tolerate this "pagan" practice. Once toleration of this practice was firmly established in the philosophy of this Aunt and Uncle, they then were able to take the next step. The next step now is obvious and today this Aunt and Uncle erect a Christmas tree when they celebrate the supposed birth of Christ in the month of December along with the rest of the culture. They and millions do so without considering to the fullest, who, what, where and when this type of a celebration and its practices come from. Just as with my Aunt and Uncle, syncretism occurred for the Israelites due to a prolonged exposure to practices and beliefs that were not found in Israel's theology, before their experience of being in exile in Babylon,

When the Babylonians fell to the Persians, the oppressive, somewhat restrictive regime began to fall with it. Because it was Babylon who had taken captive the Israelites and not Persia, perhaps the Persian rulers had diminishing interest in keeping the captives captive due to the fact that Persia was not their original captor. After all the Persian rulers' battle had been with the Babylonians, of which these "Jews" were clearly not. For a ruling King to offer freedom to a captive people is an excellent strategy for engendering favor from the captives and affirming His sovereignty over a people group. To deliver them to freedom is tantamount with being the Messiah. After all, a characteristic of the Messiah in Hebrew thought is one who has the power to deliver Yahweh's people from captivity. This is a large part of why the prophet of the Most High calls Cyrus the Mashiach (Messiah) in Isaiah 45 verse 1 as seen below where the word "anointed" has been translated back to the word used in Hebrew.

> *Thus saith the LORD to his mashiach, to Cyrus, whose right hand I have holden, to subdue nations before him; and I will loose the loins of kings, to open before him the two leaved gates; and the gates shall not be shut; Isaiah 45:1*

When the Israelites were in Persia and Cyrus had made the decree for the Israelites to return and rebuild their Temple, it may have seemed as if the pagan Persian ruler was inclined to worship the God of Abraham, Isaac, and Jacob. However history reveals this ruler was only inclined to further his own cause as it pertained to the god he worshipped, which was no god at all but was given the name Ahura Mazda, meaning wise Lord. Honoring the religions and gods of the people in his kingdom was a practice that benefited the ruler Cyrus. The benefit was realized through Cyrus acquiring support and loyalty at various levels from his subjects. A result of Cyrus' decree was that Israel as a people group were liberated and sent on their way home. They had been prospering in the Persian world due to the favor they experienced through the many years of assimilation in exile. Many of the Israelites had established businesses and entered the Kings service. In fact, Nehemiah, a well-known Hebrew, was the respected cupbearer of the king and was instrumental in the return to Jerusalem and the rebuilding of the Holy Temple. The International Standard Bible Encyclopedia has this to say of the Royal Cupbearer;

> The office of cupbearer was "one of no trifling honor" (Herod. iii. 34). It was one of his chief duties to taste the wine for the king to see that it was not poisoned, and he was even admitted to the king while the queen was present (Neh_2:6). It was on account of this position of close intimacy with the king that Nehemiah was able to obtain his commission as governor of Judea and the letters and edicts which enabled him to restore the walls of Jerusalem.[77]

The Israelites who desire to return to Judea were enabled to do so with the costs covered by the Persian ruler Darius. Darius had lived and worked along side these peoples for many years now and seems to have little, if none at all, resistance to edicting their complete liberty. Seemingly, this hard working, Hebrew people of integrity had gained much respect and trust. In actual

77 Taken from entry on "Nehemiah" in the International Standard Bible Encyclopedia

fact, they posed no threat at all to the Persian Empire and its ruler. Therefore, when Yahweh prompted the heart of Darius to liberate them, there is no mention of Darius' resistance to letting Yahweh's people go. For Darius, the release of a long oppressed and captive people had magnificent return for a politician strategizing to gain ever more power and looking to be seen as sovereign over the land. This release though did not come without cost to the people of Yahweh and to the faith of that people. After all the years of exile, some difficult but many prosperous, the returning exiles were leaving Persia with some very profound baggage. Baggage, which can be attributed to the persistent and seemingly "harm-free" exposure, to the gods and philosophies of Persia. In *Peoples of the Old Testament World,*[78] we are told this of Darius;

> Scholars disagree about whether the Achemenids were Zoroastrians. Though some scholars such as Boyce believe that all the Achemenians, including Cyrus II, were Zoroastrians, the evidence is quite inconclusive for Cyrus II and Cambyses II[(footnote 75)] The strongest case for a Zoroastrian background can be made in the case of Darius I, who mentions the god Ahura Mazda repeatedly in his Behistun inscription. Though the King focused on Ahura Mazda, Persepolis texts from Darius's reign indicate that the court also recognized numerous other gods as well [(footnote 76)]. Both Biblical and nonbiblical texts indicate that in general the Achemenian Kings not only tolerated other religions but actively sought their prayers and devotions by granting subsidies. [(footnote 77)]
>
> **Footnote 75**-Dandamaev and Lukonin, Culture and Social Institutions, 34-48; T. Cuyler Young Jr., "The Consolidation of the Empire and Its Limits of growth Under Darius and Xerxes," in CAH 4:100-101
>
> **Footnote 76**-Richard N. Frye, Religion in Fars under the Achaemenids," in Orientalia J. Duchesne-Guillemin Emerito Oblata (Leiden: Brill, 1984), 172
>
> **Footnote 77**- H. Koch, Die reliriosen Verbaltnisse der Dareiozeit (Wiesbaden: Harrassowitz, 1977); idem, " Gotter und ihre Vereherung in achamenidischen Persien,"Zeitschrift fur Assyriologie 77 (1987): 239-78

---

78 Page 122 of *Peoples of the Old Testament World;* Edited by; Alfred J. Hoerth, Gerald L. Mattingly and Edwin Yamauchi. Published By Baker Books.

It is clear Darius was a Zoroastrian; however, that does not prove that the returning exiles would have adopted a philosophy of the existence of a good and evil force from the Persian environment. To prove conclusively through one piece of information or another from history is not possible. Even in light of the book of Esther, which tells of events in the Persian community after the legislated return of the exiles by Darius, we can see the Persian influence on the exiles. In the book of Esther the King Xerxes who is Ahasuerus, is ruler over 127 provinces from Ethiopia to India. This kingdom was host to varied religions and those who were relocated there for one reason or another would eventually adopt some of the religious practices and customs of their host. It is even impossible in today's "enlightened" culture to avoid experiencing some syncretism when one culture is inundated with the practices of another culture for an extended period of time. The syncretism that occurs usually does not happen intentionally but it does happen and is often quite voluntary. That is to say, the sojourner in the host country invariably is desensitized to the practices of their host country, and will begin at some point expressing the manifest signs of assimilation. The effects of assimilation of the Hebrew culture are still manifest in that culture to the present day. In fact it is understood by ancient sages in the Hebrew culture that there was a great battle against assimilation in the 2nd century BCE. This battle is what is now remembered in the post Mosaic festival of Hanukkah. This festival came about because of the rebellion of a handful of devout "Jews" when their way of life was being ripped away from them by the wicked King Antiochus Epiphaneus in about 167 BCE.

Antiochus had passed legislation that all Jews were to stop circumcising their babies and could no longer keep the Sabbath as was commanded by Yahweh. The Jews of the Antiochus period were also prohibited from keeping Yahweh's Holy festival days and were not permitted to study Torah. The goal of the Antiochus legislation was to assimilate the Jews and thereby render their religion inactive, which as any leader with foresight knew, would eventually lead to the Jews voluntarily performing the worship practices of the state religion instead of, or at least joined together with, the faith of the Scriptures and the one true God, Yahweh.

It seems odd that an ancient culture could have such a monumental impact on the cultures that it rubs elbows with. If we were part of a kingdom that was as far reaching and influential as the Persian kingdom, we might better understand how the philosophical tentacles of that kingdom might find their way into the philosophies and religions of the varied cultures it is host to.

How far reaching was the kingdom of Medio-Persia in those days? Just how big of an impact did 127 provinces have on the known world socio-geographical constitution? A simple map from the period shows that the territory covered by the Persian Empire in the 6th century BCE was vast. The empire covered a large amount of territory and had taken on more geography than the conquered kingdom of Babylon, which was defeated by the Medes in the 6th Century BCE. Also notable is that the conquering of Persia by Alexander the great did not contain a significant expansion of the previous Persian kingdom geography. To give a head count for the number of subjects which were present in the Persian kingdom is difficult but it is easy to see the Persian influence was widespread and the philosophies which flowed out of such a tolerant yet significant empire as it related to religious thought were far reaching. As for the "Jewish" subjects that were present in Persia at the time, I have read that the numbers of Jews in Persia may have been in the area of 120, 000 around the period of Cyrus' reign which allowed for the first wave of repatriation to Judea for the Jews.[79]

The Persian exile as it pertains to the mindset of the "Jews" shows a similar result as has occurred for numerous foreigners who have immigrated to North America and then had children who grew up here. The children, upon attaining the age of 10 years old for example, would already begin to manifest signs of significant differences in their belief system. The effects of assimilation are unavoidable unless that child is rigidly guarded from "Western" influence. Through the social integration which takes place, they will exhibit the propensity to practice "Western ways" and tolerate, if not internalize and accept, Western values, morals and religious beliefs. Santa Clause may be a somewhat simplistic analogy for this idea. Many immigrants, more precisely the second generation of said immigrants, have amended their beliefs and practice to eventually include some recognition of the fantasy Santa Clause of Western Culture. Many have made Canada their home and had little interest in the Santa Clause of the Western world until they have had sufficient exposure. The parents may retain their concrete beliefs surrounding the existence of this Santa person but the growing and assimilated children invariably will come to accept into practice a belief in Santa Clause and his supposed benevolent acts.

Looking at the story of Esther, we can see the frog in the boiling water scenario was present in the post Darius Persian kingdom. The second in command to Ahasuerus was a man called Haman. Haman had the power to cause the subjects of his Lords kingdom to bow to him as he passed by. At the risk of speaking from the silence of Scripture, it does seem apparent that most people did comply with this practice. The fact that Haman was making

79 Information for the number of Jews in Persia at the time of Cyrus can be found at this web page; http://www.dangoor.com/74034.html

a stink over one man named Mordechai, who wouldn't bow to the second in command, seems to paint a picture of not many disobedient Jews in regards to the bowing to Haman policy. Generally most of the thousands of Jews in the Persian kingdom had fallen victim to the philosophies of the kingdom due to their assimilation and prosperity. After all, Jeremiah the prophet had told them that Yahweh wanted them to take wives, and to build houses and to farm land there.

> *Thus saith the LORD of hosts, the God of Israel, unto all that are carried away captives, whom I have caused to be carried away from Jerusalem unto Babylon; 5 Build ye houses, and dwell in them; and plant gardens, and eat the fruit of them; 6 Take ye wives, and beget sons and daughters; and take wives for your sons, and give your daughters to husbands, that they may bear sons and daughters; that ye may be increased there, and not diminished. Jeremiah 29:4-6*

However, these captives who were taken into exile, then raised to the status of colonized Jews, took their freedom to prosper and enjoy the land of their exile too far. They began enjoying the religion and practices of the captor. This is why when the decree from Cyrus came for the Judeans to begin returning to the Land of Israel, that eventually Nehemiah and Ezra put out a clarion call for the returning exiles to commit to the Torah, the pure faith of the fathers Abraham, Isaac, and Jacob. These inspiring spiritual and political leaders saw the state of the remaining Israelite people. Those who weren't sent to Babylon in the original captivity had allowed the faith of Yahweh to deteriorate and the Holy City of God, the place where He had placed His name, to remain a pile of uninspiring rubble. If the Jews in exile had remained faithful to the pure worship practice and form of the Torah then Ezra and Nehemiah would not have had to lead such an intentional revival and restoration to the ancient paths from the Torah. It would be one thing to have to restore proper worship due to years of neglect by the people of the Book who were always supposed to remain faithful to Yahweh, but one does not typically cease a deeply ingrained practice of a religion or ritual without replacing the one they have abandoned, to some degree. In fact, what may often occur is that because of the void left in the life of the individual or people group as a result of neglecting their first love so to speak, they are opened to another taking its place. This is likely what happened to the exiled Israelites. They were sent to exile by God as Jeremiah 29: 7 and other verses teach us.

In exile they may have lamented their captivity and the loss of many of the lives of their kin while being able to at least maintain their faith and value system in their hearts if not fully able to practice it outwardly. Even though the Persian way was to tolerate other religions, the exiles were not able to fully participate in the Temple service and associated festivals and practices, which are truly a badge of identity for the people of Yahweh. As time marched on the realization came that those in exile were going to be there for at least 70 years, until Yahweh would intervene in some form, as Jeremiah 29:10 indicates.

> *For thus saith the LORD, That after seventy years be accomplished at Babylon I will visit you, and perform my good word toward you, in causing you to return to this place. Jeremiah 29:10*

So, the exiled people begin to accept that they are to build lives in the land of their captor and to seek the peace of the city they are in. I can imagine the people of Yahweh took seeking peace a little too far. God never intended that seeking peace meant giving up seeking peace with Him. It appears that the exiles may have done just that in Babylon. For a time they remembered Zion with tears but absence did not make their hearts grow fonder and the Israelites in exile became less and less Israelitish and more and more Babylonian to Persian-like in practice and philosophy. I am not saying they completely abandoned their beliefs and practice, but for certain they were the recipients by choice of a much more destructive and subtle plot. They became syncretized in so many ways with the religion that eventually led to Judaism and to Christianity.

You see the human heart, which is said to be continually inclined to evil, is not going to do a one-hundred-eighty degree turn and cast off everything that is righteous and good at once. Nor is it going to embrace everything that is wicked and evil at once. Desensitization is not done through a wholesale abandonment of past practices in exchange for the beliefs and practices of the people with whom they are associated. A people group or individual rather picks and chooses the compromises and syncretistic options that are presented to them along the journey. This is all part of God testing our hearts so that we will eventually see we have wicked hearts and cannot exist and plan to enter His kingdom, unless there is a Messiah to intercede for us. All we need to do is accept His offer to be our Messiah and then do our honest best to obey His laws, commands, and statutes.

Do you remember when you were 11 years old? Let me take it from my perspective. I am 40 years old right now so 11 years old would be 29 years ago.

As an 11-year-old child in a family of the 1970's, we only had three channels on the television in our home. Now, I recently heard that the first cable, multi channel feed was occurring in the late fifties, but we only had three channels in our house for most of my childhood and teen life. One of those was a French channel. In those days, we didn't watch very much T.V. but I do recall the absolute horror that swept across the family room and the discussions that would ensue in social gatherings of the then Christian groups we circulated in as a family, as the topic of television programming and foul language along with questionable themes was discussed. The language and themes of the 70's were seen by the adults of the 70's, in many circles, as unacceptable and harmful and unwholesome in a variety of ways. Those groups opposed to the direction of the television entertainment industry were very unwilling to tolerate what they felt they and their families were unrighteously subjected to.

Well, fast forward to today, 2007. I don't think I need to get too involved here but just as an example of what has become acceptable in the entertainment choices of the now adult children of the parents who less than 30 years ago were offended by the presentation on their 2 plus one French channel television. It is difficult now to even imagine primetime T.V. without words like whore, ass, bitch, bastard, and others… Not to mention the violence and sexual content in most popular programming. The presence of homosexuality in almost every popular television program; sexual images and innuendo in commercials; as well as disrespect for authority; including disrespect for parents by children and teens is continually seen in programs and commercials. I was recently listening to a teaching by a Rabbi on morality when I was reminded of the years when the popular program about a Magic Genie and a US Military Officer called, *I Dream of Genie,* was on the air.

This mystically powered, simple servant of the man who rescued her from her bottle was not allowed to have her navel showing. She was told by the censors of NBC to keep it covered and therefore wore her harem trouser pulled up high enough to cover the navel. Suffice it to say, that in this present generation, 10-year-old girls are accustomed to having their belly buttons showing much of the time. This practice is almost unquestioned, and even less questioned in the older set of teen girls, up into early adulthood.

The point is that assimilation is always at work. What was not so socially acceptable at one time becomes acceptable as exposure to it continues and more and more of the people who make up the culture, accept that previously unacceptable practice, belief or ideal. A subtle and inevitable shift in a mindset is often the cause of this assimilation. It is simple to see how profound the changes can be from one generation to the next when a group of people has children in a culture that is not the culture of their original heritage. Being integrated in a society or culture with pervasive and persistent ideologies and philosophies which are different from those of one's heritage, is almost certainly going to entice a person to think less of the practices of their own heritage and accept more, those that are ever present in their current reality. The statement "when in Rome do as the Romans" may be just what many of the unwitting Jews were guilty of as it pertained to being in Persia.

We have seen from the Scripture how those with a monotheistic faith in Yahweh, held no prevailing belief in a cosmic Satan as the source and orchestrator of evil upon man, neither as individuals nor as a people group. What I am proposing for you to consider is that the period of exile was a period of tremendously profound assimilation and one that brought Israel into a realm of dualism. A realm where good could be attributed to Yahweh and evil could be attributed to a character that came to be known as Satan. I am suggesting that because the pre-exilic writings of the Israelites do not suggest there is any supernatural force in creation other than Yahweh, that a belief in a cosmic force as the propagator of evil came as a result of Zoroastrian and Persian influence. When a person migrates to a different land today and is prosperous, they will often acquire an altered belief system based on the things they are exposed to in the new land. So too did the Jewish people obtain an altered belief system which incorporated beliefs and practices that were not present in the pre-exilic faith system of the People of Yahweh. Being in exile where they prospered and came under strong influence from positive environment and host culture, assimilation could not be avoided and Israel took on many of the religious characteristics of the Persians.

The book *Too Long in The Sun* provides the following statement regarding the receptivity of the exiled Israelites towards the ruler of the Medo-Persian empire;

> ...when Cyrus, the Persian emperor, conquered an area, it was his policy to restore the worship of the resident gods. By doing this Cyrus, although a conqueror, was well received, and even looked upon as a hero: supporting the local god. This was also the case when Cyrus ordered the rebuilding of the temple in Jerusalem. To state this plainly... Cyrus told them what they wanted to hear! [80]

The above statements suggest that the actions of Cyrus would have been a strong impact in lives of the arguably monotheistic Hebrews. Via Cyrus' political moves, the Israelites would have been sympathetic towards

80 Chapter 4, pg 46 *Too Long in The Sun* by Richard M Rives, Partakers Publications. This information is also available at the corresponding web site http://www.toolong.com/medo.htm,

the benevolent ruler who allowed them such freedom. An understanding of religious thought in the Medo-Persian Empire is of great importance. It was from a climate of religious tolerance that Judah returned to Jerusalem, bringing with them traditions that had absolutely nothing to do with the worship of God. Belief in a second God as the force responsible for evil and others are the traditions condemned by Jesus when he spoke to the chief priests and Pharisees. Because of their refusal to abandon these false beliefs, they "stumbled" and failed to receive their long awaited Messiah, Jesus Christ. God will not allow the slightest pagan tradition to be combined with His worship. All such attempts are in vain!

Take note that Persia, Greece, and Rome were all interested in accumulating patriots for their empires. Each of these kingdoms did much in the way of adding philosophical content to the succeeding kingdom. They also were all quite accommodating to their citizens in order to make an environment of general safety, comfort, and well-being, which would often cause citizens to extend some measure of loyalty to the country they were being cared for and protected by. This can be seen in a study of the Hellenization of Jewish people as they participated in Greek culture under the rule of Alexander the Great after 336 BCE. Many Jews sided with their host ruler and agreed to extend loyalty to the Greek nation due to the relative security, support, and prosperity they were recipients of while in the Greek Empire. The Ahura info website discloses this information about the ancient Persian Empire;

> For more than three thousand years Persia was a melting pot of civilizations and demographic movements between Asia and Europe.
>
> Under Cyrus the Great, it became the centre of the world's first empire. Successive invasions by the Greeks, Arabs, Mongols, and Turks developed the nation's culture through rich and diverse philosophical, artistic, scientific and religious influences.[81]

We are now in a position to consider how the monotheism that was expected of the Israelites was altered by the Persian exile and the religious influences they were exposed to for generations. We know that the Israelites who were exiled to Babylon, which became Persia during their exile, were embroiled in a culture that practiced Zoroastrianism. Iran was known as Persia until 1935. Today the most common religion in Iran is Islam but Zoroastrianism is one of three other religions officially recognized in Iran.

81 http://www.ahura.info/iran/factbook.html

The other two state-recognized religions are Judaism and Christianity. All three are considered monotheistic.

Introducing Another God

Looking back to the 6th Century BC, with Judahites embroiled in a Zoroastrian culture it is recognized that the concept was taught that claims there was a good god, and there was an evil counterpart who was responsible for bad. The Israelites prospered in Persia and grew as a people-group through marrying Persians and having children. Assimilation was thorough due to the Zoroastrian principle of tolerance that was practiced in Persia. The Jewish people slowly began to accept the Zoroastrian precepts and were relatively unthreatened as the principles were generally supportive of a good life and lifestyle for the Jews. Isaiah's prophecy of King Cyrus the Messiah came to pass and King Cyrus issued a decree that the Jews could go back to Judea and rebuild their temple and practice their religion. This allowance was in line with the "*try to please as many people in the kingdom as possible*" mentality which worked well for the Persians as they ultimately received some measure of loyalty and incurred little in the way of rebellions and uprising from the subjects.

The Jewish People returned home in waves over the next few decades. The first wave returned under Zerubabbel and the returns under Ezra and Nehemiah were not many years behind. Not all Jews chose to return to Jerusalem but many who did return took with them ideas they had adopted in exile. Eventually the Temple and wall of Jerusalem were slowly rebuilt. Haggai and Zechariah prophesy and exhort the returned exiles. Jerusalem is slowly rebuilt and many of the prophets continue to address the ways of the people as not pleasing to Yahweh. The Persian idea of an evil entity opposed to the Sovereign God, who is engaged with the Sovereign in a cosmic battle, became part of many of the Jews' belief system. This concept, which was carried through right to the "Christian Era", is difficult to entirely define or identify as far as some of the specifics of the concept and how it migrated with the Hebrew people is concerned. The path this concept followed on its way to entering Christianity is very interesting but I assure you, the idea of a cosmic Satan did not originate with the theology of the pre-exilic Israelites who are commonly referred to as the Jews today. Nor did this theology or rather "demonology", get revealed to the people of God by the Creator while they were in exile.

Much of what Isaiah speaks as a testimony of the "one God and none else" was spoken to exhort the people of God to recognize He alone is worthy of worship and He alone is responsible for all the good and the evil which has been brought upon them and was ever present or ever will be. Yahweh always wants His children to understand and act in accordance with the axiom, that there is no other "God-like" being anywhere in existence. He has stated this in places other than the book of Isaiah but the context of Isaiah stating it, shows it was stated to provide some much-needed redirection to the Israelites. Proclaiming that it is Yahweh who "creates evil" would hopefully discourage them from imposing God-like abilities of the creation of evil, upon an imagined "evil God". This other God was a force that was seen in Zoroaster's vision and became part of the accepted Persian dualism that testifies falsely to the existence of at least two Gods. Below are several instances in the Scriptures where Yahweh is said to be the only God and as you read them, you may notice that the words are often shown in the first person to indicate that the Creator Himself is the one proclaiming Himself as the sole cosmic force in the Universe.

> *Deuteronomy 4:35 Unto thee it was shewed, that thou mightest know that Yahweh*[82] *he is God; there is none else beside him.*

> *Deuteronomy 4:39 Know therefore this day, and consider it in thine heart, that the LORD he is God in heaven above, and upon the earth beneath: there is none else.*

> *1Kings 8:60 That all the people of the earth may know that the LORD is God, and that there is none else.*

> *Isaiah 45:5 I am Yahweh, and there is none else, there is no God beside me: I girded thee, though thou hast not known me:*

> *Isaiah 45:6 That they may know from the rising of the sun, and from the west, that there is none beside me. I am Yahweh, and there is none else.*

> *Isaiah 45:14 Thus saith the LORD, The labour of Egypt, and merchandise of Ethiopia and of the Sabeans, men of stature, shall come over unto thee, and they shall be thine: they shall come after thee; in chains they shall come over, and they shall fall*

82 In the King James Version the word, "LORD" when seen in capital letters is originally found in the Hebrew as the four-letter name of God and can be transliterated as Yahweh. The word LORD is not the Creator's name but is a title for Yahweh. Some in Judaism and similar streams of religious movement believe it is inappropriate to attempt to pronounce the name of God and refer to it as the ineffable name of God. Here and elsewhere, I have replaced the English title LORD with the transliterated name of God, Yahweh.

> *down unto thee, they shall make supplication unto thee, saying, Surely God is in thee; and there is none else, there is no God.*
>
> *Isaiah 45:18 For thus saith Yahweh that created the heavens; God himself that formed the earth and made it; he hath established it, he created it not in vain, he formed it to be inhabited: I am the LORD; and there is none else.*
>
> *Isaiah 45:21 Tell ye, and bring them near; yea, let them take counsel together: who hath declared this from ancient time? who hath told it from that time? have not I Yahweh? and there is no God else beside me; a just God and a Saviour; there is none beside me.*
>
> *Isaiah 45:22 Look unto me, and be ye saved, all the ends of the earth: for I am God, and there is none else.*
>
> *Isaiah 46:9 Remember the former things of old: for I am God, and there is none else; I am God, and there is none like me,*
>
> *Joel 2:27 And ye shall know that I am in the midst of Israel, and that I am Yahweh your God, and none else: and my people shall never be ashamed.*

The words of Isaiah and others are clear; there is no God at all, anywhere who has any power. When Yahweh told us in Isaiah 45 that *He creates evil* but we still choose to believe that "Satan" creates evil, then we are saying there is one in the earth like God. This means that if we believe there is a "Satan" who brings evil into this world, we believe that there is another God. We can use any language we like to speak of the evil that supposedly comes from "satan". If we say he causes, brings, orchestrates, or any other verb to indicate he is responsible for the true evil in the world; we are simply dancing around the truth with semantics to justify a dualistic belief system. If Satan brings about or "orchestrates" evil, then he is the one who "creates" evil. If Satan has the power to create, then he is like God, the Creator, we then are right back in the position of calling Yahweh a liar because we have been told that there is NONE LIKE HIM.

Perhaps you have heard one of the many theories that actually try to implicate "Satan" as a creator. Albeit these theories suggest he is a creator, they state he is a creator of the perverse, and one who creates for the purposes of destruction. I came across this bizarre theory of Satan as a creator recently from a couple of religious leaders who wrote in 1992. Jason Zolot and Damien Royce wrote a work titled, "*Did God Destroy the Dinosaurs?*". In a twisted fabrication of one account on the creation of the world and the associated satanic activity as it pertains to man, Royce and Zolot postulated their conclusion that Yahweh gave Satan the ability to create. This being, who eventually became Satan, was initially just Lucifer. As Lucifer tampered with creation he turned into Satan and then set out to create creatures of violence for his amusement and the amusement of other angelic beings, many of whom ended up cavorting with Satan in his escapades of destructive behavior. Royce and Zolot go on to teach Satan eventually created the dinosaurs and turned the earth into a , *"freakish, hellish nightmare world drenched in the blood and gore of violence, death and destruction, an obscene parody of what God had intended.....His bloodlust became insatiable."*

These profoundly intelligent but deeply disturbed men go on to teach that the fallen angels at first assumed the form of the dinosaurs for fun but the exposure to abject killing and bloodshed caused them to not see physical life as anything of value. Eventually these fallen angels "*grew morally dissolute.*"

This wacky teaching by Royce and Zolot is just one example along a spectrum of ideas that suggests "satan" has the power to create.

The decision really falls to each individual. Do you believe there is another creator who at the very least has the power to create evil? Or do you believe that there is none other with the ability to create, except Yahweh, the one who is big enough to take responsibility for the good and the evil just as He stated in Isaiah 45;

> *I am Yahweh, and there is none else, there is no God beside me: I girded thee, though thou hast not known me: That they may know from the rising of the sun, and from the west, that there is none beside me. I am the LORD, and there is none else. I form the light, and create darkness: I make peace, and create evil: I the LORD do all these things. Isaiah 45:5-7*

I will say this though, as we see what the Scriptures say about the evil in the world we are soon able to conclude that there are only two options for pinning the evil on someone. Evil comes either from man and the heart inclined to do evil or from Yahweh the one who creates evil. This means that all the sin and rebellion, seen throughout the world, is not the result of demonic forces imparting themselves in the form of an evil spirit into people like Saddam Hussein or George W Bush. The bottom line is that evil came straight from the pit of their wicked hearts, the heart which is deceitful above all else. My heart is no different than any one else's in the world in that it too has the ability to produce wickedness, wickedness that some may attribute to demons and satan, but in fact, it is just the heart that is yet to be completely reformed by agreeing with God and His Messiah in all things.

Zoroastrian philosophy is widely recognized as having influenced the great monotheistic religions of the world. I use the descriptor "great" in mentioning these faiths only because they are referred to as great by many scholars, historians, and teachers. However, they would not be considered great in the eyes of the Creator or the Messiah as they propagate false doctrine as if it were true. They are faiths which have adopted and put into practice many unbiblical, and in some cases pagan rites, rituals and concepts. They have become daughters of ancient, false pagan religions by their close resemblance of form and function to the ancient pagan religions that were used as a springboard through time. Even Royce and Zolot although recognizing Zoroastrianism as just another dying religion, they rightly conclude that it was a forerunner of modern Judeo-Christianity. The ancient pagan religion of Zoroastrianism has had influence on such world religions as Judaism, Christianity, and Islam. I find it interesting that in Iran today, which is the area of ancient Persia, Islam is the official religion but the "Big 3", of which Zoroastrianism is one, are all government-recognized religions. The encyclopedia Britannica is one of a plethora of resources that clearly state the connection of Zoroastrianism with Judaism and Christianity. Here are some quotes from the encyclopedia;

Macropedia Volume 15 page 785 under the topic *Revelation*.

Zoroastrianism.

A fourth great prophetic religion, which should be mentioned for its historic importance, is Zoroastrianism, once the national faith of the Persian Empire. Zoroaster (Zarathustra), a prophetic reformer of 7th century BC, apparently professed a monotheistic faith and a stern devotion to truth and righteousness. At the age of 30 he experienced a revelation from Ahura Mazda(The Wise) and chose to follow him in the battle against the forces of evil. This revelation enabled Zoroaster and his followers to comprehend the difference between good (Truth) and evil (The Lie) and to know the one true god. **Later forms of Zoroastrianism apparently had an impact on Judaism, from the time of the Babylonian exile, and throughout Judaism , on Christianity.** *(Bold emphasis added throughout)*

Macropedia Volume 4 page 479 under the topic *Christianity.*

Only in post-biblical Judaism does the devil become the adversary of God, the prince of angels, who created by God and placed at the head of the angelic hosts, entices some of the angels into

> revolt against God. In punishment for his rebellion he is cast from heaven together with his mutinous entourage, which was transformed into demons.

In a further paragraph on this same page (479) we are told;

> Through the influence of the dualistic thinking of Zoroastrian religion during the Babylonian exile (586-538 BC) in Persia, Satan took on features of a countergod in late Judaism.
>
> On page 551 and 552 of Volume 4 under the topic Christian Myth and Legend.
>
> It was Iranian mythological concepts of the ages of the world, translated through Jewish apocalyptic views, that most influenced Christian views of time, history and man's ultimate destiny…
>
> Ahura Mazda(the Wise Lord)symbolized by light and later called Ormazd,dwelt in infinite time with Ahriman, symbolized by darkness. Ahriman, like Satan in Christianity, went against the Wise Lord. The four ages of the world created after the fall of Ahriman depict the successive stages of the struggle in finite time between the lords of good and evil for the allegiance and the souls of men.
>
> **Macropedia Volume 7 page 62 under the topic Exegesis and Hermeneutics, Biblical.**
>
> On the other hand the Iranian religious influence, primarily that of Zoroastrianism, on the angelology and eschatology (concepts of the last times) of Judaism in the last two centuries BC is unmistakable, especially among the Pharisees , (a liberal Jewish sect emphasizing piety) and the Qumran community(presumably the Essenes) near the dead sea. In the latter, indeed, Zoroastrian dualism finds clear expression, such as in the concept of a war between the sons of light and the sons of darkness, although it is subordinated to the sovereignty of the one God of Israel.
>
> **Micropedia Volume 10 page 885 under the topic Zoroaster.**
>
> Historians of religion also speculate on possible connections between Zoroastrianism and other religions, especially Judaism, Christianity and Islam.

Also Micropedia Volume 10 page 885 under the topic Zoroastrianism and Parsiism.

The ancient pre-Islamic religion of Iran that survives there in isolated areas and more prosperously in India, where the descendants of Zoroastrian Iranian (Persian) immigrants are known as Parsees, or Parsis (hence Parsiism). Founded by the Iranian prophet and reformer in the 6th century BC, this religion, containing both monotheistic and dualistic features, influenced the other major Western religions- namely Judaism, Christianity and Islam.

Micropedia Volume III page 461 and 462 under the topic, Demons, hierarchy of.

Jewish demonology was further developed in Kabbalism, a medieval mystical movement.

The hierarchy of demons in Christianity is based on various sources; Jewish , Zoroastrian, Gnostic (a syncretistic religious dualistic belief system in which matter is viewed as evil, the spirit good, and salvation as being attainable through esoteric knowledge, or gnosis) and the indigenous religions that succumbed to Christian missionizing.

Macropedia Volume 19 pages 1169 to 1171 under the topic Zoroaster we find various interesting statements;

According to the sources, Zoroaster was probably a priest. Having received a vision from Ahura Mazda, the Wise Lord, who appointed him to preach the truth, Zoroaster was apparently opposed in his teachings by the civil and religious authorities in the area in which he preached.

...; he did however place Ahura Mazda at the center of a kingdom of justice that promised immortality and bliss.

Zoroaster's teachings, as noted above, centered on Ahura Mazda who is the highest god and alone is worthy of worship.

The conspicuous monotheism of Zoroaster's teaching is apparently disturbed by a pronounced dualism: the "Wise Lord" has an opponent, Ahriman, who embodies the principle of evil, and whose followers, having freely chosen him, are also evil.

Thus say varied quotes from different contributors to the 1978 Edition of Encyclopedia Britannica. There is clear consensus as to the influence of the Zoroastrian/ Persian religion on the western religions. As with any collection of scholarly material, there is not agreement on all points surrounding the topic. Notice one quote stated the 6th century BC and another states the 7th century BC for Zoroaster's beginnings. I am not able to prove exactly the precise time of Zoroaster's existence and his vision-inspired philosophy, to do so though is not necessary to see that the "Big 3" have been influenced significantly by this ancient pagan religion.

We have taken a fair bit of time to understand the experience of the Israelites while in exile and their relation to Zoroastrianism. This information is crucial if we intend to come to an understanding of certain uses of the word "Satan" in the Hebrew Scriptures. The information on Zoroastrianism is also crucial in trying to piece together the puzzle of why *sawtawn* is portrayed in the Hebrew Scriptures as different from what we seem to see in the "New Testament". It is clear that there are two different ideas of who is responsible for evil. The idea that the Israelites generally held to before their Persian excursion was that Yahweh was responsible for "evil". Some time during and subsequently after the exile in Persia, many thought it to be some cosmic, evil adversarial force as was taught by Zoroaster to his followers.

After ingesting a lot of information about the paradigm shift of the Israelites in exile, over the past number of pages, we are now able to reconcile why two different writers, from different periods, penned the same story but wrote of different characters. One of them stating it was "God" who had caused something to happen while the other said it was *sawtawn* (translated Satan) who caused the exact same thing to happen. Understanding the view on good and evil that was planted and nurtured during the exile, allows us to reconcile the very opposite pictures we are given in two accounts of the same numbering of the tribes of Israel. Let me remind you of these two accounts where you will clearly see they are the identical account but the writer of 2nd Samuel names God as the inciter while the Chronicler is shown in English to name Satan as the inciter.

> ***2Samuel 24:1*** *And again the anger of the LORD was kindled against Israel, and he moved David against them to say, Go, number Israel and Judah.*

One solution as to why the first accounting of this incident reveals God to be the inciter is that the above verse was **written before** the exile period when all the writers of what is now called Scripture, understood that good and evil come from Yahweh for a purpose. Moreover, often the purpose is judgment and divine strategizing to get the people He is angry with to eventually turn back to Him in obedience. The next account, which was written after the exile, has the English name "Satan" as the one who incited David. Please keep the fact that the Hebrew word used means "adversary" in the front of your mind as you read.

> ***1Chronicles 21:1*** *And Satan stood up against Israel, and provoked David to number Israel.*

This verse was written after the exile period when many of the Israelites had returned from Persia and had carried with them religious concepts that they learned in exile. One solution as to why there is change in identity of the inciter when reading the English translation, is that many post-exile Israelites had adjusted their concept of God. Many came to believe Yahweh was a good God who wouldn't bring evil on the people He loves. With Chronicles being written a few hundred years after the exile we must at least consider the possibility of this writer expressing the new found perspective of good and evil in his work. I believe the writer of Chronicles is not intentionally trying to teach a lie to the reader, but in this case, he may simply be writing from what he knows. Although the writer in all probability identified with the correct understanding of the word *sawtawn* as a term meaning adversary, it is possible that what he knew about where evil comes from was based on a teaching about a false god that controls evil. It has to be a case of one or the other in this instance. Either the writer believed that God was the adversary and therefore recounts the story from 2nd Samuel 24 by describing God as *sawtawn* or the writer found himself aligned with the less palatable view and performed his own revision of the story by claiming that Satan was the one who caused David to number Israel. Again, I state that I perceive the writer was true to the Scriptures and was simply describing God as an adversary when he used the word *sawtawn* in place of the word God to identify the inciter of David. Whatever the case in this instance, we are still left with the problem that although the writer may have been referring to Yahweh as the adversary when he said *sawtawn* incited David to number the tribes, those who read his words today generally impose their cosmic diabology on this passage. Such an error includes imposing a literal Satan on his words because that is how the English has been handed down to us.

While in Persia the Israelites and subsequently the writer of Chronicles, was exposed to the "other" God, the God that was alleged to be responsible for evil. This false god paralleled Yahweh in so many ways that the exiles ingested the wrong philosophies about the true God of the Universe and began attributing evil to "the adversary". "The adversary" was actually Yahweh but in using a different term to identify the adversary, this force eventually became separate from Yahweh in the minds of the confused and was given an identity of its own. *Sawtawn* the adversary began to become *Satan* the evil archenemy of God. Whether the writer of Chronicles intended one philosophy of evil or the other matters little. What is clear is that in the period of his writing, Jews not only began Judaism, the forerunner of Christianity but Jews began to truly apply literalness to the *sawtawn* and the title of an adversary began to be used as a name of an entity.

If we base our decision about this topic on current Christian thinking which has decided there is a Satan and associated demons, then we are neglecting much of what the Holy Scriptures that were used by the apostles and the Messiah have to say. If we base our decision on reconciling the texts that are apparent contradictions, via the use of history and a cultural understanding, then we will in all probability come to the correct conclusion. The conclusion I might add, no matter how logical it may appear, still must be imbued by the Spirit of truth for one to receive it and grow in truth.

That spirit of truth is available to all humanity and all it takes to access it is an honest desire to accept the truth no matter what it looks like, where it comes from or how different it is from what we have been taught all our lives. Once we are over that hump then the truth we are receiving must be weighed against the whole counsel of God, which is contained in the Holy Scriptures, called, the "Old Testament." We see below in 2nd Timothy, the Apostle Paul reminds Timothy of the value of the "Old Testament" when he exhorts his student with words that declare it is the "Old Testament" which has led him to salvation and is given by inspiration of God.

> *And that from a child thou hast known the holy scriptures, which are able to make thee wise unto salvation through faith which is in Christ Jesus.*
> *All scripture is given by inspiration of God, and is profitable for doctrine, for reproof, for correction, for instruction in righteousness:*
> *That the man of God may be perfect, throughly furnished unto all good works. 2Timothy 3:15-17*

The Timing Of Isaiah's Words Add A Piece To The Puzzle

By now in our study, we may be getting a distinct understanding of the ancient belief of the Israelites in the area of the Sovereignty of God. In an attempt to provide another piece to the puzzle of how the concept of Satan as an "autonomous" evil entity made its way into present day religious thinking,

I would like to address the timing of the writing of the book of Isaiah. Isaiah's instruction came at a pivotal time in Israelite history during exile. Prior to the exile there was not an Israelite understanding that leant itself to an evil adversary who was going to fight against the Good God and His people until the end of time.

We have discussed at length the thought that it wasn't until exposure and assimilation into the Babylonian and Persian cultures, that Israel, or at least part of the people of Israel began to embrace a Persian doctrine of good and evil. Those who had power to propagate false doctrines adopted the concept of an evil entity that is opposing Yahweh and then imparted the same concept to the faith of Israel, which became a version of Pharisaic Judaism. Much of the religion of Pharisaic Judaism continued to morph and evolve into Christianity. There is still much to consider in the effort to prove conclusively that the Christian concept of a wicked being called Satan is one of many adopted false teachings from ancient pagan Zoroastrianism.

The doctrine of Satan is merely one of the erroneous doctrines found in much of Christianity today. I encourage you to explore carefully most of the main doctrines and practices of Christianity, which involves Catholicism and Protestantism, to understand the numerous other concepts that are mere traditions of men but have been accepted and taught as being doctrine. We will continue here to stay on the topic dealing with the non-existence of Satan.

The Prophet Isaiah is the most quoted prophet in the "New Testament" and is truly known to be one of the major prophets of Israel and Christianity. He is also one of the Major Prophets who told of the soon coming Messiah throughout his writings. We have already discussed the prophecy in Isaiah 45 of Cyrus being the Messiah in the sense of a Royal figure acting as a deliverer of the people of Judah who were in exile. As with any of the ancient Biblical writings, there are many theories and ideas of the authorship of the Book of Isaiah. Some say it is broken into two parts, some say three and I have even read of some who think there are seven distinct divisions in the book. Many scholars indicate multiple authors authored the book of Isaiah. A common theory is that three authors wrote the book and the complete contents were compiled by another party. Probably the least accepted view is that the Book of Isaiah was penned in its entirety by the Prophet Isaiah the son of Amoz, during the period of His life. It is well accepted that Isaiah contains at least two sections written by different authors at different time-periods. This acceptance does not make it so and some compellingly argue for complete authorship by the Prophet Isaiah son of Amoz. For the sake of argument, I share the following understanding from Westminster College as presented in a class called *Understanding The Bible.* Dr. Bryan Rennie identifies conclusively the different periods of the Isaiah texts and for our present study, I would like you to note the time-period that the chapters which repeatedly declare that there is one God, are written. Utilizing the work of many scholars before him, Dr. Rennie identifies these different periods as "Divisions of the Book of Isaiah".

UNDERSTANDING THE BIBLE Dr. Bryan Rennie
Religion 101[83]

The Divisions of the Book of Isaiah.

Proto-Isaiah, 1 - 39.

1. Biographical details of the life of Isaiah.
2. Assyria as major power.
3. Exile as future threat.
4. Emphasis on the judgement to come.
5. Implicit monotheism.

Before 587 in Jerusalem

Deutero-Isaiah, 40 - 55.

1. No biographical details.
2. Babylon as major power and Persia growing.
3. Exile as present suffering.
4. Emphasis on redemption.
5. Explicit monotheism.

Shortly before 538 in Babylon.

Trito-Isaiah, 55 - 66. Very similar to Deutero-Isaiah but contains evidence of the Persian takeover and the return from Exile.

After 538 in Jerusalem

Chapters 36 - 39 appear to be historical narratives edited into the book from 2 Kings 18:13 to 20:19 at a later date. Chapters 24 - 27 is proto-Apocalyptic, a literary style which developed only after the return from Exile and so is also probably a later editorial addition. Chapters 13 - 23 also appear to be later additions. This still leaves Chs. 1 - 12 and 27 - 35 as original material deriving directly from the late 7th and early 6th centuries BCE.[84]

83 Taken from http://www.westminster.edu/staff/brennie/prophets.htm, (used by permission)

84 Information taken from http://www.westminster.edu/staff/brennie/prophets.htm

The above understanding indicates chapters 40 to 55 were written shortly before 538 BC in Babylon, which had become Persia by that time. If this is so then we are better able to understand some of Isaiah's words in relation to the topic of the non-existence of Satan we are discussing. Isaiah and the Jewish exiles are in Babylon and have been adopting and accepting Zoroastrian religious concepts. Isaiah 45 was written near the end of the exile when Isaiah proclaims that it is Yahweh who is the creator of evil. Isaiah was confronting a false belief of the Persians that claimed some other god was responsible for the creation of evil circumstances. This foreign philosophy was dramatically opposed to the pre-exilic belief that there is only one God, who causes both the good and the evil to fall upon His people.

Although the ancient Israelites ascribed to a belief in other god's while not fully coming under the dominance of the gods of the nations, the entire nation of Israel was commanded to adhere to the concept of one God as is stated in Deuteronomy 4 and then again in the prayer/anthem of the Children of Israel called the Shema, meaning hear in the purest sense of actively hearing and diligently obeying, which is found in Deuteronomy 6: 4-9. Yahweh wanted Israel to diligently accept and embrace the fact that He was the only God in the universe. Below is the first line of this text;

Hear, O Israel: The LORD our God *is* one LORD

This section of the Torah has long been the first verses a young Israelite child commits to memory, often by the age of two years old. The Shema states not only who one is as an Israelite but it also states in absolutes who Yahweh is. Albert Barnes comments very insightfully in his notes on the Bible.

> *These words form the beginning of what is termed the "Shema" ("Hear") in the Jewish Services, and belong to the daily morning and evening office. They may be called "the creed of the Jews."*
>
> *This weighty text contains far more than a mere declaration of the unity of God as against polytheism; or of the sole authority of the revelation that He had made to Israel as against other pretended manifestations of His will and attributes. It asserts that the Lord God of Israel is absolutely God, and none other. He, and He alone, is Jehovah (Yahweh) the absolute, uncaused God; the One who had, by His election of them, made Himself known to Israel.*

It was not easy to pull the wool over the prophet Isaiah's eyes. He was sold-out to the concept of Yahweh's Sovereignty and oneness as the only force to be acknowledged. He understood there was no other force in existence. Therefore when the Jews were getting near the end of their exile period, Isaiah was able to give them the prophecy of King Cyrus being Yahweh's anointed and he was also able to admonish the Persian King who was propagating the dualistic philosophy, telling him that there is no force, no other god but Yahweh. It was clear by now that the Jews in exile had begun to attribute evil that was happening to them or those around them, to an evil entity. It makes perfect sense for Yahweh to send His man to tell the Jews to clean up their act before He liberates them from exile. So Isaiah gave a prophecy and a number of admonishments. Multiple times Isaiah reiterates to the Persian leaders and those who are said to be Israelites, that there is "one God and none else" but the most poignant example of Isaiah discouraging the exiles from attributing anything in their lives to any other power is seen when he tells them that Yahweh creates evil. The ancients before the exile were clear on this point. We have already looked at the concept of where evil comes from in many references which took place in the pre-exilic existence of Israel. Now however, Isaiah, speaking quite strongly I presume, is proclaiming that it is Yahweh who does "all these things". "All these things" refers to the good and the evil that has come upon the Israelites.

> *I form the light, and create darkness: I make peace, and create evil: I Yahweh do all these things. Isaiah 45:7*

It is absolutely undeniable that the reason God had Isaiah speak these words in chapter 45 is because Israel, the Jews in exile, needed to hear them. What were "all these things" Yahweh was referring to? The Jews were not denying giving credit to the Creator of the Universe for the good in their lives. However, as humans the Israelites seem to have a need to pin the bad, or evil in our lives on some identifiable source. As faithful Hebrews who were still relatively close, historically speaking, to the great wars and deliverances in Israel's history, it was simple to attribute the good that had occurred to them, to the Almighty. However, it seems the Hebrew captives were not so eager to attribute the bad to the Almighty. Crediting Yahweh for the good and the evil had been the general attitude for the Israelites throughout most of their turbulent history up until now. However, being in exile caused them to consider an adjustment to the long held belief that Yahweh causes evil to happen to His chosen people. It isn't so unrealistic to perceive how this major paradigm shift occurred for the exiles.

How would you or I respond if we were forced into exile for almost two full generations? Perhaps we too would recognize that bad happens and then begin to agree with our captor-host that someone other than the "Wise

Lord" was the hand behind the bad. The "Wise Lord" is not just a different name for the one true God, Yahweh, but is the name of the good God in a two-Deity dualistic system, which attributes evil to the bad god Ahriman, their second deity. There are many examples of a nations' drifting from what they once knew as a concrete unalterable value, to a value based on moral relativism. We only need consider how the once unacceptable public display of homosexuality has become more than tolerated in our on Western culture today. Moral relativism has been affecting the world for millennia and the Jews in exile were not immune to its insidiousness. Assimilation, which caused a two-God philosophy to flourish, was like an infection that embedded itself deep into the theosophical fibers of a once pure pattern of faith, in people that were chosen to share the morality of the Creator with the world. Now Isaiah wanted to do what prophets do best, that is speak the message of the Creator and give the exiles the opportunity to reject their syncretism, which enabled false belief in some other force, and acknowledge once again that Yahweh is the only force and the only source of all things. The Israelites were about to be delivered and in much the same way that John the Baptist was anointed to prepare the way of Messiah the deliverer, by calling all who would hear to turn to the true practice of the Faith in Yahweh. So too is Isaiah preparing Israel to be delivered by Cyrus, Gods anointed, by announcing that it would be wise to reject the palatable yet eroding ways and beliefs of the Zoroastrian concept of good and evil. Isaiah's message could not have been clearer to those who would hear it; no less than eight times in three chapters does Isaiah declare that there is only one God.

The message was profound and sadly, the message was lost to a huge segment of the returning exiles and the dualistic, two-God philosophy, became seated in the theology of many returning exiles. Returning exiles that would embrace the false message and see to it that it was embellished and enhanced in ways that would be so illogical that many were left to believe without question that those who propagated the false doctrine knew what they were talking about. What was to be a purely monotheistic culture was almost irreversibly changed by accepting and then furthering a two God theology that was never taught in the Scriptures, by the Prophets, or intended to be taught by the Creator, the only God.

CHAPTER 8

Lucifer's Fall in Isaiah 14, Explaining the Myth

It may seem difficult to accept such a seldom heard of concept as there not being any Satan. We are going to look at yet another clue that casts doubt on the idea of a cosmic satanic being and his hordes of minion demons, propagating and creating evil in the world. For the moment though, I would like to ask a serious question that many of us ought to ask ourselves. The question is; "Why do I need to believe in a Satan?" That may be a question one would hear from an atheist-apologist who is challenging a believer in God as to whether or not there is a God. "Why do you need to believe in a God?" they might ask. However, to ask, "Why do you need to believe in a Satan?" is not a question one would find them self confronted with along the path of typical human interactions. It is for this reason that I ask you to find a quiet place without the influence of your pastor, rabbi, spouse, or friends and ponder this question. "Why do you need to believe there is a Satan?"

Is it the same thing to say you *believe there is a Satan* as it is to say you *believe in a Satan*? Perhaps you notice I worded those questions differently. In one question I asked, "Why…believe *in*…", and in the next I asked, "Why….believe *there is*….?" Look at those two questions again and notice the different wording this time.

"Why do you need to believe in a God?
"Why do you need to believe there's a God?"

"Why do you need to believe there is a Satan?"
"Why do you need to believe in a Satan?"

The reason for the different wording is simple. I want you to be able to see that in conversation both ways to ask the question yield the same result. On semantics alone, it can be determined that there is a difference between the two wordings but communication is not always reliant on strict semantics. Let's explore how both questions mean the same thing.

If you ask someone the question, "Why do you need to believe there is a God?", and you also ask them, "Why they need to believe in a God?" you will see that you are asking the same question. If you do the same word switch as I just did with the question of "Satan," then no one would consider the questions to have a different meaning. Believing ***there is*** a God is likened to believing ***in a*** God. Why would someone consciously believe there is a God but say I don't believe in a God? The same thing is being said; believing there is a God is believing in a God. It is the same concept that says; believing there is a Satan is to believe in a Satan. By believing there is a Satan one is then believing that Satan does what so many attribute him to doing, that is causing evil. Therefore, if you believe there is a "Satan" who causes evil then you are believing in a Satan. I am not implying you would be placing your life in his hands in the same way many believe in Yahweh.

To admit to believing in a Satan does not mean you are admitting your reliance on Satan for your salvation. I realize there are probably only a handful of people in the world who totally reverse the roles of Yahweh and Satan and believe "Satan" to be the good guy and God is trying to annihilate the world. But I am saying, by attributing any of the things God does to a false "Satan" is not only an affront to the Creator, but shows that a person "believes" in a Satan. This unfounded but very real belief is similar to the way a child who believes there is a Santa Clause, and through the **belief of** his existence, **believes in** him. So too is having a belief that there is "Satan", to believe in him. I suppose if one believes there is a Satan, one ought to ask him or her self this question about Satan's abilities, "*If I believe there is a Satan, what do I believe he is capable of doing?*"

- Can Satan inhabit a person's soul or take on other physical forms?

- Does Satan transcend time or is he bound by time like you and I?

- Can Satan thwart God's plans in any real and effective way?

- Does Satan bring illness upon people and then lift the illness from them as a manipulative way to mess with their minds so they won't turn to God?

- Can Satan resist the curse in the garden that was placed upon the serpent who according to some is supposedly Satan?

- Can Satan tell the truth about anything at all?

- Does Satan bring death or does Yahweh kill and make alive as Deuteronomy 32 states?

All these questions need to be asked if one has decided they believe Satan exists. For to believe something exists is to believe something has power, whether small or great, the facts are that a belief in Satan must be coupled with the belief that he does certain things that only a supernatural being could accomplish. For a child to believe "there is" a Santa Clause is to believe Santa has power to perform marvelous things such as fly around the entire world in 24 hours dispensing gifts to billions of people all over the world and return at the close of Christmas to begin preparing for the next Christmas in a year from that point. Believing **there is** "Satan" is to **believe in** a Satan because one then believes he has the power to do supernatural things such as inhabit a person through "his demons" or bring evil on a city, or send a nation into exile, which we have discussed is completely an act of the sovereign Yahweh. Recall the words of the prophet Amos in chapter 3 verse 6 that teaches evil in a city is done by Yahweh:

> *Shall the horn be blown in a city, and the people not tremble? Shall evil befall a city, and the LORD hath not done it? Amos 3:6 Jewish Publication Society*

Why would someone believe there is a Satan who causes evil, when here the prophet, speaking on behalf of Yahweh, tells us when evil befalls a city it is Yahweh who causes it? I must remind you yet again that Isaiah 45:7 clearly tells us Yahweh does all the good and evil things. This of course is not referring to the evil that is sin and comes from man's heart, rather the calamitous evil that falls upon individuals or people groups. Aside from the evil which proceeds from a man's heart, nothing, absolutely nothing that is seen as "evil" is to be attributed to any force other than Yahweh. To do so means one believes in another like Yahweh. There cannot be "another" because we were told in Yahweh's own words that there is none like Him. Isaiah is not the only one to herald this vital message. We first saw this message go to the people of God when they were engaged with the multi-god Egyptian culture prior to their exodus. At that time, Yahweh proved all the man made gods to be nothing.

> *For I will this time send all My plagues upon thy person, and upon thy servants, and upon thy people; that thou mayest know that there* ***is none like Me*** *in all the earth. Exodus 9:14 JPS*

If hanging on to a cosmic "Satan" helps you feel better, well then that's sad. It is sad that many of us seem to have a need to believe in lies like the tooth fairy or that "Satan" is a living, breathing being. If you do choose to believe there is a "Satan" who is responsible for doing evil, then you in essence believe in Satan. As I have suggested above, you may not rely on this Satan as the God who could save you, but neither did the ancient Israelites who were told not to conform to the practices and beliefs of the neighboring nations, who were guilty of serving many gods. To acknowledge that there is another God who has power over anything such as the crops or the weather or illness, is to serve another God. Don't be mistaken, Yahweh never accused Israel of serving another God to the exclusion of acknowledging Him. While acknowledging some of the gods of the pagan nations, Israel still maintained the belief that there is an omnipotent all-powerful God responsible for saving them. Much like the case of the Zoroastrians, who believed in the supremacy of their God, yet attributed all the evil to another deity and were seen as serving other gods, so too was Israel seen to be going after other Gods by their acknowledgment and homage paid to other gods. We may be guilty of having a belief system that acknowledges more than one God.

This is so when we consider the pseudo-monotheistic religions of the Far East. According to the Scriptures, use of the word gods in its plural form, referred to the primary false deity of that culture and any other false deity that was believed to require appeasing or was said to be feared. The inclusion of all their deities as "other gods" shows us that if we accept the false idea of "Satan" which is a "god" developed from the concepts in other false religions, we are accepting the existence of multiple gods. Yahweh would see that same multi-god concept being adhered to in religion today, which includes a cosmic "satan," as if the participants are guilty of believing in a false "god." The Scriptures say we should have no other "Gods" before Him. Supernatural power is an attribute that belongs only to Yahweh.

Looking at the journey and experience of the Israelites, who have been called Judahites, in the exile to Babylon, which was conquered by Persia prior to the return of the exiles to Jerusalem; one is able to see why they found it beneficial and convenient to believe in "Satan." The emerging belief in a being who is responsible for the evil in their world, brought comfort to the exiled Israelites. As we have discussed in the previous chapter, they would not have to credit the evil that had befallen them, to their good and loving Yahweh. The exiles had experienced much calamity or "evil", as many would see it, and the God they had come to trust in was not capable of doing such evil to the people He loved. At least this was the thinking in their minds at the time. God was only doing what any loving parent would do to their child who continually disobeyed the parent and chose to rebel against the parents instructions and reject the request of the parent to live according to the rules that the child had agreed to abide by at one time. Eventually the parent will exercise their right to discipline that child and just may send him or her off to a type of remedial boot camp for a while for rehabilitation. In a sense, the periods of exile, which were imposed upon Israel by Yahweh, are a very serious boot camp given as a consequence upon the disobedient and rebellious nation as a result of their obstinance. Israel was responsible for their exile and whether we like it or not, both the exile of a delinquent son to a boot camp, and the exile of the delinquent nation of Israel, particularly Judah in this discussion, is done for their own good. The exile is simply a response by the Master to repeated, delinquent behavior. When in exile the wise person will look at where and why they are in exile and learn the lesson it is intended to teach them. They will learn that exile is designed to direct them back to the path of truth, and therefore they will work to get on that path and stay there if it at all has anything to do with them and their choice. And it always does.

Why Do Some Need to Believe There's A Satan?

I have had some serious introspection finding the answer to why I needed to believe there is a Satan when I first began to discover that there might not be a Satan. Uncovering your own honest answer is an essential element of beginning to see the traditionally accepted Scriptures that are said to speak of Satan, for what they were intended to be speaking of when the writer first penned them. If you are at the point where you can admit that you might need a Satan in your belief system so that there is some evil entity to lay blame on for all the bad in your life or world on, then you are at an advantage to come to understand that there is no Satan. The picture will become even more clear as we look closely at two more of the passages that are horribly misunderstood by many of those who contend that Satan does exist as a real antagonist to Yahweh and man.

The topic of "Lucifer" in the 14th chapter of Isaiah is understood by some correctly but when strong religious leaders preach or teach on Satan it is this chapter, which has been quoted for centuries by Christian theologians and laypersons, that is brought into the sermon or teaching. It is known as a hallmark verse to teach us about Satan. It is usually taught in connection with the words of the Messiah in the Gospel of Luke in which He states that He saw "Satan" fall from heaven. There is a very important question that needs to be asked regarding this statement of the Messiah and every statement in the Apostolic Testimony, the New Testament, about the devil, demons, or Satan. The question is; "What did the speaker believe about the topic when he spoke those words?" It is not difficult to understand that a first century Hebrew teacher would have been in line with the concept of good and evil taught in Torah. Messiah said the Scripture cannot be broken. The Scripture, the Old Testament, does not teach the existence of a literal Satan; therefore, Yeshua would not have been speaking about a literal Satan falling from a literal heaven when He spoke those words. Yeshua was very familiar with the Scriptural concept that tells us Yahweh brings forth both good and evil. As well as knowing that there is no other force in the universe that can orchestrate evil except the will of man and the heart of man that is inclined towards evil continually. Knowing this is helpful toward understanding why Yeshua taught us that defilement comes not from what we eat or from having unwashed hands, but from what is in our heart.

Yeshua had been confronted by a group of scholars who had seen His disciples eating with unwashed hands. The scholars were convinced that eating with unwashed hands would cause one to become spiritually and therefore ritually defiled. Yeshua knew that eating with unwashed hands held no power to defile one's spirit, therefore He told the scholars that the defilement comes from within and it is from the heart where evil comes from. The Gospels recount the moment for us.

> *But those things which proceed out of the mouth come forth from the heart; and they defile the man. For* ***out of the heart*** *proceed evil thoughts, murders, adulteries, fornications, thefts, false witness, blasphemies:*
> *These are the things which defile a man: but to eat with unwashen hands defileth not a man. Matthew 15:18-20 (emphasis added)*

Recall that Yeshua also had told Peter to get behind Him; and called Peter "Satan" at one point, therefore when Yeshua had said He saw Satan fall from heaven like lightning, was He referring to Peter as fallen from heaven? How could the Master of the Universe call a human man "Satan" in one breath, and have said in another instance that He had seen "Satan" fall from heaven? The answer to these questions lies within a more correct understanding of the use of metaphor and personification. These concepts will be addressed thoroughly later in our discussion. For now I will say, that if we think we are able to understand the Greek New Testament, without possessing a more correct understanding of the use of metaphor and personification in the era it was written, then we should also think a first century seamstress would be able to understand computer science by simply being shown a computer chip. The words of the New Testament must be studied in a more properly placed, historical context, to understand the meaning behind the words, just as the words of Isaiah which we will look at here must be located properly to comprehend all the nuance and mytho- poetic imagery that comes from the prophetic language of the period of Isaiah.

Whom or what is Lucifer in the 12th verse of Isaiah 14?

> *How art thou fallen from heaven, O Lucifer, son of the morning! how art thou cut down to the ground, which didst weaken the nations! Isaiah 14:12 KJV*

The above passage when understood in its literary and historical context is not about a cosmic being but is about a man. This famed verse used by millions as a reference that identifies Satan and his supposed origin is nothing but a very stylish writing about a great human king who was being prophesied about. The magnificent King of Babylon is said to have fallen from his exalted position as a powerful world leader. The word Lucifer is a Latin translation of the Hebrew word *"helel"* which means the morning star, or the bright morning star. This Latin translation for *helel,* was inserted by a man known as Saint Jerome when he translated the Hebrew Scriptures and produced the Latin Vulgate. In 346 CE the Hebrew word for "daystar", became Lucifer, which means "shining one" and may have been intended to state the same concept that is seen in the Hebrew. In Biblical history, "the Bright and Morning Star" has long been an appellation for a great and mighty ruler or human King. The King of Babylon was obviously not a literal star that was bright in the morning therefore we can see this term also defined as "light bringer", to be a metaphor. The metaphorical usage of the word "*helel*" placed in conjunction with the other metaphors which are intended to teach us concepts of royalty and rulership, reveal to us that a human King is being spoken of. For one to fall from heaven means they have fallen from authority or that they are no longer serving the purposes of their kingship due to the lack of wise ruling and the absence of God-honoring leadership. The New King James Version Study Bible has identified this fact as is stated in the comments on Isaiah 14 that are found in the study helps.

> Fallen from heaven is a figure of speech meaning cast down from an exalted political position.[85]

85 New King James Bible, Study Version; Zondervan Publishing

Lucifer in Isaiah 14 is referring to a human king who has lost his place as a magnificent ruler due to the pride in his heart. Verse 16 calls this fallen one a man and there are many other clear clues in the text that indicate this fallen ruler is a human being, a pagan king, and not a cosmic Satan. The International Standard Bible Encyclopedia has this to say about "Lucifer" in its entry on Astrology.

> 5. Lucifer, the Shining Star
>
> The planet Venus is more distinctly referred to in Isaiah_14:12 : "How art thou fallen from heaven, O Lucifer, son of the morning!" (the King James Version). The word here rendered Lucifer, that is, "light-bearer," is the word *helel* corresponding to the Assyrian *mustelil*, "the shining star," an epithet to which the planet Venus has a preëminent claim.

Commentaries both past and current are almost unanimous on the understanding that Lucifer in Isaiah 14 is neither speaking of nor giving a name for the "Satan" that much of religion has come to hate and fight against. Here are some testimonies from commentators on this verse containing the word "Lucifer;"

> **Isaiah 14:12** -
>
> **How art thou fallen from heaven -** A new image is presented here. It is that of the bright morning star; and a comparison of the once magnificent monarch with that beautiful star. He is now exhibited as having fallen from his place in the east to the earth. His glory is dimmed; his brightness quenched. Nothing can be more poetic and beautiful than a comparison of a magnificent monarch with the bright morning star! Nothing more striking in representing his death, than the idea of that star falling to the earth! *Albert Barnes Notes on the Bible*
>
> **Isaiah 14:12** -
>
> *"How art thou fallen from the sky, thou star of light, sun of the dawn, hurled down to the earth, thou that didst throw down nations from above?"* הילל is here the morning star (from *halal*, to shine,..... *Keil & Delitzsch Commentary on the Old Testament;Johann (C.F.) Keil (1807-1888) & Franz Delitzsch (1813-1890)*
>
> **O Lucifer, son of the morning**! alluding to the star Venus, which is the phosphorus or morning star, which ushers in the light of the

morning, and shows that day is at hand; by which is meant, not Satan, who is never in Scripture called Lucifer, ...

John Gill's Exposition of the Entire Bible; Dr. John Gill (1690-1771)

LUCIFER [LOU see fur] (*morning star*) — the Latin name for the planet Venus. The word Lucifer appears only once in the Bible "How you are fallen from heaven, O Lucifer, son of the morning! How you are cut down to the ground, you who weakened the nations!" (Is. 14:12). Literally, the passage describes the overthrow of a tyrant, the king of Babylon.[86] *Nelson's New Illustrated Bible Dictionary*

Lu´cifer (*light-bearer*), found in Isaiah. 14:12, coupled with the epithet "son of the morning," clearly signifies a "bright star," and probably what we call the morning star. In this passage it is a symbolical representation of the king of Babylon in his splendor and in his fall. Its application, from St. Jerome downward, to Satan in his fall from heaven arises probably from the fact that the Babylonian empire is in Scripture represented as the type of tyrannical and self-idolizing power, and especially connected with the empire of the Evil One in the Apocalypse.[87] *Smiths Bible Dictionary*

Lucifer

"light bringer", "the morning star": Isaiah 14:12 (*helel*, "spreading brightness".) Symbol of the once bright but now fallen king of Babylon. *Fausset's Bible Dictionary*

by Andrew Robert Fausset (1821-1910), co-Author of Jamieson, Fausset and Brown's COMMENTARY ON THE WHOLE BIBLE.

Isaiah 14:12 -

86 Ronald F. Youngblood, general editor; F.F. Bruce and R.K. Harrison, consulting editors, *Nelson's new illustrated Bible dictionary: An authoritative one-volume reference work on the Bible with full color illustrations [computer file], electronic edition of the revised edition of Nelson's illustrated Bible dictionary, Logos Library System*, (Nashville: Thomas Nelson) 1997, c1995.

87 William Smith; revised and edited by F.N. and M.A. Peloubet, *Smith's Bible dictionary [computer file], electronic ed., Logos Library System*, (Nashville: Thomas Nelson) 1997.

> Fallen - From the height of thy glory. Lucifer - Which properly is a bright star, that ushers in the morning; but is here metaphorically taken for the mighty king of Babylon.
>
> *John Wesley's Explanatory Notes on the Whole Bible*

I believe we can see in the above testimonies the clear statement that Lucifer in Isaiah 14 is an appellation literally referring to the King of Babylon. I presume you will look at the above references in their complete context. Once you do you'll find many of the above quoted commentaries and dictionaries go on to state that although this reference to Lucifer is referring literally to the fallen or falling King of Babylon, the metaphor is still referring to "Satan." However, in light of the concept of "satan" being originally a Hebrew word which means adversary, opposer or accuser, one is adding to Scripture by applying a meaning of a literal Satan to the term.

In addition, in light of the fact that there was no Satanology in the Hebrew monotheistic religion prior to the exile to Babylon, it seems presumptuous to impose a cosmic Satan as the intended metaphor onto the Isaiah reference. Rudimentary biblical scholarship will clearly teach it is not proper for the New Testament to define terms and concepts from the Old Testament but properly, the terms in the New Testament must be defined by the manner in which they are presented in the Hebrew Scripture. New Testament terms are simply Old Testament terms that are expressed in Greek words. One must find the Hebrew understanding that underlies the Greek words that are used. That is to say, the New Testament is to be defined by the Old.

For example, when the New Testament mentions the Passover we must look to the Hebrew Scriptures for the understanding of the Passover. When the New Testament expresses a concept of an unclean person, we must determine through studying the Hebrew Scriptures, just what constitutes an unclean person. How about if the Apostolic writings use a word such as Sabbath? Is it possible to interpret that word apart from how the Hebrew Scriptures define it? Although God says the Sabbath is the Sabbath, the Catholic Church Fathers have gone on record as calling Sunday the Christian Sabbath and saying that Sunday is now the day of rest for Christians.

> *On Sundays and other holy days of obligation, the faithful are to refrain from engaging in work or activities that hinder the worship owed to God.....Family needs or important social service can legitimately excuse from the obligation of Sunday rest.*[88]

---

88 Page 449,article 2185 of the Catechism Of the Catholic Church, published by Publication Service- Canadian Conference of Catholic Bishops

> *The Sabbath which represented the completion of the first creation has been replaced by Sunday...*[89]

We would be falling tragically short of sticking to true principles of understanding terms of Scripture if we agree with that Catholic doctrine, which has endeavored to change the words of Scripture. Sabbath is easily defined as the 7th day of the week, which is Saturday, when one properly defines the term through the Hebrew Scriptures. Just as with interpreting the Sabbath or the term "unclean", so too if a biblical commentator implies that the Lucifer of Isaiah 14 is the Satan who Messiah said fell from heaven, they are guilty of trying to interpret the Old Testament by using the New Testament instead of the other way around. For Scripture to remain understandable one must look at a term found in the "New Testament" and find out what that term meant in the "Old".

Satan Falling From Heaven Must Be Understood How The Old Testament Would Explain It

Although it is a slight deviation from the direct study of Isaiah and the topic of Jesus' Luke 10 statements is covered thoroughly in Volume II of *Satan, Christianity's Other God,* I would like to take a few moments and discuss the meaning behind seeing "*Satan fall like lighting*". It is beneficial to do so here as an example of the need to interpret the New Testament through the understanding found in the Old Testament. As well, it might allay some of the readers concerns that what is found in the Old Testament is contradicted or changed in the New. What did Messiah mean when He stated in Luke 10:18 that He saw Satan fall from heaven like lightening? This statement has been postulated to mean various things and explained via various concepts. Most of which typically result in adhering to the common Satanology doctrine much of the world has become accustomed to. In addition, most explanations fail to define the underlying Hebrew term for the Greek word *satanas* through the context of the Hebrew Scriptures, as it should be. Why do so many scholars divorce themselves from the Hebraic understanding of "the adversary" when it comes to interpreting and understanding what is contained in the New Testament? The first century followers of Yeshua would have heard Him speaking these words and would not have been confused as to their meaning. Whether Yeshua spoke them in Hebrew, Aramaic, or Greek, would not change the fact that the people of His day would likely

89 Page 450,article 2190 of the Catechism Of the Catholic Church, published by Publication Service- Canadian Conference of Catholic Bishops

have understood the term in either of two ways. The hearers would have understood the term "satan" through the truth of the Hebrew Scriptures or else from the understanding of the culture of their day. It is probable that both understandings were present when Yeshua spoke, but both cannot be the correct understanding. To settle this argument one might want to take a poll of the hearers of the words of Yeshua at the time that He spoke them, however that is not possible therefore we are left to consider the possibilities. Even if we were to take a poll, the facts are that the meaning of a message is decided on by the speaker and not the hearers, no matter how large or small the number of hearers is.

Possibility number one would be that some first century listeners would hear Yeshua use the term *satanas* in Greek or *sawtawn* in Hebrew or its Aramaic equivalent and conclude, as many of the first century citizens of the Roman Empire had, that Yeshua was referring to a cosmic archenemy of Yahweh, an evil celestial being with supernatural, God-like abilities. To arrive at that conclusion the hearer would have to ignore the fact that Yeshua was a Jewish Rabbi and taught true doctrine according to the Torah and the Prophets. Possibility number two would be that Yeshua is speaking of an adversary that is opposing the plan of God.

We have seen that the doctrine of Satan presented in the Torah and Prophets is a doctrine that teaches either man is the adversary called satan in English or "satan" is a descriptive term for the force Yahweh sends. A force He uses to enact his judgment on a person or people to direct them back toward being in line with Yahweh's will.

The hearer who concludes that Yeshua was referring to the casting to earth from heaven of a celestial "satanic" being would also have to reject the fact that any way you slice it, the word that Yeshua used is a Hebrew origin word. Even the Strong's concordance and Thayer's Greek Definitions tell us that the word used is from Strong's #7854 in the Hebrew. This helps to guide us to understand this term the way it is understood in the Old Testament. Below are the two words used to describe some type of an adversary or opponent as found in Strong's Concordance. Notice the last line of the second definition below. That part of the definition indicates that the Greek word Yeshua used, which we know as "Satan", is from a Hebrew word that never meant a cosmic, evil being. The first of the following definitions is said to correspond to the second, which, as I have stated, is based on the Hebrew origin that means opposer or adversary.

G4567

Σατανας

Satanas

sat-an-as'

Of Chaldee origin corresponding to G4566 (with the definite article affixed); *the accuser*, that is, the *devil*.

G4566

Σαταν

Satan

sat-an'

Of Hebrew origin [H7854]; *Satan*, that is, the *devil:* - Satan. Compare G4567.

The word in the text of Luke 10:18, is traced through word 4566 of Strong's and then shown to be originally a Hebrew word #7854. I don't think it can be stated enough that the word that underlies the Greek word *satanas* is the Hebrew word *sawtawn,* meaning adversary. Based on this fact, one would have to come to understand the Hebrew word *sawtawn,* before imposing a more contemporary understanding on the word used in this and other cases. Aside from tracing the basic linguistics of this word, one would also want to consider that Yeshua might very likely have used common phrases and words in His day. Phrases and words that were based on a very mythopoetic style of language and a culture that was well versed in speaking metaphor. By Yeshua's use of such a descriptive metaphor for the city of Capernaum just a few sentences earlier, it would follow that His reference to Satan falling would also be an understandable metaphor and used with the expectation that His hearers were able to understand it. Satan had no more literally fallen from a celestial location than did Capernaum literally fall from the geographical location known as Heaven. Notice the metaphor used to express Capernaum's reduction in political status in the following quote from Luke.

And thou, Capernaum, which art exalted to heaven, shalt be thrust down to hell. Luke 10:15

After all, was Capernaum really in heaven? Will Capernaum the geographic location, be placed in a Hell that is another supposed geographic location? It is highly doubtful on both accounts. No more was Capernaum in Heaven than was there a cosmic "Satan" as an actual entity with free will who is able to thwart Yahweh's plans, in heaven. If we are to take the words of Yeshua, the God of the Universe made flesh as truth, and allow them to bear the weight, as one would expect they should, then we must believe that He meant what He said. If Yeshua means what He said, what did He mean when He said Peter is "Satan"? The word used for calling Peter "Satan" is the same word as in Luke 10;

> *But when he had turned about and looked on his disciples, he rebuked Peter, saying, Get thee behind me, Satan: for thou savourest not the things that be of God, but the things that be of men. Mark 8:33*

Therefore, by using the literal application of metaphorical statements that has taken place, in order to devise a satanology doctrine, we then could line up some of the remarks that include the use of the word Satan in the Gospels and find a very disturbing conclusion. If Yeshua had called Peter "Satan" and Yeshua saw "Satan" fall from heaven; and to add to this , we are told "Satan" entered Judas at the last Passover Supper; then because everyone knows if A=B and B= C, C has to equal A. Yeshua has supposedly seen "Satan" fall and Yeshua has called Peter "Satan". Added to these facts is the fact that the "devil" and "satan" are thought to be one and the same and we also see that before the Last Supper that "Satan" entered Judas.

> *Then entered Satan into Judas surnamed Iscariot, being of the number of the twelve. Luke 22:3 KJV*

Considering all these references to "Satan", are we to believe that these all mean the same thing and conclude that Peter was Satan and entered Judas; and Peter fell from heaven? Christ surely wouldn't call Peter "Satan" if it wasn't true therefore, either Peter is the Satan that religion has been battling for millennia, or there is another way to understand the reference to "satan" so that Yeshua's words are still true.

Just as many have applied the word "satan" literally through the "New Testament", one must conclude in believing literally the words of Messiah that Peter the Apostle is Satan, Peter the apostle fell from heaven, and Peter the apostle entered Judas. After all, there is only one person in the entire "New Testament" who is called "Satan." Peter is called Satan by the only person who was perfect in speech and action and never spoke a lie. So either Peter is Satan; or Yeshua is a lying, name caller. If neither of those is the case, then we are misunderstanding something about what a satan is.

I hope you are getting to know me well enough by now that you can see I have suggested the "Peter is Satan" idea, in a "tongue in cheek" manner. I hope that you are able to see that I believe the problem is a lack of understanding. Peter is not the cosmic archrival of God, nor did Peter fall from heaven or enter Judas, so Messiah must have meant something other than implying that Peter is the incarnate form of a rebellious, fallen angel.

The challenge is that we must try to understand what the Messiah thought and meant by using the term "satan". The Messiah adhered to the pre-exilic concept of "the adversary", which states Yahweh creates peace and evil. The Messiah is always true to Torah and accepts the original doctrine of good and evil. The Messiah knew the Scriptures and that it is humans who oppose and at times the agents of Yahweh who act out the will of Yahweh. These are referred to as "a satan" in the Hebrew language. Knowing this helps us understand, then we can begin to perceive where the Messiah's head was at when He called Peter "Satan". Yeshua was simply calling Peter an adversary and sticking to the correct biblical understanding of the term satan. In fact, Yeshua Himself interprets for us what is meant by calling Peter "Satan".

Notice how in Yeshua explaining to Peter why Peter is being referred to as a "satan," we are able to see the Messiah's definition of Satan as it was understood in His time;

> *...,Get behind me satan for thou savourest not the things that be of God, but the things that be of men.*

A "satan" is one who is not for the things of Yahweh. Peter is rebuked by Yeshua and is called an adversary because he is not for the things of God. Messiah was supposed to go to His death but Peter, being a satan, renounced the fact that Messiah was soon to suffer many things and be killed. It was this act of disagreeing with the will of Yahweh that caused Peter to be a "Satan" to Yeshua, one who opposed the will of the Father. Thankfully, that attitude did not prevail in Peter's life as is seen in the accounts of his activities through out the gospels and letters. Peter does exhibit the actions which identify him as a true apostle of the Messiah, one who is inclined to do the Fathers will no matter what it looks like or what the cost. Peter was not the cosmic Satan of mythology but was "a satan" when he proved to be an adversary to Yeshua. The message is clear in that we are not to impose an interpretation on the words of the Apostolic writings that cannot be seen in the understanding of the same words or terms from the Hebrew Scriptures. When Yeshua makes a statement that a man is Satan or that "Satan" fell like lightning and was seen by Yeshua, we must be diligent to try to find out what He meant and how it can be seen through the Hebrew Scriptures to bring understanding. Therefore, the claim by Yeshua to see satan fall like lightening is not a reference to the daystar in Isaiah that fell from power because of his pride.

The word Lucifer in Isaiah, which is more correctly translated as "day star" according to a correct understanding of the Hebrew word, is not to be confused with the reference to the fall from heaven of "Satan" spoken of by the Messiah in Luke. Because Christ was not using the word *satanas* as a name when He spoke it, he neither would have taken the word used in Isaiah as anything more than a word referring to the King as the "morning star". Isaiah is not identifying an historical, monumental fall of a rebellious archangel. Looking at the passage from Isaiah 14, we see some highlights which testify to the nature and identity of the subject.

We first must recognize that this dissertation begins a full chapter previously with what is known as "*The Oracles Against Foreign Nations.*" The dissertation goes on for some time. If you read through from Chapter 13 without letting the chapter breaks or paragraph headings separate the body of text, the flow and intent of the text is quite clear and it carries on to chapter 17. The first full addition of Chapter numbers and verse numbering occurred in the 16th Century with the Geneva Bible. Therefore, this oracle is to be read as one long letter.

What Does it Mean to Be Fallen?

The section labeled "Chapter 14" is written about Babylon, not about some fallen cosmic being. It is part of a larger body of admonishments that are directed toward pagan nations and a political system or political leader. Men fall, rulers fall and nations fall; we are not being told of anything other than the fall of human leadership and authority. The concept of one "falling", in its euphemistical sense, has long been understood as intimating that one who had a certain position, which granted him certain rights and privileges, has made some choices and actions, which resulted in that person or nation becoming less than what it had been before it, or he had "fallen". Most of us are familiar with the phrase, "He's fallen from grace", in reference to a spiritual icon and leader who has been found out to be participating in a sexual sin or financial scandal. Fallen from heaven means virtually the same thing; a leader with power and prestige has lost that power and prestige because of his own actions that went against what God wanted. In every case in history, both biblical and secular, when a person or a nation is referred to as fallen, it is always clear the meaning is referring to a decrease in exalted status. The "fallen" one no longer possess the status or power and control position, it or he previously possessed. A fallen one loses some or all of its power and position and when we see this statement in its context in Isaiah 14, it is apparent we are seeing a reference to a political or spiritual demotion, not to a literal drop from a geographic location to a lesser or lower geographic location. A perfect example of this statement referring to "a fall" being a fall from political power, is seen in another place in Isaiah. Isaiah 21 uses the same terminology to express that the great political and world power of Babylon, which comes to represent a false religious system, is brought down by a mightier warring nation;

> *And, behold, here cometh a chariot of men, with a couple of horsemen. And he answered and said, Babylon is fallen, is fallen; and all the graven images of her gods he hath broken unto the ground. Isaiah 21:9*

One fulfillment of the prophecy of the fall from power of the King of Babylon and the fall of the nation did in fact occur at the hands of the Medes. Her fall could be seen to indicate a future fall in a spiritual sense. The empire of Rome, which had taken John the Revelator captive on the Island of Patmos, was called Babylon by first century writers as is indicated in the International Standard Bible Encyclopedia.[90] This is a helpful piece of information. It helps us to understand that when Babylon is said to have fallen in The Revelation, John is talking about the false religious system fostered by Rome that is destined to be brought down when the Messiah's kingdom becomes fully realized.

As we look specifically at the Isaiah 14 text, let's pinpoint some portions of it that indicate that this account is not of a fallen cosmic being but that it is of a fallen King of Babylon. This King believed himself to be a god and imposed the metaphorical title of the "Morning Star", known as the great light-bearer that rises before the sun in the morning, upon himself. "Morning Star" was also known as the planet Venus. This king believed himself to be a God, as did a great many of his subjects. This seems odd to the present thinking found in North American religion as so few people who attain to great status and position would ever think they are "Gods." Although we do not possess the same mindset as the ancient pagans when it comes to considering oneself a

90 Rome is designated as Babylon in the Sibylline Oracles (5 143), and this is perhaps an early Jewish portion of the book. The comparison of Rome to Babylon is common in Jewish apocalyptic literature (see 2 Esdras and the Apocrypha Baruch).
ISBE article on Babylon

God, we still might ask the question, "How could anyone think they are an actual God?" One might ask this of Anton Levay, the writer of the Satanic Bible. In his writings he repeatedly tells the reader they are a God and that the only one that should matter to themselves is them self, because they are a God. Therefore, he describes in quite graphic language, how each person should work to gratify every carnal desire and lust they have, in order to affirm and solidify the concept that he or she is God. Vexen Crabtree writes of this Autodeist belief on a web article telling of Satanism;

> **Autodeists** - we worship ourselves. The only God we can ever perceive is in our own existential world. We are each a God.[91]

Of course this sick and twisted philosophy will not sit well with the Creator of the universe but this group of so called "Satan Worshippers," has some of the clearest understanding of the history and origin of the present day contemporary understanding of Satan. In fact, a cursory view of their doctrine quickly reveals that they don't even believe in a cosmic "satan" but state quite clearly that Satan is what is inside every person and emanates from within, out of the wicked desires of the individual. Quoting again from Crabtree's article, we see this view expressed.

> *"Satan is not a real, living entity, conscious or a physical thing that can be interacted with. It is a symbol, something ethereal, something that basically doesn't exist except as an emotional attachment and personal dream. Just like Buddhists do not worship Buddha, Satanists hold up Satan as an ultimate principal rather than an object of literal worship. Satan inspires and provokes people, like all (honest) religions the ultimate point is self-help. God believers have a different opinion on what Satan is, but their opinion is a result of their religion. Satanism's Satan is much more eclectic and multicultural than to be defined by Christianity or Islam.* [92]

Hey, I am not condoning such a twisted anti-Yahweh group as this, but I do admit that I find it quite interesting to hear that the view of Satanists on Satan is not so far from a Hebraic view as would have been understood

91 http://www.dpjs.co.uk/modern.html#thesatanicbible, A Description of Satanism by Vexen Crabtree.

92 http://www.dpjs.co.uk/modern.html#thesatanicbible, A Description of Satanism by Vexen Crabtree.

thousands of years ago. They sure fall off the cart though when they begin to articulate their view of self as God.

We see then that even today, as with the King of Babylon who Isaiah was speaking about, there are those who think themselves to be gods. According to Isaiah's writing, the King of Babylon and the entire nation are in for a stern rebuke for thinking such lofty thoughts of itself. The entire dissertation begins in chapter 13 verse 1; "*The burden against Babylon...*"

This text goes on to speak of how Babylon is the glory of kingdoms and will be wiped out by Yahweh, which occurs through the use of His agents, who happen to also be pagan nations. It is interesting to note when Babylon is called "*the glory of Kingdoms*" in verse 19 of the previous chapter, it is quite a picture of the exalted status of this nation in comparison to the other Chaldean nations. And also, a clear denouncement declaring that she will be overthrown.

> *And Babylon, the glory of kingdoms, the beauty of the Chaldees' excellency, shall be as when God overthrew Sodom and Gomorrah. Isaiah 13:19 KJV*

Something, whether a human king or a nation, must be exalted to high status in some form for it to be considered as fallen at any point in its history. Babylon had a high position in the political Eastern world but the prophet unabashedly proclaims that it is about to fall.

Chapter 14 verse 4 clearly tells that this statement is a Proverb against the human King of Babylon. In verse 5, we are told the staff of the wicked is broken and so is the scepter of the rulers.

> *That thou shalt take up this proverb against the king of Babylon, and say, How hath the oppressor ceased! the golden city ceased! The LORD hath broken the staff of the wicked, and the sceptre of the rulers. Isaiah 14:4-5*

References to a "scepter and staff" are symbols of the King's power and we see that they are removed from him. Looking at verses 9 to 11, we see strong reference to this character being a human king.

> *Hell from beneath is moved for thee to meet thee at thy coming: it stirreth up the dead for thee, even all the chief ones of the earth; it hath raised up from their thrones all the kings of the nations. All they shall speak and say unto thee, Art thou also become weak*

as we? art thou become like unto us? Thy pomp is brought down to the grave, and the noise of thy viols: the worm is spread under thee, and the worms cover thee. Isaiah 14:9-11

Although the references to hell, the dead and Sheol are difficult to understand from our current cultural perspective which has a poor understanding of what Sheol was to the biblical writers, these references cannot be referring to a Lucifer who is also "Satan." They speak of "Hell" being prepared for him and indicate that there are already patrons of hell waiting in hell for the arrival of "Lucifer". This cannot be so for one simple reason. It is said this verse is speaking of the fall of Satan from heaven and supposedly happened sometime before or right around the time of creation of the world. Therefore, it would have to be placed at a point in cosmic history where there is not yet any wicked being. If hell is prepared for the fallen Satan and the dead, who is it that is in hell and is stirred up? Moreover, if Lucifer is said to be the first fallen angel; then how can there be inhabitants of "hell" waiting for "Satan's" arrival? Wasn't Satan the first of the fallen angels? Were there other creatures that rebelled against the Creator before Satan rebelled and was ejected from the presence of Yahweh? Would it not seem odd that there were either demons or dead souls waiting in hell for the fallen "Satan" to arrive? The answer to this question is found through understanding the concept as it may have been intended and understood culturally and historically. Satan cannot have entities waiting for him in hell prior to his fall to the mythological place of the dead. Hell to the ancient biblical writers was simply a metaphor for what happens to a person when they die. They simply are dead and buried with no transfer of an immortal soul to a place of eternal torture. To the many "pagan" cultures it was different. One concept was that Tartarus was the place in the subterranean parts of the earth that was reserved for those wicked people who did not receive their due punishment on Earth before they died. A Greek mindset could not reconcile that a person who was wicked on Earth simply ceased to exist upon death so they concocted the mythological "Hell/ Tartarus" that became so popular in Christian lore. The ISBE provides some insight into the word "Hell" however there is much to discuss on the topic and perhaps that will take place in later pages of this book.

Hell

shel (see SHEOL; HADES; GEHENNA):

1. The Word in the King James Version

> The English word, from a Teutonic root meaning "to hide" or "cover," had originally the significance of the world of the dead generally, and in this sense is used by Chaucer, Spenser, etc., and in the Creed ("He descended into hell"); compare the English Revised Version Preface. Now the word has come to mean almost exclusively the place of punishment of the lost or finally impenitent; the place of torment of the wicked. In the King James Version of the Scriptures, it is the rendering adopted in many places in the Old Testament for the Hebrew word *sh^{e}'ol*

We are seeing the use of language by the prophet Isaiah, which depicts in allegorical and metaphorical terms, the intensity of those nations and leaders who were eager to see the great Babylonian King fall. The words spoken are intended to paint the picture of the absolute demise of the ruler, the human ruler, of Babylon. Hell is referring to the grave, as is Sheol in verse 11. The only way "Hell" can be waiting for Lucifer to arrive, is if "Hell", which is sheol or the grave, is personified. Personification is a widely used practice today. We see it used in depicting the intensity in various maladies and situations. Such as in the idea of alcohol beckoning to an alcoholic who is fighting to be alcohol free and master his addiction; or speaking about cancer ravaging a person's body as they fight to live while undergoing intense and painful treatments or surgeries to eradicate the cancer. Here in Isaiah we see hell personified and spoken of as if it is an entity with actual desires and that is able to feel excitement. The writer was not intending these personifications to be taken literally but he wanted his statements to be understood as a euphemism to display the intense nature of the fall of the King of Babylon. If you were to narrowly escape death on numerous occasions such as being rescued from a fire or liberated from a horrific car accident or were left unharmed after a vicious tornado, and I said that "death is stalking you", there would be no doubt about the personification I am using to express my message. "Death" would not be confused for a literal physical creature. Rather you would recognize the personification in death being said to "be stalking" you. This is no different than for "the grave", or "Hell" as the English puts it, to be "excited" for the King to arrive. Hell is personified to appear as if it is a character that literally exists. In verse 9, we see that all the "chief ones" are kings of nations. This is identifying the human kings who ruled other nations that had not ascended to the level of power internationally as the king of Babylon had. These envious and equally power hungry kings were being prophesied to relish and take delight in the fall of Babylon and particularly the King of Babylon who is here called the "morning star".

In verse 10, the human King's question, in a rhetorical sense regarding the imminent weakness of this fallen king, is another indicator that this passage is referring to a man. If this passage is referring to the "cosmic satan" who is believed to have supernatural powers after being ejected from heaven, then why would human kings believe this entity will be as weak as they are, after the "fall"? Much of the present cultural belief in a Satan with power to invoke evil and possess the spirits of humans, suggests "he" has much greater power than any human does? Therefore, the descent from power that is spoken of in Isaiah 14 must be reference to Satan having his power drastically limited after the fall. However, because there is no Satan one can comprehend that this passage in Isaiah 14 is about a man. A man who has great political power would certainly become weak like the lesser kings, once his empire is ripped from him. As well, a cosmic being who is supposedly cast to earth where he is able to manifest all manner of phenomena, would not be compared to a small time king and considered as being in the same category as other human kings. It is fractured and inconsistent reasoning to believe this passage is referring to a cosmic Satan.

Verse 12, as I have already spoken of, is where the name "Lucifer" is gleaned from. Remember Lucifer is simply the Latin word for the original Hebrew word *helel*, and means the light bearer. The more correct translations use the term "morning star" or "day star". True, many versions still utilize the word Lucifer in the English translation, however, it is typically the case that these translations are based on the KJV translation which has imparted to successive translators a mindset which continues to apply the word "Lucifer" to the Hebrew term for "morning star". Why did the translators of the KJV carry the Latin word for "morning star", Lucifer, across to the English? Was it an intentional act to build this false teaching on "Satan"?

Translated incorrectly or perhaps with less than fair judgment, the use of the word "Lucifer" in Isaiah 14:12, could simply have been born out of a misunderstanding. When a translator has a belief system or a theological grid that claims that there is a "Satan", then a word choice during translation may often be made which represents that belief. I am not stating unequivocally that the choice to use the word "Lucifer" for the Hebrew word *helel* was the result of a skewed understanding of the Hebraic concept of the adversary. The translators may well have recognized that the word "Lucifer," which meant *light bearer* in Latin, was indeed referring to the planet Venus. The ruler of Babylon was believed to be the incarnate form of this God Venus, which was believed to be a God that rises before the sun in the morning. The translators may have understood, when making their word choices, that Lucifer meant "day star" or the like, and chose an analogous word to represent the power of the King of Babylon. They could have simply used the phrase, "daystar", or "morning star" but chose the Latin term that meant pretty much the same thing. Many translations of the passage in Isaiah have translated the Hebrew word *helel* more correctly. Below are selections of translations of this verse for comparison. Some of which do not use the word "Lucifer" to translate what was meant by the word *helel* in the Hebrew text.

Isaiah 14:12

(American Standard Version) How art thou fallen from heaven, O day-star, son of the morning! how art thou cut down to the ground, that didst lay low the nations!

(Jewish Publication Society) How art thou fallen from heaven, O day-star, son of the morning! How art thou cut down to the ground, that didst cast lots over the nations!

(King JamesVersion-1611) How art thou fallen from heauen, O Lucifer, sonne of the morning? how art thou cut downe to the ground, which didst weaken the nations?

(Literal Translation of the Holy Bible) Oh shining star, son of the morning, how you have fallen from the heavens! You weakening the nations, you are cut down to the ground.

(The Message) What a comedown this, O Babylon! Daystar! Son of Dawn! Flat on your face in the underworld mud, you, famous for flattening nations!

(Youngs Literal Translation) How hast thou fallen from the heavens, O shining one, son of the dawn! Thou hast been cut down to earth, O weakener of nations.

(Jeromes LatinVulgate) quomodo cecidisti de caelo lucifer qui mane oriebaris corruisti in terram qui vulnerabas gentes

These verses help to shed light on the issue and when reading the above Latin Vulgate version of the verse, we see the use of the word "Lucifer" not as a proper noun but a descriptive term, just as was intended by the Hebrew writer who originally wrote these words. The use of the more correct term for *helel* being, 'day star,' or 'morning star,' does indeed elucidate the concept which teaches "Lucifer" in Isaiah 14 is referring to the pompous attitude of the King of Babylon and not to some cosmic satan being.

Perhaps in Disney's version of the biblical story of the Exodus from Egypt, we can see how researching the culture that the story was set in, helps illuminate some of the concepts of "Kingship" at the time. At one point in the story, which is called "Prince of Egypt", the Pharaoh is recognizing that his power and authority are being challenged; it is at this point in the story that the Disney writers have Pharaoh saying, "I am the bright and Morning star." Somehow, the Disney crew knew that this term had long been a chosen appellation for the king of some ancient nation in the Near East. Although one cannot rely entirely on the story which is relayed by Disney as being completely factual, one certainly can add this thought to the process of understanding the historical usage of a term such as "morning star" by powerful kings of the ancients. After all, even a kid's cartoon, when depicting history, nature or otherwise, is often researched to represent the practice of the period as accurately as feasible.

Jerome Added the Word Lucifer in the Fourth Century

I have mentioned Jerome's Latin vulgate and could easily accuse Jerome of trying to further the "satan" concept in using the word Lucifer for the word *helel*; however, I am not certain that Jerome purposely tried to further Satan doctrine. It may be more prudent to believe that Jerome was not intending to infuse Scripture with this doctrine but was simply applying the knowledge he had of language and translating to his work. To Jerome it was likely a matter of using the Latin word, which at the time of the Vulgate translation, had the same meaning as the Hebrew word *helel.* He knew the word *helel* meant something along the lines of "son of the morning", or "morning star", as translated in so many versions of the Scriptures.

The Clues in The Text Show us "Lucifer" is a Man

We already have more than enough information to conclude that Isaiah 14 is not talking about a cosmic "satan", but let's continue to be thorough and explore the other clues found in the passage in question. What are we being told in Isaiah 14 verses 13 and 14, the oracle against Babylon and subsequently her king?

These verses are recognition of the pride of the heart of this once great nation. A nation obviously cannot have an actual heart, yet the writer writes as if this nation does. This again is an example of the poetic style of the writing that personifies things such as nations.

> *For thou hast said in thine heart, I will ascend into heaven, I will exalt my throne above the stars of God: I will sit also upon the mount of the congregation, in the sides of the north: I will ascend*

> *above the heights of the clouds; I will be like the most High. Isaiah 14:13-14 KJV*

We can see the message of these words when we look at a similar concept in Isaiah 47:10. In this passage, we are told of Babylon boasting how "she" is the only one. Babylon is metaphorically said to have raised herself up as the only god. For this reason, she is cast down, brought to nothing.

> *For thou hast trusted in thy wickedness: thou hast said, None seeth me. Thy wisdom and thy knowledge, it hath perverted thee; and thou hast said in thine heart, I am, and none else beside me. Isaiah 47:10 KJV*

We are hearing highly poetic language to describe the aspirations of this great nation and her king. So often, the words of these few verses are affixed to the satanology of the present day. If these were statements referring to a cosmic, satanic archenemy of God, then the statement of this subject being a man in verse 16 would have to be rejected.

> *They that see thee shall narrowly look upon thee, and consider thee, saying, Is this the man that made the earth to tremble, that did shake kingdoms; Isaiah 14:16 KJV*

It is a human being that is referred to in the bulk of this oracle against Babylon. Another reference to indicate that the text is dealing with only human entities is verse 16. That verse speaks of this fallen one being gazed at by those who once saw the power and might that emanated from this man's rulership. Verses 18-20 talks of the human kings of the nations being asleep in their graves but this once proud king will not join them in burial. Does this mean that Satan will not be buried like the human Kings or is this perhaps a statement informing the subject that he is going to miss out on the honor of a King's burial? It was the honor of a king to have a national memorial and royal burial after he died, however in this instance the fallen king of Babylon, known as the "morning star" and called Lucifer in Isaiah 14, would not receive this honor. He had caused the people to be slain, as verse 20 states, and due to his choice to believe himself a God and attain such an exalted position, he would be refused the funeral and burial that was typical of the kings of the nations.

It is abundantly lucid that the Isaiah 14 reference to "Lucifer" is not referring to a cosmic "satan." Understanding this verse and passage from the cultural, historical, literary, and social context, helps us to understand what was being spoken and to whom. In conclusion of the discussion on this section of Scripture, I will quote from the study notes in the New King James Version, Nelson Study Bible. The "study helps" provided in that Bible sum up the entire passage quite nicely. We are given the meaning of the word "Lucifer", the understanding of the term "fallen from heaven" as a figure of speech; the power of the poetic language that is used and the conclusion that there is no connection of this verse to Yeshua's statements of seeing Satan fall like lightning.

> Fallen from heaven is a figure of speech meaning cast down from an exalted political position. Jesus said, "And you, Capernaum, who are exalted to heaven, will be brought down to Hades" (Luke 10:15), and apparently with the same meaning, I saw Satan fall like lightning from heaven" (Luke 10:18). The name for Lucifer in Hebrew literally means "Day Star," or the planet Venus. The poetic language of this verse describes the aspiration of this brightest star to climb to the zenith of the heavens and its extinction before the rising sun. This is an apt summary of the failed goal of the king of Babylon (v.4) who wanted to grasp universal and eternal domination.
>
> Tertullian, Milton and others have linked this passage to the carreer of Satan on the basis of Luke 10:18, but the text does not specifically make this connection.[93]

Isaiah 14 is not in any way referring to the Satan who supposedly is the archenemy of the Creator of the universe and of those who follow the Messiah. In an effort to conclude who and what Satan is, it is essential that we see clearly the mention of Lucifer in Isaiah, which has often been thought to be referring to Satan, as simply referring to the once great King of Babylon and by extension the nation he ruled and the subsequent fall from power of both of them.

93 New King James Version- Study Bible; by Zondervan Publishing.

CHAPTER 9

Is Satan the Anointed Cherub from Ezekiel 28?

One day, sometime ago, I was having a conversation with an old friend and the topic of Satan came into the dialogue. I was discussing the possibility of having not seen correctly in the past and the concept of whom or what "Satan" was. After expressing a few of the views, which I had, I was told by this old friend, "If you want to understand who Satan is you have to start in Ezekiel 28." I had looked at this passage before and there had been a time when I believed it to be referring to the cosmic Satan who was so well known and so frequently fought against by many in world religions, including Christianity. I knew that many connected the concept of a cosmic Satan to Ezekiel 28. However, I saw that this passage might not be referring to Satan, the alleged archenemy of God. Knowing that this passage is a key passage in Christianity for identifying Satan, I realized I had to look at this passage again and see if that old friend of mine was right. Indeed, I needed to look at Ezekiel 28 afresh to start with, in order to understand "satan." Here is how things seemed to be when I took another look at this famous Satan passage from its contextual and historical perspective. After all, I recognized how important it is to try to understand the words of the Scriptures from the original intent of the author. Once I looked at the passage it was easy to see much of the wording used in it was not meant as a statement of who the cosmic being was, but a statement directed to a human king that intended to address the magnificent splendor of this particular ruler.

I see now that Ezekiel 28 is very similar in its imagery and message to that which is seen in Isaiah 14. After all, right in verse 2 of this passage the writer calls the entity that is being spoken to, "a man"; *yet thou art a man, and not God,*

The context is quite clear; Ezekiel is bringing a number of oracles from Yahweh against nations who have abused and in many cases fought against the nation of Israel.

If we suggest the verses in Ezekiel 28 are speaking of "Satan", and by doing so reject the immediate context of the entire section of oracles, then our ability to interpret this Scripture correctly, becomes notably diminished. What is notable is that the Prophet speaks the word of Yahweh to Ammon, Moab, Edom. Philistia, Tyre, Sidon and then finishes his oracles against the nations by delivering a lengthy collection of oracles against Egypt. If the oracle against Tyre in Ezekiel 28 is to be understood of "Satan" then how does the Prophet think it should be fit in with oracles that are specifically pointed to geographic nations and their ruling parties? It is unlikely that the oracle against the ruler and nation of Tyre should be understood in a different manner than the other oracles in the package of utterances, which are all directed to human subjects. Ezekiel was addressing people in nations who were hopefully going to understand that their nation was about to come under judgment from the Creator of the universe because of unacceptable treatment towards the Daughter of God, the nation of Israel.

We have now come through much of the "Old Testament" and we have looked at some of what we find in Isaiah regarding the concept of an archenemy of Yahweh versus the concept of an inclination to choose evil. We have discussed how the evil inclination that stems from man's heart and is sometimes the adversary, called *sawtawn* in the Hebrew, is used by the Father. The idea of evil manifesting from the heart of man as its point of origin is far from a new idea. In Genesis Chapter 6, we were told the earth would be destroyed with a flood because every inclination of man's heart was evil continually.

> *And GOD saw that the wickedness of man was great in the earth, and that every imagination of the thoughts of his heart was only evil continually. Genesis 6:5 KJV*

The wording of that verse has not gone unnoticed by scholars and particularly, the Jews who are "the People of the Book". There is a concept found in this verse that is in ancient Judaism that has been carried forward to Judaism today. This concept recognizes the evil inclination as the great fight every human has within himself or herself. This is not saying we are created entirely evil but is saying we all have an evil inclination in our foundational being which desires to choose that which is contrary to the good. The evil inclination is known as the "*Yetzer ha rah*" and the good inclination is known as the "*yetzer ha tov.*" These are often spoken as the yetzer tov and the yetzer hara. The basic concept here is that the *yetzer tov* must overcome the *yetzer ha rah.* On their web site, the Union of Orthodox Jewish Congregations of America, we are given a definition of the *Yetzer ha rah and Yetzer tov.*

> **"Yetzer" -** desire or inclination; as in "Yesh l'Adam shenai **yetzarim**," "A person has two **inclinations**."
>
> **"Yetzer HaRa" -** "evil" inclination, desire to commit sin; as in "Yoseph HaTzaddik cavash et ha-**yetzer ha-ra** shelo," " 'Joseph the Righteous' conquered his **"evil" inclination**."
>
> **"Yetzer HaTov" -** "good" inclination, desire not to commit sin; as in "Lekol echad yesh **Yetzer HaTov**," "Everyone has a **"good" inclination**.[94]

In looking at the definitions provided above, you might have noticed the first of the three definitions makes the statement that a person has two inclinations, a good one, and an evil one. I agree as regards the good and evil inclinations. In fact, I can agree with any religious group that postulates a belief that agrees with Yahweh and teaches about His truth. The good inclination will overcome the evil inclination when one uses the right tools. For the good inclination to overcome the evil inclination, one must practice righteousness out of a desire to do the right thing, which ideally stems from the heart. When the desire to do good stems from the heart, then as the choice to do good is exercised, the power one has over the evil inclination grows.

It is also understood the Torah, which means the teaching and instruction of Yahweh recorded in the first five books of the Bible, contains and is the antidote for the evil inclination.

Many of the admonishments given in Scripture are to nations that are embroiled in paganism and have rejected Yahweh or rejected and persecuted the Hebrew people of God. In the book of Ezekiel the lamentation against the human King of Tyre, oft thought to be about Satan, is not about Satan but is part of a collection of proclamations against powerful nations and leaders. The strong exhortations include six nations and The King of Tyre fits into this package as one of the strongest leaders of the richest nation. The subjects that are included in the proclamations are:

94 http://www.ou.org/about/judaism/yz.htm

Ammon, Moab, Edom, Philistia, Tyre, Egypt, King of Tyre, Pharaoh of Egypt

We are going to look at these proclamations in the context of their thousands year old cultural period and focus on the statements made to the King and Prince of ancient Tyre.

The oracle against Tyre really begins back in chapter 27. Ezekiel gives a very descriptive monologue of how Tyre has made herself perfect in beauty, in verse 3 and following of that chapter.

> *And say unto Tyrus, O thou that art situated at the entry of the sea, which art a merchant of the people for many isles, Thus saith the Lord GOD; O Tyrus, thou hast said, I am of perfect beauty. Thy borders are in the midst of the seas, thy builders have perfected thy beauty.*

Take special note of this because this acknowledgment of Tyre's pronouncement of her beauty is one of the charges mentioned by the prophet about the King of Tyre in chapter 28 verse 12. Contained in this prophecy against Tyre, which begins in chapter 27, we are given a strong statement directed to the nation as a whole, and then we are given a statement directed to the Prince of Tyre at the start of chapter 28. The fact that the oracle against the Prince of Tyre follows directly after the prophet told of the profound, virtually worldwide influence of Tyre as a nation is telling. It is intended to aid us in seeing how powerful Tyre had become and how powerful her royalty was at the time. On the cnn.com website, this is said of the ancient city of Tyre.

> UNESCO wants to raise money to preserve Tyre's ruins, as well as carry out excavations on land and under water, where there are many shipwrecks.
>
> In its heyday, Tyre headed a trading center which had a virtual monopoly of maritime trade in the Mediterranean and along the Atlantic Ocean coast from Wales to Africa.
>
> Tyre also is said to be where the alphabet was invented and later adapted by the Greeks.

> And, according to the Bible, Solomon asked Hirarr, king of Tyre, to buy wood and the services of craftsmen to build the Temple in Jerusalem.[95]

Above is only one of the many statements that speak of the impressive status of Tyre, which was known throughout the world at the time. In the Scriptures, her exalted position and powerful economical status are mentioned often. Tyre is called the crowning city in Isaiah with acknowledgement of the prosperity and success of the merchants who came from Tyre.

> *Who hath taken this counsel against Tyre, the crowning city, whose merchants are princes, whose traffickers are the honourable of the earth? Isaiah 23:8*

In Joshua 19 it is stated Tyre is strong. In first Kings Chapter 5 Tyre was noted for the skill of its artificers, and its manufactured products were famous throughout the world. The purple dye and works in bronze, which issued from Tyre were especially famous. This type of recognition should be a sure sign that Tyre was quite a great city in many ways. While the inheritances in the Promised Land are being parceled out to the Israelites in the book of Joshua, the lists of geographic locations mentioned are typically non-descriptive. However, when Tyre is mentioned the writer was certain to add the adjective "strong" when mentioning the city of Tyre. Special mention was made in numerous places of Tyres' magnificence.

The writer of Ezekiel 27 and 28 has lamented against the city of Tyre and the prince of Tyre, then he moves on to speak an oracle against the King of Tyre. This is where many will point out that it is Satan who is being spoken of by the prophet. It seems highly unlikely that the writer would leap from speaking about geographically identifiable locations and their associated ruler or rulers, into a hyper-spiritual realm to describe for us a so-called angel that used to be a resident of heaven with the God of the universe. Why does it seem to be okay in so many people's opinions to reject the context of a passage when we think it may be talking about "Satan?" Why does it seem to be accepted by so many that it is an allowable practice to take one portion of an entire thematic section of Scripture and say, "Oh this is about Satan here in this section of this chapter?" In fact, it is not okay to do either of those.

95 Taken from the article on cnn.com World News Story page titles; UNESCO hopes to save Lebanon's ancient city of Tyre. May 9, 1998
Web posted at: 4:10 p.m. EDT (2010 GMT) http://www.cnn.com/WORLD/meast/9805/09/lebanon.tyre/

The Scripture cannot be broken; it should not be piecemealed out to find a way to fit every concept and thought which can come to a human's mind. The point in Ezekiel lamenting against Tyre the great city then the prince of Tyre and then the King of Tyre, was because each of them held the opinion that they were as good as God. The city of Tyre and the King of Tyre are both spoken of as perfect in beauty. The many metaphors Ezekiel uses to elucidate for the hearer as to how grand the city, Prince and King of Tyre are, is simply a style of writing common to prophetic utterances. This style is designed to paint an understanding for the hearer that everyone hearing the oracle against Tyre's Prince and King is able to see how full of themselves they are. Is it not acceptable to try to hear the language used by the writer, as it would have been heard by the original audience? We stand to better understand the message when we can see the writer is working to provide the hearer and the subject with a vivid picture of how a city or person has raised themselves up to be as God. Many ancient rulers thought they could be as gods and believed they could ascend to the mount of the gods where they would take and give counsel from that position. The message comes clear as we hear the language used by the writer in the context of the writer's cultural and linguistic environment and setting.

In today's vernacular, we often make statements about a person who thinks he or she is better than everyone else is. Which of us has not come across an arrogant and self-inflated person in our lives who when spoken of it was with statements such as, "What, does he think he's god?" Or perhaps with the even more descriptive phase," Who died and made him King?" Often certain people and specifically people in positions of power, have a seriously over-inflated concept of their greatness. This is the case when the Prince of Tyre, who may be seen as the same person as the King of Tyre according to some commentators, is spoken against in the Ezekiel oracle. Yeshua was know as a King and Prince and it is likely that because the word *nawgheed*, translated as prince in Ezekiel 28 verse 2, means; a ruler, commander or honorable one, that the King and the Prince of Tyre are one and the same.

Before we work to dissect, some of the concepts spoken in Ezekiel 28, allow me to share a couple of comments regarding this text and regarding the passages placed proximal to Ezekiel 28. The package of prophetic utterances Ezekiel delivers to his hearers can only be seen as referring to "Satan" if the reader decides to ignore the context of the entire group of oracles. In fact, one is hard-pressed to find a quality, scholarly commentary that makes the error of lifting this particular passage out of context and imposes a concept of some "satanic" being upon it. The *Intervarsity Press Woman's Bible Commentary* speaks of the package of Scripture in Ezekiel 28 to 33 as a group of oracles against ruling nations and a warning to the prideful not to get too big for their britches.

> Oracles against Israel's most geographically immediate neighbors – Ammon, Moab, Edom, Philistia, Tyre and Sidon – are followed by a lengthy collection of oracles against Egypt. Set exactly between the oracles against six nations and the oracles against Egypt are words of promise for Israel....
>
> ...The theme of God's self-disclosure through judgment is central to this collection. In addition, the oracles serve to warn readers of the consequence of pride, conceit, arrogance, selfishness and vengeance.[96]

In John Gills Exposition of the Bible, we find these comments on the chapter in Ezekiel, which is often mistakenly said to be representing "Satan."

> **Ezekiel 28 - INTRODUCTION TO EZEKIEL 28**
>
> This chapter contains a prophecy of the destruction of the prince of Tyre; a lamentation for the king of Tyre; a denunciation of judgments on Zidon, and a promise of peace and safety to Israel. The order given the prophet to prophesy of the ruin of the prince of Tyre, Eze_28:1, the cause of his ruin, his pride on account of his wisdom and riches, which rose to such a pitch, as to make himself God, Eze_28:2, the manner in which his destruction shall be accomplished, Eze_28:7, the lamentation for the king of Tyre begins Eze_28:11, setting forth his former grandeur and dignity, Eze_28:13, his fall, and the cause of it, injustice and violence in merchandise, pride because of beauty and wisdom, and profanation of sanctuaries, Eze_28:16, next follow the judgments on Zidon, Eze_28:20, and the chapter is concluded with a promise of the restoration of the Jews to their own land, and of great tranquility and safety in it, Eze_28:24.[97]

As you see, the above commentators are not confused about the issues spoken of in Ezekiel 28. I find by looking at the context of the passage and understanding the manner in which great rulers often raised their selves in their own eyes, to be seen as deity, that this misunderstood passage is only amplifying the arrogant nature and self-aggrandizing attitude of the rulers of Tyre. Let's take a look at the statements made by Ezekiel and see if we can

96 Inter Varsity Press, Women's Bible Commentary, pg 415

97 John Gill's Exposition of the Entire Bible
Dr. John Gill (1690-1771)

understand them through the eyes and ears of someone hearing or reading the words at that time. A time where many, many kings and nations were known to come under God's judgment for their pursuit of greatness which proved to consume them with a lust for as much power, success and sovereignty that they might acquire.

As I stated, it may be that the reference to both the Prince of Tyre in verse 1 and the King of Tyre in verse 11 might both be referring to the same ruler. For our purposes, it is not necessary to decide whether these references are referring to one or two persons; however, we will look together at the text that deals with both of these titles, first the section addressed to the Prince and then the following section that is addressed to the King. I will not prolong our discussion beyond that which is necessary to adequately relay the concept, but we will include thoughts on many of the verses as we go along. There is so much to say on every verse in this passage and many commentators have done excellent work in developing an understanding of how the poetic terms utilized by Ezekiel are truly descriptive phrases, which are intended to speak of the puffed up greatness, and delusion of grandeur the Prince and King of Tyre had. Although it would be simple to just paste in large quantities of excellent commentary here, I will only toss in a little bit of those materials. I do hope that you will weigh my words in light of what we have already discussed throughout this book and you will dive in to the vast resources available, which clearly explain the entire passage of Ezekiel 28 and surrounding oracles. Although a number of commentators wrongly conclude that this passage may be spiritually referring to a, "Satan who fell from heaven", they do so incorrectly, based on only a partial understanding of what Isaiah 14 is speaking about.

The difficulty becomes even more pronounced, when a commentator sets up his conclusion on his perceptions of the message in Ezekiel 28. Most erroneous conclusions are based on the commonly accepted view that there is a separate, identifiable, tangible, cosmic archenemy of Yahweh called Satan. Titles applied to this entity who is commonly said to be thwarting the plans of God are; Lucifer, Beelzebub, and Prince of Persia, among many other monikers. They who have arrived at the wrong conclusion about Ezekiel 28 have done so because of a predetermined theological grid. They impose their predetermined belief that Satan exists onto Ezekiel's oracle against the ruler of Tyre. This predetermined belief has lead them to force this passage to fit their views instead of allowing their views to be shaped by the passage. So, just as with previous sections of miss-understood Scripture I ask that you please be patient as we look at some telling clues in Ezekiel 28, which can easily be seen to show that this passage is simply about a man or perhaps two separate men.

If This passage is About Satan then the Context Shows him to be a Man

Interpreting Scripture by taking the context of the passages is the primary rule of successful biblical interpretation. Our first explorations of this passage shape the context of the proclamation by telling us that Ezekiel was hearing a word from God and that the ruler of Tyre had better take heed because he is simply a man.

> *The word of the LORD came again unto me, saying, Son of man, say unto the prince of Tyrus, Thus saith the Lord GOD; Because thine heart is lifted up, and thou hast said, I am a God, I sit in the seat of God, in the midst of the seas; yet thou art a man, and not God, though thou set thine heart as the heart of God: Ezekiel 28:1-2 KJV*

Reading verse 2 may be far enough for some individuals to look, in order to see that this passage is about a man, "***yet thou art a man".*** The very text uses the Hebrew word *awdam,* which is understood to mean a "human being". If this passage is indicating that the prince of Tyre is Satan, then "Satan" has to be a human being. When the word commonly translated as "satan", is used properly to identify an adversary, a human being can be a Satan but is not "the satan". In the true understanding and sense of the word, a human being is a "satan" as in the case of Yeshua calling Peter "Satan". That use of the word satan means one who is not for the things of God but is for the things of men.[98] The fact is that this verse in Ezekiel is speaking of a human being and not "Satan" and that is pointed out clearly in verse two when the subject of the text is called "a man".

Verse 3 is often pointed at by many who mistakenly conclude that the statement, "*no secret can be hid from thee*, is a statement referring to "Satan".

> *Behold, thou art wiser than Daniel; there is no secret that they can hide from thee:*

Again, the conclusion on this matter for many flows out of a pre-decided stand that there is a Satan who is opposing the Creator. Therefore, many force

98 Matthew 16:23 KJV
But he turned, and said unto Peter, Get thee behind me, Satan: thou art an offence unto me: for thou savourest not the things that be of God, but those that be of men.

this passage and others that we will look at, to fit their concept of a being called Satan. Perhaps if we take this verse alone we might be able to see and accept their conclusion but the previous verses just told us that the subject is a man; so what could be meant by this verse? Are we just going to ignore the context of this passage, as it is set within a group of oracles against the nations? Should we not work to find understanding within the context of a passage? To apply understanding to this verse in context we need to be aware of the unrivalled power of the city of Tyre and its ruler's power, which we have previously touched on in our discussion. Mention of this great economic power is frequent in history and the Scriptures. Zechariah, who was a post-exilic prophet, mentions Tyre and we are shown yet again that she, that is Tyre, was well situated geographically and was prosperous economically. To assist in understanding the status of this city and the significance of its geographical area, we note John Gills comment on the following verse in Zechariah.

> *And Tyrus did build herself a stronghold, and heaped up silver as the dust, and fine gold as the mire of the streets. Zechariah 9:3 KJV*
>
> **Zec 9:3 - And Tyrus did build herself a strong hold**,.... Tyre was built upon a rock, and was a strong fortress itself, from whence it had its name; and, besides its natural defence, it had a wall one hundred and fifty feet high, and its breadth was answerable to its height (e); but yet, as it could not defend itself against Alexander the great, who took it; so neither against the Gospel of Christ, which found its way into it, and was mighty to pull down strong holds in a spiritual sense:
>
> **and heaped up silver as the dust, and fine gold as the mire of the streets**; the riches of these cities, especially Tyre, are often made mention of; they were famous for their wealth, being places of great trade and merchandise; see Isa_23:2 all which were to be holiness to the Lord, and for the sufficient feeding and durable clothing of them that dwell before him, Isa_23:18 his ministers. [99]

As for this amazing subject having knowledge of secret things, we need to know how it is possible for the subject to have such an ability to know secrets if he is just a man. The particular Prince of Tyre who is the "Prince" in the sense of being Tyre's foremost ruler is also called the King of Tyre later. He would have been so well networked in order to get himself to such an exalted status that indeed it would be difficult to keep secrets from him

99 John Gill's Exposition of the Entire Bible
Dr. John Gill (1690-1771)

in the ancient world. His network of informants and information gatherers and deliverers would be large. The depth that the King's informants would be associated with the culture and society, both political arenas and non-political connections, would be seen as this ruler being in a position where "nothing" could be hidden from him. Daniel was himself privy to many secrets including the information that revealed the King's plan to kill all the wise men in the kingdom during Daniel's time. True too, Daniel received secrets of the Most High, as an interpreter of dreams, but it is doubtful that the statement in the verse in question is depicting the Prince of Tyre as one who had mysteries revealed to him. Certainly, this Prince knew of Daniel and of Daniel's unsurpassed wisdom and favor in the land of his captor. It is believable that this pompous Prince thought of himself as one who was wiser than Daniel was. When you read the reference to Daniel made by Ezekiel in the verse below, consider that it is likely the ruler of Tyre was aware of the great Daniel. Daniel was hailed as very wise and sagacious during and after the period wherein he counseled the Persian rulers. The statement of the Prince being wiser than Daniel may simply be a challenge to the self deifying monarch who was not so much being said to be wiser by the prophet but was sarcastically being indicted for his pride which moved him to think himself wiser than Daniel. The prophet is speaking tongue in cheek to the ruler in a way that is similar to addressing a cocky teenager by saying, "*You think you're so smart.*" If the princes' claim to be God is correct, he should be wiser than Daniel. However, Daniel was so well renowned in Babylon for his wisdom that this prince would be unlikely to be wiser than Daniel would, unless he was in fact a God as his self-claim indicated. Further to the concept of "secrets," we can see that the "secrets" revealed to Daniel is a different word than the "secrets" being referred to as being revealed to the Prince. Often times an English translation of one word such as "secrets" has two very different Hebrew words underlying it. This is apparent when we assess the common interpretation of the English word versus the idea that was meant by the Hebrew words originally used. This is the case for the word "secrets" found in Ezekiel 28 and Daniel 2:28. Note the different word reference numbers in the following two verses that mention secrets.

> *Behold,[2009] thou[859] art wiser[2450] than Daniel;[4480, 1840] there is no[3808] secret[**5640**] that they can hide[6004] from thee: Ezekiel 28:3 KJV+*

> *But[1297] there is[383] a God[426] in heaven[8065] that revealeth[1541] secrets,[**7328**] and maketh known[3046] to the king[4430] Nebuchadnezzar[5020] what[4101, 1768] shall be[1934] in the latter[320] days.[3118] Thy dream,[2493] and the visions[2376] of thy head[7217] upon[5922] thy bed,[4903] are these;[1836] Daniel 2:28 KJV+*

The use of the word secret in Ezekiel 28 is the word *satham*, and means to shut up or to keep closed. The word used in the statements made by Daniel is a very different word for secret, it is *raz*. This Hebrew word means a mystery, or like the English translation indicates a "secret" that can only be known by Daniel and who he tells. Now the book of Daniel uses both Hebrew words where we are given the English translation "secret" but they have a different meaning to a Hebrew listener. It makes sense to see that the word used in Ezekiel 28 for the secrets that are not kept from the Prince is not the same as the mystery type of secrets that were revealed to Daniel by Yahweh. Daniel was shown mysterious things from God contrary to the type of "secrets" that the King was able to gain knowledge of. The "secrets" that the King was able to uncover were simply messages and information that would be shut up or closed to the King under normal circumstances. The King found out the "secrets" of men through the use of men who were his informants.

One final note on this concept is that we are told, "There is no secret "**they**"_can hide." The word "**they**", is also kept in the Jewish Publication Society Bible and is referring to a specific group of people. In the context of what is to happen to the ruler of Tyre, and that it is through strangers and then the uncircumcised that destruction comes, the "they" here is referring to, for lack of a better term, the Prince's contemporaries, associates and enemies. This statement is not referring to the mysteries of Yahweh that are known by a cosmic "satan"; otherwise, an attribute of omniscience is being applied to Satan.

We find an interesting note in John Gill's thoughts on this princes' self-vaunting Gill tells us that a number of ancient versions render this statement as an interrogation of the prince of Tyre. Gill goes further to tell us how the statement of *"there is no secret that can be hidden"* from the prince, was speaking of the inside track this powerful and influential ruler had, when it came to collecting and extorting knowledge. Knowledge that would enable him to protect himself and to grow his kingdom further.

> **Eze 28:3 - Behold; thou art wiser than Daniel**,.... That is, in his own opinion; or it is ironically said. The Septuagint, Syriac, and Arabic versions, render it by way of interrogation, "art thou not wiser than Daniel?" who was now at the court of Babylon, and was famous throughout all Chaldea for his knowledge in politics, his wisdom and prudence in government, as well as his skill in interpreting dreams. The Jews have a saying, that
>
> "if all the wise men of the nations were in one scale, and Daniel in the other, he would weigh them all down."

> And perhaps the fame of him had reached the king of Tyre, and yet he thought himself wiser than he; see Zec_9:2, antichrist thinks himself wiser than Daniel, or any of the prophets and apostles; he is wise above that which is written, and takes upon him the sole interpretation of the Scriptures, and to fix the sense of them:
>
> **there is no secret that they can hide from thee**; as he fancied; he had sagacity to penetrate into the councils of neighboring princes, and discover all plots and intrigues against him; he understood all the "arcana" and secrets of government, and could counterwork the designs of his enemies.[100]

Although somewhat difficult to understand, Gills commentary goes on to explain his understanding of this passage and sees this ruler representing the anti-Christ. Gill like so many other commentators, is seeing these passages correctly for the most part, but he and others continue to make them fit their pre-determined and previously learned concept of a "satan being".

Leaning entirely on John Gills understanding of this passage would be foolhardy; however, his commentary is one of the premiere commentaries of his period, which does an excellent job in assisting us in understanding the history, and culture of the period in which certain Scriptures were penned. Please do take time to search out numerous other commentators and historians. You will likely be delighted to find the majority of them will lead in the same direction as John Gill has gone by seeing the Prince of Tyre as a real human who was self–exalted and would therefore, ultimately be judged. Even commentators who believe in a cosmic Satan know that the Ezekiel 28 passage is not referring to Satan. For now though, when the sum of all the parts is considered and we add the previous thoughts contained in this book to the equation, we are lead to a correct understanding of the absence of a "Satan" as a cosmic, antagonistic, supernatural, archfiend of man and God. The next verse in Ezekiel 28 provides more to help in identifying the subject of Ezekiel's statements.

> *With thy wisdom and with thine understanding thou hast gotten thee riches, and hast gotten gold and silver into thy treasures: Ezekiel 28:4 KJV*

Looking at half of this verse it is easy to see it as a reference to Satan, however, the remainder of this verse tells of the wealth of this ruler. Earthly riches are the possessions of humans and not to be seen as the possessions of a "Satan" who is supposedly a celestial spirit being. Ezekiel 28 tells of the

---

100 John Gill's Exposition of the Entire Bible

physical riches that were acquired by the subject in question. The types of riches spoken of are very much identifying the riches of a human. If then this passage in Ezekiel is in fact about Satan then he must be a human according to the prophet's understanding. Why would any one give any credibility at all to some supposed "Satan" attempting to thwart Yahweh through his influence on human kind, thinking him to be a supernatural being if he is just a wealthy man as Ezekiel 28 testifies to? It is unreasonable and would simply be satanological suicide to acknowledge the context of this passage about a man and think that Satan is represented here. If one believes this passage is about Satan, the context forces the conclusion that he is a human being who can acquire wealth in the forms a human would acquire wealth. A belief in Satan cannot stand up under scrutiny when it is seen here that the subject of Ezekiel 28 is but a man and therefore must not be a cosmic Satan possessing human riches and supernatural power. This passage is simply about a human ruler who has become extraordinarily rich. The next verse clarifies this understanding by referring to the economic activities of this human ruler. The term *traffick* in the verse is without doubt a reference to the trade activities of the great merchant city of Tyre.

> *By thy great wisdom and by thy traffick hast thou increased thy riches, and thine heart is lifted up because of thy riches: Ezekiel 28:5 KJV*

We will see further on in this text a reference to the merchants of Tyre and this particular Hebrew word does indeed breakdown to mean trade and by extension refer to economic activities which generate vast amounts of wealth, power and control in the ancient world. Coupled with this concept is the statement that it is due to the material wealth of the Prince of Tyre that his heart is lifted up. So many in biblical scholarship claim it was because of Satan's pride that he lifted himself up but this verse tells us it is due to riches that the subject's heart was lifted up. Again when held up against the light of the full counsel of Yahweh on this issue one would not be able to contend that this particular statement is speaking of Satan. Verse 5 then confirms that the profound wisdom of the Prince of Tyre aided him in major commerce that made him rich and it is those riches that are pinpointed, as the cause of the pride of his heart. The Prince of Tyre, as with virtually all Royalty of the ancient non-Hebrew and polytheistic nations, thought himself to be a God.

> *Therefore thus saith the Lord GOD; Because thou hast set thine heart as the heart of God; Ezekiel 28:6 KJV*

Looking back, on the Pharaoh of Egypt, we are reminded of God judging the Pharaoh at the 10th plague because Pharaoh and his subjects believed Pharaoh was a God. Due to this self-deifying belief of the ruler Yahweh proved Pharaoh was impotent to stop death from coming upon the land and particularly from killing the first born of everyone who refused to obey the God of the universe in applying lambs blood to the doors of their dwellings. The first-born of Pharaoh would too be seen as a God and Yahweh, after demonstrating His power as the only sovereign and supernatural Deity in the universe, ended His demonstration by mocking one final false god and went as the death Angel through Egypt killing thousands of first-born. The God of the Hebrews aptly proved that He was the only One, the only God in existence and anything else, including those supposed Gods who were responsible for evil in the eyes of Pharaoh and his people, were in fact nothing in the most literal sense of the word. Yahweh said they are nothing and they are "no gods" and now He had proved it. It would have been a paradigm shift for the Egyptians and even for many Hebrews, to come to the realization that there is only one Power and all this time the concepts of the existence of other supernatural beings had been a farce. Any other supposed power source was simply non-existent and just because the people believed in these other sources so intensely and sincerely, did not make them real.

The Egyptians, who are said to be the forefathers of "magic", were the echelon and pinnacle of skilled slight-of- hand entertainers and illusionists. The only real power they possessed was the power of deception and intuition coupled with exceptional charisma to draw people into believing their charade. Utilizing these powers and possessing a great commitment to devising methods of presentation to appear as if they somehow controlled the energy forces and natural forces that are under the control of Yahweh, these Egyptian magicians exercised a somewhat inexplicable, hypnotic control over the minds of the general populous, as well as over much of the leadership of their day. You may find it interesting to engage yourself in a study of the paranormal and supernatural phenomenology in order to gain some clarity on practices that have deceived multitudes into thinking that there are men who possess supernatural powers.

Many Hebrews and Egyptians had a strong belief in mysticism and magic as they were far from the scientific age that was able to explain that which was previously inexplicable. This belief was affirmed to them often while they were intermingled with other nations and their Egyptian sojourn was not any different. The Egyptians demonstrated the "magic" arts frequently and the Hebrew people were not immune to the deception of their tricks. Taking time for an exploration of the magic arts of the Egyptians in the court of Pharaoh and other ancient "magic" practices would be interesting, as we would learn that the Egyptian magic was no more than clever trickery, ingenious science, and deceptive illusions. That discussion will perhaps be for another time. I will say however, in books such as the "*History of Magic*" by Ennemoser and other encyclopedic volumes, it is shown that it is probable the "magic arts" of the Egyptians were clever tricks, schemes and hypnotic suggestions that fooled the masses regularly.

In 1924, Harry Houdini wrote a book titled "*A Magician Among the Spirits*."[101] In this book Houdini, arguably the world's greatest illusionist tells how he spent thirty years compiling a library of phenomenology in an effort to determine if he would be able to contact his departed mother. Houdini went so far as to design a secret code with his mother before she passed away in an effort to know it was she contacting him from the beyond if there was ever an apparent dialogue with the dead mother. After many years of research and encounters with spiritists and illusionists, Houdini concluded there was no such thing as contacting the dead, manipulating, or communicating with spirits or for that matter, any real psychics. Houdini had spent time with many of the world's most renowned persons of psychic phenomenon and somewhat surprisingly, one by one they shared with Houdini precisely how they plied their trade and that they in fact had no supernatural ability. Even today, the incredible entertainers David Blaine and Chris Angel have told interviewers that they possess no supernatural ability. Blaine, Angel and Houdini all realize that the greatest reason people sincerely believe in supernatural phenomenon is because of the excellence and flawlessness with which magicians deliver their product. In addition, and more importantly, there is the strong desire of the audience to see magical acts yet not believe they can be fooled. These "magicians" are not tapping into the forces of some type of phenomenal energy. So here, I state yet another large and difficult to believe declaration for some; magic is not real on any level where it is believed to be the use of supernatural forces that brings forth its mind-bending results! Whether it is present day "phenomenon" or the mystical acts of the ancient Egyptians, magic is simply demonstrations that trick the mind and fool the willing and unwilling alike. Although being entertained by magic is most certainly enjoyable, there is no magic demonstrated at the hands of men that is truly a display of supernatural abilities or powers. Allow me to direct you to the James Randi Foundation web site to aid in your search if you are interested in exploring the issue of magic a little more, *http://www.randi.org/research/index.html*.

101 Publishers: Harper & Brothers New York and London 1924 ISBN 0-8094-8070-0

"The Amazing Randi", as he is called, is a forerunner in debunking the claims of phenomenologists and those who say they are psychic or paranormal. Randi in fact, for a number of years, has had the "One Million Dollar Paranormal Challenge."[102] What he has done is put up a million dollar prize money for any one who is able to prove under moderately controlled circumstances, that he or she possesses supernatural abilities. Thus far, Randis' million dollars is still accumulating interest in his own account and he has seen many of the world's most renowned spiritists and psychics unable to or unwilling to accept his challenge. Others have failed miserably when they are bold enough to engage Randis' organization and try their hand at earning a quick million dollars. Of course, as with any monumental failure of someone who believes completely they are able to do something "special" and then find out they fell short of their own and others expectations, there is always an excuse as to why there was no documented success. That Randi negates the truth of the Scriptures and the validity of the Messiah Yeshua and His sacrifice is hopefully not a reason for some of us to abjectly resist investigating his claims and work.

With a bit of perspective on magic as it pertained to the ancients and understanding that, we can see that not only does the belief in something not make it real but that the Pharaoh's and the ruler of Tyre's belief in themselves as "*a God*" only opened themselves up to be judged by Yahweh. Therefore, we can move on in the passage. Ezekiel continues with his prophecy against the prince of Tyre and before you read the next verse ask yourself the question, "If there is a Satan, who is being referred to in this passage, and how can swords of war as administered by human beings do damage to a spiritual being called Satan?

> *Therefore thus saith the Lord GOD; Because thou hast set thine heart as the heart of God; Behold, therefore I will bring strangers upon thee, the terrible of the nations: and they shall draw their*

102 The JREF website offers this information and history for the Million Dollar Challenge. **1.1. What's the history of the Challenge?** The Challenge started in 1964 when James Randi put up $1,000 of his own money to the first person who could provide objective proof of the paranormal [1]. Since then, the prize money has grown to the current $1,000,000, and the rules regarding the Challenge have gotten more and more official and legal. It is vital that you understand this fact before you apply. The contract signifies your willingness to adhere to the Challenge rules. If you do not feel that you can abide by the rules, you should not apply, because NO rules will be circumvented on your behalf. So don't even ask. *Information taken from http://www.randi.org/research/faq.html#1.1*

swords against the beauty of thy wisdom, and they shall defile thy brightness. Ezekiel 28:6-7 KJV

Verses 6 and 7 are easy to unpack in light of the fact that there is no Satan. Many will stop at verse 6 which states, "thou hast set thine heart as the heart of a god." Stopping at this point with the conclusion that this verse is referring to "Satan" is shortsighted as verse 7 brings us right back to the theme and context of verse 6. After all, how could a cosmic "satan," be affected by the swords of humans as verse 7 speaks about? The prophet is warning the ruler of Tyre that other nations will draw their sword against the mighty Tyre and "defile its brightness." Tyre and her Prince will suffer at the hands of warring nations just as any other human entity would. This is to say Tyre will not look so good after God is done with it, as purposed through the attacks from other nations. Surely, we are able to see the use of a strong tongue in cheek term that emphasizes an attribute of the subject with seeming flattery. Even today, people use similar derogatory, tongue in cheek remarks if they are in a dialogue with a person who has come up with a smart idea and seems to be overtly proud of themselves. Can you hear a statement like this being said to such a person?

"Oh you certainly are the bright one in the gang aren't you?"

The statement acknowledging Tyre's brightness, and how the collective consciousness of Tyre is such that it is said to have set its heart as if it was God, is a statement that is meant to focus on how this great city thought so highly of itself. It is definitely not a statement referring to "Satan".

As discussed previously, this passage is in no way to be connected to the Isaiah 14 passage, except to equate it as an oracle against a King and Nation, such as is found in Isaiah 14. We are seeing the use of very common poetic language to express how Tyre has out shone the other nations in respect to its economic strength and pursuits for a long time. In comparison to many other nations in the world at the time of this utterance of Ezekiel, Tyre far surpassed others in power, wealth, and prosperity, according to common perception and according to the view of both the prince and king of Tyre. By all accounts, the brightness of Tyre was exceeding when compared to the less successful nations existing in the same world of Tyre.

The Pit is not the Hell of Popular Religious Thinking

Verses 8, 9 and 10 are not intended to depict an ultimate geographical kingdom in hell of a cosmic satanic being.

> *They shall bring thee down to the pit, and thou shalt die the deaths of them that are slain in the midst of the seas. Ezekiel 28:8 KJV*

Sure verse 8 seems to imply, by way of mentioning the "pit," that this may be about "Satan." However, "the pit" is not referring to a place known by us today as "Hell." The pit simply meant the place of the dead at the time of a person's completion of their life. The place of the dead was understood to be a place where nothing happened anymore for the dead person. The deceased simply did not exist any longer in a living form. The whole concept of Hell as a place of torment for the wicked dead was never a Hebraic idea. This concept developed over time and the long and short of it was that it is an ancient mythological belief, which, much like the belief in Satan, found its way into contemporary thought through millennia of cultural melting pots. Assimilation and syncretistic religious beliefs and practices were the vehicle by which "the pit" came to be thought of as a place of eternal torment for the wicked dead. To say the ruler of Tyre will go down to the "pit" is just another way of telling that the Prince of Tyre will die.

Most Ancient Rulers Were Believed to Be Gods

Verse 9 is asking the Prince of Tyre, "Is it going to work for you to tell the one killing you that you are a God?" The prophet answers quickly by stating once again that the Prince is a man, a human being,

> *Wilt thou yet say before him that slayeth thee, I am God? but thou shalt be a man, and no God, in the hand of him that slayeth thee. Ezekiel 28:9*

The prophet goes on in verse 10 to talk of the fact that this human ruler is going to die by the hand of other human strangers, by being specific in his wording found in verse 10. Wording that assigns a death that is intended for humans, to the subject of the prophecy.

> *Thou shalt die the deaths of the uncircumcised by the hand of strangers: for I have spoken it, saith the Lord GOD. Ezekiel 28:10 KJVA*

Declaring the death of this ruler in terminology applicable to a human is a certain indication that this subject is but a man. The question of verse 9 asking if this ruler is going to tell his slayer that he is a god is rhetorical and poignant. If the Prince, who thinks himself a god, is in fact a god then informing the one who is to slay him, of his status as a god, should stop the plans of the killer from taking the life of the prince. Obviously, the prophet who is making this statement on behalf of the only God is mocking to some degree, the drastically mistaken concept of the Prince that he is a "God." There is really no mistaking this information and thus seeing this reference to a "man" as a reference to the "Satan" of popular lore or medieval fear mongering is a grave error in interpreting the Scriptures.

Can a human being kill Satan? If he did exist then there would be no way that a human could take the life of the supposed Prince of Darkness. Therefore, as for the representation we have in the early verses of Ezekiel 28, it is shown that "Satan" is not even identified in this passage for this passage is about a human man who happens to be the ruler of a magnificent nation and privileged to a very unique position.

So far, there is no Satan in Ezekiel 28 and next we will look at the ideas of verses 11 to 19. We will be presented with a few other difficulties but I am confident that using the same, solid method of trying to understand Scripture, through the properly located historical, cultural, linguistic, social, and literary context we will find a better understanding of the message. We will be able to realize that the King of Tyre, whether this is the same as the Prince of Tyre or not, is just another human man, there was, and is no intent of the author as inspired by the Creator, to have the hearer impose a cosmic "satan" onto his words.

> *Moreover the word of the LORD came unto me, saying, Ezekiel 28:11 KJV*

As we engage together in a look at the next 8 verses in Ezekiel, I want to remind you that I am not dissecting the issue of whether the Prince of Tyre and the King of Tyre are intended to refer to the same person in Ezekiel's oracle. As stated previously there are differing opinions among scholars as to the identity being singular or plural. Some have tried to imply that the beginning verses about a "prince" in this chapter are indeed about a human but beyond verse 11 we are then being told specifically about "Satan". It is prudent to remind the reader that the Messiah, Yeshua, often called Jesus, was both a Prince and a King. He is the King of Kings and the Prince of Peace. With that understanding, it is possible to see the Prince and the King of Ezekiel 28 as one and the same. As for my purpose at this time, I only wish to help explain that whomever these verses are referring to, whether they are regarding two individuals or one, they can clearly be seen as not referring to a cosmic "satan". Just as the previous verses here and the passage in Isaiah 14 about the King of Babylon, are referring to a human ruler, so too is this passage in Ezekiel 28 speaking of a human ruler. It seems that an error is made by those who do not consider all the verses in the passage or the overall context. Taking one or two verses such as a verse that talks about someone being in Eden for instance and stating that the verses refer to a cosmic Satan, while neglecting to weigh the literary context of the verse is called "proof-texting". Proof texting is taking a verse or passage out of context in order to buoy up a theological position, and this practice is the product of weak integrity and refusal to administer honest weights and measures to scriptural interpretation. The practice of proof-texting can be used to prove anything in Scripture. Proof-texting has led to grave errors in doctrine and has become an acceptable form of teaching the masses, incorrectly I might add, how to be a follower of the Messiah. The practice of proof-texting is most notable in mainstream Christianity and can be heralded as the reason for the thousands of differing forms and streams of Christianity.

Christianity is little different from ancient Gnosticism. Gnosticism was so diverse in form and practice that the ends of the spectrum were very far apart. On one end, we could see rigid, ascetic type of Gnostic-Christian who would continually live in self-denial of all pleasure. The other end of the spectrum would consist of the completely self- gratifying and indulging Gnostic-Christian. This latter type of believer understood the soul to be separate from the physical body and therefore the physical man could do absolutely anything he or she pleased as it was their soul/spirit which would remain pure and thus be accepted by the Master. A Gnostic was one who believed they had an esoteric or secret knowledge of God and His Messiah and through that, would be able to enter the Kingdom of God. The Gnostics, much like present day Christianity, were very diverse in their views of God and how to serve and worship Him. They had many styles of worship that were not practiced by followers of the God of the Scriptures. This manner of practicing worship can only come through the error of proof-texting, to extract those ideas and doctrines which complement a person's or group's concept of how and when to worship the Creator. A search for the truth will consider all the Scripture, which is the full counsel of God. A search will not stop just because one finds the answer they are looking, particularly if there are still apparent contradictions in the Scripture and the New Testament. Using the full counsel of God is the only way to bring out a correct conclusion and doing so can be accepted as rightly dividing the word of God. Therefore, as we finish up with Ezekiel's statements to the ruler of Tyre we will be careful not to extract only those phrases that might prove our point and we will continue to use Scripture to define Scripture as well as assessing history, context, and language appropriately.

Wasn't Satan the Most Beautiful Angel at One Time?

Considering the foregoing thoughts on proof-texting, let us begin to assess the remaining verses in this passage in a way that holds to the literary form, style, and context of the writer. We resume now, by looking at verse 12 of Ezekiel 28.

> *Ezekiel 28:12 KJV*
> *Son of man, take up a lamentation upon the king of Tyrus, and say unto him, Thus saith the Lord GOD; Thou sealest up the sum, full of wisdom, and perfect in beauty.*

We have already spoken of the idea of the wisdom of the ruler of Tyre. The wisdom reference is connected with the ability to be a huge economic power generating wealth and riches. "Full of wisdom," does not have to refer to a Satan who possesses qualities of a supernatural genius. We see "perfect in beauty" as something other than referring to a supernatural being called "Satan", who so many say was the most beautiful of all the angels that Yahweh had created. The phrase "perfect in beauty" and similar phrases can be seen elsewhere in Scripture. They are a metaphor for an exalted status or profound prosperity and position among other comparable physical entities such as kingdoms and lands.

In Lamentations 2:15 the term "perfection of beauty" is a statement of derision and mocking made in reference to the city of Jerusalem by her enemies after the city had been the recipient of some measure of destruction that was due to a judgment by Yahweh for her wicked and sinful ways.

> *All that pass by clap their hands at thee; they hiss and wag their head at the daughter of Jerusalem, saying, Is this the city that men call The perfection of beauty, The joy of the whole earth? Lamentations 2:15*

Zion is called the "perfection of beauty" in Psalms 50:2. The nation of Israel who was rescued by Yahweh is said to have relied on her "perfect beauty" which came from Yahweh. Found in Ezekiel 16, Yahweh is accusing His chosen nation, Israel of playing the harlot. Israel, once given such favors and prosperity by the Creator, began to forget to whom credit for the favor and prosperity was due. It was solely due to Yahweh's kindness and love for her that she had any favor at all. The tale is quite sad but Yahweh Himself speaks of the "perfect beauty," which He had given Israel. The phrase, "perfect beauty," as used by Ezekiel is intending to state a very prosperous and favored status of a person or nation. The phrase refers to a person or nation who would be looked upon by others and envied for its uniquely favored position. We see the phrase used again in Ezekiel 27 just as the lamentation against Tyre begins. The prophet uses the phrase twice in the early part of his prophecy against Tyre and is giving the hearer information regarding the unparalleled status of the city of Tyre. At the beginning of the lamentation, Tyre is imaged as a beautiful ship. "Perfect in beauty" is another manner of stating the similar concept about the King being in Eden, the garden of God. This place was so pristine and ideal in the sense that it, the Tyrian Empire, was admired by all who gazed upon it. Due to the magnificence of the city it was referred to as "perfect in beauty" and had so many amazing attributes, it was called the "garden of God."

Thy borders[1366] are in the midst[3820] of the seas,[3220] thy builders[1129] have perfected[3634] thy beauty.[3308] Ezekiel 27:4 KJV+

The men[1121] of Arvad[719] with thine army[2428] were upon[5921] thy walls[2346] round about,[5439] and the Gammadims[1575] were[1961] in thy towers:[4026] they hanged[8518] their shields[7982] upon[5921] thy walls[2346] round about;[5439] they[1992] have made thy beauty perfect.[3634, 3308] Ezekiel 27:11 KJV+

"Perfect in beauty" as used in Ezekiel and elsewhere is simply more poetic language, intended to describe the exquisite appearance and prosperous position of this great ancient city.

Thy borders are in the midst of the seas, thy builders have perfected thy beauty. Ezekiel 27:4

The men of Arvad with thine army were upon thy walls round about, and the Gammadims were in thy towers: they hanged their shields upon thy walls round about; they have made thy beauty perfect. Ezekiel 27:11

Tyre was a city that was built on an island rock and was viewed by the surrounding nations and peoples as the pinnacle of all cities. Keil and Delitzsch say this about the city;

Eze 27:1-11 -

The lamentation commences with a picture of the glory of the city of Tyre, its situation, its architectural beauty, its military strength and defences (Eze_27:3-11), and its wide-spread commercial relations (Eze_27:12-25); and then passes into mournful lamentation over the ruin of all this glory (Eze_27:26-36).[103]

Why was the King Said to Be in Eden?

Moving on to verse 13, we arrive at the challenging statement of this ruler being said to have spent time in Eden. Looking carefully at the information we can determine that once again, these words do not apply to a mythological Satan.

> *Thou hast been in Eden the garden of God; every precious stone was thy covering, the sardius, topaz, and the diamond, the beryl, the onyx, and the jasper, the sapphire, the emerald, and the carbuncle, and gold: the workmanship of thy tabrets and of thy pipes was prepared in thee in the day that thou wast created. Ezekiel 28:13 KJV*

A little historical context regarding the passage shows how statements made in chapter 28, which are interpreted by some as to be referring to "Satan," are made elsewhere. The statements that are made elsewhere clearly refer to nations that do not have any supernatural elements contained in their character but the undertones imply metaphorical, mythological attributes.

It was a practice of ancient kings in this region to also be considered to be priests. You might recall the priests of Yahweh were given a breastplate with 12 precious stones representing the 12 tribes of Israel. Keil and Delitzsch provide this information on costly jewels that are referenced in verse 13;

> *Costly jewels were his coverings, that is to say, they formed the ornaments of his attire. This feature in the pictorial description is taken from the splendour with which Oriental rulers are accustomed to appear, namely, in robes covered with precious stones, pearls, and gold.* [104]

Adornment with extravagant jewelry was not an unheard of practice for the priest/king of other nations and the fact that nine stones are spoken of here where as 12 are spoken of in the Septuagint, indicates the priestly imagery. The 12 stones spoken of in the Septuagint are identical with the

103 Keil & Delitzsch Commentary on the Old Testament
Johann (C.F.) Keil (1807-1888) & Franz Delitzsch (1813-1890)

104 (Keil & Delitzsch Commentary on the Old Testament; Johann (C.F.) Keil (1807-1888) & Franz Delitzsch (1813-1890)

stones of the High Priests robe from Exodus 28. A look at the first statement in this passage speaking of the King being in Eden could easily be seen to speak of Satan. Particularly if one ascribes to the erroneous belief that Satan was the serpent in the garden with Adam and Eve. The only teaching that many have been taught in their life, is that the "serpent" from Genesis chapter 3 in the Garden of Eden story is in fact "Satan" or a literal snake inhabited by "Satan." Once again, if we are diligent, we are able to see other references to Eden in Scripture, which are undoubtedly poetic references about the premium qualities of a geographic location. There are a number of times in Scripture and out of Scripture that the poetic imagery and tone is undeniable. If one takes the time to read through the entire book of lamentations and particularly the lamentation against Egypt, in chapter 31 they will see "Eden" is used as a poetic reference. For the moment though, take a look at the references in the following verses which speak of a geographic location as if it is as lush and fertile as Eden is:

> *And they shall say, This land that was desolate is become like* ***the garden of Eden****; and the waste and desolate and ruined cities are become fenced, and are inhabited. Ezekiel 36:35 KJVR*

> *For the LORD shall comfort Zion: he will comfort all her waste places; and he* ***will make her wilderness like Eden****, and her desert like the garden of the LORD; joy and gladness shall be found therein, thanksgiving, and the voice of melody. Isaiah 51:3 KJV*

> *A fire devoureth before them; and behind them a flame burneth: the land is* ***as the garden*** *of Eden before them, and behind them a desolate wilderness; yea, and nothing shall escape them. Joel 2:3 KJV*

Clearly, the reference to Eden is not intended to place someone back in the garden with Adam and Eve but it is used to say how beautiful an environment is, was, or will be. The statements found in Ezekiel 28, which are thought to refer to a fallen Satan, are not isolated occurrences of such implicative statements. There are other statements made by the prophet that indicate the magnificence of a ruler's status. The writer does so by relating the lofty history of the ruler to the metaphorical position of being in Eden at one time. Any occurrence where this happens and the reader considers the subject of the statement to be the fallen Satan is not being consistent in interpreting Scripture. This reference in Ezekiel to the King being in Eden simply means that he had things really good for a while, pretty close to a perfect situation if you will.

Ezekiel 31 Also tells of a Pharaoh Being in Eden, Does that Mean the Pharaoh is Satan?

In Ezekiel 31 verses 7 to 9, we are given a picture of how powerful and exalted the Pharaoh of Egypt was. Upon looking at these verses, one could conclude either of two things. One, that the Pharaoh was in the Garden of Eden just as the King of Tyre supposedly was if the belief that Ezekiel 28 is about Satan is ascribed to; or two, the Pharaoh had a far-reaching dynasty, having many provinces and cities under his rule. The Pharaoh's political might is referred to in the statement about his branches and is the cause for the envy by all the other "*trees in the garden of God*." If we use the same literal understanding commonly used for the King of Tyre/Satan, the fact that the verse states the trees of Eden envied the Pharaoh, would mean that Pharaoh was also in Eden. As the verse below makes known, Pharaoh was among the trees of Eden in some sense of the meaning.

> *To whom art thou thus like in glory and in greatness among the trees of Eden? Ezekiel 31:18*

However, it is clearly indicated in the form, style, and context of these lamentations that the other trees in Eden the garden of God that envied Pharaoh, must be understood as other competing and less powerful nations and or rulers. Unless we allow Scripture to interpret Scripture we fail to rightly divide the word by imposing some manner of mystical meaning on the King of Tyre prophecy. We then add error to error by not imposing that same meaning on the lamentation against Pharaoh in chapter 31. This is such an important connection that I decided to place the lamentation to Egypt and Pharaoh in front of you to help you better see just how telling this connection is. Seeing how the Pharaoh's greatness is mentioned and the cedars in the garden are shown to be in close proximity to the Pharaoh, thus placing him in the Garden of Eden also, should help us to be fair in assessing whether or not Ezekiel 28 is about the supposed cosmic Satan.

If you aren't inclined to read all 18 verses at this time, then take a look at verses 7, 8, 9 and then at verse 18. Doing so should help you to see the point I am making. The point is, that the terminology thought to be speaking of Satan elsewhere, is only poetic language applied to the subject. The poetics are employed in order to express just how overwhelming the magnitude of the subject's rule was.

Ezekiel 31:2-18 KJV

2 *Son of man, speak unto Pharaoh king of Egypt, and to his multitude; Whom art thou like in thy greatness?*

3 *Behold, the Assyrian was a cedar in Lebanon with fair branches, and with a shadowing shroud, and of an high stature; and his top was among the thick boughs.*

4 *The waters made him great, the deep set him up on high with her rivers running round about his plants, and sent out her little rivers unto all the trees of the field.*

5 *Therefore his height was exalted above all the trees of the field, and his boughs were multiplied, and his branches became long because of the multitude of waters, when he shot forth.*

6 *All the fowls of heaven made their nests in his boughs, and under his branches did all the beasts of the field bring forth their young, and under his shadow dwelt all great nations.*

7 *Thus was he fair in his greatness, in the length of his branches: for his root was by great waters.*

8 *The cedars in the garden of God could not hide him: the fir trees were not like his boughs, and the chesnut trees were not like his branches; nor any tree in the garden of God was like unto him in his beauty.*

9 *I have made him fair by the multitude of his branches:* ***so that all the trees of Eden, that were in the garden of God, envied him.***

10 *Therefore thus saith the Lord GOD; Because thou hast lifted up thyself in height, and he hath shot up his top among the thick boughs, and his heart is lifted up in his height;*

11 *I have therefore delivered him into the hand of the mighty one of the heathen; he shall surely deal with him: I have driven him out for his wickedness.*

12 *And strangers, the terrible of the nations, have cut him off, and have left him: upon the mountains and in all the valleys his branches are fallen, and his boughs are broken by all the rivers of the land; and all the people of the earth are gone down from his shadow, and have left him.*

13 *Upon his ruin shall all the fowls of the heaven remain, and all the beasts of the field shall be upon his branches:*

14 *To the end that none of all the trees by the waters exalt themselves for their height, neither shoot up their top among the thick boughs, neither their trees stand up in their height, all that drink water: for they are all delivered unto death, to the nether parts of the earth, in the midst of the children of men, with them that go down to the pit.*

15 *Thus saith the Lord GOD; In the day when he went down to the grave I caused a mourning: I covered the deep for him, and I restrained the floods thereof, and the great waters were stayed: and I caused Lebanon to mourn for him, and all the trees of the field fainted for him.*
16 *I made the nations to shake at the sound of his fall, when I cast him down to hell with them that descend into the pit: and all the trees of Eden, the choice and best of Lebanon, all that drink water, shall be comforted in the nether parts of the earth.*
17 *They also went down into hell with him unto them that be slain with the sword; and they that were his arm, that dwelt under his shadow in the midst of the heathen.*
18 *To whom art thou thus like in glory and in greatness among the trees of Eden?* ***yet shalt thou be brought down with the trees of Eden unto the nether parts of the earth:*** *thou shalt lie in the midst of the uncircumcised with them that be slain by the sword. This is Pharaoh and all his multitude, saith the Lord GOD.*

The Day of His Creation

There is yet another statement made in verse 13 of chapter 28 that requires some explanation. Verse 13 speaks of the "*day of his creation*".

> *Thou hast been in Eden the garden of God; every precious stone was thy covering, the sardius, topaz, and the diamond, the beryl, the onyx, and the jasper, the sapphire, the emerald, and the carbuncle, and gold: the workmanship of thy tabrets and of thy pipes was prepared in thee in the day that thou wast created. Ezekiel 28:13*

The notable statement made in the above verse is the musical reference about "*the workmanship of thy tabrets and pipes*". This very misunderstood description is frequently seen as referring to Satan being the leader of worship in the heavens prior to his alleged fall. However, this is not so and the writer of Ezekiel was again using expressions which would have identified to the original hearers who this prophecy was against.

It was the custom of many kings in the orient to be coronated with the accompaniment of splendid music and much celebration. The hearer of Ezekiel's words would by no means think he believed the subject of his lamentation is a celestial, anthropomorphic being, who is a talented musician.

An important question to ask here is; how would the original hearers of these statements have understood Ezekiel's words? The hearers would know of the manner in which Kings were crowned and would call to mind how grand the musical display was during this ancient ceremony. The phrase "the day he was created", is referring to the day this King was coronated. The day that Yahweh appointed him to become the ruler of this particular nation is referred to as *the day of his creation.*

It seems highly unusual that Yahweh would have bestowed such honor through a great cosmic concert, upon an angelic being that was only designed to serve Yahweh and would ultimately rebel against the Creator. How could this term indicate a Satanic being who received a majestic introduction into his cosmic existence? It seems unlikely that God would have held such a glorious inauguration for a mere angel that was designed to be a loyal servant of the Creator. We are being told of the magnificent day of the coronation of the human King of Tyre, which took place with splendid musical accompaniment. The only parallel I can see in the Torah or gospels is at the announcement of the birth of Yeshua the Messiah. We are told of quite the musical announcement by the angels. The announcement of Yeshua the King being born in Bethlehem (see Luke 2:13-14 below[105]) seems to connect to how the King of Tyre would have been announced in the day that he was created, which means the day he was made king. Kings were known to be "created" by means of a grand musical ceremony and celebration. The understanding that pomp and ceremony occurred in the day a king was created is an understanding that is heard from many commentators. The Keil and Delitzsch commentary puts it well:

> The service (תכאלמ, performance, as in Gen_39:11, etc.) of the women is the leading of the circular dances by the odalisks who beat the timbrels: "the harem-pomp of Oriental kings." This was made ready for the king on the day of his creation, i.e., not his birthday, but the day on which he became king, or commenced his reign, when the harem of his predecessor came into his possession with all its accompaniments. Ezekiel calls this the day of his creation, with special reference to the fact that it was God who appointed him king, and with an allusion to the parallel,

105 And suddenly there was with the angel a multitude of the heavenly host praising God, and saying, Glory to God in the highest, and on earth peace, good will toward men. Luke 2:13-14

underlying the whole description, between the position of the prince of Tyre and that of Adam in Paradise[106]

Ezekiel is not writing of the day Satan was created in this passage, rather he was telling of the magnificent beginnings of a powerful and extraordinary King's reign.

The Anointed Cherub.

As we study this passage considering its historical, linguistic, and cultural position in literature, we come to the point where there is a reference to an anointed cherub on the mountain of God walking amongst the stones of fire. In verse 14 of this passage many people conclude that we are being shown how special and close to the Holy One, Satan was, prior to his fall.

> *Thou art the anointed cherub that covereth; and I have set thee so: thou wast upon the holy mountain of God; thou hast walked up and down in the midst of the stones of fire. Thou wast perfect in thy ways from the day that thou wast created, till iniquity was found in thee. Ezekiel 28:14-15 KJV*

If certain verses in Chapter 28 are referring to Satan then Ezekiel 31 is also referring to Satan and the Pharaoh of Egypt was also in the Garden of God, Eden. After all, we are told that no tree in the Garden of God was as beautiful as the Pharaoh. These verses speak very similar metaphor about Pharaoh as was spoken about the King and Prince of Tyre. They laud the Pharaoh's greatness as being beyond compare and show how he was envied by others that were with him in Eden.

> *Son of man, speak unto Pharaoh king of Egypt, and to his multitude; Whom art thou like in thy greatness? Ezekiel 31:2 KJV*

> *The cedars in the garden of God could not hide him: the fir trees were not like his boughs, and the chesnut trees were not like his branches; nor any tree in the garden of God was like unto him in his beauty. I have made him fair by the multitude of his branches: so that all the trees of Eden, that were in the garden of God, envied him. Ezekiel 31:8-9 KJV*

---

106 Keil & Delitzsch Commentary on the Old Testament
Johann (C.F.) Keil (1807-1888) & Franz Delitzsch (1813-1890)

It might be helpful for our present discussion, and to make note of for future dialogue in this book, some understanding of the word "Eden" that is found in the International Standard Bible Encyclopedia (ISBE). The entry in the ISBE on Eden informs us that the word "Eden" came into use as a metaphor for a paradisiacal environment and does not always mean entirely the Garden environment of Adam and Eve;

> Moreover, the climate was such that clothing was not needed for warmth. It is not surprising, therefore, that the plural of the word has the meaning "delights," and that Eden has been supposed to mean the land of delights, and that the word became a synonym for Paradise.[107]

It seems to be a regular occurrence by Christian interpreters to suggest that because Ezekiel 28 talks about its subject being in Eden that the subject it is talking about must be Satan. However, consistency of interpretation is cast to the wind when interpreting Ezekiel 31. There is not one Christian commentator that I have come across who will say, when reading the lamentation against Egypt and the Pharaoh; "*Oh Pharaoh must have been in Eden too because the verse says so.*" No one seems to see the statement by the prophet that Pharaoh was "*great among the trees of Eden*" as a statement proclaiming that Pharaoh was in Eden. Yet certain people automatically believe that the similar statement made to the King of Tyre in Ezekiel 28 is telling about Satan in the Garden of Eden. The reference to Pharaoh, being in the Garden of Eden must be reconsidered in accord with an ancient understanding of the phrase to reveal that the discussion is about a human. So too must the reference to the king of Tyre being in Eden be recognized to be speaking of a human.

I have mentioned it briefly already but we will look further at another place where chapter 28 informs us that it is discussing a human and not Satan. This is seen when the prophet states in verse 10 that the subject will die the death of the uncircumcised. By mentioning dieing as the uncircumcised, we see an explicit reference to a human attribute. After all, common belief about the Satan of Christianity is that he will be tortured forever after Christ returns and therefore he is not seen as dieing. For one to die they must be human in this instance.

> *Thou shalt die the deaths of the uncircumcised by the hand of strangers: for I have spoken it, saith the Lord GOD. Ezekiel 28:10 KJV*

107 International Standard Bible Encyclopedia; under the entry "Tyre"

Being called uncircumcised is figurative language to indicate one's disdain toward another man or group of men. Erdmann's New Bible Commentary Revised, tells us the Phoenicians practiced circumcision. Therefore, to be thought of as residing with the uncircumcised when dead was shameful, involving a dishonorable position in the realm of the dead, called *Sheol* in Hebrew.

It has been spoken of before in this book and I restate it again here that Sheol is a term that simply refers to the grave. The following bible commentary makes note of some other fascinating information that helps in understanding Ezekiel's thoughts of the King of Tyre, as he paints the picture of a once exalted ruler soon to be rendered impotent. The writers of the commentary say:

> Ezekiel seems to have adopted for his threnody a popular story, presumably current in Tyre as well as elsewhere, of a primal being who dwelt in the garden of God in splendour and purity but was subsequently driven out through pride; so shall the King of Tyre shortly fall from his glory. It looks like a highly mythological version of the story in Gn.3, but the prophet does not hesitate to use it since it was well known and admirably suited to his purpose[108]

The above bible commentary acknowledges the prophet's use of a readily recognizable tale from mythology as a means to relay his message to the hearers. A critical look thus far, at what has been poetically and metaphorically spoken about the Prince of Tyre and the King of Tyre has shown that the statements of this lamentation are not intended to refer to anything other than human rulers. Being aware of that fact, we cannot honestly take the next thought of Ezekiel out of its context and claim he is now referring to a cosmic fallen being who was once the most beautiful, musical, favorite angel of God. Is there another way to understand Ezekiel's statement about someone *walking in the midst of stones of fire*? How would terms such as "anointed cherub", and "stones of fire" have been understood by the hearers?

The "*anointed cherub that covereth*" is simply referring to the King as one who was placed in a position of guiding and protecting the people in his kingdom by God. In a poetic sense the King of Tyre was to be "covering", that is protecting, those who he had the rule over. He was called "anointed" because he was placed in the position by Yahweh. Any ruler who abuses his position and power, and acts in ways not pleasing to the Creator will and

108 **The New Bible Commentary** Revised: D Guthrei, J.A. Motyer, A.M. Stibbs, D.J Wiseman, Erdmann's Publishing Co.
1970 Intervarsity Press

must answer to the Creator. We are given here a picture of a ruler who was placed there by God and now is recklessly indulging himself and subsequently his kingdom, in prideful behavior that comes before a fall. The fact of the King being placed to protect those under his rulership, is seen a little more clearly in the wording used by the Douay-Rheims 1899 translation of the Bible which speaks of the ruler protecting;

> *Thou a cherub stretched out, and protecting, and I set thee in the holy mountain of God, thou hast walked in the midst of the stones of fire. Ezekiel 28:14 DRB*

This 1899 Douay-Rheims version uses language that is more intelligible for our present age by stating the King's role of being a stretched out cherub is that of "protecting". The words that come next clearly state that it was Yahweh who placed the King of Tyre in his position. God says, *"I have set you so"*. Sadly, the King of Tyre is only one of many kings and rulers who very quickly forgot the fact that Yahweh is the one who raises kings to their office. The reference we have seen in Ezekiel 31 to the trees of Eden being envious of Pharaoh is a reference to all the other kings who were also appointed to their positions by Yahweh. It is when a ruler begins to believe in himself and become over confident in his own ability and position that Yahweh chooses to prove how insignificant the man is. God displays to the ruler and the ruler's adoring nation that virtually worships their ruler, that their King is not a God but just a man. He does so using kings, kingdoms, and people to humble a pride filled nation and ruler. Therefore, when they fall into the downward spiral of the sin of pride, Yahweh is the one who brings their fall to pass. It is interesting though to recognize that the merciful Creator always gives warning to the one He is soon going to bring down to the pit and then He uses another heathen nation to administer His judgment by bringing the sword against the offending nation. If you have a difficult time understanding how "God" could do this then you are not alone. It seems as if we have no control over what happens to us when Yahweh sends a warring nation against one that is ready to be judged. I too wished I comprehended this practice of the Mighty One at a deeper level, however for the present I am comfortable looking at and accepting the "I will" statements of Yahweh in the Scriptures.

What are the "I will statements"? These statements are those which start out with Yahweh speaking through a prophet to tell a people or nation that if they don't straighten up and start honoring Him with their heart and actions, then He says "I will bring destruction on you" or "I will send calamity" or I will drive you out" or "I will scatter you." Here is but a few examples from the Scriptures.

> *Thus saith the LORD, Behold,* ***I will bring evil*** *upon this place, and upon the inhabitants thereof, even all the curses that are written in the book which they have read before the king of Judah: 2 Chronicles 34:24 KJV*

> And the LORD said, **I will destroy** man whom I have created from the face of the earth; ... Genesis 6:7 KJV

> For I will pass through the land of Egypt this night, and will smite all the firstborn in the land of Egypt, both man and beast; and against all the gods of Egypt **I will execute judgment**: I am the LORD. Exodus 12:12 KJV

> And I **will set my face against you**, and ye shall be slain before your enemies: ... Leviticus 26:17 KJV

> Then my anger shall be kindled against them in that day, and I will forsake them, and I **will hide my face from them**, and they shall be devoured, and many evils and troubles shall befall them; ... Deuteronomy 31:17 KJV

> Behold, **I will stir up the Medes against them**, ... Isaiah 13:17 KJV

The examples are multitudinous in the Scriptures and you may find it interesting to see just how many times it is God whom is the one bringing the evil upon the offending group.

Ezekiel 28 verses 14 and 15 tell about the prestigious position that was bestowed upon the King of Tyre. This King was coronated with brilliant pomp and ceremony and was anointed by the Creator to rule in an equitable manner, protecting the people and ultimately honoring the Creator who bestowed the responsibility upon him. However, this pride filled King honored himself and took on the title of "God"; therefore, Yahweh set out to cause his fall.

Who is an Anointed one?

It is understood from Scripture that any ruler who is lifted to a position of being the Ruler, is placed there by Yahweh and is therefore known as the anointed one. All the Kings of Israel were called *Mashiach* in Hebrew, that is to say "anointed" In English. In fact, the Kings of Israel were subject to a ceremony where they had oil poured on them at which time they were referred to as being anointed. That means they were chosen by the King of the Universe to rule according to His will. Once chosen and appointed any ruler of any nation has the choice to rule according to Yahweh's ways or to essentially make themselves their own god and rule according to their own ways. This is what the anointed cherub, the King of Tyre was guilty of and why he was going to be removed, brought down to the pit. It was the God of the Universe who anointed the King and set him in his position as protector but why might he be said to be on "the mountain of God? Could this mean that he was Satan and walked in Heaven with God at one time before his fall?

> *Thou art the anointed cherub that covereth; and I have set thee so: thou wast upon the holy mountain of God; thou hast walked up and down in the midst of the stones of fire. Ezekiel 28:14*

That this ruler was said to be *on the Mountain of God*, was simply an allusion to the mythology about the geography that surrounded the Tyrian location. This location, because of it being up on rock was thought by mythologians to be a mountain of the Gods. Many Ancient Near Eastern cultures had a sacred mountain where it was thought the divine council of the culture would convene and make decisions. If this King of Tyre, who thought himself to be a god, had been in the divine council and literally walking on the mountain of God in heaven as was thought to be the case according to the mythology of the day, then surely he would have the connections to be able to avert his destruction.

Alas, averting his destruction would not be possible and his supposed position as one who partakes in meetings of divine council was nothing more than a meaningless farce. A farce of epic proportions as it led to the demise of the once great King of Tyre. The Creator had anointed this king for a purpose and now because of his pride and a heart that thought he was a god, he lost his authority and his kingdom. After all, Tyre was such a renowned city throughout many biblical periods but it continued to abuse the prestige and favor afforded it by Yahweh. The ancient interpretive commentary on the Scriptures known as the Targum states that the phrase "*thou art anointed for a kingdom*", has to do with royalty and a regal position.

Tyre and its rulers are flatly told of their demise and the profound and intense mythopoetic imagery and language used was full of meaning which in all probability was completely understandable to the recipients of the lamentation at the time. The language and style used by the prophet is common in ancient writings that describe powerful ancient regions. The *Nelsons New Illustrated Bible Dictionary* expresses the concept of how this prosperous and pompous city received numerous prophecies against her. Tyre had been in good relations with Israel during the reigns of David and Solomon, but eventually became a willing and active participant in human trafficking through the purchase and sale of Israelites as slaves. Through understanding the nature of this city, we are better equipped to understand the prophet's message to this region and her human rulers.

> ***Tyre in Prophecy.*** Several prophets of the Old Testament prophesied against Tyre. They condemned the Tyrians for delivering Israelites to the Edomites (Amos 1:9) and for selling them as slaves to the Greeks (Joel 3:5–6). Jeremiah prophesied Tyre's defeat (Jer. 27:1–11). But the classic prophecy against Tyre was given by Ezekiel.
>
> Ezekiel prophesied the destruction of Tyre (Ezek. 26:3–21). The first stage of this prophecy came true when Nebuchadnezzar, king of Babylon, besieged the mainland city of Tyre for 13 years (585–572 B.C.) and apparently destroyed it. However, Nebuchadnezzar had no navy; so he could not flatten the island city. But losing the mainland city was devastating to Tyre. This destroyed Tyre's influence in the world and reduced her commercial activities severely.
>
> The second stage of Ezekiel's prophecy was fulfilled in 332 B.C., when Alexander the Great besieged the island city of Tyre for seven months. He finally captured it when he built a causeway from the mainland to the island. Hauling cedars from the mountains of Lebanon, he drove them as piles into the floor of the sea between the mainland and the island. Then he used the debris and timber of the ruined mainland city as solid material for the causeway. Hence, the remarkable prophecy of Ezekiel was completely fulfilled.[109]

As mentioned, the "anointed cherub" is no more than a reference to the fact that a human King was placed in his position by Yahweh and he was to perform the act of protecting those who were left under his rule.

> *Thou art the anointed cherub that covereth; and I have set thee so: thou wast upon the holy mountain of God; thou hast walked*

---

109 Ronald F. Youngblood, general editor; F.F. Bruce and R.K. Harrison, consulting editors, *Nelson's new illustrated Bible dictionary: An authoritative one-volume reference work on the Bible with full color illustrations [computer file], electronic edition of the revised edition of Nelson's illustrated Bible dictionary, Logos Library System*, (Nashville: Thomas Nelson) 1997, c1995.

> *up and down in the midst of the stones of fire. Ezekiel 28:14 KJV*

This protection would have indeed been extended to the subjects of his kingdom according to their nationality but would also have been expected to be extended to the Israelites. Through the abuse of international relations and economic power this kingdom had chosen to pursue its own desires and selling, rather than protecting Israelites, which was in her view, a means of garnering yet more wealth and power.

The Holy Mountain of God is Not Speaking of A Place in Heaven

We need not be confused into thinking the Holy Mountain of God is either in heaven or in Eden and that Satan once walked upon it before he fell from heaven. The "*holy mountain of God*" is explained well by the Keil and Delitzsch commentary, which addresses the mythology behind such a statement very adequately.

> The idea of a holy mountain of God, as being the seat of the king of Tyre, was founded partly upon the natural situation of Tyre itself, built as it was upon one or two rocky islands of the Mediterranean, and partly upon the heathen notion of the sacredness of this island as the seat of the Deity, to which the Tyrians attributed the grandeur of their state.[110]

In an internet article, which tells of the moon-god religions of the ancients, we are given some valuable historical information to enlighten us as to the amazingly intricate and ritualistic ceremony of the anointing of the King of Tyre. The impressive ritual was fully designed and intended to install the king as a God and to show that the God was the King. Verse 15 of Ezekiel 28 is in view here when Ezekiel mentions the day this King was "created".

> *Thou wast perfect in thy ways from the day that thou wast created, till iniquity was found in thee. Ezekiel 28:15 KJV*

The *ancientdays .net*, excerpt below tells of the grand ritual where a King was created.

110 Keil & Delitzsch Commentary on the Old Testament
Johann (C.F.) Keil (1807-1888) & Franz Delitzsch (1813-1890)

> We have an example of religious ritual connected with the "divine kingship" system much closer to Jericho than Ugarit is. In Tyre, at a little later time (ca. 1000 BC but also probably before), the king went through the dramatic Enthronement Ritual on New Year's Day each year. The ritual lasted probably eight days. New Year's Day was the greatest day of the year. In the Tyrian Enthronement Ritual on that day, the king of Tyre acted out the resurrection of the god Melcart by going with his retinue of priests and officials to a place east of the city. Then at sunrise, in the first moments of the New Year, he came with majestic procession, attended by hosts of worshippers, through the eastern portal of the temple and ascended the sacred throne. "In all this the king played the role of the god. The king was the god and the god was the king. And having played this role once . . . the king remained ever thereafter a divine being, a god, a god in human form, 'Epiphanes'" (J. Morgenstern, *Journal of Biblical Literature* LXXX: 69. See also J. M. in *Vetus Testamentum* 10:152-157)[111]

I could continue to share with you still more history and commentary which affirms the fact that all the terms in chapter 28 of Ezekiel, about the Prince or the King of Tyre, are not intended to refer to a cosmic Satan. The entire body of material delivered as a prophetic message by Ezekiel is intended to apply common imagery of mythological, non-existent entities to the King and Prince. The references to ancient biblical images is a method of enhancing the imagery and performs the dual function of punctuating the point that the ruler being prophesied against is not "all that". Verse 15 is saying of the King that he was on the right path at the time Yahweh placed him as King of Tyre. Then, just as Adam was doing alright in his magnificent beginning as the first man and ruler of all animals and keeper of Eden only to choose iniquity, so too this King had iniquity enter him which results in his destruction.

> *Thou wast perfect in thy ways from the day that thou wast created, till iniquity was found in thee. Ezekiel 28:15 KJV*

The next verse tells us again, like the Prince of Tyre spoken of earlier, that it was because of economic wealth that this iniquity was found in him.

> *By the multitude of thy merchandise they have filled the midst of thee with violence, and thou hast sinned: therefore I will cast thee as profane out of the mountain of God: and I will destroy thee, O covering cherub, from the midst of the stones of fire. Thine heart was lifted up because of thy beauty, thou hast corrupted*

111 Excerpted from internet web page http://www.ancientdays.net/mooncity.htm

> *thy wisdom by reason of thy brightness: I will cast thee to the ground, I will lay thee before kings, that they may behold thee. Ezekiel 28:16-17 KJV*

The iniquity in question is not to be thought of as that of a jealous heart in a cosmic Satan being. The iniquity is because the king and his kingdom had become untouchable and through the pride of his greatness, violence was in his midst, sin was the result. Now the king is rejected as king over the area of Tyre which was thought of as a mountain where the gods met to confer. This king is no longer worthy to maintain his position as the chosen, anointed, protector of this kingdom so out he goes from the stones of fire which as John Gill informs us by quoting an ancient rabbi named Kimchi, happen to be the followers of God;

> Kimchi paraphrases it,
>
> "from the midst of the saints who are the Israelites, comparable to stones of fire;"

We Tend to Believe What We are First Taught

It is easy to understand the phrase, "I will cast thee . . . out." Everyone knows this phrase does not mean God will grab this king by the literal scruff of his neck as one would do to an obstinate cat walking across the kitchen counter and fling him out the back door. So why do we have such great difficulty in seeing the other phrases surrounding the cast out phrase as speaking idiomatically and poetically? I think the answer is simple, we have been told what to think the meaning of Ezekiel's statement is. In addition, anyone who tries to undo a concept that was first taught to a student will tell you, the very fact that this concept was taught first, makes the removal of said erroneous concept as difficult as extracting a sliver that has migrated beneath the skin and been closed in. The wrong concept is deeply embedded in the substructure of their belief system and it doesn't seem to matter whether or not that first taught concept was correct or incorrect. It takes a lot of intentional hard work and some serious jack hammering.

It is so difficult to make the shift from error to truth when a person has an entrenched belief. This is due to the simple fact that we generally believe what we have been taught first. That is why hearing some of what I am sharing doesn't sit right with "your spirit". That is why some of what I am sharing may cause you to feel a little confused. That is why I am asking that you take what

I am sharing and prove it to yourself whether it is right or wrong. Simply abandoning a pursuit of truth because it doesn't "witness" with you as many might say, is probably another way of saying, "Hey, I'm comfortable in the beliefs I have already accepted, I don't want to do the work to see if my reality was wrong…must resist change…change is bad."

Let me just say, for the one who decides to work to uncover the gold nugget or excavate the hidden treasure they will find that if only in themselves, they have done a good thing and didn't let feeling become their master when truth and error hangs in the balance. As for the stones of fire at the end of verse 16, it is not clear exactly what they are but it is clear what they are not. One suggestion by Kimchi, as given us by John Gill, is that the stones of fire that the King was walking amongst are the children of Israel who were in his kingdom.

> *and I will destroy thee, O covering cherub, from the midst of the stones of fire.*

We see the term appears in only verses 14 and 16. It has, at no time been attached to a place or representation of a satanic dwelling. Eden did not have any type of a stone of fire as far as can be perceived by scholars and there is no indicator that heaven, where "Satan" was supposedly dwelling prior to his alleged casting down to earth, had stones of fire for "Satan" to walk up and down upon. So what could the stones of fire be? It may be that due to the connection of the phrase to the mountain and the mention of this king walking up and down in the midst of these is referring to a mythological concept of approaching a mount of divine council. Recall the burning mountain Moses encountered when he received the Torah from Yahweh on Mt Sinai. That the stone of the mountain was said to be on fire might be considered as being along the lines of stones of fire that are representative of a mountain of God. Well it is conceivable that any reference to a "mountain of God" would mean that the one who was a part of that supposed divine council would be able to approach the area likened to the Hot Zone. This is one explanation for the meaning of the stones of fire and although this meaning still may require more understanding and explanation, it easily fits with the context of the mythopoetic ideas expressed by Ezekiel. The stones of fire and the thought of them referring to Satan walking either in Hell or in Heaven, in no way fit the context of this verse.

In further addressing verses 17 and 18, we are able to draw now on the concepts understood in other verses from Ezekiel 28 and elsewhere. Here are verses 16 to 18 of Ezekiel 28;

> *16By the multitude of thy merchandise they have filled the midst of thee with violence, and thou hast sinned: therefore I will cast thee as profane out of the mountain of God: and I will destroy thee, O covering cherub, from the midst of the stones of fire.*
> *17Thine heart was lifted up because of thy beauty, thou hast corrupted thy wisdom by reason of thy brightness: I will cast thee to the ground, I will lay thee before kings, that they may behold thee.*
> *18 Thou hast defiled thy sanctuaries by the multitude of thine iniquities, by the iniquity of thy traffick; therefore will I bring forth a fire from the midst of thee, it shall devour thee, and I will bring thee to ashes upon the earth in the sight of all them that behold thee. Ezekiel 28:16-18 KJV*

For a moment or two, let's talk about the last sentence of verse 18. The verse ends proclaiming that the subject of the verse will be laid before kings, that they, the human kings, will behold the one who was newly removed from his position. What a clear statement this is, to be spoken to a human king who is being told of his fall from power. The fact that this king is to be seen by other kings when he is destroyed, which is stated as being "*cast to the ground*", is quite purposely meaning this king is merely a human king brought down. Verse 18 goes on to make reference to the concept that a king of Tyre was also a priest. Notice the Creator is not saying the king has defiled Yahweh's sanctuaries but that the king has defiled his own sanctuaries. I am not 100% certain of all the activities of the sanctuaries in Tyre but I do know that for a king/priest to be accused of defiling already pagan sanctuaries would be a very serious accusation. These sanctuaries had sacrificial and sexual, ritualistic cultic behavior. Although Yahweh abhorred what was going on in the pagan sanctuaries He makes it clear through the prophet that the king has even done worse than what was typically practiced by the king/priest in similar situations.

How could one see this message as a message that refers to Satan, when once again we are told it is the merchant practices and commerce that brought the king to the place of economic might? The term *traffick* used in verse 18 is a term that means commerce and merchant activities. This activity was one of the things Tyre was renowned for and the trade value of this city on an easily defended mountain-like position was monstrous. The entire Ancient Near East was aware of Tyre's ability to control world markets. Tyre was impenetrable in economy and in military; that was until Yahweh decided to allow it to be penetrated. The following verse in Ezekiel 26 reminds us of the literal merchandising which came from Tyre. The word for merchandise is the same word translated as "traffick" in Ezekiel 28.

And they shall make a spoil[7997] of thy riches,[2428] and make a prey[962] of thy merchandise:[7404] and they shall break down[2040] thy walls,[2346] and destroy[5422] thy pleasant[2532] houses:[1004] and they shall lay[7760] thy stones[68] and thy timber[6086] and thy dust[6083] in the midst[8432] of the water.[4325] Ezekiel 26:12 KJV+

The destruction that will come from the midst of this king is a result of the pride of the king. The Targum of Jonathon puts it this way:

"I will bring people who are strong as fire, because of the sins of thy pride they shall destroy thee

People will be enlisted by God as His vessels of destruction to annihilate the King. As with so many once exalted rulers, this king will reap the consequences of his pride and sin through his sin blinding him and perhaps blinding those who are part of his government. With the King and his counsel blinded, there would then be inroads into his kingdom for annihilation to come. Betrayed trust and acts of sedition will be a huge factor in bringing this King and his kingdom to its knees. The "fire from his midst" will be the result of his sin. The plan of God will bring a "fire" through internal conflict and betrayal from within the kingdom that is only quenched when the kingdom is destroyed. This City will be a great place for fishermen to hang their nets on for drying, at some point in the future. Seaside rocks were often a place that fishermen spread their nets to dry. The end of this city will be, for the near and far future, so complete that all who knew of her once unparalleled greatness would be astonished at her now historical demise as verse 19 below speaks about in the classic biblical manner of prophesying using the economy of words.

All they that know thee among the people shall be astonished at thee: thou shalt be a terror, and never shalt thou be any more. Ezekiel 28:19 KJV

What we have seen in walking through this passage of misunderstood Scripture, which has been said to speak of the "Satan" of Christianity, is this;

We are now able to see the Prince of Tyre and the King of Tyre are both human beings and may very well be different terms for the same ruler. As stated even if they are not the same person, neither of the lamentations against them is to be interpreted as speaking of a cosmic Satan. The rulers that are lamented against here in Ezekiel are true historical personalities. The rise and fall of them was orchestrated by Yahweh and the prophet's message was spoken in terms that would have easily been understood by the culture of Ezekiel's time. There is no difficulty in understanding the imagery painted by Ezekiel when one invests the time to understand a little about the culture, language, and mythology that would have been understandable at the time. We are able to see that there is no Satan here in Ezekiel. Moreover, as far as believing this passage to be accepted as speaking of a cosmic Satan, I would confidently say one must take a mystical leap and add to the text if they are to find Satan in Ezekiel 28. The whole of Ezekiel 28 is about human men and verse 12 sufficiently proves the point that the subject is only another human who has submitted to his own pride and evil inclination instead of embracing the opportunity to serve the only Creator. The King of Tyre is just a man who is called to account for his choices.

Ezekiel 28:12
Son of man, take up a lamentation upon the king of Tyre, and say unto him

CHAPTER 10

The Satan in Job, Human Adversary or Evil Incarnate?

The topic of whether or not Satan exists is not one that can be casually glanced at. One cannot merely take a cursory view of some of the common Scriptures that are from the scant armory of ammunition used to prove there is a "satan." It would be impossible to fully explore the topic of "Satan's" existence or absence of existence without taking a good look at the book of Job. I would like to lay out the concept of how Satan has traditionally been seen in the book of Job, and then I will submit the concept of how Satan should more correctly be viewed when considering that ancient document. After that, I will delve into an explanation of some of the passages and concepts that help us to understand exactly what is the situation with the Satan in the book of Job. Allow me to remind you that this concept, that is the concept of a cosmic archenemy of Yahweh not existing in the form of a being called "Satan," is not a new idea. Some seem to think this idea is birthed from rabbinic Judaism however, if one looks at the post-exilic development of Judaism, one will see that it was Rabbinic Judaism and its mystical brother Kabbalism, which cemented the false idea of a cosmic "satan" into the religion of the Jews, which then became a tenet of the religion of the Muslims and Christians. Therefore, it is not from Rabbinic Judaism that the thought of Satan not existing springs from, rather it is centuries before post-exilic Judaism took form that the Jews testified to there being only one God and no other such as a cosmic Satan. The belief in other Gods did exist for the Hebrew people at times during their adventurous history; however, the predominant perspective that was to be held by the chosen people was that there truly is only one God, only one being that is supernal, celestial, and ethereal.

In his 1929 book titled, "*Origin of the Church and Synagogue*" author and scholar, Kaufman Kohller outlines many concepts and practices that the Jews adopted as a result of their Persian exilic experience. Although Kohler does a fine job of pointing out those practices and beliefs that came from exile, he does not make it his job to conclude that a true follower of Yahweh is to reject these additions to the faith of Israel. Kholler is in all likelihood coming from the perspective of so many of the Rabbinic sages through out the centuries. It is not far fetched to say Kholler, because of his ingrained belief system which I refer to as "his grid," accepts the concept that says Torah Scholars and Rabbis are allowed to alter the Faith of Israel at numerous and varied fundamental levels, in order to move with culture and current trends.

True, many of the practices of Judaism are founded on the Torah and stand up clearly to the litmus test of analyzing said practice through the light of the Torah. But, and there seems to always be a great big but; all through Israel's history they were exhorted to not add to or take away from the Word of Yahweh, that Torah. All through Israel's history, they were told not to learn the way of the nations and all through her history Israel was told by Yahweh and his prophets to keep commands of the Torah in the manner He wanted them kept from the beginning; that is without adding doctrines of men and teaching them as commandments. The Israel of God has continually fallen short of the injunctions that God has placed on her as a people who are supposed to be His faithful. Here is a short list of some of the additions Kohler identified as coming out of Persia only to become "foundational" in post-exilic Judaism. Notice that demonology was a late addition to the faith of the Jews known as Judaism and one should not consider the turning from the demonology of the Persians as an anti-biblical Judaic behavior.

> **Pg 45...**Thus the entire Messianic hope of Judaism underwent a change, while at the same time the Jewish angelology and demonology was formed under Perso-Babylonian influence.
>
> **Pg 50**...In post exilic time the use of the name Yahweh became more and more restricted and finally withdrawn from common use...
>
> For the people at large the name *Adonai,* "The Lord," was introduced as a substitute both in the reading and translation of the Scriptures, as is shown by the Septuagint and the Targum.
>
> **Pg 58**... Apparently the first benediction introducing the Shema, which directly refers to the Deutero-Isaianic verse: " the Former

of light and Creator of all things"- the term *Ra*, "evil," being intentionally changed, in order not to have evil ascribed to God- was brief, as the Shema itself was originally brief and only gradually extended, as were also the Benedictions.

Pg 63...It seems, then, that under Persian influence the Hasidim introduced the wearing of the Teffillin[112], which had been used before as amulets, as a religious practice based upon the scriptural passage, and also made it a rule not to walk four ells without them.

Pg 168... But since the Scriptures do not indicate a place of punishment for those found wicked in the divine judgment or a place of reward for those found righteous, the Apocalyptic writers borrowed their ideas from the Persians.

Pg 203...The Babylonian captivity was the crucible from which emerged the Synagogue, a house of God for the people, a religious democracy.

Pg 273...[speaking about the Gnostic Christians which is the Christianity of today Kohler says]... Their system was a combination of Babylonian and Persian systems, a dualism of light and darkness, or of life and death, in which however the Persian predominated, inasmuch as the Babylonian star deities were turned into evil powers and the mother goddess *Ishtar* into a demon *Namrus*, the consuming noon heat, who, in opposition to the Jewish religion, was given the name of *Ruah Di K'dusha,* "the Holy Ghost."[113]

The above small list of changes that occurred as a result of Persian influence contains the Shema; the synagogue system; teffillin[114]; heaven and

112 Teffillin are the ceremonious, religious armband and head band with attached box, which are wrapped in a symbolically prescribed order upon the head and arm of the observant Jew. The attached box on the headband contained select Scripture passages. The concept of these amulets is derived from Exodus 13(and elsewhere) where a passage about keeping the feast of unleavened bread ends with saying; *"And it shall be for a sign unto thee upon thine hand, and for a memorial between thine eyes, that the LORD'S law may be in thy mouth: for with a strong hand hath the LORD brought thee out of Egypt."* *Exodus 13:9 KJV*

113 The Origins of the Synagogue and The Church. By the Late Kaufmann Kohler; Published by New York, The Macmillan Company 1929

114 Teffilin are the adornments worn by observant Jews during prayer. Also called phylacteries, these adornments include a headpiece with a leather box containing passages of

hell as the destination for the dead; and demonology/angelology which is so prolific in thought today.

Is it any wonder the God of the Universe came to earth as the Messiah to die and to teach the correct application of the Torah? So much has been added to the Torah by man that true faith in the God of Israel remains hidden away under the mountains of traditions. Traditions that were borrowed and learned from non-God fearing nations.

It seems to me that the Israelite people, because of their exposure to Persian influence, were robbed of the true message and manner of the Torah and through that were rendered as prisoners. As a result of their Persian sojourn, what was to be an exclusively monotheistic Torah keeping faith of Israel, was subject to the addition of laws, commands, precepts, statutes, and doctrines, by those who were supposed to be teaching the true faith. They in essence could not remove themselves from the situation or the false religious ideas that became pervasive to their culture and faith because of their situation.

We have talked previously at length about the Persian influence but it becomes clear when looked at critically that the real hold of the Persian influence came as a result of leaders of Israel adopting false doctrine from Persia and her religion. Clearly if the leaders and people abjectly refused to accept any practice or idea that wasn't completely Torah based, they would have not become blind and deaf. It seems as if there was a bit of a catch 22 going on, The Israelites were told to prosper in exile, they got close to their captors and then were influenced and seduced by her captors ways. Those who would have had the leadership strength to guide Israel safely through the melting pot society of theology and mythology appeared to have misused their leadership, whether wittingly or not, to implement additional doctrines and concepts into the faith of Israel. Just before Isaiah tells us of the people being robbed, spoiled, and trapped in snares, he tells us that the servant would come to make the Torah honorable. The blatant disregard that was displayed in Persia/Babylon and beyond was a major contributor to the furthering of a false religious system developing called Judaism. Judaism was and is a precursor to Christianity and the practice of adopting concepts from other cultures has been rampant in both major streams of Christianity, Protestantism, and Catholicism. As Kaufman Kohler points out, the "Jews" of Judaism were really in a large part a product of their environments. In addition, it becomes apparent that the Christianity of today, which has Judaism in its direct lineage, is also a product of the Persian religious system with many adaptations and

---

Scripture on small parchment, and an armband of kosher leather that is wrapped around the left arm in a specific and ceremonious fashion.

adoptions of varied philosophies and doctrines along the winding path to today. History reveals that many of the practices and beliefs of Christianity and Judaism are not found to be prescribed in Scripture. Moreover, we have not found "Satan" evident in any of the Scripture we have discussed yet.

Is "Satan" then to be found in the book of Job? After all, doesn't it say right there in plain English, *"Satan was among the sons of God."*? In addition, does it not also say that Satan "*was going to and fro throughout the earth*"? Well it is true, it does say that, but does it mean a cosmic Satan with the power to roam about freely looking for some trouble to get in, where he might cause one of Yahweh's children grief and pain in hopes of getting them to curse God and die? It seems that that is exactly the case when the English words are read and taken literally but a deeper look brings much doubt of the literalness of this writing to the surface. Here is what is likely going on in the book of Job. Understand that for anyone, including me, to dogmatically say this is exactly what was occurring in Job, why it was occurring, and who the "satan' was or what the "satan" is would be a mistake. The minutiae of details which are given and the even greater minutiae of details which are absent from the story of Job make it impossible to give a complete and 100% accurate interpretation of all that is and is not contained in Job. It is quite possible though to be dogmatic at this point, on what the teaching in the wisdom book of Job is not about. I would be bold enough to state that the Book of Job is not about a man Job who becomes the target of an evil archenemy of God. The book of Job is not about a spiritual nemesis to man and God, who threatens the complete destruction of all who are Job's and all that is Job's. To be clear, the book of Job, when wisely viewed against the backdrop of the entire Scriptures, is not teaching us that "Satan" is always looking for a target and has to ask the God of the universe what he can do to cause someone grief. One writer elucidates the unlikeliness of such a situation when he says this in his article on the *Implausibility of Satan;*

> ...is Satan constantly asking God, "hey God, can I, like, shoot massive pain through Joe's body and see if that turns Joe against you?" And God says, "No, Satan, you may not." And then Satan asks, "well--can I, like, kill Joe's baby and see if that turns him against you?" And then God says, "Oh, okay, Satan, I guess you can do that." You might think I'm being sacrilegious but the point is that, although some theologies may sound logical when you read them in a book, when you try to take them off the pages of the book and see how they work in actual practice, they are exposed as just being pat answers that have no real value.[115]

115 **The Implausibility of Satan;** Paul Doland http://www.secweb.org/index.aspx?action=viewAsset&id=310

I agree with this writer on this point. He adeptly makes the point that the existence of a counter–God called Satan, who begs God for opportunities to afflict the faithful, is implausible. There are so many inconsistencies and incongruities in common "Satanology" that one need not investigate it for long to see it is very suspect as a theological doctrine or teaching. It has been easy for contemporary scholars and spiritists who think Satan is a spirit being to be contended with, to impose their evolved concept of this spirit being onto ancient texts of the Bible. Texts which were never intended to instruct us in that manner.

When looking at Job while having the information that "satan" is the English translation for the Hebrew word for adversary or one who opposes or accuses, we can come to a more clear and sensible conclusion as to what is being taught in Job. The fact that the word *sawtawn* is only either a messenger sent from Yahweh; or a human man acting in an adversarial manner; or the rebellious nature which is inherently present in the spirit of every human being; it is easy to conclude that the story of Job is not supporting the commonly understood idea of "Satan". In Job's story, we are given the opening lines of the tale and promptly we are told of Job's righteous standing.

> *There was a man in the land of Uz, whose name was Job; and that man was perfect and upright, and one that feared God, and eschewed evil. Job 1:1 KJV*

Why is it so easy to understand that this statement does not literally mean Job is perfect? Most understand it to speak of Job's maturity and desire to do the best he could for God always. If understanding the terminology that states Job is perfect is so simple, should we not be able to understand the use of the term

"*sawtawn*" translated as "Satan" in the English text? Study will show that the wording used is intended to mean something different from a literal "Satan" entity. In the Hebrew as it appears in all Hebrew texts we have the term "*ha sawtawn*." The fact *sawtawn* is preceded by "*ha*", which means "the", shows us that it is a common noun, and refers to a title of someone or something and not a proper noun that would indicate the name of someone or something. This is represented fairly in Young's Literal Translation of the Bible by being translated as "the Adversary";

> *And the day is, that sons of God come in to station themselves by Jehovah, and there doth come also the Adversary in their midst. Job 1:6 KJV*

So, just as Job can be called "perfect" and not literally be perfect, then the English word "Satan" potentially could be meaning something other than the cosmic Satan we have been told it means. In his article titled, *The Satan,* Bill Long writes about translation of the word;

> **Standing behind the translation "Satan" in almost all translations is the Hebrew word *hasatan*.** In Hebrew the "*ha*" is the definite article. **If we were, therefore, to take the name directly over into English it would be "The Satan."** Every time the word is used in the first two chapters of Job (an amazing 12 times), the creature is called *hasatan.* Never once is it called "*satan.*" **Thus, as any good translator must do, you must render what you have. It is "The Satan." Therefore, the word *hasatan* is more of a *title* than a proper name, more of a *designation* than an appellation.**[116]

Another element of ancient culture that is being taught in this writing is that the servant Job is one who regularly brings sacrifices to Yahweh.

> And it was so, when the days of their feasting were gone about, that Job sent and sanctified them, and rose up early in the morning, and offered burnt offerings according to the number of them all: for Job said, It may be that my sons have sinned, and cursed God in their hearts. Thus did Job continually. Job 1:5 KJV

Verse 5 of chapter 1 is teaching us there is a sacrificial system of some type and because Job is perfect and upright as the story reveals, He would be sacrificing as a priest or through utilizing a priest of the Most High. This therefore would likely occur at some type of a temple that is approved by Yahweh or at least at some place where there is an altar approved by Yahweh.

Scholars disagree on the exact period of Job and the exact dating of when the story was written and I will not be developing an argument to show when this book was written or the events it seems to speak of took place. It is however easy to conclude that the story of Job, whether real or allegorical, did not occur before Esau was alive. Esau was the son of Isaac whose story comes some time after the flood of Noah in the book of Genesis. A clan called the Temanites eventually surface as a clan that is the descendants of Esau. Now in the story of Job one of Job's "counselors" was a Temanite. This means he would have to have been of the line of Teman. The first Teman who

116 *The Satan,* Bill Long, May 29,2005; http://www.drbilllong.com/MoreJobEssays/TheSatan.html

appears in Biblical history is the grandson of Esau. Esau had a first son named Eliphaz who is not the Eliphaz of Job. Then Eliphaz had a son named Teman. This Teman may or may not be the one who is referred to in the mention of Eliphaz the Temanite but there is no previous option so at least through this and the other characters mentioned in Job, we know that the story of Job took place no further back than 2 generations this side of Esau. A third point to draw from the ancestral references is to aid us in believing that the horrific tale of the destruction of Job's family and wealth is about real people and truly would have occurred somewhere in history. Job being called perfect, is described for us as one who fears Yahweh and one who shuns evil or turns off evil. If the text describes what it means to be "perfect" then can we too allow the text to define what it means to be "*ha satan*?"

Job as a sacrificer is seen according to chapter one where we see Job going off to make sacrifices on behalf of his children;

> *And it was so, when the days of their feasting were gone about, that Job sent and sanctified them, and rose up early in the morning, and offered burnt offerings according to the number of them all: Job 1:5*

It is possible that Job performed the service of sacrifice on his own but more likely is that Job employed the services of an approved priest, as was the practice for the ancients from periods long before Job's story came to us. Some may not be aware of the presence of priests during the period represented in Job's story, however, long before the Hebrews were instructed to build the Temple in a specific fashion and maintain personnel in specific priestly offices, nations all over the known world operated with established Temple environments that incorporated priestly personnel. Priests of Yahweh were present at the time of Abraham, which was before Job's time. The King of Salem, who blessed Abraham, was a priest according to the account in Genesis seen below.

> *And Melchizedek king of Salem brought forth bread and wine: and* ***he was the priest*** *of the most high God. Genesis 14:18 KJV*

Now Job would take his sacrifices before the Lord and offer them with a pure heart. It is often thought that to say someone comes before the Lord here in the book of Job means that there is an audience in heaven where the Creator resides.

We first see the phrase in the writing of Job in chapter 1;

> *Now there was a day when the sons of God came to present themselves before the LORD, and the adversary came also among them. Job 1:6*

The term "before the LORD", as we have it in the English will be considered in depth further on in this chapter. It is a term that speaks of someone, a physical human being, coming into the presence of Yahweh. In Genesis 19 verse, 27 Abraham is said to get up early in the morning at the place of the previous evening's sacrifices where he is said to have been "before the Lord". We are told Nimrod was a mighty hunter "before the Lord" and in the Exodus period, Moses is told that the Israelite males must go up to the tabernacle three times a year to appear "before the Lord". Exodus 30 verse 8 shows us the place in the tabernacle where Aaron was to burn incense unto God, was known as a place that was "before the Lord". In the later history of Israel, the term "before the LORD" is a term to indicate coming to the Temple to worship or offer sacrifice. The prophet Zechariah tells of a time when many people from many nations will go to the Holy city Jerusalem that is known to be the geographic location of the temple and there they will pray "before the Lord".

> *Yea, many people and strong nations shall come to seek the LORD of hosts in Jerusalem, and to pray before the LORD. Zechariah 8:22*

As indicated, Job was one who sacrificed regularly and as the priest of his clan perhaps in the same manner that Jethro, Moses' father in law was a priest of his Midian clan, he brought sacrifices on behalf of his children who may have sinned and require that blood be shed for them. The connection to Job being a sacrificer and the term "before the LORD", is enough to lead us in a direction to see whom the sons of Elohim which came before Yahweh in Job's story were. They were not angels but were men, who were either going to the "temple" or designated sacrificial precinct that was administrated by a priest or they were gathering to worship, "before Yahweh", in some other place. Either way, we are not necessarily seeing the picture of angelic beings, with one of them being Satan. If the case was that Satan had entered heaven to talk to Yahweh after he was supposedly cast out of heaven then we should be asking; "hey, why is Satan back in heaven?" How could this cosmic monster be entering the heavenly court to talk to Yahweh face to face? The picture is just not there when we are given information of what other picture may be discerned from this text. If Satan was evil and was ejected from Heaven, how is he able to get back in to heaven where God is? Especially since iniquity cannot stand in the presence of God.

> *Thou art of purer eyes than to behold evil, and canst not look on iniquity: wherefore lookest thou upon them that deal treacherously, and holdest thy tongue when the wicked devoureth the man that is more righteous than he? Habakkuk 1:13 KJV*

So let me suggest that what we are shown in the writing of Job is a picture of human men gathering before the Lord at the Temple, or elsewhere. They are called the "sons of God" as are all who are His children. One of the men is opposed to Job for some reason. This one is said to be "ha sawtawn" the adversary, as the text says. Probably one of the following two things is going on in bringing about this situation. It is very possible we are seeing that a human adversary is jealous of Job and tells his friends, the sons of God, that Job is only so prosperous because Yahweh has a wall around him and therefore is favoring Job. This human adversary is allowed by the Creator to afflict Job as a test because Yahweh will prove to Job and all who are near that Job is serving Him out of love and not because Yahweh is seen as some kind of deified sugar daddy. In the story, Job never once blames all his calamity on "Satan." Job knows that good and evil come at the hand of Yahweh and he makes this abundantly clear when he admonishes his wife for her part in encouraging Job to curse God and die.

> *But he said unto her, Thou speakest as one of the foolish women speaketh. What? shall we receive good at the hand of God, and shall we not receive evil? In all this did not Job sin with his lips. Job 2:10 KJV*

The telling of this tragic tale is not told through simple historic prose or documentation, rather the style of writing known as *Wisdom Writing* is used. One of the purposes of this *Wisdom Writing*, called *Aggadah* in Hebrew, is to teach us that good and bad can happen to every human being on the planet regardless of how "perfect" one is. The adversarial force that came against Job is not a cosmic archfiend but is most probably other men. The second possibility for explaining the situation in Job is that Yahweh sent an angel of some celestial variety to enact the affliction on Job. However, in my view it is most plausible that a jealous contemporary of Job performed the evil acts that befell Job.

There are numerous assertions as to who or what the satan in Job is. Saadiah Gaon a 9th century translator, biblical scholar and philosopher states that this "satan" in Job was a man who envied Job and was not a cosmic monster as other of his contemporaries suggest. We can find reference to Saadiah Gaon's remarks made on the *monstropedia.org* website.

> Not all Rabbinic commentators agreed on Satan's spiritual nature. Rabbi Saadia Gaon, an [9th] century philosopher and scholar, wrote in his commentary to the Book of Job that Satan was simply a human being who resented Job's righteousness and called upon God to test him. This interpretation rests on a literal reading of the Hebrew word שטן or "adversary", which Saadia claims refers only to the intentions of the individual in question and not to any spiritual or supernatural status[117]

Other sources are available to direct us to a correct understanding that the "adversary" who accused Job was just an envious worshipper of God. Jealousy and envy causes many problems according to the Scriptures and the Apostles, who agreed that jealousy and envy do damage to people. The letter from the apostle James makes mention of what results from jealousy in James 3:16, he says; *For where envying and strife is, there is confusion and every evil work.* The Proverbs teach us how inexorable jealousy is and it is next to impossible to withstand it.

> *Wrath is cruel, and anger is outrageous; but who is able to stand before envy? Proverbs 27:4 KJV*

We find the following understanding on the Key Bible Lessons web site that explains well the thought of Job's adversary being a human being;

> THE 'SATAN' OF JOB
>
> This leaves only the record in Job where the word 'Satan' occurs (but there again, the AV has the revealing term 'adversary' in the margin). The introduction of the orthodox personal Devil theory into the Job picture is totally incongruous. This 'Satan' or 'adversary' was 'among the sons of God' (the worshipers) who came to 'present themselves before the Lord' (Job 1:6). To picture the traditional Devil in such a situation is an absurdity, and betrays a very low concept of God.
>
> To see it for what it really says - an adversary of Job, a professed worshiper of God who was jealous and envious of Job's favor with God - is perfectly natural and reasonable, and is the picture anyone would get if it were translated correctly. To suppose that God would negotiate and argue with a supernatural personage almost as powerful as Himself - as traditional theology would have us think - and give him power to bring God's faithful servant

117 Excerpt from Article titled *Satan* in Monstropedia; http://www.monstropedia.org/index.php?title=Satan

> Job to the very gate of death, illustrates the depth of confusion to which popular religion has sunk.[118]

In the above excerpt we see that the writer identifies the "adversary" in Job as a human being who may well have been a worshipper of God but became envious of Job and therefore took on the role of adversary, which we see translated as "satan", bringing trouble upon Job that caused Job to experience great suffering.

THE ADVERSARY IS A HUMAN WHO IS FILLED WITH JEALOUSY

Evidence suggests that the "satan" in Job was a human adversary acting out of a heart of jealousy yet still under the sovereign allowance of the Creator. Where else is the adversary a human, or an inherent, rebellious propensity to choose evil in man? There are a number of instances in Scripture where the adversary is an "angel". The majority of uses in the "Old Testament "where the Hebrew word for "angel", which is *melek,* is used, it is clear that the word is speaking of a human being, as is the case in Job. It is entirely possible that the majority of references to "angels" in Scripture are human beings. The lesser probability when the word angel appears in Scripture is that the messenger being spoken of is a supernatural being such as a celestial messenger from above. Because we see the word "angel" in the English translation does not have to mean it is a spirit being that can fly through the heavens and perform tasks on earth then fly back again for the next assignment. This is a difficult concept for one who is convinced that angels are everywhere and working all the time to orchestrate human affairs and bring messages from Yahweh. Based on the fact that Yahweh is the omniscient sovereign who is present everywhere all the time as the non-physical "Holy Spirit," it is then possible that He is the entity directing all human affairs without controlling the will of a human which has to make a choice. Although He is not moving each of us as if we were pawns in a chess match, he certainly does have an effect on humanity and can direct some of our choices as was seen in 2 Samuel 24 when Elohim was angry and caused David to number the tribes of Israel. By somehow setting up the path so David would choose to number the tribes of Israel, a path was opened up for God to render a needed judgment. That said, is there any reason a person who has been stirred by the Creator's Spirit to perform an action or behavior, whether wittingly or unwittingly, would

118 Excerpt from article; Bible Teaching about the Devil – 2, found at http://www.keylessons.com/reader.py?l=19

not fit into the definition of a *mawlawk*? An angel (*mawlawk)* can simply be a person who is acting out of a prompting from God to move in a certain direction or speak a certain word. Being as how there are human "angels" in Scripture, it makes perfect sense to be open to the idea of a Satan being a human too. So, are there human "satans" in the Scriptures?

We know that in the New Testament when Peter desired the things of man instead of the things of God, the Messiah Himself called Peter a Satan. In the Old Testament, there are numerous occasions where "the satan" is a human and numerous occurrences of a satan coming from God. In the book of Numbers, we see the adversary is manifested by Yahweh because God is angry with Balaam. In other places, we are told of an "evil spirit" which comes from The Lord upon certain individuals. It is difficult for many to try to separate what is called "an evil spirit" that comes from God, from being connected to a "satan" under the present day concept of Satan and evil spirits. Even if one were to say that the evil spirit was not Satan but was just one of his many minions then one would still have to deal with the fact that the evil spirit is said to come from God in every case that "satan" appears in the Old Testament. Below are a few examples that show the "evil spirit" is from Yahweh. These verses are among many that firm up the position that the so-called "bad demonic spirits from Satan" are in fact not bad demonic spirits but are methods and modalities Yahweh uses to accomplish His will. The "lying spirit" is included in this list for your discernment as well. I have added emphasis to the verses that show that Yahweh sends the evil spirit.

> *Then **God sent an evil spirit** between Abimelech and the men of Shechem; and the men of Shechem dealt treacherously with Abimelech: Judges 9:23 KJV*

> *But the Spirit of the LORD departed from Saul, and an **evil spirit from the LORD** troubled him. 1Samuel 16:14 KJV*

> *And the **evil spirit from the LORD** was upon Saul, as he sat in his house with his javelin in his hand: and David played with his hand. 1Samuel 19:9 KJV*

> *Now therefore, behold, the **LORD hath put a lying spirit** in the mouth of all these thy prophets, and the LORD hath spoken evil concerning thee. 1Kings 22:23 KJV*

> *Now therefore, behold, the **LORD hath put a lying spirit** in the mouth of these thy prophets, and the LORD hath spoken evil against thee. 2Chronicles 18:22 KJV*

There are a significant number of occurrences in the Bible that demonstrate "the satan" to be a human being. In many verses the Hebrew word "*sawtawn,*" is translated as "adversary". These examples, which I cite below, truly represent what a "satan" is in the Hebrew Scriptures. The following list shows the use of the Hebrew word "sawtawn" in each verse but translate it as "adversary." I have added emphasis and placed the English word "satan" into the text to show how one reads it differently if the translated word is not correctly chosen by the translators.

> 1Samuel 29:4 KJV+ And the princes[8269] of the Philistines[6430] were wroth[7107] with[5973] him; and the princes[8269] of the Philistines[6430] said[559] unto him, Make this fellow return,[7725, (853), 376] that he may go again[7725] to[413] his place[4725] which[834, 8033] thou hast appointed[6485] him, and let him not[3808] go down[3381] with[5973] us to battle,[4421] lest[3808] in the battle[4421] he be[1961] an **adversary[7854(]satan**) to us: for wherewith[4100] should he reconcile[7521] himself[2088] unto[413] his master?[113] *should it* not[3808] *be* with the heads[7218] of these[1992] men?[376]

> 2Samuel 19:22 KJV+ And David[1732] said,[559] What[4100] have I to do with you, ye sons[1121] of Zeruiah,[6870] that[3588] ye should this day[3117] be[1961] **adversaries[7854](satan)** unto me? shall there any man[376] be put to death[4191] this day[3117] in Israel?[3478] for[3588] do not[3808] I know[3045] that[3588] I[589] *am* this day[3117] king[4428] over[5921] Israel?[3478]

> 1Kings 5:4 KJV+ But now[6258] the LORD[3068] my God[430] hath given me rest[5117] on every side,[4480, 5439] *so that there is* neither[369] **adversary[7854] (satan)** nor[369] evil[7451] occurrent.[6294]

> 1Kings 11:14 KJV+ And the LORD[3068] stirred up[6965] an **adversary[7854] (satan)** unto Solomon,[8010] [(853)] Hadad[1908] the Edomite:[130] he[1931] *was* of the king's seed[4480, 2233, 4428] in Edom.[123]

> 1Kings 11:23 KJV+ And God[430] stirred him up[6965] *another* **adversary,[7854] [(853)] (satan)**Rezon[7331] the son[1121] of Eliadah,[450] which[834] fled[1272] from[4480, 854] his lord[113] Hadadezer[1909] king[4428] of Zobah:[6678]

> 1Kings 11:25 KJV+ And he was[1961] an **adversary[7854] (satan)** to Israel[3478] all[3605] the days[3117] of Solomon,[8010] beside[854] the mischief[7451] that[834] Hadad[1908] *did*: and he abhorred[6973] Israel,[3478] and reigned[4427] over[5921] Syria.[758]

> Psalms 109:6 KJV+ Set[6485] thou a wicked man[7563] over[5921] him: and let **Satan[7854] (adversary)** stand[5975] at[5921] his right hand.[3225]

With perhaps the last verse in the above list as the only one in question, all the examples given are instances where a human being is called a "satan". We see *sawtawn* translated as adversary correctly on a number of occasions because that is the correct translation of this Hebrew word.

It is interesting to note that if in fact there is a "Satan," his name has remained unchanged through at least three language changes to get to the English. In Hebrew, it is *sawtawn*, in Greek it is *satanas*, which comes from the Hebrew; and in English of course, it is "*satan.*" There has been no trouble bringing the supposed name of the archenemy of "God" across barriers of language without altering it significantly from the original pronunciation. The power of a myth to stay current is incredible. The fact that Satan has not undergone a name change, unlike the name Jesus which has been changed from Ieseus which in turn was changed from Yeshua, testifies to this satan-myth being developed and passed on from a huge misunderstanding and wrong interpretation of the meaning of the word satan. Meanwhile we have extensive evidence from Scripture and history that the "satan" was not ever to be understood as the name of a cosmic being.

The previously quoted verses showed that a "sawtawn" is a man and it is clearly revealed the propensity to be an adversary can be situated in what is known to be the spirit in man. The "spirit" of man, called the "*ruah*" in Hebrew, refers to man's personal attitude and intentions with the word bearing the nuance of a force that influences. This is not particularly referring to a spiritual entity within a man but is understood by the Ancient Hebrews as man's character. We can think of this term in the same way as we might think when we hear a person being spoken of as having a gentle spirit or a humble spirit; or perhaps an angry spirit. It is to be understood more as the description of a person's character rather than identifying the presence of a supernatural entity inhabiting a person. Knowing that "spirit" does not necessarily mean some type of an ethereal being which is sent to inhabit a human man but may more likely describe the behavior of the person, helps us understand what an "evil spirit" is. When speaking of an "evil spirit" being sent to a person we are to recognize that person has been guided by the Creator in such a way that he or she no longer has a heart that chooses to live in a holy and pleasing manner. A manner that is in accordance with acceptable behavioral patterns of one who is submitted to God. Hence, an evil spirit was sent from Yahweh.

Imagine if you will, a young man who enters the realm of Christian leadership. This young man intends to serve "God" and lead His people in the ways of his understanding of the Word of God. At the outset, to give the benefit of the doubt, this young man has good intentions to do what is right and to honor and obey the Creator as he was taught from his pastoral schooling and church upbringing. This could be seen as a man of integrity and seems to have a spirit of holiness about him. As things go, he is a very charismatic individual and soon is the pastor of a thousands-big super-church and is broadcasting services across the globe on a satellite TV station. Early thirties, married, two children, successful and financially secure, all because of his ministry. The key words in the last sentence are "his ministry". As with any church leader, he is quick to claim it's "the Lords" ministry and that he is only the vessel. This story could go any number of ways; perhaps a counseling situation goes a little too far and the pastor gets involved sexually with his little lost sheep, or although he is financially secure this pastor has a hankerin' for the green stuff and takes a little more than his share on a semi regular basis. Alternatively, maybe the sermon preparation on Thursdays was cut short one day by a "coincidental" appearance of a pornographic image on the internet while preparing. Now Pastor "golden boy" is visiting pornographic websites on an almost regular basis. This young man is in deep mental, emotional, and spiritual trouble but he is supposedly still leading "Gods people." I think as with many young professional church leaders, this pastor's intention was pure enough off the start and pride, compromise or selfishness crept in. Now, no longer serving "God" through his ministry, but regularly serving himself he no longer could be considered as exhibiting a '"holy spirit" but in essence he has received an "evil spirit." Could one say this evil spirit was from Yahweh? I think so. For it was Yahweh who placed the opportunities for choice in the path of this self-aggrandizing pastor who was poor at self-assessing and unable to bridle his evil inclination. It is highly doubtful that Yahweh actually sends a type of a ghost-like entity into this man and through that, imparts an evil spirit to him. What type of a God just throws a powerful force into a weak human being to turn the human evil? Wouldn't that fly against his architectural design of humanity to allow us free choice? We won't engage in the free will discussion here but rather try to see the point as we think about the Pharaoh of the Exodus.

The King, we are told hardened his own heart a handful of times when the judgments came upon his kingdom, and then we are told, "God hardened the heart of Pharaoh." What does it mean that God hardened Pharaoh's heart?

It is possible that God just goes "ZAP" and now Pharaoh no longer has even the potential to agree with the Creator because his heart is hard. However, I think that a God who created humans with the ability of choice would not make such a forced change to a human creature, but allows the choices of our hearts to bring about that change all on our own. That change, due to Yahweh's influences, is referred to as God hardening the heart. It makes sense that Yahweh after offering a way out over and over again to Pharaoh or anyone, would eventually stop giving chances for the hard hearted to go

Yahweh's way. After numerous rejections of the grace, love, and mercy of the Father, the Father simply leaves a rebellious human to their own devices. Refusing to do things God's way, the Father leaves us to prove to ourselves that we are truly in control and allows us the chance to see the outcome of running the show our own way.

Letting a person run their life without receiving God's direction and assistance is a little like what can happen when a child is being taught to ride a bicycle for the first time. It often happens with the child's father trotting alongside for a number of attempts to help the child stay balanced and off the pavement. After a few wobbly attempts, the child insists that the dad let go and he do it by himself. The father tries, without breaking the little guy's "spirit", to coax his child to continue accepting his help. Well, the child was simply too strong in his pleas and the father, knowing what the result would likely be, reluctantly allowed the little cyclist to go it alone. The father would ultimately be right, but he allowed his son to attempt a solo ride without his protective hand guiding his son's progress. The father let go of the seat and the child's wobbly start looked promising, however in a few novice pedal strokes the child crashed into a bush coming to a quick stop and fell to the ground. Suffering only a few minor scratches, the rider sheepishly turned back to the father and readily accepted his stabilizing hand on the next attempt.

If we relayed this story using biblical imagery and language, perhaps one could say that the child's father, in releasing the child to his own designs, sent the child an evil spirit. The "evil spirit" in this scenario was simply the act of letting the child be the master of his own destiny, if only for a poignant moment. Like the pastor that was spoken of above or the Pharaoh, the child started out with the guidance of the Father but out of his or her own desires each one ended up separated from the protective and guiding presence of the Creator and thus were susceptible to an "evil spirit from the Lord". An "evil spirit" when found in Scripture, always comes from Yahweh. A more understandable way to express this concept might be to say; due to the response to the circumstances that are presented to an individual, one has a greater inclination towards choosing and then receiving evil, when God places them in various defining situations.

Thought in the Apocalyptic Period Helped to Create the Satan of Today

Sawtawn was a common noun originally before it was transformed to a proper noun as the term passed through different cultures. The word should have kept its original meaning as it moved through time but it was altered because of a skewed concept of evil that flourished during the Apocalyptic period. A period where literature was produced to explain all manner of theological concept and done from the framework of a culture that had been given to mythology. The Apocalyptics were a truly Hellenized people and highly creative in their writing. This trait is particularly evident in the leaders and teachers of that religious culture. A culture that flourished under Greek and then Roman rule in the 400 years after coming out of the Persian exile. One writer points to the meaning of the word *sawtawn* as it should be seen in the story of Job.

> The word 'satan' as used in many English Bibles, and in the book of Job, is a transliterated word from the Hebrew that means 'adversary' or 'opponent.' It can mean 'the adversary' or 'the opponent' as in Job, with the definite article 'the.' Sometimes it means 'accuser' as 'a prosecutor in a trial,' The word is a title. It is NOT a proper name as 'Satan.' Saddam is an adversary (a satan) to George Bush, but the opposite is also true; Bush is a satan to Saddam. Interesting enough the adversary in Job is a 'messenger' (Angel) of Yahweh (Job 1:6). So also in Job this satan was performing his properly appointed role as the 'adversary' of Yahweh. He is performing under the complete control of Yahweh, for in the above passage of Job, it indicates very clearly that Yahweh gives this adversary 'limited' power and authority to bring affliction (bad or evil) to Job.[119]

It seems the reason the pronunciation of the word "Satan" moved through the linguistic labyrinth virtually unscathed is that it was a term describing a concept and behavior, not an actual name. The transition of the term from one language to another was virtually seamless as it described a concept and there was no word to adequately articulate the concept of "adversary" that was held by the original word *sawtawn.* Therefore, when an adversary was described by the Hebrew word *sawtawn,* the same adversary would have been described by the Greek word *satanas* and the English word "*satan.*" There is more for us to consider about the word *sawtawn* and its derivatives. It often falls to the revisionists as the ones responsible for taking a solid concept such as the word *sawtawn,* which is a common noun, and infusing it with new and not previously accepted meaning to create something drastically different from what was originally intended.

---

119 http://assemblyoftrueisrael.com/Questions/Thewordsatan.htm

The word "*sawtawn*" (Strong's 7854) has a minimal change to represent the plural form of this word. It is Strong's 7853 (seen below), as mentioned earlier in this book;

> **H7853** *saw-tan'* A primitive root; to *attack*, (figuratively) *accuse:* - (be an) adversary, resist.

The following verses use a plural version of the Hebrew word for "satan" and in each of the following examples, once again the "satan" is always human and never divine. Emphasis is added.

> Psalms 38:20 KJV+ They also that render[7999] evil[7451] for[8478] good[2896] are mine **adversaries;[7853] (satans)** because[8478] I follow[7291] *the thing that* good[2896] *is*.

> Psalms 71:13 KJV+ Let them be confounded[954] *and* consumed[3615] that are **adversaries[7853] (satans)** to my soul;[5315] let them be covered[5844] *with* reproach[2781] and dishonor[3639] that seek[1245] my hurt.[7451]

> Psalms 109:4 KJV+ For[8478] my love[160] they are my **adversaries:[7853] (satans)** but I[589] *give myself unto* prayer.[8605]

> Psalms 109:20 KJV+ *Let* this[2063] *be* the reward[6468] of mine **adversaries[7853] (satans)** from[4480, 854] the LORD,[3068] and of them that speak[1696] evil[7451] against[5921] my soul.[5315]

> Psalms 109:29 KJV+ Let mine **adversaries[7853] (satans)** be clothed[3847] with shame,[3639] and let them cover[5844] themselves with their own confusion,[1322] as with a mantle.[4598]

> Zechariah 3:1 KJV+ And he showed[7200] me (853) Joshua[3091] the high[1419] priest[3548] standing[5975] before[6440] the angel[4397] of the LORD,[3068] and Satan[7854] standing[5975] at[5921] his right hand[3225] to **resist[7853] (satans)** him.

Once again, all but perhaps the Zechariah reference listed above is referring to human beings as the adversaries/satans, and even Zechariah can be shown to be a vision that contained human adversaries. We will discuss the Zechariah "Satan" in chapter 11 but for now, we can acknowledge the many occurrences of "satan" as a human being in the Scripture. So knowing that in most cases the "satan" is a human, is it possible to find if the "satan" may perhaps be a human being in Job? Shouldn't we be eager to take the meaning of the original Hebrew word and try to understand how and why it was used here? In the Hebrew text, the article "the" is placed before the word for adversary. This indicates that we are dealing with a title for a character. Too quickly, we default to our belief system, which has taught us that this character is in fact Satan. However, there are many clear clues in the story of Job that tell us that it is Yahweh who does the evil to Job. Moreover, this evil was done for the most part, at the hands of men. Amelia Wilson expresses the point in her 2002 book with the idea that this story may in fact be a real occurrence but told with somewhat of a literary license in order to emphasize a point. Her book gives us a history of images and ideas about the devil and how they formed in the public imagination. Amelia says;

> "The Satan in the story of Job is really a device in a traditional Jewish allegorical tale- Aggadah-used to illustrate a concept. Such Aggadic stories abound in the Talmudic literature and the frequent parable told by Jesus to his followers are in the same tradition.[120]

The use of overemphasized and utterly embellished components in wisdom literature is so frequent in this ancient story telling that many have taken every aspect of the tale as literal. As Wilson stated above, Yeshua employed this technique in His teaching and even admitted to His disciples that He taught in parables. The reason being is that those not following Him would be incapable of understanding His meaning because they were unfamiliar with His personal style of teaching. If you have ever been the fifth wheel in a group of really tight friends who spend all their time together, then perhaps you might understand how an "outsider" might feel when listening to Yeshua. It is common for the fifth wheel guy to not get the humor or understand the passion or intensity behind the statements and stories of members of the core group. It is no fault of the fifth wheel's but he or she simply lacks the exposure to the form, style, and mannerisms of those in the group. This difficulty in "getting" someone is particularly notable when a student in university walks into a professor's class two or three times and then, when sitting with other students from that class, concedes to the group the difficulty they are having in comprehending what the prof is trying to teach. They may state their complaint by saying; "I don't get him."

Of course, what is meant by this student is that as a learner, he is having a difficult time connecting to and understanding the prof. Typically, there is another student or two who have had this professor in a previous class or semester, and they may respond something like this. "I never got him either for the first month but after I got to know him a little better he started to

120 From pg 39 of "The Devil," Amelia Wilson; 2002 PRC Publishing Ltd.

make sense." The prof was really never being "senseless", it was just that the student who was a new initiate to the prof and his style of teaching, eventually began to understand the prof as the student figured out the profs delivery techniques coupled with the profs body language, voice inflection and tone. All the pieces came together for the confused student when he received further understanding of the professor's almost undetectable, sarcastic, and dry wit. We see the same thing going on with Yeshua and those who get to know Him and how He teaches and we should see Aggadah in a similar manner. Aggadah can be explained variously and one explanation that is fairly comprehensive says;

> **A**ggadah (Hebrew, narrative) is rabbinic teaching which is not halakhah[121] and which (is) stories, legends, history, and witticism. The rabbis themselves state that the aggadah is not authoritative and insist that no halakhah may be derived from aggadot, but it is held in high esteem concerning insight and piety. This is emphasized by the comment, "Do you want to know him who created the world?" read the aggadah. Aggadic literature was developed in Palestine from the era of the second Temple until the end of the Talmudic period.
>
> Within the literature are expressed ideas and sentiments of the tannaim and the amoriam and draws on old myths and legends as well as popular teachings. For example, Rabbi Hillel was supposed to know "the conversations of trees and clouds, and of the beasts and animals," while Rabbi Meir was said to have known 300 fox fables.
>
> Discourses on the rabbinical biblical teachings were preserved, and sermons apparently were delivered at Festivals, after the reading of the Torah scroll in synagogues on occasions of family joy and sorrow and at other public functions. Such discourses preserved in aggadic literature were subsequently employed (by) later rabbis.
>
> In aggadic history of the literature some of the accumulative additions seem highly fanciful to later readers. For example, the contrast between Esau and Jacob in Genesis 27:22 is seen as a contrast between Esau's and Jacob's descendants, namely the Romans and the Jews.

121 Halakhah is the Hebrew word meaning to walk and is most often a reference to the rules and commands that an observant Jew lives his faith by, or the way a religious Jew walks out his or her faith.

> Theological doctrines as well were discussed, and sages attempted to answer such questions as to whether the heavens or the earth were the first to be created, how proselytes should be treated or whether Israel's salvation was dependent on prior repentance. Much later mystical speculation also is drawn from aggadic teaching.
>
> Although the aggadah lacked the authority of the halakhah it was the literature from which evolved over a period of nearly a thousand years the treasury of Jewish thought and feelings which formed the Hebrew people.[122]

Understanding the nature of Aggadah allows the reader to glean the intended message from the story being told. Other stratagem used to aid comprehension would be perhaps to get to know the teacher or speaker of the story of Job; however, the fact is that we are unable to get to know the original speaker who spoke and penned the words of the book of Job thousands of years ago. Therefore, either we are left to adopt customary interpretations and understanding of the book of Job or we can try to do better, knowing that we may or may not be dealing with an actual occurrence that has been told to emphasize a point and not to teach us of literal characters. It may or may not be safe to presume that Job's story actually happened to some degree, and I am aware there are many who say the entire story is an allegory or a myth. Some even allege that Job's story is simply a retelling with different characters of an ancient mythical account of a suffering worshipper of the pagan gods. I, for now, will lean toward the probability of this being an occurrence which truly happened and that a lesson is to be gleaned from this tale that is "embellished for emphasis". Who's to say that we are not reading a well-written weave of truth and larger than truth words and ideas when ingesting this story? Perhaps it is so that Job existed and Job did suffer the trials depicted in his tale. It is not unusual that such mythical and poetic imagery might be added to the story to bring home the point that the teller wants to make.

Pictures of the human activity being the adversary in Job's affliction are numerous. In Chapter 1 verse 8 we are told it is the sons of God coming before Yahweh. Most see this as a group of angels and "Satan" standing before Yahweh. This would be acceptable but first off, if "Satan" existed and had a heart to make a choice to do evil at one point and rebel, then how can he stand in the presence of the Almighty and remain. There is no sin or wickedness in Heaven at the throne of the Almighty. There is no possible way

122 http://www.themystica.com/mystica/articles/a/aggadah.html

to reconcile that sin cannot be in the presence of Yahweh in Heaven and yet allow the one who is supposedly the epitome of sin into the heavenly court. The psalmist considers this in Psalms chapter 5;

> *For thou art not a God that hath pleasure in wickedness: neither shall evil dwell with thee. Psalms 5:4*

We are the Sons Of God

Reading the above verse it is sensible to conclude that one who is the embodiment of sin would not likely be found in the presence of Yahweh in heaven. It is excessively convenient for erring theologians to simply flip a concept on its proverbial head in order to make a piece of their theology fit the distorted puzzle they call their belief system. Either Yahweh allows sin in heaven or He doesn't. We can't flip back and forth on this one. Knowing that evil cannot come in the presence of God and that the character of Satan is said to be the epitome of evil, then it is not possible for there to have been a Satan in the story of Job that literally went and stood in the presence of Yahweh. The adversary was in the presence of God or "before the Lord" and therefore we can ask who was it that came "before the Lord" if the verse is not talking about angels and Satan? In this tale, we are told those who come before Yahweh are "**sons of God**", including the satan. If humans are sons of God then who, are the "sons of God" in Job's story?

> *Now there was a day when the sons of God came to present themselves before the LORD, and Satan(the adversary) came also among them. Job 1:6*

One might also ask; "Hey, don't I become a son of God when I choose to follow the Messiah?" The answer is; Yes. You do become a "son of God" when you choose to follow the Messiah. Of course a female becomes a daughter of God and the two groups combined then are the children of Yahweh. A son of God is at times still called a "son of God" even when they become a prodigal and choose to go against the Father's wishes as the prodigal son in the Gospels did. Note the following list that represents who a "son of God" is according to the apostles.

> But as many as received him, to them gave he power to become the sons of God, *even* to them that believe on his name: John 1:12 KJV

> For as many as are led by the Spirit of God, they are the sons of God. Romans 8:14 KJV

> For the earnest expectation of the creature waiteth for the manifestation of the sons of God. Romans 8:19 KJV

> And because ye are sons, God hath sent forth the Spirit of his Son into your hearts, crying, Abba, Father. Galatians 4:6 KJV

> That ye may be blameless and harmless, the sons of God, without rebuke, in the midst of a crooked and perverse nation, among whom ye shine as lights in the world; Phillipians 2:15 KJV

> Behold, what manner of love the Father hath bestowed upon us, that we should be called the sons of God: therefore the world knoweth us not, because it knew him not. 1John 3:1 KJV

> Beloved, now are we the sons of God, and it doth not yet appear what we shall be: but we know that, when he shall appear, we shall be like him; for we shall see him as he is. 1John 3:2 KJV

According to the apostle's teachings as seen above, humans are "sons of God" here in this physical life. The first time the term "son of God" appears is in Genesis.

> *That the sons of God saw the daughters of men that they were fair; and they took them wives of all which they chose. Genesis 6:2 KJV*

Some might have been taught that understanding a term or word according to the "first mention" of it in Scripture is how to apply an interpretation to further appearances of that word or term. This practice is referred to as "The Rule of First Mention." This is generally a good practice however, the Genesis 6 account that first mentions the sons of God is mistakenly taught by many to be speaking of the fallen angels who had sex with human women and created a race of giants. These "sons of God" are said to be essentially, wicked demon-people but the term is really referring to human sons of Elohim. One should be careful to not rigidly apply that guideline of the Rule of First Mention in every case. There is an instance here where a reference to an earlier son of God precedes those sons of God mentioned in Genesis 6. The rule of first mention can be applied in essence by knowing that Adam was the one who was first referred to as a son of God, rather than applying the rigid use of the practice, which requires only the first written uses of the term be used to define further uses of the term. Adam, being the first human, was called a "son of God" as we are told in the genealogy given us by Luke in the gospel that bears his name.

> *Which was the son of Enos, which was the son of Seth, which was the son of Adam,* ***which was the son of God.*** *Luke 3:38 KJV*

The Sons of God Can't be Demon Angels

Even under the erroneous doctrine that the sons of God in Genesis 6 are demons that had intercourse with women, one can find that Adam being the first human, was the first one referred to as a "son of God", identifying references to "sons of God" in the future as human. Any good commentary will bare this out for you but to give you a little fodder on this topic, one of the better arguments against the idea of the sons of God being fallen angels goes like this;

If the "sons of God" from Genesis 6 are fallen angels, having sexual intercourse with human women, then that blows apart the belief that angels have no gender or sex organs and possess no power to create anything. If in fact they are ejaculating into human women in Genesis to "create" a super species of demon-man, then they are in fact creating and have creative powers that are only possessed by Yahweh. Only humans were given the command and procreative blessing to be fruitful and multiply. If the fallen angels had in fact undertaken to have sexual relations with human women resulting in some form of procreation, are then the fallen angels still procreating with human women today? It is highly unlikely, as angels then must possess sex organs in a form similar to humans. In well-known medieval lore, we can find mention of the *incubus and succubus*, demons that were supposedly capable of procreating with humans. Monstropedia tells us about both of these fictitious entities;

> In medieval legend, a **succubus** (plural *succubi*; from Latin *succuba*; "prostitute") is a female demon that seduces men (especially monks) in dreams to have sexual intercourse. They draw energy from the men to sustain themselves, often until the point of exhaustion or death of the victim. From mythology and fantasy, Lilith and the Lilin (Jewish), Lilitu (Sumerian) and Rusalka (Slavic) were succubi.[123]

123 From article titled *Succubus* on Monstropedia, http://www.monstropedia.org/index.

> In European medieval legend, an **incubus** is a demon in male form supposed to lie upon sleepers, especially on women in order to have sexual intercourse with them. They are also believed to do this in order to spawn other incubi.[124]

Aside from the belief that fallen angels can have productive sexual relations with women, is the curious perspective that claims in Genesis that these sons of Elohim are angels that fell and that they took human wives. That belief is gleaned by some from verse 2 of Genesis chapter 6.

> *That the sons of God saw the daughters of men that they were fair; and they took them wives of all which they chose. Genesis 6:2 KJV*

If they are "angels" who married women, then Yeshua must have misunderstood the role of angels when He told us that there will be no marrying for men in his kingdom and alluded to that being like the angels as not marrying.

> *For in the resurrection they neither marry, nor are given in marriage, but are as the angels of God in heaven. Matthew 22:30 KJV*

Of course Yeshua did not misunderstand, because He knew that the sons of God in Genesis were not fallen angels seeking to copulate with humans, motivated by the evil plot to form a race to take down the Creator's precious humans. The period spoken of was one of depraved human behavior in human history that saw strong men taking any woman they pleased and doing with them as they wanted. Because of this unmitigated depravity, Yahweh destroys the earth and all human beings except Noah and his family. God enacts this judgment because of the inclination of mans' heart which is always evil. Yahweh does not indicate that the wickedness has anything to do with apostate angels and their inter-species relationships. As I said, there are lots of excellent resources available to help you unpack this false concept and see it truthfully, but before we go on with Job, take a look at where else and what else is a "son of God" as we see in the International Standard Bible Encyclopedia in the article *The Sons of God.*

---

php?title=Succubus.

124 From article *Incubus* on Monstropedia, http://www.monstropedia.org/index.php?title=Incubus

> in Luke 3:38 it is applied to the first man; and from the parable of the Prodigal Son it may be argued that it is applicable to all men. It is applied to the Hebrew nation, as when, in Exo_4:22, Yahweh says to Pharaoh, "Israel is my son, my first-born," the reason being that Israel was the object of Yahweh's special love and gracious choice. It is applied to the kings of Israel, as representatives of the chosen nation. Thus, in 2Sa_7:14, Yahweh says of Solomon, "I will be his father, and he shall be my son"; and, in Psa_2:7, the coronation of a king is announced in an oracle from heaven, which says, "Thou art my son; this day have I begotten thee." Simply put, a son of "God" is not an angel nor is it an angel who has fallen from Heaven, but a "son of God" is always pertaining to humanness.

The "sons of God" in Job then are mere humans as is every other son of God in the Scriptures. The term is used of Yeshua to identify that He took on human form. From this point we can move forward to see that the sons of God, known to be men, came "before the Lord" as was the common practice of men engaging in a temple-like setting.

BEFORE THE LORD

Our question of who and what the Satan is in the book of Job is unanswerable without understanding what is the meaning of the phrase "Before the Lord". What does it mean to "come before the Lord"? Does it really mean to be present in Heaven in front of the throne or court of Yahweh? Could it perhaps be a term with a different meaning, which needs to be understood through looking in the Old Testament? It all gets very simple when we use Scripture to define Scripture. How on earth could a shepherd or a fisherman understand what Yahweh was trying to say if He kept giving new meanings to the terms found in His word? New words and terms that had no prior understanding that could be found in previous writings. It would be like living with a bipolar father in-law who is next to impossible to understand because he doesn't remember what he said yesterday and you know the meaning of what was said today will change the next time he speaks. No, I assure you, Yahweh is not like a bipolar father in-law. The words that come from God are able to be understood by a child. This is why He provides a way to determine the meaning or intention for a phrase or a word that remains consistent. If he leaves His words with no available manner of understanding the meanings, then He is a God of confusion.

It is so easy serving a God who doesn't keep changing but is stable where things He says are always simple to keep in order. When Yahweh states for instance that a "son of God" is a human man, He will not change the meaning to become a term for an angel who wants to destroy humanity. God is a consistent God and His consistency is proven over an over again. We will see it again as we consider further the phrase "**before the Lord**". A phrase that is thought by some to refer to being in attendance in Heaven.

Following are uses of "before the Lord" to look at, and then we will talk about how this phrase refers to an actual physical visit to a place right here on earth, where worshippers convene to engage Yahweh. Engaging Yahweh is often done at that place through His priests. I have added emphasis to the pertinent words in the passages below where we can see that "before the Lord" is always connected to the Earthly Temple.

> *For I will cast out the nations before thee, and enlarge thy borders: neither shall any man desire thy land, when thou shalt go up to* ***appear before the LORD*** *thy God thrice in the year. Exodus 34:24 KJV*

> *But when* ***Moses went in before the LORD*** *to speak with him, he took the vail off, until he came out. And he came out, and spake unto the children of Israel that which he was commanded. Exodus 34:34 KJV*

> *And they brought that which Moses commanded before the tabernacle of the congregation: and all the congregation drew near and* ***stood before the LORD****. Leviticus 9:5 KJV*

> *The censers of these sinners against their own souls, let them make them broad plates for a covering of the altar: for they* ***offered them before the LORD****, therefore they are hallowed: and they shall be a sign unto the children of Israel. Numbers 16:38 KJV*

> *Three times in a year shall all thy males appear* ***before the LORD*** *thy God in the place which he shall choose; in the feast of unleavened bread, and in the feast of weeks, and in the feast of tabernacles: and they shall not appear before the LORD empty: Deuteronomy 16:16 KJV*

> *Then all the children of Israel, and all the people, went up, and came unto the house of God, and wept, and* ***sat there before the LORD****, and fasted that day until even, and offered burnt offerings and peace offerings before the LORD. Judges 20:26 KJV*

> *And Solomon went up thither* ***to the brasen altar before the LORD****, which was at the tabernacle of the congregation, and offered a thousand burnt offerings upon it. 2Chronicles 1:6 KJV*

Clearly in the above examples "before the Lord" means to be in the Temple, the place where He has placed His name. This phrase spoke of one person or many persons attending at the Temple to pray, worship, sacrifice or petition Yahweh. We know from history that the physical Holy Temple, which was constructed on earth, was not immune to entry by human adversaries. A cosmic Satan might not be given the privilege of presenting himself in the pure environment of heaven but an adversarial human was not prevented access to a temple environment because of his desire to be adverse. It is true that the Temple environment was frequently visited by people who intended to be less then sincere in their worship of the Creator. There were indeed many non-believing Pharisees and Sadducees, who performed functions in the Temple during the time of the Messiah's earth walk. Looking at both possibilities for understanding the phrase "*Satan also came among them to present himself before the Lord,*" it is most probable that the one whom is called Satan and is the supposed embodiment of sin, did not come into the Heavenly court after being cast down by Yahweh. It is acceptable that there was a human person who was an adversary, as the word meant to Job and questioned Job's relationship with Yahweh. Job 1 verse 6 can be seen to tell it thusly;

> *Now there was a day when the sons of God came to present themselves before the LORD, and the adversary (A man) came also among them. Job 1:6*

A man who opposed Job came along with the men who arrived at the area that is considered the Temple, at the time of Job's story. This human adversary was bent on seeing Job taken down a few notches, probably because of his jealousy towards job. For goodness sakes, even today I have been involved in conversations that circle around a certain individual and their prosperity. It has happened more than once that the equivalent of Job's adversary's statements have been made by someone who was jealous of another's prosperity and apparent favor.

One example of what was heard might be seen in the following statement; "*Dan sure is doing well, I wonder what he did to get so blessed... I heard he cheats on his taxes every year.*" The accusation may or may not be true but the "Satan" making that statement (the one opposing he who is prosperous), who has been talking with the "sons of God", really is speaking against the legitimacy of the prosperity of someone within their circle of acquaintances and friends.

The accuser in a situation such as this is having difficulty dealing with the fact that he himself is not as prosperous as the person he is accusing. At times, it is a part of present day conversations that we will hear the adversary trying to malign the prosperous one's commitment to the Creator by suggesting something like this: *"So-and-so probably wouldn't even care about God if God hadn't made him rich."*

The accuser or the "Satan", is truly being an adversary to Job, he is not being an archenemy to Yahweh. It may be that Yahweh wants to reveal through the prosperous one's suffering how loyal this one is to the Creator regardless of his situation. There is more than one purpose to be seen in Job's suffering. A dual purpose of the suffering of Job would be to glorify Yahweh in proving that He is worthy of Job's loyalty even when He is the cause of Job's tribulation while another purpose may be to reveal the wickedness in the heart of the accuser. This accuser would witness the resolve of the one who is the target of his attacks, to not turn from serving the Creator amidst the terrible "injustices" brought upon him. When we ponder the thought that the accuser is a man that is used to test a seeming undeserving victim, we see how any one of us can be in the role of the accuser. Admittedly I myself have spoken judgmental words in the past about a person I have been jealous or envious of in some way. The accuser is the same as the adversary, which is the same as being called by the familiar term "Satan".

Thus far, in Job, we can see the sons of God as men and the "adversary" (Satan) is another man who is envious of Job. These men came to the Temple or its equivalent in the days of this story, and are either talking amongst themselves, or the adversary announces his view of Job's supposedly insincere relationship with Yahweh, to the presiding priest. The priest would have been a man of authority and may be the one speaking on behalf of Yahweh in this account as the priests of God did often when acting in their appointed role. This priest, as a true servant of their God, is acting in the authority of God and is able to send the accuser/adversary away to afflict Job. This human affirmation of Job spoken to the adversary is as if Yahweh Himself had spoken and it is an affirmation that asserts that Job will not turn from Yahweh no matter what happens to him. Yahweh is in the practice of using the hands of men to enact His will. This is seen in situations such as is found in the Book of Jeremiah when Yahweh tells a king of a pagan nation that he will be His battle-axe to bring judgment and destruction on Babylon and Chaldea.

> *Thou art my battle axe and weapons of war: for with thee will I break in pieces the nations, and with thee will I destroy kingdoms; Jeremiah 51:20*

The adversary is allowed to afflict Job in ways that men opposing one another in that day might do. The fact that it is men doing harm to Job is revealed in how Job himself sees "wicked men" as the ones whose hands it was whereby his troubles were brought to pass. Job states this in chapter 16:

> *God hath delivered me to the ungodly, and turned me over into the hands of the wicked. Job 16:11*

The Story of Job is Wisdom Writing, Writing Not Intended to be Interpreted Literally

For the scenario to have played out with evil intentioned men being the adversary of Job, complements the truth being taught by this wisdom book. This story is likened to the style found in many of the wisdom writings, writings designed to teach us a deeper philosophical concept often using images that are not to be literally applied. Much is written about wisdom literature and the forms and styles it displays in how it is distinct from other Hebrew writings and in contrast to Greek thought. Beside the book of Job, we are informed that Psalms, Proverbs, Ecclesiastes, the Song of Songs (also known as the Song of Solomon), The Wisdom of Solomon, and Sirach (also known as Ecclesiastics) are also wisdom writings from Hebrew literature. Wikipedia teaches us the following about this genre of writings;

> ***Wisdom literature** is the genre of literature common in the Ancient Near East. This genre is characterized by praise of God, often in poetic form, and by sayings of wisdom intended to teach about God and about virtue...*
>
> *...The key principle of wisdom literature is that whilst techniques of traditional story-telling are used, books also offer wisdom, insight and 'truths' about the nature of life and our reality. The interest of the material is in the ethical training of the individual, which is pleasing to God, on earth. Nationalistic overtones, state, or even governmental recommendations are deemphasized in favor of instructing the average man and woman.*[125]

That a temple environment is being indicated in Job is buoyed up by the opinion of scholars who understand the term "before the Lord" as a term that is not intended to speak of celestial courtroom activities. This opinion is

125 Excerpt taken from article titled *Wisdom Literature* at http://en.wikipedia.org/wiki/Wisdom_literature

found in an article titled; *Garden Of Eden: A Prototype Sanctuary.* We are told there that the term "before the Lord" means to be in a temple environment or place where a sacrificial altar is known to be. The following quote from the article references Donald Parry's book and a book by Menahem Haran, a commentary that is highly recommended as a model presentation of biblical scholarship to an educated lay audience.

> This term is referring to a convening of men at the Temple or its parallel. Menahem Haran (*of the Hebrew University in Israel)* has argued that the phrase "*before the Lord*" (*lipnê Yahweh*) indicates a temple setting. He writes that "in general, any cultic activity to which the biblical text applies the formula '*before the Lord*' can be considered an indication of the existence of a temple at the site, since this expression stems from the basic conception of the temple as a divine dwelling-place and actually belongs to the temple's technical terminology.[126]

Many examples of the term "before the Lord" are shown in Haran's work to be references to a temple or altar environment, such examples are;

> ..., it was quite usual for people to visit the temple and prostrate themselves before the Lord there on all the holy days all the year around (Isa.I:12-15 ; Ezek. 36:38 ; Lam.I:4; 2: 7 *et al*), including the New Moons and Sabbaths (Isa. 66:23 ; Ezek. 46: 1-3); as we shall see further on, whole families would even assemble at local sanctuaries at special times specifically appointed for them.[127]

> A Levite who lives in the provinces and wishes 'with all the desire of his soul' to come to the chosen place may do so and become in every respect a priest, 'like all his brethren the Levites who stand there before the Lord' (Deut. 18: 6-7).[128]

126 Garden of Eden: Prototype Sanctuary
Donald W. Parry, in *Temples of the Ancient World.* Donald W. Parry and Stephen D. Ricks eds., (Salt Lake City: Deseret Book and FARMS, 1994.): 126-152. Mr. Parry quotes from Menahem Haran's work*Temples and Temple Services in Ancient Israel.* The above quote used by Mr.Perry can be found on page 26 of Manahems work.

127 Temples and Temple-Services in Ancient Israel, Menahem Haran; pg 292 originally published Oxford[Oxfordshire]; Clarendon Press

128 ibid. page 61

> Only in the case of Josiah's reform was the covenant first made with Yahweh by the king and the people, in the temple court, 'before the Lord'.[129]

It is simple to perform a survey of the Scriptures to find how the term "before the Lord" refers to the area of a temple or altar environment. Haran has done so, wonderfully in the book quoted from above. We are however, given other clues in the context of the book of Job that the sons of God and the adversary in Job had access to a Temple or altar environment. The tale reveals in chapter 1 verse 5 that Job is one who sacrifices to Yahweh when Job is said to be making sacrifice on behalf of his children. This lends credence to the idea that the men had access to and were at the temple when the accuser voiced his concerns and was engaged in a dialogue with the priest or perhaps at the very least engaged in an internal dialogue with the Creator. We must consider the possibility that the dialogue we are privileged to hear in the book of Job is a dialogue that takes place in the mind and heart of a man. It is possible that we are reading a conversation that is in the form of an internal dialogue with the Creator. Internal dialoguing happens often by people who are grappling with a difficult situation or issue and need to communicate their grapplings with the God they believe in. There are many who have had internal dialogues with Yahweh when they are working through a difficult choice that is before them and it is entirely possible that through the message contained in this form of wisdom writing we are let in on how the accuser's internal dialogue played out. A dialogue that contained thoughts and responses from the still small voice of the Almighty.

Should Satan be Walking up and Down if He was Cursed to Go on His Belly Forever?

Looking at verse 7 in chapter 1, we find another subtle clue to lead us to the understanding that this "adversary" in Job is not the cosmic Satan of common lore. The text has the accuser answering to Yahweh, upon being asked where he has been, that he has been walking up and down in the earth.

> *....Then Satan answered the LORD, and said, From going to and fro in the earth, and from walking up and down in it.*

This is a valuable statement to aid in dispelling the lie that the serpent in the garden was "Satan". (I know I have yet to discourse at length on the

129 ibid page 136

serpent in the garden so please look ahead to chapter 12 if you must, to the chapter titled, *Understanding the Serpent in the Garden.*)

The presumptions about the serpent in the garden being either a real serpent or a manifestation of Satan, forces us to consider that the serpent was cursed to go about on his belly forever. If the serpent was a manifestation of Satan in Genesis 3 then we should realistically expect that Satan was cursed to go on his belly; yet in this situation in Job it appears that Satan is not on his belly at all rather he is walking upright in the earth. Why is Satan not crawling on his belly as the curse of Yahweh consigned him to in the story of the fall of man? According to the view that says the serpent is Satan, we see in Job chapter one that "Satan", is not on his belly. Other instances occur where this supposed curse on "Satan" is ignored. One such occurrence would be when the "Devil" takes Yeshua up to the pinnacle of the Temple.

> *Then the devil taketh him up into the holy city, and setteth him on a pinnacle of the temple, Matthew 4:5*

If this devil in the above verse is Satan the serpent as some purport, then he should not be walking to and fro or up and down in the earth in abject contrast to Yahweh's curse on him. Neither should he be taking the Messiah to the pinnacle of the Temple in what must only be perceived as a situation where Satan the serpent is ambulatory, definitely not crawling or slithering on his belly. This serpent, who is Satan, should be depicted as slithering along the ground. On another vein, what if the serpent was only inhabited by "Satan" as some claim? Is it not heinously unjust of Yahweh to curse a poor serpent who undoubtedly had no choice in the matter of being possessed by "satan"? Does it not seem odd to anyone that "satan", arbitrarily inhabited this upright, walking creature, and now this innocent creature is cursed forever to no longer be able to walk upright? Did a snake choose to submit to the supernatural power of a cosmic rebel and embrace an opportunity to serve the anti-God force that had no input into the creation of the serpent? A simple creature who was under the dominion of man and God would not be found to be worthy of an eternal curse if it was used as a pawn for Satan. Why curse a snake when the bad guy is Satan? This concept too is implausible. I know Yahweh is sovereign and can do anything He wants, but He cursed Adam, then Eve, then the serpent. Why didn't God curse Satan, if it was "Satan" who entered the serpent? Should the serpent really be held responsible for how he was taken over and used by Satan?

This story has been misunderstood and misrepresented to depict that a supposed fallen angel who is trying with great fervor to thwart Yahweh's plans, abuses his power and possesses a snake in order to destroy humanity but does not get a curse himself. That just is not right. Neither Satan being the serpent nor Satan inhabiting the serpent fits with Yahweh's truth. We will discuss this topic on the serpent, Satan and the behavior in the Garden of Eden in depth in chapters 12 and 13.

Continuing on in Job, we are told in chapter 2 verse 10 that the evil as well as the good comes from God and is to be received by Job. This is told to Job's wife by the suffering man himself. Self-testimony ought to be heeded if Job was truly an upright man.

> *But he said unto her, Thou speakest as one of the foolish women speaketh. What? shall we receive good at the hand of God, and shall we not receive evil? In all this did not Job sin with his lips. Job 2:10 KJV*

Although recognizing that bad things coming from God may seem like a logical conclusion to some, there are many who say that this statement is no more than indicating that God allowed the evil to come on Job because "God is in control of everything even the actions of Satan". Indeed Yahweh is in control of everything but the "satan" He is in control of is not a cosmic archenemy, rather it is nations, leaders and other persons who have been chosen to be the adversarial force Yahweh requires at any particular moment to see that His will is done.

Receiving good and evil at the hand of God, refers to the fact of there being only one supernatural entity who administers evil and good. Job is clear on the fact that there is no being other than Yahweh and the dialoguing he does with his friends and wife we are shown that no one in the story considers Job is being attacked by an anti-God, evil entity. The way Job makes a statement about receiving good and evil, informs his wife and us the present day hearers, that everything good and evil that happens to man originates from the hand of the Father. Job is not claiming the evil he has received was from a cosmic being opposed to God, who conceived of this evil towards Job and convinced the Creator to allow it. Job knows implicitly that Yahweh conceived of the evil that befell Job. Job also knows that Yahweh has a very good reason for applying evil to Job but that God may not be telling what the reason is at this time. The axiom remains that when this type of evil and calamity occur, it is God who has done it. Remember in Amos 3:6 we are told that evil happens in a city because Yahweh has done it not just allowed it.

> *Shall a trumpet be blown in the city, and the people not be afraid? shall there be evil in a city, and the LORD hath not done it? Amos 3:6*

Interesting dialogue ensues all throughout the book, including the words from Job and all the speeches and unwanted counsel from Job and his friends. In all this dialogue about Job's difficult situation, not one of them blames a cosmic "satan" for Job's trouble. In fact, in Chapter 6 verse 4, Job states the poison, arrows, and terrors are from the Almighty. Job knows how Yahweh is capable of pouring out calamity and destruction on any person in the world. Job is unwilling to deny that his anguish comes from the Most High stating that these painful arrows are coming from God.

> *For the arrows of the Almighty are within me, the poison whereof drinketh up my spirit: the terrors of God do set themselves in array against me. Job 6:4 KJV*

The Jamieson, Fausset and Brown Commentary, understands Job's words as recognizing from whom his horrible situation had come.

> **Job 6:4 - arrows . . . within me**--have pierced me. A poetic image representing the avenging Almighty armed with bow and arrows (Psa_38:2-3). Here the arrows are poisoned. Peculiarly appropriate, in reference to the burning pains which penetrated, like poison, into the inmost parts--("spirit"; as contrasted with mere surface flesh wounds) of Job's body.
>
> **set themselves in array**--a military image (Jdg_20:33). All the terrors which the divine wrath can muster are set in array against me (Isa_42:13).[130]

In Chapter ten Job indicates that it is Elohim who is contending with him and that it is Yahweh who is hunting Job but God shows Himself to be marvelous upon Job.

> *For it increaseth. Thou huntest me as a fierce lion: and again thou shewest thyself marvellous upon me. Job 10:16 KJV*

It seems that even though Yahweh is the one who has done these terrible things to Job, he still has an element of marvel in verse 16, at the fact that everything comes from this work of Yahweh. The method and manner of the afflicting performed on Job by Yahweh, although calamitous, was a thing to marvel at. Job knowing it was coming from his God was not reticent to recognize the marvelousness of the Creator even in the way the Creator

130 Robert Jamieson, A. R. Fausset and David Brown Commentary Critical and Explanatory on the Whole Bible

afflicted. John Gill notes this well, in his commentary on this portion of Job's dialogue.

> **and again thou showest thyself marvellous upon me**; or, "thou returnest (f) and showest", &c. after he had afflicted him in one way, he returned and afflicted him in another; and he not only repeated his afflictions, but devised new ways of afflicting him, uncommon ones, such as raised admiration in all beholders, as things rare and uncommon do: Job's afflictions were surprising ones; to be stripped at once of his substance, servants, children, and health; and it might be more wonderful to some, that God, so gracious and merciful as he is, should afflict in such a severe and rigorous manner; and especially that he should afflict so good a man, one so just and upright as Job was, in such a way: and it was even marvellous to Job himself, who was at a loss to account for it, not being conscious to himself of any gross enormity he had committed, or of a sinful course of life, or of any one sin he had indulged to, wherefore God should come forth "against" (g) him as an enemy, in so terrible a manner: so some render the particle.[131]

The above quote adds clarity to the point that God is even marvelous in how he dismantles a person's material life for purposes that are far greater than those which can be comprehended by the recipient.

> *For it increaseth. Thou huntest me as a fierce lion: and again thou shewest thyself marvellous upon me. Job 10:16*

You may notice that Job uses the imagery of a Lion to tell of Yahweh hunting Job.

Not just any lion, but a "fierce lion". A connection can be seen in Scripture to the metaphor of a lion and how personification of sin and evil is done by referring to it in terms representative of a hunting lion. Looking way back in Genesis when Cain kills able Yahweh confronts Cain and tells Cain that if he will not do well and overcome sin, then sin couches at the door waiting to overtake Cain.

> *If thou doest well, shall it not be lifted up? and if thou doest not well, sin coucheth at the door; and unto thee is its desire, but thou mayest rule over it.' Genesis 4:7 Jewish Publication Society*

131 John Gill's Exposition of the Entire Bible
Dr. John Gill (1690-1771)

The word used in the Hebrew to describe sin waiting to overcome Cain is a Hebrew word that carries with it the nuance and meaning of a lion waiting to pounce on its prey. The verse shown above is from the Jewish Publication Society translation and better aids in displaying the use of the word "couches" than what is found in the King James Version. This translation may be a more accurate translation of the original Hebrew word[132] as it is able to guide the reader to more closely recognize the association of this wording with a lion who is after its prey. It is entirely possible the imagery used by Job would be seen as Job understanding God better than most at the time. Job understood that it is the God of the Universe who tests man, and the imagery used, likens Him to a powerful, decisive, and intense Lion. It is apparent that we cannot take the words of Job literally here as Yahweh is not actually hunting Job in the same way a Lion in the African jungle would hunt a gazelle and then pounce at just the right moment sinking his teeth into the gazelle's back. Job's statement is again, more poetic imagery, used to express how he believes the Creator is actually the one bringing all this trouble on him.

Job was called a *perfect and upright* man who resists evil in chapter 1. To be called such by the Creator it makes sense that Job would therefore have had a profound relational knowledge of who Yahweh is and how God operated. Job knew the Sovereign God of the Universe was putting all these calamities upon him and realized that this God tests his children at times and often doesn't give a concise reason as to why. If man fails then, it is entirely possible Yahweh will continue to allow sin to perform its destructive process in much like the manner in which sin is personified in the statement made to Cain saying that it will desire him and overcome him if he does not overcome it. We have then the star of the story of Job saying in these verses that God is the contender and the hunter, not Satan;

> *I will say unto God, Do not condemn me; shew me wherefore thou contendest with me. Job 10:2 KJV*

> *For it increaseth. Thou[God] huntest me as a fierce lion: and again thou shewest thyself marvellous upon me. Job 10:16 KJV*

So far, there is not a literal cosmic Satan to be found if we are to understand the affliction of Job the same way Job understood it. Job said his

---

132 The original Hebrew word is #7257 in Strong's Exhaustive Concordance :râbats *-raw-bats'*
A primitive root; to *crouch* (on all four legs folded, like a recumbent animal); by implication to *recline, repose, brood, lurk, imbed:* - crouch (down), fall down, make a fold, lay (cause to, make to) lie (down), make to rest, sit.

afflictions came from God. The text of Job's story continues to reveal whom and what, is the originator and vehicle of his unparalleled trials. Another small but observable clue is in chapter 12 verse 16. In verse 16, we are told that the deceived and the deceiver both belong to God.

> *With him is strength and wisdom: the deceived and the deceiver are his. Job 12:16 KJV*

If the Deceiver Is Satan, then Why is the Deceiver Yahweh's?

We also must consider who it was that was responsible for deceiving Job. Wasn't "Satan" called the deceiver in the "Bible?" Here for some reason Job tells us that the deceiver belongs to Yahweh. If the deceiver is Yahweh's that means that the deceiver is doing Yahweh's will. How could a deceiver be Yahweh's and continue acting like a rogue force, determined to defeat God? Here again the negative aspects of this universe, which some would claim are evil that comes from Satan are said to be God's. And being as that they are God's, these unsavory aspects alluded to here as coming from *the deceived* and *the deceiver,* ought not to be attributed to any one else. Of course, as was discussed earlier, we humans have the capacity to rebel and be an active force of wickedness in this world. Often times even our choices to rebel are enhanced, shall we say, by God, because we have chosen to not "do well" initially. In the same way "God" caused David to number the tribes of Israel back in 2 Samuel 24 because He was planning a way to administer a judgment on David and his Kingdom, so does Yahweh stir up the heart and mind of man to have His purposes performed. God influences his created to move in a way that leads one to make a choice by placing an opportunity to choose in front of that created man or woman, as was done in the Garden of Eden when God caused the tree of the knowledge of good and evil to grow. Many times the option chosen by man is a choice for evil.

Job's speech continues by declaring a number of the things Yahweh is responsible for as it pertains to humanity. The speech discloses knowledge about judges, princes, kings, the mighty nation and the heart of the chief of the people of the earth. There is no one that Yahweh does not have rule and reign over. We also get the sense here that Job knows there is not one entity that is not being used for the plan of the almighty, even to the point of God being the reason for the person who is groping in darkness without light as Job declares in chapter 12.

They grope in the dark without light, and he maketh them to stagger like a drunken man. Job 12:25 KJV

There is no indication of another supernatural being that is responsible for causing the confusion of those who Job speaks of as staggering like a drunken man. If we are to think like Job then when we see a brother or sister of the human race not following Yahweh and doing works of unrighteousness then we are to understand that they are in their staggering position because the Most High had orchestrated their life. The situations that brought that person to the point of "groping in darkness without light" were all brought to pass by Yahweh not Satan. Job knows well enough to give credit where credit is due, that is in part why he was called "perfect and upright" by God, therefore Job recognizes who is running the show.

Job is not just stating bad things happen because God allows them to as some who believe there is a Satan claim. Job is 100% clear on the fact that all things happen as if they directly flowed from the Fathers hand and Job knew the Father utilizes everything to bring about His plans. That would include the "adversarial" characters that are human beings. Also included are the "adversarial" celestial manifestations that have been mistaken as being an archfiend of the Creator sometimes being Yahweh Himself. This mistaken identity has caused Yahweh's delegates to be thought of as demons that are bent on thwarting God's plans and destroying humanity to prevent them from returning to the Creator. Oh but there's more!

Look in the following verse at whom Job believes would kill him if in fact there were any slaying performed on Job. Once again, it is not some "satan" character but the One and Only Creator of the Universe is to be the force doing the slaying as far as Job knows.

Hold your peace, let me alone, that I may speak, and let come on me what will. Wherefore do I take my flesh in my teeth, and put my life in mine hand?
***Though he slay me**, yet will I trust in him: but I will maintain mine own ways before him. Job 13:13-15 KJV*

In the above verse, Job is defending his integrity to his so-called friends who have become counselors with little insight into the facts of Job's affliction and why it is occurring. Job's friends are trying to find a reason in the suffering Job is going through, by claiming Job's actions and sins as the reason. Many of us who have suffered various and extended maladies have received similar misplaced counsel from friends and family from time to time. Counsel that suggests our suffering is the result of our sins. Neither Job nor his friends attribute Job's trials to a cosmic archenemy of Yahweh and although this is correct, they errantly blame Job as the one who brought all these trials upon himself. This is unwarranted counsel according to Job and in defense of his integrity; he says even if the God of the universe kills me I will still trust in Him. Job unequivocally states that God might decide to kill him but because Job knows any killing that is to be done is the Creator's prerogative, Job faithfully proclaims that he will still trust in the God of the Universe. He then persists in explicating his understanding of where these trials came from, in chapter 16.

> *He teareth me in his wrath, who hateth me: he gnasheth upon me with his teeth; mine enemy sharpeneth his eyes upon me. Job 16:9 KJV*

Here we are told that Yahweh has made Job weary, that it is God who is tearing Job in His wrath. At this point Job tells us that he believes God hates him. What a horrible shock it would be to believe the God of the Universe hates you. Job seemingly "takes it like a man", which is a colloquialism that has long held the meaning most know it to have today. In fact, it appears that phrase comes from the story of Job when Yahweh decides to speak to the afflicted man and says to "*gird yourself like a man and I will answer you*" in Chapter 38 verse 3.

How Could God Hate Job?

The Hebrew word for "hate" conveys the meaning of describing the activity of one lurking for or persecuting Job. Looking at the word Job uses which is translated as "hateth" in the English, we see it is very similar to the word for "adversary", number 7853 and 7854. This related word, which we see translated as "hateth", is Strong's number 7852 and is the Hebrew word "*saw-tawm*." This word does not mean "hate" in the present English sense of the word but speaks of one lurking after or persecuting another. Perhaps this simple chart below of the three words I am talking about as defined in the Briggs, Driver, Brown Lexicon, will be helpful to see the way God hates Job is not a seething, reviling type of hatred but is an adversarial persecuting manner of treatment rendered to Job by Yahweh.

H7852	H7853	H7854
שׂטם	שׂטן	שׂטן
śâṭam	śâṭan	śâṭân
BDB Definition:	**BDB Definition:**	**BDB Definition:**
1) to hate, oppose oneself to, bear a grudge, retain animosity against, cherish animosity against	(Qal) to be or act as an adversary, resist, oppose	1) adversary, one who withstands 1a) adversary (in general - personal or national) 2) superhuman adversary 2a) Satan (as noun proper)

As seen in the above chart, the Briggs Driver Brown Lexical work conforms to most major lexicons that choose to concretely define the word *sawtawn* as Satan and call it a proper noun. This is an error in translation however, it is not possible to alter all lexical works from time past that say they properly depict the Hebrew word *sawtawn*, which is simply not intended to be translated as a proper noun. Alternatively, we can take the information we have before us today and work around the error of major linguists and translators who have conformed to the revisionists' interpretation and adopted the word *sawtawn* as the name of Satan. It is commonly understood that the word did not become a popular name until the New Testament period. Monstropedia provides this etymological insight to the word Satan and its synonym "Devil";

> The nominative *satan* (meaning "adversary" or "accuser"), and the Arabic *shaitan*, derives from a Northwest Semitic root *šn*, meaning "to be hostile", "to accuse". In the New Testament, Satan is a proper name, and is used to refer to a supernatural entity that appears in several passages.
>
> The most common synonym for Satan, "the Devil", entered Modern English from Middle English *devel*, from Old English *dēofol*, from Latin *diabolus*, from Late Greek *diabolos*, from Greek, "slanderer", from *diaballein*, "to slander" : *dia-*, *dia-* + *ballein*, "to hurl"; which ultimately derives from PIE *gʷel-*(meaning "to throw"). In Greek, the term *diabolos* (Διάβολος), carries more

negative connotations, meaning "slanderer", or "one who falsely accuses". [133]

Human Enemies Deliver the Affliction

In verse nine of chapter 16, Job recognizes the fact that Yahweh has placed this blight upon him and now God's plan has Job's enemies causing grief for Job. Job says, "*Mine enemy sharpeneth his eyes upon me*". Grief from human enemies is part of the meaning of the words in the King James Version, which say Job's enemies are sharpening their eyes on him. Job understood very well that Yahweh was the one responsible for the horrible situations he is subjected to but in that understanding, Job is realizing that God is working through Job's enemies as a vessel for the tragedy he has encountered. We are given a clear statement from Job that it is humans who are called his enemies that are presenting Job with the distress in his life. We can see below that verse 11 identifies these men as ungodly and wicked.

> ***God hath delivered me to the ungodly**, and turned me over into the hands of the wicked. Job 16:11 KJV*

Who does Job say it was that delivered him to the ungodly? Is Job aware of whom it was who handed him over to the wicked? Yes, Job is aware. He states it was God who passed Job off to the ungodly and handed him over to the wicked men. Unless the context of this passage is ignored, one cannot conclude that the terms "ungodly" and "wicked", in this text refer to Satan and his alleged "demons". The context of these few verses clearly places men as the enemies who actually have become the physical afflicters of Job.

> *He teareth me in his wrath, who hateth me: he gnasheth upon me with his teeth; mine enemy sharpeneth his eyes upon me. They have gaped upon me with their mouth; they have smitten me upon the cheek reproachfully; they have gathered themselves together against me. God hath delivered me to the ungodly, and turned me over into the hands of the wicked. Job 16:9-11 KJV*

Ignoring the context of the above verses is easy to do for those who are already convinced that Satan exists and want that statement by Job to fit a firmly cemented idea that it is a cosmic, archenemy of man and God who is employed as the afflicter of Job. Even though setting a preconceived

133 Excerpted from, "http://www.monstropedia.org/index.php?title=Satan"

understanding on the shelf while exploring the context of a verse will perhaps cause a little discomfort for the searcher, it will ultimately cause us to come to the truth. Then we will be equipped to decide if we need to change our concept or if we can continue to force the words of Scripture to change and therefore suggest God has changed. Again, in verse 13 of this chapter Job speaks the truth of who is responsible for his journey of strife. Using the imagery of a military leader employing the skilled archers to inflict damage upon the target with their masterful stealth and accuracy, Job testifies to the Almighty being the employer of the inflictors.

> *I was at ease, but he hath broken me asunder: he hath also taken me by my neck, and shaken me to pieces, and set me up for his mark.*
> *His archers compass me round about, he cleaveth my reins asunder, and doth not spare; he poureth out my gall upon the ground.*
> *He breaketh me with breach upon breach, he runneth upon me like a giant. Job 16:12-14 KJV*

Who are the "He" and "His "in these verses talking about? The "He" and "His" in these verses is not referring to an imaginary being called "satan." The "He" and "His" are talking about Yahweh who is the only responsible party for Job's affliction. There were human forces and potentially even divine forces used in the affliction of Job, however, there is not a cosmic, Satanic force used, and Job is completely aware of that. I wonder if Job ever thought that the hearers of Job's tale would pin Job's afflictions on a being that was constructed in the minds of confused men? The fact that a Satan has been constructed is a testimony to theologians of this age who so readily accept interpretations handed down by men who have simply adopted a Greco-Roman style of adding mystic meaning to text they do not comprehend. Their form of mystical interpretation postulates a cosmic dualism that is unacceptable to Yahweh

When Yahweh brought the Israelites out of Egypt and took them to the Mount Sinai to give them His Torah, He wanted them to clearly understand that He was the One who rescued them from their polytheistic stupor. You see, in Egypt, most of the Israelites had learned to accept the false idea of other deities who had control over aspects of creation. The manner in which the Hebrew people learned false doctrine and worship practices in their Egyptian exile was similar to the learning process through assimilation, which occurred in the Babylonian/Persian exile. Eventually the Israelites' belief system moved away from the practice of equitable, monotheistic worship. Although they had their own national deity known as the God of Abraham, Isaac, and Jacob at the time, they all too readily accepted the idea of the Egyptian hierarchy of "gods." Therefore, once they arrived at the mountain and the God of the Universe told them who He was in a fiery, thundering, smoking introduction, He emphasized that He was the One who brought them out of Egypt. Yahweh had literally destroyed all the Gods of Egypt, which "were no Gods", as we spoke about earlier in chapter 5. Just as Yahweh did not want His actions of the destruction He placed on Egypt, including His actions as the "angel of death" credited to the false gods of Egypt, so too did neither Job nor Yahweh want anyone today to pin Job's catastrophes on anything or anyone other than the God of the Universe. Job knew this and if we look closely at Job's understanding then we can see how simple it was to the perfect, upright Job who shunned evil. Reread the last few verses above that we looked at in chapter 16 and you will see how difficult it is to convince yourself that Job believes it is any one else , other than Yahweh, who is doing this to him. I have heard a lot of good arguments but not many have taken Job's own belief system into account, which is an absolute must if we desire to see what Job understood about his sufferings and who he attributed them to.

Chapter 19 of this story is equally explicit in sharing the truth of who is dismantling Job's life. We may have been thrown off the trail of the reality of who is the source in Job's tragedy by the use of the word "Satan" in the start of his story, but the amount of proof contained within the text of the story reveals who the real minister of destruction is. This should be proof enough to see that most of Christianity has misunderstood the idea of a "Satan" coming after Job as a process that was simply allowed by God but acted out by another cosmic entity. This misunderstanding keeps people believing a lie, and will and has, ultimately diminished their understanding of the true God. To have a diminished understanding of the Only God is to be missing out on knowing Him in the way He wants to be known. There will come a time when all who are willing and have an open and humble heart, will see and hear that there is only One God, only one way to that God and only one life in which to accept Him on His terms. Those terms include giving Him credit for the good and the evil in the lives of man. Remember Job's own words to his wife about accepting good and evil at the hand of Elohim.

> *Then said his wife unto him, Dost thou still retain thine integrity? curse God, and die. But he said unto her, Thou speakest as one of the foolish women speaketh. What? shall we receive good at the hand of God, and shall we not receive evil? In all this did not Job sin with his lips. Job 2:9-10 KJV*

It's All God And Only God

Job does not falter halfway through the story when he once again states who it is that is working at doing him in. There are at least 8 verses in chapter 19 that tell us in Job's own words, that it is none other than the Creator who is administering what we might call "evil" to Job. The highlighted portions in the verses below clearly identify God as the one applying pressure and strife to Job.

Job 19:6-12 KJV

6 *Know now that* ***God hath overthrown me****, and hath compassed me with his net.*

7 *Behold, I cry out of wrong, but I am not heard: I cry aloud, but there is no judgment.*

8 ***He hath fenced up my way*** *that I cannot pass, and* ***he hath set darkness in my paths.***

9 ***He hath stripped me of my glory,*** *and taken the crown from my head.*

10 ***He hath destroyed me*** *on every side, and I am gone: and* ***mine hope hath he removed*** *like a tree.*

11 ***He hath also kindled his wrath against me****, and he counteth me unto him as one of his enemies.*

12 ***His troops come together, and raise up their way against me****, and encamp round about my tabernacle.*

13 **He hath put my brethren far from me**, and mine acquaintance are verily estranged from me.

Job 19:21 KJV

21 *Have pity upon me, have pity upon me, O ye my friends; for* ***the hand of God hath touched me.***

How can anyone conclude that it is Satan who is doing the afflicting on Job? Understandably, one might be a little mislead due to the conversation we are presented with at the outset of the story of Job. This opening conversation seems quite conclusive that there is in fact a Satan chatting with the Almighty about the righteous Job. However, when we accept the idea of a lesson being taught through this conversation, as opposed to a literal occurrence being recounted, then we can see things differently. We are then able to reconcile all the other evidence in Job that lucidly points to Yahweh as the one performing the afflicting of Job. Seeing Job as the wisdom writing that it is one can understand that the God of the Universe is not simply allowing some "Satan" being to have his way with Job. The evidence is overwhelmingly supporting of the fact that Job is experiencing his tribulation through the King of the Universe who is utilizing the men in Job's life.

If any one of us were to sit down and really think through who or what has been our adversary along the path of life we would likely see it has been other humans who have foisted adversity upon us. If not other humans, then it has been ourselves who have invited adversity into our lives through the choices we have made. Too many of us who have walked this earth have not taken responsibility for being the reason for adversity which ultimately came through the actions of some human agent. Perhaps it was a testing or perhaps it was a judgment, no matter what reason it happened, we must take responsibility for how we have brought it upon ourselves and if we have not brought it upon ourselves we ought to be diligent to respond appropriately. An appropriate response would be to trust that God has a reason for the adversity and to ask the question, "What is it I am to learn from this move of God in my life?"

Believe this, that Yahweh does move in the lives of His people, he may be moving in your life right now and it may not be pleasant. When God moves in a life, it may be a move that brings us to our knees in humble submission to the King of the Universe. Just because it sometimes causes pain and hurt doesn't mean God is not doing it. The result of the affliction that comes from God is often that the recipient becomes willing to acknowledge all God's ways and seek to do His will steadfastly. The verses we just looked at from Job are unequivocally stating that God is the one performing the entire calamity that has and is coming upon Job. Amos 3 has told us if there is calamity in a city or by extension in a man's life, then God is the one who caused it. Verse 31 of this chapter in Job really puts it straight. This poor persecuted and broken man is asking that his friends or "counselors," would have pity on him instead of railing against him. His friends implying that he is some kind of a stubborn, arrogant, fool who has brought this upon himself, did not comfort Job. Job tells his "counselors" to pity him because "it is the hand of Elohim who has touched him". It is not some radical and virtually uncontrollable, nefarious, fallen angel, but the only One with power to afflict is the one touching and afflicting Job.

> *Have pity upon me, have pity upon me, O ye my friends; for **the hand of God hath touched me.** Job 19:21 KJV*

Wouldn't it be easier to exist through a trial if once we had searched our hearts and asked Yahweh to search our hearts and find any wicked way within us we could rest on a belief which recognizes we control only our own choices and responses to life, but Yahweh controls life?

It is guaranteed, if you begin to adopt a philosophy similar to this then anything that comes upon you can be walked through with a measure of peace that is elusive for many during trials. A Simple application of this philosophy might look like this. If bad stuff is happening, look inside to see if your heart is right with Yahweh. Then, humble yourself and ask for his forgiveness and deliverance. Once that is accomplished, whether something in your mind stood out as being in opposition to God's will for your life or not, acknowledge God is the source of your affliction and ask Him to give you the strength and wisdom to journey through it. Next, accept that what you are going through is because Yahweh wants you to be going through this. His ways are not our ways and He does nothing without a purpose.

In Job's questioning he also makes mention of how the wicked are prospering. This is somewhat confusing to Job who is a child of Yahweh. Job is a pretty clean living guy by all accounts and even by the accounts of the Creator, as seen in chapter one of this book where Job is said to be blameless. In verses 8 and 9 of chapter 21, Job makes mention of how the wicked are having children who are not being decimated and in fact are being "established", as Job puts it. As well, Job makes note of the fact that the houses of the wicked are safe and the inference that follows is that the rod of Elohim that has brought calamity upon Job is not even touching the wicked. To Job, as it would seem to many, it doesn't make sense. The good guy is being smacked and the bad guy keeps living it up unscathed and no one is raining on the wicked guy's parade. Here is how Job puts it:

> *Wherefore do the wicked live, become old, yea, are mighty in power?*
> *Their seed is established in their sight with them, and their offspring before their eyes.*
> *Their houses are safe from fear, neither is the rod of God upon them. Job 21:7-9 KJV*

Job in essence is posing a question asking; why do I get the "rod of God" ripping apart my life when the wicked are not even tickled by it let alone beaten into submission? Now these are not the exact words of Job but the concept is abundantly represented when we consider Job's line of questioning and the information he supplies in his heart-rending discourse. Going into all the feeling and thoughts of Job at this time is unnecessary and is a task that can better be undertaken by someone else. As mentioned earlier, there has been a multitude of commentaries and books written that have covered the subtleties of Job's thoughts and feelings. However, for our purposes we only need take note that once again we are shown Job knows his rotten hand in the great poker game of life, was dealt by the Creator. Job also knows that the Creator can stack His deck any way He wants to because the House always ends up on top. In the wisdom of King Solomon, said to be the wisest man to walk the earth outside of the Messiah, we are told how this "good to the wicked and bad to the righteous" plays out sometimes;

> *There is a vanity which is done upon the earth; that there be just men, unto whom it happeneth according to the work of the wicked; again, there be wicked men, to whom it happeneth according to the work of the righteous: I said that this also is vanity. Ecclesiastes 8:14 KJV*

Solomon knew how it worked. He knew that sometimes what one would expect to be the earthly justice upon a wicked man actually happens to a just man. Conversely, Solomon figured out that often stuff that would be thought to happen to a just man here on earth is happening to a wicked man. As it goes, sometimes bad things happen to good people and good things happen to bad people. I don't like it any more than Job did, but it just is.

Yahweh Vexes Job's Soul

As we move through the book of Job looking for major clues to who it is that is afflicting Job, we hear Job say that Yahweh is vexing his soul.

> *Moreover Job continued his parable, and said, As God liveth, who hath taken away my judgment; and the Almighty, who hath vexed my soul; Job 27:1-2 KJV*

Even after all the prodding and bemoaning by Job's friends who attempt to make Job see that he himself is responsible for the wicked that he has suffered, Job continues to faithfully expound about the character of Yahweh to his friends by saying "God liveth". In declaring that "God liveth," Job is proclaiming the sovereign attribute of the Almighty. In this statement, we are able to recognize that Job is delivering more truth about his situation and that it is God who is inflicting the damage. Job knows that to declare to his friends that "God liveth" is to let them know that Job himself is not furious with the Creator, nor is Job diminishing Yahweh's absolute right to do whatever He desires with His creation, including Job himself who is pretty high ranking in the weekly top forty of righteous servants of the Almighty. Job was called blameless and righteous by God. The possibility for all men to be deceived exists but even considering that fact, we do not see Job taking a big moral or theological backslide in this story. All we know for now is that Job has the approval of the Creator and could be considered to be somewhat of a saint.

In considering the testimony of the key player in this unfolding drama, we must take seriously the claim heard from Job stating that the God of the Universe has "vexed his soul".

TWO POSSIBILITIES FOR UNDERSTANDING THE STORY OF JOB

Although in the first two chapters of Job we see the word "Satan" in the English, which is really "adversary" in Hebrew, we must try to remember that the type of literature that is represented by Job, is writing known as Aggadic or wisdom writing. Because this story is designed to teach us a concept and not to espouse facts and specifics, a seemingly literal conversation may not necessarily be literal but simply may be a literary method of depicting either of two possibilities. The first is that this conversation represents an internal conversation between a human adversary present at the temple environment and Yahweh. Or the second which would be; a literal conversation between a human adversary who came to the temple environment with other human "sons of God" and is railing against Job to the Priestly representative of the Most High. The adversary here is likely doing this out of jealousy and envy of Job and Job's prosperous life. Either way we decide to view this initial conversation in the text of Job's story, our perspective must be reconcilable with the rest of Job and the statements in Job that clearly say the evil comes from God.

Somehow, in all this, most people considering the story of Job often slip back into the idea that contends; "Well God **allowed** it to happen to Job." Or, "God **allowed** Satan to afflict Job." Let's be sensible about the whole matter; is it really the manner of the Creator to be convinced by a fallen angel who was cast out of Heaven forever because of his pride and rebellion, to allow him to hammer Job with destruction of family, finances, and health? Why is it so simple for common Christianity to accept this distorted view of the Creator? Is the need to believe their God could not do bad to people so strong for so many, that they have to blame the uncomfortable and trying portions of their life on a cosmic Satan? Do we believe Yahweh is so weak that He cannot be held responsible for the unpalatable afflictions that may come upon them? What kind of control then does the God of the Universe have if He can be convinced by a fallen angel to allow that "angel" to rip apart the life of a servant of the Most High? How in the world do we then expect that this fallen Angel is not continually trying to convince the Creator to "let him "test" any person who is diligently serving God? Moreover, how can we expect that God will not be convinced by Satan repeatedly to allow him the delight of attacking any one of us or our family members?

The idea of an angel who is the epitome of sin and rebellion and who once was the crowning creation of Yahweh, being kicked out of Heaven because of pride, and then is allowed to enter into heaven again whenever he feels like "coming before the Lord", is absolutely absurd. If this is the case, then Yahweh doesn't really place much value on the fact that sin cannot be in his presence as Habakkuk 1:13 says; *Thou art of purer eyes than to behold evil, and canst not look on iniquity:.*_

Is this the God that says, "*I make peace and create evil*" or is it the God that only makes peace? Isaiah 45:7 declares the former. If the thoughts and statements in Job are all to be believed to be true, then we have to view the conversation with "the adversary" at the start of the story differently than the traditional understanding. Otherwise, we have to view all the statements which acknowledge God as the one responsible for the activity which virtually destroyed the life of Job, as meaningless words and lies. By looking at the sum of all the parts and setting another possible understanding of this story in front of us, we then should be able to comfortably dismiss the afflicting of Job as being the act of a cosmic, archenemy of God. We should be able to realize the potency of this tale as a teaching aid. A story delivered through the medium of writing that incorporates common literary tools and styles, as they would be used in the distant past. To ponder for a moment that if society were to continue to advance and then exist in 3 or 4 hundred years from now those present at that time might very well be confused by some of the language, images and cultural practices which are readily understandable to us who are engaged in them today.

The long and short of it is that one cannot understand an ancient writing or work without working to understand much of the culture and styles of writing or presentation that were understood in the age they are exploring.

All that said, there is still more in this book of Job to attest to the fact that there is no other cosmic entity but the Creator who performed these unsavory acts on poor Job.

Nearing the end of Job's story, we are confronted with the words of yet one more man to give counsel to Job. Elihu is the name of this final human counselor. I say "human counselor" because Job is yet to receive counsel from the Creator, who is not a human. If you look at the last chapter of Job, this counselor is not lumped in with the three friends of Job who dispensed counsel that was not acceptable nor glorifying to God. Eliphaz, Bildad and Zophar are said to have not spoken right of Yahweh. In Verse 7 of chapter 42, we hear this;

> *And it was so, that after the LORD had spoken these words unto Job, the LORD said to Eliphaz the Temanite, My wrath is kindled against thee, and against thy two friends: for ye have not spoken of me the thing that is right, as my servant Job hath. Job 42:7 KJV*

Job's counselors are accused by the Creator of not speaking right of Yahweh. God on the other hand affirms Job as speaking correctly. This would be such a powerful vindication for the deeply afflicted Job. If these words of the Creator are true then we can rule out Job's persecution from God as being the result of speaking ill about Him. Looking carefully at the story and then weighing Yahweh's words spoken to Job, there is some indication that even though Job had been called perfect, he still was being dealt with by the Father for certain aspects of his attitude. Some of these aspects of Job's appear to have been aspects that may have been arrogant or aspects that seemed to show Job presumed he had figured out God's workings.

It is in Elihu's words that we see a defense of Yahweh's actions against Job. This can be understood in it's simplest form by Elihu saying, don't think you fully understand the ways of God because the Creator is far to profound and perfect in his judgments and justice for a human to really make complete sense of it. This is the reason Elihu says to Job, Elohim thundereth things that we cannot comprehend in chapter 37.

> *God thundereth marvellously with his voice; great things doeth he, which we cannot comprehend. Job 37:5 KJV*

In verse 7 of this chapter, we are told God controls the hand of all men and we are given the reason God does so. The reason is to enhance the potential for all men to know His works.

> *He sealeth up the hand of every man; that all men may know his work. Job 37:7 KJVA*

What we are hearing is that even a situation of evil coming upon a man by the actions of another man, is controlled, "or sealed up" as it is put in this chapter, by the Almighty. It is interesting timing that the statement from Elihu in this wisdom book is immediately followed by the words of Yahweh. Perhaps Yahweh finally heard some counsel from a friend of Job that had value and then God decided to punctuate the wisdom with His statement to Job.

I am not in a position today to dogmatically say that when Yahweh spoke to Job He was speaking audibly in a comprehensive language with detectable sound that was heard by the ears of Job. It may be that we are in fact given the script of a literal conversation. Conversely, I am not in a position today to dogmatically say that this conversation, which we are let in on between Job and the Master, is an inner conversation that went on inside of Job. It is difficult to be dogmatic in stating that either this conversation was an external conversation or that it took place deep in Job's heart and mind. We all are capable of understanding that there is not really a potential for humans to have a conversation in his or her literal heart. However, no matter whether we use physiological terminology or ethereal concepts to explain the manner and location of this conversation, it is entirely possible that the conversation between Job and Yahweh had been an "internal" dialogue. We all have the ability to comprehend euphemism and metaphor such as this in language today, so why is it so difficult to comprehend these kinds of poetical words found in ancient writings? As I said, I am not intending to be dogmatic on this issue but please consider the possibility based on the following reasoning.

We are given the words of Elihu, which are a powerful testimony to Job that the Creator is about His business, and we humans are only able to faithfully accept the Creator's dealings with limited understanding. The type of arrogance that comes with believing one understands implicitly the workings of the God of the Universe is definitely not seen as humility before Yahweh. Elihu expresses this sentiment so eloquently that the following words of God we are presented with could very likely have been serious and deep introspection on behalf of Job, similar to the silent prayer of a person who is connecting to Yahweh. I know through experiential knowledge that when I have been challenged by my wife or a brother or sister or a friend on an action, attitude or behavioral pattern which displays a less than honorable and "godly" attribute, I often will reflect on the words of the "counselor". I often will sit before the Father to try to hear His mind on the matter. I am quite certain that I have not heard an audible, detectable voice from Yahweh but I am certain that because He has used one of His children to speak words that prick my heart, He then ministers or "speaks" if you will, to my heart. I believe what may be happening in those moments is that the Spirit of the Creator is drawing out of my innermost being, words or understanding, which have been deposited in me simply by walking through life trying to serve Him. The Father has used an obedient servant to deliver a message to me in a timely and effective manner. After the delivery of the message, presuming my heart is softened to receive a prompting that directs me towards self-assessment, I am able to productively reflect on the situation. If I am being honest with myself and consequently being honest with my God, I will likely begin changing my attitude to exhibit a demeanor or behavior which is more in line with the Father's will for my life. It may sound a little complicated, but there are few who can deny that they have worked through some type of an inner dialogue in their life. There are many who at least say they have listened to that still, small voice deep within. An almost undetectable reasoning and prompting that caused them at some point in their life to change one aspect or another of who they are and how they may be functioning as a human being, a unique creation designed to relate to the Creator, to other humans and to serve the Master out of love for Him.

In a great many of movies or stories where the character in the story is at a crossroads of sorts in making a significant decision the story uses a soliloquy to let us in on the self-talk or inner conversation this character is having with themselves. The listener or reader is then fully apprised of the character's process to come to a conclusion on a decision or difficult situation. Perhaps this is the type of concept found in the wisdom book of Job. Perhaps knowing of the possibility of this type of an inner dialogue in Job's life may help you accept the possibility that the dialogues in this story between Job and God are not literal, physical conversations. One way or another, Job did receive some rebuke from Yahweh and Job's reply was appropriate in that he recognized the need to maintain a humble acceptance of whom God is and how He operates.

When All is Good Again the Evil is Said to Have Come from God

We are getting near the end of looking at Job and the "satan/adversary" found in this book. Overall, like any good wisdom writing of the period, this book of Job is no exception in that it concisely concludes the tale with a final dissertation from the Creator and a response from Job, which shows Job's heart. Job ends up a changed man by his experience and from those things that he has heard in his spirit from and about the Creator. Our main character speaks humble words that claim he now knows Yahweh does things that Job and therefore we today if we are learning from this wisdom book, are too wonderful and full of meaning for us to understand. We are humans and He is not. The Creator holds too much knowledge, power, wisdom, justice, and truth for a created being such as a human to understand. Upon admitting this, Job repents in dust and ashes. This is an act of serious humility and contrition. This act displayed Job's heart of repentance. Many who engage in a discussion around the story of Job, miss the fact that Job repents. It is a common theme in the judgments of Yahweh that they are designed to bring humans to repentance and to reveal to the human being, their true heart. If Job had nothing to repent of, as some may conclude based on the early description of Job as being perfect and upright, then he would not have repented in dust and ashes. However, through the actions of Job we can conclude that repentance was required and if we understand repentance was required then we may be able to conclude that Job had some sin in his heart that needed to be revealed and dealt with. Be it a sin of pride or arrogance matters little for our purposes. The fact is that God gave Job suffering in place of a life and position of comfort. He was given a position of strife and anguish. Job was given a judgment that included suffering. This evil was at the hand of Elohim as Job had told his wife in chapter 2. This evil or judgment brought the desired response. It changed Job's heart, and even though he was in the "weekly top forty" in the eyes of Yahweh, he still needed to tweak certain aspects of his life, heart, and understanding of the Creator. Said simply in biblical shoot from the hip style, Job is tested and judged, Job repents and Yahweh restores Job....mission accomplished... the plan worked.

The closing chapter and more specifically in the final 10 verses, we see how Job had spoken words of repentance from his heart and Yahweh receives sacrifices and prayers from Job on behalf of Job's erring "counselors." Then we are told how many of Job's friends came to Job to bemoan what had happened to him. In the closing of this story we are once again told where the "evil" that happened to Job came from. The friends of Job come together with Job's family to comfort him for all the evil that the Lord had brought upon Job;

> *Then came there unto him all his brethren, and all his sisters, and all they that had been of his acquaintance before, and did eat bread with him in his house: and they bemoaned him, and comforted him* ***over all the evil that the LORD had brought upon him****: every man also gave him a piece of money, and every one an earring of gold. Job 42:11 KJV*

The above verse is irrefutably saying all the evil that Job suffered was brought upon him by Yahweh. It would be irresponsible after seeing all the reference and testimony in the book of Job that explicitly blames the evil Job received on Yahweh, for us to continue to attribute the evil to Satan. It is simply incorrect to adhere to the mainstream view of Satanology, which translates the Hebrew word for adversary into the name for Satan when a human sent by God is generally the adversary that is being spoken about. By mistranslating and misunderstanding the term for a human adversary, we risk ascribing what God has done, to some fabricated, nonexistent, and therefore powerless cosmic being. It is abject denial, of the full counsel of the Scripture's perspective on a Satan, to continue to impose a contemporary understanding of Satan on the terms we are seeing in Job. Particularly in light of Job himself, testifying his woes had come from the hand of Yahweh. This sure agrees with the thinking and statement of Isaiah 45:7 that told us Yahweh makes peace and creates evil.

Either these acts of evil upon Job were direct actions from Yahweh or they possibly were administered through the hands of Job's human adversary and his agents that had questioned Job's uprightness at the outset of the Job saga. Seeing that the wicked done to Job does not have to be seen as coming from a mythological being invented by man, called "Satan," gives us the opportunity at least to explore the potential of these acts being the work of men's hands. In the first chapter, just prior to Job's family being killed by a combo of invaders and natural disasters we are told;

> *And the LORD said unto the adversary, Behold, all that he hath is in thy power; only upon himself put not forth thine hand. So Satan went forth from the presence of the LORD. Job 1:12*

If some wish to believe that Yahweh actually said to a cosmic Satan, "Here, take everything of Job's and go ahead and kill his family", then why would one trust that Yahweh is not continually relinquishing his rule over their life and giving His beloved children over to an evil supernatural being? Particularly because Job was blameless and upright and certainly was less deserving of being destroyed by Satan than many of us. This kind of a story line, which has a Sovereign Creator literally giving the heads of the innocent to an evil force or being, is intended to express in graphic imagery the point that it is Yahweh doing the acts to the innocent. It appears possible that this story is in fact a parable of the most potent form. We have a story with some very powerful actions occurring to destroy the life of a good man but the details of the acts are not plentiful. In the absence of detail, we can start to lean in the direction of understanding the story as a parable intended to teach Israel about their God. Job's story educates the people of Israel to the fact that they are supposed to continue seeing Yahweh as the only God in control of everything, even though calamity has struck. After Job loses all his children, he worships God and we are then told that God was the one who has taken away from Job;

> *Then Job arose, and rent his mantle, and shaved his head, and fell down upon the ground, and worshipped,*
> *And said, Naked came I out of my mother's womb, and naked shall I return thither: the LORD gave, and the LORD hath taken away; blessed be the name of the LORD.*
> *In all this Job sinned not, nor charged God foolishly. Job 1:20-22 KJV*

What are we supposed to learn from seeing Job worshipping the Creator after the tragedy that he has just been subjected too? Among many things that are worthwhile to take from Job's story, I would submit that we are to learn how that no matter what befalls man; it is because Yahweh has perpetrated it. King Solomon was no stranger to this principle when he wrote in the book of Ecclesiastes that evil stuff falls on good men at times.

> *There is a vanity which is done upon the earth; that there be just men, unto whom it happeneth according to the work of the wicked; again, there be wicked men, to whom it happeneth according to the work of the righteous: I said that this also is vanity. Ecclesiastes 8:14 KJV*

Perhaps seeing the anguish of Job due to the loss of his family is understandable. Perhaps it is understandable that this man was so extraordinarily righteous, that he just took what Yahweh did to him and didn't think anything of it. Perhaps we can justify Job's exceptional response to his tragedies by thinking he believes the cause of his pain is Satan. It is possible though, to understand the tragedies of how Job's children died can be attributed to natural disasters and to human men who came as invaders. This seems possible and if Job truly had an enemy or a human adversary of influence and power out to get him, then the attacks on his family may well have been orchestrated in a similar fashion to John Gotti taking out a hit on another mob family by contracting the services of a street gang. The fact is, we are given very little detail of the actual outworking of Job's sufferings as they pertain to other men being the perpetrators of said suffering. Therefore, it is plausible when we are honest with recognizing just how little detail is given us in the story of Job's tragedies, that God may have employed more than one method against the righteous Job and the men that God used as ministers of pain.

Job Received Boils

Perhaps it is true that men are responsible for the actual physical hands behind the inflicting of Job but you might ask, what about the boils that the English versions say were afflicting Job? These boils surely must have been an attack of Satan like the English text says.

> *And the LORD said unto Satan, Behold, he is in thine hand; but save his life.*
> *So went Satan forth from the presence of the LORD, and smote Job with sore boils from the sole of his foot unto his crown. Job 2:6-7 KJV*

There we have it, according to the English translation of this verse, Satan gave Job boils. Some might contend that it is not possible for man to give another man boils. Aside from transmitting an infectious disease or launching an ancient version of biological warfare, I generally agree that it is unlikely for one man to have the ability to place boils upon another. I sincerely doubt there would have been biological warfare used on Job by his adversary. What then could the boils have resulted from? Some may claim that "Satan" had the power to place boils on Job but the Hebrew doesn't claim the boils came from a cosmic Satan just that the adversary was responsible for the boils. In the absence of a cosmic Satan as is taught by the Scriptures, there has to be another explanation for the boils Job received. Let us consider a different possibility.

Let me ask you, if you saw a friend with a rash all over their neck and arms and they were asked what happened would you understand their answer if they replied," My laundry detergent gave me a rash."?

Of course, there is no question that there is nothing spiritual about that rash but it is purely a physical reaction to the soap the clothes were washed in. Alternatively, how about if they answered when asked how they acquired the festering rash; "I got this rash thanks to Johnson and Johnson!" Simple enough, we know Johnson and Johnson did not come to their house and somehow infect your friend's skin so that they would break out in a rash. Let me ask another one, have you ever been so burdened with stress that you break out in a rash or boil-like sores? Do you realize that it is possible to break out in boils or a rash when you are under a stress overload? I have seen it happen with stressed out men and with small children as well as others and it is very uncomfortable. How about a parent who is stressed out and say, "My kids give me a headache!" In the instance of Job's boils, what we are seeing poetically blamed on "Satan," is likely no different from a stress response manifesting itself physically on Job as boils. Neither Job nor his wife blamed Satan, but Mrs. Job wanted Job to curse God and die to which Job had a ready response;

> *Then said his wife unto him, Dost thou still retain thine integrity? curse God, and die.*
> *But he said unto her, Thou speakest as one of the foolish women speaketh. What?* ***shall we receive good at the hand of God, and shall we not receive evil?*** *In all this did not Job sin with his lips. Job 2:9-10 KJV*

Job said, "Hey woman, the evil is coming from God, watch what you're asking me to do."

Of course, I am paraphrasing, but the boils that many say are from a cosmic Satan based on the English rendering of the word for adversary, are actually from Yahweh. I would say even at that, they are not a direct act from Yahweh but just the process of stress taking its toll on Job's body. It is a creative conclusion to decide that a physical illness, condition, or malady is from a supernatural Satan who possesses the power to make a person sick. If in fact there is no Satan then the reader must come to another conclusion or at least be open to there being another possibility for what caused Job's boils. Some proposed options for the cause of Job's boils are; Satan who doesn't exist sent boils, or wicked adversarial opponents of Job enlisted some manner of biological or chemical warfare against Job, or the boils were the physical manifestation of the stress and negative state that Job was in for possibly quite some time. Remaining in a negative or stressful state for a period of time might manifest in physical ailments such as headaches, insomnia, intestinal difficulties, skin rash, boils, or other conditions. Due to the lack of specifics in the story, one can be creative in postulating how exactly Job ended up with boils from his experiences. I think the important point to make here is that as long as one sees that a non-existent cosmic Satan had nothing to do with Job's boils, then a sensible pursuit of another possible answer will bode well for the seeker.

If it were so that a Satan existed who could impart disease to a human, then why do the Scriptures repeatedly acknowledge Yahweh as the source of physical illnesses and such? I have myself at times in the past blamed illnesses and conditions of physical malady on "Satan", when I used to believe what I was wrongly taught about the "evil one." I soon learned that the things that others and I were experiencing could be attributed to the result of other physical stimuli in my or our life at the time. I will share more later on this part of my journey but as a former "intercessory prayer warrior", I at one point in my life was praying against Satan because of the difficulty I was having with achieving quality sleep. Much to my chagrin, as I reduced my stress and busyness in my life, I was able to reclaim valuable sleep and realized I needed to look at the physical reasons for my dilemma, not try to attach some spiritual reason to it. I will say that in the years I practiced "intercessory prayer", blaming a satanic force for things such as a cold or a backache became the norm. I am still somewhat embarrassed to explicate the depths of this deception in my life at that time but I will mention certain aspects about that leg of my journey from time to time in this work.

As for Job and his tragedies, including the boils, I would suggest strongly that all that happened to Job, besides the natural disasters which some erroneously say are also controlled by "Satan", could very easily be attributed to human hands and are a natural response to stress from the intensities of life that Job was experiencing.

I am not postulating a new idea, just one or should I say one more, that has been veiled in centuries of mixed and confused theology. Confused theology that has been propagated by the false religious system of our time. The belief in a cosmic Satan and the associated belief that claims Satan causes sickness is error compounded upon error that started thousands of years ago. When I am reminded that the Messiah was not a Christian according to the common understanding of what it means to be a Christian and how Christianity is generally practiced, I find it easy to question the teachings of Christianity. Especially in light of the fact that so much of what Christianity professes as accurate biblical teaching and doctrine, cannot be proven by the Scriptures that Christ used. If the Messiah were to stroll through our towns and cities today, he likely wouldn't recognize Christianity today as a product and outcome of the way His apostles walked out their faith and worshiped the Creator. Christianity today is the outcome of edicts by the Roman Empire from the 2nd to fifth centuries. For us to stand back and accept the idea of a cosmic, supernatural Satan, being the active cause of the affliction of Job would be to reject the real power that stands behind Job's afflictions. If we are careful to assess the story apart from our predetermined perspective on the issue of Satan, we can clearly see that the source of affliction is simply an "adversary" in the form of a human man and the power behind that "evil" is not a "satanic" force that is in opposition to the God of the Universe. The force behind the affliction of Job is the God of the Universe. To accept the truth of the words of Job and understand the use of the Hebrew word for "adversary" as a word to represent that which is an oppositional force to Job, is to effectively reduce "Satan" to what he truly is in relation to Job. Satan, or should I say satan, is a human adversary. The wisdom writing of Job is in line with the rest of the Hebrew Scriptures in that it supports the concept that there is only one God and that an evil cosmic force said to oppose man and God does not exist.

CHAPTER 11

Zechariah's Vision, What Was the Satan He Saw?

Have you ever had a dream? I don't mean a dream to take your family to Disneyland or a dream you could some day whisk your spouse off in a private jet to Paris for a romantic dinner. I'm not talking about the type of dream a person has that is made up in their mind and is intended to help them escape from reality for a moment or two but in actual fact will probably never come to pass. For instance, the other day the lottery was promising a prize of 35 million dollars. I have to be honest with you I did take a few seconds out of my busy day to dream what I would do with 35 million dollars. The dream did not last long and wasn't the kind of dream that has the characteristic epiphany qualities to redirect one's life toward a focus of pursuing the dream. My few seconds of dreaming about having 35 million dollars did not consume my thoughts, nor did it at all lend me to believe that winning 35 million dollars might actually happen to me. So, after a few ideas popped into my head of what I would do with all that money, they then left my focus of attention and I went on with my day and my life. This is definitely one type of dream many are familiar with or have experienced. However, when I asked you if you have ever had a dream, I was referring to the more ethereal concept of the dream. The type of dream you have when you're sleeping and according to sleep-researchers, the kind of dream that occurs during the stage of sleep that occurs just before you begin to wake up and enter a conscious level of activity.

Think about a dream you've had. In this dream, did you perhaps see a tree or a bridge? Maybe this dream contained images of an animal or a coworker or perhaps it was the kind of pizza dream many people have and in it, the co-worker is an animal. How about a dream that had images of a bird or a park with a child playing? Did your dream contain any of those images? There's a chance your dream contained images of you or someone in the dream being chased. It may be that you have a had a dream where you are late for work or showed up at an exam in university and you not only are un-studied for the test but there are only minutes remaining to complete the exam which was to have been a three hour test. Do some of us have dreams of our children going missing or getting hurt? Have you ever had a dream that you were trying to run but you could barely move your feet and legs because they were either so heavy or seemingly stuck to the ground? How about a dream where you are falling? Many people have those types of dreams periodically throughout life but are in reality not literally falling from a high precipice.

If you take all the dreams you have had in your lifetime, analyze the content and characters in the dreams, then sit down, and make a list of all the literal components of your dreams, how big would the list be?

I remember when I was about 10 or eleven years old, I had a dream where I was sitting on the curb at the edge of the sidewalk one day and shuffling my feet through the leaves that had collected in the gutter. I looked down and there was a twenty-dollar bill in the dirt. In my dream, I remember the feeling I had when I found the twenty-dollar bill. I was so excited. Twenty dollars was a sizable amount of free money for an eleven year old in 1978. In the morning, I woke up and was actually, physically looking for the twenty dollars I had found. Knowing how fantastic of a treasure that amount of cash was to me I logically searched the typical places I would have stashed the loot upon returning home with it. Alas, there was no twenty to be found and when I sufficiently inspected every sensible spot that I might have placed my find, I conceded that the twenty-dollar bill find must have been a dream and I let it go. Logic prevailed and to this day, although the feeling I recall from the instance when I woke up to hold the found money was palpably real, I don't question that the whole thing was a dream. Conclusion on this type of a dream would be that it meant nothing and I should move on, or each of the components, such as the debris, the money, and me, the character, all had meaning that could be related to some other aspect of my life. The dream about the found money as a child was not a literal situation, neither were the components of the dream literally representing physical realities. All components of the dream were not actual concrete real-world experiences, situations, or material icons; that is all but me as the main character in the dream. Therefore, the type of dream I am talking about is the kind that happens in your mind at a time of rest when you are not consciously controlling your own thoughts. I am quite certain that any person reading this book can attest to the fact of having a "dream" in their sleep at least once in their life if not regularly. My dream about the twenty-dollar find happened almost thirty years ago and I still know today that it was a dream and that the components of it were symbols representing something I still do not know of.

My list of literal dreams that I have personally had is small. In fact, I might say that my list of literal dreams is almost countable on one hand. Another dream that I have had and am inclined to accept as being literal went like this. One night during sleep, I dreamt I was contacting a certain person. The senior Pastor of the church I used to attend who used to be a significant influence in my life. Due to theological differences, this person and his board of directors kicked me out of the church he was leading some months before I had the dream that I would meet up with him. After a few complaints by loyal members of the church that I was challenging their beliefs, I was sent a registered letter to my home. The letter informed me I was no longer permitted to attend services unless I had the written permission of the pastor or board of deacons. The whole story and reasons for me being excommunicated from this church are long and involved so I will save that discussion for the future perhaps; for now let me say that the dream I had was a dream where I ran into this person, whom I'll refer to as Merv. When I woke, I felt that I would be seeing this person in the next couple of days. The next day as my wife and I were stopping by Wal-Mart™ my dream came to mind and I became certain that I was going to run into Merv any moment. My wife and I went different directions to gather items for about five minutes and when we met, she told me she had just seen Merv by the tills. I told her that I expected to run into him here today because of my dream. While speaking those words to her I felt that I was supposed to see Merv personally, thus confirming my dream. Well, as I was sharing these thoughts with Ellah my wife as we were walking down the aisle, within about five steps of her telling me she just saw Merv, I looked to my right and there he was about ten feet from the end of the isle where I was now standing. At that point, I went over and said hello, providing the greeting I believed was appropriate based on the understanding I had from the dream of me running into Merv. At that chance meeting there was nothing of any great significance that occurred. I did however invite Merv to get together to discuss some of our theological differences. Sadly, this highly paid Pastor decided that God had told him to no longer discuss differences in theological views and that he was right and I was in the wrong. This is an example of what I would call a dream that was to be taken literally. I dreamt of running into Merv at an undefined location, then within the next day, the dream came true and I did run into Merv.

The dream did involve me having contact with Merv but in the dream this contact did not happen in a Wal-Mart™. Therefore, in this instance the concept and the characters were literal. It is always a little spine tingling when someone has a dream of a future event. It would be nice to be able to say that you or I was able to identify clearly the complete meaning of every dreamed situation and character but that is just not the case. I am confident though that there is only one Creator and one being who knows the end from the beginning, so in the event that a person is questioning the meaning and reason for a certain dream I would counsel the dreamer that their dream which tells of future events, must be from Yahweh for one reason or another. The reasons then are to be explored by the dreamer with the aid of wise counsel and the aid of the Father's Spirit. Moreover, the incidents depicted often must be waited on as a dream about the future is only fully confirmed at the point of its occurrence when the future becomes the present, due to the passage of time.

As I said, my list is small and I would be surprised if there are many out there who do a dream accounting and conclude that they have had many literal dreams. If dreams were by nature literal then there would be no need of interpretation, nor would there be any mystery and then we would be able to remove the Creator, Yahweh, from the picture altogether, beyond the point of perhaps He being the one who has given a person their dreams. Daniel says it well in the book of Daniel when he is asked to interpret the King's dream. Daniel, one of the wisest men in all of Babylon, tells the King that it is Elohim who reveals things to him:

> *Daniel answered in the presence of the king, and said, The secret which the king hath demanded cannot the wise men, the astrologers, the magicians, the soothsayers, shew unto the king; But there is a God in heaven that revealeth secrets, and maketh known to the king Nebuchadnezzar what shall be in the latter days. Thy dream, and the visions of thy head upon thy bed, are these; Daniel 2:27-28 KJV*

When trying to delineate between dreams and their counterpart, visions, it often may be presumed that one or the other is more meaningful and at times more comprehensive because of the level of consciousness of the recipient at the time of the dream or vision. We need not split the proverbial hair on the difference in the technical aspects between the two; however, it is simply fair enough to state that both dreams and visions are of the same substance. Dreams are often placed in the same category as visions in the Scriptures according to the International Standard Bible Encyclopedia;

> In all time dreams and their interpretation have been the occasion of much curious and speculative inquiry. Because of the mystery by which they have been enshrouded, and growing out of a

> natural curiosity to know the future, much significance has been attached to them by people especially of the lower stages of culture. Even the cultured are not without a superstitious awe and dread of dreams, attaching to them different interpretations according to local color and custom. Naturally enough, as with all other normal and natural phenomena for which men could assign no scientific and rational explanation, they would be looked upon with a certain degree of superstitious fear. ...
>
> Thus, dreams are to the sleeping state what visions and hallucinations are to the waking state, and like them have their ground in a distorted image-making function. While the source of the materials and the excitant may not be the same in each case, yet functionally they are the same.[134]

Notice in the above ISBE quote that dreams and visions are considered to both have their ground in distorted image making. Sometimes it is difficult to delineate if a dream or a vision in Scripture has occurred and if this has occurred at night while the one having the vision or dream is asleep, or if it has occurred during the waking hours. Suffice it to say, that both sleeping and waking visions occur in Scripture. It appears that these types of visions, which often seem like fairly dramatic experiences that find the person having the vision in a trance like state, do not occur with great regularity to the individual. The record displays the visions as happening a lot but the fact is, there is a large quantity of time between the visions and therefore the volume of visions that occur is not that great. A misunderstanding of dreams and visions has led many to wrong conclusions as to their meaning. Near the end of the chapter, we will consider the significance of a culture being shaped by its stimulus and how it has a propensity to adopt mystical concepts that those in the culture are exposed to. First, we will discuss how Zechariah's visions are not literal and the word "Satan" is not meant to imply the Satan of ancient lore.

The book of Zechariah has eight visions or dreams which we are given an account of in the Hebrew Scriptures. These eight visions appear to be given to Zechariah in the night, which may indicate they are dreams he received while sleeping. We will not read through them all together but I highly recommend you do so at some point to assist you in comprehending the context of these visions. Let's talk about the context of these visions for a while. I am not able to put it as well as some of the brilliant scholars who have taken the task of dissecting the entire work of Zechariah and communicating the main themes

134 ISBE reference under entry on Dreams, Dreamers

and purpose of Zechariah's writings. The Fausset and Brown commentary says much of the context of this book and I offer their insight from their commentary below as an aid in understanding a little about Zechariah and the book that bares his name.

In the last paragraph of the following reference, I have highlighted and underlined one statement. The statement is saying that the visions of Zechariah are of a symbolical nature. Too many individuals and groups with a sincere desire to believe in the God of Abraham, Isaac, and Jacob have applied literal meaning to symbolic images. This error has left many lacking in understanding more clearly, the message the prophet is intending to relay to the hearer. It is crucial that one bare in mind this fact; that Zechariah is delivering symbolic, prophetic utterances, therefore imposing a literal attribute to every single symbol or character is not going to bring the reader to the truth intended in his writing. True some of the characters may be literal, such as the mention of Joshua the high priest in chapter 3 and 6, however, the use of a literal character is more likely intended to imply a moral or allegorical concept. We have previously discussed briefly, mytho-poetic language. And here, as with all the prophets, we are able to see mytho-poetic language used in this writing. Therefore, we must try to understand the poetical and symbolical nature of the writings of Zechariah.

Numerous scholars and commentators acknowledge the rich imagery of this prophet's statement and see clearly the connection of literary statements that are called Chaldaisms, to the delivery of the prophetic message. A Chaldaism is an idiom or peculiarity in the Chaldee dialect that would have been readily understood for its metaphorical intent by those familiar with the Chaldean culture and language as those who Zechariah was speaking to would have been. Therefore, before we forge ahead to explore how the Satan in Zechariah's vision was not a literal entity we can consult the information from a well known commentary to assist us with background information on Zechariah the man and his writings. Please notice the commentators below are careful to iterate that all eight of Zechariah's visions are symbolical.

> **Zechariah** - THE name Zechariah means one whom Jehovah remembers: a common name, four others of the same name occurring in the Old Testament. Like Jeremiah and Ezekiel, he was a priest as well as a prophet, which adapts him for the sacerdotal character of some of his prophecies (Zec_6:13). He is called "the son of Berechiah the son of Iddo" (Zec_1:1); but simply "the son of Iddo" in Ezr_5:1; Ezr_6:14. Probably his father died when he was young; and hence, as sometimes occurs in Jewish genealogies, he is called "the son of Iddo," his grandfather. Iddo

was one of the priests who returned to Zerubbabel and Joshua from Babylon (Neh_12:4).

Zechariah entered early on his prophetic functions (Zec_2:4); only two months later than Haggai, in the second year of Darius' reign, 520 B.C. The design of both prophets was to encourage the people and their religious and civil leaders, Joshua and Zerubbabel, in their work of rebuilding the temple, after the interruption caused by the Samaritans (see Introduction to Haggai). Zechariah does so especially by unfolding in detail the glorious future in connection with the present depressed appearance of the theocracy, and its visible symbol, the temple. He must have been very young in leaving Babylonia, where he was born. ...

...The prophecy consists of four parts: (1) Introductory, Zec_1:1-6. (2) Symbolical, Zec_1:7, to the end of the sixth chapter, containing nine visions; all these were vouchsafed in one night, and **are of a symbolical character.** (3) Didactic, the seventh and eighth chapters containing an answer to a query of the Beth-elites concerning a certain feast. And (4) Prophetic, the ninth chapter to the end.[135]

The Jamieson, Fausset and Brown commentary does a good job at elaborating on the visions of Zechariah. Theirs is just one of many commentaries which correctly discern that what Zechariah sees in his visions and relates to the audience is symbolical and thus not to be taken literally as so many have chosen to do with the image of an adversary that is called Satan in English translations of the Scriptures.

Each of Zechariah's visions was replete with the subtleties of symbolism and the intentionalities of symbols. Zechariah was a prophet who followed the model of previous prophets and, in a true Ancient Near Eastern philosophical and image infusing style, used many symbols to relay his message to the people. This message, which is delivered from Zechariah, may have been imbued with mystical cosmic images by a complete and ultra-spiritual impartation to Zechariah, or, as Yahweh seems inclined to do, the visions may have come to Zechariah's mind through the use of imagery and stimulus that he had been exposed to in the past. It is usually the case the things we have seen, heard, smelled, or touched in our life, are the elements in our dreams that mean something other that what the element itself actually is. This manner of a man receiving a vision respects the emotional and physical limitations of a human being. True some have and will receive vision that may overwhelm

135 Robert Jamieson, A. R. Fausset and David Brown Commentary Critical and Explanatory on the Whole Bible

them because of the unfamiliar or intense imagery contained in the vision. We see this appearing to be occurring in Daniel's vision where he actually lay "sick" for a time after the divine impartation.

> *And the vision of the evening and the morning which was told is true: wherefore shut thou up the vision; for it shall be for many days.*
> *And I Daniel fainted, and was sick certain days; afterward I rose up, and did the king's business; and I was astonished at the vision, but none understood it. Daniel 8:26-27 KJV*

However, this response from a recipient of a divinely imparted vision does not appear to be the norm throughout Scripture, nor does it appear to be the state we find Zechariah in after his vision experience. It may be, as I am purporting, that Zechariah was given these visions in concert with the imagery he already had been made familiar with through past experiences or stimuli. Not all visions are direct downloads of brand new material from the Creator. Therefore, to be clear, the elements of Zechariah's vision could have been from something that was brought to mind from the library of images that was catalogued in his head. This concept is not new and the ancients accepted the potential for diversity in the way "visions" came to humans

As John Gill notes, the Targum speaks wisely about Zechariah's dreams. The Targum is an Aramaic translation of the Hebrew bible, with commentary from the perspective of the Second Temple period to a few hundred years into the common era.[136] The Targum gives us a paraphrase of the starting words of Zechariah in chapter one verse one. The paraphrase that is presented depicts

136 **Targum**
From Wikipedia, the free encyclopedia; http://en.wikipedia.org/wiki/Targum

A **targum** (plural: *targumim*) is an Aramaic translation of the Hebrew Bible (Tanakh) written or compiled in the Land of Israel or in Babylonia from the Second Temple period until the early Middle Ages (late first millennium). (Targum is also the name used for a dialect of Hebrew that was spoken by Jews in Kurdistan.)
As translations, the *targumim* largely reflect rabbinic (i.e. midrashic) interpretation of the Tanakh. This is true both for those *targumim* that are fairly literal, as well as for those which contain a great many midrashic expansions.
Aramaic was the dominant language or lingua franca for hundreds of years in major Jewish communities in the Land of Israel and Babylonia. In order to facilitate the study of Tanakh and make its public reading understood, authoritative translations were required.

the various possibilities of how the vision came to Zechariah and it is stated by Gill as follows;

> **came the word of the Lord unto Zechariah**; that is, "the word of prophecy from before the Lord", as the Targum paraphrases it; which came to him, either in a dream, or in a vision, or by an impulse on his mind;[137]

The eight visions are listed below. As you read the following synopsis and explanation of each of the visions which Zechariah had, one cannot miss the vibrant images that accompanied these visions. We should pay close attention to the images in the vision as it becomes abundantly clear that the images given are not to be understood as literal entities.

> 1) The vision of the horses (Zechariah_1:8-11).
>
> *I saw by night, and behold a man riding upon a red horse, and he stood among the myrtle trees that were in the bottom; and behind him were there red horses, speckled, and white. Then said I, O my lord, what are these? And the angel that talked with me said unto me, I will shew thee what these be. And the man that stood among the myrtle trees answered and said, These are they whom the LORD hath sent to walk to and fro through the earth. And they answered the angel of the LORD that stood among the myrtle trees, and said, We have walked to and fro through the earth, and, behold, all the earth sitteth still, and is at rest. Zechariah 1:8-11 KJVA*

This vision is teaching the Father's special care for and interest in his people and Yahweh tells of His intent to rebuild the Temple, which has been all but forgotten by the returning exiles. This vision contains images of horses of different color. These horses and riders are understood as references to the different aspects of the work on the earth, which proceed from God. It is possible to see the reference to the four horses with riders on them, as depicting something other than celestial beings. Some scholars conclude that angels take on the form of a human man because the being that is called "an angel" in one place of the text is referred to as a man in another portion of the text. The more likely situation is that in this instance as in so many other instances the Hebrew word *mawlawk* is referring to a human messenger. Verse 10 above shows clearly that a man is called an angel. "*And the man that stood among the myrtle trees answered and said...*" Because it is acceptable for

137 John Gill's Exposition of the Entire Bible, Dr. John Gill (1690-1771)

Scripture to not necessarily impose one meaning of angel upon the other, full license is given for the English language to call that man an angel.

In the above verse the Hebrew word, "*mawlawk*'" is translated as angel however in numerous instances the same word is translated as "messenger". One hundred and ten times(110 times) we see "*mawlawk*" as "angel or angels," and 98 times we find the word translated as "messenger or messengers" with yet four times being translated as "ambassadors". Most references where we find the Hebrew word "*mawlawk*" are in fact referring to human beings. It is therefore likely in this instance the reason Zechariah first calls the messenger in his vision a "*mawlawk,*" only to later let us know he is a "man", was because he was speaking to a human. Zechariah calls the messenger a "man" likely due to the fact that the prophet was engaged in a spiritual conversation with a human man who is acting as a "messenger" for the Almighty. It is not unusual for a person to be called a "*mawlawk*" as the Hebrew does and then in English translate *mawlawk* with the word "angel" while all the while referring to a man. A New Testament example of a man being referred to as an angel is found in the letter to the Hebrews verse 2 chapter 13 where the audience is instructed to not forget to entertain strangers because they may unwittingly be entertaining angels.

> *Be not forgetful to entertain strangers: for thereby some have entertained angels unawares. Hebrews 13:2 KJV*

The context of most uses of "angel" in both the Hebrew Scriptures and the Christian New Testament indicate the "angel" is a human. It seems a little odd that one could be in the presence of an angelic being but not be aware of that being actually being an angel. To indicate to the hearers that they might not know of an angelic presence is to tell them that they are spiritually deadened in some way. Conversely, to not recognize that a stranger who comes from a foreign country is a messenger could easily happen in a culture that was bustling with travelers of differing nationalities regularly. I am not dogmatically stating that angels are a non-existent creature and creation of God, I do however see ample evidence to believe that the number of celestial beings in the Scriptures and New Testament is far less than many have come to accept.

It is suggested in Psalms 78 and 103 that there are an order of spiritual beings designed specifically to do Yahweh's pleasure. The angels of Psalm 78 are said to be evil and sent by God and those of Psalm 103 are noted for doing His commands

He cast upon them the fierceness of his anger, wrath, and indignation, and trouble, by sending evil angels among them. Psalms 78:49 KJV

Bless the LORD, ye his angels, that excel in strength, that do his commandments, hearkening unto the voice of his word. Psalms 103:20 KJV

In actual application though, it is possible that even these verses are referring to human beings or groups of humans. For now though, I will not claim unequivocally, that all the angelic activity represented in Scripture or the Apostolic writings is not the result of actual celestial angels. As well, I am not able to state resolutely that the activities credited to celestial Angels that takes place presently in the world, are just manifestations of the omnipresent God of the universe. I reserve postulating a conclusion for another time and concede that some inexplicable and explicable activities could possibly be angelic manifestations. I will however state that God can be everywhere all the time in any form if He so chooses. If Yahweh can be everywhere all the time and can be anything such as a burning bush or a pillar of fire, then it is absolutely possible that the Omnipresent One can be manifesting an aspect of Himself as an angel at one time and place or as a million angels at another time and place. Because He is not bound by time, space, or physical laws, He could be a million, million angels all over the earth and universe and still be the God who sits on the throne in heaven all at the same time. At any rate, I have not completely understood that mystery and am quite content knowing that either situation could be the case as long as the God of the universe is in control I can wait to understand all the mystery surrounding Him, until He decides to reveal all the answers to us.

As for Zechariah's first vision, do we have to believe that the horses and riders represent four literal horses and riders? On the other hand, could those divinely imparted images be referring to perhaps the swiftness of the indignation of Yahweh on those who are keeping His house from being rebuilt in Jerusalem? Those who are the recipients of God's judgment are seen as the myrtle trees, as the final verses in this account seem to indicate.

I saw by night, and behold a man riding upon a red horse, and he stood among the myrtle trees that were in the bottom; and behind him were there red horses, speckled, and white. Zechariah 1:8

The Jamieson, Fausset and Brown Commentary does an excellent job in suggesting a possible interpretation of these images so I won't go any further into explaining the potential for these images to be recognized as symbols referring to something else. What I would like to do is provide you with some commentary on the remainder of the visions of Zechariah so you can better see we are dealing with imagery that is poetic and symbolic in the vision of the *sawtawn,* adversary. The comments below are given with segments of the passages that contain the entire vision. I encourage you to read each vision completely when you find time. This will add context to the concept of each vision

2) The four horns and four smiths (Zec_1:18-21).

Then lifted I up mine eyes, and saw, and behold four horns. And I said unto the angel that talked with me, What be these? And he answered me, These are the horns which have scattered Judah, Israel, and Jerusalem. And the LORD shewed me four carpenters. Then said I, What come these to do? And he spake, saying, These are the horns which have scattered Judah, so that no man did lift up his head: but these are come to fray them, to cast out the horns of the Gentiles, which lifted up their horn over the land of Judah to scatter it. Zechariah 1:18-21 KJV

This vision is in no way taken literally by the reader. It is not teaching us that Yahweh is sending four actual animal horns and four carpenters to do a work in Israel. The message that the prophet is delivering is probably along the lines of Israel's foes having finally been destroyed. In fact, what is depicted through this utterance is that the foes have destroyed themselves. There is no longer any opposition to building God's house. Even a cursory look at this vision reveals that there is nothing literal here; however, it is easy to see how one could misunderstand the concept if one is not diligent to explore what the prophet is saying.

3) The man with a measuring line (Zec_2:1-13).

I lifted up mine eyes again, and looked, and behold a man with a measuring line in his hand. Then said I, Whither goest thou? And he said unto me, To measure Jerusalem, to see what is the breadth thereof, and what is the length thereof. And, behold, the angel that talked with me went forth, and another angel went out to meet him, And said unto him, Run, speak to this young man, saying, Jerusalem shall be inhabited as towns without walls for the multitude of men and cattle therein: Zechariah 2:1-4 KJV

Please take note of the fact that all of the visions that Zechariah relays to the hearer take place on the same night. The date is given as the twenty-fourth day of the eleventh month in the second year of King Darius' reign. This vision of the man with the measuring line was aimed at teaching that God will restore a population of His children to Jerusalem and that He would protect and dwell in Jerusalem as soon as the Temple, the place of His holy habitation, was rebuilt. The city itself will expand until it becomes a great metropolis without walls. The boundary of the inhabitants of the Holy geographic location will be larger than what was currently perceived at the time of the return from exile when Zechariah delivered his visions. Yahweh will be the protector of the city by being a metaphorical wall of fire around it. There is no indication elsewhere that there was ever or ever is to be a literal wall of fire around the Holy City.

4) Joshua, the high priest, clad in filthy garments, and bearing the sins both of himself and of the people (Zec_3:1-10).

And he shewed me Joshua the high priest standing before the angel of the LORD, and Satan standing at his right hand to resist him. And the LORD said unto Satan, The LORD rebuke thee, O Satan; even the LORD that hath chosen Jerusalem rebuke thee: is not this a brand plucked out of the fire? Now Joshua was clothed with filthy garments, and stood before the angel. And he answered and spake unto those that stood before him, saying, Take away the filthy garments from him. And unto him he said, Behold, I have caused thine iniquity to pass from thee, and I will clothe thee with change of raiment. Zechariah 3:1-4 KJV

This vision represents the huge statements that are in question regarding the existence of "Satan". I would like to address it in a moment, but for now let me mention a couple of the notable symbolic images and the fact of them not being intended as literal entities. The High Priest is indeed referring to Joshua who had returned from exile and was to take the office of High Priest in the rebuilt temple. The first significant metaphorical symbol we are given is from Yahweh to Zechariah. Yahweh tells us that Joshua is a "*brand plucked out of the fire*". We can easily ascertain that this does not mean Joshua is a literal firebrand, but it is more properly understood in the metaphorical sense. It is speaking of the value of the character being referred to and because Yahweh recognized that value, He purposely hand picked Joshua as the soon to be High Priest of the Temple. Yahweh, rather than letting the "fire brand" extinguish, chose to keep the proverbial fire of this man going by taking him from the dwindling fire before the fire is out. As a "fire brand", Joshua will be used to rekindle the Temple service and cause to ignite again a commitment to righteousness in the returning exiles.

Next in verse 3 of the vision account we are told of the filthy garments Joshua is clothed in. I suppose it is possible that Joshua the High Priest truly was wearing filthy clothes; however, the end of this chapter adds clarity to the symbol of filthy clothes through the mention of the sin of the land. The angel of Yahweh tells Joshua, as seen in the vision, to walk in Yahweh's ways and to take care of the Temple, and then Joshua will be given a place to walk among the other priests and workers or Levites in the Temple. Further on in verse 9, Joshua is told that the iniquity of the land will be removed in one day. Therefore, the references to the sins in this chapter buoy up an explanation of the image of Joshua the High priest in filthy clothes. Had he truly been in filthy clothes then no priestly duties would have been undertaken by him to this point in the historical Temple reconstruction by the returning exiles. The image of the filthy clothes is a sign of the sins of the people being the responsibility of the High Priest Joshua. Quite prophetic and anti-type in nature is this picture as the name *Joshua* is *Yehoshua* in Hebrew. The Messiah's name, *Yeshua* which many claim is the name Jesus, is linguistically connected to this name *Yehoshua*.

The filthy clothes on Joshua in the vision may also be intended to represent his sin. There is a connection in Ezra that helps clarify what is spoken about here. In Ezra chapter 10, we are introduced to the sin of this Joshua, which is depicted as filthy clothes in Zechariah's vision. The exiles had returned to the land of Israel from Persia and many of them, including Joshua, had taken pagan wives who did not turn to the God of Abraham, Isaac, and Jacob but maintained their heathen ways. Much of the problem with that scenario was that the heathen ways of the wives and mothers would in turn be passed on to the children. The wives/mothers were the primary teachers of faith to the children in that day. Now the men who had married pagan wives did divorce, or put them away as the text tells us but this was definitely a proverbial soiling of the garments. This is particularly so in the case of the High Priests. A High Priest was commanded to not marry a woman who had been the wife of another, but he was to marry a daughter of Israel who had never been married. It is important we recognize that Joshua was placed in a position of authority in the Temple and therefore was recognized as having some responsibility for not only his own action but also the actions of the people. As the responsible minister for the people, Joshua's leadership in the recently returned group of Yahweh's children is emblematic of the responsibility Yeshua, the Great High Priest, took upon Himself in regards to the sin of the world. The Joshua to Yeshua correlation is not an absolute parallel however, the distinct similarities based on the office of each are difficult to deny. The following excerpt from the ISBE (International Standard Bible Encyclopedia) speaks of Joshua's position and following that excerpt is a verse from the book of Ezra that indicates Joshua was in fact a priest.

> **Joshua (3)**
>
> Son of Jehozadak (Hag_1:1, Hag_1:12, Hag_1:14; Hag_2:2, Hag_2:4; Zec_3:1, Zec_3:3, Zec_3:6, Zec_3:8, Zec_3:9; Zec_6:11 form (b)) and high priest in Jerusalem, called "Jeshua" in Ezra-Nehemiah. His father was among the captives at the fall of Jerusalem in 586 BC, and also his grandfather Seraiah, who was put to death at Riblah (2Ki_25:18 ff; 1Ch_6:15).(ISBE)[138]
>
> *Ezra 10:18 KJV*
>
> *And among the sons of the priests there were found that had taken strange wives: namely, of the sons of Jeshua the son of Jozadak, and his brethren; Maaseiah, and Eliezer, and Jarib, and Gedaliah.*

In the above verse, the one called Jeshua is in fact the Joshua of the Zechariah chapter 3 vision. He is stated as being one of the priests who had taken a pagan wife, thus causing him to be categorized as having "filthy garments" in Zechariah's vision.

Now we jump to the main point of understanding this vision of a supposed "Satan" in the heavenlies acting as an accuser. What we are being given in this account is a story of disenchanted and perhaps jealous men who are not only trying to prevent the re-construction of the Temple but are accusing Joshua of sin that negates him from his leadership position. These men are the adversaries in a similar fashion as the adversaries who came against Job. The adversaries in this situation attempt to discredit the one who is to be given the position of power. By pointing to his sins of the past, they attempt to prove his unworthiness to act as the High Priest.

The era of return from exile was rife with many pretentious, power mongers, who wanted to further their own cause and prevent others from advancing in authority. Particularly at this point in Israel's history when the people were returning from exile and lobbying was ongoing for position of leadership as these coveted positions were being reinstituted. It is sad to see that some who returned to Jerusalem acted as adversaries or "the satans", and tried to prevent construction of the temple and inauguration of the High

138 From International Standard Bible Encyclopedia under the Entry "Joshua(3)"

Priest. Even today when a new president is about to be elected or is elected, various accusations are made by his contemporaries, which are aimed directly at impugning the new president and maligning his character. The accusations are intended to get the electorate to believe he is not worthy to attain the office of President. This type of adversarial activity today is somewhat socially acceptable because it is said to be propagated by a leader's "critics".

In the days of the return from exile when Joshua and the governor Zerrubabbel were key players in the national re-institution of a system of governance that involved the Temple and its associated service, the critics were called "*sawtawn*". They are better known in English today as adversaries and are improperly affixed with the pro-noun "Satan". Here, in this vision, there is no satanic archenemy standing in the throne room or heavenly court accusing Joshua. We are seeing a symbolical and metaphorical scene played out where Zechariah sees images that reveal there are human forces opposing the plan of Yahweh for Joshua and the reconstruction of the Temple.

Zechariah's vision containing images familiar to his mind was no more literal than was Joseph's dream of bushels of wheat bowing low to his own bushel in Genesis. The vision of chapter 3 is not to be taken as literal any more than the rest of the visions of Zechariah. The Hebrew word *sawtawn,* used in the first and second verses of this chapter, never meant a cosmic archenemy of Yahweh or man but meant someone who opposes and resists Yahweh, or a human who is part of the plan of Yahweh. In fact the word "resist" in verse one of chapter 3 which tells us what the adversary is doing in Zechariah's vision to Joshua, is also the word "sawtawn"(Strong's 7853) when spoken in the Hebrew but somehow was not translated as "satan" or adversary when the Hebrew text evolved into today's English version. The verse may be read like this; I have highlighted the words "satan" and "adversary" and please note that both are the word *"sawtawn"* and in fact mean adversary.

> *And he shewed me Joshua the high priest standing before the angel of the LORD, and the* ***adversary****(7854) standing at his right hand to* ***satan(resist*** *7853) him. Zechariah 3:1*

Please take note of this point because it is a crucial point in understanding why there is an adversary accusing Joshua. Although the Hebrew word in Zechariah 3 is "sawtawn" and means adversary, once again it has been mistakenly translated as "Satan" in English. By being translated as Satan, we are given a false understanding that there is a cosmic archenemy of Yahweh standing in His presence. The false understanding intimates that Satan is trying to prove Joshua is a sinner and should not be given the office of High Priest. What is believed to be depicted here also has been understood as Satan using the past failing of Joshua as a reason to prevent the further re-construction of the Holy Temple in Jerusalem. Joshua's filthy garments represent his own sin and in fact, he is not literally wearing filthy garments. Again, we must accept the symbols as symbols and come to understand the concept they represent instead of imposing a literal sense to them. The chapter 3 vision is given to Zechariah so that as the prophet, he can inform Joshua and Zerrubabbel of the oppositional movement that is afoot as they re-construct the temple and install Joshua as High Priest. The work of a prophet of God is intended to bring light to a situation where Yahweh is moving and working. It would be encouraging for Joshua to hear that even though he had fallen short of the standard of Torah by sinning and marrying an unconverted pagan wife in exile, because of his act of repentance through divorcing her, he would be cleansed and acceptable to Yahweh. Joshua would thus metaphorically be seen as having clean garments placed on him for service and charge of the Temple. Once in charge of the Temple Joshua is seen in the vision to then have crowns placed on him. The following verses use the metaphorical terminology of apparel to depict Joshua's status change from unworthy to serve Yahweh in the Temple, to being fit for service because of the Creator's cleansing process.

> *Now Joshua was clothed with filthy garments, and stood before the angel.*
> *And he answered and spake unto those that stood before him, saying, Take away the filthy garments from him. And unto him he said, Behold, I have caused thine iniquity to pass from thee, and I will clothe thee with change of raiment.*
> *And I said, Let them set a fair mitre upon his head. So they set a fair mitre upon his head, and clothed him with garments. And the angel of the LORD stood by. Zechariah 3:3-5 KJV*

Why would anyone try to take away from the beauty of the message in this vision by making this passage to focus on "Satan?" Isn't it a tragedy to have missed the point that these visions of Zechariah's, just like almost every vision in the Scriptures, were not literal and truth is ebbed away from the message by imposing a literal understanding on these visions. Even though the elements of the vision are not all to be taken as literal, the concept may still be "literal" and most assuredly is literal in this case. Joshua was not to heed the accusations of his "adversaries" because Yahweh himself had accepted Joshua. As well, the warning of opposition to Zerubabbel's leadership in Temple reconstruction was necessary. This opposition came at the hand and design of Sanballat and can be read about in the Book of Nehemiah. Joshua and Zerubabbel had already built the altar of Yahweh and this Sanballat and his friends wanted a piece of the pie when it came around to construction time. Zerrubabbel did not allow them to join the building program and Sanballat got sour about it. It is entirely probable that the "adversary" as seen in Zechariah's vision of Joshua the High Priest before the angel of Yahweh is in fact Sanballat and his cronies.

This would follow the understanding of the rest of the Hebrew Scriptures that either the "adversary" or a "satan" can be an angel acting in an adversarial manner as sent from Yahweh, or it can be a human person (also an angel) acting in an oppositional manner when the will of the Father is being worked out.

In coming to a close on the discussion on the Zechariah concept, I will briefly cover the remaining visions of Zechariah's big night. By now, you should be able to quickly conclude that none of these visions were or are literal. For posterity, I will employ the comments from another writer. He has posted his commentary on the internet under the title, "*Zechariah's Eight Visions for Israel*" by Clarence Wagner.[139]

> **5. The Gold Lampstand and the Two Olive Trees (Zechariah 4)**
>
> *Meaning: Israel as the light to the nations under Messiah, the King-Priest.*
>
> In this vision, Zechariah saw a gold lampstand with a bowl of oil at the top, from which seven channels continually supplied the seven lights on the lampstand. Then, there were two olive trees standing on each side of the lampstand with two gold pipes that continually supplied golden oil to the bowl.
>
> Zechariah asked the meaning of the lampstand with seven lights, and was told, "These seven are the eyes of the Lord, which range throughout the earth" (v. 10b). And of the olive trees, "These are the two who are anointed to serve the Lord of all the earth" (v. 14). The whole vision is connected to Zerubbabel, the governor of Judah, and the rebuilding of the Temple.
>
> **6. The Flying Scroll (Zechariah 5:1-4)**
>
> *Meaning: The severity and totality of divine judgment on sin in Israel.*

139 "*Zechariah's Eight Visions for Israel*" by Clarence Wagner http://www.ldolphin.org/zech-wagner/

The last three visions have to do with the administration of judgment on sin in Israel, and on the Gentile nations who have not responded to the God of Israel. In the sixth vision, Zechariah saw a flying scroll, 30 feet long and 15 feet wide (9.0 x 4.5 meters). Interestingly, it is the exact dimensions of the tabernacle, perhaps indicating that the message on it was in harmony with God's presence in the midst of Israel. The scroll was not rolled up, but flying open so that both sides could be read.

The angel explained to him what it meant: "This is the curse that is going out over the whole land; for according to what it says on one side, every thief will be banished, and according to what it says on the other, everyone who swears falsely will be banished. ... It will enter the house of the thief and the house of him who swears falsely by My Name. It will remain in his house and destroy it" (Zech. 5:3-4).This vision is a call to righteousness in Israel, and the scroll represents the Word and Law of the Lord that judges the sinful. God desires that His people and His land, the place of His past and future habitation, be holy. It has been suggested that the fullness of this vision can only be accomplished when the Messiah comes, for only then can divine judgment on sin be so rapid and complete.

7. The Woman in a Basket (Zechariah 5:5-11)

Meaning: The removal of national Israel's sin or rebellion against God.

In this vision, Zechariah saw an ephah, which is a measuring basket for grain and other household commodities. The basket represented "the iniquity of the people throughout the land." (v. 6). When the lid was lifted, inside the basket sat a woman. The angel said that the woman represented wickedness, and he pushed the wickedness back into the basket and shut the lid (v. 8). This is not to suggest that women are wicked. Rather, the Hebrew word for wickedness is in the feminine form, and the "woman" was wickedness personified. Then, Zechariah saw two women with the wind in their wings like a stork, and they lifted the basket up into the air between heaven and earth.

When Zechariah asked where the basket was being taken, he was told: "To the country of Babylonia to build a house for it" (Zech. 5:11). Babylon is the place of ancient and future idolatry and rebellion against God, so an apt location for the removal of idolatry from Israel. Putting wickedness and idolatry back in Babylon also sets the stage for her final judgment (Rev. 17-18).

8. Four Chariots (Zechariah 6:1-8)

Meaning: Divine judgment on Gentile nations.

Then Zechariah saw four chariots coming out from between two bronze mountains. In this instance, the bronze mountains could symbolize the righteous, divine judgment of God against sin (Rev. 1:15; 2:18) meted out by chariots of war going out into the world. The first chariot had red horses, the second black, the third white, and the fourth dappled all of them powerful. It has been suggested that the colors represent: red = war and bloodshed, black = death, white = triumph, and dappled = pestilence.[140]

After looking carefully at the visions of Zechariah, one is compelled to conclude that these visions are not intended to be interpreted literally. As with visions in general in the Scriptures, we are to endeavor to hear them for their intended concept and instruction without using the images in them to design doctrine and entrench theology. I remind you that one is hard-pressed to find any vision in the Hebrew Scriptures, which is a completely literal view of actual events and characters. Visions in the Scriptures are from Yahweh and are one of his vehicles to provide part of the inside story in a given situation to the recipient. Visions are tools, which are part of the toolbox of the Creator that are designed to prick the heart of the recipient and those who are privileged to be let in on the content of the vision by the recipient. Visions are designed to deliver a particular message with an intensity that is greater than one could display without the assistance of the Divine Creator. Visions are some of the most misunderstood and abused segments of Scripture and of Christian and other religion's spiritual portfolio. It is my intent to understand visions and dreams in a way that does not jade the interpretation with my own pre-conceived ideas or agenda, but to eliminate the prejudices and biases of the fleshly analytical mind as much as is humanly possible when trying to understand a dream or vision. That done it is my intent to allow the Spirit of the Creator, Yahweh to remove prejudices and biases beyond that which is humanly possible. Although the spirit of the prophet is subject to the prophet according to 1 Corinthians 14:32, the Creator can aid the human spirit to go beyond that which is capable of the human mind and spirit on its own. For the spirit of the prophet to be subject to the prophet would mean that there is to be no ecstatic prophetic utterances which are done out of a state of altered consciousness as if the prophet is not a participant in the prophecy but has been taken over by a spiritual force and simply used as a "speaker." There is no

140 *Zechariah's Eight Visions for Israel*" by Clarence Wagner http://www.ldolphin.org/zech-wagner/

force that abducts the will of a human and uses that human as an unwitting megaphone. Each person who speaks what they believe to be the words of the Creator is doing so as an act of his or her own will. Certainly, there are some who place themselves in such a deep hypnotic state that they appear to have been taken over and used as a mouthpiece for their deity. However, each one of them is in reality speaking from their own self-altered consciousness and ultimately by their own will. Paul speaks it thus;

> *For ye may all prophesy one by one, that all may learn, and all may be comforted. And the spirits of the prophets are subject to the prophets. 1 Corinthians 14:31-32 KJV*

The ecstatic utterances that occur today in some charismatic churches are simply a repeat of ages old Gnostic practices. In the Gnostic variety of worship, the "oracle", which was the woman of prophecy sought after for a word of prophecy, would give herself over to the frenzy of ritualistic music filled worship and while in a frenzied state would utter unintelligible sounds, which were said to be a message from God. At times the worshippers present at a Gnostic worship gathering would give themselves over to the frenzy and all manner of "messages" would supposedly emanate from their mouths with the belief that this utterance was coming forth from the spirit of God and the one uttering was now no longer in control. This is totally a separate and large topic itself, but I encourage you to explore it as it is a deep deception that flows through many Charismatic and non-charismatic religious sects.

In summary, Zechariah was a prophet who received visions that were given to edify the returning exiles and particularly the leadership as seen in Joshua the High Priest and Zerubabbel the governor of Judea. Zechariah was not given a vision of a literal, cosmic, archenemy of Yahweh called Satan, which showed up in heaven. If there were a "Satan", he would not have access to heaven as seems to be the case if Zechariah's visions are taken literally. Satan would not be allowed access to the court of God due to the fact of him supposedly being the embodiment of pure evil and his supposed ejection long before the time of Zechariah. It is quite an inconsistent belief to think that Satan was ejected from Heaven long ago and although evil is not allowed in the presence of Yahweh, Satan is said to come into God's presence repeatedly.

What Zechariah saw was images that depicted an adversarial person or group opposed to the reconstructing of the Temple and to the leadership that Yahweh had chosen for the Temple. These adversaries tried to use the past sin of the High Priest Joshua in their case against him to eliminate him from office by maligning his righteous standing, which Yahweh restored after Joshua's repentance. These "satans" tried to implicate him as one who was unworthy to act in the position of Israel's representative in the Holy temple. Although Zechariah the prophet was one of the returning exiles from Babylon/Persia, he was not submitting to the dualistic philosophy of the Zoroastrians, which taught there is a good god and evil god that was engaged in a cosmic war to destroy the good god and His followers.

Zechariah would have been well aware that the Hebrew word "sawtawn" meant adversary and therefore when it was used in relating his vision to the hearer he would have had no confusion over a mythological and superstitious, pagan concept of a supernatural evil force which we are told today is "Satan." As for Zechariah's part in supporting the argument of a cosmic "satan", it is very different from what Zechariah understood and was relaying to the hearer. There is no cosmic "Satan" in Zechariah and for our part in understanding that the English reference to 'Satan" simply is referring to a human adversary; I think it is fair to say that "satan" is not found in Zechariah chapter 3. It may be helpful for you to read the entire chapter of Zechariah 3, as you now may see it for the "vision" it was intended to be seen as. While reading the vision below, ask yourself how the elements in the vision might have been understood by the prophet Zechariah as well as those with whom he shared this vision. What follows, is the focus text for this chapter with the Hebrew word *sawtawn* translated by using the English word "adversary". I have added emphasis to aid the reader in understanding the message more closely, to how it was intended by the writer.

Zechariah 3:1-10

1 *And he shewed me Joshua the high priest standing before the angel of the LORD, and the* ***adversary*** *standing at his right hand to resist him.*

2 *And the LORD said unto the* ***adversary****, The LORD rebuke thee, O* ***adversary****; even the LORD that hath chosen Jerusalem rebuke thee: is not this a brand plucked out of the fire?*

3 *Now Joshua was clothed with filthy garments, and stood before the angel.*

4 *And he answered and spake unto those that stood before him, saying, Take away the filthy garments from him. And unto him he said, Behold, I have caused thine iniquity to pass from thee, and I will clothe thee with change of raiment.*

5 *And I said, Let them set a fair mitre upon his head. So they set a fair mitre upon his head, and clothed him with garments. And the angel of the LORD stood by.*

6 *And the angel of the LORD protested unto Joshua, saying,*

7 *Thus saith the LORD of hosts; If thou wilt walk in my ways, and if thou wilt keep my charge, then thou shalt also judge*

my house, and shalt also keep my courts, and I will give thee places to walk among these that stand by.

8 *Hear now, O Joshua the high priest, thou, and thy fellows that sit before thee: for they are men wondered at: for, behold, I will bring forth my servant the BRANCH.*

9 *For behold the stone that I have laid before Joshua; upon one stone shall be seven eyes: behold, I will engrave the graving thereof, saith the LORD of hosts, and I will remove the iniquity of that land in one day.*

10 *In that day, saith the LORD of hosts, shall ye call every man his neighbour under the vine and under the fig tree.*

Considering How a Culture Comes to Accept Mystical Concepts.

It is needful that we briefly discuss the widespread acceptance of mystical beliefs and concepts. Seeing how a culture is shaped by the stimulus it is presented with, brings clarity to the issue. In many ways our culture's form of Christianity and spiritualism has become so hyper-spiritual that some automatically ascribe a cosmic and celestial concept to things in the Scripture which perhaps have a more down to earth reality, when understood in the light of the culture where it was written. This is not surprising as generally, we are a culture that claims, and I am speaking of North America particularly, that we are Christian. Although there has been a move to expressing skepticism about religion and religious teachings for a number of years now, there remains a very large segment of people who adhere to a belief in Satan. The Barna Research Group states that in 2006 more than half of adults (55%) say that the devil, or Satan, is not a living being but is a symbol of evil. That leaves 45% of adults with a belief in a literal Satan. Barna also says that in 2006 45% of born again Christians deny Satan's existence, which is significant in that out of a Christian group the belief in Satan is 10% higher than the general population. We are also told that slightly more than two-thirds of Catholics (68%) say the devil is non-existent and only a symbol of evil. (2006). Out of Catholics alone there remains a large group of those who actually see Satan as a real entity.

In another recent poll by the Harris polling group, the Reuters News Group reports that the belief in hell and Satan out numbers the belief in evolution for Americans. Reuters reports;

Poll finds more Americans believe in devil than Darwin

Thu Nov 29, 2007 5:56pm EST

By Ed Stoddard

DALLAS (Reuters Life!) - More Americans believe in a literal hell and the devil than Darwin's theory of evolution, according to a new Harris poll released on Thursday.

It is the latest survey to highlight America's deep level of religiosity, a cultural trait that sets it apart from much of the developed world.

It also helps explain many of its political battles which Europeans find bewildering, such as efforts to have "Intelligent Design" theory -- which holds life is too complex to have evolved by chance -- taught in schools alongside evolution.

The poll of 2,455 U.S. adults from Nov 7 to 13 found that 82 percent of those surveyed believed in God, a figure unchanged since the question was asked in 2005.

It further found that 79 percent believed in miracles, 75 percent in heaven, while 72 percent believed that Jesus is God or the Son of God. Belief in hell and the devil was expressed by 62 percent.[141]

Aside from the specific belief in Satan, there seems to be clouding of concrete beliefs when one considers how many meaningless superstitions prevail in people's lives. North America generally claims to be "Christian" and in 2006, a whopping 71% of American adults believed in God according to Barna's research, when described as the all-knowing, all-powerful, perfect Creator of the universe who rules the world today. According to *adherents.com* 85% of Americans claim to be Christians.

Even amidst this large sampling of people who say they believe in God, there still exists huge numbers who are found to believe in all types of spiritual power and things like ghosts and mediums, possessing a wide array of superstitions that supposedly can affect our lives in various ways. These beliefs are just a couple of examples that are found amid multiple, illogical superstitions, such as blowing on the dice before they are rolled in a game of

141 Reuters News, November 29, 2007, by Ed Stoddard; http://www.reuters.com/article/lifestyleMolt/idUSN2922875820071129

monopoly to aid in acquiring a number that will get you to the Boardwalk space when you want to purchase it.

It is not difficult to point the finger of accusation at pop culture and media as the source and teacher of so many of our superstitions and beliefs. In the book, *Believing in Magic the Psychology of Superstitions*, by Stuart A Vyse, we learn that if we are to be honest we can see how so many have submitted to the training in spiritual things, which has been passed down by the media and pop-culture. This training has betrayed us because we are now all but incapable of setting down our understanding because we already have a comfortable acceptance of a thought or topic. Our acceptance becomes our truth and this prevents us from honestly exploring a potentially opposing view. The belief that other forces affect our lives but can be controlled to some degree if we are attentive to the details and nuances that play into our superstitions is common in a culture that has so many superstitions and mystical beliefs. One article speaks of the prevalence of superstition thus;

> An exclusive survey conducted for American Demographics by research firm Market Facts, indicates only 44 percent of us are willing to admit that we're superstitious. The remaining 56 percent are "optimistically superstitious," meaning we're more willing to believe the good over the bad. For example, 12 percent of those who say they don't buy into the folklore, do believe that knocking on wood brings good luck. What's more, 9 percent of those who don't believe in superstitions do, however, accept that finding a penny brings good luck. Nine percent of non-believers also say the same of a four-leaf clover, while 11 percent give credence to kissing under the mistletoe.
>
> Of the 44 percent of Americans who admit to being superstitious, 65 percent say they are "only a little," 27 percent are "somewhat," and 8 percent are "very" superstitious. Interestingly, while women comprise 60 percent of all superstitious persons, 64 percent of the "very" superstitious are male. In another twist, more younger people buy into the folklore than their older counterparts: 64 percent of adults aged 18 to 24 are at least a little superstitious compared with 30 percent of those 65 and older.[142]

Superstition seems to develop from a lack of correct and critically determined information, coupled with the desire to add explanation to

142 Excerpt from SNAPSHOTS OF TODAY'S CONSUMERS; toplines: Tempting Fate – by John Fetto October 2000 http://findarticles.com/p/articles/mi_m4021/is_2000_Oct/ai_67001162/print

otherwise poorly understood situations, events, or concepts. This type of behavior has led to grave misinterpretations of otherwise explainable events and concepts and often is enhanced by generational transmission that more often than not, goes unquestioned. As it goes, I will tend to believe what my Father believed and he, unless questioned, will tend to believe what his Father before him believed. These varied transmissions remain unproven as to the efficacy of that which has been passed down. We have fallen victim to this type of behavior in the area of understanding the visions of the Bible. What has generally been passed down to successive generations has quite readily been accepted as unquestionably accurate.

Angel of The Lord is Often The Priest

Quite often we understand visions in a manner where we over spiritualize the images in the vision and remove any potential for the images to represent something completely understandable. We reject the context of the writing and refuse to consider the time and place where it was written. For instance, the book of Zechariah and elsewhere refers to the "angel of the Lord", which is believed by most to speak of a celestial form and figure but it may simply be a reference to a priest.

> *And they answered the angel of the LORD that stood among the myrtle trees, and said, We have walked to and fro through the earth, and, behold, all the earth sitteth still, and is at rest. Zechariah 1:11 KJV*

What was discussed in the previous chapter (Chapter 10) on the "sons of God" in Job, as men coming before the Lord to what would have been a temple environment that included priests, can be brought to mind when assessing the phrase "angel of the Lord". It is well known that priests are called angels at times. According to the wording in Malachi, the priest was at times referred to as an "angel" and therefore an "angel of the Lord" could be a temple priest. In the following verse, the English word "messenger" is in fact the Hebrew word "*mawlawk*", which is translated as angel in many instances. A comment from Albert Barnes follows the verse below.

> *For[3588] the priest's[3548] lips[8193] should keep[8104] knowledge,[1847] and they should seek[1245] the law[8451] at his mouth:[4480, 6310] for[3588] he[1931] is the messenger[4397(angel)] of the LORD[3068] of hosts.[6635] Malachi 2:7 KJV*

> **For he is the messenger (or angel) of the Lord of hosts -** Malachi gives to the priest the title which belongs to the lowest order of the heavenly spirits, as having an office akin to theirs; as Haggai does to the prophet, Hag_2:11. …
>
> ….most truly is the priest of God called angel, i. e., messenger, because he intervenes between God and man, and announces the things of God to the people; and, therefore, were the Urim and Thummim placed on the priest's breastplate of judgment, that we might learn, that the priest ought to be learned, a herald of divine truth."

It is entirely acceptable to speak of a priest as an angel. Therefore it is entirely acceptable where an "angel of the Lord" is in a story, to sometimes recognize that particular angel as simply a human priest or a designate of Yahweh, appointed to pass on a message or preside over a particular situation with a view to see that God's will is done.

The Changing use of the Word *sawtawn* Through Apocalyptic Literature-a Word Becomes a Name

Seeing that the visions of Zechariah are not depicting a literal Satan and that the adversary was likely a human force just as likely as an angel of the Lord can be recognized as a human priest, we are left to explore the grammatical nature of the word translated as Satan.

In understanding proper grammar, we are able to recognize where a proper noun is used and where a common noun is used. In the English text of this verse where the Hebrew word "sawtawn" has been translated as "Satan", the word somehow evolved or had a metamorphosis that caused it to be translated into a proper noun. The word *sawtawn* eventually was written with a capital letter when it was translated into English, thus being rendered "Satan". The Hebrew word is not to be considered a proper noun and it is in fact to be heard as a common noun. The difference in the use of the word as a proper noun instead of a common noun has forced a word that describes an adversarial behavior of a person, to become the name of an entity. As the Scriptures were transcribed and translated the bias of the translators crept in and they viewed the word "*sawtawn*" as the name of the archenemy of the Creator and therefore imbued it with the proper noun status. In essence, it was because of a revisionist theological bias, which led the translators to translate a word that was not ever intended to refer to a cosmic, satanic being into the name of a cosmic satanic being, thus calling him Satan.

The name Satan itself is not even recognized as being used to identify a supposed archenemy of Yahweh until the book of Enoch was written. This was claimed to have been about the 2nd century before Christ. We find a major shift in thinking when the Apocalyptic writings of the post-Persian exile period are examined. Many of which are difficult to determine an accurate and conclusive date of their writing. Some find ample evidence to give the book of Enoch a date as recent as the pre-Christian period, which places a 2nd century CE writing on the book. The International Standard Bible Encyclopedia explains the dating of the book of Enoch in its article on Apocalyptic Literature. The book of Enoch is a post-exilic, apocalyptic text that appears to have been written to try to make sense of the world and bridge the Mosaic Torah-based outlook of life, with the more eclectic spiritualistic style of life that was present in the profoundly Greek environment of the day. The writer of the Book of Enoch is not Enoch the pre-Mosaic bible personality. The book of Enoch was written by an author at a much later time and place than that which Enoch the man existed in. The book of Enoch is considered a pseudepigraphic text.

Do you know what a pseudonym is? It is where someone is given a different name than his or her real name. A pseudepigraphic book then, is one where a person has composed a written work and claims what they have written is by the person who they named it after. *The Pseudepigrapha* then, are a collection of books or religious writings written by individuals who then attached the name of another to their writings to enhance the value of their writings. The value was and often still is magnified because people believe the writing is inherently connected to the person who the writing was named after. The book of Enoch is one such instance where the writer affixed the name of a well-known biblical figure in an attempt to bring credit to his writings. With written literature not exactly prolific in the time of the postexilic revolution, those who were able to put together a document that supposedly shed light on some difficult to reconcile concepts found in the Scriptures, would find readily acceptance of the information contained in their document.

The world at the time of the writing of the Book of Enoch was greatly Hellenized. The writer of the book of Enoch is known to not have been a practicing Jew but a Hellenized Jew. This type of a writer wrote from the perspective of the Greeks and the Greek religious philosophy and concepts. In Richard Lawrence's' 1883 translation of the Book of Enoch from the Ethiopic version, we find mention of Satan only a few times but all mentions of this entity are preceded by the mention of impious angels. Of interest to us on this topic is that in the footnote of Mr. Lawrence's translation of that passage we are told that "Satan" was not known to be a name by the Hebrews. Seemingly, this transition did not take place until the period Enoch was written. Chapter

40 verse 7 is translated thus; take note of the footnote attached to the term "impious angels".

> The fourth voice I heard expelling the impious angels, (40) and prohibiting them from entering into the presence of the Lord of spirits, to prefer accusations against (41) the inhabitants of the earth. Enoch 40:7
>
> (40) **Impious angels.** Literally, "the Satans" (Laurence, p. 45; Knibb, p. 128). Ha-satan in Hebrew ("the adversary") was originally the title of an office, not the name of an angel.[143]

The reason the book of Enoch and others like it seem to support the idea of a Satan and attached concepts of angelology and demonology, is because the writer had been deeply integrated into the Greek culture and was attempting to explain Hebraic spiritual ideas using Greek philosophy and thinking. The esoteric knowledge and multi-God belief system of the Greeks had a major impact on those who allowed themselves to be seduced by such a deep spiritual culture with so many varied understandings of the spirit world. This resulted in writers like the writer of Enoch adopting the "Satan" philosophy of the culture and adapting it to typically Hebraic ideology, an ideology that recognized One God through whom good and "evil" flowed.

Until at least the period represented by the writings of the book of Enoch, the word "satan" in Zechariah was not seen as a name for a cosmic entity by the Children of Yahweh but would have been understood as referring to a human opposition or adversary. The English words may seem to say one thing, but we should not merely ***read*** the words to show ourselves approved, we are told to ***study*** to show ourselves approved. There is a large difference between simply reading the words versus actually studying the words that are found in Zechariah or anywhere in the Scriptures. As we can see, careful study will reveal the fact that Zechariah has not delivered a message of a cosmic Satan through relaying the visions of his head. What is found in Zechariah is a description of adversarial men who intended to be in opposition to the work of Yahweh and therefore can be called the satan. The images found in the visions are simply contemporary symbolical elements that would have been applicable to the situation that was occurring. A situation where the High Priest was appointed and the Temple was reconstructed but human adversaries once again entered the picture to oppose these advances, as the satan always does.

---

143 Richard Lawrence's' 1883 translation of the Book of Enoch from the Ethiopic version; http://www.johnpratt.com/items/docs/enoch.html

CHAPTER 12

The Serpent In the Garden: Understanding the Foundations of Why We Believe a Myth.

In all stories about the fall of man that have come down through the ages there is none so well known as the Biblical account of Adam and Eve and the serpent in the garden that is said to have caused their fall. The beginning of all sin and suffering is often attributed to the monumental event that is believed to have taken place in the Garden of Eden. An event that took place sometime around 6000 years ago according to chronology that calculates the ages and numbers which are provided in the Scriptures.

The story has been told for generations and has either been believed to be wholly literal or believed to be wholly allegory; a mere tale to deliver a message that speaks of mankind's potential to choose to sin. When taken as wholly literal this tale of ancient origin is commonly seen as a true story about a man and woman that were created by the Creator. In the process of performing their assigned duties in their garden paradise abode, they were tricked by a creature that may have been inhabited by Satan or may have been Satan himself as some suggest.

Acceptance of such a story at face value is often the practice of a biblical literalist and is not easy to agree with entirely, while contrariwise, the dismissal of the story as purely lore is equally as difficult to accept from the other end of the spectrum. The issue then could be debated with no resolve for hundreds of years, as has been the case with this ancient tale up until this point. It may be possible to enjoy the both/and perspective on the Adam and Eve tale involving the serpent in the Garden. This tale may very well have content that is both allegorical and literal. The appearance of a serpent in the story has done little to add understanding to either side of the debate but remains a multi-interpreted conundrum that seems to speak of a nefarious force, yet is difficult to pin down. In this present age however, it seems plausible to submit a comprehensive answer to the question of whom or what the serpent in the garden was. Looking at this perplexing puzzle through multiple modalities of instruction and information such as history, archeology, and linguistic studies, does much to direct a query towards a possible solution to the question. That question being, "Who or what is the serpent in the garden?"

In this chapter, we will be employing not only the aforementioned means to reach a conclusion but we shall be challenged to incorporate some logic and some philosophy. This is necessary in order to unearth an answer that lays forth a conclusion, which upholds a true monotheistic ideology. In exploring the topic of who or what the serpent in the garden was, there is no better place to begin than at the start of the book of Genesis. Genesis is the document, that has for centuries, held the words of this ancient story in somewhat of a vault that locks out man's understanding. This is so, not because the words are incomprehensible, but due to the prolific, popular views, which themselves are somewhat incomprehensible for various reasons and ideological inconsistencies.

Following is the first verse of the book of Genesis and a lengthy thesis to explain that the serpent in the garden is not what most think it to be. Answers to the question of the serpent being a real serpent, or a manifestation of Satan are not easily gleaned from the language of Genesis but diligence in study will prevail and a more acceptable solution to the question will be submitted in the following pages.

Genesis 1:1

In the beginning, Elohim created the heaven and the earth.

Well ----that seems easy enough to understand doesn't it? No need to question who it was that did the creating or what was created. It is so nice and simple when the words in the text of Scriptures are easily understood. It is not so nice when the words of Scripture are full of metaphors and concepts from a cultural period that we have long lost and forgotten. So often the ancient metaphors that are written in Scripture are so far from the modern reader's line of reasoning that we are prevented in part from understanding them. Often times reading Scripture can leave us with the same patchy understanding as one might experience after reading a Newspaper from across the world.

Unless the writer provides a complete context to the story and fully articulates every aspect, nuance, and image of his or her story, the reader automatically places images and ideas from his or her own mental library into the writer's description. This practice is a normal and helpful process for the reader because it enables the reader to get more out of the story than if the entire writer's tale had not invoked any images for the reader.

We read the Scriptures in a very similar manner, where we see what the writer is imaging through a pre-set library of images in our mind. When a word or phrase is used to describe a character or situation our mind goes to work to complete the image to help us to attain a comfortable level of understanding. Although, the images in the mind of the news story reader may help the reader to avoid the confusion that comes from a complete lack of understanding, they are in all likelihood inaccurate images that were developed out of the library of images that have been inserted into the mind of the reader over his or her lifetime. If the reader were transported to the time and place of the story and was able to perceive with their own eyes and mind the same scenario that the writer shared through the written word, they would understand clearly the situation. What the reader would actually see and what the writer intended to be seen might be quite similar. The reader would probably be happy to see the images as the images were intended to be seen but would also have many words and phrases come to mind to express the scenario in a way that would be more comprehendible to that reader if the story were to be re-written.

It would be interesting to have a group of people read a story from the news in another part of the world and then ask them to describe the images that came to mind while reading. Upon receiving the descriptions from the participants, it would undoubtedly be illuminating to then a show a video of the same story and compare the descriptions of the participants with the images that are displayed on screen. It is not likely that a comparison of the images presented to the images described by the participants, would result in exactness of similarities. The participants might find themselves stating that they pictured that all wrong and then have a sense of enlightenment upon receiving the true pictures in their minds to replace the misinformed and uninformed images, which they had previously described in detail.

Thankfully, for most news stories today we are privileged to have the aid of photographic images along side the story. A picture is truly worth a thousand words when it is presented in place of written details describing a scene. A picture of a scene brings much greater clarity to the story than is being told in writing alone and provides imagery that is often unattainable by words alone. Wouldn't it be great if we had pictures of the first few chapters of Genesis? In the absence of pictures, mental images differ from hearer to hearer. The stories of Genesis have been interpreted in picture, by thousands of illustrators and writers for centuries. The imagined scenes that have been put to paper are not necessarily accurately represented in the images that are portrayed. Any story that has accurate pictures of the scenes it writes of becomes vivid to the reader. Sadly, the stories of Genesis and much of the Scripture lack the vividness that would be found had there been accurate pictures available to add to the written version of the story.

One is hard pressed to accurately perceive of the images related to a written story when they are deprived of a concise image to visualize and store in the memory. This image association works in two ways. If I say, "Don't think of a flower", you automatically have an image of a flower come to mind. Your image might be of a different flower than hundreds of others but you very likely did have an image of some type of flower. The other modality this functions in is if I tell you a story about a beautiful bouquet of flowers that sits on the mantle of a warm country home, filled with the sweet scent of roses. In reading that story, one is very likely to have had a picture from their image library in their mind of the roses sitting on the mantle. The image may be even clearer because the sense of scent was brought into play when the aroma in the home was spoken of. Whether we are given a negative instruction to not think of something or something like a rose is merely suggested, a typical person has images come to mind. We are very much subject to suggestion and what comes to mind from reading the words of Scripture is no different. All the suggestions we have received from images one has seen, that were supposedly depicting a certain story, are conjured up in the mind every time the story is reiterated. If a picture of the rose or bouquet were available to be viewed, the reader would then have all their own mental images replaced with the image that is presented to them in the picture. Once shown the picture, the image of that bouquet is now perceived accurately as it is not an image drawn from a mental library that is readily available to apply images to any written description that a person reads. As an example to help make the point that accuracy of mental images is compromised in the absence of clearly discernable pictures, I will simply quote a few headlines below. Take note of what images come to mind, including any details involved. Don't think too hard but pay attention to any mental pictures that come to you as you read the words and the short description of the article.

South Africa: Zuma Trial Heightens Rape Awareness

One of South Africa's most celebrated musicians added her voice to the chorus lamenting the government's failure to tackle the country's tragic rape problem. By **Eugene Soros**.

Charles Taylor Faces Court in Sierra Leone

News of Taylor's arrival in Freetown spread like wild fire during harmattan, the dry and dusty wind that blows out of the Sahara along the northwest coast of Africa. By **Roland B. Marke**.

Senegalese Musician Honors African Leaders

When most African music icons are looking to the West for fame and glory, Senegalese rap musician Didier Awadi is concentrating his efforts on igniting Africa's visions and aspirations. By **Eugene Soros**.

Malaria at a Crossroads

Over the course of the past 4,000-plus years, this mosquito-borne disease has slowly insinuated itself into human society. Its effects are both far-reaching and complex. From an IRIN in-depth report.

These are just four examples from African news in May of 2006. They are headlines and teasers from the internet website WorldPress.org. http://www.worldpress.org/Africa.htm.

The images that come to mind for most of us may be similar but the details we could put into the images will be vastly different. Where one person would have a mental picture of swarming mosquitoes while reading the last of the above example news stories, another person may imagine a mosquito "biting" the arm of a young child. Still another may not imagine mosquitoes at all but may picture the emaciated body of a sick mother close to the point of death with her baby in her arms, too weak to cry. Because I do not know much about Malaria, the mental picture I had when I first read this was of military workers going through the region wearing white masks and spraying for mosquitoes. Forgive my ignorance on this issue but I don't even know if they have ever sprayed for mosquitoes in Africa. After writing down the mental image I had of the above Malaria story I clicked on the link to see if my mental images correlated to the picture provided.[144]

---

144 Image and caption can be found at http://www.worldpress.org/Africa/2293.cfm. Caption with photograph says the following;
Most of the hundreds of thousands of children who die from malaria every year are under the age of five. Almost 90 percent are from sub-Saharan Africa. (Photo: Cris Bouroncle / AFP-Getty Images)

The picture on the website revealed a child sick in bed who appears to be near the point of death. The sick child is being attended by his mother who is stroking the child's face and there was a younger sibling in the picture kneeling near the foot of the bed. The article tells of Malaria as significantly affecting pregnant mothers, infants, and young children. The images in the online photo were similar at best to some of the images I had in mind when reading the headline but there is no way I could have accurately depicted this picture until I saw it. The point is, the words in a story do bring forth images for the reader but unless the words are absolutely, explicit and fully descriptive, the reader will stand a good chance of entertaining inaccurate images. We are going to encounter this same problem when reading the words of the Scriptures.

As I was researching for this book, while discussing some of the concepts with my own family, I saw first hand the propensity of people to apply images that are in their mental library to written stories that come into their path. This replacement imaging happens readily within the mind's eye of most who read stories from the Bible when they do not have the privilege of knowing helpful information surrounding the context of the tale. The story of the Serpent in the Garden is not exempt from this process and some in my family have become aware that it is difficult to see something differently when the way it is written has engendered the same images for so long. In a telephone conversation recently, my mother asked me if I could rewrite the Adam and Eve with the serpent account from Genesis, in a plain understandable text for her. We were discussing the literal nature of the writing versus the metaphorical nature of the writing and the words before her on the pages of Genesis were too potent and image invoking for her to move past. Mom therefore could barely perceive of a different message than the one she had in mind from the years of this message being taught, indoctrinated, and reaffirmed. Mom could only see a real snake slithering in a real tree actually speaking to Eve and convincing her to take the fruit. The picture Mom had in her mind of the fruit was clearly an apple. Of course there was more detail in the images Mom saw in her mind's eye than just an apple, but I saw a little more clearly how deeply embedded the images we have "seen" our whole life are, when we read a Bible story that has never had any Polaroids to go along with it. I told my Mom I would write about the serpent story soon and although I will pass along the following "re-writing" to my Mother long before any of you read this book, I submit the following for your discernment. I call it a conceptual and contextual paraphrase of the Serpent in the Garden story. I will go into great detail to explain my understanding, after the "re-writing" Of Genesis 3 seen below. I will just mention before we go any further, that those inclined towards Bible worship, known as bibliolatry, will have a very difficult time reading a paraphrase such as I am presenting below. However, if you can trust that you will not be agreeing to a change in the words of the Holy Bible and try to be opened to the potential of finding more truth, then perhaps you will read through the following information with greater ease. As you read the following re-writing of the serpent in the garden account, please understand I am attempting to express what I have come to comprehend is the concept Moses was relaying when he reworked an ancient serpent myth that was common in his culture. The myth was depicting a decision made by the story's characters to choose evil and disobedience as opposed to good and obedience.

The retelling of the ancient story in the manner that I have submitted below is an analytical paraphrase and is not intended to replace or add to the words of Scripture, only to assist in explaining the meaning of the words of an ancient and difficult to understand story.

Genesis 3, A paraphrase to Aid in Understanding;

Now the subtle desire in the heart of man was one thing that Yahweh had made which He chose not to control. All the beasts of the field did not posses this innate potential to choose evil known as the evil inclination, only man and therefore this evil inclination was more subtle than anything else Yahweh had created. Beasts of the field are given instinct where man has been given an ability to choose.

One day as the woman was tending the garden, a thought came to her while tending the tree of the knowledge of good and evil. She noticed how pleasant looking the fruit on the forbidden tree was and started to wonder why the Creator, who loved her and gave man so much, would want to keep man from eating the fruit of this "forbidden" tree that looked so delicious. With that in mind she asked the question to herself; "Did God say man shall not eat of every tree in the garden?" Knowing this was not a very safe line of questioning to pose to oneself, the women began wrestling within herself. She said, "No, how can I think that? God told us that we are allowed to eat of the trees of the garden."

As she looked at the trees and pondered, she continued her thought. Reminding herself , "God said that the fruit of the tree in the midst of the garden was not eatable." By thinking so she then took the next step of justifying wrong choices and added to that command of God's. The evil inclination within her was already weakening the good inclination. Adding to God's words was done by the simple embellishment of the words of the Creator, saying; "God said we can't even touch it or we'll die."

The woman had now claimed that any contact with the tree would kill. The Creator said to eat from the tree would bring death but the woman was saying that to simply touch the tree would bring death. By changing what God had said she was in for a world of trouble. When she spoke this to herself, she reasoned that it was ridiculous to think God would kill her just for touching the fruit of that tree, so she rationalized that it was OK to touch the fruit. Because she had changed God's command in her own mind and saw that she didn't die when she touched the fruit, she was able to convince herself that God must have meant something else.

Wanting to eat this fruit that looked so pleasing she thought, "I didn't die when I touched the tree so I'm pretty sure we won't die if we eat from the tree in the midst of the garden, the reason why God is keeping us from it is that He must want us not to be like Him."

Going on with her internal dialogue she thought, "He is the one making the rules and obviously He is demanding we don't touch or eat that fruit because then we will be like Him. It is entirely likely that because He is protecting that forbidden tree He knows we will be like Him if we eat it. Yes, if we eat from that tree then we will be like God, knowing good and evil, I can't understand why He wouldn't want this pleasure for me. I bet if I touch it that I can better decide if I should eat it or not. Then I will decide if it's worth eating so my eyes will be opened."

After a brief period of wrestling within herself and sorting through the internal dialogue over whether or not to eat the fruit of the forbidden tree, the woman's conscience became sufficiently weakened and the subtle, evil inclination took over. The woman could not help but be almost drawn to the tree and its fruit. The fruit smelled and looked delicious and it was something new she had never tried before. It was such a nice looking fruit too.

It was clear to her, after putting some thought into it, that this tree would help her get where she wanted to go by making her wise like God. Seeing the tree in this way, that by eating from it the woman stood to benefit greatly, she had become morally weak in this area and actually reached up and plucked a piece of fruit from the tree. She quickly realized that she had touched the fruit and was still alive so she began to listen to the part inside her that often tries to justify and rationalize wrong choices.

In her mind she had wrongly concluded that God had said that if you "touch the tree it would kill you". Although really He didn't say, "you touch it you die," the woman worked to rationalize her desires and changed the word God spoke to Adam, and then she ate of the fruit she was holding. She ate the fruit without dieing instantly, and then gave some to her husband who was with her. He was with her but remained silent not knowing or perceiving the internal battle she was having which brought her to the place of making this bad decision.

Now that both the man and the woman had broken God's rule and disobeyed willingly, they felt different. Up until this point in their short existence the potential to choose wrong was in them but it was never an issue because they had not acted on it. For the first time they felt a feeling that is common to most people who intentionally choose evil and submit to the craftiness of the evil inclination and the way it causes man to rationalize and justify their wrong actions. This shame, brought on by their sin, opened a crack in their spirit where the evil thoughts and desires found a place to pervade their thoughts more and more. So much so that they even felt ashamed that they were naked. Their physical nakedness was a huge symbol representing that their righteousness was stripped away because of choosing sin, sin that brings death. No, they didn't die that moment, but the choice to sin ultimately leads to death if the sin is not paid for or "covered". Therefore, when the man and woman saw that they were physically naked they were ashamed. They certainly were not familiar with this new feeling of uneasiness but being physically naked truly represented their inner man, which now was exposed as being without perfect obedience.

They were no longer innocent, possessing righteous hearts of the first man and woman created. To cover up the outward reminder of their inner sinful choice and resulting feeling of shame, they made themselves aprons to cover their bodies. Almost as soon as they had made their best attempt to make a covering for their shame, they heard their Creator starting to question their whereabouts. It was as if their own consciences were working overtime to bring them to the point of admitting their failure and repenting. As if Adam and Eve hadn't done enough to try to cover up the shame from their sin by making clothes out of leaves, now they were working harder to avoid the detection of their error by hiding in the trees of the garden. They now felt unrighteous because they were no longer in the pure state of existence that they started in and were hiding amidst created things which were still in the state of purity they were created in. Then, almost as if Adam and Eve were really getting away with their sin, the Creator who knew where they were, called out to give them a chance to turn back to Him. He said, "Where are you?"

Although it was a weak response, Adam said, "I heard your voice and I was naked and afraid so I hid myself."

Adam said this knowing that he had hid himself because his whole world was spiraling down around him due to the choice to disobey and sin. The knowledge that he disobeyed the instructions to not eat from the tree in the midst of the garden brought all kinds of never before felt emotions. Adam and Eve felt fear that came from the feelings of remorse and disappointment for what they had done. The threat of loss often brings fear and Adam knew loss would be the result of his actions. Adam had no power to take back what he and Eve had done and just make it all go away.

The fear was magnified because of the unknown. The unknown factor was the question of how their perfect life would now change, that life could never be the same now that Adam and Eve the sinners have this experiential knowledge. The fear that there will be a consequence for their behavior but the extent of which was also unknown. After all, now they "knew" good and evil because of the experiential knowledge they had from choosing evil by disobeying.

Yahweh replied to Adam with a question. Knowing full-well that Adam and Eve had eaten from the forbidden tree and were now reacting in shame to their self destructive choice, he asked Adam, "Who told you that you were naked'?

Of course, the Creator knew no one had told Adam and Eve they were naked but through this rhetorical question God was letting Adam know that He, the Creator knew Adam and Eve had realized their shame because they had made a conscious choice to disobey the main rule the Father had given them.

Being very straight forward Yahweh then asked Adam, "Did you eat from the tree that I told you not to eat from?"

Feeling trapped and too weak from his own shame to own up to his own choices, the man Adam blamed his sin on someone else. Adam was unable to take responsibility for his choice to disobey so he blamed it on Eve. Worse still, he twisted it to lay some of the blame on the Creator Himself. Adam answered, "The woman **you** gave me to be with me, she passed me some fruit from the forbidden tree, and I ate it." Even this weak attempt at blame shifting by the man fully implicated him because in his attempt to avert consequences he admitted that he knew the fruit the woman was handing him was from "the tree", meaning the one that was forbidden. The Creator questioned the woman now, "What have you done?" He asked the woman.

In response to the confrontation by her Creator, the woman told Yahweh that it was this internal desire to be wiser, which drove her to make that choice, it wasn't really the choice she wanted to make. The woman said, "It was almost as if she couldn't control her self."

Yahweh knew she was speaking of the inner desire she submitted to when she rationalized eating the fruit, thinking that to be as God would help her and her husband. Yahweh then explained the subtle nature of that part of man, which deceives man through rationalizing and justifying wrong desires and actions.

Yahweh said that this active potential for sin that is latent in humans would be continually present. He continued that the "evil inclination" in man would almost have a will of its own, with a personality whereby it acts in a stealth-like manner inside of man. What is referred to as a serpent is the evil inclination that is always ready to rationalize and justify sin. This potential to sin was part of created man and now was activated when the man and woman made a choice to disobey. It would not disappear at the death of the first man Adam and the first woman Eve; it would carry on to the children and grandchildren of the woman throughout time.

Although the propensity to disobey and justify sin is present and active in man, there will be a seed of the woman, the Messiah, who will perform a work at one point in history. The Messiah's work will all but eliminate this active potential to choose sin. By living a sinless life and dieing unjustly only to be resurrected, the Spirit of Messiah will be available to provide the strength to overcome the sinful desire.

This "seed" of woman will perform this work, which will benefit all humankind but the active potential for sin will still hold some sway over the heart of man. The Messiah's work will limit the evil inclination of man; but because of man having knowledge of good and evil, it will still be strong enough to prevent man from always choosing righteousness and obedience to the Creator. So essentially the Messiah will bring back a greater potential for righteousness by being an acceptable sacrifice which covers our past sin, but because this potential for sin has overrode the potential for righteousness in this inaugural instance in the garden, there will still be times when sin is the result of mans choices.

Once Yahweh had dealt with the aspect of the human's heart and mind, which can choose evil, He sadly had to deliver a consequence for disobedience to the man and woman. He said to the woman; "Sin choices affect everything and from now on, bearing children will be fraught with difficulties and discomfort which would not have been part of bearing a child had disobedience not been your choice. Because you reasoned in yourself and decided to pluck the fruit that was forbidden and eat it and then hand it to your husband, it appears you think it is OK to make unilateral decisions. This being so, from now on you are going to have a part of you that would like to control your husband and be the boss of him. This will make for a challenge in life for you and your husband. As a couple, you will have to continually work to be lovingly and mutually submissive. If only you had considered this when you began convincing yourself it was acceptable to eat that fruit and didn't consult with your partner.

After delivering the consequence to the woman for her choice, the Creator said to Adam, "Because you were paying more attention to the garden and your surroundings than you were to what your wife's needs were, you Adam will have to work hard to live comfortably pretty much until you die and return to dust in your grave. Had you been paying attention to her you would have seen how obvious it was that she was moving in an unsafe direction when she was assessing the forbidden tree. It would have been better if you were not just "with her", but actually being attentive to her. The ground will no longer produce abundance so simply but will require unpleasant work to gain produce from it. It will no longer yield so easily under your hand but it will be cursed with unfavorable thorns and thistles to slow you down. This, more time-consuming work environment will cause you to have to fight like crazy and be intentional to give the attention to your wife that she needs. You will strive to give her more attention as you should have this day when you were paying more attention to your work than to your wife.

So, even though they were cursed because of their actions Adam knew they had to go on and make the best of it. As a symbol of his intention to provide for His wife and work together with her through what might prove to be a challenging life where bearing

> children will be challenging to say the least, Adam said that his wife would be the mother of all living and called her "Eve."
>
> Then Yahweh, seeing the resolve for man to accept his consequence and move forward in the challenges ahead, trusting still in the Creator to care for him, made clothes out of animal skins for Adam and Eve to cover themselves. This act showed Adam and Eve the Father still loved and cared for them and represented that because of their choice to sin it was necessary there be death to cover it. This was realized in the death of an animal to provide the covering for their naked bodies that were now exposed because of disobedience.
>
> After the new wardrobe was given to man Yahweh said, in a poetic way to emphasize his multiple facets and sovereignty, "Because man has experienced evil as a result of their choice to disobey, man has become like one of us, knowing good and evil, it is not allowable for him to eat of the tree of life and live forever." The edict of the Creator meant that humankind could not proceed and possess the gift of never dieing a physical death. Through their choice to sin, they have quickened the aspect of their spirit that is designed to inspire them to make a choice to both obey and love their Creator or disobey and loose immortality. It is vital that this choice to love their Creator is actually a choice and not some mechanical preprogrammed response. If they eat of the tree of life in this state, then they will not only be immortal but will be immoral. I must continue on with the plan to ensure there is no immorality and sin in the perfect kingdom of Yahweh."

The analytical paraphrase you have just read admittedly is only one way to hear what the words of the Genesis passage are saying. It is difficult to know for certain what the conversations and attitudes of Adam and Eve were in the Garden. However, the account as presented above shows much greater logic than is found in a traditional, literalistic view. The above version provides an explanation for a poetical manner of writing as would have been done by the writer of Genesis to an ancient culture. Thinking that there was a serpent who slithered into the lives of Adam and Eve and outsmarted them because it was supposedly inhabited by the spirit of "Satan", offends the senses when one tries to consider the logic of such a literal interpretation.

The point alone of a spirit of "Satan" inhabiting another created object goes against all the statements Yahweh made which claim there is "none like him." If there exists a supposed Satan, who has the ability to inhabit the spirit of a creature, then "satan" is like God and God then becomes a liar. There cannot be any entity that can "fill" a person or creature, except The Holy Spirit of Yahweh the Creator.

What happened next was Yahweh sent the man and woman out from the perfect environment, which is to say they are not going to be allowed to enjoy paradise until the sin of theirs is atoned for. So, out they go and they cannot come back to eat of the tree of life. This consequence comes because the Father and Creator has allowed the subtle potential for man to choose sin to be strong enough in the heart of man, that entry by sinful man to paradisiacal immortality is prevented. Man is unable to receive the immortality of paradise until such a time as the plan for the ages is complete and the seed of the woman has fully put an end to sin, the sin that stems from the sinful desire of the heart of man.

The only way man can eat of the tree of life is through obeying the commandments the Creator gives them. God's commands must be obeyed out of a sincere heart of love for the Creator and His Messiah, the promised seed of the woman. The Tree of Life is protected now but man can find his way back to paradise eventually and enjoy the gift of immortality.

The Tree of Life is not gone forever but it is up to man to follow Yahweh's plan and to eventually arrive at the point where he may once again have the right to the Tree of Life. A verse in Revelation reveals what John thought about returning to the tree of life. He unabashedly declares that those who do God's commandments will be those who eat of the tree of life. Keep in mind that Adam and Eve were the first to ever go against the command of God.

> *I am Alpha and Omega, the beginning and the end, the first and the last.*
> *Blessed are they that do his commandments, that they may have right to the tree of life, and may enter in through the gates into the city. Revelations 22:13-14 KJV*

The above paraphrase of Genesis 3 is not intended to replace the words in the Torah but to explain what was to be relayed by the writer. The last words of Revelation 22:14 are quoted to help bring attention to the Tree of Life, which is available to all who keep the commands of the Creator. The Tree of Life will be part of "Paradise" once again according to what is read in Revelations. The wording I used to expand on some of the thoughts in Genesis is wording which could be used to describe any parable-like story.

Yeshua of Nazareth is known to have taught in parables and therefore when we read a parable in the Apostolic writings, we know the characters are not literal. The probability of the story in the garden, or at least parts of it being like a parable, which is full of metaphor and non-literal meaning, is high.

In the above re-telling, we see that Eve is not talking with a serpent but she is talking with herself, in the sense of an internal dialogue. She is battling that part of the human being that we all battle from time to time. Eve is fighting against her own internal desires. It is the flesh or rather her desires that Eve is battling against. One's desires often lust against the spirit. Paul spoke of this perpetual struggle in his letter to the Galatians;

> *For the flesh lusteth against the Spirit, and the Spirit against the flesh: and these are contrary the one to the other: so that ye cannot do the things that ye would. Galatians 5:17 KJV*

James also tells us that out of our own lusts we are drawn away. James the apostle knew the origin of our sin choices was not from the evil desires of a satanic salesman but that the origin of our sinful choices was from the desires and lusts that lay inside of us.

> *But every man is tempted, when he is drawn away of his own lust, and enticed. James 1:14 KJV*

Is it Possible That the Evil Inclination in Man is "good?"

In the above retelling of the serpent in the garden account, I tried to express the story in such a way so as to help the reader understand that the serpent character, which is read in Genesis 3, is a metaphor for the latent sin-potential in humankind. The serpent represents the subtle nature that was created within man from the beginning. A nuance of human character that is the driving force behind sin choices. Every human being on earth has a desire to choose good and a desire to choose evil but where do those desires come from?

There has been a debate for centuries as to whether the human infant is born into sin or if sin is learned. To engage in that debate here would undoubtedly be engrossing and would not be solved by simply assessing and adhering to the typical arguments found on both sides of the debate. Where the debate falls short of being successful on either side is when it fails to recognize that man was created with a potential for both evil and good. Man is not so much either born with sin or born without sin, but man is born with the profound ability and potential for both. Yahweh created man with both the ability to choose good and the ability to choose evil. Interestingly, if one believes the following statements in the bullet points below, then one must believe Yahweh placed the potential for good and evil inside of man and that both of those attributes are good. This is seen by noting that it was only after man was created that Yahweh said, "It is very good"; Genesis 1:31 "*And God saw every thing that he had made, and, behold, it was very good*". Where He otherwise said, "it is good" for that which was created on the previous five days.[145] In using logic to discern the truth the following points must be considered when finding a way to accept that the evil potential in man was imparted to man at the point of creation and that it is not an attribute that was foisted on man by an evil cosmic deceiver. Here then are some points to add to the equation.

- Neither "Satan" nor anyone can create anything because there is none like Yahweh;

- After man was created with the potential for good and evil, Yahweh saw all that He had created and said, "It is very good." inferring that the potential for evil was "good".

All of the other creative efforts of the Creator brought only the remarks that acknowledge the product of His work as, "It is good." However when man was created we heard the Creator saying, "It is very good!"

Now, if Yahweh created man with the potential to choose good or evil and said the entire creation was very good, then the potential in man to choose evil must be "good". Is it possible that Yahweh is saying that the "*yetzer ha ra*" which is known as the evil inclination in man is "good?" If it is true as I am positing that Yahweh did create man with the potential for both good and

145 And God saw the light, that *it was* good: and God divided the light from the darkness. Genesis 1:4 KJV
And God called the dry *land* Earth; and the gathering together of the waters called he Seas: and God saw that *it was* good. Genesis 1:10 KJV
And the earth brought forth grass, *and* herb yielding seed after his kind, and the tree yielding fruit, whose seed *was* in itself, after his kind: and God saw that *it was* good. Genesis 1:12 KJV
And to rule over the day and over the night, and to divide the light from the darkness: and God saw that *it was* good. Genesis 1:18 KJV
And God created great whales, and every living creature that moveth, which the waters brought forth abundantly, after their kind, and every winged fowl after his kind: and God saw that *it was* good.
Genesis 1:21 KJV
And God made the beast of the earth after his kind, and cattle after their kind, and every thing that creepeth upon the earth after his kind: and God saw that *it was* good. Genesis 1:25 KJVA

evil and then said "it was very good," then it must be that the evil inclination is good in His eyes. I am not saying that when man chooses evil it is a good thing. Rather, I am saying the ability and potential to choose evil as well as good is good.

According to Yahweh, choice is good.

Man's evil choices are part of the acceptable plan of the Creator to redeem man. If man were incapable of choosing evil then man would not need a redeemer and would not need God at all. However, throughout life man must learn to choose the good and refuse the evil. Shades of the necessity for man to learn to refuse evil are found in a prophecy about a uniquely anointed child who is spoken of to come by Isaiah. It is believed that this prophecy is about the Messiah but an application to all men can be made.

> *For before the child shall know to refuse the evil, and choose the good, the land that thou abhorrest shall be forsaken of both her kings. Isaiah 7:16 KJV*

Man does not acquire this potential to choose sin as he grows, but the potential to choose sin is inherent. He was created with it and it is an attribute of human beings that needs to be managed and balanced. This balance takes place by man coming to understand what righteousness is. This learning process presents man with the option for righteous choices as well as having the option for wicked choices. We humans are neither inherently good nor inherently evil, we are inherently both, and this is what differentiates us from the animal kingdom. We have the privilege of choosing our behaviors in life where animals have only the ability to act on instinct. That is unless you are to train a monkey or like creature to choose between two objects, then it appears you are endowing that creature with the gift of free choice. However, that animal is not choosing between good and evil on a conscious plane because that animal does not know the difference between good and evil. It would be senseless to argue that animals do not have the power to choose because certainly some are trained to choose. This choice is not based on the animal's autonomous free will. Free will is an attribute that is a unique aspect of humanity, which allows us to choose between good and evil. Rather when an animal makes a choice, it is either out of instinct or out of a programmed response through training.

In the Book, *"Classical Christianity and Rabbinic Judaism"*, the authors recognize the inherent ability man has to make choices in the daily walk of life. The authors I quote below use a term you may or may not be familiar with.

The term used below is *"halakah"* and has a meaning of walking. Halakah is translated as "walk" in the Scriptures. This use of it is a typical Hebraic use and is always referencing how one walks out their faith.

> *The halakah embodies in norms of behavior deep reflection on the meaning of human nature. Endowed with autonomous will, man has the power to rebel against God's will, and it follows that rebellion lurks as an ever-present possibility.*[146]

Was the Serpent Motif New to Moses?

To understand the fact that we as humans are created with the power to choose good or evil carries us a long way from the place where we are abdicating the responsibility for our sin choices to some mythic satanic being. I use "mythic" in reference to this being here, because the serpent in the garden has been a mythic or mythological figure for ages before the account of the serpent in the garden story was written into the Torah. In fact Moses, who is the alleged and commonly accepted writer of the book of Genesis, had spent forty years in Egypt and became learned in all the wisdom of Egypt we are told in Acts.

> *And Moses was learned in all the wisdom of the Egyptians, and was mighty in words and in deeds. Acts 7:22 KJV*

This learning would have included an in depth understanding of all the gods of Egypt, which included the serpent.

To put it plainly the serpent as it was spoken of in many ancient myths was a mythological creature that was said to be full of wisdom and protected the "tree of life". Is it plausible that Eve would blame a literal snake for tricking her into disobeying God? It is a huge ideological leap into mythology to rationalize such as a phenomenon. A phenomenon that claims that a creature man had named and man was ruling over, was the character that actually deceives a human being. The humans were the top of the intellect chain and unless the serpent was a literal serpent with unbelievable intellect, or the serpent was "Satan" posing as the serpent or appearing as a "shining one" as some teach; then this "serpent" must have been a literary tool used to teach some other point.

We know with almost concrete certainty that the writer of Genesis was a Hebrew and in all likelihood was the great Hebrew leader Moses. Without

146 Classical Christianity and Rabbinic Judaism by Bruce D. Chilton and Jacob Neusner, p. 92. Baker Academic: A Division of Baker Publishing, 2004

debating that fact, we can see Moses was able to use this myth involving a serpent, in writing the story of the beginnings and fall of man. Although there are crumbs of a serpent-to-Satan relation left in Judaism today, the pre-Judaism faith in Yahweh (God) was not akin to interpreting the serpent in the garden as Satan or any other literal entity.

Moses, as many great writers today, played off a very commonly understood concept and mythological story to tell the Israelite people about their beginnings. Moses knew his kinsmen had been in Egypt for hundreds of years and because of their connection to Egypt would understand the connection Moses was making to the ancient serpent myth. The serpent was hailed as divinity in Egypt and any connection made to this "divine" creature would have held with it the understandability that was commonly associated with the attributes of this creature/god. Egypt was not the only culture to possess a belief in the serpent as a subtle intelligent representation of divinity, almost every ancient culture throughout time has held a similar belief. Therefore, the Moses, who was the prophet of the only God, carried this story with him. Moses was allowed by the Creator to incorporate the mythopoetic imagery familiar to the people of the day, into the creation account. An ancient story that had all but been lost and forgotten by the Hebrew people while in a centuries-long enslavement in Egypt. Relating a necessary story in terms that were comprehendible and connectable to well understood ancient mythological themes was instrumental in expressing the profound nature of the fall of man in the Garden of Eden, known as Paradise.

Satan Grows in Imaginations Over Time

As was said earlier, we humans automatically place the pictures that have been given us through various modalities of stimulus throughout life, into the text of Scripture and other written works. For many of today's believers in "Satan" and "Hell", the ideas they posses are really second-hand beliefs. Historically there have been many submissions of unique and equally incorrect images and writings about Hell and Satan. Looking at the historical evolution of these ideas is immensely valuable in coming to a correct understanding of Satan. Jeffrey Burton Russell discloses explicitly how the formation of the concepts and images of the devil have been evolving throughout history as a result of personification of evil by past generations. Russell says:

> *The historical approach observes the origins of the concept, sketches its early lines, and shows its gradual development through the ages down to the present. The concept of the Devil is found in only a few religions. There was no idea of a single*

> *personification of evil in ancient Greco-Roman religions, for example, and there was and is none in Hinduism or Buddhism. Most religions- from Buddhism to Marxism- have their demons, but only four major religions have had a real devil. These are Mazdaism (Zoroastrianism), ancient Hebrew religion (but not modern Judaism), Christianity and Islam. Through these four religions, the tradition of the Devil can be defined.*[147]

Many of the well-known images, specifically of Satan, which have taken up residence in the minds of many, have roots in the descriptions and subsequent artistic works of two pieces of famous literature. These are the famous works by Dante Alighieri and John Milton. We will talk about Dante's Inferno in a little while; as for John Milton, it was in the 1600's that he wrote a famous poem called *Paradise Lost*. This work of John Milton has been acknowledged as a primary source for instilling many of the images one brings to mind today when the serpent and the Garden of Eden are spoken of. The Wikipedia says this in its entry on the epic poem *Paradise Lost.*

> ***Paradise Lost*** (1667) is an epic poem by the 17th century English poet John Milton. It was originally published in 1667 in ten books and written in blank verse. A second edition followed in 1674, redivided into twelve books (mimicking the division of Virgil's *Aeneid*) with minor revisions throughout and a note on the versification. The poem concerns the Christian story of the Fall of Man: the temptation of Adam and Eve by Satan and their expulsion from the Garden of Eden.[148]

Paradise Lost is very creative writing indeed but what Mr. Milton has failed to do in his writing which sadly is not always read as fiction poetry but is taken as non-fiction by so many, was to separate the use of ancient myth and mythopoetic language that is read in the Scriptures, from what is real and literal. Mr. Milton apparently decided at one point in his choice for belief system that this satanic spirit realm and its accompanying hell was a factual and literal group of beings and places. His writing reflected his belief, and through that choice of a belief he was forced to concoct or fabricate if you will, in a hodge-podge fashion, an entire spiritual system in which was contained the main component of the supernatural Satan. I state this as somewhat of a presumption in that it seems Milton's work was not intended to be complete fiction but he articulated it as true and literal to a large degree.

147 From page 4, The Prince of Darkness; Radical Evil and the Power of Good In History by Jeffrey Burton Russell Copyright 1988 Cornell University Press

148 http://en.wikipedia.org/wiki/Paradise_Lost

Through this belief system Milton has done what countless other hyper-spiritual individuals have done through the ages, and from my experience, do so presently in constructing their own game and set of rules. The manner in which the spiritually minded have developed their own system of operating within the faith practices they adhere to is very much like creating a new game based on an original that had its own established set of rules. If you sit down today and invent a brand new game, such as a board game or a sporting-type event, it is you the creator, who establishes the rules. The game itself may be inspired by another similar game but because you are the designer, you get the privilege of defining the rules and parameters that are built into the game.

For instance, there are numerous word games on the present board game market. Most of us have played or heard about "Scrabble™". Scrabble™ is an excellent game that allows each player to possess up to seven tiles with varied letters on each tile. The player is asked to place his tiles in the acceptable fashion according to the rules on the playing board and in so doing composes a word, which scores him a number of points. The total of points varies depending on the letters used, and the placement of the tiles. The player may acquire a double or triple letter score or a double or triple word score. Board games that are similar to Scrabble™ are numerous and one such game that comes to mind is Boggle™.

Boggle™ is a word building game where the letters are all placed on dice in a 4 by 4-square pattern. When the dice are shaken and then settled in place in the 4 by 4 pattern, the player then attempts to find as many words in the presenting letter combination within a short period. The game of Boggle™ accepts the National Scrabble Associations Dictionary to settle disputes on questionable words. Beside board games that were built in part from a concept seen in an existing game are electronic games. One type of word game that is of the electronic variety has taken the notion of building a game from the concept seen in another game to the digital world yet the creator of the game was free to define the rules and parameters of play;

> **Mumbo Jumbo 1.0.2.3** by Tamera A Shaw-McGuire
>
> A twist on the popular Scrabble(TM) game. Use the tiles on the board to find words up to seven letters. Use the bonus squares to receive more points. You can play this game online using the Tams11 lobby found at www.tams11.com.

The number of games taken from concepts seen elsewhere is vast and in each of the games, the designer has implemented his own rules. If you try to play any of these games by different rules, you in essence are actually coming up with a new game. The whole point of the designer placing rules and parameters on "his" game is so that it is unique and different from all the other games in some ways. The designer is now in a sense the one who controls how the game is played, that is if the player agrees to play according to the prescribed rules. John Milton seems to have done this very thing by creating images and concepts to go along with his belief system, which includes a cosmic "Satan". He took an existing concept and reworked it, adding elements and concepts so it became a completely new way to see Satan and Hell but still based it on concepts that developed long before his time. Milton launched his concept of Satan and Hell off another concept drawing inspiration from a previous work. In so doing, Mr. Milton has established the rules for his game; only in this instance, the game is not physical but spiritual. In developing his concept, he made it unique from previous concepts but drew from much available thought that pre-existed himself. The rules he decided to play by are uniquely his and because they are all in the spiritual realm, which is, for the most part intangible, they become unchallengeable.

These are the rules that he seems to play by and because he is convinced that this is how to play this spiritual game he is able to remain in control and appear that he has a form of Godliness in the concept of "Paradise Lost" as it relates spiritual forces to the reader. Milton is not the only one who has compiled a treatise on the concept of a cosmic "satanic" being who thwarted God's plan to establish an eternal Paradise at the beginning of creation. As I mentioned another writer who may have been a catalyst at embedding a false notion of "Satan" and "Hell" even further in the psyche of humankind is a man named Dante. For your reading pleasure and as an aid in understanding some of the origins of the highly evolved, present day concept of "Satan" and "Hell" please peruse the following synopsis of the poem, which is more of a book, titled *"The Divine Comedy"*. The most famous segment of the entire work is called *Dante's Inferno.* Here follows excerpts of the poem as synopsized on the internet encyclopedia Wikipedia. The poem is the transmission of a vision of Hell that Dante claimed to have had. The following explanation and synopsis provided by Wikpedia is far more concise than any that I might provide for you. Please note the remarks of the contributor who supplied the poem to Wikipedia. We are told that this poem has had such a great influence *"that it affects the Western Christian view of the afterlife to this day."*

> ***The Divine Comedy*** (Italian: ***Commedia***, later christened "***Divina***" by Giovanni Boccaccio), written by Dante Alighieri between 1308 and his death in 1321, is widely considered the central epic poem of Italian literature, the last great work of literature of the Middle Ages *and* the first great work of the Renaissance, and one of the

greatest of world literature. Its influence is so great that it affects the Western Christian view of the afterlife to this day.

The poem begins on Good Friday of the year 1300, a significant holiday, "In the middle of our life's journey" (*Nel mezzo del cammin di nostra vita*), and so opens in medias res. Dante is thirty-five years old, half of the biblically alloted age of 70 (Psalm 90:10), lost in a dark wood (perhaps allegorically, contemplating suicide--as "wood" is figured in Canto XIII), assailed by beasts (a lion, a leopard, and a she-wolf; allegorical depictions of temptations towards sin) he cannot evade, and unable to find the "straight way" (diritta via) to salvation (symbolized by the sun behind the mountain). Conscious that he is ruining himself, that he is falling into a "deep place" (basso loco) where the sun is silent ('l sol tace), Dante is at last rescued by Virgil after his love Beatrice intercedes on his behalf (Canto II), and he and Virgil begin their journey to the underworld.

Dante passes through the Gate of Hell, on which is inscribed the famous phrase, "*Lasciate ogne speranza, voi ch'intrate*" or "*Abandon all hope, ye who enter here*".[1] Before entering Hell proper, Dante and his guide see the Opportunists, souls of people who in life did nothing, neither for good or evil. Mixed with them are the outcasts, who took no side in the Rebellion of Angels (among these Dante recognizes either Pope Celestine V, or Pontius Pilate; the text is ambiguous). These souls are neither in Hell nor out of it, but reside on the shores of the Acheron, their punishment to eternally pursue a banner, and be pursued by wasps and hornets that continually sting them while maggots and other such insects drink their blood and tears. This symbolizes the sting of their conscience.

Then Dante and Virgil reach the ferry that will take them across the river Acheron and to Hell proper. The ferry is piloted by Charon, who does not want to let Dante enter, for he is a living being. Their passage across is unknown since Virgil forces him to let them across, but Dante faints and does not awake until he is on the other side.

Virgil guides Dante through the nine circles of Hell. The circles are concentric, each new one representing further and further evil, culminating in the center of the earth, where Satan is held, bound. Each circle's sin is punished in an appropriately revengeful way to fit the crime. The nine circles are:

> First Circle (Limbo). Here reside the unbaptized and the virtuous pagans, who, though not sinful, did not accept Christ. They are not punished in an active sense, but rather grieve only their separation from God, without hope of reconciliation. Limbo includes fields and a castle, the dwelling place of virtuous souls of wisdom, including Virgil himself. In the castle Dante meets the poets Homer, Horace, Ovid, and Lucan. (Canto IV)
>
> All of the condemned sinners are judged by Minos, who sentences each soul to one of the lower eight circles. These are structured according to the classical (Aristotelian) conception of virtue and vice, so that they are grouped into the sins of incontinence, violence, and fraud (which for many commentators are represented by the leopard, lion, and she-wolf[3]). The sins of incontinence — weakness in controlling one's desires and natural urges — are the mildest among them, and, correspondingly, appear first:

Dante's poem goes on in magnificent detail to speak of no less than 9 descending circles and some of those with various zones that are even more deep, dark and dire than the upper levels of the Hell. The final zone of the final circle, zone 4 of Circle 9 depicts the place for the worst sinners that ever have or will exist. Dante speaks of this tortuous place and then closes his poem/vision in the following fashion;

> Zone 4 (Judecca): Traitors to their lords and benefactors (Canto XXXIV). This is the harshest section of Hell, containing Satan. Satan is depicted with three faces, each having a mouth that chews a prominent traitor. Satan is waist deep in ice, and beats his six wings as if trying to escape, but the icy wind that emanates only further ensures his imprisonment (as well as that of the others in the ring). The sinners in the mouths of Satan are Brutus and Cassius, who were involved in the assassination of Julius Caesar (an act which, to Dante, represented the destruction of a unified Italy), and Judas Iscariot (the namesake of this zone) for betraying Jesus. Judas is in the center mouth, and alone among the three has his head inserted into the mouth.
>
> The two poets escape by climbing the ragged fur of Lucifer, passing through the center of the earth, emerging in the southern hemisphere just before dawn on Easter Sunday beneath a sky studded with stars.[149]

149 The Divine Comedy can be viewed at; http://www.divinecomedy.org/divine_comedy.html. Excerpt provided above can be viewed at; http://en.wikipedia.org/wiki/The_Divine_Comedy

Both Dante and Milton, although excellent writers, are guilty of prejudicing their writings based on forgone errant conclusions of the concept of a "satan" and a "Hell." Your guess is as good as mine as to whether or not they were intending that their writings become a part of forming the collective consciousness of society for centuries to come. Perhaps, in a style similar to Dan Brown and his book the *Davinci Code*, both Milton and Dante may have professed that their works were not to be taken as fact but were fictional works, which were composed to entertain the masses. Dan Brown has stated that his work is intended to be fiction although it does in fact contain some fact. So too perhaps, did the aforementioned writers make the same claim. Nonetheless, Milton's and Dante's impact through their ingenious work certainly has some parallels to the impact Dan Browns "fictitious" work has had on religious thought today.

As I said, your guess is as good as mine and it may be true that Dante and Milton set forth to develop a work that would be used to inform the readers of their day what they believed Hell and Satan to be. By extension, a large segment of society today, which was future to Dante and Milton, has the common belief in a cosmic "satan" and his abode. The Harris poll quoted in Reuters News, November 29th, 2007, claims 62 percent of Americans believe in Satan and Hell. Perhaps these historical writers were hoping to impart their theology which spoke of the abode of the wicked upon their death, to all those who might read their works in the future. Regardless of the writer's intentions, both of these works have proven to be a major piece of the puzzle in understanding the composition of beliefs in our culture today. Their writing has definitely helped to form the contemporary concept of the supposed archenemy of God and the Hell the enemy rules over. In addition, regardless of their intent, both Dante and Milton are guilty of placing concepts in the hands of society that they themselves had adopted from previously known concepts. Both these gifted writers wrote through the eyes of their predetermined understanding of the concept of Satan.

Because of a propensity for much of culture to accept hyper-spirituality and the concept of spiritual men and women having special insight into the "spiritual realm", both Dante and Milton garnered much support for the concepts explained in their works. Although both men were writing through an incorrect, pre-determined understanding of unproven concepts, they were able to write their own rules. Because most people will not question the "spiritual" visions and dreams of others, Dante and Milton were allowed to play by their own rules to their games and get others to play by the same rules without recognizing when and how those rules were developed. We see in this a clear picture of the evolution of a belief or ideology. Persons of influence developing *theo-spiritual* ideas based on preconceived or previously available concepts is a grievous occurrence which has taken place with great regularity throughout history and has affected many. The practice of studying long-held church doctrines, as opposed to rightly dividing and studying the Scriptures from a properly placed historical context, has led many brilliant men and women astray into further doctrinal error. This typical shortfall and misunderstanding has been the error of many writers and teachers who have put forth works that have added to the forming of contemporary thought about "Satan" and "Hell".

It is little different to say that one could write a book about the tooth fairy and her escapades and then have readers all over the world believe that the tooth fairy is real. Readers would fully embrace the tooth fairy idea and believe that she truly does come at night, undetected to reach under young children's pillows. It would be ludicrous to think that the readers would believe the tooth fairy literally does remove a carefully placed, sub-pillow tooth and place the currency of the respective country in its place. Along with the acceptance of a myth as fact, one must weigh the factor of time into the equation. This plays a big part in how a belief comes to be cemented in the societal psyche. The longer a myth is told the more rooted into the human belief system it stands to become. Regarding the heartfelt belief of a myth as it pertains to theology there can be no more profound and true axiom than to say that a lie told long enough becomes the truth.

The entire cycle of people designing their own spiritual reality, which I have made analogous connection to one designing their own game or games, continues to happen over and over again, as time moves on. Dante and Milton both did it when they created their own reality wrapped in spiritual and pseudo-scriptural concepts. They presented it articulately and convincingly to a culture that was not privileged to access of information. Because it appeared to be their experiences; and one cannot argue the significance of another's experiences in determining that person's belief system, their spiritual flavor was accepted and began more and more to be the rules by which others formed their belief systems. Along with that process, the established concept became a template for others to fabricate their own "spirituality" which cannot be challenged by another who is only a bystander able to observe individuals as they play by their own rules. This is such a deeply rooted Gnostic concept in our culture that it is acceptable and has become today what is known as Christianity. With over 33000 different flavors of Christianity that have developed since the first century, one can see where one game inspires another and another and another. Down to the present age, we are seeing such diversity in the explanations and understanding of supposed "satanic" activity that it is difficult, but not impossible; to trace the evolution of these fabricated concepts.

The family tree of similar but unique theological ideas and concepts continues to grow and ultimately the original rules for the spiritual game are no longer used, and possibly forgotten altogether. Recognizing the origin and original parameters of true faith though is different than feeling the need to determine the process of the evolution of a board game which begets numerous knock offs and look-alikes. The true faith, if in fact was started by the Creator of the universe who is perfect in all His ways, is more consistent than the creators of various games are. If in fact there is a true faith that is designed by the one God who Created the heavens and the Earth and all that is in them, then it seems reasonable to believe that He would not make a game with rules that needed constant revision and evolution to make them better. His faith has no need of fundamental change. Unless one can reconcile all the apparent contradictions in the entire bible as we have it today and come up with a faith-based stand that allows for a perfect unchanging Creator, they will be left floundering with seemingly unanswerable questions about who God is and how He desires to be served and worshipped.

The idea of one constant format for a game, or to be more specific, a pattern of worship and obedience to the Creator that is intended for all time, is far more comprehendible than an ever-changing set of rules, which are altered by humanity, as time marches on.

Every child has played a game with a few friends where the rules keep changing every time the game is played and often changed during the game. This makes it impossible for the players to establish a concrete relationship within the game and to the game itself. There is no difference with the evolving spirituality that many allege has its roots in the Bible. These alterations appear to be done in an effort to create a God who is palatable and not convicting of our rebellious desires that reside in our hearts. The pattern of worship and obedience, which one chooses, can be referred to as ones "spirituality." It is this spirituality that should have endured, being more consistent as a rule instead of evolving from one concept to another. As well, it is this inconsistency and evolving truth, which has brought us to the point in contemporary belief systems, where the most common beliefs about of the serpent in the garden contain the notion either that "Satan" is the serpent or that "Satan" inhabited the serpent for his evil manipulative game.

For our pursuit to be closer to being considered exhaustive, I hope to answer the following very important questions. The questions are;

- Is the serpent in the garden Satan?

And

- Is the serpent a literal snake that is inhabited by Satan and then used by Satan to tempt Eve?

Other topics that will be discussed are;

- What style of writing is the story of the serpent in the garden?
- Is the writer of the story, who is thought to be Moses, speaking literally or figuratively or both?
- When did the serpent come to be understood incorrectly by readers as being Satan, the cosmic entity?
- In addition, we will consider how this story applies to our lives if we are no longer able to see all the components in the story as literal components and characters.

CHAPTER 13

Answering The Serpent In The Garden Questions

Now we shall go on to consider the first question posed in the previous chapter.

Is the serpent in the garden "Satan?"

The short answer is, No!

If as some say the serpent was in fact Satan who had taken on the form of a serpent, then we are back at the place where we are ascribing supernatural attributes to an entity other than Yahweh. If it is true that there is a God and He calls himself Yahweh in the Torah or as some pronounce it Yehovah; then; it also must be true when He says that "He is God and there is none else", as well as when the God of the universe says, "there is none like me" in Exodus chapter 9.

> *For I will at this time send all my plagues upon thine heart, and upon thy servants, and upon thy people; that thou mayest know that there is none like me in all the earth. Exodus 9:14 KJV*

If there is "none else," this means there are no other entities with supernatural powers. This would include all the false Gods that the Egyptians and many of the Hebrews had come to believe existed and believed possessed supernatural power. The statement, "*there is none like Me*" was made by Yahweh in the context of referring to the Egyptian gods who were given homage by the Israelites and the Egyptians. If we understand even a few of the thoughts the Egyptians had on the topic of the gods of Egypt and that these gods included supposed deities who enacted evil upon humans, then we have to include "satan" as being the same as one of those gods.

It is a well-known historical fact that Ancient Egypt had hundreds of Gods as we discussed in chapter 5. Egypt was not as close to a monotheistic belief system as was Persia. Many of these gods were believed to have the ability to incarnate themselves or to manifest themselves as different animals and objects. It was highly common to accept and believe that certain gods caused good to come upon or happen to humans and other gods caused evil to happen to man. It was also a belief that some gods cause both good and evil to happen. The fact that Yahweh decided to free His people from Egypt and show them that He is the only God and there is none else, was His instruction to the people. Yahweh wanted to teach the people that they are not to believe in the gods of Egypt. Yahweh wanted His chosen people to not only come out of Egypt physically but to come out of Egypt spiritually too. After spending multiple generations in Egypt, the Hebrew people had learned about, and in many ways come to believe in the false gods of Egypt. Yahweh referred to these supposed forces that were believed to possess ability to affect and control matters here on Earth as "Gods" Even though they were imagined forces that didn't really exist, Yahweh referred to them as "Gods" because they were given the place of God in the minds of the people. Early on in the story of the Exodus, we hear the Creator announce that those entities that are assumed to possess power in the eyes of the Egyptians are "gods".

> *For I will pass through the land of Egypt this night, and will smite all the firstborn in the land of Egypt, both man and beast; and against all the gods of Egypt I will execute judgment: I am the LORD. Exodus 12:12 KJV*

If people attribute any power, control or supernatural ability to a being such as is the case in believing their exists a cosmic entity that is able to manifest himself as a snake, then those people have made that entity into a God. In effect, the bulk of Christianity, much of Judaism and the majority of Islam believe in another God and are therefore not truly monotheistic. Their other God is "Satan". Although the other God is a distortion of a concept that is found in the Scriptures, having this god in one's theological, belief system places them in a category where the Creator might say that they are following another God. The original precept attached to the word *sawtawn* was designed to represent an adversary in human form, or perhaps an adversarial force sent from the Creator. At times, the adversary is the active force of wickedness that originates and is inherent in man. The one who believes there is a "Satan," believes there is another God.

One important thing that needs to be addressed here is that I am not stating that a person is not a believer in the true God of the Universe by believing in the other god called Satan. Somewhat to the contrary, the belief in another God does not preclude one from believing in the One God of the Universe. If you or I believe in a Satan, which fits the definition of another God in Yahweh's eyes, we are guilty of adding a God to a true monotheistic belief system and now have two gods in our portfolio. Much like the Hebrews in Egypt still thought of the God of Abraham, Isaac, and Jacob as the Almighty God but acknowledged other "gods" which were fabricated by the Egyptians or their predecessors, so too do many today claim that Yahweh is the Almighty God but consciously acknowledge some type of a literal Satan.

Most people when confronted with the concept that suggests they are saying there is another God if they believe there is a Satan are quick to defend their beliefs by saying that "Satan isn't a God". This hasty defense is based on their definition of a "God" and not necessarily Yahweh's definition. The person, who defends their belief in Satan, cannot see that by believing in a "Satan" they are saying there is another God. Yahweh is not stupid, He knows that the one who believes in a Satan being is not equating the power of "Satan" with the power of Yahweh as if both Gods possess the same amount of supernatural power. However, the ancient Israelites did the same thing. They began believing there were other supernatural forces that were deities and accepted them alongside the God of the Universe. The Ancient Israelites, believed some of the Egyptian gods were responsible for evil yet they were careful to not ascribe the same power and prestige as Yahweh had, to the other gods. Yahweh still chastised and admonished them for worshipping the "gods" of Egypt and other nations throughout their history. Here are a couple examples from the Scriptures of the One God admonishing the Israelites to avoid following the other gods and secondly, telling them that once they have chosen to neglect serving Him that He would scatter them and they will serve other "gods". Keep in mind that even though these "gods" did not really exist, Yahweh still referred to them as Gods because of the power they were thought to possess by the Israelites.

> *And it shall be, if thou do at all forget the LORD thy God, and walk after other gods, and serve them, and worship them, I testify against you this day that ye shall surely perish. Deuteronomy 8:19 KJV*

> *And the LORD shall scatter thee among all people, from the one end of the earth even unto the other; and there thou shalt serve other gods, which neither thou nor thy fathers have known, even wood and stone. Deuteronomy 28:64 KJV*

The Scriptures seemingly consider any other conceptual entity that is given the slightest homage by the children of Israel as if it is another God to them. Therefore, when Yahweh sees man claim Satan exists and affects humanity by using his supernatural abilities, then Yahweh sees man as having another God.

The Ludicrous Concept of Allowing Another God to Exist

Granted there are varying levels to how much "power" and recognition is attributed to Satan as far as evil and influence on human matters goes. However, even believing on a tiny scale that there is a supernatural being with the ability to shape-shift, that is take on the form of a created being such as a "serpent", means one is guilty of believing in another God. There is nothing; no power or force in the universe, which is of a supernatural nature that is in opposition to the Creator of the Universe. If there were another oppositional power, the Creator of the universe would destroy it hastily and not share His ability to supercede nature, with anything. It is senseless to think that there exists a supreme and sovereign Creator, who created humanity to share His world with, and desires the devoted affection and worship from humanity, yet refuses to destroy the entity that inexorably pursues the allegiance of the fragile humans. In addition, barring the wholesale receipt of humanity's allegiance to Satan, this evil being will do his best to try to destroy humanity. It would seem that if this is the case and God allows Satan to continue to offend, then this God is senseless and weak and is not then the God of the Universe but simply a co-regent and is relegated to share power with some other force.

Do we understand the implications of such a claim? If you or I had a paperweight on our desk and began to believe that the lifeless paperweight was bringing harm upon us, causing people to do evil against us, giving us nightmares, inhabiting the souls of gang members who commit violent murders, and appearing in different forms to try to trick well-meaning people into rejecting God; then clearly we would be seen as regarding that lifeless paperweight as a God. Whether you use a small "g" or a capital "G" makes no difference. By giving anything else the powers I mentioned regarding the paperweight, it is considered a God. Claiming there is a supernatural being on the loose trying to overcome the Almighty is stating that there is more than one God. It also portrays a limited potency of the God of the universe. If there is any force that can limit Yahweh in any way, then that force is indeed a God and the God that claims, "there is none else" is a liar. Satan has become a God in Christianity. As much as Satan has existed as a real entity, he might as well have been a paperweight, because according to Yahweh the concept of Satan is completely lifeless.

Would Your Father Put Up With Relentless Attacks on Your Family?

Could you imagine even on a physical level, if a father and husband were subjected to such opposition while trying to live at peace with his family? Imagine the Father and His family was subject to continued harassment and attempts to steal His family away by a much weaker neighbor or acquaintance. All the while, the Father had the power to stop this adversarial person but chose to let His family endure the harassment until he was good and ready to do something. This is the essence of what many are saying the world and humanity are going through by believing there is a Satan. Yahweh is the Father, we are His family, and many believe there is an adversarial force working to destroy the family and bring down Yahweh. This twisted logic is absolutely disassociated from the character of Yahweh the God of the Universe.

The one and only God gave man the choice to activate the evil that is inside man through creating man with a free will. Wouldn't Yahweh the Almighty God be seen as a weak and impotent God or at the very least, an uncaring and manipulative God if the false idea of an oppositional force was true? Understanding the term "supernatural" to mean, one who can override or move in realms which are above nature and supercede natural laws at will, allows us to see the blatant disrespect for the fact of Yahweh being the only God. Webster's 1918 dictionary of the English language defines "supernatural" thusly:

> **Supernatural**
>
> **SUPERNAT'URAL**, a. [super and natural.] Being beyond or exceeding the powers or laws of nature; miraculous. A supernatural event is one which is not produced according to the ordinary or established laws of natural things. Thus if iron has more specific gravity than water, it will sink in that fluid; and the floating of iron on water must be a supernatural event. Now no human being can alter a law of nature; the floating of iron on water therefore must be caused by divine power specially exerted to suspend, in this instance, a law of nature. Hence supernatural events or miracles can be produced only by the immediate agency of divine power.

Why would the God of the Universe give any other created being the ability to supercede nature? If one supercedes nature, would they not be seen as a God as a result? We do not serve a weak and insensible Creator. He is not in the business of imbuing rebellious creatures with super-powers which enable them to "be like God" when Yahweh has clearly said there is none like Him.

> *For I will at this time send all my plagues upon thine heart, and upon thy servants, and upon thy people; that thou mayest know that there is none like me in all the earth. Exodus 9:14 KJV*

Moses also testifies to the fact that there is no other "god" or supernatural force in the universe.

> *Or hath God assayed to go and take him a nation from the midst of another nation, by temptations, by signs, and by wonders, and by war, and by a mighty hand, and by a stretched out arm, and by great terrors, according to all that the LORD your God did for you in Egypt before your eyes?*
>
> *Unto thee it was shewed, that thou mightest know that **the LORD he is God; there is none else beside him.** Deuteronomy 4:34-35 KJV*
>
> *Know therefore this day, and consider it in thine heart, that Yahweh he is God in heaven above, and upon the earth beneath: there is none else. Deuteronomy 4:39 KJV*

To believe that the serpent in the garden is "Satan" is to believe there is another God and then we would be calling Yahweh, the God of the universe a liar.

If this serpent is a manifestation of Satan, then one must believe there exists another god and Yahweh is a liar; or that one has sorely misunderstood God's words.

A Word for Serpent is "nachash" Among Other Words.

Perhaps we might find some answers to our search by looking at the word used for serpent in the book of Genesis. The word for serpent in Genesis and elsewhere is the Hebrew word "*nachash*". This word is a word that is easily understood in context, to mean a snake. The word meaning, according the Briggs, Driver, Brown Hebrew Definitions is:

nachash

1) serpent, snake

1a) serpent

1b) image (of serpent)

1c) fleeing serpent (mythological)

Part of Speech: noun masculine

A Related Word by BDB/Strong's Number: from H5172

Conceivably this particular use of a word that means serpent could be accurate in relaying the message of some type of a snake in the garden. However, biblical writers often spoke of snakes, serpents and the like to relay a message that could be enhanced using the imagery and metaphor that the serpent portrayed. Remember Dan, one of the tribes of Israel? Dan is called a snake in Genesis chapter 49. Another example of a speaker employing the imagery that serpents carried in the minds of the hearer is seen when Yeshua called a group of the unbelieving Pharisees a "brood of vipers!" Neither of these uses was of literal intent yet after one reads the serpent in the garden story, they all too often conclude that it is literal. Do we too easily pick and choose what we believe is literal because of the desire to impose our theological conclusion backwards onto the pages of the Torah? Because the word literally means "snake" does not mean we have to see the story as containing a literal snake that spoke to Adam and Eve. After all, a literal word was used of Dan and the Pharisees.

The use of "snake" imagery in the story is in all probability done to teach a point, which did not include the belief in a literal talking snake. If Moses wrote this part of the Torah that speaks of the "serpent", and if "satan" was a real force to be reckoned with, then why did He choose to describe this force in the garden as a serpent? Would Moses not have wanted the children of Israel to know that this "serpent" in the garden was in fact "Satan" disguising himself to fool Eve? Moses wrote down these words for all Israel to hear some time after his encounter with Pharaoh's magicians where Yahweh turned Moses' staff into a snake and the Egyptian slight of hand artists mimicked Moses' feat with a very similar production. In the encounter with the Egyptian magicians, the word used for "serpent" is the Hebrew word "*taneem.*" There are only three times that the word *taneem* is translated as serpent or serpents. These occurrences are all when Moses and Aaron hook up with the Egyptian magicians.[150] Moses and Aaron were clear on what a snake was. After all, God had told Moses that his staff would become a snake and then the result was that it became a *taneem.* Wouldn't it be simple for Moses to have used the word "*taneem*" when writing about the serpent in the garden, if He wanted the Israelites to believe the serpent in the garden was a snake? It seems that he would. The Hebrew people could easily associate the "*serpent/taneem*" of the Pharaoh Court incident, with the "serpent/nachash" of Genesis, if only the same word was used.

Well Moses did not use *"taneem"* so perhaps Moses was not intending for the Israelites to think of the serpent in the garden as a real snake or serpent. Some might ask if it is possible that Moses used *"nachash/serpent"* in telling the serpent in the garden story because He wanted the Israelites to connect it with Satan? This is a good question and is one possible line of reasoning; however, Moses may have a different purpose in mind by using a word other than the word for snake that was associated with the rod that changed. The same word that the Israelites had heard connected with the rod into the serpent scenario that Moses and Aaron displayed in Pharaoh's court did not get used because Moses was not intending to have the hearers think of a literal snake appearance in the garden when he passed on the story.

Because Moses chose the word *nachash* in Genesis instead of taneem, indicates that Moses wanted to teach the Israelites something else. Could it be he used the word *nachash* because He was referring to "Satan"? Some think so but I highly doubt it, because Moses was the one telling the Israelites "*there is one God and none else*". Had the writer of Genesis actually taught the Israelites that there is a Satan who has powers like God, he would have been no different from the other polytheistic, national leaders of his day. He would have been guilty of teaching that there is another God and therefore been guilty of the charge of false prophet.

Aside from that, if the "*nachash*" was not a snake or "serpent" but was an appearance of "Satan" then why was there a curse on this "nachash" believed to be "Satan", which did not take effect? Ethelburt Bullinger, a scholar who makes the incorrect conclusion that the serpent is "Satan", gives information

---

150 Uses if the word *taneem*: **H8577**
tannîyn / tannîym
Total KJV Occurrences: 27
dragons, 15
Deu_32:33, Job_30:29, Psa_44:19, Psa_74:13, Psa_148:7, Isa_13:22, Isa_34:13, Isa_35:7, Isa_43:20, Jer_9:11, Jer_10:22, Jer_14:6, Jer_49:33, Jer_51:37, Mic_1:8
dragon, 6 Psa_91:13 (2), Isa_27:1, Isa_51:9, Jer_51:34, Eze_29:3/**serpent, 2** Exo_7:9-10 (2)/
monsters, 1 Lam_4:3/**serpents, 1** Exo_7:12/**whale, 1**Job_7:12 (2)/**whales, 1**Gen_1:21

on the meaning of the word "*nachash*". He claims the word means brass or copper in the ancient Chaldee language and renders it "shining one", suggesting that the *nachash* was Satan.

> The Hebrew word rendered "serpent" in Gen. 3:1 is *Nachash* (from the root *Nachash*, to *shine*), and means *a shining one*. Hence, in Chaldee it means *brass* or *copper*, because of its *shining*. Hence also, the word *Nehushtan*, a piece of brass, in 2Kings 18:4.

Bullinger has endeavored to provide information that helps to understand the word used in Genesis 3 for serpent, as referring to something shining but lexical works do not ratify his definition of "shining one" as being correct. Bullinger also, makes some other assertions in his document titled *The Serpent in Genesis 3;* found in his Companion Bible notes, which we will address later but for now we will address a different question. If the *nachash* is not a serpent but is Satan in a manifest form, then why is there evidence in the Bible of Satan not being affected by the curse placed on him?

In the Genesis account, a curse is rendered that conscripts the serpent to eat dust and to crawl on his belly from that moment on. Why are there numerous instances in the Bible where the "serpent" who is said to be Satan by Bullinger and others, did not appear to adhere to the curse placed upon him in the garden?

The curse I am speaking of is in Genesis 3;

> *And the LORD God said unto the serpent, Because thou hast done this, thou art cursed above all cattle, and above every beast of the field; upon thy belly shalt thou go, and dust shalt thou eat all the days of thy life:*
> *And I will put enmity between thee and the woman, and between thy seed and her seed; it shall bruise thy head, and thou shalt bruise his heel. Genesis 3:14-15 KJV*

If theologians like Bullinger are willing to see the serpent in a literal sense that defines the serpent as Satan, then should they not expect that Satan is only able to go upon his belly eating dust as the curse proclaimed? It seems odd that one can decide that either the serpent is literally a snake or literally Satan, yet not consider the curse placed upon the subject in the same literal regard. Never bringing into question the issue of why this subject that is cursed by God seems to be unaffected by the God of the Universe in subsequent appearances of this Satan. Clues to direct us in a path of understanding that debunks a literal view of either the serpent being a snake inhabited by Satan or the serpent being Satan himself are plentiful, right within the text of the

Bible. All we have to do is be careful to look for these clues and weigh the evidence against the evidence for literalness.

Notice the serpent that is called the "*nachash*" is placed in the same category as the other animals. This "*nachash*" as I have mentioned, is believed by some to be Satan who has taken on the form of a snake. Once cursed it is told it will go on his belly all the days of his life. Therefore, if the serpent is in fact Satan, then we should see the product or result of the curse by Yahweh on Satan. If the "serpent" is "Satan" and "Satan," is not seen crawling "upon his belly," then Yahweh becomes a lying god and proves impotent in the realm of administering justice through curses. Coupled with that Satan then proves powerful enough to override the God of the Universe. Under the "serpent is Satan" theory, we see that Yahweh has told "Satan" he was to "*go on his belly all the days of his life*". Yet there are no instances in the entire Bible that display Satan on his belly. Instead, every instance where Satan is believed to be found in the Bible, he is always spoken of as being ambulatory or supernaturally transporting himself. Because the belief that postulates the serpent equals Satan is based on a literal translation of Genesis 3, we must continue to use equal weights and measures and then believe that the curse is also literal. It is interesting to see the hermeneutical back flips some take to conclude that the serpent is literally referring to a snake or Satan and then claim the curse portion of the story is figurative, asserting that the curse represents a concept. It is conveniently suggested that the curse means "Satan" will have to sneak around and try to overcome man who is made from the dust, by tricking him. The musing by some goes further and the curse of the serpent eating dust is said to be fulfilled in the instances when Satan is shown to be overcoming man. The thinking is that man is the dust and Satan dominating man is as if Satan is eating the dust.

Neither the idea that the serpent is Satan nor the idea of an allegorical understanding for the curse are possible, here's why. If the serpent is literally "Satan" and is subsequently cursed by Yahweh to go on his belly forever then why is it that when this character called Satan in Job appears, he is not shown to be on his belly but is "*going about to and fro in the earth and walking up and down in it.*"? If the Satan in Job is that Satan from the garden then he is obviously oblivious to and not subject to the curse of Yahweh. One who is not subject to the curse of the Creator must be either equal to or greater than the Creator. Is it possible for that which is created to reject a curse of the Creator? I do not believe there is any one or thing equal to or greater than the Creator who dwells in heaven, and presented Himself in the flesh as Yeshua a couple of thousand years ago. If Satan was cursed to go about on his belly then he should not rightfully be seen walking.

Another account of this supposed "Satan" character, where he is seen to be ambulatory and definitely not going about on his belly, is in the story of the Messiah being tempted in the wilderness. If this tempter of Messiah is the literal cosmic Satan who received a belly travel curse in the garden, then he is clearly ignoring the curse to go about on his belly all the days of his life. It is insensible to think that the Messiah followed a slithering Satan up to the top of a high mountain. If the serpent is Satan and the devil is Satan in Matthew 4, then Satan is said here again to not be subject to God's curse, and right in front of God Himself.

> *Again, the devil taketh him up into an exceeding high mountain, and sheweth him all the kingdoms of the world, and the glory of them; Matthew 4:8 KJV*

The story of Christ being tempted by "the devil" is dealt with in Volume II of *Satan, Christianity's Other God!* when the Apostolic Writings that appear to tell of a cosmic satan, are explained. In that work, details are presented to understand who or what the "devil" in the story is. The case is built revealing the adversarial force encountered by the Messiah as one of two things. The force expressed by the word "*devil*" in Matthew 4 is either a human adversary that is testing Yeshua or it is the desires of the man Yeshua that are being brought into submission by Yeshua as he deals with the draw of power that is often present in a man who is on the doorstep of coming into his purpose in life. Every man struggles with the evil inclination over various things. Because Yeshua was tempted in all things like us, it is conceivable that the term "the devil" was a metaphor for His own desires as a man. Desires that many men on the doorstep of a powerful ministry have, that draw them in a direction that is not good. Full treatment of this topic is reserved for Volume II as I have stated.

For now, it is plain to see that if in fact the tempter of the Messiah was the cosmic "satan" who was the "*nachash*" in the garden, then he once again was immune to the curse of the Creator that relegated him to belly dwelling for his whole existence. It is not indicated in the text that this "devil" who is supposed to be satan the serpent or "*nachash*", was eating dust and going about on his belly. If one is to accept the curse to go about on his belly as an allegory or metaphor indicating a clandestine manner in which the supposed Satan was going to go about his business, then a few serious questions need to be asked because when Satan tempts Jesus he is not on his belly.

If Satan is real and is the "serpent", a second instance in Scripture where Satan is not acting in accord with the curse to be upon his belly is seen in the book of Job. When asked by Yahweh in the book of Job as to his whereabouts, it seems odd that his answer is in no way indicative of a secret and stealth like pursuit of the man Job who would be considered then to be the "dust" to be "eaten" by this allegedly once glorious creature. Just as the curse that said of the serpent, "*thou art cursed above all cattle, and above every beast of the field; upon thy belly shalt thou go, and dust shalt thou eat all the days of thy life:*" was a metaphor employing poetic language, so too is "*the serpent*" a metaphor. The serpent of Genesis 3 is an ancient metaphor written into an ancient story that employs poetic language. The writer may very well have chosen to use a word that could literally be heard as "snake" but just because a word can be literally translated as one thing or another does not relegate this word to being the literal thing the word alone is defined as. If you are to say that your friend is a real bear when he wakes up in the morning, that doesn't mean that he is literally a fuzzy grizzly bear. Serpent does not speak of a literal snake in the Genesis 3 passage.

Licking the dust is not a real practice.

Every day in our life and work, we hear words and use words that are not to be defined literally in the contexts that they are used. For instance, I work with a group of men who spare no linguistic expense when they decide to deride a fellow worker for a particular unpalatable pattern of behavior. I have heard many co-workers speak of another co-worker as a "boot-licker" or an "asshole" but everyone hearing, knows these terms are describing a characteristic behavior pattern and not the physical characteristics of the ill-favored co-worker. I have yet to meet a literal boot-licker or asshole and unless one is unrealistic in their interpretation of common vernacular, all are able to perceive what is meant by the speaker.

Does then a boot-licker have to literally lick boots, any more than does one who is said to "lick the dust" have to literally lick the dust? Understanding the prolific use of metaphor in all languages of all periods leads us to be able to recognize that there is no actual dust licking taking place by anything. We are able to gain insight by finding other examples of how the metaphorical terms of Genesis 3 are used. There are other uses in Scripture of very similar terminology to that used in the curse on the serpent. Looking at these instances will benefit in directing us towards accepting the fact that the curse on the serpent in the garden was neither a curse on a cosmic Satan nor a curse on a literal serpent.

In the Psalms, David offers a prayer for Solomon. In his prayer, he asks Yahweh to make it so Solomon's enemies are completely subdued and enter into absolute submission to him. This is represented with the phrase "*lick the dust.*"

They that dwell in the wilderness shall bow before him; and his enemies shall lick the dust. Psalms 72:9 KJV

In the book of Isaiah, we are given a prophecy that tells just how greatly the veneration of the God of Jacob and His people will be in the future. The idea is expressed by the similar phrase "Lick up the dust of thy feet." Again, in this instance the term is intended to express the posture of the people who are brought into submission to God and God's people. Being close to the ground in a bowed low posture to honor a king or people group is the picture this euphemism is portraying.

And kings shall be thy nursing fathers, and their queens thy nursing mothers: they shall bow down to thee with their face toward the earth, and lick up the dust of thy feet; and thou shalt know that I am the LORD: for they shall not be ashamed that wait for me. Isaiah 49:23 KJV

John Gills commentary provides a little insight into this practice of "licking the dust."

and lick up the dust of thy feet; the allusion is to the eastern nations, especially the Persians, who, in the adoration of their kings, used to kiss the ground they stood on, and seemed to lick, if they did not, the dust that was about them; and it expresses the very low submission of kings and princes to the church, and their high veneration of it; their willingness to do the meanest office for the good of it, and their great regard and affection for the meanest of its members, the dust of Zion; see Psa_72:9,

Remembering the deeply poetic and mythopoetic language of the prophet Isaiah, we are able to understand the use of many of his terms in their correct sense. That is a sense that is referring to something drastically different than the literal words might indicate. Notice how the term "dust shall be the serpent's meat" is used in Isaiah 65.

The wolf and the lamb shall feed together, and the lion shall eat straw like the bullock: and dust shall be the serpent's meat. They shall not hurt nor destroy in all my holy mountain, saith the LORD. Isaiah 65:25 KJV

The poetic imagery found in this passage is all too often taken as literal. Many preachers will catapult his message off this or the like passage in Isaiah 11 to talk of how glorious "heaven" will be when the wolf and the lamb are feeding together. The propensity to take literally the kind of poetic imagery we see in books such as Isaiah is difficult to resist. Many seem to want to believe in a type of magical fairyland paradise, where animals, which are normally adverse to cohabitating, begin an existence where they are at peace and no longer a threat to each other. This may be a nice idea and may very well be part of the renewed Earth where Messiah is reigning, but it is not necessarily the picture Isaiah was depicting.

If we work to reconcile "Old Testament" theology with "New Testament" theology then we will soon see Earth was made for man to inhabit and "Heaven" wasn't. Notice the following verse that expresses how many people have ascended to "Heaven." We are told in the Gospels that Christ ascended to heaven; this was the point where He resumed His heavenly office from His throne in Heaven. It appears from the following verse the only one who has been in the flesh who is in heaven is the Messiah, the King of the Universe. He is the only one who has immortality, at least up until the time Paul wrote these words to Timothy.

> *That thou keep this commandment without spot, unrebukeable, until the appearing of our Lord Jesus Christ:*
> *Which in his times he shall shew, who is the blessed and only Potentate, the King of kings, and Lord of lords;*
> ***Who only hath immortality,** dwelling in the light which no man can approach unto; whom no man hath seen, nor can see: to whom be honour and power everlasting. Amen. 1Timothy 6:14-16 KJV(emphasis added)*

Part of the reason we fall short of understanding these poetic images such as are found in Isaiah and Genesis is because we have removed ourselves, or been removed from even being remotely close in culture and geography to the time where these metaphors were clearly understood as metaphors. Many scholars have done excellent work on the metaphors and idioms in the Scriptures. One such scholar is George Lamsa. In His book "*Idioms of the Bible Explained*", Mr. Lamsa assists the reader in recognizing the metaphors as metaphors. Through his work, we are taught the unique position of present day Near Eastern regions. The region Lamsa references still employs Aramaic as their daily language. Lamsa is an Aramaic Scholar and as with any scholar who put forth theories that are contrary to mainstream understanding of other scholars, there is some controversy around his work. I will not argue for Lamsa on all fronts, but I will say I have yet to find another scholar who so clearly illuminates much of the Near Eastern idioms and does so through experiential knowledge. According to Lamsa and his supporters, he grew up using the Aramaic language and therefore understanding the Aramaic terms and idioms from the cultural, linguistic, and historical perspective. I am careful to mention the historical perspective because, if one studies the Near Eastern Aramaic speaking peoples in the period Lamsa gleans understanding from, one would find they have progressed slowly in comparison to other cultures that are near them and therefore they were a fine example in that state, of an historical perspective on language and idioms.

George M Lamsa was a world-renowned Bible translator and commentator. He was born in 1892, was raised in an Aramaic speaking community, which had maintained many of the customs that were present at the time of Christ. Lamsa died in September of 1975. He has done a huge amount of work in interpreting the idioms of the bible in the light of a culture that is more closely connected to the culture Yeshua walked in than any culture seen today. I suppose it makes sense to talk to a British man if you want to understand the British culture and their particular idiomatic usage of different words and phrases. Why not consider the insight from an Aramaic man such as Lamsa who provides a perspective relative to Aramaic culture? This perspective is of great importance when trying to understand the Gospels that tell of Yeshua because the culture Yeshua functioned in was an Aramaic culture. Examples of a few of the idioms Lamsa explains are;

> From Ezekiel 30:18-**"The day darkened and a cloud shall cover."**
> Meaning; *Impending disaster and sorrow*[151]
>
> From Isaiah 60:16- **"Thou shalt suck the breast of kings."**
> Meaning; *You shall drain the wealth of kings.*[152]
>
> From Jeremiah 8:21—**"I am black."**
> Meaning; *I am ashamed, I am sorrowful.*[153]

The above references are but a few of the metaphors Lamsa explains in his book titled "*Idioms in the Bible Explained and A Key to the Original Gospels.*"

I have mentioned "metaphors" often in this writing and there are many other sources available to provide the reader with a list of metaphors, common and biblical, and their associated definitions of which I won't list here. Metaphor use is and always has been a common tool of communication. If one does not understand the metaphors of his or her culture then one is destined to

---

151 "*Idioms in the Bible Explained and A Key to the Original Gospels.*", George M Lamsa, Harper Collins Publishing

152 ibid

153 ibid

misinterpret a large amount of what is spoken in the culture. Think for instance if there were not a common understanding of such colloquial terminology as; "Cat got your tongue?", "You suck!" , "Boy did we have a blast at the shaker!", "He hit the roof when he found out his car had been repossessed.", "It's raining cats and dogs." Or, "My dogs are killing me!"

These, again are a few examples of how simply metaphor can be interpreted if one is knowledgeable of the culture and context of the metaphor's use. In regards to common metaphors, one available resource is "*Renton's Metaphors, A dictionary of over 4000 Picturesque Idiomatic Expressions*" The forward in the book says this;

> WHAT IS A METAPHOR?
>
> "A cynic once defined a metaphor as "a simile with the words of comparison left out".
>
> Less frivolously, the Concise Oxford Dictionary puts it as the "application of a name or descriptive term to an object to which it is not literally applicable".
>
> The word is derived from two Greek roots - *meta* (with, after) and *pherein* (bear) - which, in combination, denote "transfer" (of meaning).
>
> Many metaphors involve colourful analogies. Every day one talks of "missing the bus", of "being in the same boat" as someone else, of "getting down to brass tacks", or of "not having a crystal ball".
>
> People are always "getting a feather in their cap", "earning brownie points", "building bridges", "clasping at straws", "muddying the waters", "cutting the Gordian knot", and "missing something by a whisker".
>
> For the most part such figures of speech involve combinations of words sounding very familiar to their audience, and their non-literal use is quite subconscious."

Reading the above statement from Renton, shows us how unquestionable it is to state that we communicate using metaphors. Metaphor use takes place in not only our own culture but also it is the way of communication in all cultures. Idiomatic usage of terms and phrases are "a dime a dozen" to use a metaphor. The Scriptures are no different as we have discussed and Lamsa went to work to define the idioms and metaphors in the Bible. A fairly simple Biblical idiom for present day culture to understand as a statement that does not mean what the words literally say, is seen when Yeshua celebrates the Passover with His disciples on the night he was betrayed. Yeshua calls the wine that is being consumed at the Passover, His blood and tells the disciples to drink it. In essence, He is saying, "**drink my blood**". Imagine taking these words literally. Some have, and doing so has led them to accusing the believers in Messiah of being cannibals. This metaphor is found in Mark 14:23-24;

> *And he took the cup, and when he had given thanks, he gave it to them: and* ***they all drank of it****.*
> *And he said unto them,* ***This is my blood*** *of the new testament, which is shed for many.*

Very different from actually meaning that the disciples are to consume the blood of their Master as some kind of ceremonial libation, we learn from Lamsa of a more sensible and culturally understandable meaning for this statement. Of this idiom, Lamsa teaches the meaning to be about absorbing Yeshua's teaching;

> **Drink my blood Mark 14:24**
>
> *"Make my teaching a part of your life. Be willing to suffer for my truth. Think of me when you celebrate the Passover"*[154]

As I said, it is not difficult to extract a meaning other than the literal meaning of the words given us by Mark. When one starts to go through the "Old" and "New" Testaments it is possible to clearly see the numerous metaphors and idioms which were used. Sadly, it is difficult to establish exactly what could have been meant unless we attempt to connect the words in the metaphor to their cultural origin and meaning. This is what Lamsa has endeavored to do. Isolating a statement to derive a meaning is never a good practice and most of the metaphors that are used in the Scriptures and New Testament can be located elsewhere in the Bible thus providing insight into the meaning of many of the misunderstood metaphors.

Finding a metaphor that is used one place in the Bible, used in another place, will always enhance the understanding and can be found to alter the often rigid, literal interpretation that is imposed on it. We have already looked at the metaphor of the serpent "eating dust" after it was cursed in the garden.

154 George M Lamsa, Idioms in the Bible Explained and A Key to the Original gospels. Pg 56

This metaphor is not restricted to the passage in Genesis 3 but is found elsewhere in Scripture. Exploring the meaning of the term found elsewhere can shed much light on what was meant in the garden of Eden story. As I have shared, this term appears in similar form in a few places in Scripture. Lamsa gives a meaning for it as we see it below in Isaiah 65.

> *The wolf and the lamb shall feed together, and the lion shall eat straw like the bullock: and dust shall be the serpent's meat. They shall not hurt nor destroy in all my holy mountain, saith the LORD. Isaiah 65:25 KJV*

Clarity is added to the prophet's words by Lamsa in identifying the phrase used here and in Genesis 3 as meaning the following;

> **Dust shall be the serpent's meat. Isa 65:25**
>
> *"The oppressor shall be reduced to poverty, humbled."*[155]

To be true to the culture and the literary styles of the writers of Scripture, one should give full consideration to the many metaphors and idioms as we read them in both the Scriptures and the Apostolic writings. It is certain that Yeshua Himself taught in parables. As a Hebrew man in a Hebrew culture many of His parables contained metaphors that must be understood in their relation to the time and space Yeshua existed in. If the King of the Universe employed such broad use of parables and metaphors, could not have Moses been capable of a similar teaching style? I believe he in fact did teach using this style and the account of the serpent in the garden is not to be considered differently than other writings from that period or from that of a style familiar to other biblical writers. Moses used available imagery from the cultural milieu of myth and metaphor to teach the Children of Israel.

We see another reference to dust-eating serpents, in the book of the prophet Micah. The prophet is admonishing and exhorting a depraved group of people who had moved far from living in a manner that was acceptable to Yahweh. In describing how they will come crawling back to Yahweh with their "tails between their legs," to use another metaphor, the prophet tells the people they will be humbled and out of their depravity will fear Yahweh and turn back to Him.

---

155 ibib pg 34

> *They shall lick the dust like a serpent, they shall move out of their holes like worms of the earth: they shall be afraid of the LORD our God, and shall fear because of thee. Micah7:17 KJV*

Sure, it appears that a snake is licking the dust when it juts its tongue out to probe the environment; however, Micah is expressing how the rebellious people will most assuredly be humbled by God. Micah is not suggesting that serpents eat dust or that the subjects of his statements will truly sample dust with their tongues any more than the writer of the Serpent in the Garden story was suggesting that a literal snake would dine on dust. Neither the term "serpent", which is translated from the Hebrew word *nachash,* nor the phrase "eat dust", are to be taken literally.

The facts are; the "*nachash*" who was cursed in the garden is not referring to "Satan." If there was a real "Satan" who was given a curse by the Almighty, why do we have depictions of this character in the Scriptures as being unaffected by the curse placed upon it? Allow me to reiterate.

If Satan is the "*nachash*", he is neither crawling on his belly nor is he acting stealthily in instances where he appears in the Scriptures that are commonly believed to be about a cosmic Satan. If this serpent was Satan, then he should have been forcibly submitted to be crawling on the ground for all his days because God had cursed him to do so. How then is it that when Job and Yeshua encounter "Satan" there is no indication that he is crawling on the ground eating dust?

This is so because the serpent in the garden, which is a "nachash", is not "Satan". How then did this serpent metaphor come to be a reference to a clever aspect of humanity's psyche you might ask? The most likely explanation based on the people of Israel's place of residence, is that the metaphor was borrowed from Egyptian lore. This well-known lore contained discernable meaning to the Hebrew people who came out of Egypt.

The story was telling of a time in history at the beginning of the world when purity was the norm and then the evil inclination, spoken of as the serpent by Moses, was activated through self-deception and subsequent disobedience. This selfish act of Adam and Eve in the garden became known as the original sin. Contrary to popular opinion, the first sin was not the act of eating the forbidden fruit, but was the practice of changing the words of the Creator as we see Eve did. If one looks carefully at the story it would seem that the first sin was when Eve changed the words of Yahweh when she said, "God said we cannot even touch it or we will die." Yahweh's words were, "*you're not to eat of the tree of knowledge of good and evil.*" He had said nothing about touching it. Expanding on the commandment of the Creator is the same as adding to it; by adding to it a person is changing it and thus guilty of changing God's word. In the account given we see that Eve's words expanded on God's command when He said; "*…thou shalt not eat of it.*" Genesis 2:17

The words of Yahweh are still being changed to this day by multitudes of so-called Scripture teachers and leaders who are as guilty as Adam and Eve of adding to the words of God. Is it any wonder Yahweh gave a command not to add to the words of the Torah in Deuteronomy 4 and 12?

> *Ye shall not add unto the word which I command you, neither shall ye diminish ought from it, that ye may keep the commandments of the LORD your God which I command you. Deuteronomy 4:2 KJV*

> *What thing soever I command you, observe to do it: thou shalt not add thereto, nor diminish from it. Deuteronomy 12:32 KJV*

As was mentioned above, the serpent myth was an ancient myth that far preceded the time of Moses' ministry to the Chosen People of Yahweh. This myth is found in many cultures and was also found in some form in Egyptian lore, where Moses was raised. It is absolutely plausible to think that Moses knew the tale well as did the Hebrew people who had assimilated so deeply into the Egyptian culture. Of Moses, we are told he was learned in all their wisdom. To be "learned" in all the wisdom of the Egyptians is tantamount to having a working knowledge of all the myth and lore as well as the academic information available to the most educated royalty of the Egyptians. The writer of the book of Acts teaches us of Moses' great knowledge and understanding of Egyptian wisdom.

> *And Moses was learned in all the wisdom of the Egyptians, and was mighty in words and in deeds. Acts 7:22 KJV*

For Moses to be spoken of as learned in all the wisdom of the Egyptians does not have to mean he practiced all of the Egyptian religious mysteries his entire life. Just to clarify, the word I am quoting here is "*learn-ed*", meaning one who has acquired knowledge of a matter through education. Consider this; I may study Aboriginal culture and religion in Canada where the aboriginal peoples have a deep history replete with incredible amounts of mysterious legends and practices. The mystery and legend facet of their cultural history and journey goes along with the true stories of persecution and strife. By studying this people's history, culture, and religion, one becomes learned in all the wisdom of the Aboriginals. Being learned in the ways of this people does not mean participation in their ceremonial and religious practices such as "sweats"[156] and smoking sweet grass and pay homage to the "Spirit of the Forest " or the "Great Eagle Spirit." However, it does mean I can use their stories and legends to communicate to a people group who are able to understand the meaning of the stories due to a prolonged exposure to these legends and culture. I would not necessarily be practicing the aboriginal ways but I would posses an intimate understanding of them. Being learned in all the wisdom of the Egyptians, as was the case of Moses, does however lead us to the question; did Moses practice the Egyptian religious mysteries among other things that were common to the Egyptian culture? It would be unrealistic to expect that a child, who has been adopted as a son of the Pharaoh's daughter, would not be practicing and consequently learning the faith of the household he was raised in. Picture a small child taken into the home of the Queen of England. No matter whether this child was "adopted" at a very young age or in the early to late childhood years, this child would be considered a full resident of the Queen's house. Would not this child be trained in the manners, practices, and ways of the Queen's royal Household? It is doubtful this adopted child would be encouraged to participate in a religious lifestyle or otherwise that would not be familiar to the Queen's household. This would be very similar in the Royal Palace and household of the King of Egypt, Pharaoh. It is likely that this child Moses did not have the opportunity of a thorough upbringing in practicing the faith of the God of Israel. Moses therefore would have participated in Egyptian religious practices as he was taught them by those of his adoptive household.

Was Moses Practicing the Hebrew or the Egyptian Religion?

Moses was not afforded a full initiation into the faith of Israel due to the early age at which his mother placed him in the Nile. An argument may surface to try to claim that Moses was experienced in the Israelite faith practice prior to being separated from his birth mother once weaned. Some may adhere to such an argument as a means to reject the notion of Moses' knowledge of Egyptian lore. This argument states that the infant Moses was in essence given back to a Hebrew nursemaid and that because she was his mother Yochabel, he would have been trained to know the faith of Israel.

It is true, Moses was placed with his mother to be nursed until weaned, and there is therefore an argument that should be considered when one proposes that Moses did not have a working knowledge of the faith of Israel while in the House of the Pharaoh. Exodus chapter 2 tells us the birth mother

156

did nurse the baby and when he was grown, the child became the son of Pharaoh's daughter who called the child Moses, which refers to the child being drawn from the water. From there the discussion of how old Moses was at the time he was weaned and entered the palace of Pharaoh, begins to take form. According to some, he may have been weaned before five years of age while according to others the ancient meaning of the terminology could indicate Moses was an older child when "weaned". If the latter is the case it seems that the term "weaned" means Moses may have had some foundational teaching from his mother on the facts of who the God of Abraham, Isaac, and Jacob is. The ISBE provides insight into the term "weaned."

> **Wean**
>
> wen: "To wean" in English Versions of the Bible is always the translation of (גּמל, *gamal*), but *gamal* has a much wider force than merely "to wean," signifying "to deal fully with," as in Psa_13:6, etc. Hence, as applied to a child, *gamal* covers the whole period of nursing and care until the weaning is complete (1Ki_11:20). **This period in ancient Israel extended to about 3 years,(*emphasis added*)** and when it was finished the child was mature enough to be entrusted to strangers (1Sa_1:24). And, as the completion of the period marked the end of the most critical stage of the child's life, it was celebrated with a feast (Gen_21:8), a custom still observed in the Orient. The weaned child, no longer fretting for the breast and satisfied with its mother's affection, is used in Psa_131:2 as a figure for Israel's contentment with God's care, despite the smallness of earthly possessions. '[157]

For our purposes, it matters not whether Moses was weaned at 1 year, 3 years or older, so we needn't debate the question any longer. The fact remains that this child was adopted into the Pharaoh's palace at a young age and would have been fully integrated into the mystery religions and the wisdom of the Egyptians. These mysteries would have included the ancient serpent myth that was pervasive in Egypt and most other cultures of the ancients. Egypt specifically was in the practice of recognizing the serpent as the official symbol of authority and wisdom, both religious and civil. Pharaohs usually wore the golden serpent on their head and the snake represented the patron Cobra goddess of lower Egypt. All who were Israelite would have been quite familiar with the meaning behind not only the staff of Moses being turned into a serpent under the control of Moses' hand but also of the meaning of a serpent that was spoken of in a story involving the beginnings of man.

157 From entry "Wean" in the International Standard Bible Encyclopedia.

It is easy to understand why Luke, the writer of the book of Acts stated the depth of Moses' learning as it pertains to the Egyptians. Luke recognized what happens to a person who spends his childhood and almost 30 years of his adult life, living in a very seductive, profoundly "spiritual" culture. Moses, the grown man and leader of a liberated nation from Egypt, would have understood the Egyptian religious philosophy and he also would have knew that the Hebrew people, of whom he was one, would also be able to understand and relate to the Egyptian religion and its corresponding concepts and philosophies.

The Egyptians had many gods and Moses was fully educated in all of them with all the myths that were affixed to them. In so understanding, Moses would not be reticent to utilize the mythological imagery and language that would be understood by the Hebrew ex-slaves. Moses' intention was to teach them their lost history and relate in vivid images the origins of them as a people. It is arguable for some that Adam also might be a mythological character not truly existing and one may find a case to support that argument quite convincing. However, seeing the genealogies in the Scriptures and "New Testament," that speak of Adam and the line that sprung from him, give cause to believe that the man Adam was a real character. The proof can only be found in the Scriptures, therefore the best argument and the worst argument both depend on one's level of belief in those ancient writings. Nevertheless, we do perceive that Moses was a wise and learned leader. He did not hesitate to employ an already understandable serpent myth motif to educate Yahweh's people on the first man and woman's choice to sin. One could say that Moses placed Adam and Eve into an already recognizable serpent myth. Today we value timeless stories such as Winnie the Pooh and the Legend of King Arthur. Both stories make use of a real person that is placed into a mythological or imagined tale. Christopher Robin was a real person and although somewhat difficult to find, information on the character of King Arthur being a valiant warrior can be found in tracing the origins of that tale. Perhaps this Arthur was not a literal king but the legends that have grown up around this mysterious leader certainly do speak an amazing message. Persons of real physical form are often inserted into mythical tales in order to establish a connection between the story and the listener and deliver a meaningful message. So it is probable that Moses did likewise with the real Adam and Eve.

The serpent myths have been found in virtually every culture. Many, who hear a serpent myth from an ancient culture, assume these ancient serpent myths are based on a retelling of the writings of Genesis and the serpent in the garden. Perhaps that assumption is an error that is based on the assumption that the text of Genesis was transmitted some time before Israel spent time in Egypt. It is more likely that these serpent myths themselves predated the writing of Genesis and the Hebrew enslavement in Egypt by many generations. Considering that Moses wrote the Torah, which includes Genesis, one must also consider when he might have penned that work. It is not possible that Moses did so until after the Nation of Israel received the Ten Commandments at Mount Sinai.

These famed commandments and the story of their revelation is a major part of the Torah. It is the Torah that contains the story of the serpent of Genesis, and because Moses was the writer of it, it chronologically was written after Moses left Egypt. This type of serpent story was not a brand new story line that came into existence upon the revelation of the Ten Commandments. The fact is that many ancient cultures had already transmitted serpent myths to the successive generations that grew from them. Scholars date the Exodus from Egypt and the subsequent giving of the "Ten Commandments", to hundreds of years after the Great Flood of Noah. This places the writing of Genesis in a period that was familiar with an already ancient storyline about a mythological serpent. The story Moses was employing in his instructions to the Israelites contained much more Egyptian and Sumerian lore than you or I could imagine. The serpent motif was mythology that was carried along from generation to generation in the familiar process of myth transmission.

The ancient Sumerian and Acadian cultures for instance were vibrant cultures long before the Israelites had a connection to Egypt and lived through the Exodus from Egypt. Predating the writing of the Genesis account, these cultures, which existed as far back as 2000 years before Christ, both had serpent myths that spoke of a mystical serpent known to be a god of sorts, which interacted with humanity at the earliest point in history.

Integration and Assimilation Have Dire Consequences to a Visiting Culture

Even by the most conservative scholarship, we are told that the Book of Genesis was written many years after the Hebrew exile to Egypt. If this is the case then the ancient serpent myths were even more entrenched in the minds and understanding of the unwittingly, integrated Hebrew people. Integration of cultures can often benefit the assimilated people, but in the end, most cultures who experience integration adopt philosophies of their host culture. The Children of Israel would have been no exception as was foretold would happen in Deuteronomy.

> *And the LORD shall scatter thee among all people, from the one end of the earth even unto the other; and there thou shalt serve*

other gods, which neither thou nor thy fathers have known, even wood and stone. Deuteronomy 28:64 KJV

Part of the consequence of Israel's rebellion and disobedience was their being scattered and becoming like the nations where Yahweh scattered them. This is a fact of Israel's history after the Exodus and one could reasonably expect the cultural integration to have affected them negatively while in their Egyptian captivity. One result of this period of captivity would have been a strong familiarity with the ancient serpent myth. Familiarity with the serpent motif was not necessarily a bad thing but clearly was an important piece of lore for them to understand. Soon after they left Egypt, they would receive a story of man's beginnings, which would only make sense to the liberated Israelites because they were familiar with the meaning of the serpent mythology. The ancient Sumerian religion contained one such serpent myth. Sumerian history is said to span the years from approximately 3200 BC to around 1750BC when it disappeared as it was taken over by other cultures in the area. This culture predated Moses and the Exodus by hundreds of years according to most chronologies. As a frame of reference we are told the date of the Exodus by four different scholar/chronologists. The dates identified by these scholars are as follows; Poole 1652 BC; Hales 1648 BC; Unsen 1320 BC; Usher 1491 BC. Presuming any one of these dates is accurate, easily places the Sumerian myth long before Moses wrote the Torah. For Moses to have written the Torah would have had to have taken place during the 40 years in the wilderness because according to Scripture Moses was 80 years old when he led the children of Israel out of Egypt, then at 120 years old he died. Therefore, it is highly probable that Moses' writing of the creation account and the serpent story was following a literary myth concept from an even more ancient culture than the ones he had been living in.

The Sumerian culture had great influence on the Ancient Near Eastern religion, which was the birthplace of the Israelite religion. That is not to say the Israelites mimicked or modeled the Sumerians but that many of the concepts that were present in Sumerian religion did in fact receive a type of divine refinement once the Israelites were introduced to Yahweh during their wilderness experience after the Exodus. Sumerian mythology's strong influence on Ancient Near Eastern Religion can be seen in the areas of sun, moon, and star-worship. Other areas included a divine hierarchy of gods and epic myths that included dying gods and resurrected gods. The *New International Version Archeological Study Bible* by Zondervan Publishing tells of a serpent myth, which was present in Sumerian religion. The myth that I will explain shortly, is found in what is called the Epic of Gilgamesh. In that myth, there are some similarities to the serpent in the garden account of Genesis chapter 3. The Archeological Study Bible has this to say;

> The snake of the Sumerian Epic of Gilgamesh is somewhat reminiscent of the serpent in Genesis 3 in that it deprives the hero, Gilgamesh, of immortality. While Gilgamesh is bathing in a pond the serpent robs him of the plant of Rejuvenation which, if eaten would have granted him eternal life. The serpent devours the plant and is rejuvenated as it sheds its old skin. Gilgamesh, however, is consigned to die as a mortal.[158]

This is one serpent myth from the ancients and Moses, being privy to all the wisdom of the Egyptians, would have not only known of this epic but would have also had a keen awareness of the Egyptian serpent myth of the god Osiris, known by many as Ra. This myth spoke of a demon serpent that attempted to throw the world into darkness by trying to overthrow the great god Ra each day. In Mesopotamian lore, the serpent myth has the serpent opposing humans and gods in their epics such as the renowned *Enuma Elish, Inanna and the Huluppu Tree,* as well as others. An ancient *Ugaritic* myth contained a seven-headed serpent named Lotan who was a component of their Baal–Anat Cycle where Baal and Anat defeat the "twisting serpent". The name of this serpent "*Lotan*" has a connection to the *Leviathan* that is mentioned in the Bible and is prophesied to become a notable oppositional force once again in the end times.

At any rate, the serpent of Genesis 3 is written in a literary form that can very much be equated with the adversarial serpents of all of the ancient myths. The Archeological Study Bible concludes its article titled, *"Serpent Motif in Other Ancient Near Eastern Literature"* with these thoughts;

> "Although the serpent or sea monster motif in the Bible reflects the fact that biblical writers incorporated well-known images from the ancient world into their writings, other Biblical material clearly demonstrates that these inspired authors did not accept the mythology behind the Mesopotamian or Egyptian Stories."[159]

As you see above, the serpent motif is understood as a common image in the ancient world and the writer of Genesis was writing in a similar fashion as other biblical authors in that he uses images from mythical lore such as the serpent to tell his story. The writer never intended for a literal understanding

158 NIV Archeological Study Bible, the Zondervan Corporation. Pg 8

159 NIV Archeological Study Bible, the Zondervan Corporation. Pg 8 "The Serpent Motif in Other Ancient Near Eastern Literature"

of his work and those who were closest in time to the penning of the Garden of Eden story would also, not have believed the story to be a literal account in its entirety. The entire allusion to a serpent as well as the curse on the serpent is metaphor. The curse that is assigned to the "serpent" is aimed at teaching us that there is a subtle, active potential in humanity to disobey and sin. The assignment given the serpent; *upon thy belly shalt thou go, and dust shalt thou eat all the days of thy life*, was identifying that the ever-present sin potential of humans will always be active as long as man exists on the earth. The story does go on to give allusion to a time when the Messiah finally destroys man's desire to choose wickedness through bringing in righteousness. We are told that the seed of the woman will crush the serpents head and in so hearing, we are made aware that there will come a time when the active, potential to sin in humans will be obliterated and rendered powerless.

The time when this sin potential is brought to nothingness is referenced in the book of Revelation where the wickedness of man is spoken of using several commonly used apocalyptic metaphors.

> *And he laid hold on the dragon, that old serpent, which is the Devil, and Satan, and bound him a thousand years, Revelation 20:2 KJV*

Our present culture has been basted in a mystical understanding of these words for so long that it is extremely difficult for most to see the words of the above verse any different than that they are referring to a literal Satan who they believe to be the serpent from Genesis. If we know that the language used by the Old Testament writers was highly poetical and borrowed many images, then we ought not to be shocked to find that the first century vision of John, the one that we know as the book of Revelations, is also profoundly poetical. The *serpent*, that *old dragon*, *satan* and the *devil*, are not references to a literal being but they are references to the very thing that the serpent was reference to in the Old Testament. What better way for an apocalyptic vision to relate the obstruction of the sin nature. The sin nature is rendered impotent because of the presence of righteousness when the Messiah rules the earth. This is a far better depiction of the subduing of wickedness than to imbue it with fantastical images of a messenger coming down from heaven and having a key that seemingly opens a locked pit. This is suggested to be a pit of pain and suffering, which no one or nothing could ever come out of due to the bottomlessness of the pit. The fecundity of John's mind, enveloped by a divine vision, was truly amazing. So much so that the absolute vital nature of the message was relayed through the use of enhanced graphic images. Images such as a dragon being cast from the sky, which is an image intended to express the sin nature being brought into submission to Christ. In this reference in Revelation all four terms are referring to the active potential for humans to sin in the flesh and how they will be rendered inoperative under the reign of Messiah's righteousness. Each of these terms will be explained fully in the section on Revelations near the end of Volume II of *Satan, Christianity's Other God.* We are so far removed from the culture and mindset of the writer of Revelations that I will go into much detail in order to explain the use of, *dragon, that old serpent, the devil, and satan.* There it will be discussed how these misunderstood terms bare out to be references to human attributes, qualities, or entities. One clue that is provided by another prophetic writer is where Ezekiel uses the term "dragon". In Ezekiel 29, the Egyptian Pharaoh is a dragon. Calling the Egyptian Pharaoh a "dragon" is simply another example of the use of mythopoetic language to state how the Pharaoh of Egypt has a bent to go against the God of the Universe and His people. The label "dragon" is often affixed to a false religious system, as is the case in Revelations and in Ezekiel. When spoken of as a dragon, the Pharaoh is being seen as a powerful oppositional force to the plans and ways of the only God.

There are many clues to aid us in identifying the old serpent, the dragon, satan, and the devil as references to the active potential to sin which manifests in man and in governmental rulers. This subtle potential is readily personified because it brings deception to a pinnacle in a man because of the fleshly desires. Man is often enticed to compromise good by these completely human forces, submitting to the sin nature.

Sin is not chosen because an active supernatural source that is probing and tempting, but because of our innate desire to rebel. Remember, it is the heart that is deceitfully wicked above all else. Jeremiah 17:9 has taught us this. This means desire to sin and deceit comes from the heart of man and no place else. James the apostle says it well in chapter 1 of his letter to the scattered believers that our own desires are the cause of sin:

> *But every man is tempted, when* ***he is drawn away of his own lust****, and enticed.*
> *Then when lust hath conceived, it bringeth forth sin: and sin, when it is finished, bringeth forth death. James 1:14-15 KJV*

You might ask how is it possible to conclude that the Satan idea as it pertains to the serpent in the garden is not as literal as many of us have been taught in our lifetimes. It seems it is very possible and likely when we truly consider how metaphor and mythic images were employed by ancient writers. If I observe a dirty, cheating lawyer, help get a murderer acquitted in a dramatic courtroom battle and I then refer to that lawyer as a snake, there is not one person within ear-shot who would take me literally and perceive that the lawyer is an actual reptile. When utilizing the wisdom and discernment that is afforded us by the Creator it is possible to conclude that although the Hebrew word "*nachash*" is definitely a word used to refer to a snake, perhaps we are not to take this word to mean an actual serpent but to hear it as meaning what the serpent represents. Many scholars will concur that *nachash* does indeed mean a serpent or snake. Smith's Bible Dictionary shows us this;

> **Serpent**
>
> **Serpent.** The Hebrew word, **nachash**, is the generic name of any serpent.[160]

The Snake Was the Smartest Beast in the Garden, is it Still the Smartest?

We have discussed how the serpent is not to be understood as Satan but we need to consider the question; Is the *nachash a* literal serpent in this story? That Moses made use of the serpent myth as a teaching tool can be seen in the curious reference in the story, telling us that the serpent was "more subtle than all the beasts of the field that God had created". What does it mean to be more subtle? The Hebrew word "*arum*" occurs 11 times in the Scriptures. Eight times it is translated as "prudent"; 2 times as "crafty"; and once as "subtle" as we see it in Genesis chapter 3.

> *Now the serpent was more subtle than any beast of the field which the LORD God had made. And he said unto the woman: 'Yea, hath God said: Ye shall not eat of any tree of the garden?' Genesis 3:1 JPS*

In the above verse we see that the serpent was more subtle than any beast of the field, however, the text does not call the serpent a beast, it just states that it is more subtle than the beasts of the field. With this in mind we are able to preclude the serpent as a beast of the field and therefore eliminate that verse as a proof for the serpent being a literal snake. If the "serpent" is not a beast of the field but is more subtle than all the beasts there then is the possibility that the "serpent" is a reference to the evil inclination in man. An inclination that is indeed more clever than any beast because man's evil side

160 Smith's Bible Dictionary by Dr. William Smith (1884)

seems always able to justify and deceive one into choosing evil. In this we can see how Jeremiah was accurate in saying that the "*heart is deceitful above all things, and desperately wicked.*"

Considering further the acclaimed intellect of the serpent in the Garden, we will address a few points on the matter. First of all, if the serpent is a snake as some suppose, then it was the most cunning, crafty, and prudent of all the beasts of the earth. This attribute was present in the serpent while the serpent was in the garden before the serpent was cursed by Yahweh. So unless there was a curse on the exalted intellectual status of the snake in the garden we should expect to see the serpent as the craftiest, most cunning and prudent creature of the field today. I am no herpetologist[161] and if I were, my penchant for snakes and serpents would probably inspire me to hail the brilliance of the creature and announce it as one of the smartest animals around, that is if the snake was the most "subtle." However, I have yet to find any herpetologist or animal science specialist who flatly states the snake is the most cunning of all the beasts of the field. The point is, that if the snake was the most intelligent creature while in the garden and was not shown to have had its intelligence removed by a curse, then the snake should still be known to be the smartest animal of the animal kingdom.

An article on a Petstation.com FAQ about reptile training answers the question of how smart snakes are. The excerpts provided below give an answer to the snake question and then in the following question we are told tortoises are smarter than snakes. This opinion shows that a snake is not smarter than all the other animals and is then unable to be said to be more subtle than all the beasts of the field.

> ***TAMING AND TRAINING YOUR REPTILE***
> BY VALERIE HAECKY…
>
> **Q: How smart are snakes?**
>
> Not very! The animals they eat are a lot smarter than they are (provided they are alive). They can learn certain associations, though. Most notably, if you always drop food into the cage, the snake will associate opening the cage with the coming food and eventually bite the first thing that comes in when the lid opens, including your hand.

161 Herpetology; the study of snakes.

Q: How smart are turtles and tortoises?

A lot smarter than snakes. Turtles can learn a lot of little things and routines, given enough time and food rewards.[162]

Some scholars profess that the serpent must have walked on legs of some type in an upright fashion prior to the curse it received but few if any address the attribute of the serpent that claims it was the most "subtle". Once again, if the snake was real and the fact was as it is stated that it was the most "subtle", would it not stand to reason that the subtlety, which is indicated as being superior intellect, should still be possessed by the snake today. Yes it should, unless Yahweh had cursed the characteristic of "subtlety" in the serpent.

Aside from that, if the serpent truly was a serpent and truly was as brilliant as we are led to believe, then how could this ingenious creature display such stupidity in going against not only the man who had charge over it but pitting himself against the one and only Creator? It is near impossible to ignore the unreasonable and illogical perspective of such an idea that suggests a snake that was supposed to be profoundly crafty would be so stupid as to think it could outsmart the Creator. At any rate, the serpent that was the most subtle in the garden is not the most subtle today, as it should be due to its intellect being left intact after the garden episode story, a story that is so often confused as being a literal account. God is not typically in the practice of imparting silent curses that alter a creature's inherent characteristic. At some point in the Scriptures God speaks all the curses that took affect on His subjects. Some construe the curse that relegates the serpent to crawl along the ground forever as meaning that the snake once walked upright and had legs at one time. God proclaimed three curses in the garden but none of these curses was aimed at the intellect of the serpent. One therefore could reasonably expect that because the serpent is not the most intelligent creature today that there must have been a curse on its intelligence spoken in the story. However, there is no curse found in the story and therefore we need to explore why the serpent is not still the most intelligent creature alive.

It is safe to conclude that the serpent is not the most cunning creature in existence today because the serpent in the garden was not a literal serpent. The presence of a "serpent" in the story we are exploring is but an ancient metaphor, a metaphor representing man's ability to deceive himself and others.

162 http://www.petstation.com/reptame.html Taming and Training Your reptiles, by Valerie Haecky

The Serpent is not An all-Bad Embodiment of Evil!

In exploring the metaphor of the serpent a little further, we might ask; "If the serpent is not the most cunning of all creatures today, what then is?" My suggestion is that based on the meaning of the word "subtle", there is a characteristic of man that fits the description of being a "serpent". A characteristic that is more cunning and clever than any beast of the field. It becomes clear that there is nothing more "subtle" than the part of the human character that works to deceive and lead one into self-deception. There is an inclination in the human psyche that will work overtime to manipulate, justify, blame, and generally formulate crime and evil. The "serpent in the garden" is a metaphor for the aspect of the human psyche and the collective human potential to choose evil. A characteristic that is innate in every human, often bringing each person to rebel against the good and to convince oneself to practice evil. The serpent is not to be seen as an aspect of the human composition that we can eradicate entirely in this life, but overcoming what the serpent represents is the goal. The "serpent" as metaphor can represent many things, and those can be either beneficial or detrimental.

A serpent in mythology was considered a character that had some power to control good and evil. Overcoming the inherent potential for evil and wickedness that is represented by the serpent is the goal. Examples of a positive meaning for the serpent metaphor are seen all through the Bible. The Messiah tells us to be "*wise as serpents*" in Matthew 10:16. Yahweh told Moses to place a brazen serpent on a pole in Numbers 21:8 and have the Israelites look up to it to effect healing in those who were suffering from fiery serpent bites. Jacob called Dan a serpent in the blessing that was given in Genesis 49:17. If we are being consistent and are ascribing a literal interpretation to the serpent in the garden, we then should ascribe a literal interpretation to the tribe of Dan as a serpent. There is none who will contend that when Dan is called a serpent in Genesis it is anything other than a clearly understood expression, which was not intended to be interpreted literally.

> *Dan shall be a serpent by the way, an adder in the path, that biteth the horse heels, so that his rider shall fall backward. Genesis 49:17 KJV*

What more proof does one need than to see that a serpent is a dynamic metaphor that can be either positive or negative in its application, than to hear the Messiah refer to Himself as being "lifted up as the serpent in the wilderness was lifted up so that all men could come to him"?

> *And as Moses lifted up the serpent in the wilderness, even so must the Son of man be lifted up:*
> *That whosoever believeth in him should not perish, but have eternal life. John 3:14-15 KJV*

As we can see above, even the Messiah being lifted up on the tree when He was crucified has a positive connection to a serpent, based on the comparison drawn by John above. Bernard Simon tells of the serpent motif as a metaphor with a multiplicity of meanings, often depending on the context said metaphor is used in. Simons writes;

> The scaly reptile can be a symbol of both death (as in the fall of man) and life (the brazen serpent). Its supposedly sinister character, with its attendant menace, brings about fear and its mysterious and duplicitous nature has led human beings to opposing assessments. On the one hand, it is thought of as evil and the cause of death and on the other it is believed to embody beneficial, and even divine, powers. It was as the wise one, in this beneficent form, that various sects of Gnostics in late antiquity adored the godhead in the form of a serpent.[163]

Sure there are numerous meaningful interpretations of the serpent metaphor in the Bible and ancient cultures; however, one interpretation that would not be found in the ancients would be to interpret the presence of a "serpent" in an ancient tale as being a literal snake. Likewise, one would be hard-pressed to find the ancients who were closest to the telling of the serpent myth stories, interpreting the character of the serpent as being a manifestation of the literal Satan.

The mystical interpretation of the metaphor and poetic language found in the "Old Testament" that has been predominant in Christianity, is a product of Hebrew thinkers becoming Hellenized in their thought. The Greek manner of thought was so mythically and mystically based, that all things were given a metaphysical meaning and the Old Testament was even reinterpreted at one point by Philo who was a student of Plato. The result was a mystical, Neo-Platonic understanding of a body of literature that was meant to be understood through a Hebraic view.

In "*Pagan and Christian Mysteries*" a book that contains a collection of Papers from the Eranos Yearbooks[164], Hanz Leisegang speaks of the theology

---

163 From the *Essence of the Gnostics,* by Bernard Simon. Pg 139 Copyright Arcturus Publishing, 2004

164 In 1933 in a secluded villa on the mountainous shore of Lago Maggiore, in Ascona, Switzerland, a group of scholars, organized by the inspired Olga Fröebe-Kapteyn, gathered

of Orpheus, Museaus, Hesiod, and Homer. These men posited concepts of a cosmos permeated by divine forces. In his essay, Leisegang says this of Philo;

> In course of time this solar pantheism became enriched with other ideas from various sources, and Philo made it into a universal metaphysic mystery of light, in terms of which he even re-interpreted the Old Testament. From him this philosophy of light passed into Neo-Platonism and into Christian theology, continuously gathering new life from the Greco-Oriental Zeitgeist.[165]

The above excerpt from the essay titled *Mystery of the Serpent,* tells how Philo's metaphysical adaptation of the Old Testament was carried into Christian theology. Certainly there are many things in the Creator's realm that are difficult if not impossible for us to explain with our finite reasoning and intellect, but these things and the experiences that flow from them need not be imbued with a metaphysical explanation that incorporates mystical thinking and fantastically imagined explanations. The gloss of the entire metaphysical re-interpretation of the Old Testament, and the same goes for the New Testament, is that the theology of the Greek minded mystics, which included a Satan theology, became a construction. In essence, the constructed theological interpretation was an afterthought of spiritual experiences. The men who influenced the thought that would continue to evolve in a dangerously metaphysical direction were the great thinkers who had a perceived need to explain difficult biblical concepts. However, they felt the need to use otherworld elements in doing so. In short, Philo, who was the most significant re-interpreter, and others since, have adopted a reinterpretation principle of the Old Testament that is based on a metaphysical belief system. This mystical style, that employs many mythologically based concepts, is far removed from the intent of the authors and of the Creator who inspired them.

The Hebraic view understood mythopoetic language and metaphor in the allegorical intent of the language. Greek thinking understood mythopoetic

---

around C. G. Jung to discuss the research topics they were involved in whether in psychology, religion, anthropology, or the classics. At this conference, the first of the Eranos Conferences or in German, Tagung, a unique tradition was born. And the Eranos Conferences have continued up to this day. They have united some of the most unusual thinkers and personalities of this century with the in-depth research of lesser-known scholars. Until this day the Conferences continue to provide a fertile opportunity for meetings and creative discussions.

165 Pagan and Christian Mysteries Copyright 1955 by Bolingen Foundation Inc. Excerpt from the Essay titled, "The Mystery of the Serpent" by Hans Leisegang pg 28

language and metaphor as referring to something literal. The Hellenized concept of the Hebrew Bible ascribed metaphysical images and concepts to the Old Testament stories such as the story of Job being afflicted by God and by human adversaries in his life. As well as this shortcoming in interpretation, these formative theologians misunderstood the metaphors, idioms, poetic language, and mythopoetic language that the Biblical record presents. Far too many concepts from Scripture that were misunderstood were explained with ideas that sprung from mans' imaginations and fabrications,

The Bible is filled with allegorical and metaphorical statements. Here are some more examples that are easily understood by the hearer and not confused as literal statements. No one has a problem with Judah being called a lion's whelp (Genesis 49:9); or Zebulun being said to be as a foal and an ass's colt (Genesis 49:11). Other metaphors that have not been misconstrued to imply a literal aspect to the subject are; Issachar as a strong ass (Genesis 49:14); Naphtali as a hind {A red deer -- one that is fully grown} (Genesis 49:21); Joseph as a bough {branch or limb of a tree} (Genesis 49:22); Benjamin as a wolf (Genesis 49:27); All the tribes as a lion (Numbers 23:24; 24:9); Gad as a lion (Deut. 33:20); Dan as a lion's whelp (Deut. 33:22); Yeshua as a Lamb (Throughout the Book of Revelation); Israel as a speckled bird (Jeremiah 12:9); A nation of the East as a ravenous bird (Isaiah 46:11); Preachers as fishers (Jeremiah 16:16); Pharaoh King of Egypt as a young lion and a whale (Ezekiel 32:2); a flock as men (Ezekiel:34:30-31) and Herod as a fox (Luke 13:32).

Agreeing that the serpent in the garden that is represented in many myths throughout history is either a literal serpent or a metaphysical Satan, is like believing that the term "he stopped on a dime" truly means there was a dime on the ground and the person came to rest in a stopped position on top of a shiny 10-cent coin. The literal thinker who places a metaphysical twist on concepts that he doesn't understand, becomes well versed at applying mystical interpretations to just about any situation and metaphor. A person given to that mode of thought might take the well-known "stopped on a dime" metaphor and force it to mean there is a supernatural force incorporated or represented by the dime. Thinking in a manner that is consistent with the metaphysical interpreter of a statement that is a metaphor allows one to come up with an inanely ludicrous idea about a metaphor's meaning such as could be said of the above metaphor "stopped on a dime". There is of course no limit to the directions such an interpretative style might take a thinker as the possibilities are only limited by the interpreter's imagination. One possible way to place a mystical meaning on the phrase "he stopped on a dime" might be to suggest that the dime equaling 10 and 10 being the number of ordinal perfection, means that their was an active supernatural power working in the dime, which caused the one needing to stop urgently, to come to an abrupt halt. The ancient Greek philosopher Philo was adept at applying mystical meaning to otherwise mundane or non-mystical terms, phrases, and occurrences. Employing the Philoian, metaphysical style of interpreting words joined together that are nonsensical when the sum of the individual words is considered, can easily place a ridiculous mystical meaning on an otherwise easily understood colloquialism. Obviously, you and I both know that the dime, just because it represents the number 10, played no part in a person being able to stop abruptly. It is as ridiculous to assert such a mystical belief on the phrase "he stopped on a dime" as it is to assert that a metaphor from Genesis that says the serpent was more subtle than all the beasts of the field means that there was a genius snake hanging around Adam and Eve.

These types of mystical and metaphysical assertions have been a blight on truly understanding the serpent in the garden story, for hundreds of years. The story however, must be found to make sense but in the absence of any real understanding, that locates the elements of the story in their proper place in history and lore, one often makes up a meaning for the elements and passes that idea on to others who essentially give the idea wings.

The only way to reconcile the entire concept of the serpent in the garden is to realize the impact that myth and poetic imagery had on the literature of the Bible. The authors of the Bible were imparted with divine wisdom from the Creator to disseminate wisdom in conceptual form so that it is accessible to anyone who intellectually and spiritually ingests the story. The teaching of the necessary concepts was not absent of cultural and historical considerations. All great teachers through Eastern and Oriental history have employed a similar style of instructing the faithful. The teacher's role is not to explicate the historical facts with such specificity that the hearer becomes exempted from engaging in the learning process. Contrariwise, the teacher wisely used symbols and myth, allegory and ambiguity, in his or her teaching in order to lead the learner to the truth that was being taught.

The Bible generally gives few facts when relating a story. In light of the lack of details, it is the basic concept of the story that is to be discerned, and one ought not get caught up in focusing on minutiae of detail. The lack of facts and the use of mythical language still allow the reader or hearer to glean the underlying truths that are represented and intended by the story. However, when a person or group is far removed in time from an historical situation, it is not uncommon for imaginary stories to rise up in an attempt to explain these vague narratives. The small points and details of these narratives often become somewhat misunderstood, because the original writer is not available to provide clarity. If one realizes that the original writer need not be present because the purpose of relating and relaying a story is to express a truth and not to give all the details, then the present reader stands a better chance at gleaning a more accurate message from the narrative. Provision of the vague narrative by the Biblical writers was done in a way that was intended to aid the hearer in understanding the lesson or truth that is to be found within the story. Yes detail is important, however simply by its absence, it is apparent that detail must not be necessary in so much of the Biblical writings, otherwise the Creator of the Universe who inspired the writer would have included a lot more detail than we have today.

If the serpent is Satan, then Satan is a God

Two very strong points to consider about what is believed regarding the serpent of Genesis 3 are as follows: If the serpent in the Biblical narrative found in Genesis is literal, then it should still be the most subtle creature on the earth today. The second is this; if the serpent is "Satan", as some posit, then we are seeing him as a God and are guilty of idolatry. What does it mean to see Satan as another God? I am not saying we are seeing him as "The God", which is Yahweh. And I think it is clear that most who believe in Satan cannot be said to be putting him on the same level as Yahweh. However, simply by believing he is capable of doing supernatural things, one is seeing him as "a God". This then identifies one as a dualist if not a polytheist to some degree. Polytheism and dualism are insidious when they are elements of a faith walk in Yahweh and His Messiah. The diversity of interpretations is vast and many, many interpreters of the serpent in the garden story have imposed concepts onto the story, which are simply not there. The concept that some today have of the serpent as a real creature that was one time walking upright and now must crawl along the ground has evolved over the ages to contain additions that would have not been conceivable to the first hearers of the story. Another interpretation that has been constructed from ancient myths is that the serpent was Satan and was jealous of man. In wanting man to be out of favor with God, the serpent is said to have tricked the man via the woman, into taking and eating the fruit. Other mystical and metaphysical ideas that have been added go so far as to claim that Eve had sex with the serpent. This is a completely fabricated Gnostic idea. In an internet article, *Serpent Gnosticism, Apostasy of All Ages; Source of the Female Priestess,* we are told about the Gnostic belief in a sexual relation between the serpent and Eve.

> The Gnostics used women priestess who would teach man the secret knowledge. Because sex was a part of the Babylonian ritual, it was taught by the Gnostics, that Eve had sex with the serpent and Cain was the serpent's seed. The Gnostics taught

> that Cain was the good seed and that is why he was not to be killed for the murder of Abel, whom the Gnostics taught was not a true brother of Cain. Abel was seen as a child born by the power of the bad GOD who had cursed Adam and Eve during a temper tantrum and drove them from paradise.[166]

An idea that I have addressed previously is that "Satan" is said to have actually inhabited the serpent. This idea is not represented at all in the Genesis 3 passage.

Scholars Project Their Present Beliefs Back Onto the Pages of the Old Testament

As one writer puts it, it was not until a Satan theology was established that scholars added new meaning to Old Testament passages based on their present theological understanding. This occurred in part because it gave the believer the ability to simply proclaim things he could not understand as "spiritual". Men began to define things they did not understand with yet other things they did not understand and often say it cannot be understood; do you understand? That's right, these men were confused in their understanding and then manufactured fairy tales that pronounced the confusion; from then on it seems no one could understand anything as making sense. A brilliant way to insulate the scholars by suggesting that they were the only ones who could understand the truly spiritual things.

It is far simpler to create a mystical interpretation of a mythopoetic or metaphorical allegory than it is to seek to understand it from its historical, social, cultural, and linguistic perspective. Creating a mystical interpretation of an ancient biblical narrative is not a wise practice and in so many ways can be seen to be simply agreeing with fictional Jewish fables.

The Jewish fables of the first century were amazing stories that reduced the practical aspect of the Torah and prophets' teachings to a type of Jewish myth. Paul the apostle taught against believing these myths and fables.

An example of a Jewish myth circulating some time before and around the time of Christ was a tale that taught about the Noah flood story. This myth sews unbelievable elements of imagined and metaphysical concepts into the Biblical account. In so doing, the people who received these myths through popular storytellers, believed these nearly incomprehensible, mythological accounts of these stories. In a letter to Titus that was said to be

166 Article found at , http://jesus-messiah.com/w-preach/wp-nt-17.html

written by Paul, we hear Paul warning his listener to not give heed to these fables that are a cause of men turning from the truth.

> *Not giving heed to Jewish fables, and commandments of men, that turn from the truth. Titus 1:14 KJV*

Louis Ginzberg recounts the Jewish myths in his work, *The Legends of the Jews, Volume I.* I am amazed at the vast number of Jewish Fables that have been catalogued and provide here only an excerpt from "*The Flood*" in *Bible Times and Characters from the Creation to Jacob.*

> The difficulties were increased when the flood began to toss the ark from side to side. All inside of it were shaken up like lentils in a pot. The lions began to roar, the oxen lowed, the wolves howled, and all the animals gave vent to their agony, each through the sounds it had the power to utter.
>
> Also Noah and his sons, thinking that death was nigh, broke into tears. Noah prayed to God: "O Lord, help us, for we are not able to bear the evil that encompasses us. The billows surge about us, the streams of destruction make us afraid, and death stares us in the face. O hear our prayer, deliver us, incline Thyself unto us, and be gracious unto us! Redeem us and save us!"[38]
>
> The flood was produced by a union of the male waters, which are above the firmament, and the female waters issuing from the earth.[39] The upper waters rushed through the space left when God removed two stars out of the constellation Pleiades. Afterward, to put a stop to the flood, God had to transfer two stars from the constellation of the Bear to the constellation of the Pleiades. That is why the Bear runs after the Pleiades. She wants her two children back, but they will be restored to her only in the future world.[40]
>
> There were other changes among the celestial spheres during the year of the flood. All the time it lasted, the sun and the moon shed no light, whence Noah was called by his name, "the resting one," for in his life the sun and the moon rested. The ark was illuminated by a precious stone, the light of which was more brilliant by night than by day, so enabling Noah to distinguish between day and night.[41]
>
> The duration of the flood was a whole year. It began on the seventeenth day of Heshwan, and the rain continued for forty days, until the twenty-seventh of Kislew. The punishment

> corresponded to the crime of the sinful generation. They had led immoral lives, and begotten bastard children, whose embryonic state lasts forty days. From the twenty seventh of Kislew until the first of Siwan, a period of one hundred and fifty days, the water stood at one and the same height, fifteen ells above the earth. During that time all the wicked were destroyed, each one receiving the punishment due to him.[42] Cain was among those that perished, and thus the death of Abel was avenged.[43] So powerful were the waters in working havoc that the corpse of Adam was not spared in its grave.[44] [167]

Another story that is seen to be a "Jewish Myth" is the well-known *Eve Myth*. This myth has many forms and is so convoluted it is difficult to identify one concise and authoritative version of the myth. A synopsis of this myth is as follows;

> Gnostic scriptures said Adam was created by the power of Eve's word, not God's. Adam's name meant he was formed of clay moistened with blood, the female magic of ***adamah or "bloody clay."*** He didn't produce the **Mother of All Living** from his rib; in earlier Mesopotamian stories, he was produced by hers. The biblical idea was a reversal of older myths in which the Goddess brought forth a primal male ancestor, then made him her mate - the ubiquitous, archetypal divine-incest relationship traceable in every mythology. Furthermore, Gnostic scriptures said Eve not only created Adam and obtained his admission to heaven; she was the very soul within him, as Shakti was the soul of every Hindu god and yogi. Adam could not live without "power from the Mother," so she descended to earth as "the Good Spirit, the Thought of Light called by him **"Life"** (Hawwa)." She entered into Adam as his guiding spirit of conscience. "It is she who works at the creature, exerts herself on him, sets him in his own perfect temple, enlightens him on the origin of his deficiency, and shows him his (way of) ascent." Through her, Adam was able to rise above the ignorance imposed on him by the male God.[168]

This was a Gnostic Myth that did much to undermine a Hebraic view of the Scriptures. In *Pagan and Christian Mysteries,* Leisegang's essay tells of the practice of drawing a serpent between the thighs at the crotch level to

167 The Legends of the Jews by Louis Ginzberg, Translated from the German Manuscript by Henrietta Szold. Volume I, Bible Times and Characters from the Creation to Jacob (can be viewed at; http://philologos.org/__eb-lotj/default.htm)

168 The Woman's Encyclopedia of Myths and Secrets, *Barbara G. Walker*

bring fertility to the practicer. Elaine Pagels discusses an idea that Eve had sex with the serpent in the garden. Many authors gain a clouded perspective by adopting the Gnostic Scriptures as an authoritative source that unfolds the truth of the Hebrew Scriptures. They who do so seem to put themselves in the camp of those who believe the serpent was literally present in the Garden of Eden. Once smitten by the Gnostic bug many lose the ability to discern the story as a mythical representation of the internal compulsion man has to disobey. The story as told in Genesis, discloses the subtleness of the evil inclination Eve had, which she eventually succumbed to a short time after she was created.

At any rate, I find the work of Elaine Pagels refreshingly informative. Her ability to explicate the depth of ancient myths and the fact that they do relate to the Genesis account of the serpent in the garden, brings a learner a long way towards recognizing how incorrect it is to adopt a literal understanding of the story. As far as the Eve myth goes there are many documents that claim Eve, known as Sophia in some versions of the story, was the creator of Adam and through her, Adam had life. On page 66 of "*Adam, Eve, and the Serpent Myth*," Pagels refers to a text called "*Reality of the Rulers*", which tells of what happened when Adam first recognized Eve. Adam noticed Eve's spiritual power and did not see her only as a marital partner.

> And when he saw her, he said, "It is you who have given me life: you shall be called Mother of the Living [Eve]; for it is she who is my Mother. It is she who is the Physician, and the Woman, and She Who Has Given Birth."

Pagels tells how the *Reality of the Rulers* went on to explain how Adam was told by the Creator to not hear Eve's voice any longer, and after losing contact with the spirit, the woman Eve eventually reappeared to Adam in the form of the serpent. The mythical account goes on and on but seems to have a basis on the flawed belief that the serpent is a literal serpent, which is not probable according to what we have discussed thus far

To accept that the serpent in the garden is a literal serpent stops short of recognizing the impact of myth on the biblical writers and reveals a failure in consistent interpretation and as well as displaying an inconsistency in a belief system. I am not intending to engage in a discussion to discredit the work of Elaine Pagels, however, Pagels appears to have based some of her conclusions on a preconceived acceptance for the authority of the Gnostic writings. It seems she makes conclusions in support of a literal interpretation of the serpent in the garden story.

The manner in which we have been given the story of creation in the Genesis account is a manner that incorporates both literalness and metaphor. How can it be both? Is it much different from if I was to say, "I stopped by the grocery store before the long weekend, the store clerks were rude animals and the line ups were a million miles long." Well, in understanding the acceptable literary style of the biblical writers and understanding the God of the universe's desire to give us profound truth not providing explicit detail in many of the instances, one can then look for the truth contained in the story. The truth might be that there was a literal creation of the universe, Earth, and humans. The humans were given everything and the Creator wisely placed the good and evil before humans. At some point, humans chose to submit to their evil inclination and disobeyed the Creator.

What was the Fruit?

An example of how ideas that are incorrect become entrenched in our minds is seen when we consider the "forbidden fruit" that Eve ate. We have for the most part as a "Christian" culture, come to believe the "fruit" which Adam and eve ate of was an apple. Where did this detail come from? The type of fruit is not a detail that is provided in the Genesis account. The possibility of parts of this account being myth can be realized by noting things such as the "fruit" not being identified by the writer. Just as the belief that the serpent was Satan has evolved over time, so too has the idea of the fruit Eve ate being an apple, evolved through the course of time. A period where many of today's philosophies and beliefs went through a process of "refinement" occurred during the Renaissance. This period of ego inspired reconstructionism, not only altered for all time many concepts but many concepts and interpretations were birthed which began to be accepted as fact. This in part was due to an inability to understand the mythological ideas, which must be placed back into their culture to gain understanding. The apple itself is known to have had an interesting metamorphosis from its original unidentified species of fruit as is mentioned in the excerpt below.

> In Northern Europe, the unnamed "Forbidden fruit" became considered a form of apple, because of a misunderstanding of the Latin "malum", where malum as an adjective means evil, but as a noun means apple. The larynx in the human throat, noticeably more prominent in males, was consequently called an *Adam's apple*, from a notion that it was caused by the forbidden

> fruit sticking in Adam's throat as he swallowed, and the name has stuck.[169]

The same Wikpedia article on Adam and Eve expresses similar thought on the potential for an ancient story such as this to contain myth, intent on representing fundamental truths.

> Nearly all modern Christian and Jewish scholars of today consider Adam and Eve as an example of religious myth focussing on the teaching of perceived fundamental truths. In their interpretation, the story's purpose is to convey the importance and truth of sin and human rebellion in their traditions, regardless of historical accuracy. All, some, or none of the actual events of the narrative may have actually happened, or been embellished.
>
> Adam and Eve are often considered as real historical people, as Genesis 5:4 records Adam within a geneaology. In the New Testament, Paul references Adam and Eve many times, especially contrasting Adam with Jesus where Paul writes "just as sin entered the world through one man." This seems to support a historical Adam as many theologians interpret Adam's sin as a historical event that changed humankind. However, Paul could be merely using the myth as a teaching method. Others view Adam and Eve as metaphorical for every person when they first sin and God seeks them out. Those who hold this view point out that *adam* can also be translated *humankind.*
>
> The Age of Reason prompted Christians to interpret the Bible as strict history rather than historical myth; William Whiston was one such early scholar. James Ussher calculated Adam and Eve's life at approximately 4,000 BC, basing on the Genealogies of Genesis and Table of Nations.[170]

Notice the last paragraph in the above reference that mentions "The Age of Reason". This appears to reference a time when the confusion and discomfort brought on from the difficulty in understanding a story in the Bible was too great for the scholars of the day. To add to our understanding the information provided by Wikipedia tells this of the Age of Reason;

---

169 From article titled "Adam and Eve" on Wikpedia. Article can be found at; http://en.wikipedia.org/wiki/Adam_and_Eve#Mythological_connections

170 From article titled "Adam and Eve" on Wikpedia. Article can be found at; http://en.wikipedia.org/wiki/Adam_and_Eve#Mythological_connections

> 17th century philosophy in the West is generally regarded as seeing the start of modern philosophy, and the shaking off of the medieval approach, especially scholasticism. It is often called the "Age of Reason" and is considered to succeed the Renaissance and precede the Age of Enlightenment. Alternatively, it may be seen as the earlier part of the Enlightenment.[171]

Because of this advance in philosophical thinking, the "Reasoners" began imposing literal ideas on much of the mythological and mythopoetic language and stories in the Scriptures. You know what they say, "If you tell a lie long enough it becomes truth". Well we have been told the lie that the Adam and Eve and the serpent story is accurate history in a literal sense for a long time and the vehemence with which most who adhere to this concept, is acute. Most people who need to hang on to their belief of this falsehood refuse to fully investigate the matter. If only they would take seriously the exhortation to *"prove all things and hold fast that which is good*"[172] in this controversial area, then the pursuit of truth and knowledge might bring to light a new perspective on an age-old lie. To "prove" means to test and examine with a view to affirm it as truth utilizing wise discernment. There is not much of a better reason to read this book than to show that you are eager to prove the truth in your belief system. We should jump at the opportunity to rightly divide the word of God and stop resting on our second-hand beliefs that have never been proven by most souls who have entertained and accepted those beliefs over the course of modern history.

Many of us base our belief in a Satan on what we have been told from others, such as religious leaders and pop culture. It is not very complementary to human intellect to think we have swallowed a great big pill that is just a deeply twisted folk-tale, postulating that there exists another entity with supernatural power in the universe. This present age has been encouraged in its belief in a supernatural evil force with a fervor that could only be brought about through the mass media. The Barna Research Group addresses the belief in the supernatural on their web site as it is found in today's teens.

New Research Explores Teenage Views and Behavior Regarding the Supernatural

January 23, 2006

---

171 http://en.wikipedia.org/wiki/17th_century_philosophy

172 *1 Thessalonians 5:21 Prove all things; hold fast that which is good.*

> (Ventura, CA) - If the spiritual world is elusive and controversial, one certainty is the prevalence of the supernatural dimension in mass media. Supernatural beings, stories, and themes have invaded America's entertainment choices - from movies (such as *Underworld, The Sixth Sense, The Exorcism of Emily Rose*), to television programs (*Buffy the Vampire Slayer, Ghost Whisperer*), to books (*Harry Potter, Goosebumps*), and video games (*Doom, The Darkness*).
>
> The nation's most media-drenched consumers are well aware of these portrayals of the supernatural: more than four out [of] five teenagers say they have witnessed supernatural themes in media during the last three months. This insight comes from a new report issued by The Barna Group that examines teens' media exposure to the supernatural world, as well as a variety of other aspects of teens' experiences and perceptions of the immaterial realm, including their participation in psychic and witchcraft activities, their beliefs, and their influencers. [173]

The assertions of the presence of supernatural forces such as Satan, are in essence claims that there is another god. The other God is perceived as always attacking humans in some form and desires to destroy or take over the God of the Universe.

Looking at the "serpent in the garden" story, a person who has already decided to believe there is a Satan and his minions of demonic angels, will likely be brought to the conclusion that the serpent is Satan or was at least inhabited by Satan. Saying the serpent in the garden is "Satan" is the result of a post biblical effort to explain a Scripture through views and beliefs that were taken on from other cultures. From cultures that were not Hebraic in their thinking or understanding. It is metaphysical thinking and the literal interpreting of non-literal terms that has brought us to the point that we see the serpent as "satan" and for some they see "Satan" as the party responsible for all the evil and wickedness in the world. If there is a God, is He not able to shoulder the blame or credit, call it whatever you like, for both the good and evil that we often see in the world? How can an almighty God, who is in control of everything, defer power over "evil" to a supposed rebellious being? In light of the entire Old Testament Scriptures, it is not correct to attribute evil and wickedness to any other source than these few things;

- Evil is sent from Yahweh as in the "evil spirit on Saul."

173 Article and links available at, http://www.barna.org/FlexPage.aspx?Page=BarnaUpdate&BarnaUpdateID=216

- Evil is an active force of wickedness that comes from man's heart.

- The adversary, which is often interpreted as "Satan", can be a manner of divine dispatch from Yahweh used to affect humanity in some form, as appears to have been the case in the story of Balaam cursing Israel found in Numbers 22.

- The adversary, which is the word "*satan*" in most cases, can be another human being as is the case in 1 Samuel 29 where King Achish was going to war and was told by his princes to not let David and his men join them lest they end up becoming a "*satan*/adversary" to them. See the example of the word being translated as adversary highlighted below from the book of 1st Samuel.

And the princes[8269] of the Philistines[6430] were wroth[7107] with[5973] him; and the princes[8269] of the Philistines[6430] said[559] unto him, Make this fellow return,[7725, (853), 376] that he may go again[7725] to[413] his place[4725] which[834, 8033] thou hast appointed[6485] him, and let him not[3808] go down[3381] with[5973] us to battle,[4421] lest[3808] in the battle[4421] he be[1961] ***an adversary[7854]*** *(satan) to us: for wherewith[4100] should he reconcile[7521] himself[2088] unto[413] his master?[113] should it not[3808] be with the heads[7218] of these[1992] men?[376] 1Samuel 29:4 KJV+*

The only way to find a literal cosmic Satan in the serpent in the garden account is to accept the interpretation of those who failed to understand the text through its cultural and historical context. Why is it so difficult to accept the use of literary devices such as employing metaphor and mythical lore to enhance the learn-ability of a lesson? Moses was dealing with 2 to 3 million Israelites when Yahweh gave him the reigns to leadership. Moses was wise enough and connected enough to his culture and the Egyptian culture to not even question whether the use of a metaphor representing the potential to sin in man would be understood by the Israelites. The Israelite people were to be a light unto the nations. Instead, what had been happening was the Israelite people went into captivity on more than one occasion where they then became a part of the culture in which they were captive. It is not uncommon for the captive to become, in practice, like their captor. As Israel moved through history she and those who were supposed to lead her in her worship, lifestyle and belief system, not only learned the ways of the environment they found themselves in; but they eventually lost the ability to understand the cultural perspective of the stories in the Scripture.

Instead of the more Hebraic understanding of their heritage advancing slowly and steadily, the Israelite mindset and Hebraic understanding of ancient texts from the period of their cultural setting, slowly receded as each generation became a little less connected to their history. Their history was one that included the use of ancient stories with powerful meanings and nuances. Instead of slow steady growth in numbers of followers who were able to understand the ideas that were flowing from the Israelite culture, the number of followers shrunk. Later in Israelite history, Hellenization appeared to become the last straw on this proverbial camel's back. As a result of Hellenization, practically the entire "Jewish" culture adopted practices and beliefs that came from a Greek and later, a Greco-Roman view of the unseen world. A fictitious world with its plethora of gods and spirits, who were thought to play into the lives and affairs of the mere human. Ancient Israelites never saw the serpent in the garden as "satan" and neither did the ancient Israelites believe the cause of sin and wickedness in the world was anything other than from the choices they made. These choices originated from the place within man which is know today as the evil inclination, the "*yetzer ha ra*".

The serpent in the garden is really a representation of the rebellious evil inclination, which was present in Adam and Eve at the point of creation. Yahweh had to have created man with this ability to choose. Another belief as to where the ability or potential to choose evil came from is the belief that it originated as an act of some other entity. Making this other entity out to be the creator of humanity's potential to sin, is to make it a God. Once again, we are right back at the point where we have to see that to believe there is another force that can cause man to sin by introducing this characteristic into the "psyche" of man, is to say there is more than one God. This may be seen by some as blasphemy to credit God for the evil that is believed by many to originate from Satan.

However, Isaiah taught us that God makes peace and creates evil, and Amos stated that if there is evil in a city Yahweh is the one who has done it. (see Isaiah 45:7 and Amos 3:6)

There may be many reasons that some may want to call me a heretic but where do I sit on being a blasphemer and a heretic for claiming there is no "Satan" and for stating that evil comes from either man's wickedness or is sent by Yahweh? Well, to answer that question I have to ask you to be honest in your assessment of what we have seen thus far in the Word. So far, I sit with the Messiah and His Word, which are the Holy Scriptures. These Scriptures do not teach or reveal a cosmic "satan" at any point. These Scriptures do reveal that man is responsible for all the wicked choices that proceed from his heart and therefore we need a Messiah to redeem us from sin so we can **choose** to sin no more.

THE NACHASH IS SAID TO BE SATAN ACCORDING TO BULLINGER

Soon we are going to get into the controversial texts of the "New Testament". Before we do that I would like to spend some time specifically addressing the teaching of Ethelbert Bullinger. A teaching that claims the serpent in the garden is actually "Satan". Understanding how Bullinger is mistaken on his conclusion is meaningful to our entire discussion on the topic of whether or not a cosmic Satan exists. The conclusion that the *nachash* (serpent) in the garden was a manifestation of Satan has been accepted by untold thousands. This teaching has been handed down from theologian to layman virtually unchallenged over the years. To accept the Bullinger theory as fact without carefully dissecting the various claims made in his teaching leaves a lot of room for the errors in the theory to continue to move forward in theology. Many of the points made by his theory are based on a presumption. The presumption lies in presuming that some of the beliefs connected to the theory and add strength to the argument, are completely correct. As we are about to see, Bullinger, while somewhat of a genius in many ways, has forced his conclusion to line up with his beliefs about a literal Satan, rather than striving to determine if his beliefs can be conclusively supported by Scripture. When discerning the truth in a matter of interpreting Scripture and when attempting to rightly divide the word of God, we will always land on our feet if we avoid making Scripture fit into our predetermined belief system and try to ensure our belief System fits in with the Scriptures. Addressing Bullinger's theory on the serpent in the garden may be unnecessary for some. However, his theory is such a well published and repeated argument that most of us will benefit by assessing it and dismissing it. The amount of ancillary information that I will share whilst confronting Bullinger's theory will prove to be worthwhile even for those who might be modestly interested in it. So before we begin to asses the theory of Mr. Bullinger, let's briefly consider who Ethelbert Bullinger was.

Ethelbert William Bullinger (December 15, 1837 - June 6, 1913) was an ordained Anglican clergyman, Biblical scholar, and dispensationalist theologian. E.W. Bullinger was noted broadly for three works: *A Critical Lexicon and Concordance to the English and Greek New Testament* (1877) for his ground-breaking and exhaustive work on *Figures of Speech Used in the Bible* (1898) and as the primary editor of *The Companion Bible* (published in 6 parts, beginning in 1909 ; the entire annotated Bible was published posthumously in 1922) These works and many others remain in print (2006). Bullinger's understanding of the Genesis serpent is included in these works and goes under the title *The Serpent of Genesis 3.* I encourage you to explore Bullinger's teachings to get a feel for what an excellent Bible scholar he was. Because *The Serpent in Genesis 3* work by Bullinger has had so much influence on the false understanding of this text, I would like to explore this teaching. We will look carefully at sections of this teaching and focus on various aspects of Bullinger's well-accepted teaching on the "*nachash,*" said to be the "shining one."

Perhaps I can assist you in answering the question, "Why you shouldn't believe Bullinger, after all, Bullinger does lay out a convincing argument?" [174] I agree, his argument is convincing, so without repeating large portions of what we have already discussed in this chapter, I will simply tell you where Bullinger has erred in postulating the doctrine that says Satan is "the serpent in the garden." Dr. Bullinger begins his article titled; "*The Serpent of Genesis 3*" with these words;

> In Genesis 3 we have neither allegory, myth, legend, nor fable, but literal historical facts set forth, and emphasized by the use of certain Figures of speech.

The entire Scriptures are replete with allegory, myth, legend and fable, and the use of all of these forms of written communication can be found in the Genesis 3 account. It is simply not true that we have literal historical fact in the Genesis 3 account. It is true that figures of speech are used for emphasis. Although the emphasis is not towards the "facts" in the story but the figures of speech are used to emphasize the nature or concept of the story. The meaning of the word "*nachash*" is said by Bullinger to be from a root Hebrew word that means, "shining one." Other Scholars argue the case that the Hebrew word "*nachash*" does not mean, "shining one," as can be seen by a study and an investigation of the word. Bullinger tells us the word "*nachash*" is interchangeable with the word "seraph" which means "burning" or "fiery". In Numbers 21, we see both words used as you will see by reading the text. There we read of the story of the Hebrew people wandering in the desert and receiving a judgment of God upon them where they are bitten by fiery serpents. Moses seeks Yahweh on the matter and is instructed to make a serpent out of brass and to hoist it up on a pole for the afflicted Hebrews to look at. The story tells that when this icon is gazed upon by a Hebrew person who has been bitten by the fiery serpents that they will recover. This is the very serpent that was destroyed hundreds of years later by Hezekiah during

174 Quotes in this section from *The Serpent in Genesis 3,* Appendix 19 from the Companion Bible, By Ethelburt Bullinger can be viewed at, http://www.ovrlnd.com/Teaching/serpentofgen.html

the reform under his reign when he was restoring true biblical worship to the Israelite people, which can be read about in Second Kings chapter 18.

When Yahweh commanded Moses to make a "*seraph*" which is to say make a fiery snake, we are told Moses responded by making a "*nachash nechosheth*" a "snake of brass".

> And the LORD[3068] said[559] unto[413] Moses,[4872] Make[6213] **thee a fiery serpent,[8314]** and set[7760] it upon[5921] a pole:[5251] and it shall come to pass,[1961] that every one[3605] that is bitten,[5391] when he looketh upon[7200] it, shall live.[2425] Numbers 21:8 KJV+

> And Moses[4872] made[6213] a **serpent[5175] of brass,[5178]** and put[7760] it upon[5921] a pole,[5251] and it came to pass,[1961] that if[518] a serpent[5175] had bitten[5391 (853)] any man,[376] when he beheld[5027, 413] the serpent[5175] of brass,[5178] he lived.[2425] Numbers 21:9 KJV+

The constructed snake of brass was indeed shiny and was indeed a snake. Why was Moses told to make a *seraph* but then went ahead and made a *nachash-nechosheth*? Did Moses disobey Yahweh by making something that was not what the Creator prescribed or was Moses complying with the non-specific request of the Creator by designing an icon which was shiny and was a serpent, thus fitting the parameters of a general request by the Creator? Because Moses made a "brass serpent" when God told him to make a "fiery" does not mean that "fiery" and "brass" mean the same thing only that one of the characteristics of brass is "fiery". Yahweh wanted something fiery constructed and Moses knew that gleaming brass would suffice as a representation of the fiery quality Yahweh was looking for in his latest object lesson.

We see that Yahweh described a characteristic of a symbol that Moses was to make and then we are shown that Moses made this symbol out of brass and that it was a snake. The different use of words here does not indicate '*seraph*' and '*nachash*' are interchangeable, but it indicates that Moses constructed a snake which by manner of it being brass could symbolize the "*seraph*" or the snakes that had been biting the Israelite people because of their rebelliousness and the subsequent judgment from the Father. Take note when looking over the following verses that the "*seraph*" is Strong's number 8314 and the "*nachash*" which was made from brass is #5175.

> *And the LORD[3068] said[559] unto[413] Moses,[4872] Make[6213]* ***thee a fiery serpent,[8314]*** *and set[7760] it upon[5921] a pole:[5251] and it shall come to pass,[1961] that every one[3605] that is bitten,[5391] when he looketh upon[7200] it, shall live.[2425]*

> *And Moses[4872] made[6213]* ***a serpent[5175] of brass,[5178]*** *and put[7760] it upon[5921] a pole,[5251] and it came to pass,[1961] that if[518] a serpent[5175] had bitten[5391 (853)] any man,[376] when he beheld[5027, 413] the serpent[5175] of brass,[5178] he lived.[2425] Numbers 21:8-9 KJV+*

As I have stated, the symbol on the pole, which Moses had made, was a "snake", as indicated by the word "*nachash*". This snake was made out of a shiny material seemingly to emphasize the burning bites of these fiery serpents that had plagued the Israelites.

On a side note, notice whom the evil is coming from in this situation. The Israelites would have been foolish to blame Satan or some other God for the judgment that came upon them. Once again, "evil," in the form of biting serpents this time, came from God.

To make an English comparison in wording, the concept of receiving a general instruction that is then complied with in a specific manner plays out something like this….

Let's say my wife really enjoys spicy food and requests that I make her a spicy, chicken dish for supper. Although she did not explicitly specify what type of "spicy chicken dish" she wanted, it was clear to me that there were some parameters to her general request but the specifics were left up to me. If I then went and made "Sweet and Sour" chicken, I would not be acknowledging the request for "spicy chicken." I understand then, the desire for a spicy dish, and now it is my responsibility to make it happen. Off I go to the kitchen where I cook up a storm for the next hour, and just as I finish cooking my Mother in law calls on the telephone to chat. She asks what I am doing and I tell her that I just finished making supper for Ellah because she had made a special request. The obvious question that comes next is, "Oh my, what did you make her?" My answer is, "Buffalo wings and Cajun drumsticks."

Both dishes are chicken and both dishes are spicy so I had complied with my wife's request to make her some "spicy chicken". Is it correct then to say that spicy means the same thing as Cajun drumsticks and Buffalo wings or does spicy simply describe a predominant characteristic of Cajun wings and Buffalo drumsticks?

If we use the Bullinger method of deciding different words are interchangeable because they are both references to the same thing, we are apt to make many mistakes in applying our understanding to words and terms. Had I made spicy beef then I would have failed to comply with the request of my wife. When she said she wanted a spicy chicken dinner; she was describing the characteristics of a dish, not what specifically the dish was. I responded by making spicy drumsticks and wings, not by making creamed chicken or popcorn chicken. Neither did Moses respond to Yahweh's request by making a stone or a wooden serpent on a pole, rather he made a shiny serpent on a pole. The words "spicy chicken" are not interchangeable with "Buffalo chicken wings". Using Bullinger's logic one could say that a Buffalo is a chicken. Moses was asked to make a "serpent" and he complied by making a serpent that was shiny. The Creator did not state explicitly for Moses to make a "shiny serpent", but Moses was on track when He used his creative license to construct a serpent that was shiny upon being asked by Yahweh in a general sense, to construct a "serpent".

It would be daft to now say, spicy chicken is interchangeable with Cajun drumsticks or Buffalo wings, they being one and the same; or to claim a snake is interchangeable with the phrase, "shiny brass artifact." *Nachash* is not a word that is interchangeable with *seraph.* In Genesis 3, the *nachash* is a metaphor because it speaks of a snake motif and in Numbers 21, the *nachash* is a real brass snake used to represent real biting snakes in the wilderness.

We are not to derive an implicit connection of the words and equate them to mean the same thing as Bullinger has claimed, when we see that the serpent on the pole was indeed shiny. This word *nachash* is not generally said to mean shiny as Bullinger contends by forming a connection to a different word that informs of the quality of shininess of a brass snake that was made by the hands of man under the prescription of God. Moses did make a *"snake/ nachash"*, which the text describes is made from a shiny material called brass. Moses complied with Yahweh's request and Moses knew that the snake of brass would adequately portray the symbol of the fiery serpents that had been biting the Israelites. To claim interchangeability of *nachash* and *saraph* is simply a very clever way to force a pre-conceived concept into a passage of Scripture that was a little confusing to some because of the different terms used.

Here is how Bullinger puts it in his commentary;

> But when the LORD said unto Moses, "Make thee a fiery serpent" (Numbers 21.8), He said, "Make thee a *Saraph*", and, in obeying this command, we read in verse 9, "Moses made a *Nachash* of brass". *Nachash* is thus used as being interchangeable with *Saraph*.

Bullinger's claim that the word *nachash* means, "shining one", is not substantiated by many. There are few linguistic scholars who will state that *"nachash"* is a word that means shining. The lack of connection to the word *"nachash"* and *"nachosheth"* is apparent. The words *nachash* and *seraph* are two different words and one word which can indicate something shiny because of its meaning of "copper or brass" does not become the same as or interchangeable with the word for serpent, *"nachash"*. The word *saraph* is more intended to speak of the shining luminescence of a thing in some instances than it is to speak of the burning. To an ancient Hebrew, there was no doubt that something burning was in fact shining. In the Book of Isaiah we are told of the vision the Prophet has that revealed six-winged creatures in a heavenly setting. The word used to describe these creatures was *seraphim,* which is a word to describe their brilliant appearance, and was understood as meaning shining. The shining symbol that Moses constructed to represent the poisonous snakes that cause burning by their bites was a snake that shone because it was constructed out of shiny brass. When Moses was told to make a shiny symbolic image to represent the snakes that had been biting the Israelites, He had the good sense to fabricate a serpent out of brass. Moses' good sense to interpret Yahweh's request with the appropriate image when asked to make a "seraph" to indicate a biting, poisonous, serpent, should not force the reader to equate the word *nachash* as being interchangeable with *seraph.*

On a web forum, we find a short discussion on the topic. I will present it in its entirety but I recommend you consider doing your own research to find out that Bullinger has missed the mark on this one and appears to have pressed his concept into a mold not intended to fit either a snake or a " Satan." In his work on this topic, we are confronted with a brilliant man who allows himself to impose upon the Scriptures a meaning that the man himself desires to exist in a passage. Had Bullinger been able to dismiss the age-old belief in a cosmic "satan" I am sure his work on this topic would have been more accurate. To decide that *nachash* means *seraph* and *seraph* means *nachash* is far too convenient of a theological leap intending to make one's belief fit the Scripture instead of finding out if the Scripture fits one's belief. Below then, is the discussion I mentioned which addresses some of the issues with the erroneous Bullinger concept.

> Posted: Mon May 08, 2006 6:26 pm Post subject: The 'Nachash' of Genesis 3
>
>> Hello. I'm new to the boards, so I'm happy to "make your acquaintance."
>>
>> Question: Does anyone have any idea as to the etymology of 'nachash', normally translated "serpent"? There is some debate over whether the "serpent" of Gen. 3 was or was not a literal serpent. What is the etymology for nachash? I've read from some sources that it originally meant "shining

one," and that perhaps Gen. 3 should be translated to say that Eve encountered "the Shining One."

Any takers . . . ?

Thanks,

Andy

Posted: Mon May 08, 2006 8:14 pm Post subject:

Andy:

I believe the idea originated with E.W. Bullinger in his Companion Bible. You can get it from him first hand on a website which contains all of the appendices from that work.

Bullinger has a tendency to force things a bit in his interpretations, and his treatment of nachash is no exception. In my evaluation, his proposal doesn't pass the test

Posted: Wed May 10, 2006 6:45 pm Post subject: Re: The 'Nachash' of Genesis 3

[quote="derksen"]Question: Does anyone have any idea as to the etymology of 'nachash', normally translated "serpent"? There is some debate over whether the "serpent" of Gen. 3 was or was not a literal serpent. What is the etymology for nachash? I've read from some sources that it originally meant "shining one," and that perhaps Gen. 3 should be translated to say that Eve encountered "the Shining One."[/quote]

The same word for "serpent" is used in Exodus 4:3 and 7:15 to speak of Moses' rod turning into a snake. It is also used in Numbers 21 to speak of the serpents that bit the people as well as of the serpent of brass that Moses lifted up to bring them healing.

Interestingly, this is one of those words that happens to have a separate and unrelated meaning (much like our English word "trunk") -- it can speak of divination.

John Stevenson

Posted: Fri May 12, 2006 7:27 am Post subject:

While E.W. Bullinger claims that the Hebrew word for serpent (nachash) comes from the word 'to shine' (nagahh), I can find not a single lexical work that defines the verb 'nachash' as "to shine," but rather 'to enchant', as he himself admits at the end of his work titled; "The Serpent of Genesis 3". The verb meaning "to shine" is, "nagahh".

This sloppy morphology in my view is an attempt to force the connection between the serpent in Genesis 3 with 'Helel ben shachar', the shining one, son of dawn in Isaiah 14. As a 'cross-reference', those who advocate such an interpretation attempt to employee 2 Corinthians 11.14; "And no marvel; for Satan himself is transformed into an angel of light."

See how easy that is? If we know Satan transforms himself into an 'angel of light' and we can make the Genesis 3 serpent mean 'shining one', then we can make the connection to the shining one in Isaiah.

Wow!!! What creativity!!!

Agrammatos kai Idiotas

MJS

Posted: Mon May 22, 2006 2:29 am Post subject

Quote:

Interestingly, this is one of those words that happens to have a separate and unrelated meaning (much like our English word "trunk") -- it can speak of divination.

We could perhaps add תֶשחְנ (nəhosheth, copper/bronze) to the collection of meanings for this root. (Moses's brass serpent in Numbers 21:9 is an interesting pun: תֶשחְנ שַחְנ, nəhăsh nəhōshěth.)

If one wanted to make out a connection between serpents and shining, I would have thought that this would be a better place to start, rather than a root as far from שחנ as חגנ[175]

175 The bible forum discussion can be seen at http://forum.bible.org/viewtopic.php?t=4478&sid=6721af503bbe3e66b49f56063869579f#top

The person posting on this forum named "MJS" in the above discussion ends their comment, seemingly tongue in cheek. The comments state that knowing "satan" transforms himself into an angel of light; it is easy to make the serpent of Genesis 3 into "satan." The final comment of this commenter is, "*Wow!!! What creativity!!!*" I whole-heartedly echo MJS's proclamation by agreeing that Bullinger, and for that matter, any scholar who decides to equate words and derive connections when the linguistics do not indicate a connection, is being very creative. Creativity, when used to fabricate theological position, becomes a bane to those who practice it and to those who accept the false teaching that comes from it. Use of a descriptive word to paint a picture of a desire does not license the scholar or the hearer to explicitly equate it with a different word combination describing the specifics of an object. "Nachash" and "seraph" are not interchangeable as Bullinger purports. He claims "*nachash*" means snake or serpent and "shining one" and is connected to the Hebrew word for "shining". It seems that this is not so and *nogah* is the Hebrew word for "shining." Used 19 times in the Scriptures *nogah* is translated as shining, brightness, bright, and light. Examples of this are clear, Isaiah 4 and Habakkuk 3 display the word. I have highlighted it below.

> And the LORD[3068] will create[1254] upon[5921] every[3605] dwelling place[4349] of mount[2022] Zion,[6726] and upon[5921] her assemblies,[4744] a cloud[6051] and smoke[6227] by day,[3119] and the **shining[5051]** of a flaming[3852] fire[784] by night:[3915] for[3588] upon[5921] all[3605] the glory[3519] *shall be* a defense.[2646] Isaiah 4:5 KJV+

> The sun[8121] *and* moon[3394] stood still[5975] in their habitation:[2073] at the light[216] of thine arrows[2671] they went,[1980] *and* at the **shining[5051]** of thy glittering[1300] spear.[2595] Habakkuk 3:11 KJV+

The word *nachash* is shown to be connected to the concept of a whisperer or one who uses enchantments. Understanding the subtle nuances typical of a metaphorical term used by an ancient Hebrew writer, the word *nachash* can be seen as speaking of something that is itself subtle, sinister, and able to go somewhat undetected. This connection would allow us to more closely identify the serpent in the garden as being a force that propagated lies such as the evil inclination. The evil inclination is definitely somewhat of a whispering enchanter that was present in Adam and Eve prior to when they were given a choice to obey and to not eat of the tree of knowledge of good and evil or disobey and taste it.

If a person does not even have a potential to disobey then why would the Creator even have to tell them not to disobey. Placing the choice in front of the first man and women is proof enough that there was a potential to sin, an evil inclination, already hard wired into humanity from the moment they were created. As far as what the word *nachash* means, we have a choice whether or not to believe Bullinger's theory, which may affirm a belief in a cosmic "satan" that we already have. Or we can accept the testimony of other ancient Hebrew sources that disagree with Bullinger's view. Thus far, I have not found any ancient Hebrew source, which says "*seraph*" is interchangeable with "*nachash.*"

I am not interested in vilifying Ethelbert Bullinger and if it comes across that way that is not my intent. Thousands of men and women have done great scholarship in many areas of Biblical studies. I have learned a lot from them and will continue to glean of their wisdom, including from Bullinger. It is true however, that many of these scholars have done similar to Bullinger in taking a preconceived understanding of a concept and finding a way to fit it into Scripture. If a person squeezes a meaning of a term or a word that they have learned in the past, into Scripture, the fact is that they are then not speaking according to Scripture but speaking according to their own hearts and minds. Isaiah 8:20 teaches us, *if they do not speak according to the Torah and the testimony then there is no light in them.* The law and the testimony as would have been understood by Isaiah's contemporaries when he penned that verse, was known as the Torah. Bullinger and countless others have decided to speak things that don't exist in the Torah, such as the serpent in the garden, being "Satan."

The serpent in Genesis 3 was not believed to be Satan until such a time as a belief in a literal cosmic Satan had been adopted and accepted. It was when Satan came to exist in the minds and theology of the teachers who were guilty of adopting ancient mystical ideas, that the Satan-God was imposed on the Genesis serpent.

Bullinger also claims the "serpent" connection of 2 Corinthians 11:3, where the English words say the serpent beguiled Eve, is an instance that aids in firming up the argument that the "*nachash*" in the garden was "satan." The error here is in not seeing how the "serpent" metaphor Paul employs is simply a reference to the minds of those Paul is speaking to. The personification of a part of the mind of man as a serpent has led many to believe that the serpent is a literal entity but Paul connects it to the mind in the following verse. The serpent beguiling someone is the same as the mind being corrupted according to Paul.

> *But I fear, lest by any means, as the serpent beguiled Eve through his subtilty, **so your minds should be corrupted** from the simplicity that is in Christ. 2Corinthians 11:3 KJV*

It is the intentions in the mind of man that is the "serpent". Paul is in essence personifying the evil inclination in man that subtly justifies action and behaviors, and invokes an internal dialogue until one has sufficiently convinced him or herself to sin. We will discuss the typical and very regular personification of sin and the *yetzer hara* as it is displayed in the Greek "New Testament" in Volume II, but for now please hear what Paul is saying. A paraphrase of this verse might be as follows;

> *I am afraid just as Eve gave in to her own inherent desire for rebellion when she mulled things over and justified them in her mind, so I fear that you will let your minds get corrupted by talking yourselves into a more complicated form of this faith walk in Christ, also deceiving your own minds.*

To some, the statements made by Paul about the adversary being transformed into a messenger of light become a roadblock that prevents them from clearly understanding that Paul was not intending a literal application of the metaphor. Bullinger's work incorrectly makes a connection to "satan" being called an "angel of light" in 2nd Corinthians chapter 11 as being a reference to what he calls "a shining one" in the garden. He states;

> The Nachash, or serpent, who beguiled Eve (2Cor. 11:3) is spoken of as "an angel of light" in v. 14. Have we not, in this, a clear intimation that it was not a snake, but a glorious shining being, apparently an angel, to whom Eve paid such great deference, acknowledging him as one who seemed to possess superior knowledge, and who was evidently a being of a superior (not of an inferior) order?[176]

He and others are missing the point that, the active force of rebellion in man does masquerade as righteous at times, hence it is a "light" in the metaphorical sense. However, Paul's use of the word *satanas* in the Greek text comes from the Hebrew word for "adversary", which we have discussed previously. This time Paul is warning the hearer that there are "adversaries" who are human men that are subverting the truth. These are appropriately called "Satan" just as Peter the apostle was called "Satan" by the Messiah when he opposed the things of God.

176 http://www.ovrlnd.com/Teaching/serpentofgen.html

For[1063] such[5108] are false apostles,[5570] deceitful[1386] workers,[2040] transforming themselves[3345] into[1519] the apostles[652] of Christ.[5547]

And[2532] no[3756] marvel;[2298] for[1063] Satan[4567] himself[846] is transformed[3345] into[1519] an angel[32] of light.[5457] 2Corinthians 11:13-14 KJV+

The adversarial force that Paul is speaking about can definitely appear to be a messenger of truth, which is here called "an angel of light". Both are men speaking lies that are almost undetectable, and our own minds can appear to be "light" at times, deceiving us with lies that are masquerading as truth. It is either other men and their words or the thoughts of our own mind that appear to be "light" and deceive us. The following verses demonstrate this principle;

For they that are such serve not our Lord Jesus Christ, but their own belly; and by good words and fair speeches deceive the hearts of the simple. Romans 16:18 KJV

And Jesus answered and said unto them, Take heed that no man deceive you. Matthew 24:4 KJV

But the unbelieving Jews stirred up the Gentiles, and made their minds evil affected against the brethren. Acts 14:2 KJV

Now as Jannes and Jambres withstood Moses, so do these also resist the truth: men of corrupt minds, reprobate concerning the faith. 2 Timothy 3:8 KJV

Let no man deceive you with vain words: for because of these things cometh the wrath of God upon the children of disobedience. Ephesians 5:6 KJV

Bullinger also misses the truth of the issue when he claims the King of Tyre in Ezekiel 28 is a supernatural being, saying that he represents the supernatural Satan. We have discussed in Chapter 9 that the King of Tyre was a human king who received no different admonishment from the prophet than had many other kings in the Scriptures. Carrying the King of Tyre concept further, Bullinger states the verses describing the King can only be understood of the "mightiest and most exalted supernatural being that God ever created". Here we see a practical admission that Bullinger believes there is "one like God". He admits this by referring to the subject found in Ezekiel, as a mighty, exalted supernatural being (See quote below). Only

Yahweh is mighty and to be exalted but Bullinger confesses that he believes "Satan" was mighty and exalted. How is it possible the only God worthy of worship was so foolish as to create a being as mighty and exalted as "Satan"? It can be found that He did no such thing and once again, it appears that the misunderstanding Bullinger has, is based on foregone conclusions that are drawn from other erring instructors of the Word.

It seems Bullinger believes that Satan fell from Heaven, as many have falsely believed is depicted in Isaiah 14. Recall if you will that Isaiah 14 is a prophetic oracle about the fall from power of the "morning star" who was the King of Babylon, not about a creature named "Lucifer." Lucifer is simply a Latin word for "light bringer" and refers to the King who thought himself to be like the god Venus, which was the planet that rose on the horizon just prior to the sunrise each day. Here are Bullinger's words that identify him as a believer in more than one god. Bullinger ascribes God-like attributes to the Satan that he believes is the serpent in the garden.

> There is more about "the king of Tyre" in Ezekiel 28. 11-19 than was literally true of "the prince of Tyre" (verses 1-10). The words can be understood only of the mightiest and most exalted supernatural being that God ever created; and thus for the purpose of showing how great would be his fall. The *history* must be true to make the *prophecy* of any weight.[177]

Yahweh did not create a being that was mightier and more exalted than all the other beings He had created. Aside from the fact that there is nowhere in Scripture that indicates God made a super-angel, it makes no sense for Yahweh to have done something like this, only to have this supposed creature abuse his position out of what many say was motivated by jealousy.

In *The Serpent in Genesis 3* by Dr. Bullinger, his purpose is to prove that the serpent is not a literal snake as is thought by many. He seems to move in this direction because of a long held belief in a cosmic Satan and the subsequent perceived need to find Satan in the story of the fall of man. There is no mention of Satan at all in the Genesis account of creation and the serpent, however, in the following quote from Bullinger we see that he presumes that Satan is referred to in the Genesis 3 story.

> When Satan is spoken of as a "serpent", it is the figure *Hypocatastasis[[178]]* or *Implication*; it no more means a snake than

177 The Serpent of Genesis 3, By Dr E Bullinger

178 *Hypocatastasis* is more intense than metaphor. It is the figure that is a comparison by

> it does when Dan is so called in Genesis 49.17; or an animal when Nero is called a "lion" (2 Timothy 4.17), or when Herod is called a "fox" (Luke 13.32); or when Judah is called " a lion's whelp". It is the same figure when "doctrine" is called "leaven" (Matthew 16.6). It shows that something much more real and truer to truth is intended. If a Figure of speech is thus employed, it is for the purpose of expressing the truth more impressively; and is intended to be a figure of something much *more real* than the letter of the word.[179]

The above statement is correct in testifying that the serpent in the garden is more than a figure of speech and is intended to express a profound truth. The truth though is not as Bullinger concludes, wherein he is bent toward seeing the "*nachash*" as "Satan". To claim the serpent is Satan is to say this supposed Satan has the power to become incarnate. Incarnate can mean simply becoming concrete or taking on a fleshly form to become real. To be sure, the ability of an evil angel to manifest in any form he chooses at any time is a power God has. Possessing such a power would then make one to "be like God". Can Satan take on different forms like the God of the Universe? Believing Satan can manifest in diverse forms as Yahweh can, is an admission that there are two Gods in the universe. If one believes with their heart, mind, soul, and strength that Yahweh is the only God, then one would be diligent to seek out to prove there is no Satan, thus declaring the existence of only One God. Bullinger's efforts to find the truth of the serpent in the garden story stopped short of trying to understand the ancient use of mythological imagery and metaphors to deliver a message that is "truer to truth."

Also employed in Bullinger's article are references to Hebrews 2:14 and 1 John 3:8. We will discuss these also in detail during our "New Testament" discussions in Volume II of *Satan, Christianity's Other God!* For the moment I will say that Bullinger must have failed to study the tense, voice and mood of the language of those verses. Both of those verses indicate an action performed by Messiah, which is already being played out or put into action. The tense of those verses is not indicative of a time yet to come when Messiah will destroy the works of evil. It is like a football game that is completed and the players have retreated to the locker room and are heard bantering about

---

implication. Calling a messy eater "Pig," instead of comparing the messy eater with a pig by saying he is **like** a pig, or even that he **is** a pig, is *hypocatastasis* where the comparison is just implied. One person says to the other, "Pig!" and the person spoken to gets the idea that they are a pig. Although the comparison is implied, the meaning is effectively communicated.

179 From "The Serpent in Genesis 3" By Dr. Bullinger. (footnote on hypocatastasis is added by the writer)

their opponents. "We kicked their asses!", the players may proclaim, yet no one hearing that would believe that the winning team is yet to accomplish the "ass kicking". It would be clear to all hearers that the "Ass Kicking" was accomplished and now the results of that victory will be realized in the player and team stats, as well as the overall position heading towards the playoffs. Not to mention, the next time the losing team hits the field for practice, they may find themselves motivated to play harder and smarter. Possibly improving their performance through the use of intense physical drills.

To his credit, we receive the sensible argument by Bullinger of the implausibility of the "serpent" being literally a snake, by recognizing that it is unlikely that the "serpent" could actually speak audible human language. I agree with Dr. Bullinger here but as you read his quote, I would like you to consider the question; how could "Satan" become incarnate according to Dr. Bullinger in whatever form he supposedly took in the garden or as a messenger of light, yet not have the power of miracles to cause a snake to speak? Does it make sense however, that Satan could incarnate Himself in a manner like God but was absent of the supernatural power to cause a serpent to appear to be speaking? It would seem that manifesting himself in the garden would be a far more potent miracle than to speak through a literal serpent.

> It is wonderful how a snake could ever be supposed to speak without the organs of speech, or that Satan should be supposed able to accomplish so great a miracle.
>
> It only shows the power of tradition, which has, from the infancy of each one of us, put before our eyes and written on our minds the picture of a "snake" and an "apple": the former based on a wrong interpretation, and the latter being pure invention, about which there is not one word said in the Holy Scripture.[180]

Bullinger has claimed that Satan was the "mightiest and most exalted supernatural being" and that he is "wiser than any other living creature" and by implication, he is saying that Satan has the power to take on other forms. How could a scholar of Bullinger's caliber conclude all of those items and yet not think this "mighty supernatural" creature could cause a serpent to speak? This must be because Bullinger was bent on making this serpent fit the "fallen angel" theology he and millions of others had come to believe instead of searching out Scriptures like Isaiah 14 and Ezekiel 28 in the cultural and historical context of which they were written (see chapters 8 and 9 for the

180 From "The Serpent in genesis 3" By Dr. Bullinger.

discussion on these concepts). I too do not think that a literal serpent is being spoken of here but there must be an error in thinking to conclude such a thought and then use that conclusion to advance the theory that the serpent is actually Satan himself appearing as a shiny angel.

Bullinger finishes his article by trying to put forth an idea, and I am paraphrasing, that this evil being "Satan," whom Bullinger and others blame so much evil on, is not involved in the lives and activities of the criminal and deviant segment of our society. Bullinger asserts that this supposed archfiend of the God of the Universe is only after the teachers of the Scriptures. I cannot imagine why the "evil one" would keep his minions from exercising their wicked devices, which are intended to thwart the will of the Father and harm created humans through encouraging crime and deviance, onto feeble humans. A point made in his article that indicates Satan is not at work in the criminal elements of society, is stated thus;

> We are not to look for Satan's activities today in the news, or the courts; but in the pulpit, and in professors' chairs.

Bullinger is in the same place as many other scholars by espousing beliefs that are inconsistent. If in fact this theory of Bullinger's does seem meritorious to some, then perhaps those who affirm Bullinger's "*nachash*" theory ought to explore all of the intricacies of each of Bullinger's statements and the Scripture references he uses, instead of accepting his dogma cart-blanche. The blind acceptance of this teaching may place the recipient in the position of being seen as the blind following the blind in this area.

It is quite certain there is no 'Satan" in Genesis 3 and that the serpent is not a literal serpent in this account as I have explained. The serpent in Genesis 3 is not a "shining one" as some believe, but is the subtle, evil inclination in the human heart as the metaphor suggests. Although misunderstood by countless scholars, this ancient serpent metaphor was understood by the Hebrews who came out of Egypt, the audience whom the message of the Serpent in the Garden was first written to.

Could Adam be "the serpent" acting as an adversarial force?

Before we come to the end of Volume I, I would like to present one more possible understanding of who the adversary is, in the garden situation. I submit this to you with trepidations and ask that you only consider the concept and not perceive that this is a rigid and dogmatic understanding of who the adversary in the garden was. Perhaps some can see I am only submitting it because there is a remote chance, based on what we have learned about the adversary being a human, that this "position" I am about to suggest could possibly be correct.

Based on the conclusions that the "adversary/satan" of the Old Testament is often a human character; and that the serpent in the garden is metaphorical terminology that is intended to represent a concept of wickedness latent in humans, then it might be possible that Adam is "the serpent". It is possible the serpent Adam, is the force behind the choice for wickedness.

It is interesting to note Eve's surroundings and the wording patterns of the account as we have it. Eve is in the garden tending it and although it is often thought she was alone the text indicates that she was not. The text tells us that Adam was with her.

> *And when the woman saw that the tree was good for food, and that it was pleasant to the eyes, and a tree to be desired to make one wise, she took of the fruit thereof, and did eat,* ***and gave also unto her husband with her****; and he did eat. Genesis 3:6 KJV*

It is clear from the text that Adam was with Eve. To begin a long philosophical discussion on what it meant to be "with" Eve at this juncture, might be inhibiting to articulating the point. However, the word *im,* "with", is translated as against, among, beside, before, between, accompanying, more, and reason. Assuredly, the translators chose accurately by choosing to use "with" for expressing Adam's proximity to Eve when she decided to eat the fruit of the forbidden tree. Let me pose a few questions to help get to the explanation I am moving towards that suggests Adam might have been the "serpent".

- How did sin enter the world?
- Through whom did sin enter the world?
- Is Adam credited with sin entering the world or is Eve credited with sin entering the world?

- Who received the commandment from Yahweh to not eat of the tree in the midst of the garden?

- Was it not the man, Adam's responsibility to correctly transmit Yahweh's command to the woman if in fact he received it from the Creator?

These questions, if answered according to the texts we have available in the "Bible," will help us to see the potential for a human to have been the "adversary" in the garden. The answers are; that sin is said to have entered the world through man not Satan and Adam was that man. Eve was not credited in the Scriptures or Apostolic writings of being the one who sin entered the world through only that she was beguiled by the serpent in Second Corinthians 11 verse 3 (who was possibly a *human deceiver*). [181] Adam was credited with sin entering the world in Romans 5 verse 12. And it was Adam who received the command to not eat of the forbidden tree in Genesis chapter 2 verses 15 to 17. Adam would have passed the information on to Eve; therefore, he was the only reliable source to pass on the instructions to Eve. In being that source, he was in the perfect place to put Yahweh's words together in a slightly different way so as to cause Eve to entertain something that was not said by God at all.

When we are told in Genesis 3 that *the serpent was more subtle than any beast of the field that the LORD God had made,* the traditional view is to assume the writer is talking about how smart and deceptive the snake is. We

---

181 1st Timothy 2:14 is a verse that will often be used to identify Eve as the first sinner, particularly by those inclined towards male dominance in culture. This verse in its context is intended to address the Jewish myths of the day that said Eve was created first and then she created Adam whom she then proceeded to deceive into believing was created first. It is a Gnostic creation myth and the intent of Paul's words to Timothy was to deny that Eve was created first. Paul is simply advocating the creation order and denouncing a myth by saying Eve was the one who was deceived and was not created first. In so doing Paul was able to make his stand on the Genesis account being the accurate account of creation and that the Jewish fables were wrong. Note in the text that Paul precedes the statement by announcing that Adam was created first. The words "*and Adam was not deceived*", are not a defense against the fact that Adam sinned in the garden because elsewhere we are told sin entered the world through one man and that in Adam all men die. They are words stated to combat the error that claims Adam came second and Eve deceived him. Eve was said in mythical lore to be pure and divine but Paul felt the need to inform Timothy and those hearing his letter, that Eve is just a human and did enter into transgression, not sinless as the myth that many were inclined to believe, suggests. The verses in question here are referenced below.

1Ti 2:13-14 *For Adam was first formed, then Eve. And Adam was not deceived, but the woman being deceived was in the transgression.*

have discussed the idea of the snake's intelligence earlier in this chapter but we need to consider the meaning of the word "subtle". Is it possible that this word can be used to refer to a human quality or characteristic?

The word "*arum*" which has been translated as "subtle" in the King James Version, can mean cunning. This word can also be used in a positive sense to indicate prudence or prudent behaviors. As we discussed earlier, the pre-exilic "Jewish" understanding about man was generally that man inherently had the "*yetzer-ha ra*" and the "*yetzer ha tov*" at work inside of him. That is, the "evil inclination" and the "good inclination." It is not a new concept to see that man was created complete and the potential for sin was already programmed in and not added to man at a later time because of the tragedy of the "original sin". The potential for sin had to already be present for man to actually choose the sin action. Paul says sin is in his members and James said we sin because of the lust in us, both recognizing that sin starts from the inside of man and not from an external influence with supernatural powers. Paul and James' statements are quoted below.

> *Romans 7:23 KJV*
> *But I see another law in my members, warring against the law of my mind, and bringing me into captivity to the law of sin which is in my members.*

> *James 1:14 KJV*
> *But every man is tempted, when he is drawn away of his own lust, and enticed.*

Both Paul and James understood that the potential to sin is something inside of man and not from an external "demonic" influence. They clearly say, the law of sin is in my members and that the active force that draws man into sin is **his own** lusts. Neither of these pillars of the Faith is indicating that "Satan" is doing anything to cause man to choose sin. Therefore, either Yahweh created man like an obedient robot without the ability to choose volitionally to serve and obey the loving Creator, or man was created with this potential to sin This potential is referred to as the law of sin by Paul and as one's own lusts by James. If the former is the case, then the "*yetzer ha ra*" did not exist until Adam and Eve chose to eat from the forbidden tree. This implies that the "evil one" called "Satan" was able to place the potential to sin inside the psyche of Adam and Eve. That the potential to choose disobedience would have been imparted to humans by Satan in the garden just before Adam and Eve decided to eat of the forbidden fruit, does not agree with a one-God philosophy. Man was not in a position to inherit the potential to sin after man had been created "complete". The only plausible explanation is that

Adam and Eve, and therefore every human which follows, had the potential to choose sin, called the "*yetzer ha ra*", hardwired from the factory so to speak. Why so many are content with believing the potential to choose sin is an after market innovation which came to be part of humanity at the hands of the archfiend and nemesis of Yahweh is beyond me.

It is however understandable, that the desire humanity seems to have which causes us to accept an ideology that states our problem of making evil choices at times is because of a fallen angel called "Satan". This false ideology states that evil and evil choices are not mans' fault completely. It is convenient to take the focus and blame for our sins, off our selves, and see them as occurring because of man being persuaded to give in to some evil force that is attacking them. Adam and Eve both had a potential to disobey before they ate from the forbidden tree in the garden. Had they not had the potential to sin God would not have had to tell them to not eat from that tree. Adam and Eve are just as much the originators of their own sin then as you and I are the originators of our sins today. The "satan" is not an external force but an internal drive that must be overcome as we endeavor to serve the Creator. The Scriptures and the "New Testament" outline for us that anyone who goes against the will of the father is seen as a satan. Whether called Satan or a devil, both terms can describe one who is for the things of man instead of the things of God. The Messiah gave his definition of what a satan is when he spoke to Peter on one occasion and on another, when he said one of his disciples is a devil. All who heard Him knew he was indicating that one of the present company was being an adversary And opposing the things of God.

> *But he turned, and said unto Peter, Get thee behind me, Satan: thou art an offence unto me:* ***for thou savourest not the things that be of God****, but those that be of men. Matthew 16:23 KJV*

> *Jesus answered them, Have not I chosen you twelve, and one of you is a devil? John 6:70 KJV*

So Messiah was calling those who were for the things of man, if even for a moment, Satan. Of course if the "Devil" is "Satan" as is typically taught and we accept that there exists a cosmic Satan, then we now have the problem of deciding why both Peter and the soon to be betrayer, are identified as the Satan, the cosmic evil one. That cannot be reconciled within the context of the traditional understanding of this "satan" being. However, when one understands the concept that "satan" and "devil" are terms intended to describe an attitude, attribute, or behavioral pattern of a human or a system of governance, then we are able to comprehend how both Peter and Judas could be called the "devil/satan."

Therefore, if we are following the thought process, we see that at times, "the satan," is referring to a human opposing God's will, plan and commandments. We also see that the serpent in the garden is referring to a characteristic in humans of justifying the choice to sin. There is another point I am to make in this developing line of reasoning; it is that sin entered the world by one man, that man is Adam. The following verses indicate how sin entered through a man, not a "Satan" and how death, which is a result of the humans' sin, appears to have originated with Adam.

> *Wherefore, as by one man sin entered into the world, and death by sin; and so death passed upon all men, for that all have sinned: Romans 5:12*

> *For since by man came death, by man came also the resurrection of the dead.*
> *For as in Adam all die, even so in Christ shall all be made alive. 1Corinthians 15:21-22*

If the above statements from the Apostolic writings are valid, then it appears the actual original sin is being credited to Adam and not Eve. Many say this is so because Adam was responsible to protect Eve from the "satanic" lies that persuaded her to touch the forbidden fruit and then eat it. This is a convenient way to get around a difficult verse implicating Adam as the sinner of origin instead of Eve, which seems to be seen in the text of Genesis 3. If sin came in through Adam, but we seem to see Eve as the first one to sin in Genesis, then maybe we are missing something. Is it possible that because the "serpent" represents the justifying self-talk or inner spirit of man; and human beings were created with a potential to choose disobedience, and the adversary that we see called "the satan" in the Scriptures is often a man; then it could be that Adam is the one speaking to Eve? It may be possible that Adam is the "serpent" or the one providing the influencing force to sin. After all, he was "**with**" Eve when she took the fruit. Let's recap a few points in this regard.

- Adam was with Eve in a physically proximal sense,
- the serpent can represent a subtle force,
- an adversary can be a man;

and

- death and sin entered the world through the man Adam.

It is possible then that indeed, the serpent/adversary in the story was Adam.

Consider further that Adam was with Eve yet spoke nothing to the supposed snake that was lying to Eve. Why don't we see Adam speaking up and telling the lying serpent whom he has dominion over, to leave his wife alone? At least Adam should be seen correcting the lies of the serpent. This can be answered by suggesting the serpent is not representing Eve's evil inclination but that Adam was the subtle force that coaxed Eve into disobedience.

Could it be possible that the writer of the origin of man's fall, who wrote using mythical images and concepts, made a point to tell us Adam was **with** Eve, in an effort to point to Adam as the one who talked Eve into taking from the tree of knowledge of good and evil? After all, Adam was very quick to blame Eve for giving him the fruit when he was right with her. Adam would have heard the conversation between the serpent and Eve, so why didn't Adam point to the serpent as the party responsible for making him sin instead of defaulting to Eve? Being with Eve surely Adam would have seen the serpent if one actually existed in physical form. And Adam would have had to be a fool to not lay blame on the serpent or Satan. However, he chose to blame Eve instead of a serpent for his failings.

Part of the explanation for this behavior can be seen by hearing a story of two kids responsible for breaking a window. It is not uncommon to persuade another to do something bad and then skirt being blamed for it even though it was your idea.

> There were two 10-year-old boys playing in the schoolyard after school. No one was around and the boys were out chucking rocks into the tunnel slide on the play structure. All the teachers' cars were gone from the parking lot and the boys had the whole place to themselves. Eric and Chris never usually got into much trouble but today would end differently. Eric had a big rock in his hand when he turned to Chris and said, "Have you ever smashed a window with a rock?"
>
> "No I haven't," said Chris, "I don't even like to throw stones close to the school or my mom will get mad."

These boys were all alone and Eric said with a little mocking tone in his voice, "What's your mommy gonna do, is she gonna spank you if you throw a stone at the school?"

Chris continued his argument with Eric and was hearing himself as he talked, the picture of his mom getting mad for throwing a stone close to the school just didn't make his mom look too cool and that played into Chris' feelings about himself. Chris looked at Eric and then said, "No, mom won't spank me, she probably wouldn't even really get mad if I threw a rock near the school"... so he tossed a rock a little more than passively and it hit the brick school wall then fell harmlessly to the ground.

In the wall, facing the boys there was a window for the janitor's room within throwing distance and it started to look more like a target than something to avoid aiming at. Not really considering the consequences, they started throwing rocks against the school wall and began landing them closer and closer to the window. Eric said to Chris, "What do you think will happen if you hit that window?"

Well as it goes with little boys, once a hint of a challenge is mixed with a bit of senselessness there is almost no turning back. Chris threw the rock and saw it heading for the window, his cringing was mixed with his strong desire to start running but as he began turning to flee, he heard the thud as the rock bounced off the brick about two feet from the window and fell to the ground. The relief Chris felt was a typical first feeling after that kind of suspense. The kind of suspense you feel waiting to hear the crashing glass sound from a rock you had just thrown that you can't call back.

Then Eric says, "Ha! You missed!"

"Yeah lucky for me." replied Chris.

Eric taunted Chris, "why don't you take one more shot?.... ah forget it you probably don't have good enough aim!"

Without even thinking now, Chris had a rock in his left hand that he hadn't dropped yet and he flipped it to his throwing hand and let er' fly. The excitement was palpable as the rock soared straight for the window and crashed through the top corner sending glass tinkling to the ground.

"Whoa....nice shot!" Eric yelled while Chris bent down to the ground and grabbed another stone, which he tossed to Eric and said, "Bet you can't hit it!"

Eric cocked his arm and hurled his rock as hard as he could; it bounced off the window ledge and ricocheted up, smashing out the rest of the window. The boys took to the hill; so to speak, I mean they were really booking it, over the burm and into the bushes to hide, before someone saw them. Alas, it was too little too late for these young, scandalous boys. It just so happened that the principal had ridden his bike to work that day and had not yet left for home. Stopping from work in his office after hearing the first smash, the Principal had gotten up to look out the window onto the playground. He was just in time to see the two boys run over the small hill and into the bushes. So, out he went to call after them. Meanwhile in the bushes the boys were anxious, afraid, and excited all at the same time. I guess neither of them thought they had it in them to throw so far and actually take out a window. If they could describe it, they might say it was an oddly invigorating and somehow liberating feeling to destroy something just because they could. Then along came the Principal.

"Boys, where are you?' He called." ...No answer.

"Boys, come out right this minute or I'm going to call the police!"

All of a sudden this was serious, the boys felt weak, and like crying and running all at the same time. They realized they still had some rocks in their pockets so they dumped them out and slowly walked out of the rustling bushes. As they came into view of the Principal, he recognized who they were, Eric and Chris. His first thought was one of surprise at seeing these two, normally good boys, at the scene of this event.

"Eric, Chris, come here," called the Principal.

The boys made their way over the little hill and slumped toward the principle.

Now that they were in front of the Principal, they knew they were in BIG trouble. The Principle looked at them and said, "Eric, did you smash that window?"

Eric knew it was coming, but oh how he wanted to avoid having to answer that question, he knew there was no way out so he said, while pointing his finger at Chris, "He gave me the rock!"

That response seemed to be planned out all along; get Chris his buddy to aim for the window and then maybe Eric didn't have to shoulder the blame for the damage. Good plan but the principal could see the guilt all over Eric's face so he turned to Chris and said, "Chris, why would you do something like that?"

Chris was red faced and scared, not worrying too much about anything except a way to point blame elsewhere. Just like most kids, when they are blamed for something they're not totally responsible for, they look to deflect the blame onto something or someone else in an attempt to avoid punishment. Fear of punishment is a big motivator to cause a guilty person to spin their story. All he could think of at that time was, "I don't know, I wasn't thinking I guess." Glancing over to Eric he continued, "Something just kind of told me to try to hit the window." The Principal wasn't surprised at the feeble answer coming from such a pathetically sad looking kid. It was obvious to the Principal that neither of these boys wanted to take the blame for their actions.

As he pondered for a few seconds he remembered a report he had received from Eric's teacher last year, that Eric had been getting the other kids in his class to place sticky-tack inside the shoes of their girl classmates over the course of about two or three days. The little girls were running around the school with dirty sticky-tack stuck to their socks for a few days. Looking at the boys, the Principal somehow started to think that Eric might have tricked, cajoled or deceived Chris into throwing rocks at the window. He soon realized Eric had been the one putting the idea of throwing rocks at the window in Chris' head. The principal also realized they were both responsible for their actions but understood Chris wouldn't have thought so seriously about smashing a window if Eric hadn't led him to do so.

As the whole story came out, the Principal's instincts proved true. The boys were both punished accordingly and Eric and his parents had to talk with the school Guidance Counselor to see if there was something going on which caused Eric to get himself and others into trouble. The sticky tack incident and now the broken window made two infractions for Eric. Hopefully there would be no more, but that would be up to Eric I guess. Both Eric and Chris were busted, even though they tried to blame something or someone else for their actions.

In this story, of Eric and Chris, even though it seems like a simple tale, we see that Chris was deceived by Eric but Eric was the one who influenced the offense to take place. Although Eric was not the one who grabbed Chris' arm and flung it towards the window, Eric was still the one who brought the sin into play by setting things up so his evil desire was satiated but still found a way to blame the actual action on someone else.

If we could get into Paul the Apostle's mind when he wrote the letters to the Romans and the Corinthians, we would find that he was aware the Scriptures do not teach a "Satan" doctrine and therefore, the serpent in Genesis was neither a literal snake nor a manifestation of Satan. Yahweh did levy some curses on the serpent but that curse was upon the evil inclination of man. The part of man's psyche that would always do battle against the good in man would not reign supreme in the heart of man. Man would ultimately choose good more readily than evil. Thus rendering the aspect of Adam that was bent towards evil to be subservient to the aspect of Adam that is inclined towards good. We see it today that any one of us in all of the human race, can force the "serpent" in us into submission, by exercising our will to choose good.

As was said, in the story of the broken window, Chris was deceived. Perhaps Eve was deceived in the same way by the one with her and she then submitted to the evil inclination that justifies sinful choices. In Eric and Chris' story, the serpent could be said to be the metaphorical representation of Eric's persuasive powers to influence Chris to choose wrong. This particular anti-good force happened to be in the form of his buddy Eric. Eric therefore is equated as being the serpent. Without dividing Eric into two aspects of a human being, the "*yetzer ha ra*" and the "*yetzer tov,*" suffice it to say this boy was not intrinsically evil and to be seen as a "Damien" type, destructive and demonic being. He could however be seen as the "serpent," an aspect of humanity that works in man to justify rebellion. Eric, at least for this time, did not yield to the good side but chose evil, which was his rebellion. His survival instinct became selfish and fearful of being caught and then punished. He decided to blame Chris as the reason he rebelled.

With that in mind one can see how it is possible that Adam and Eve were together in the garden and Adam influenced Eve to first touch and then taste the fruit just as Eric was with Chris when he was influenced to shatter a window. Adam, being the one through whom death came into the world to all men, asking in a leading sense, if they would die by eating of every tree in the garden. Eve replies to Adam, who was acting as a "serpent" or "adversary" if you will, "*We can't even touch it!*" Adam persists, now reasoning in himself, "*As if we can't touch it, Yahweh created it, we won't die.*" After reasoning with himself that no one is going to die by touching the fruit, he expresses his feelings to the woman. Along with those feelings Adam adds a little more to nudge the boundaries that are in place, He effectively says, "*We probably will be like God if we eat it, he made it, it has to be good.*"

By his actions of opposing God's plan and being an adversary to Eve, Adam was the "serpent". To be specific, at least his innate potential to choose disobedience can be seen as the serpent. He was with Eve. He was the one who had received the prohibition to eat of the forbidden tree. Adam was to have properly passed this information on to Eve and was to have been her support when she might be tempted to sin. There was no literal snake or Satan "the Shining One", in the garden. If there was, Adam would have corrected the misspoken command when the Serpent asked, *"Did God say you mustn't eat of every tree in the garden?"*

By Adam being with Eve and apparently not speaking up at the appearance of one who was challenging the words of the Creator, leaves the story open to suggest that Adam was the one with the influence, "the serpent." This only means that he behaved in a cunning manner, a manner that deceived the woman and was then seen to be attempting to insulate himself from blame by making it look like the woman was responsible for making him eat the fruit.

As for how the curse pertains to this version of the story; each of these curses is more full of meaning and metaphor than I am prepared to discuss fully now. If the "serpent" was Adam though, then the curse of eating dust and going about on its belly still contains a factor that is applicable to the situation. The curse that proscribes the serpent to crawl on its belly forever, tells us the "subtle" and cunning part of the human psyche will forever be subject to the will of the human when the human-will to choose good is exercised. The nuance of this curse suggests the evil inclination will have less power over the human than the good inclination and therefore is metaphorically said to be "eating dust". The evil inclination is reduced in its place in the human spirit but will not be a quality that is completely subdued by the human will. Effort must be employed to subdue the penchant for evil in man's heart. A heart that is continually inclined towards evil from its youth according to Yahweh. The numerous opportunities to choose evil that are placed in front of us today are always able to be overcome by the "good" in us but these opportunities will have a draw to them that is subtle and difficult to resist. The "serpent" will be subdued and maintain that position of necessary submission when the human being makes an effort to overcome, by refusing the evil and choosing the good.

Is Adam the serpent of Genesis 3? It is plausible that he is when all things are considered and one resolves the issue that the serpent is definitely not a real snake nor is the serpent a literal manifestation of a supernatural Satan. As I stated a few paragraphs ago, I am only considering the possibility of Adam being the adversarial influence to Eve and I ask that you consider it further to make your own conclusions.

The Importance of the Ancient Serpent Mythology Connection

Through the use of the serpent in the garden story, Moses was teaching the Israelites a timeless lesson from their ancestry, using well-understood mythology and the associated images. Moses and the Children of Israel had been in Egypt for a number of successive generations. In order to elucidate this concept a little more it is helpful to understand the depth of the serpent mythology in Egypt. The serpent as divinity was a fact for those steeped in Egyptian culture and it would have been a reasonable consideration for the Israelites who had been assimilated to some degree over the hundreds of years of their sojourn. Aspects of the serpent's divinity are found in the story of Genesis 3. Recognizing the relation to the telling of the story by Moses is vital to comprehend how a myth was being reworked to aid the Hebrew people in learning the message of truth. I would like to share some excerpts from an excellent article on the serpent mythology, called "*The Divine Serpent*" by Robert T. Mason.

> **Egypt**
>
> **When we come to the snake as a divinity in Egypt, we need look no further than the great crowns worn by the divine Pharaoh. No matter which crown, the Blue crown, the informal crown or the great double red and white crown we examine we will find the snake god of Lower Egypt present. Even when the vulture god of Upper Egypt is missing, the asp, or Egyptian cobra, is there. The serpent, in Egypt, has a varied career, the Uraeus, or cobra, and other mythical snakes are all considered quite differently. The spinal cord was symbolized by the snake and the Uraeus serpent coiled upon the foreheads of the Pharaoh represented the divine fire which had crawled serpent-like up the tree of life.**
>
> **Page 8**
>
> **The Uraeus, or asp, is a benevolent guardian god, a tutelary god of the delta region of Egypt. This is probably where this snake was most often found. Even today the swamp-like areas of the Nile delta is home to the Egyptian cobra. This snake was also connected to the god Horus, and therefore**

with the living Horus, who is seen incarnate in the Pharaoh. The Uraeus rules by day, and therefore is also connected to the sun god Ra, who is also a god of Pharaoh. It is not an accident of history that the legendary Cleopatra chose to be joined to the Egyptian cobra, the asp, by being bitten by the serpent. She is identifying the goddess Isis, whom she represented, to the sacred Uraeus who was her protector and who would lead her into eternal life in the western land.

When we come to night and darkness, the crocodile becomes supreme. Ra, the sun god of Heliopolis is diminished. The solar ship has entered the realm of night and encountered darkness. The crocodile, in Egyptian legendary, is seen as an aspect of the serpent rather than a separate creature. There are places in the world where the great saurians are not seen as serpents, but as a completely separate genus of creature. The Americas would serve as an example of this, but in Egypt and other Africa nations which were influenced by Egypt, the crocodile is a serpent, no matter in what form it is depicted.

In the original Egyptian creation story we find a serpent and the primordial egg, which contained the "Bird of Light". In Chapter 175 of the Book of the Dead we find the prophecy that when the world returns to its original chaos, the hidden aspect of the supreme god, Atum, will become the new serpent. There is a text I found in the "Coffin Texts" [I.161 ff] which contains Atum's description of himself:

" I am Atum, the creator of the Eldest Gods,

I am he who gave birth to Shu,

I am that great he-she.

I am he who did what seemed good to him,

I took my space in the place of my will.

Mine is the space of those who move along

like those two *serpentine circles"* [emphasis mine]

Page 9

Before the boat is the great serpent Ankh-neteru, and twelve amikhiu gods, taking hold of the tow line, enter this serpent at the tail, and drawing the god in his boat through the body of the serpent, bring him out at his mouth.

During his passage through the serpent Afu Ra is transformed into Khepera [the ancient god associated with the creation of the world] and is now towed into the sky by 12 goddesses."

The Egyptians also adopted the ancient Persian god Azhi Dahaka, the sky serpent who formed all of the observable heavenly planets. So, in one sense powerful gods of both light and darkness are seen as serpents. This may have some connection to the linking of the snake to the moon in the mythological and psychological areas.

This identification is intensified because of the waxing and waning of the moon, demonstrating the death of the old and the rebirth of the new and forever young.

One of the chief powers of this darkness is the serpent god Apep, who tries to swallow the sun ship. Apep [or Apepi or Apophis] is the great primordial serpent who lived in the waters of the celestial Nile [the Milky Way] and is considered the serpent of chaos and destruction. A mighty struggle took place and when the sun appeared in the east the next day prayers of thankfulness were offered that Ra was triumphant and the sun would continue to shine. Just imagine what chaos a solar eclipse would cause!

The serpent Apep is seen in two other forms, or traditions. The first was most likely the crocodile and was called *Typhon*, or dragon. Two other serpents divinities mentioned in Egyptian mythology are *Nehebkau,* a serpent with human arms and legs. This fearful god, once he was tamed by Ra, became his faithful servant. The other serpent god is *Am-Mut,* the 'eater of souls'. The other, and more extensive is as Set, or Seth, or Sethos. This is a half-crocodile, half -human creature who becomes important in the Egyptian pantheon. The serpent Typhon is the youngest son of Gaea and Tartarus in Greek legend. He was taller than any mountain, and had great wings, eyes of fire, hands made of dragons, and a lower body composed of vipers. He and Echidna gave birth to Hydra, Cerberis, Chimera and the Nemean lion. The Egyptian Typhon was a more simple serpent lord.

Again, it is important to note here that the dragons we have included in this study are only those dragons which are seen as serpentine. The classic European dragon which looks more like a mammal with wings, like the Griffin, are excluded. The Egyptian and Chinese dragon concepts depict them as serpents, as does the Greek. [I will speak more of dragons when I write of the Asian serpents]

Page 10

The Isis cult lasted into the Christian era as an active mystery cult. But, the original priesthood of the serpent god, Set, in ancient Egypt survived for twenty-five recorded dynasties (ca. 3200-700BCE) It became one of the two central priesthoods of predynastic times, the other being that of HarWer (Horus the Elder).

When the Egyptians abandoned the mines in the Timma Valley (about nineteen miles north of the Gulf of Aqaba) during the Egyptian decline of the twelfth century BCE, the Midianites converted the local temple into a Midianite shrine. In the makeshift Holy of Holies of the shrine, modern excavators have found only one religious object. They found a molded copper serpent with a gilded head, the ancient symbol of life and fertility of the Middle East. This would indicate that the Midianites had a serpent god or goddess in their pantheon. Again, we see echoes of Biblical stories here.

Before we leave Egypt we must briefly mention two other aspects of the divine serpent; Nehebu-Kau is the great snake under the world and upon which the world rests, and there is a winged serpent found in hieroglyphs which may be the ancestor of our Mesoamerican Quetzalcoatl.[182]

Mr. Mason does excellent work in the field of following and explaining serpent mythology and the divine connections that are apparent. The Egyptian attitude toward serpents definitely played into the level of understanding that the Israelites would have possessed as they left Egypt and went on to receive the Torah of Yahweh through the servant Moses. Through many, many eras and continuous exposure to different world views, Christianity and many of the religious counterparts to Christianity have come to accept *cart blanche*, that the "serpent in the garden" is a literal serpent in the garden. Alternatively,

182 "The Divine Serpent" by Robert T Mason. The website where this article can be read in its entirety is; http://www.geocities.com/Athens/Delphi/5789/serpent.htm

as we have discussed, many have come to believe that the "serpent in the garden" is a cosmic "Satan." A large contributor to this confused conclusion is the misunderstanding of Egyptian and other mythological references to the serpent. In short, adaptation of mythology has yielded this result.

Egyptian influence is not the only influence on current thought that has aided in defining present day perceptions of the serpent and "satan." In "The Mystery of the Serpent" by Hans Leisegang, we are told of the Pietroasa treasure. This was a treasure discovered by peasants in 1837 CE, in northwestern Romania. The treasure has been the object of looting, and conflict until recently when it has found a permanent home in Romania's National History Museum in Bucharest. Like any early CE treasure, the Pietroasa treasure has been followed by legends that enhance the excitement of this treasure to those willing to believe the legends. Legends such as, any snake being buried with the treasure, wherever a piece of it lies, remains alive. According to Dr Marius Constantinescu, the curse that would be expected to transfer to the liberator of this treasure is placed on the snake instead. Another is the legend that flames shoot from the ground every August to reveal where remains of unearthed treasure can be found. The interesting aspect of this treasure for our present discussion is regarding the number of pieces that displayed ideas of serpent divinity. The treasure is said to be from the 4th Century CE and although not nearly as ancient as the archeology that reveals Egyptian beliefs in serpent divinity, we are able to comprehend the vibrant serpent mythology, which was abounding in the early centuries of this Common Era. Cults such as Orpheus and Dionysius are replete with practices and rituals that have been brought across into "Christianity" in forms that closely resemble the original practices by the cult worshippers. Perhaps had we not had the advantage of the scientific field of archeology, we would not see the ancient understanding of things such as the "serpent," motif revealed. Knowledge that was previously unavailable to scholars has been brought to light and sheds much understanding on ancient religious beliefs. Beliefs that have evolved to a place of acceptance today seated comfortably in many of the worlds greatest religions. Along with unearthing of artifacts that expressly portray ancient serpent motif, we are slowly dissolving the distant connection we have to understanding Hebraic terms, and Hebraic thought and philosophy. This historical misunderstanding has been the primary cause of such misguided literal interpretation of serpent mythology and subsequent integration of the erroneous concepts that are now so deeply rooted into Christianity and other religions. Leisegang writes:

> Thus the Etruscan lamp, the alabaster bowl, and the golden bowl from the Pietroasa treasure are united by a common

> bond. They all bear witness to the mysteries, to the diverse yet always interrelated forms of the original Orphic-Dionysian cult. And the development whose beginnings can still be discerned in these magnificent pieces- which have come down to us but by a fortunate chance-extends beyond antiquity, deep into the Christian world.[183]

The influences, which brought us as a culture to accept the serpent and the garden experience of Adam and Eve that we are so familiar with, are multiple. For far too long many of us have taken the words in the text of Scripture and affixed our own ideas and inventions with their diverse and ethereal meaning, which cannot be proven through any means. Is it possible to see the story of the serpent in the garden through different glasses? After being taught for so long what we have come to accept as truth, is it even possible for most of us to try on different glasses? All I can do is encourage you to not just ask questions but to also look for answers. Answers which don't lessen or diminish the sovereignty and wonder of the Creator of the Universe but answers which help in reconciling more of the inconsistent beliefs we seem to be trapped by with an almost nonchalant resignation. Questions which when answered, will undoubtedly aid in reconciling apparent contradictions in the Scriptures and New Testament.

Is the serpent in the garden a literal serpent? Does the serpent represent a concept that points at the human heart as being the origin of sinful thought, action, and persuasions? Is it possible that Adam is the serpent? As I said earlier, it is plausible that the writer of Genesis, in his ancient metaphorical style of writing, was intending to express the view that indicated a man was the adversary. However, I will not dogmatically state it is so at this time. Adam may or may not be seen as the serpent insofar as I am able to prove conclusively. I will state that the serpent in the garden must be either Adam or a metaphorical reference to the human psyche, which actively considers and justifies disobedience.

In the letter to the Romans we see that beyond simply telling us the "law of sin was in his members" because he sometimes found himself to be a human who sins; Paul was relating that he was acutely aware of the internal struggle of man. Paul recognized that man had to battle down the occasional and sometimes persistent desire to sin. Paul knew a cosmic Satan was not a part of existence and his words in Romans describe the same thing I have been speaking about in saying that sin dwelleth in him. Paul says;

---

183 From, Pagan and Christian Mysteries, pg 68 "The Mystery of the Serpent" by Hans Leisegang

> *Now then it is no more I that do it, but sin that dwelleth in me. For I know that in me (that is, in my flesh,) dwelleth no good thing: for to will is present with me; but how to perform that which is good I find not.*
> *For the good that I would I do not: but the evil which I would not, that I do. Now if I do that I would not, it is no more I that do it, but sin that dwelleth in me.I find then a law, that, when I would do good, evil is present with me. Romans 7:17-21 KJV*

Paul has told us sin and evil is something that dwells in him. As an influential teacher and leader in the first century, he did not teach of a "being" called Satan who was tempting and trying to cause man to choose sin. Paul admitted that sin was his own problem and in admitting it, was able to overcome sin to a certain extent. Paul owned the sin. Adam and Eve in the garden, whether the serpent is Eve's *yetzer ha ra* or the serpent was referring to Adam acting in an adversarial role by leading Eve to touch and then eat the fruit, are two humans who are fully responsible for their choice. They chose to disobey and this was a choice that affected humanity forever. Reading Genesis Chapter 3 with this understanding does much to place the Creator God in the position of being the only supernatural being controlling the universe and entering into the lives of humans. Reading Genesis chapter 3 with this perspective does much to liberate man to responsibly make choices without believing a fabricated, cosmic "satan" is persuading them. Being liberated in this manner helps man to see that the full responsibility for all his choices to disobey is completely born by what is in man's heart already. Reading and understanding any Scripture in a way that exalts Yahweh as the only God and does not allow another false or mythical God to be constructed by a tainted belief system, truly proclaims that there is no other God but the I Am God of Creation.

Please read the serpent in the garden account with the perspective I have endeavored to impart in the previous pages. Perhaps you will see how Yahweh hoped we would see this true story as a story with profound truths. A story with mythical undertones that was to be passed on to us in order to transmit the message about the problem of sin, to all of humanity. That problem is humanity's' oldest problem and is the fact that we all have a part of us that desires to rebel. Not all of us desire complete rebellion but if even on a minute level, the rebellious nature exists in every human being and we are capable of justifying anything if we want it bad enough.

The forbidden fruit, called the *tree of the knowledge of good and evil*, is placed in front of us by the Creator, because he wants us to have the privilege of choice and to ultimately learn to choose good. It is hoped that we will learn to choose the tree of life so that at some point in time, we will be able to live with him forever, having only One God, in the truest sense of The Word.

Genesis Chapter 3 - King James Version

1 *Now the serpent was more subtil than any beast of the field which the LORD God had made. And he said unto the woman, Yea, hath God said, Ye shall not eat of every tree of the garden?*

2 *And the woman said unto the serpent, We may eat of the fruit of the trees of the garden:*

3 *But of the fruit of the tree which is in the midst of the garden, God hath said, Ye shall not eat of it, neither shall ye touch it, lest ye die.*

4 *And the serpent said unto the woman, Ye shall not surely die:*

5 *For God doth know that in the day ye eat thereof, then your eyes shall be opened, and ye shall be as gods, knowing good and evil.*

6 *And when the woman saw that the tree was good for food, and that it was pleasant to the eyes, and a tree to be desired to make one wise, she took of the fruit thereof, and did eat, and gave also unto her husband with her; and he did eat.*

7 *And the eyes of them both were opened, and they knew that they were naked; and they sewed fig leaves together, and made themselves aprons.*

8 *And they heard the voice of the LORD God walking in the garden in the cool of the day: and Adam and his wife hid themselves from the presence of the LORD God amongst the trees of the garden.*

9 *And the LORD God called unto Adam, and said unto him, Where art thou?*

10 *And he said, I heard thy voice in the garden, and I was afraid, because I was naked; and I hid myself.*

11 *And he said, Who told thee that thou wast naked? Hast thou eaten of the tree, whereof I commanded thee that thou shouldest not eat?*

12 *And the man said, The woman whom thou gavest to be with me, she gave me of the tree, and I did eat.*

13 *And the LORD God said unto the woman, What is this that thou hast done? And the woman said, The serpent beguiled me, and I did eat.*

14 *And the LORD God said unto the serpent, Because thou hast done this, thou art cursed above all cattle, and above every beast of the field; upon thy belly shalt thou go, and dust shalt thou eat all the days of thy life:*

15 *And I will put enmity between thee and the woman, and between thy seed and her seed; it shall bruise thy head, and thou shalt bruise his heel.*

16 *Unto the woman he said, I will greatly multiply thy sorrow and thy conception; in sorrow thou shalt bring forth children; and thy desire shall be to thy husband, and he shall rule over thee.*

17 *And unto Adam he said, Because thou hast hearkened unto the voice of thy wife, and hast eaten of the tree, of which I commanded thee, saying, Thou shalt not eat of it: cursed is the ground for thy sake; in sorrow shalt thou eat of it all the days of thy life;*

18 *Thorns also and thistles shall it bring forth to thee; and thou shalt eat the herb of the field;*

19 *In the sweat of thy face shalt thou eat bread, till thou return unto the ground; for out of it wast thou taken: for dust thou art, and unto dust shalt thou return.*

20 *And Adam called his wife's name Eve; because she was the mother of all living.*

21 *Unto Adam also and to his wife did the LORD God make coats of skins, and clothed them.*

22 *And the LORD God said, Behold, the man is become as one of us, to know good and evil: and now, lest he put forth his hand, and take also of the tree of life, and eat, and live for ever:*

23 *Therefore the LORD God sent him forth from the garden of Eden, to till the ground from whence he was taken.*

24 *So he drove out the man; and he placed at the east of the garden of Eden Cherubims, and a flaming sword which turned every way, to keep the way of the tree of life.*

WHAT'S NEXT FOR *SATAN CHRISTIANITY'S OTHER GOD*

Thank you for taking the time to read Volume I of *Satan Christianity's Other God*. Our study however, is far from complete. I encourage you to look forward to Volume II, which will carry on from where we left off.

In Volume II, there will be a discussion on the famed encounter by King Saul with the Witch at Endor. The evidence in the text and information contained in historical and cultural examinations will reveal that the woman with a familiar spirit, the witch of Endor, was no more than a ventriloquist who plied her trade of cold reading. Cold reading is a well-known psychic practice that has the "psychic" extracting information from the participant and playing off the subtle body language of that participant in order to make statements that the psychic seemingly could not know, unless he or she had some supernatural powers.

Volume II will spend significant time outlining exactly what the New Testament is and what it is good for. Both Paul and Yeshua did not use anything other than the Hebrew Scriptures as their handbook of doctrine. The New Testament has been broiled in controversy for hundreds of years and now it is time to see it placed in its proper position in the anthology of ancient writings that are claimed to be God's Word, or Scripture. Convincing evidence will be presented that shows how the New Testament only testifies of itself as "letters". There is no internal evidence identifying the New Testament as Scripture in the sense that the Old Testament is Scripture. In addition, neither does the Old Testament suggest that the idolized Apostolic writings are Scripture.

There is nothing quite as difficult nor as illuminating, as determining the underlying Hebrew meaning to all of the Greek writings found in the New

Testament. Once again using the Bible the Messiah used as the source book for understanding the words of the New Testament, Volume II explains how the New Testament came to be revered as equal to the Bible Christ used. It is also explained how it is possible to continue to use the New Testament as a guide book of sorts, for difficulties encountered in walking out the faith of Yeshua.

Where many scholars say to throw out the New Testament because it is unreliable and contradicts the Old, Volume II of *Satan, Christianity's Other God* proves diligent to reconcile the apparent differences and supports the validity of the Apostolic writings. These writing are credible witnesses to the period Yeshua walked the earth and the time shortly thereafter. Recognizing the rich metaphorically based Greek language and mindset for what it is, allows the student to discover the meanings of Hebraisms that are written in Greek language. Volume II also explores the connection Greek terms such as *satanas, daimon, and diabolos* have to the readily understood Hebrew concepts that underlie them.

In Volume II, the reader will experience for the first time, a fresh understanding of dozens of New Testament passages that for a long time have been thought to be about a cosmic Satan. Commentary is provided for every passage in the New Testament that uses the words; *devil, Satan, Demon, unclean spirit* and the like. No stone is left unturned and if you are inclined to use the "Well what abouts…" to point to a New Testament passage that you think confirms the existence of Satan, you will want to explore the commentary on the Apostolic Writings first. Answers are presented for every difficult passage and concept. Without upsetting the message or power of the words of the New Testament, Volume II of *Satan, Christianity's Other God* promises to give a lot of answers where previously answers have been inconsistent and difficult to accept in the light of there being only One God in the universe.

In the second volume of this title, the reader will receive hundreds of proofs from Biblical writings and history that a literal Satan was not taught by the Apostles or the Messiah. The reader will go away with a strongly affirmed belief that if there is a Sovereign God as the Scriptures and the Apostolic writings claim, He did not create a supernatural cosmic entity called Satan that rejected the glory of heaven and fell to Earth to torment the faithful.

The conclusion is, that there is One God and none else. Just as Yahweh claimed in His written word.

BIBLIOGRAPHY

Satan, Christianity's Other God
by James R. Brayshaw
www.scog.ca

1. A Commentary on The Revelation Of John – George Eldon Ladd, *William B. Eerdman Publishing 1972*
2. A Guide to The Prophets – Stephen Winward, *John Knox Press 1977*
3. A Magician Among the Spirits – Harry Houdini, *Harper and Brother 1924*
4. Adam Clarke's Commentary on the Bible - Adam Clarke, LL.D., F.S.A., (1715-1832)
5. Albert Barnes' Notes on the Bible - Albert Barnes 1798-1870
6. Associations, Synagogues, and Congregations – Philip A. Harland, *Augsburg Fortress 2003*
7. Believing In Magic-The Psychology of Superstition – Stuart A. Vyse, Oxford *University Press 1997*
8. Bible Guide – Prophets of Israel (1) Isaiah – George Knight, *Lutterworth Press and Abbingdon Press 1961 and 1962*
9. Bible Guide – Prophets of Israel (2) Jeremiah and Ezekiel – William Neil, *Lutterworth Press and Abbingdon Press 1964*
10. Bloodline of the Holy Grail – Laurence Gardner *Fair Winds2002*
11. Catechism of the Catholic Faith – *Canadian Conference of Catholic Bishops*
12. Commentary Critical and Explanatory on the Whole Bible - Robert Jamieson, A. R. Fausset and David Brown
13. Encyclopedia Britannica – 15th Edition, *William Benton 1943-73 – Helen Hemingway 173-74*
14. Every Prophecy of the Bible – John Walvord, *Chariot Victor Publishing 1999*
15. Galatians, A Torah Based Commentary on the Book of Galatians – Avi Ben Mordechai, *A Milleniaum 7000 Publication 2005*

16. Gods and the One God – Robert M. Grant, *The Westminster Press Philadelphia 1986*
17. Gospel Light – George M. Lamsa edited by James Magiera, *A.J olman Co. 1939 & The Aramaic Bible Society 1995*
18. How Our Bible Came to Be – H.G.G. Herklots, *A Galaxy Book 1954*
19. Idioms of the Bible Explained & A Key to The Original Gospels – George M. Lamsa, *Harper Collins 1985 originally published 1931*
20. Jesus Through The Centuries – Yaroslav Pelikio, *Yale University Press*
21. John Gill's Exposition of the Entire Bible - Dr. John Gill (1690-1771)
22. Josephus The Complete Works – Translated by William Whiston A.M., *Thomas Nelson Publishers*
23. Keil & Delitzsch Commentary on the Old Testament -Johann (C.F.) Keil (1807-1888) & Franz Delitzsch (1813-1890)
24. Kooks By Donna Kossey, *Feral House 1999*
25. Occult and Supernatural Phenomenon , D. H. Rawcliffe, *Derick Ridgeway Publishing 1952 (original title) The Psychology of the Occult*
26. Origins Of the Synagogue and Church – Kaufman Kholer - posthumously 1929 *The Macmillian Company New York*
27. Peoples of The Old Testament World – Alfred J. Haerth; Gerald L. Mattingly; Edwin M. Yamouchi, *Baker Books 1994*
28. Scofield Reference Notes (1917 Edition) by Cyrus Ingerson Scofield (1843-1921)
29. Skeptic - *Volume 7 Number 4 1999*
30. Surpassing Wonder – Invention of the Bible and Talmuds – Donald Harmon Akenson, *McGill Queens University Press 1998*
31. Synopsis of the Old and New Testaments - John Nelson Darby (1800 - 1882)
32. Temples and Temple Services in Ancient Israel – Menahem Haran, *Eisenbrauns 1985 2nd print 1995*
33. The Bible And the British Museum – Ada R. Habershon, *Morgan and Scott Ltd.1909*
34. The Birth Of Satan: Tracing The Devil's Biblical Roots, T.J. Wray and Gregory Mobley, *New York: Palgrave Macmillan, 2005*

35. The Dead Sea Scrolls, A New Translation – Wise, Abegg, and Cook, *Harper Collins 1996*
36. The Devil – Amelia Wilson, *PRC Publishing CO.2002*
37. The Element Encyclopedia of Secret Societies – John Michael Greer, *Harper Element 2000*
38. The Epic History of Good and Evil, *http://www.satan4u.8m.com/history/history.html*
39. The Essence of the Gnostics – Bernard Simon, *Arctarus Publishing Ltd. 2004*
40. The History of Magic Volumes 1 and 2 – Joseph Ennemoser, *University Book,1970*
41. The History of the Devil and the Idea of Evil from the Earliest Times to the Present Day– Paul Carus, *Open Court Publishing Co.1900 and Dover Books 2008*
42. The History of the Devil, G. Messandé, *Newell, London, England, 1996*
43. The IVP Woman's Bible Commentary – Katherine Clarke-Kroeger and Mary J. Evans –*Inter Varsity Press 2002*
44. The Mentor Dictionary of Theology and The Bible – Richard J. Daigle and Frederick R. Lapides, *New American Library 1973*
45. The New Bible Commentary Revised – W.B. Eerdmans Press, IVP 1970
46. The New Covenant – Commonly Called The New Testament – Vol. 1 – Willis Barnstone, *Riverhead Books NY 2002*
47. The Old Enemy, Satan And The Combat Myth, Neil Forsyth, *Princeton:, Princeton University Press, 1989*
48. The Origin Of Satan - Elaine Pagels, *Vintage Books 1996*
49. The Prince of Darkness – Jeffrey Burton Russell, *Cornell University Press*
50. Too Long In the Sun – Richard M. Rives, *Partaker Publication 2002*
51. Vincent Word Studies - Marvin R. Vincent, D.D.
52. Who Wrote the New Testament- The Making of the Christian Myth – Burton L. Mack, *Harper Collins Publishers 1999*
53. Word Pictures in the New Testament - Archibald Thomas Robertson

54. OTHER SOURCES

The number of other sources, including audio, video, internet articles, periodical articles, digital books and varied research-based web sites, are too numerous to list in this biography at this time. The amount of thought and conjecture from literally hundreds of "teachers", which directed the author towards a research-based conclusion that marshals documentary evidence for contentions, is virtually innumerable and has proven invaluable. The list of which could take up a volume in itself.

INDEX

B

C

D

E

F

G

H

I

L

M

N

O

P

R

S

T

U

V

W

Y

Z